Honoring Tradition, Embracing Modernity

Honoring Tradition, Embracing Modernity

A Reader
FOR THE
Union for Reform Judaism's
Introduction to Judaism Course

Edited by
Rabbi Beth Lieberman and Rabbi Hara Person

UNION *for*
REFORM JUDAISM
Building Communities. Reimagining Jewish Life.

CCAR
Press

10 9 8 7 6 5 4 3

CCAR Press, 355 Lexington Avenue, New York, NY 10017
(212) 972-3636
www.ccarpress.org

Contents

Contents • ix

Acknowledgments

The Central Conference of American Rabbis is proud to join forces with the Union for Reform Judaism in publishing this resource guide for the Reform Movement's Introduction to Judaism classes. The Movement's Introduction to Judaism classes play an essential role in strengthening our communities, and we are honored to make these important resources available to the Intro teachers and students, as well as to those who sponsor them.

There were a number of individuals whose hard work, creativity, and goodwill made this project happen, whose passion for teaching and learning in community allow us all to reach across community divides and unite as a vibrant, inclusive, and open people. We are particularly grateful to Rabbi Leora Kaye and Rabbi Beth Lieberman for their thoughtful work in bringing this resource to fruition, and to all the writers and editors whose work is included here. Many thanks also to Rabbi Steven Fox, Chief Executive of the Central Conference of American Rabbis, Rabbi Rick Jacobs, President of the Union for Reform Judaism, April N. Baskin, Union for Reform Judaism's Vice President of Audacious Hospitality, Frieda Hershman Huberman, Union for Reform Judaism's Manager of Introduction to Judaism and A Taste of Judaism®, Rabbi Danny Moss, former CCAR Rabbinic Intern, and Joy Wasserman, Union for Reform Judaism's Coordinator, Introduction to Judaism and A Taste of Judaism®, Chicago.

Rabbi Hara Person

Chief Strategy Officer,
Central Conference of American Rabbis

Publisher, CCAR Press

Dear Learner,

Welcome to the next stage of your journey! This sourcebook, which contains some of our tradition's greatest teachings, can be used in many ways. It is designed for you as you seek to deepen your knowledge of Judaism—its wisdom, its practices, its beliefs, its customs, its people and our story—with the goal of helping you to understand what being part of a Jewish community might mean for you or someone close to you.

Thank you for choosing *Introduction to Judaism* as your gateway to our magnificent heritage.

Sincerely,

April N. Baskin
Vice President of
Audacious Hospitality,
Union for Reform Judaism

Rabbi Hara Person
Chief Strategy Officer,
Central Conference of
American Rabbis
Publisher, CCAR Press

Unit I

BEGINNINGS

What Is Judaism?
Who Are the Jewish People?

On The Jewish People

RABBI RACHEL TIMONER

1

Liberal Jews in our era treasure our autonomy and are ambivalent about the authority of God and Torah. No one is going to tell us what to say, what to do, or what to believe. Though we want the benefits of community, we are wary of the demands it may place on us. Furthermore, those of us in America live in a society in which freedom is defined in direct contrast to obligation, instead of in partnership with it.

But let's face it: we have not yet learned how to be free. It is one thing to throw off authority. It is another to realize freedom. Freedom requires conscious choice, and choice is its own burden. How do we choose well? Using which values? Having chosen, do we commit and follow through? How and when do we reevaluate our choices? The number and scope of choices in a day is overwhelming. Without a framework, we flail. So we look to a mix of external norms and institutions from the surrounding culture—the Protestant work ethic, the American dream, parenting trends, to name a few examples—to make choices for us. Shouldn't the wisdom of our own people have at least as strong a voice? Once we realize that we've traded one system of external authority for others, we find that the treasure we are seeking is under our own hearth. We are yearning for guidance. We are yearning for coherence. If chosen, covenant, mitzvah, and Torah are as relevant and sacred to us now as they ever have been.

Covenant is the choice to commit to a Jewish way of life in relationship with Jewish community: to study it, question it, and reinterpret it, but to choose Jewish text and tradition—the threethousand-year-old conversation of our people with God—as a framework for our lives. Within this framework, a mitzvah is a call for action that requires a carefully considered response. Perhaps the response is to try to live the mitzvah for a period of time. Perhaps the response is commitment to the mitzvah, or rejection of it, or a "not yet." New mitzvot might be identified and adopted, old mitzvot might be reinterpreted or adapted. Decisions are made with care, lived out, and reevaluated in time. In this way, mitzvot become living expressions of our Jewish values, a thoughtful effort to learn the discipline of acting on our highest ideals. Through it all, Torah is our sacred guide. Those who study it know that it endlessly reveals insights about the meaning of life. Gershom Scholem teaches, "The Torah turns a special face to every single Jew, meant only for him [*sic*] and apprehensible only by him, and a Jew therefore fulfills his true purpose only when he comes to see this face and is able to incorporate it into the tradition" (Scholem, "Revelation and Tradition as Religious Categories in Judaism," 295).

Autonomy is a lonely fiction. Covenant, mitzvah, and Torah are the modern liberal Jew's way to journey toward freedom.

2

I put
יהוה
before me always. (Psalm 16:8)

You are not the center of the universe.
Remembering that is the beginning
of being religious.

What is the center of the universe?
That is the question of being religious.

Putting that question
and what's found there
— the Ineffable,
יהוה

before you always,
deliberately, repeatedly,
that is being religious.

You lift up the fallen . . . and are faithful to those who sleep in the dust.
—*(Birkat G'vurah, Amidah)*

Having faith is different.
Having faith (*emunah*) is trusting that
when everything comes apart
and you fall,
you will be caught.

From generation to generation we will tell of your greatness.
—*(K'dushah)*

If you're a religious Jew you testify
through words (*t'filot*) and actions (mitzvot)
to what you found
when you went asking
about the center of the universe.
You do so in chorus with your people,
singing through time.
You do so to remind yourself
that you are not at the center,
and What Is.

3

Any way you look at it, the Jewish people has a unique vocation among all nations. This does not make us superior. It only makes us singular. (The same can be said of every other tribe and nation on earth.) No other people shares our ancestry, our history, our Torah, our culture, our traditions, or our obligation.

You do not have to believe in God or Torah to believe in the unique vocation of the Jews. You only have to believe in history. Whether because, as the Torah teaches, God lifted us out of slavery in order to form an eternal covenant with our people; or because we witnessed, perished in, and survived the Holocaust; or because of a myriad of other defining moments in our story, the Jewish people is unlike any other. And we have a specific job to do.

We are here to remind the human race that the world we live in is not good enough, that human dignity, justice, and peace are possible on earth, and that we are needed to transform the world that is into the world that should be. As Tal Becker of the Shalom Hartman Institute wrote, "The Biblical imperative of being 'a kingdom of priests and a holy people' (Exodus 19:6) compels you not only to ask how can I be better tomorrow than I was today, but also to believe that constant improvement is possible" (Becker, "iEngage: How to Be an Optimist in the Middle East").

The prophets describe a messianic age when there will be dignity for the poor and justice for the oppressed (Isaiah 11:4), an end to all war among nations (Isaiah 2:4), harmony with nature (Isaiah 4:2), and an utter lack of fear (Micah 4:4).

I believe that human beings are capable of continual improvement and that the messianic age will be its result. If that day is guaranteed through God's will, we are needed as God's partners to make it real. If that day is not guaranteed by God, well then, it depends on us. Either way, I agree with Franz Kafka, who wrote: "The Messiah will come only when he is no longer necessary" (*Parables and Paradoxes, 81*).

4

On that day, God will be One and God's name will be One.
—*Aleinu* (based on Zechariah 14:9)

If our vision is to coexist in harmony with the other nations of the earth, if we dream that someday all will see that the many gods known to humanity are diverse faces of One and the same, we have a lot of work to do.

It begins with knowing each other. Organized dialogue in which churches and synagogues compare and contrast beliefs and values is important, but so are college friendships, neighbors walking the dogs together, sports teams, and book groups. What we need are real relationships of trust that enable Jews to know non-Jews, and non-Jews to know Jews, to ask each other honest questions over a cup of coffee or at the water cooler. We need safe friends with whom we can clear up misunderstandings, share perspectives, learn, and teach.

But in order to effectively field the questions of our non-Jewish friends and neighbors, to be able to explain the nature and origin of our holidays, theology, mitzvot, and customs, we have a lot of learning to do. To explain synagogue practice and life-cycle events, the role of Torah in our lives, the range of movements in contemporary Judaism, and our relationship with Israel, we first need to become Jewishly literate ourselves.

The Jewish people are not merely a faith community. We are a nation, a people, a collection of tribes. Exchange with adherents of other religious traditions is important, but equally important is dialogue with other ethnic, social, and cultural groups within the societies in which we live.

The most important question is not whether Jews are obligated to participate in intergroup dialogue. The most important question is, given the ubiquitous interaction between Jews and non-Jews: What is the nature of the dialogue already taking place? How effectively are Jews able to represent our own story and practice? What are non-Jews learning about Judaism from their Jewish friends, and what should they be learning? What should Jews be learning from non-Jews that will better equip us to understand and respect the other?

There are two goals here: (1) to educate ourselves to be able to represent Judaism and the Jewish people, and (2) to build greater trust and understanding between Jews and non-Jews so that we can create a future of peace and mutual respect.

Source: Rabbi Rachel Timoner, in *Lights in the Forest: Rabbis Respond to Twelve Essential Jewish Questions*, ed. Rabbi Paul Citrin (New York: CCAR Press, 2014), 213–217.

Jewish Religious Pluralism

Rabbi Joan S. Friedman

"Pluralism: 1. A condition or system in which two or more states, groups, principles, sources of authority, etc., coexist."[1]

Today there exist multiple ways of being a Jew, each of which claims to be *a* correct, or the correct, way. What is the Reform Jewish perspective on this reality? Do Reform Jews think that Judaism can legitimately be conceptualized and lived in multiple ways? If so, do Reform Jews think that there are limits to the ways Judaism can be legitimately conceptualized and lived? Or do Reform Jews think that there is, in fact, one right way, and that pluralism exists only because it is impossible to suppress or eliminate the wrong ways?

It may seem paradoxical that a movement grounded in a universalist approach to religion ("We recognize in every religion an attempt to grasp the infinite, and in every mode, source or book of revelation held sacred in any religious system the consciousness of the indwelling of God in man"[2]) should care about which forms of Judaism are, or are not, correct. But, of course, any group must define itself both by who it is and by who it is not, who belongs and who does not. *Religion* is a human creation. A religious community is a group of people who all implicitly or explicitly share a world view and a way of life rooted in something

---

1. https://en.oxforddictionaries.com/definition/pluralism. Accessed 22 September 2016.
2. "The Pittsburgh Platform," http://ccarnet.org/rabbis-speak/platforms/declaration-principles/. Accessed 23 May 2016. This 1885 document was an attempt by nineteen American rabbis to define the essential principles and beliefs of Reform Judaism and was accepted as such by most Reform Jews until the 1930s.

—text, story, whatever—that they regard as authoritative. *Pluralism* becomes a religious issue when, for any number of reasons, members of the community develop some variations in the shared understanding. This raises questions: How much variation is legitimate? At what point does a variant differ so greatly from the original that it has become something else? And who determines that?

A historical perspective on Judaism shows us how Jews have dealt with pluralism in the past. All Jewish religious expression rests on one fundamental premise: that God and the people Israel made a formal agreement (a *b'rit*, covenant) at Mt. Sinai, in which God gave them a set of laws by which to live, embodied in the Torah, and promised blessing and protection in return. Jews are *b'nei b'rit*, members of the covenant, and Jewish life is lived out within a covenantal nexus of God, Torah, and Israel. Everything else is contingent and mutable. Even the very definitions of *God*, *Torah*, and *Israel* are dynamic, to a degree. Determining what is Judaism and what is not Judaism is not a new endeavor, and it has never been a simple one.

Sometimes mutability is due to historical contingency, those fascinating "what ifs:" What if the Romans had not destroyed the Temple in 70 CE? What if, in the eighth century, the caliph in Baghdad had not granted authority over Jewish life in the vast Muslim empire to the rabbis, thus ensuring that the Babylonian Talmud would acquire its authoritative status? What if the *Shoah* had not taken place? Historical contingency, however, does not reduce the importance of intra-Jewish dynamics – not only spirited polemical and ideological debates, but also trends created out of myriads of individual decisions. What constitutes a "Jewish" world view in any era is the result of a constant sifting of possibilities – a dynamic interaction, evident only in hindsight, among Jews, their inherited authoritative tradition, and their cultural "now." In any given time and place Jews consciously and unconsciously gravitate toward ideas and concepts that cohere with or build upon their existing world view. Thus the vast majority of first- and second-century Jews rejected the religious view of the small group that created the theological innovation that eventually became Christianity because it did not cohere with their existing understanding of Jewish life. Conversely, when the Zohar, the central text of *kabbalah* (Jewish mysticism), was printed in the 16th century, *kabbalah* spread like wildfire among Jews everywhere because it did cohere, i.e., it "made sense" to them as a way to add meaning to their lives.

"Rabbinic Judaism" became the Jewish norm through the complex interaction, over centuries, of historical contingency and Jews gravitating toward what made sense to them and gravitating away from what didn't. The rabbinic interpretation of the God-Torah-Israel covenantal nexus held that God had revealed at Sinai not only the Written Torah (i.e., the Pentateuch) but also the Oral Torah, the way of interpreting the written commandments and applying them to daily life. At Sinai God had also designated Moses as the first *rabbi*, the original arbiter and interpreter of Torah law; the rabbis of every generation were his authoritative successors in the "chain of tradition."[3] Covenantal life, therefore, was what the rabbis determined it to be, and for them it meant fulfilling the commandments of the Written Torah as expounded in the Oral Torah. "Oral Torah" eventually became a vast written corpus comprising the Mishnah, the Talmud, the medieval codes of Jewish law, and much more, all of which make up the *halakhah* (literally, "way," but commonly used to mean "law").

In some ways pre-modern Jewish society was pluralistic. There are distinctive regional liturgical customs, for example. There were controversies among rabbis over the use of philosophy to interpret Torah, and controversies over mystical theologies and practices, but ultimately most of these were judged to fall within acceptable ranges of the God-Torah-Israel nexus. The halakhic practices of Ashkenazic (northern and eastern European) Jews and Sephardic (Spanish and Portuguese) Jews diverged enough that Rabbi Moses Isserles of Cracow had to add copious annotations to the Shul an Arukh, the great digest of law published by Sephardic rabbi Joseph Karo in 1575, to adapt it for use by Polish Jewry. Even asidism, the eighteenth-century mystical-pietist movement, and its opponents reached a *modus vivendi* despite the disruptive force of the former.

However, this pluralism had a definite limit: All these Jews accepted the rabbinic way of interpreting Torah as normative. One Jew might conceive of God as the Aristotelian First Cause and another insist that God was the mystical unknowable Infinite; but as long as they were not violating the *halakhah* (e.g., eating pork, doing business on Shabbat, failing to circumcise a son, marrying and divorcing in ways not in accordance with Jewish law), they remained members in good standing of the covenant community. State recognition of a separate Jewish community reinforced this normative Jewish life. The Jewish, Christian, and Muslim legal systems all recognized *Jew* as a legal category, and Jewish communities enjoyed varying degrees of internal self-government, for which *halakhah* was essential.

Modernization, however, called into question every aspect of traditional Jewish life, including the very nature of the covenantal community; the meanings of

---

3. *Pirkei Avot* 1:1. See also B. *Bava Metsia* 59b

God, Torah, and Israel; and their hitherto unbreakable linkage. Enlightenment intellectuals advanced the idea of a state in which religion was irrelevant to citizenship. The state's law governed citizens' behavior, but citizens' consciences were free to believe what they wanted in matters of "faith." Wherever Jews were emancipated, the separate Jewish community came to an end and Judaism was reconceptualized as a "religion" in the model of Protestantism.[3] Reconceptualized Judaism's function was to offer ethical guidance and spiritual uplift – not to regulate either the individual body or the social body.

Many emancipated Jews simply abandoned Judaism, like immigrants to a new country who come to see their native culture as backward and unattractive. Others tried to find some way of maintaining a Jewish life, but again, like immigrants in a completely new environment, much of that life seemed to make no sense, or clashed with the values and mores of the new society. Acculturated laypeople who desired a style of worship appropriate to modern sensibilities created new houses of Jewish worship, which they called "temples" to distinguish them from traditional synagogues. These laypeople did not think about the theological implications of their rejection of most of the commandments. However, when a critical mass of traditionally educated rabbis acquired university educations and realized the extent of the intellectual gap between their beloved tradition and modern knowledge, they created *Reform Judaism*, an intentional reinterpretation of the God-Torah-Israel covenantal nexus.

Jews entered the mainstream of European society precisely at the time and in the places where new ideas about truth were upending centuries of received wisdom. Nineteenth century Europeans were certain that virtually all elements of human culture evolved over time in a linear progression, from "lower" to "higher," from less advanced to more advanced, from primitive and superstitious to enlightened and rational; and that their own time, place, and civilization constituted the pinnacle of human achievement. Universities studied the natural and the social worlds "scientifically," i.e., critically, rather than accepting the truths of the past. Scholars particularly valued the "scientific" study of history, certain that it would reveal truths about the present. Documents were a crucial element of this process, with the result that texts handed down from the past and hitherto revered as divinely revealed were now regarded as human artifacts subject to critical analysis.

---

4. See Leora Batnitzky, *How Judaism Became a Religion: An Introduction to Modern Jewish Thought* (Princeton: Princeton University Press, 2011), especially the Introduction and Chapter 1.

Jewish scholars applied this critical approach to the study of Jewish texts, calling it *Wissenschaft des Judentums*, the "science of Judaism." Rabbis like Abraham Geiger (1810-1874), the main intellectual progenitor of Reform, were certain that the disconnect between Judaism and rational, progressive modernity was the result of the centuries of oppression. Ghettoization had distorted Judaism's natural evolution, but now the critical study of the history of Judaism would reveal the principles according to which Judaism should be properly reformed in the present.[5]

Other academically trained rabbis shared Geiger's commitment to modern scholarship but not his willingness to see all of Judaism's sacred texts as historical artifacts. The differences among these rabbis – over how much of Judaism was divinely revealed, and over which laws could be changed, and how – led to the emergence of three strands of modern Judaism in the nineteenth century: Reform, Positive-Historical (later known as Conservative), and Neo-Orthodoxy (later called modern Orthodoxy). Though they were very different, they all differed from the "traditionalists" who completely rejected all elements of modern thought.

To Geiger and his fellow Reformers, however, *all* the other approaches were merely varieties of "Orthodoxy" – all equally unwilling to allow Judaism to evolve as it should. *Geiger and his reforming colleagues did not think they were creating an alternative form of Judaism that would coexist with Orthodoxy, because they were certain that their studies* proved *that all forms of Orthodoxy would naturally disappear as modernity progressed.* As Isaac Mayer Wise (1819-1900) explained, Orthodoxy was incompatible with "the understanding and consciousness of the nineteenth century" because "the orthodox principle [is] that religion must be in conflict with reason."[6]

5. Abraham Geiger, "A General Introduction to the Science of Judaism," in Max Wiener, *Abraham Geiger and Liberal Judaism: The Challenge of the Nineteenth Century* (Philadelphia: Jewish Publication Society, 1962). See also Michael A. Meyer, "Abraham Geiger's Historical Judaism," in *New Perspectives on Abraham Geiger*, edited by Jakob J. Petuchowski (Cincinnati: Hebrew Union College Press, 1975); and "Religious Ideology" in Michael A. Meyer, ed., *German-Jewish History in Modern Times*, vol. II (New York: Columbia University Press, 1997), 138-151.
6. Isaac Mayer Wise, *American Israelite* Vol. 15, no. 4, 30 April 1869, p. 4, and quoted in James G. Heller, *As Yesterday When It Is Past: A History of the Isaac M. Wise Temple* (Cincinnati, 1942), 3; both cited in Heller, *Isaac M. Wise*, 553-555. See also Kaufmann Kohler, "The Concordance of Judaism and Americanism (1911)," in Paul Mendes-Flohr and Jehuda Reinharz, eds., *The Jew in the Modern World: A Documentary History*, 3rd edition (New York: Oxford University Press, 2011), 525-526, originally published as "American Judaism," *Hebrew Union College and Other Addresses* (Cincinnati: Ark Publishing Company, 1916).

Wise was the great organizer and popularizer of Reform in the US, but the radical Kaufmann Kohler (1843-1926) who drafted the Pittsburgh Platform, was largely responsible for the intellectual core of American Reform Judaism until the 1920s. Kohler insisted that Reform was not a movement within Judaism but rather its inevitable, scientifically verifiable next stage: "Reform is no principle in itself; *progress* is....There is no such thing as an Orthodox or a Reform Jewish science. Science has neither color nor party. Historical study is the study of *progress*."[7] In other words, the founding generations of Reform Judaism believed that their form of Judaism was *the* correct one, and that history would bring about the inevitable switch to Reform among all Jews.

This sense of historical certainty had a geographical aspect as well. Western Europeans looked down on the backward, "oriental" peoples to the east and south of them. Even as western European Jews tried to defend Russian, Romanian, and Ottoman Jewry from persecution, they shared this western contempt for these "oriental" varieties of Judaism. American triumphalism reinforced this perspective. Just as Americans in general viewed their country as a higher stage of nationhood than the states of old Europe, so American Reform leaders viewed America as the place where Judaism would evolve into its highest form. They were certain that America's environment would lead east Europeans to abandon traditionalism and embrace Reform. As American Reform rabbi Max Landsberg confidently assured his rabbinical colleagues in 1894, "To our Jewish brethren who are not yet redeemed from the influence of medieval persecutions, and believe, that Judaism must necessarily be clothed in oriental garments, we are the pioneers who carve the way which, sooner or later, they will all surely follow; we are their torch-bearers."[8]

Reality, however, did not conform to expectations. Yes, modernity led more and more Jews to doubt that God had commanded them at Mt. Sinai not to eat bacon cheeseburgers or lobster salad; but joining a Reform temple was not the inevitable next step. Many Jews found that other ways of being Jewish—Conservative Judaism, or various forms of cultural identity—made more sense to them. And some chose to remain Orthodox. Nevertheless, most twentieth-century Reform Jews shared the conviction that Orthodoxy was incompatible with modernity and would inevitably disappear.[9] In the meantime, however, Reform

---

7. Kaufmann Kohler, "A United Israel," *Central Conference of American Rabbis Yearbook* [henceforth *CCARY*] vol. 8 (1898): 87, 89-90.
8. Max Landsberg, "The Duties of the Rabbi in the Present Time," *CCARY* vol. 5 (1894): 122.
9. See Solomon B. Freehof, *Reform Jewish Practice and Its Rabbinic Background* (Cincinnati: Hebrew Union College Press, 1944), Introduction; see also Joan S. Friedman, *"Guidance, Not Governance": Rabbi Solomon B. Freehof and Reform Responsa* (Cincinnati: Hebrew Union College Press, 2013), 187ff.

had never denied that Orthodoxy was a *valid* form of Judaism, so Reform Jews readily cooperated with Orthodox and Conservative rabbis in all sorts of institutional settings.

Orthodoxy, however, has had a lot of difficulty cooperating with Reform, because it never accepted Reform as a valid form of covenantal living. Reform rejects the Orthodox insistence that "Torah" in the God-Torah-Israel nexus must mean that all the laws of the Torah were divinely revealed and still in force, and that they must be interpreted only according to the views of Orthodox rabbis down to this very day. From an Orthodox perspective, Reform (and Conservatism, as well) went too far in revising the God-Torah-Israel covenantal nexus.

Historical contingency has influenced how this intra-Jewish conflict of ideas plays out today. Orthodoxy has experienced a resurgence since the Shoah, greatly facilitated by its privileged position in the State of Israel, where the state gives the Orthodox rabbinate control over all Jewish religious affairs. The Israeli rabbinate has used its political power for years to try to stop the spread of Reform Judaism in the Jewish state and in struggling Diaspora communities where Israeli assistance comes with Orthodox strings attached.[10] Only in the United States do the majority of religiously identified Jews declare an identification with Reform or Conservative Judaism.[11] "The Guiding Principles of Reform Judaism," http://ccarnet.org/rabbis-speak/platforms/guiding-principles-reform-judaism/. Accessed 23 May 2016. The size and influence of the American Jewish community gives Reform Jews a seat at the transnational Jewish table; but Reform is increasingly compelled to use that seat to fight for recognition as a legitimate form of Judaism, as evidenced by the struggle over space for non-Orthodox prayer at the Western Wall.[12]

10. See these resolutions of the Central Conference of American Rabbis: "Disestablishment of the Chief Rabbinate of Israel, http://ccarnet.org/rabbis-speak/resolutions/all/chief-rabbinate-disestablishment-of-1981/; "Support for Religious Freedom in Israel," http://ccarnet.org/rabbis-speak/resolutions/all/freedom-in-israel-support-for-religious/; "The Israel Supreme Court's Affirmation of Non-Orthodox Conversions in Israel," http://ccarnet.org/rabbis-speak/resolutions/all/israel-supreme-court-s-affirmation-of-non-orthodox-conversions-in-israel/; and numerous other resolutions on "Religious Freedom" and Religious Pluralism" in Israel, http://ccarnet.org/rabbis-speak/resolutions/all/. Accessed 7 June 2016.
11. *A Portrait of Jewish Americans: Findings from a Pew Research Center Survey of U.S. Jews* (Washington, DC: Pew Research Center, 2013), http://www.pewforum.org/2013/10/01/jewish-american-beliefs-attitudes-culture-survey/, 10. Accessed 8 March 2016.
12. Clashes as Non-Orthodox Rabbis Bring Torah Scrolls into Western Wall," *Haaretz* English edition, 2 November 2016. http://www.haaretz.com/israel-news/1.750459. Accessed 5 November 2016. See also Helen Chernikoff and Naomi Zeveloff, "Western Wall Prayer Deal Crumbling as Rivals Stage Dueling 'Provocations,'" *The Forward*, 16 June 2016. http://forward.com/news/israel/342783/western-wall-prayer-deal-crumbling-as-rivals-stage-dueling-provocations/. Accessed 10 October 2016.

Jewish religious pluralism, however, is about more than the Reform/Orthodox struggle. It is also about how Reform defines the boundaries of what constitutes Judaism. Reform makes distinctions and draws boundaries based on an informed and critically reflective understanding of the continuity of Jews and Judaism through history – in other words, by applying the process we described at the beginning of this essay: reflecting on what coheres with what has been the Jewish understanding of the God-Torah-Israel covenantal nexus.

From a Reform perspective, any form of Judaism that is about *Jews* responding to *God* by living a life rooted in the teachings of the *Torah* is a legitimate form of Judaism. We do not read even the most extreme anti-Reform traditionalist out of the Jewish community. Ultra-Orthodox, Orthodox, Conservative, Reconstructionist, Renewal – each in its own way agrees with the Reform movement's 1937 statement that "Judaism is the historical religious experience of the Jewish people."[13] Crucially, we no longer hold to the simplistic nineteenth century view that there is a single "scientifically" correct form of Judaism.

We do, however, exclude variations that are at odds with the historical Jewish religious experience. We categorically reject all the so-called "messianic Jewish" groups, because their belief in Jesus as divine and as savior places them utterly beyond the boundaries of Judaism.[14] The Reform movement also rejects Humanistic Judaism. While many individual Reform Jews may hold views similar to those of the Humanists, the Reform movement itself does not embrace this form of Judaism, because it dismantles the God-Torah-Israel covenantal nexus by eliminating God.[15]

It is important to underscore that Reform also adheres to the historic Jewish legal principle that Jewish status is permanent and cannot be revoked or lost. A Jew who abjures Judaism and adopts another religion is a "transgressor," but

13. "The Guiding Principles of Reform Judaism," http://ccarnet.org/rabbis-speak/platforms/guiding-principles-reform-judaism/. Accessed 23 May 2016.
14. "Deceptive Proselytization of Jews," *CCARY* vol. 96 (1985): 241. See also Responsum #5759.2 "Baptism and Jewish Status," and Responsum #5758.11, "On Patrilineal Descent, Apostasy, and Synagogue Honors," in Mark Washofsky, *Reform Responsa for the Twenty-First Century*, vol. I (New York: CCAR Press, 2010), e-book. In the early twentieth century many Reform Jews were attracted to Christian Science; in 1912 the CCAR declared that formal affiliation with that church also put a Jew outside the pale of Judaism. *CCARY* vol. 22 (1912): 229-236.
15. For an overview of the matter see Dana Evan Kaplan, *American Reform Judaism: An Introduction* (New Brunswick: Rutgers University Press, 2003), 54-55, and Friedman, *"Guidance, Not Governance,"* 251-252. See also Eugene Mihaly, "Qualifications for Membership in the Union of American Hebrew Congregations (Cincinnati: Beth Adam, 1990), and "Responsum #5751.4, "Humanistic Congregation," in W. Gunther Plaut and Mark Washofsky, eds., *Teshuvot for the Nineties* (New York: CCAR Press, 1997).

still a Jew.[16] In the pre-modern world apostate Jews were "banned"—excluded from the Jewish community. In the modern world, when identities—including religious identities—are increasingly fluid, individual Jews sometimes choose to adopt spiritual practices or beliefs from other traditions. Ethical Culture, Christian Science, Unitarian-Universalism, and Zen Buddhism have all attracted modern Jews over the last 150 years. Reform rabbis are saddened when Jews neglect or disdain their own spiritual heritage while looking elsewhere, but prefer to decide on an individual basis whether a person has crossed the line from interest to a formal commitment that would lead to their exclusion from Jewish religious life, usually after consultation with the Responsa Committee, the committee of Reform rabbis that offers guidance on questions of Jewish practice on the basis of precedents in traditional rabbinic sources.[17]

In conclusion, then, we can say that Reform Judaism exists comfortably within the reality of a pluralistic Jewish world, and is confident that in both its openness to religious pluralism and its recognition of limits to that pluralism, it is consistent with historic Jewish tradition.

Source: Rabbi Joan S. Friedman, "Jewish Religious Pluralism," from *A Life of Meaning: Embracing Reform Judaism's Sacred Path*, ed. by Rabbi Dana Evan Kaplan (New York: CCAR Press, 2017).

16. *Yisrael af al pi shechata Yisrael hu*, "A Jew who has sinned nevertheless remains a Jew." Babylonian Talmud, *Y'vamot* 47b and Rashi, s.v. *de'i hadar be*; Babylonian Talmud, *Sanhedrin* 44a; Maimonides, *Mishneh Torah, Hilchot Isurei Biah* 13:17; *Shulchan Aruch, Yoreh Dei-ah* 268:2; *Maggid Mishneh* to *Mishneh Torah, Hilchot Yibum V'chalitzah* 1:6, s.v. *mi sheyesh*; *Mishneh Torah, Hilchot Ishut* 4:16.
17. See the numerous relevant references at http://www.ccarnet.org/rabbis-speak/reform-responsa/index/. Accessed 10 October 2016.

On the Jewish People

RABBI EVAN MOFFIC

Covenant is the sustaining idea of Jewish life. It connotes a sacred relationship, a commitment between God and the Jewish people. It began with Abraham. It was affirmed by Moses in the Exodus from Egypt. And it was sealed with the entire people through the giving and acceptance of the Torah at Mount Sinai. It is sustained through the practice of mitzvot. To live by the covenant is to make the Torah sacred and to make ourselves and our community sacred.

Yet, sacred does not mean frozen. The covenant is dynamic. It is not fixed by one time and place. It is rooted in the past, yet evolves into the future. We are meant to hear the word of God in the present tense. We are meant to listen for its message for our time. Martin Buber expressed this as follows: "The eternal revelation is here and now. I do not believe in a self-definition of God prior to the experience of human beings. . . . The eternal voice of strength flows, the eternal voice sounds forth to us now" (Buber, *I and Thou*, 84–85).

Buber's conception may sound mystical, but it is also eminently practical and relevant for us today. Rabbi Jonathan Sacks paints a picture of what Buber's conception means in action in a beautiful story about an encounter he had. Rabbi Sacks was the chief rabbi of Great Britain from 1990 to 2013, and his work included several cutting-edge questions of medical ethics. In this capacity, he met with Lord Robert Winston, one of the world's leading researchers on in vitro fertilization, embryo development, and the human genome.

During their visit in Lord Winston's office, Sacks noticed a copy of the Five Books of Moses, wedged between volumes of the latest scientific research. In addition, several volumes of commentary, along with a prayer book, sat near them.

Even though he is a cutting-edge scientist pushing the boundaries of life, Lord Winston is a deeply religious man whose faith guides him in the critical work he does. For him, the covenant is ongoing, continuing to guide his work and values.

So it is with us. We do not live *in* the past. Rather, we live *with* the past, drawing from the accumulated wisdom of our tradition in order to build a better future. We see our lives as part of a journey that began before us, continues after us, and is carried forward by and through us. That is what it means to be part of a covenant.

Source: Rabbi Evan Moffic, in *Lights in the Forest: Rabbis Respond to Twelve Essential Jewish Questions*, ed. Rabbi Paul Citrin (New York: CCAR Press, 2014), 197–198.

A Statement of Principles
for Reform Judaism

ADOPTED AT THE 1999 PITTSBURGH CONVENTION
CENTRAL CONFERENCE OF AMERICAN RABBIS
MAY 1999—SIVAN 5759

Preamble

On three occasions during the last century and a half, the Reform rabbinate has adopted comprehensive statements to help guide the thought and practice of our movement. In 1885, fifteen rabbis issued the Pittsburgh Platform, a set of guidelines that defined Reform Judaism for the next fifty years. A revised statement of principles, the Columbus Platform, was adopted by the Central Conference of American Rabbis in 1937. A third set of rabbinic guidelines, the Centenary Perspective, appeared in 1976 on the occasion of the centenary of the Union of American Hebrew Congregations and the Hebrew Union College-Jewish Institute of Religion. Today, when so many individuals are striving for religious meaning, moral purpose and a sense of community, we believe it is our obligation as rabbis once again to state a set of principles that define Reform Judaism in our own time.

Throughout our history, we Jews have remained firmly rooted in Jewish tradition, even as we have learned much from our encounters with other cultures. The great contribution of Reform Judaism is that it has enabled the Jewish people to introduce innovation while preserving tradition, to embrace diversity while asserting commonality, to affirm beliefs without rejecting those who doubt, and to bring faith to sacred texts without sacrificing critical scholarship.

This "Statement of Principles" affirms the central tenets of Judaism—God, Torah and Israel—even as it acknowledges the diversity of Reform Jewish beliefs and practices. It also invites all Reform Jews to engage in a dialogue with the sources of our tradition, responding out of our knowledge, our experience and our faith. Thus we hope to transform our lives through *k'dushah*, holiness.

God

We affirm the reality and oneness of God, even as we may differ in our understanding of the Divine presence.

We affirm that the Jewish people is bound to God by an eternal (*b'rit*), covenant, as reflected in our varied understandings of Creation, Revelation and Redemption.

We affirm that every human being is created (*b'tzelem Elohim*), in the image of God, and that therefore every human life is sacred.

We regard with reverence all of God's creation and recognize our human responsibility for its preservation and protection.

We encounter God's presence in moments of awe and wonder, in acts of justice and compassion, in loving relationships and in the experiences of everyday life.

We respond to God daily: through public and private prayer, through study and through the performance of other *mitzvot*, sacred obligations—(*bein adam la Makom*), to God, and (*bein adam la-chaveiro*), to other human beings.

We strive for a faith that fortifies us through the vicissitudes of our lives—illness and healing, transgression and repentance, bereavement and consolation, despair and hope.

We continue to have faith that, in spite of the unspeakable evils committed against our people and the sufferings endured by others, the partnership of God and humanity will ultimately prevail.

We trust in our tradition's promise that, although God created us as finite beings, the spirit within us is eternal.

Torah

We affirm that Torah is the foundation of Jewish life.

We cherish the truths revealed in Torah, God's ongoing revelation to our people and the record of our people's ongoing relationship with God.

We affirm that Torah is a manifestation of (*ahavat olam*), God's eternal love for the Jewish people and for all humanity.

We affirm the importance of studying Hebrew, the language of Torah and Jewish liturgy, that we may draw closer to our people's sacred texts.

We are called by Torah to lifelong study in the home, in the synagogue and in every place where Jews gather to learn and teach. Through Torah study we are called to (*mitzvot*), the means by which we make our lives holy.

We are committed to the ongoing study of the whole array of (*mitzvot*) and to the fulfillment of those that address us as individuals and as a community. Some of these (*mitzvot*), sacred obligations, have long been observed by Reform Jews; others, both ancient and modern, demand renewed attention as the result of the unique context of our own times.

We bring Torah into the world when we seek to sanctify the times and places of our lives through regular home and congregational observance. Shabbat calls us to bring the highest moral values to our daily labor and to culminate the workweek with (*k'dushah*), holiness, (*m'nuchah*), rest and (*oneg*), joy. The High Holy Days call us to account for our deeds. The Festivals enable us to celebrate with joy our people's religious journey in the context of the changing seasons. The days of remembrance remind us of the tragedies and the triumphs that have shaped our people's historical experience both in ancient and modern times. And we mark the milestones of our personal journeys with traditional and creative rites that reveal the holiness in each stage of life.

We bring Torah into the world when we strive to fulfill the highest ethical mandates in our relationships with others and with all of God's creation. Partners with God in (*tikkun olam*), repairing the world, we are called to help bring nearer the messianic age. We seek dialogue and joint action with people of other faiths in the hope that together we can bring peace, freedom and justice to our world. We are obligated to pursue (*tzedek*), justice and righteousness, and to narrow the gap between the affluent and the poor, to act against discrimination and oppression, to pursue peace, to welcome the stranger, to protect the earth's biodiversity and natural resources, and to redeem those in physical, economic and spiritual bondage. In so doing, we reaffirm social action and social justice as a central prophetic focus of traditional Reform Jewish belief and practice. We affirm the (*mitzvah*) of (*tzedakah*), setting aside portions of our earnings and our time to provide for those in need. These acts bring us closer to fulfilling the prophetic call to translate the words of Torah into the works of our hands. In all these ways and more, Torah gives meaning and purpose to our lives.

Israel

We are Israel, a people aspiring to holiness, singled out through our ancient covenant and our unique history among the nations to be witnesses to God's presence. We are linked by that covenant and that history to all Jews in every age and place.

We are committed to the (*mitzvah*) of (*ahavat Yisrael*), love for the Jewish people, and to (*k'lal Yisrael*), the entirety of the community of Israel. Recognizing that (*kol Yisrael arevim zeh bazeh*), all Jews are responsible for one another, we reach out to all Jews across ideological and geographical boundaries.

We embrace religious and cultural pluralism as an expression of the vitality of Jewish communal life in Israel and the Diaspora.

We pledge to fulfill Reform Judaism's historic commitment to the complete equality of women and men in Jewish life.

We are an inclusive community, opening doors to Jewish life to people of all ages, to varied kinds of families, to all regardless of their sexual orientation, to (*gerim*), those who have converted to Judaism, and to all individuals and families, including the intermarried, who strive to create a Jewish home.

We believe that we must not only open doors for those ready to enter our faith, but also to actively encourage those who are seeking a spiritual home to find it in Judaism.

We are committed to strengthening the people Israel by supporting individuals and families in the creation of homes rich in Jewish learning and observance.

We are committed to strengthening the people Israel by making the synagogue central to Jewish communal life, so that it may elevate the spiritual, intellectual and cultural quality of our lives.

We are committed to (*M'dinat Yisrael*), the State of Israel, and rejoice in its accomplishments. We affirm the unique qualities of living in (*Eretz Yisrael*), the land of Israel, and encourage (*aliyah*), immigration to Israel.

We are committed to a vision of the State of Israel that promotes full civil, human and religious rights for all its inhabitants and that strives for a lasting peace between Israel and its neighbors.

We are committed to promoting and strengthening Progressive Judaism in Israel, which will enrich the spiritual life of the Jewish state and its people.

We affirm that both Israeli and Diaspora Jewry should remain vibrant and interdependent communities. As we urge Jews who reside outside Israel to learn Hebrew as a living language and to make periodic visits to Israel in order to study and to deepen their relationship to the Land and its people, so do we affirm that Israeli Jews have much to learn from the religious life of Diaspora Jewish communities.

We are committed to furthering Progressive Judaism throughout the world as a meaningful religious way of life for the Jewish people.

In all these ways and more, Israel gives meaning and purpose to our lives.

(Baruch she-amar v'hayah ha-olam).

Praised be the One through whose word all things came to be.

May our words find expression in holy actions.

May they raise us up to a life of meaning devoted to God's service And to the redemption of our world.

Source: "A Statement of Principles for Reform Judaism: Adopted at the 1999 Pittsburgh Convention, Central Conference of American Rabbis, May 1999<em dash>Sivan 5759," CCAR, http://ccarnet.org/rabbis-speak/platforms/statement-principles-reform-judaism/

Jewish Ethics and Values

Midrashic Thoughts

Said the roman procurator Turnus Rufus to Rabbi Akiva: "Whose acts are greater, those of human beings or those of God?"

Rabbi Akiva answered: "The deeds of human beings are greater."

Surprised, Turnus Rufus asked, "But can you create the heavens and the earth?" Akiva replied, "Do not speak to me of what is beyond the reach of humankind. Speak of what is available to human beings."

Akiva then brought to Turnus Rufus wheat stalks and cakes, raw flax and fine linen. "The wheat and the flax are the work of God," said Akiva, "but the cakes and the linen were made by human beings. Are they not superior?"

So our Sages taught: "All created things require refining and improvement. The mustard seed needs to be sweetened; the lupine needs to be soaked; the wheat needs to be ground, and the human being needs to be repaired."

The world that is given into our hands is still incomplete. Go forth, then, and work to make it better.

—Based on Midrash *Tanchuma*, *Tazria* 5
and Midrash *Genesis Rabbah* 11.6

Commentary

"The deeds of human beings are greater." Rabbi Harold Schulweis sees this statement as affirming the partnership of God and humanity, and reflecting two dimensions of the Divine: *Elohim*, Giver of the natural world, and *Adonai*, the godliness implanted within us. He writes:

"How do I understand Akiva's response? Is it a denigration of God? By no means. Akiva is here rejecting the split thinking of either/or. Either God or man. Either above or below. Either *Elohim* or *Adonai*.

"What Akiva insists is that both are involved in the benediction of creation. God and humanity. In the *motzi* benediction (*Baruch atah, Adonai, Eloheinu melech haolam, hamotzi lechem min haaretz*), *Elohim* is revealed in sun, seed, water, and soil— the raw material that none of us has created. Still the raw sheaf of wheat is inedible. One needs to have God-given human intelligence, human competence, and purpose to till the soil, to pull the weeds, to water the ground, to grind the wheat, to bake the bread. The *motzi* blessing expresses appreciation of the transaction between God and person that transforms sheaves into bread."

TURNUS RUFUS. A Roman governor in Judea during the 2nd century CE. Rabbinic literature presents debates between him and Rabbi Akiva. In some cases, these dialogues reflect our Sages' wrestling with issues that troubled them; questions placed in the mouth of a Roman leader allow the Rabbis a safe way to articulate their own doubts and struggles. Here, the discussion centers on whether it is proper for human beings to interfere with the order of creation—for example, by circumcising a child. Akiva's answer affirms that humanity is empowered and, indeed, enjoined to engage actively and creatively with the world.

RABBI HAROLD SCHULWEIS, 1925–2014.

Source: Rabbi Edwin Goldberg, Rabbi Janet Marder, Rabbi Sheldon Marder, and Rabbi Leon Morris, eds., *Mishkan HaNefesh: Machzor for the Days of Awe*, vol. 2, *Yom Kippur* (New York: CCAR Press, 2015), 163.

Rava taught: When we are led in for Judgment in the next world, we will be asked these questions:

1. Did you conduct your business honestly?
2. Did you set a time to study?
3. Did you leave a legacy for future generations?
4. Did you have hope in your heart?
5. Did you get your priorities straight?
6. Did you enjoy this world?
7. Were you the best you could be?

Among the Righteous of the Nations: Wallenberg

Wallenberg—
no smaller than his myth
Real, ideal, handsome,
big-hearted, pushy-for-Life, tireless—
all of those

At long last
I don't have to expect
someone will write a book before I die
tearing apart his Image
like they did to the Kennedys and King

Hype and wishful thinking, exaggeration won't touch him.
He was, indeed, what he was.

The beggar who has been sitting and sleeping
on the same bench in the park
day after day,
surrounded by paper bags stuffed with her belongings,

has now become a donor:
feeding with crumbs the pigeons and sparrows
in a broad circle about her.

RAVA TAUGHT. Adapted from Ron Wolfson (b. 1949), based on Talmud *Shabbat* 31a.

AMONG THE RIGHTEOUS OF THE NATIONS. By Danny Siegel (b. 1944). Raoul Wallenberg (1912–1947?) was a Swedish diplomat and humanitarian who served in Nazi-occupied Budapest during World War II. By issuing protective passes and hiding Jews in "safe houses" designated as Swedish terri-tory, Wallenberg saved tens of thousands of Hungarian Jews from deportation and death.

THE BEGGAR. By Charles Reznikoff (1894–1976).

Source: Rabbi Edwin Goldberg, Rabbi Janet Marder, Rabbi Sheldon Marder, and Rabbi Leon Morris, eds., *Mishkan HaNefesh: Machzor for the Days of Awe*, vol. 2, *Yom Kippur* (New York: CCAR Press, 2015), 377.

On Our Humanity

Rabbi Denise Eger

> Rabbi Akiva would say, "Beloved is humanity for we were made in the image of God. And doubly beloved are we for God made it known to us that we are made in God's image."
>
> —*Pirkei Avot* 3:14

Judaism teaches that humanity was created in the image of God. This principle, known in Hebrew as *b'tzelem Elohim* comes directly from the Torah. In Genesis 1:26–27 the text tells us:

> God now said, "Let us make human beings in Our image, after Our likeness; and let them hold sway over the fish of the sea and the birds of the sky, over the beasts, over all the earth, over all that creeps upon the earth." So God created the human beings in [the divine] image, creating [them] in the image of God, creating them male and female.

This is a most profound statement. Human beings are godlike. Not gods themselves, but fashioned after the image of God. We know what human beings look like, but what does God look like? Are we to infer that God has limbs and a face? Or is there something else being taught by these passages?

Our rabbis and our teachers rejected the idea of the physical resemblance between humankind and God. In fact, God rejects this as well in the Ten Commandments: we are told, "Make no graven images" (Exodus 20:4). We are not to represent God in any physical form, not with carvings, drawings, or idols so prevalent in our worlds, both ancient and contemporary. But our rabbis and sages did teach that human beings can strive to have god-like qualities. They base this on a passage in our Torah, "You shall be holy, for I, the Eternal your God, am holy" (Leviticus 19:2).

Judaism has embraced this ideal of a God we cannot see but a God we can feel and come to know through our study of Torah, through our performance of our sacred responsibilities—a God who has a relationship with the community of Israel and the world. God is found in the way we fulfill the mitzvot. So as we "Remember the Sabbath day and keep it holy" (Exodus 20:8) or obey "You must have completely honest weights and completely honest measures" (Deuteronomy 25:15), we are striving to live in the image of God.

This story from the Talmud frames the meaning of *b'tzelem Elohim*, being made in the image of God:

> Rabbi Chama, son of Rabbi Chanina, said: What does the Torah mean when it says, "You shall walk in the ways of *Adonai*" (Deuteronomy 13:5)? Can a person really walk in the shadow of the Divine Presence? Rather, it means that you should imitate the ways of God. Just as God clothed the naked (as it says: "And God made garments of skin for Adam and his wife and clothed them" [Genesis 3:21]), so you shall clothe the naked. Just as God visited the sick ("And God appeared before Abraham" [after his circumcision] [Genesis 18:1]), so you should visit the sick; just as God buried the dead (as it says: "And God buried Moses in the valley" [Deuteronomy 34:6]), so you should bury the dead; and just as God comforts the grieving (as it says: "After the death of Abraham, God blessed Isaac his son" [Genesis 25:11]), so you too should comfort the grieving. (Babylonian Talmud, *Sotah* 14a)

The meaning of *b'tzelem Elohim* means striving to live a life of fairness, justice, compassion, understanding, and holiness. These are the attributes of the Divine One that humanity can live by.

Source: Rabbi Denise Eger, in *Lights in the Forest: Rabbis Respond to Twelve Essential Jewish Questions*, ed. Rabbi Paul Citrin (New York: CCAR Press, 2014), 92–94.

On Our Humanity

RABBI STEPHEN LEWIS FUCHS

Being created in God's image certainly does not mean that we look like God. It means that of all the creatures on earth, we have the most godlike powers. It means that we human beings are in charge of and responsible for life on this planet. It is an awesome responsibility with which God has entrusted us.

God charges us in Genesis 1:28:

פְּרוּ וּרְבוּ וּמִלְאוּ אֶת הָאָרֶץ וְכִבְשֻׁהָ וּרְדוּ בִּדְגַת הַיָּם וּבְעוֹף
הַשָּׁמַיִם וּבְכָל חַיָּה הָרֹמֶשֶׂת עַל הָאָרֶץ.

*P'ru urvu u'milu et haaretz v'chibshuha urdu bidgat hayam uv'of
hashamayim uv'chol chaya haromeset al haaretz.*

My rendering of this passage is: "Be fruitful and multiply and fill up the earth and take responsibility for it. And rule compassionately over the fish of the sea, the birds of the air, and all the living things that creep on the earth."

My translation reflects the midrashic teaching (*B'reishit Rabbah* 8:11) that we human beings stand midway between God and all the other animals on earth. Like the animals, we eat, drink, sleep, eliminate our wastes, procreate, and die. But in a godlike way, we have the power to think, analyze, communicate, and shape our environment in a manner far beyond other creatures.

In the afternoon service for Yom Kippur in *Gates of Repentance* (415) we find a magnificent liturgical expression of what it means to be created in the divine image:

We were unlike other creatures.
Not for us the tiger's claws,

the elephant's thick hide,
or the crocodile's scaly armor.
To the gazelle we were slow of foot, to the lioness a weakling,
and the eagle thought us bound to earth.
But You gave us powers they could not comprehend: a skillful hand,
a probing mind . . .
a soul aspiring to know and fulfill its destiny.

Being created in the divine image means that we humans are the only creatures on earth who can mine iron ore from the side of a mountain and turn the iron into steel. From that steel, we forge the most delicate of instruments with which to operate on a human brain or an open heart, or we use that steel to make weapons whose only purpose is to kill and maim. Being created in God's image means we have awesome, earth-enhancing, or earth-shattering power.

God's hope in creating us in the divine image is that we use our power to help create on this planet a more just, caring, and compassionate society than exists today. But we—not God—will decide if we choose to do so or not.

Source: Rabbi Stephen Lewis Fuchs, in *Lights in the Forest: Rabbis Respond to Twelve Essential Jewish Questions*, ed. Rabbi Paul Citrin (New York: CCAR Press, 2014), 98–99.

On Our Humanity

RABBI JUDITH SCHINDLER

1

Being created in the image of God gives us human rights. The Talmud teaches that all human beings were created from one human being so that no person can say, "My ancestor is greater than yours" (*Sanhedrin* 37a). The Sages add that we were created "from the four corners of the earth—yellow clay and white sand, black loam and red soil—so that the earth can declare to no part of humanity that it does not belong here, that this soil is not its rightful home" (*Yalkut Shimoni* 1:1). We were created as equals. Each one of us is deserving of our God-given humanity, dignity, and equality.

Being created in the image of God gives us responsibilities. We are required to honor the image of God in all human beings and create a world that supports, rather than subjugates, the stranger in our midst: the one who is unknown to us or the one whose difference seems strange. Race, religion, weight, ability, sexual orientation or identification, and country of origin are just a handful of the differences that create the colorful quilt of our congregations, country, and world.

Being created in the image of God gives us creativity. Genesis requires us to be co-creators and partners with God in completing Creation.

Being created in the image of God means we must strive to actualize that which is godlike in ourselves. In our sacred texts, God embodies the ideals for which we strive. God pursues peace. God demands justice. God acts with mercy.

Rashi teaches that being created in the image of God means that we are endowed with the qualities of understanding and discernment. May we develop these traits. Nachmanides notes that being created in the image of God reflects

37

our immortality. May we work not only for the present but for the future so that our labors on behalf of others and the lessons we teach our children live on. The midrash teaches that God originally created human beings with two faces and then divided them (*B'reishit Rabbah* 8:1). Just as we can see God in the seventy faces of each and every verse of Torah (*B'midbar Rabbah* 13:15–16), so too can we see a God in the face of every human being. Being created in the image of God means we are inextricably bound to all creation, for God dwells in everyone and everything.

2

In God's image, male and female, God created the first human being. The concept of gender is woven into our image of God and into the fabric of Creation. As a sacred text, Torah binds us together as Jews and inspires us to live by the highest ideals. As a humanly authored text, Torah portrays God according to its contemporaneous understanding of gender. As one example, Torah identifies God as *rachum*, "compassionate." The root letters form the word *rechem*, which means "womb," thereby connecting God to the image of a mother, nurturer, and creator of life. Elsewhere, God is described as Adonai Tz'vaot, meaning "God of hosts or armies," reflecting a male militaristic God who protects His people and roots out evil. God commands not only the heavenly hosts but also the earthly armies who fight on God's behalf.

The kabbalists teach that the Hebrew name *Adam* for the first human being comes from the Hebrew *adameh*, meaning "I will be like," from Isaiah 14:14, which reads, "I will be like the Most High." Adam strives to make himself like God, and all of us who are descended from him strive for the same. We have human bodies with godly souls. To be fully human is to actualize the potential with which we were created. We are not meant to limit our aspirations of embodying only the female attributes of God if we are woman or the male attributes of God if we are man. Today, we see sexes crossing traditional lines of work and ways of being. Women can be soldiers and scholars, and men can be healers and homemakers. Being human means mirroring the full spectrum of God's attributes (*midot*).

I am a fraternal twin, and in a small way, my birth was likened to that of the first human being. Male and female, my brother and I were brought into this world. While we joke that we are polar opposites, our differences are never related to gender. It was our social, academic, and professional paths that varied.

According to Rashi, the *tzeila* that was taken from man to create the first woman should be translated as "side" rather than the more commonly used "rib." Man and woman were two sides of one being and then divided. The wholeness (*shalom*, שָׁלוֹם) for which Jews strive cannot be achieved by acting alone. Bringing perfection to our world is not about realizing one's own specific gender traits but rather about collaborating with others to maximize God's worldly reflections. Our goal is to nurture within ourselves those traits, whether traditionally male or female, that will help us better our world and be effective partners in completing Creation.

3

Living in a southern city with hundreds of churches, I hear the terms "grace," "love," and "salvation" regularly spoken at social events. In Christianity, these attributes are God's gifts, which from the human perception may be undeservedly given. One needs to deeply desire them, and God will respond as a parent who unconditionally loves, forgives, and saves a child. Even the most hardened criminal need only repent in his heart and these divine rewards will be attained. In Judaism, God's attributes of justice and mercy both come into play. As Moses and the Israelites learned after committing spiritual adultery by building the Golden Calf, God's forgiveness, grace, and love must be earned through our actions of repentance and repair (*tikkun*). Being rewarded for the good we have done, rather than being punished for the pain we have caused, is based on our actions.

Living in the South has taught me about "southern grace," which entails hospitality, etiquette, and appearing your best: writing thankyou notes and offering up sweet tea. In all religions, but especially Judaism, God demands more. When the prophets of our faith approached God in petition (as in Abraham's plea to save the innocent of Sodom), they prefaced their request with the phrase *im matzati chein b'einecha*, "if I have found favor [literally, 'grace'] in Your eyes." God's grace is earned through actions of justice and goodness.

In Judaism, salvation is not about saving souls but about saving our world. The title of Rabbi Robert Levine's book, *There Is No Messiah and You're It*, captures our human responsibility for bringing about deliverance. I believe that merely praying for a savior and waiting for salvation will get us nowhere. We can open doors as a gesture of hospitality; we can open doors as a ritual act as we do for Elijah at Passover; or, we can truly open doors to the oppressed so that their rights are attained, and to the hungry and homeless so that the structures that perpetuate economic inequity are rebuilt on the foundation of justice.

Love, in Judaism, likewise finds its primary expression in human beings rather than emanating from God. Love, like prayer, requires reaching out in three directions. We must reach inward and love ourselves. We much reach outward and love others. We much reach upward, not in the literal direction but in spiritual aspiration, and love God by loving God's Creation and by bringing the ideals of our religion into reality.

4

In Genesis, God created *Adam*, the first human being, from *adamah*, the earth. God then breathed the breath of life into that first individual. Our bodies, our physical and genetic composition, were formed by our biological parents. Our souls were given to us by God and nurtured by those who raised and taught us. Just as the ark is the sacred vessel that houses our Torah, so is the body the sacred home to our soul. Both the Torah and our souls transcend time.

Albert Einstein is often cited for quoting the law of conservation of matter and energy: "Energy cannot be created or destroyed, it can only be changed from one form to another." I believe that the energy that forms our soul does not die. As a rabbi, I accompany congregants on their end-of-life journey. With them, I walk to the edge. I witness their bodies weaken as their souls remain strong until their last breath. Reflecting Einstein's theory, I believe the energy of a person's soul doesn't die. It lives on in the universe. Perhaps it returns to God. Perhaps, as the mystics of the Kabbalah teach, it makes another *gilgul*—another circle through life as it lives, learns, and strives for godliness.

While one's soul living on after one dies is a matter of faith, living on through the legacy we leave is matter of fact. I rely on both when it comes to keeping alive the spirit of my own father, Rabbi Alexander Schindler, of blessed memory. Rabbi Yochanan said in the name of Rabbi Shimon bar Yochai, "Every scholar who is quoted in this world, his lips whisper from the grave" (Babylonian Talmud, *Y'vamot* 96b–97a). Among the many ways that my father's words live on are through his teachings that people continue to quote. Through the transformative Interfaith and Outreach Initiative that he envisioned in 1987 as president of the then-UAHC (now URJ), he is brought to life every day in synagogues across the globe. On a mystical level, too, my father's soul speaks to me. My father was my teacher and mentor, who taught me how to craft sermons and eulogies and how to be a rabbi. When exhaustion overcomes me and I don't know how to find the words to soften the pain of those experiencing a tragedy or inspire a congregation on a holy day, a divine energy and my dad's energy move me forward. In the same way that we can connect with God as a wellspring of healing and strength, so can we connect with the soul energy of our loved ones after their breath/soul (*n'shamah*) leaves them and returns to its Source.

Source: Rabbi Judith Schindler, in *Lights in the Forest: Rabbis Respond to Twelve Essential Jewish Questions*, ed. Rabbi Paul Citrin (New York: CCAR Press, 2014), 132–137.

Not More Than My Place,
Not Less Than My Space

How do I balance the desire to be acknowledged
while making space for others to shine?

RABBI LAURA GELLER

The morning service of the High Holy Day begins with *Hineni* ("Here I Am..."), a prayer that points to a challenge in my life. Composed by an anonymous cantor in Eastern Europe, it reflects the anxiety the *hazzan* (cantor) feels on the Days of Awe in the face of the awesome responsibility of being the *shaliach tzibor*, the community's emissary in prayer. It opens with the words, "How can I, with so little merit, stand before God to plead for the people...." The prayer seems to be about humility. But the way it is generally prayed seems just the opposite. The ark is opened; the congregation stands. The cantor enters from the back of the sanctuary and begins to sing, calling attention to himself or herself.

What does humility really mean? How can you find the right balance between acknowledging how little merit you truly have and calling attention to yourself?

One way, says Rabbi Simcha, Bunim of Psischke (1765–1827), is to always carry two notes in your pockets. The one in the right pocket reads: "The world was created for my sake." The one in the left pocket reads: "I am but dust and ashes." Humility is the space between those two extremes.

To get this balance right in my own life, I have begun to study Mussar, a Jewish spiritual practice rooted in the Bible but mostly developed in 19th-century

Lithuania. Its goal is to help an individual work on his or her own individual character or soul traits *(middot)* in order to become more holy. Each of us is challenged by specific *middot*. Noticing those challenges unveils our own personal spiritual curriculum.

Humility is a *middah* at the center of mine.

In his book *Everyday Holiness,* my Mussar guide Alan Morinis points to the teaching of the 11th-century Spanish Jewish philosopher Rabbi Bachya ibn Pekuda that "... humility is a primary soul trait to work on because it entails an unvarnished and honest assessment of who you are." Morinis explains: "The ego provides the lens through which we see all of life. To be arrogant or self-deprecating distorts our approach to life. Humility stands on a foundation of self-esteem, and is defined by how much space you occupy. Being humble means occupying your rightful space, which can be physical, verbal, emotional, financial, and so on."

Humility challenges come up every day. Some seem small, such as deciding whether to be the first to speak up at a meeting or to wait for others to start the conversation; choosing to respond to another person's story with a story of my own, or being mindful of what that other person might need from me at the moment. Others seem bigger; what motivates a decision to write an article or give a public lecture or agree to serve on the Board of Directors of a community organization?

* * *

Sometimes we can gain insights into ourselves through the confessions of others. Several years ago, a much-loved Jewish physician shared with me her deep disappointment upon learning that *Los Angeles* magazine had not included her on its list of the city's 100 best doctors. "I know it doesn't matter," she confided, "but it still feels as though I am not being seen for how good a doctor I really am. I feel hurt, angry, and a little envious of those who made it onto the list. Is it wrong or arrogant of me to want to be publicly acknowledged for my hard work?"

I suggested she view the question through the lens of the Jewish teaching that each of us is imbued with a *yetzer tov* (inclination for good) and a *yetzer hara* (inclination for bad), both of which are necessary for us to be successful. The 11th-century Jewish philosopher Maimonides taught that "without the *yetzer hara,* no one would marry, build a house, or seek a profession." This point is also made in a cautionary tale from the Talmud. Once the ancient rabbis captured the *yetzer hara* and sealed it up in a chest. All of a sudden, hens stopped laying eggs. We learn from this story: "If you kil this spirit, the entire world will be destroyed" *(Yoma* 69b).

That same *yetzer hara* part of her that desired public recognition also accounted for the drive, ambition, and commitment that led to her helping so many others. Without this impulse, she would never have gone to medical school, never endured her internship and residency, never rushed out in the middle of the night to deliver a baby.

From a Jewish perspective, ambition is a positive value. It follows that there is nothing wrong with wanting to be noticed, acknowledged, and seen—or, in the language of Mussar, claiming "not less than my space."

This, however, is only half of the equation; it must be balanced with "not more than my place."

***

Like the doctor, I am prone to "list envy." For the past several years, *Newsweek* magazine has published a list of the 50 most influential rabbis in America I'm not on the list. It's true that many talented, influential, and deserving rabbis also haven't made it. Still. not being on the list is...so public!

I rationalize that the list criteria are not those by which I would hope to be measured. Points are awarded for notoriety, media mentions, and size of constituency and not for spirituality, activism, being present in people's lives . . . Friends don't care if I am on it. My family teases me about my desire to be included. My congregants don't seem to notice. Such lists are not a real measure of who I am as a rabbi or what impact my work has had on my community. The Mussar work then challenges me to ask: What motivates wanting to be on someone's list? It cautions, in the words of the contemporary Mussar teacher Rabbi Shlomo Wolbe, "One who craves attention from others has not yet found himself. He is unaware of his true worth."

Maybe it is my *yetzer hara* that induces me to want to make the list—the same *yetzer hara* that served me well when I was one of the first women to become a rabbi. In those early years, when even the idea of a woman rabbi was resisted by many, my ambition to be successful and acknowledged (along with a sense of humor) helped me overcome the many stumbling blocks that might otherwise have seemed insurmountable. As a pioneer, I was often invited to sit on boards, participate in conferences, and do media interviews on the role of women in Judaism. Was it my *yetzer hara* that enjoyed the challenge? On one memorable radio show, the unsympathetic host asked, "What is more important—your Judaism or your feminism?" I paused, then shot back: "And what is more important to you—your heart or your liver?" Silence. I was never invited back on the program.

Today, some 30 years later, women in the rabbinate are not a novelty but the norm, and thankfully we are no longer compelled to justify our existence as spiritual leaders. I am still ambitious, but the goal of my ambition has changed. It is no longer about proving anything to anyone. Now it is about creating a congregation that really makes a difference in people's lives. And to do that, I need to get the balance right—"not more than my place; not less than my space." Creating that congregation requires making space for my talented colleagues to share their gifts; it means finding and empowering lay leaders to share in crafting and implementing our vision for the community. If I don't get that balance right, it will never happen.

Through my *Mussar* work, I have discovered three strategies to help me find balance. The first is to look at what I actually have accomplished over the years. For me, the real measure of success is my congregation having become a community I would join if I weren't the rabbi. The Shabbat morning *minyan* is my prayer community. I pray there every week whether I am leading services or not. My congregation nurtures me spiritually and it makes me proud and grateful. Gratitude, noticing the abundance already present in my life, is an antidote for wanting more of a "place" than I actually need.

The second strategy is to seek out honest friends and mentors who don't flatter me, but rather open my eyes to see myself as I really am, with all my strengths and weaknesses. These friends and mentors have gently pushed me to keep learning and growing. They have supported me as I stretched out of my comfort zone to participate in continuing education programs ranging from a summer Hebrew intensive at Middlebury College in which the next oldest student was half my age, to the Institute for Jewish Spirituality, which introduced me to meditation and the power of silence. Good friends lovingly critique my sermons. They challenge me to ask tough questions about my priorities and about whether I am living up to the goals I have set for myself as a rabbi. They help me clarify what is the "place" I aspire to occupy and they help me assess where I am. They keep me honest and don't let me take myself too seriously.

The third and most important strategy is to not lose sight of whose list really matters and the criteria to make it on that list. A hint comes from the 4th-century talmudic sage Rava. He imagines (in BT *Shabbat* 31a) that after our death we are called to account for our lives by answering these questions:

1. Did you conduct your business affairs faithfully?
2. Did you set aside time to study Torah?
3. Did you have children (or care about children)?
4. Were you hopeful about the future?

5. Did you debate wisely?

6. And did you live your life with consciousness of the presence of God?

Translating Rava's questions into more contemporary language, the criteria to make the list that matters are: Do I treat other people kindly? Do Jewish tradition and learning enrich my life? Have I nurtured my family? Have I worked to repair the world? And how compassionately do I listen to people who disagree with me? In other words, have I crafted a life worthy to be lived in the presence of God?

If I have, then I will have made it onto the only list that matters. God's list.

Source: Rabbi Laura Geller, "Not More Than My Place; Not Less Than My Space," *Reform Judaism,* Spring 2011.

Tzedakah

Giving *tzedakah* is an important mitzvah. We are commanded to use our resources to provide decent lives for ourselves and our families and to help make the world a more just and compassionate place. Judaism teaches that everyone, even the poorest member of society, has the responsibility to give *tzedakah*.[1] While *tzedakah* is often translated as "charity," it is derived from the Hebrew root *tzadi-dalet-kuf*, which means "justice" or "righteousness." It is such a central Jewish value that we are supposed to seek out opportunities to perform this mitzvah and not wait passively for them to appear.

One classic description of this concept is Maimonides's Eight Levels of *Tzedakah*.[2] This "ladder" ranks the different levels of *tzedakah*, with the highest level being the first in this list and going in descending order:

- Giving an interest-free loan to a person in need, forming a partnership with a person in need, giving a grant to a person in need, or finding a job for a person in need, so long as that loan, grant, partnership, or job results in the person no longer living by relying upon others.
- Giving *tzedakah* anonymously to an unknown recipient via a person (or public fund) who is trustworthy, wise, and can perform acts of *tzedakah* with your money in a most impeccable fashion.
- Giving *tzedakah* anonymously to a known recipient.
- Giving *tzedakah* publicly to an unknown recipient.
- Giving *tzedakah* before being asked.
- Giving adequately after being asked.
- Giving willingly, but inadequately.
- Giving "in sadness" or giving out of pity. (It is thought that Maimonides was referring to giving because of the sad feelings one might have in seeing people in need, as opposed to giving because it is a religious obligation. Other translations say, "Giving unwillingly.")

Helping someone to achieve independence and therefore no longer needing to be a recipient of *tzedakah* is the highest level. Giving sadly or unwillingly is the lowest level but is still a valid form of *tzedakah*. This ladder in many ways acts as a summary of Jewish teachings on *tzedakah*. While some levels are higher than others, all fulfill the obligation inherent in the mitzvah of *tzedakah*.

The verse *Tzedek, tzedek tirdof*, "Justice, justice shall you pursue" from the Torah (Deuteronomy 16:20), is interpreted by the midrash to mean that we are supposed to perform the mitzvah of *tzedakah* where we are, but we are obligated to also pursue opportunities beyond our immediate environs. Because of the additional emphasis on helping beyond one's own circle, it has come to mean not only giving direct aid to the poor but also supporting an array of causes and organizations involved in *tikkun olam* (repairing the world), which could include both direct service and advocacy. Therefore, *tzedakah* can also mean supporting those organizations and causes that perpetuate Jewish life and create a more just, peaceful, and compassionate society.

For many, the observance of the sacred days of the Jewish calendar prohibited acts of *tzedakah* on those days, as giving gifts of money or supporting causes were considered to be work and therefore not appropriate activities. However, an expanded concept of *m'lachah* (work) and *m'nuchah* (rest), *oneg* (delight), and *k'dushah* (holiness) suggests that for some people, observance of the sacred times is enhanced by acts of *tzedakah*, especially when doing so is understood as a subcategory of *tikkun olam* and *g'milut chasadim* (acts of loving-kindness). This is derived from the Mishnah: *Al sh'loshah d'varim haolam omeid: al haTorah, v'al haavodah, v'al g'milut chasadim*, "The world stands on three things: on Torah, worship, and deeds of loving-kindness."[3] Since study and worship are essential to our observance, it would seem natural that an act of *g'milut chasadim* would also complete and enhance our observance.

Therefore, Shabbat, the Festivals, and other sacred days, outside of communal worship hours, are very appropriate times for special acts of *tzedakah*. Ideally they ought to be tailored to the specific values most connected to the sacred day. A time-honored custom is for each household to have a *tzedakah* box, or perhaps even multiple *tzedakah* boxes, and to deposit money before candle lighting or beginning the observance of the sacred occasion. The members of the household can then determine where to give the money.

Specific occasions can engender conversation about where money might be donated to mark the ideas and values that are commemorated by the day. For example, for Yom HaAtzma-ut (Israel Independence Day), money could be donated to an Israel-related cause. On Yom Kippur one might donate food or the money that was not used that day (because of the fast) to feed the hungry. But beyond the giving of money, since Sukkot is a time of thanksgiving for the bountiful harvest, a time of hospitality, and a reminder of the fragility of providence, one might collect food for distribution to the poor, or volunteer to prepare or deliver meals to hungry. Participating in a rally on Sukkot afternoon to preserve the quality of the air and water that make bountiful harvests possible would be considered by some an appropriate observance of the festival. The possibilities are endless. The key to understanding the concept of *tzedakah*, and incorporating it into our observance on the sacred days themselves, is to consciously perform these acts *lichvod Shabbat*, "in honor of Shabbat," and *lichvod Yom Tov*, "in honor of the festival." Part of observance is to recognize the unique character of each sacred day.

Source: Rabbi Peter S. Knobel, ed., *Mishkan Moeid: A Guide to the Jewish Seasons* (New York: CCAR Press, 2013), 162–164.

Somebody's Child

DEBORAH GREENE

If there is among you a poor man, one of your brethren…you shall not harden your heart or shut your hand against your poor brother, but you shall open your hand to him, and lend him sufficient for his need, whatever it may be.

—Deuteronomy 15:7-10

Before I drove into Boulder yesterday to meet a friend for lunch, I checked the supply of food donation bags in my car. I knew that as I drove around the city, there would be ample opportunities to offer them to people in need.

As I came off of the parkway, two young men stood along the side of the road, cardboard signs in hand. The traffic light was red and I was at the end of the line of cars, so I rolled down my window, caught the attention of one of them, and offered him two bags of snacks—one for each of them. He smiled graciously, complimented me on my "beautiful smile," and offered me blessings for my kindness.

We chatted a bit, and by the time I reached the stop light, it had turned red again. The second gentleman, who had remained by the light, apologized that I had to wait for the light again because of the time spent chatting with his friend. I quickly told him that he owed me no apology. I was glad to be able to slow down, offer the bags of food, and share a moment of kind conversation. He thanked me again for the food.

"People don't always realize that sometimes we don't eat anything at all for two days or so," he said.

"I can't imagine how hard that must be," I answered. "Truly, I'm glad to be able to do my small part to change that, at least for today."

His friend had come back to his side by now, and the three of us continued to chat.

"We made these bags as a family," I told them, "ensuring we're always able to help someone who's hungry."

To which he responded, "Sometimes people forget that I'm somebody's child too. Thank you for seeing that."

Each time we put a little food and drink into the hands of those who are struggling, I'm always struck that it is *they* who—without fail—offer *us* their blessings. We who are blessed with ample food, drink, warmth, and shelter, receive the blessings of those with so little to give.

It really should be the other way around.

Indeed, it is we who can bestow blessings: a kind word, a smile, spare change, food, and drink. Although doing so won't substantially alter the lives of the men and women we encounter, such acts reflect our belief that we *all* are created *b'tzelem Elohim* (in God's image). And, by carrying a spark of the Divine spirit within us, each of us truly is "somebody's child" for we are all God's children. It is in this way that we must see—really see—one another, and what I strive to do whether I'm volunteering for the Boulder Outreach for Homeless Overflow program at Congregation Har HaShem or offering food donations to those in need.

In the end, don't we all want to be seen as part of the human family? To be offered a warm smile and to have our struggles acknowledged? Don't we all want an outstretched hand, and an escape from judgment about where we are in life and how we got there? Can we ever truly believe that we know somebody else's entire story simply because we glimpse a single chapter?

I'm somebody's child, too. And I have children of my own. And when they look out at the world, I want them to view it with open eyes and open hearts.

Our little bags containing fruit cups, nuts, cereal bars, crackers, water, and more, won't change things. Neither will the evenings we spend setting up blankets and handing out food to our homeless neighbors. Rather, they're small, temporary answers to a much larger issue.

But when I reflect on my experience yesterday, I believe that in those shared moments, each of us was changed, and that the humanity fostered in our exchange offers glimmers of hope for the future.

Source: Deborah Greene, "Somebody's Child," ReformJudaism.org blog, February 25, 2016, http://www.reformjudaism.org/blog/2016/02/25/somebodys-child.

Holiness, Mitzvot, and Justice in Jewish Time

RABBI JONAH PESNER

Holidays are for celebration. The Hebrew word for a Jewish festival is *chag*; the verb *lachgog* means "to celebrate." But what about *holy days*? Perhaps this is a better English term to express what the Torah calls *mikra-ei kodesh* than the standard "holidays." Indeed, the biblical text refers to the most ancient Jewish festivals with these words, which are difficult to translate. *Kodesh* may be more familiar— holy, meaning that which is distinct from the everyday, that which approaches the divine. We declare our festivals sacred, or holy, over a cup of wine by reciting *Kiddush*. The word *mikra-im* (which becomes *mikra-ei* when connected to another modifying word like *kodesh*) relates to the verb "to call" and "to read." It is taken from the ancient tradition of calling the community together for public gatherings to read aloud the law and conduct rituals. Taken together, *mikra-ei kodesh* are literally a call to gather in holiness.

So Jewish holy days aren't just for celebration; they are making holiness. But how? What does it mean to bring holiness into the world by observing our festivals? One way is to understand them as a call to action, animating the Jewish vision of justice in the world. The deeper meanings of Jewish holy day observance can be discovered by paying special attention to the themes of social justice that run through them.

One of the most meaningful memories I have of Sukkot was the year we shared it with Reina Geuvara. Reina is a Latina, Catholic woman who lives and works in Boston as a janitor. She and her coworkers were leading a campaign to demand living wages. At the time, economists explained that it would be hard to live in the Greater Boston area on less than fifteen dollars an hour; these often invisible workers who cleaned at night were paid less than eight dollars an hour, with no health insurance. Their plight truly tested the ancient biblical call "Do not oppress your workers nor wrong them" (Leviticus 19:13).

As part of their campaign, the janitors met with clergy and leaders of diverse congregations to tell their stories and ask us to help call attention to their conditions. They invited us to join them at meetings with building owners and cleaning contractors, to make the moral case with them. These visits were inspiring, as we joined across lines of race, class, and faith to collectively call for the just treatment of those who toil on our behalf.

As they invited us, we invited them. We explained that during the festival of Sukkot, Jews gather in temporary huts decorated with fruits of the harvest. We articulated the Jewish value of blessing God for the bounty and told the story of wandering in the wilderness after our exodus from bondage. Finally, we taught them the tradition of *ushpizin*, the practice of welcoming guests into the sukkah. We could think of no better way to fulfill the mitzvah of *ushpizin* than connecting their redemption to our own.

I will never forget how they cried on the bimah as they stood under the protection of the sanctuary and told their stories to our packed congregation. They were moved by our story of the wilderness, themselves feeling like modern Israelites. Desperately poor, they still joined us in thanking God for all that we have. We cried with them as the translator told the stories of their struggles.

Our tradition offers various paths to holiness, all of which are connected to the mitzvot (commandments). Every time we bless God for giving us the commandments, we acknowledge that "God makes us holy" through them. The mitzvot fall into two categories: ethical and ritual. Most often we think of the ritual mitzvot of holy day observance: lighting candles, blessings over wine and bread, shaking a *lulav*, and many more. How often do we think of the ethical mitzvot related to our festival celebrations? Giving *tzedekah* is one act of righteousness that fulfills a critical commandment on a holy day. But it is only a place to begin.

The stories, themes, prayers, and rituals of each holy day call us to traditional and creative ethical mitzvot that provide diverse and meaningful opportunities to celebrate through acts of justice. Achieving holiness—approaching a place that is a reflection of the Divine—demands no less. God must be as concerned with our ethical actions as with our ritual observances.

In fact, the origins of our festivals generally reflect stories of a repair of an injustice or a recognition of goodness. The obvious examples include Pesach, the master-story of redemption, or Purim and Chanukah, tales of victory in the face of likely destruction. Every holy day has deeper, subtler themes as well. Shavuot is the story of a community standing together, committing to live in covenant. It challenges the modern Jew to question how well we are living in covenant with those around us, locally and globally, many of whom suffer in poverty or with other afflictions. The sweet but profound story of Ruth and Naomi, poor and "other," set during a period of harvest, is a powerful reminder of the fragility of the most vulnerable among us, Jew and non-Jew alike.

Perhaps the best, most important example is Shabbat. In his groundbreaking and inspiring masterwork, *The Sabbath*, Abraham Joshua Heschel describes Shabbat as a cathedral in time. He understands Judaism as a religion in which we discover holiness by marking time, rather than physical space. We say blessings before our actions to elevate them; we live according to the rhythm of daily, weekly, and yearly occasions marking various moments of holiness. During the week, he writes, we work on the creation of the world; on Shabbat we celebrate the work of Creation.

Heschel is well-known for his statement that marching with Dr. Martin Luther King, Jr. was "praying with his legs." As much as Heschel understood Jewish ritual as a way to mark holiness in time, he also understood the underlying call to justice. Shabbat is not merely a ritual category in which we elevate time through prayers; it is an ethical category that seeks to elevate humanity itself. Initially, it is a reminder that to be a free human person with agency and dignity is to be able to refrain from work. We were slaves in Egypt, and we had no Sabbath; Shabbat is a reminder of the true meaning of freedom. This truth applies not only to all human beings, but also to the animal kingdom and the earth itself, all of whom enjoy Shabbat.

On a deeper level, Shabbat is a taste of a world redeemed—the world as it *should* be. It is a glimpse of the world for which we pray throughout our liturgy. It is also a call to action, for though we taste perfection in the sweetness of Shabbat, we know that it is but a taste. When the candle of *Havdalah* is extinguished in the wine, the hiss is a sad sound, as we know we live in the world as it *is*. To honor Shabbat, to fulfill the mitzvot, to heed God's call, is to tirelessly pursue justice in order to help create the repaired world we know it *should* be.

There are times when we celebrate Shabbat through prayer and ritual. And there are times when our sacred obligation to seek justice demands that we celebrate, as Heschel taught, by praying with our feet. Every year, the "pride" rally in our community would fall on Saturday, and lesbian, gay, bisexual, and transgender Jews and their allies would have to choose whether or not to participate. One year, on the eve of a significant legislative fight for marriage equality, my congregation made an important decision: we would honor Shabbat through study, ritual, celebration, and then pray with our feet by marching for justice. Leaders planned a Shabbat worship service, Torah study, and lunch, followed by a march to the pride rally. Longtime Jewish activists came for Shabbat, some for the first time in years, if ever. They wept with pride, not only in their sexuality, but that their Jewish community was fighting with them. We created holiness in time, through meaningful ritual and action for justice.

There are too many examples of the applied, living intersection of celebration of Jewish time through justice to list. Every Jew and community will discover creative ways to fulfill the ethical mitzvot of the festivals. Here are some key questions to help envision action for justice to honor our holy days:

- What are the moral and ethical implications of the *story* the holy day recounts?
- What are the *historical contexts* of the festival and corresponding themes of injustice?
- What symbols and images embodied in the *rituals* reflect our commitments to righteousness?
- What calls to action are implicit within the language of the particular *prayers*?
- What are the traditional ethical *customs* associated with each festival? What are modern approaches to practice them?
- What are the implications for justice found in the traditional *texts* read and studied on the festival? What are other ancient and modern texts are appropriate to lift up the themes of justice relevant to the holy day?

In addition, it is important to ask the following:

- What are the compelling local and global challenges that deserve attention at this particular sacred moment?
- What role does Israel play in the festival, and how can our observance both be supportive of, and strengthen our relationship, to the Jewish state?
- What is the role of world Jewry and the broader global community in the holy day?

- What opportunities exist for *tzedakah*, direct service, or political advocacy related to those issues and appropriate for the sacred occasion?
- How can our observance foster stronger relationships, not only among Jews but with our sisters and brothers of all backgrounds?
- What can we do as individuals, children, families, and wider communities?

This call to seek justice is nothing new for Jews. Many individuals, families, and synagogues have found creative ways to live out the underlying values of our holy days through social action. Indeed, the historical origins of our holy days were acts of repair, as ancient generations sought to draw closer to God as a more righteous community through ritual.

What is new is the question of what *we* will do. The challenge to us and to the next generation is: Will we make our holidays true holy days? Will we bring holiness into the world by elevating our fulfillment of ethical mitzvot alongside our rituals? If we do, not only will we keep our Jewish observance relevant in our lives and impactful on our world, we will also bring about a more just world. That must be what God wants of us, as it is written, "You know what is demanded of you: only to do justice, love mercy, and walk humbly with your God" (Micah 6:8).

Source: Rabbi Jonah Pesner, "Holiness, Mitzvot, and Justice in Jewish Time," in *Mishkan Moeid: A Guide to the Jewish Seasons*, ed. Rabbi Peter S. Knobel (New York: CCAR Press, 2013), 135–140.

Unit II

CREATING A JEWISH LIFE
IN TIME

The Jewish Calendar
and Shabbat

Source Texts

Genesis 2:1–3

[1]Completed now were heaven and earth and all their host. [2]On the seventh day, God had completed the work that had been done, ceasing then from all the work that [God] had done. [3]Then God blessed the seventh day and made it holy, and ceased from all the creative work that God [had chosen] to do.

Exodus 20:8–11

[8]Remember the Sabbath day and keep it holy. [9]Six days you shall labor and do all your work, [10]but the seventh day is a Sabbath of the Eternal your God: you shall not do any work—you, your son or daughter, your male or female slave, or your cattle, or the stranger who is within your settlements. [11]For in six days the Eternal made heaven and earth and sea—and all that is in them—and then rested on the seventh day; therefore then Eternal blessed the Sabbath day and hallowed it.

Mishnah Shabbat 7:2

The main classes of work are forty save one: sowing, plowing, reaping, binding sheaves, threshing, winnowing, cleansing crops, grinding, sifting, kneading, baking, shearing wool, washing or beating or dyeing it, spinning, weaving, making two loops, weaving two threads, separating two threads, tying [a knot], loosening [a knot], sewing two stitches, tearing in order to sew two stitches, hunting a gazelle, slaughtering or flaying or salting it or curing its skin, scraping it or cutting it up, writing two letters, erasing in order to write two letters, building, pulling down, putting out a fire, lighting a fire, striking with a hammer, and taking out from one domain into another. These are the main classes of work: forty save one.

Moses Maimonides, *Mishneh Torah,* Laws of *Shabbat* 30:2–3, 5, 7–9, 14

(2) What constitutes honor of the Shabbat? One must wash his face, hands, and feet with hot water on Erev Shabbat, in honor of Shabbat. He should then wrap himself in a fringed garment and sit in a dignified way awaiting the arrival of the Shabbat, as if he were going to greet the king. The early sages used to gather their students on Erev Shabbat, enwrap themselves and exclaim: "Let us go out to greet the Sabbath bride."

(3) Included in the honor of Shabbat is the donning of clean garments. One's weekday clothing should be different from one's Shabbat clothing. . . .

(5) A person must set the table for a Shabbat meal on Friday night, even if he feels no need for more than a minimal amount of food . . . in order to honor the Shabbat, a person must arrange his house while it is still daytime, light candles, set the table, and make the bed. All of these things constitute honor of Shabbat.

(7) What constitutes delighting in the Shabbat? This is explained by the Sages to mean that one should prepare rich foods and sweet drinks for Shabbat consumption, each person according to his means. Praiseworthy is the one who spends much for Shabbat and for the preparation of numerous tasty dishes.

(8) One who was raised in luxury and wealth such that every day was like Shabbat must nevertheless prepare different foods for Shabbat than he eats during the week.

(9) A person is obligated to eat three meals on Shabbat: an evening meal, a morning meal, and an afternoon meal.

(14) Cohabitation is regarded as one of Shabbat's delights.

The Cycle of the Jewish Year

As the earth rotates upon its axis, night becomes day, and day turns once again into night. As the earth revolves around the sun, autumn gives way to winter, winter yields to spring, spring blossoms into summer, summer once again becomes fall. The moon also exhibits cyclical changes, waxing and waning at regular intervals. The rhythmic movements of the celestial bodies divide the endless flow of time into days, months, and years. By monitoring these repetitions, we have established a calendar to measure the passage of time. The calendar rules our lives, telling us when to work and when to rest, differentiating special days from ordinary days.

As Jews living in the Diaspora, two calendars regulate our lives: the civil and the Jewish. For us the days, the months, and the years bear two dates and two distinct rhythms. This volume, *Mishkan Moeid: A Guide to the Jewish Seasons*, is designed to help Jews feel more clearly the flow of Jewish time.

Every day of the week points toward Shabbat—day of rest, day of joy, day of holiness. Every month begins with Rosh Chodesh, the marking of each new month. Each year begins in the fall with Rosh HaShanah. The blast of the shofar ushers in the New Year, announcing the season of repentance. Yom Kippur follows with its daylong fast and majestic liturgy. We confess our sins and become reconciled with God so that we can begin the new year free from accumulated guilt. Then Sukkot, the joyous celebration of the harvest, reminder of the ancient journey of our people to the Land of Israel, arrives rich with agricultural symbolism.

However, soon fall becomes winter, and the dark nights are illuminated by the brightly burning lights of Chanukah, recalling for us the heroic Maccabees and our people's long struggle to remain Jewish. As winter nears its end, we read the Purim story from the *M'gilah*, and we revel in the miracle of our physical survival despite the numerous attempts to destroy us. Tu BiSh'vat arrives in the middle of winter with its promise of rebirth, reconnecting us to both the natural world, and the Land of Israel.

Spring liberates the world from the grip of winter, and we recall our liberation from Egyptian bondage. We gather at the seder table to recite the words of the Haggadah, to eat the symbolic foods, and to renew our commitment to the liberation of all humanity. From Passover we count seven weeks to Shavuot. During this period, on Yom HaShoah, we mourn the death of six million Jews slaughtered by the Nazis, and mourn again for Israel's fallen on Yom HaZikaron, but our grief gives way to rejoicing when we join in the celebration of Israel's rebirth on Yom HaAtzma-ut.

The counting ends with Shavuot, the festival that celebrates Revelation. We stand as at Mount Sinai with our ancestors, again receiving Torah and entering into the covenant with God.

Summer is soon upon us, and on Tishah B'Av we recall the tragic destructions of the Temples and two periods of sovereignty over the Land of Israel as we lament the historical suffering of our people. Then—the dark mood turns to anticipation as we enter the month of Elul and prepare again to greet the New Year, with Rosh HaShanah.

Mishkan Moeid: A Guide to the Jewish Seasons, like *Gates of Mitzvah*, proceeds from the premise that mitzvah is the key to authentic Jewish existence and to the sanctification of life. This book, too, was conceived to help Jews create Jewish responses to living and to give their lives Jewish depth and character. As Reform Jews, our philosophy is based on the twin commitments to Jewish continuity and to personal freedom of choice.

The edifice of Jewish living is constructed of mitzvot. As a building is constructed one brick at a time, so is a significant Jewish life. Our Sages recognized that the observance of one mitzvah leads to the observance of others. As Ben Azzai said, "One mitzvah brings another in its wake." The secret of observing mitzvot is to begin.

Source: Rabbi Peter S. Knobel, ed., *Mishkan Moeid: A Guide to the Jewish Seasons* (New York: CCAR Press, 2013), 3–4.

The Jewish Calendar

Rabbi Alexander Guttmann

In order to appreciate fully the meaning of the Jewish holidays— their relationships to the seasons, to historical events, and to each other—it is necessary to have a basic understanding of the Jewish calendar. One often hears people remark, "The holidays are early this year" or "Reform Jews don't celebrate the second day." From where did the Jewish calendar come? How does it work? What is its significance for us?

The main purpose of the Jewish calendar is, and always has been, to set the dates of the festivals. Our present calendar has its roots in the Torah, but it has been modified by Jewish religious authorities through the ages. The principal rules were established by the Sages and Rabbis of antiquity and were supplemented by medieval scholars. In Talmudic times the regulation of the calendar was the exclusive right of the Jewish leadership in the Land of Israel, particularly that of the *nasi* (patriarch). Since that time, such regulation has been regarded as a task of crucial importance for the observance of Judaism.

The Structure of the Jewish Calendar

The point of departure in regulating the Jewish calendar is the biblical law "Observe the month of Aviv and offer a passover sacrifice to the Eternal your God" (Deuteronomy 16:1). Passover, therefore, must fall every year in the spring at the time of Aviv (specifically, the appearance of the ripening ears of barley). And so, each year the ancient Jewish authorities watched for signs of the approaching spring. If these signs were late, they added an extra month of thirty days (called Adar II) to the year, before the Passover month. Once the time of Passover had been established, the dates of all subsequent festivals would be determined based on whether an extra month (a second Adar) had been added.

In the Bible, the Hebrew months are lunar (i.e., each month begins with the "birth" of the new moon). However, since festivals such as Passover and Sukkot had to occur in the proper agricultural season (i.e., according to the solar year), it is obvious that the Jewish calendar must be lunar-solar. This means that the lunar year (approximately 354 days) and the solar year (approximately 365 days) had to be harmonized and adjusted to each other, a complex process that was meticulously refined by the ancient and medieval Rabbis.

The Jewish day has 24 hours and starts in the evening. The length of the lunar month is traditionally calculated as 29 days, 12 hours, and 793 parts of an hour (divided into 1080 parts). This is the time span between one new moon and the next. Since it is impractical to start a new month at varying hours of the day, the Sages of antiquity ordained that the length of the month should alternate between 29 and 30 days. Since the lunar month is somewhat longer than 29 days and 12 hours, the remainder is taken care of by making the months of Cheshvan and Kislev flexible, that is, they can both have either 29 or 30 days.

The introduction of a permanent Jewish calendar became increasingly urgent after Jews began to spread throughout the world. As Jewry dispersed, regular contacts with the Jewish leadership in the Land of Israel, which had the sole privilege of regulating the calendar, became more and more difficult. The most important step in this process of permanent calendar reform was the adoption in the eighth century CE of a nineteen-year cycle of "intercalation" (i.e., harmonization of the solar and lunar calendars). The adoption of this cycle made the actual physical observation of the new moon and the signs of approaching spring unnecessary. This cycle of nineteen years adjusts the lunar year to the solar year by inserting into it seven leap years (i.e., the additional thirty-day month of Adar) in the following order: every third, sixth, eighth, eleventh, fourteenth, seventeenth, and nineteenth year.

In the Bible, the months are most frequently designated by ordinal numbers. However, there are references both to such ancient names as Ziv, Eitanim, and Aviv and to some of the now customary names Kislev, Tevet, Adar, Nisan, Sivan, and Elul, which are of Babylonian origin. But, it is only since the first century CE that the Hebrew calendar has employed the now traditional month names of Nisan, Iyar, Sivan, Tammuz, Av, Elul, Tishrei, Cheshvan, Kislev, Tevet, Sh'vat, and Adar.

AD, AM, BC, BCE, and CE

The Jewish tradition of counting years since the creation of the world has its roots in early Talmudic times, but it was not adopted authoritatively until several centuries later. In biblical times, dates were referred to as being "two years before the earthquake," "the year of the death of King Uzziah," and so on. In Talmudic times, we find instances of dating from the creation of the world, but this was adopted as *the* Jewish method only much later, as a response to Christian dating.

It was in the eighth century that Christians began to date their documents generally as AD (*anno Domini*, "the year of the Lord"), and so it is hardly a coincidence that in the eighth and ninth centuries we find more and more Jewish documents dated "since the creation of the world" (sometimes referred to as AM, *anno mundi*, "the year of the world"). Obviously, calculating dates based on Christian theological principles was not acceptable to Jews; nevertheless, it was not until the twelfth century that dating "since the creation" was accepted by Jews universally.

Only a minority of Jews today would take the traditional Jewish date as being literally "since the creation of the world." Most of us accept the findings of science indicating that our world is billions of years old, rather than some fifty-seven hundred. But the date that changes each year with Rosh HaShanah is a convenient reference point to the beginnings of Jewish history and relates us to a venerable tradition.

Jewish texts often use the designations BCE (before the Common Era) and CE (Common Era) with the civil year to avoid any dating related to Christianity. To determine the Jewish year for a given civil year, the number 3,760 is added; conversely, to find the civil year for a given Jewish year, 3,760 is subtracted. Of course, since the Jewish year changes with Rosh HaShanah, the number to work with from Rosh HaShanah to December 31 is 3,761.

The Second Days of the Festivals

The greatest change that the Rabbis made in the festival calendar was the addition of a day to each of the holidays ordained in the Torah, except Yom Kippur. This was done in the early Talmudic period (i.e., first century CE). Compelling circumstances at that time forced the Rabbis to make this change.

Not only was the confirmation and sanctification of the new moon—and therefore the new month—the duty of the authorities in the Land of Israel, referred to historically as Palestine at that time, but theirs was also the task of communicating the dates of the new moons to every Jewish community. This was a task of vital importance, as the new moon determines the dates of the festivals. At an earlier time, the new moon (i.e., the first of the month) was communicated to all the Jews in Palestine and the Diaspora by kindling flares on hilltops. However, after the Samaritans kindled flares at the wrong time to confuse the Jews, the news about the new moon had to be communicated by messengers. The change was introduced by Judah HaNasi (ca. 135–200 CE).

Since it often happened that the messengers did not arrive in time at the places of their destination outside of Palestine because of road hazards, wars, or political upheavals, a second day was added to the holidays for the Jews in the Diaspora. This ensured that one of the two days on which they celebrated the festival was indeed the proper holy day. In Palestine the addition of these "second days" to the festivals was not necessary because the news about the sighting of the new moon, proclaimed in Palestine,[11] reached every part of that land in due time, that is, prior to the dates of the festivals. The exception was Rosh HaShanah, which falls on the first day of the month of Tishrei, making timely communication about this new moon, even in Palestine, impossible.

During the Talmudic period, a stable, scientifically determined calendar was adopted, and so the pragmatic need for second days disappeared. But the Palestinian authorities did not abolish these extra days of observance for Diaspora Jews (nor the second day of Rosh HaShanah for Palestinian Jews) because of the Rabbinic principle that we "may not change the custom of [our] ancestors."

Reform Judaism, from its very inception, abolished the second days of the festivals[14] and returned to the observance of seven oneday festivals as ordained in the Torah: the first day of Passover (Leviticus 23:7 and elsewhere), the seventh day of Passover (Leviticus 23:8), Shavuot (Leviticus 23:21), Rosh HaShanah (Leviticus 23:24), Yom Kippur (Leviticus 23:27), the first day of Sukkot (Leviticus 23:35), and Sh'mini Atzeret (Leviticus 23:36), though some Reform congregations have since returned to a two-day observance of Rosh HaShanah. However, except for the second days, Reform Judaism has always celebrated the festivals according to the traditional calendar. In effect, this means that Reform Jews today celebrate the festivals according to the religious calendar observed in the Land of Israel.

Source: Rabbi Alexander Guttman, "The Jewish Calendar," in *Mishkan Moeid: A Guide to the Jewish Seasons*, ed. Rabbi Peter S. Knobel (New York: CCAR Press, 2013), 5 –9.

The Possibilities of Shabbat

An artist cannot be continually wielding the brush. The artist must stop painting at times to freshen the vision of the object, the meaning of which is to be expressed on canvas. Living is also an art. The Shabbat represents those moments when we pause in our brushwork to renew our vision of the object. Having done so, we take ourselves to our painting with clarified vision and renewed energy.

Mordecai M. Kaplan

What Can Shabbat Mean?

We begin with a story:

> Looking out the window on a weekday morning, the Chasidic teacher Nachman of Bratzlav noticed his disciple Chaim rushing along the street. Reb Nachman opened the window and invited Chaim to come inside. Chaim entered the home, and Nachman said to him, "Chaim, have you seen the sky this morning?"
>
> "No, Rebbe," answered Chaim.
>
> "Have you seen the street this morning?" "Yes, Rebbe."
>
> "Tell me, please, Chaim, what did you see in the street?"
>
> "I saw people, carts, and merchandise. I saw merchants and peasants all coming and going, selling and buying."
>
> "Chaim," said Nachman, "in fifty years, in one hundred years, on that very street there will be a market. Other vehicles will then bring merchants and merchandise to the street. But I won't be here then, and neither will you. So, I ask you, Chaim, *what's the good of your rushing if you don't even have time to look at the sky?*"

The world of today, like the world of the eighteenth-century rebbe, is busy and often frantic. Schedules overwhelm us; our electronic devices run 24/7. We seem to be ruled by outside forces, so that "the sky" and an appreciation of life's broader purpose pass us by daily. Our lives are often consumed in activity without any feeling for the joy of the moment.

Shabbat is the vehicle by which Judaism addresses this dilemma. It is a time for stepping back from the busyness of life to gain perspective on the meaning of life.

Shabbat is an opportunity for "time out" from the pressures of the workweek. It allows us to make time for those people and experiences that matter to us most.

To give the day what Judaism calls a sense of *k'dushah*, or holiness, we refocus our activities. That may simply mean changing pace for dinner on Friday evening. However, as this book will suggest, Shabbat offers many other ways for stepping outside the realm of our usual lifestyle.

The Book of Exodus offers a model for Shabbat observance with a twofold description of what God did after creating the world. Exodus tells us that on the first Shabbat, "God rested and was refreshed" (31:17).

In our terms, God's "rest" signifies that Shabbat involves stopping weekday activities in order to leave behind our weekday mind-set. At the same time, Shabbat rest is meant to be more than mere relaxation. It is a means to the end of "refreshing" ourselves.

As Rabbi Mordecai M. Kaplan teaches, "The Shabbat represents those moments when we pause in our brushwork to renew our vision." We make the day an occasion for freeing ourselves from weekday restraints in order to become the fully human persons we want to be.

And yet Shabbat is more than a private time for introspection. Shabbat is more than a pleasant day away from the office. Shabbat is an intrinsically Jewish experience, which means that the rest and refreshment of Shabbat take on an added dimension because they are structured in a Jewish fashion. Shabbat allows us to deal with the turmoil of contemporary life in the context of Judaism.

In our society, where the pace of life is hectic and where the moral ground shifts so rapidly, Shabbat is important because it can anchor us weekly in ceremonies and values sanctified by centuries of Jewish life.

Shabbat reminds us that Jews need never stand alone. We can always draw on our roots in the Jewish experience, our connections to other Jews, our relationship to Torah, and the *b'rit* (covenant) with God.

Source: Rabbi Mark Dov Shapiro, ed., *Gates of Shabbat: A Guide for Observing Shabbat* (New York: CCAR Press, 2016), 1–3.

M'nuchah and *M'lachah*

On Observing the Sabbath
in Reform Judaism

Rabbi Mark Washofsky, Ph.D.

If someone were to ask us for a concise, standing-on-one-foot definition of the Jewish Sabbath, we would probably reply that it is a day of "rest" (*m'nuchah*) on which one is to abstain from "work" (*m'lachah*). We would say much the same about the major festivals (*chagim* or *yamim tovim*) as well. But if someone asked what those concepts mean to us, as *Reform* Jews, the answer would be much less obvious. Jewish tradition defines the words "rest" and "work" in a very specific way. The Rabbis of old developed that definition into a complex, highly detailed system of rules, principles, and exceptions that fill two Talmudic tractates, nearly two hundred chapters of the great halachic code the *Shulchan Aruch*, and constitute the bulk of what Orthodox Jews mean when they speak of *sh'mirat Shabbat*, the *observance* of the Sabbath.

Our Reform Movement has largely abandoned that system, and we have never replaced it with a single, "official" alternative definition of "work" and "rest." In some ways, of course, this is a positive thing. The absence of an authoritative Reform standard for Shabbat observance allows individuals and congregations to arrive at definitions of *m'nuchah* and *m'lachah* that are meaningful to them. On the other hand, this plethora of personal and local standards might create the impression that we, as an organized movement, are unable to speak with a unified voice about this essential element of Jewish religious life.

That impression is incorrect. I would argue that the Reform Movement, particularly in recent decades, has framed a coherent teaching about Shabbat and Festival observance. This teaching, to be sure, has not been laid down as a code, a set of detailed rules. Rather, in good Reform fashion, it takes the form of guidelines that offer direction to individuals and communities seeking to make their own decisions. It consists of three major elements.

The first element is the publication of books by the Central Conference of American Rabbis, beginning with *A Shabbat Manual* (1972), devoted in part to "the recovery of Shabbat observance" in the Reform Movement, which was later replaced by *Gates of Shabbat* (1991), and the inauguration in 2007 of the Union for Reform Judaism's "Shabbat Initiative." These publications and programs, which demonstrate that *sh'mirat Shabbat* is a major item on our movement's religious agenda, have afforded leading Reform Jewish thinkers the opportunity to express their notions of Shabbat observance, and to consider what *m'nuchah* and *m'lachah* ought to mean in our time. Rabbi W. Gunther Plaut, for example, defined Shabbat as a form of "protest" against the endless struggle and competition that characterize workday human existence. The prohibition of work—which he defined as the abstention from every activity that could be considered "usefully competitive"—affords the individual the opportunity for self-fulfillment: "doing nothing, being silent and open to the world . . . [is] sometimes more important than what we commonly call useful."

Rabbi Arnold Jacob Wolf wrote in a similar vein: "The 'work' that is forbidden by Jewish law on the Sabbath is not measured in the expenditure of energy. It takes real effort to pray, to study, to walk to synagogue. They are 'rest' but not restful. Forbidden 'work' is acquisition, aggrandizement, altering the world. On Shabbat we are obliged to be, to reflect, to love and make love, to eat, to enjoy." And Rabbi Eric Yoffie emphasized the value of Shabbat observance for "our stressed-out, sleep-deprived families": "Our tradition does not instruct us to stop working altogether on Shabbat; after all, it takes a certain amount of effort to study, pray and go to synagogue. But we are asked to abstain from the work that we do to earn a living, and instead to reflect, to enjoy, and to take a stroll through the neighborhood. We are asked to put aside those BlackBerries and stop gathering information, just as the ancient Israelites stopped gathering wood. We are asked to stop running around long enough to see what God is doing." These writers, among others, point to the continuing relevance of the Torah's instruction concerning *m'nuchah* and *m'lachah*. Our Sabbath, they remind us, cannot truly be "Shabbat" unless we take seriously the demand that we rest and abstain from work on that day.

The second element comprises writings that take these insights to the next logical level. If *m'nuchah* and *m'lachah* are still relevant to us, how might we Reform Jews, who no longer hold strictly to the traditional definition of those concepts, realize them in our personal practice? One such essay, in Rabbi Mark Dov Shapiro's *Gates of Shabbat*, suggests three alternative models of Reform Shabbat observance. "The walker" follows Rabbinic tradition and abstains from driving and the use of money on Shabbat as a means of devoting the day to prayer, study, family, and conversation; "the museumgoer" engages in activities that, while they may run afoul of traditional prohibitions, bring "honor" to the Sabbath and refresh the soul; and "the painter" regards Shabbat as a day to pursue creative activities that affirm our sense of human freedom. These models differ in their details, just as individuals and their needs differ one from the other. What unites them is their conviction that Shabbat observance is central to Reform Jewish life and their invitation to each Reform Jew to construct his or her Shabbat in accordance with that conviction.

The third element includes a series of Reform responsa, advisory rabbinical opinions on issues of Jewish practice, written over the last thirty years to address questions concerning activities that Reform synagogues ought or ought not to schedule on Shabbat. Basing themselves upon two broad conceptual foundations—the Reform Movement's renewed commitment to the importance of Shabbat observance and the value of Jewish tradition as the indispensable starting point of our thinking—the responsa urge that congregations refrain from engaging in activities on Shabbat that, however laudable, tend to violate traditional understandings of the sanctity of the day. These decisions speak specifically to congregational fund-raising efforts that involve commercial activity and to social action projects that entail physical labor. These acts are indeed mitzvot, but then, so is Shabbat. To the extent that we take Shabbat seriously, we should view it not simply as a convenient day on which to do good things but as a mitzvah in its own right, which makes its own legitimate demands upon our attention and which does not give way before other mitzvot unless those causes are emergencies that cannot be addressed on another day of the week.

As I have noted, these Reform Jewish teachings concerning Shabbat observance come not in the form of fixed rules but of general guidelines. Another way to describe them is that they represent an ongoing conversation in our movement over the nature of *sh'mirat Shabbat*. As is the case with all such conversations, we may never reach an absolutely final conclusion. As a movement that prizes individual freedom, we do not seek to impose solutions; rather, we encourage every

Reform Jew to arrive at standards that are meaningful to him or her. But to have a conversation at all requires that we speak a common religious language, that we approach the issues within a framework of shared understandings; otherwise, we are not a community at all but a collection of individuals speaking incomprehensibly to (or past) each other. The statements, suggestions, and decisions summarized here offer that sort of framework. Hopefully, they can be of help to us as we continue to explore just what we Reform Jews mean when we speak of *m'nuchah* and *m'lachah*.

Source: Rabbi Mark Washofsky, "*M'nuchah* and *M'lachah*: On Observing the Sabbath in Reform Judaism," in *Mishkan Moeid: A Guide to the Jewish Seasons*, ed. Rabbi Peter S. Knobel (New York: CCAR Press, 2013), 126–129.

The Possibilities of Shabbat:
Questions and Answers

Shabbat sounds wonderful, almost too good to be true. What if it doesn't mean as much to me as it does to some other Jews?

It is quite possible that Shabbat is not as high a priority in your life as it is in the lives of some Jews. Your Shabbat may not in any way resemble the ideal Shabbat described in books. But that does not matter at this point. What matters is that you begin wherever you are. Many options for interpreting and observing Shabbat exist.

The meaning of Shabbat is not a given. It grows as you begin to encounter Shabbat from wherever you find yourself now.

Where do I begin if I'm a novice?

Begin simply. Look over the possibilities and choose one or two ways to observe Shabbat. Starting with candlelighting on Friday night is one of the easiest ways to enter Shabbat. Whatever you choose, remember you don't need to restructure your entire lifestyle in one weekend! Just give yourself some time to experience Shabbat and the day will begin to take shape.

Even at that, don't be surprised if your "new" Shabbat also changes with time. You should continue to grow as a Jew so that Shabbat takes on greater meaning with the passing years. The process of "making" Shabbat is truly lifelong.

Should all the prayers be recited in Hebrew?

It is not necessary to read Hebrew in order to begin your observance of Shabbat. Hopefully, your enriched experience at home and in the synagogue will at some point lead to your learning to read and understand Hebrew if you cannot yet do so.

Everyone in our home works. How can we find the time to prepare for Shabbat and make the day different?

If your days are already so full that finding time for any new activity, let alone Shabbat, seems unrealistic, you will probably not find time for Shabbat by simply hoping some "open" moments will appear on the weekend calendar. The open moments will appear only if you decide in advance that *you want to make them appear*. In other words, you will need to "make time" for the time to observe Shabbat.

That might involve starting to think about Shabbat as early as Monday. Early in the week you may need to place Shabbat on your calendar and not schedule other activities; perhaps choose a Friday evening menu or plan a special activity suitable for Shabbat day. When Friday evening actually arrives, try an experiment to help yourself get started. For a set period of four weeks, commit yourself to a particular ritual like the Friday evening *Kiddush*. Promise yourself to do the *Kiddush* under almost all circumstances.

That discipline might be just what you need to begin to make the *Kiddush* a habit. After four weeks, even if you do once again become "too busy" for *Kiddush*, you may discover that your familiarity with the *Kiddush* has made it into something you miss. You will find yourself making time for the *Kiddush* because it has become a natural part of your life.

By the way, the welcoming of Shabbat from candles to challah does not take much time. It can take as little as five minutes to say the blessings, or somewhat more time if you complement the blessings with singing and the other possibilities presented in this book.

On Friday and Saturday most of the world seems to be at restaurants or shopping. There isn't much support out there for starting the weekend in a Sabbath way. What can I do about this?

You are right. We don't live in a world that is conducive to Shabbat. The cars and trucks keep running and the stores are full on Friday night and throughout the day on Saturday. Making Shabbat is like trying to create a sanctuary of quiet in the midst of unrelenting noise.

In a way, Shabbat is countercultural. There is very little support in our world for a day or even an hour of reflection and renewal. Your family and your friends may also not be interested in Shabbat. If so, you may want to explore Shabbat first in the synagogue, where a community supporting Shabbat already exists. You may find strength and warmth in a place where there literally is a "sanctuary."

In due course, you may be able to take some of your Shabbat spirit home. With some preparation, you can make Shabbat with family and friends.

The truth is, however, that even those who seem to have Shabbat worked out always feel some tension. The draw of the secular world remains even when the rewards of Shabbat are very real and quite holy.

I'm a single person. How can I have Shabbat?

Shabbat, or Judaism for that matter, does not have to be a family affair. The Shabbat message about reclaiming time for yourself or exploring your relationship with prayer and Jewish study is very much directed to individual, adult Jews.

If you want to reposition technology for a day, if you want to nurture your health and soul, or if you want to reconnect to Judaism, Shabbat can be your gateway. You can engage the day on your own. (For example, the Friday evening dinner blessings can most definitely be done by an individual of either sex; *Shulchan Aruch, Orach Chayim* 263:2, 271:2.) Alternatively, you can arrange to spend Friday evening or any part of Saturday with friends or the larger Jewish community. And don't be shy about exploring a nearby synagogue (or two) for prayer, learning, or just plain sociability. Depending on where you live, you may also find an independent prayer group (minyan) or Jewish social group (*chavurah*) that will happily welcome you.

However you proceed, the essence of Shabbat is still very much yours as a single, Jewish adult.

I'm retired. What can Shabbat mean for me when I am more or less "free" every day?

Yes, you are in a way "free." If you no longer work to make a living, you no longer have to follow a business schedule. Even with family and volunteer commitments, weekdays are probably more open than they ever were. Your lifestyle is more relaxed.

But Shabbat isn't meant only for busy workers who need a day off. Thus even if retirement allows you to feel less stressed when Friday evening arrives, Shabbat can "work" for you because it brings you something that other days don't. Shabbat connects you to Jewish ceremonies and Jewish history. It's about roots and heritage. Light candles and Shabbat introduces beauty and a sense of the sacred around your dinner table. In a world where we often spend more time in front of a computer screen than we wish, Shabbat can bring you out of your home and into the community. Attend a synagogue service. Breathe in the serenity of that sacred space. Exercise your mind in a group conversation about the Torah portion. Spend time with other people.

You might consider Shabbat as the day for thinking about why your other days matter. Rabbi Abraham Joshua Heschel, who wrote extensively about Shabbat, taught that Shabbat is a day "to turn from the results of creation to the mystery of creation; from the world of creation to the creation of the world."

I'm not a religious person. How can I relate to Shabbat?

Shabbat belongs to all Jews. For some people, the focus may be on ritual. Blessings welcome Shabbat on Friday. Services on both Friday evening and Saturday morning are meaningful and important. Others, like you, may feel differently. You may wonder about your belief in God. The language and customs surrounding prayer may be unfamiliar. That doesn't mean, however, that Shabbat can't be part of your life. In fact, if you want to take back your time, Shabbat is the perfect vehicle for doing so.

On a broadly spiritual level, on a cultural level, think of Shabbat as your Jewish resource for renewal. Draw on the ceremonies that do speak to you. Look further into this guide for creative ways in which Shabbat might help you step away from your weekday routines. You will find readings of all different kinds later in this guide that may offer you language for who you really are as a Jew.

Since there isn't only one Shabbat, you are most welcome to find a way to make a Shabbat that is really yours. (By the way, it's not inconceivable that some of the religious language that now seems opaque to you will in time become meaningful.)

My partner is not Jewish. How do we observe Shabbat?

If your partner is willing to join you in exploring Shabbat, the two of you should definitely begin the process together. Shabbat's promise of renewal and refreshment is in one sense as universal as can be. Beyond that, Shabbat allows so many possibilities for observance and enjoyment that it can act as a powerful mechanism for giving your home and relationship a Jewish ambience.

Source: Rabbi Mark Dov Shapiro, ed., *Gates of Shabbat: A Guide for Observing Shabbat* (New York: CCAR Press, 2016), 4–9.

Welcoming Shabbat

Come, my beloved. Let us go out to meet the bride. Let us greet Shabbat.

—From the sixteenth-century song *L'cha Dodi*

Jewish tradition compares the arrival of Shabbat to the arrival of an important guest. In the sixteenth century, the Jewish mystics of Safed in the Land of Israel took this imagery so seriously that on Friday afternoons they would dress in white as if they were going to a wedding. As the sun set and Shabbat began, they would go to the outskirts of their town to "welcome the Sabbath bride."

To this day Shabbat is referred to as both a bride and a queen. The understanding is that in order to greet Shabbat properly, special preparations must be made.

Preparations

According to the Rabbis (*M'chilta*, *BaChodesh* 7 to Exodus 20:8), the commandment to prepare for Shabbat is implied in the Ten Commandments as they appear in the Book of Exodus, "Remember the day of Shabbat and keep it holy" (20:8). How does one "remember" Shabbat? The answer is that one remembers Shabbat by keeping it in mind and anticipating it as the days of the week go by.

The Talmud (*Shabbat* 119a) also relates that everyone in the community became involved in preparing for Shabbat. Even the leading rabbis stopped their weekday activities early enough on Friday to participate in preparing meals, gathering wood, and getting out proper dishes for Shabbat.

In our day, too, stopping early and preparing for Shabbat can be the first steps in observing Shabbat. This can involve shopping for appropriate Shabbat food earlier in the week, baking or buying challah, and preparing the special meal often associated with Friday evening.

At the same time, preparing for Shabbat need not only mean logging hours in the kitchen. In fact, in this era when our daily schedules are so very full, a complicated dinner menu may prove to be an obstacle to Shabbat rather than an incentive. Because of that, some people may concentrate their efforts on welcoming Shabbat in areas other than cooking. Consider the following possibilities for enhancing the beginning of your Shabbat:

Purchase flowers to beautify your table for Shabbat. If children are involved, let them accompany you and help choose the flowers.

Use different dishes for the Friday evening meal. When it comes to the *Kiddush* over the wine, try to use cups that are specifically set aside for that purpose. Even though standard wineglasses and weekday dishes will suffice, special tableware is more appropriate, because it draws on the Jewish custom of *hidur mitzvah*—the belief that the spirit of any celebration is enhanced when it is carried out as beautifully as possible. By the same principle, you can make your meal special by using attractive linens or moving the meal to the dining room.

Dress differently for the Friday evening meal, if not all of Shabbat day. The Talmud (*Shabbat* 119a) recommends this practice. A clean shirt (white is a traditional Shabbat color) for everyone at dinner might set the tone. Some people, when they purchase a new article of clothing, wait for Shabbat to wear it for the first time. (You might appreciate one family's related custom: On Friday morning, they change their sheets. There is something special for them about having clean sheets on the bed when Shabbat finally arrives.)

If children are present, let them help as much as they can in preparing. Children might set the table, put out the Shabbat ritual items, or create decorations for Shabbat. Children could also choose music for Friday afternoon and evening or select a special board or video game to play or some books to read together.

Open your home to guests. Ideally, no one should have to observe Shabbat alone. Judaism even understands the act of *hachnasat or'chim* (hospitality) as a mitzvah, or commandment, which means that by sharing Shabbat with someone outside your family, you are giving extra Jewish significance to the seventh day.

Be intentional about technology. Although the spirit of Shabbat suggests that you can best experience the special day by unplugging from the electronic devices that are so much a part of our lives, there may be another path. What if you were to use technology as a way of connecting with the people you love? Instead of cooking or preparing for Shabbat on your own, use a FaceTime or Skype connection with someone you care about and prepare food together. You might stay connected too for the candle blessing and household blessing on Friday evening. Share these moments with someone who can't be with you in person but can be present "online." Singing along with a recording of the Shabbat blessings or Shabbat songs may also be very helpful. For some people, "unplugging" is essential to Shabbat; for others, staying plugged in partially might be part of creating a meaningful Shabbat.

Be there. For those who are just beginning to approach Shabbat, being home for dinner may constitute *the* major change of pace. Leaving work in time to prepare the meal or at least be present when the rest of the family eats may mean thinking about Friday's schedule one day or possibly several days in advance. It may mean breaking a series of old work habits in order to make space in your life for a new Jewish commitment.

By the way, there is another way Jews can begin Shabbat. In some communities a worship service called *Kabbalat Shabbat* takes place in the early evening (often around six o'clock). This service precedes Shabbat dinner. If your Shabbat comes to include this service, your "being there" will mean making time to be part of this service before the Erev Shabbat meal.

Finally, when you think about Shabbat, it is important to remember that Shabbat extends beyond Friday. Celebrating Shabbat can involve making room in your schedule for the many aspects of Shabbat that extend through Friday night and into Saturday.

Tzedakah—Charity

It is customary to make charitable donations just before Shabbat arrives. This can be done at your table with everyone present putting some change in a suitable collection box (*pushke*). Every few weeks you can then have a discussion as to where the *tzedakah* money collected ought to go.

In some households, family members save the requests for donations that they receive in the mail. When the family discusses how to distribute its *tzedakah*, these requests are brought to the table so that the entire family can decide which organizations ought to receive support.

If you celebrate Shabbat with friends, you can invite them to do the same. As you sit around the table, you can form your own *tzedakah* community.

Further Options

Consider adding to your Shabbat experience by trying some of the following. They can be done at any point in the Shabbat rituals.

A Special Prayer or Reading
One or more of those present can write their own Shabbat thought or prayer. It can be as simple as a brief wish for those around the table that evening. Others can participate at the table by reading a poem or a relevant article.

Something Good
Each person (from preschoolers to grandparents) completes this phrase as you go around the table: "Something good happened to me this week. It was . . ."

Proud Time
Looking back on this past week, each person completes this phrase: "I'm proud that I . . ."

Gratitude
Looking back on this past week, each person completes this phrase: "I'm grateful that . . ."

More Discussion Starters
You could also invite those at your table to respond to any one of these open-ended questions:

• Can you share a memory of an occasion with family or friends when it felt as if something holy was taking place?
• Which person in your life practices what he or she preaches?
• Which teacher, coach, rabbi, or cantor has had the most impact on you and why?
• What is the most important lesson your parents taught you?
• What is the most important lesson you learned from a grandparent?
• Why might it be that Shabbat is the only holiday included in the Ten Commandments?
• Do you have a favorite prayer? Which one is it and why?
• What is your favorite Jewish food? Why?
• What does Shabbat peace mean to you?

Some of these questions could work for your household; others, perhaps not. Feel free to create your own if you wish.

The Past Week
Without using any of the ideas above, you might simply invite those at your table to reflect on some of the events of the past week.

Source: Rabbi Mark Dov Shapiro, ed., *Gates of Shabbat: A Guide for Observing Shabbat* (New York: CCAR Press, 2016), 13 –17.

Establishing Definitions for Work and Rest on Shabbat

For the contemporary Jew who wants to observe Shabbat, there is probably no greater challenge than maintaining the spirit of Shabbat beyond Saturday morning. The problem is that if you have already made *Kiddush*, sung the various songs, and been in synagogue to pray and study (or even if you haven't managed to follow Shabbat thus far), your next step is not a given. That is because on Saturday afternoon you enter a time period without prescribed rituals. To sustain the mood of Friday evening and Saturday, you therefore cannot fall back on the performance of ceremonies.

Instead, you are left to address the basic premise of the seventh day, which is that it is supposed to be "a day of rest." This means that if you want Shabbat to be different from other days, Saturday afternoon becomes the time for deciding what you can do beyond ceremony in order to make the concept of rest a reality.

To do this, you need to remember that Jewish tradition means something quite specific when it uses the term "rest" in connection with Shabbat. Resting on Shabbat doesn't involve merely taking the day off or sleeping late. The *absence* of activity alone does not create Shabbat. On the contrary, Shabbat is very much associated with involvement in friendship, community, prayer, and study. The day that brings "rest" and peace is potentially full of stimulation.

So what, then, does Jewish tradition mean when it directs us to "rest" on the seventh day?

Jewish tradition says very little about the nature of that rest. Instead, it emphasizes the opposite—it specifies in detail what activities are *not* appropriate for Shabbat. These activities are defined as *m'lachah* (work) and are explained at the end of this section. You can see there how, under the category of "work," the tradition goes to great lengths to prohibit numerous activities that are perceived to be intrusions on the spirit of the seventh day.

Apparently, the Sages who first grappled with the meaning of Shabbat rest decided that their primary task was to create some open space in the week in order to let rest take place. Like foresters who want to clear an opening in the forest, the Sages took the Torah's injunction against work on Shabbat and used it to build a fence that held back anything resembling weekday occupations and diversions.

Shabbat became the protected clearing within the week when whatever was not work could blossom.

If you are now ready to move forward with your own Shabbat observance, this is the scenario you face in defining "rest." On the one hand, you need to respond to the significance that Judaism places on prohibiting "work." You must consider which weekday activities traditionally prohibited on Shabbat you will avoid.

On the other hand, you need to ask yourself what you will do to fill the space created by the abstentions that you make. What will you do *positively* on Shabbat to keep the spirit of the day alive?

When you read through the examples and especially when you try to apply the categories of work and rest to your own Shabbat, you will find yourself trying to resolve the tension between what you will and will not do on Shabbat. You may also be dealing with the tension between treating free time on Shabbat like free time on any other day as opposed to making free time on Shabbat into something unique. These very worthwhile tensions are the creative dynamic out of which you can fashion your Shabbat observance.

Source: Rabbi Mark Dov Shapiro, ed., *Gates of Shabbat: A Guide for Observing Shabbat* (New York: CCAR Press, 2016), 91–92.

More Thoughts on the Meaning of "Work" and "Rest"

It Takes Real Effort

The "work" that is forbidden by Jewish law on the Sabbath is not measured in the expenditure of energy. It takes real effort to pray, to study, to walk to synagogue. They are "rest" but not restful. Forbidden "work" is acquisition, aggrandizement, altering the world. On Shabbat we are obliged to be, to reflect, to love and make love, to eat, to enjoy.

—Arnold Jacob Wolf

Being Fully Aware

[The Sabbath means] being fully aware of the apple tree but having no judgments, plans, or prospects for it.

—Harvey Cox

> It is permissible to make plans for good deeds on the Sabbath . . . one may arrange alms to the poor on Sabbath. . . . One may transact business that has to do with the saving of life or with public health on Sabbath, and one may go to synagogue to discuss public affairs on Sabbath.
>
> —*Talmud, Shabbat* 150a

Reform Judaism clearly allows for a broad definition of work and rest on Shabbat. What is the position on work and rest of the *halachah* (legal system of traditional Judaism)?
The injunction against *m'lachah* (work) on Shabbat is presented several times in the Torah. For example, in the context of the Ten Commandments, the

Torah says, "Six days you shall labor and do all your work, but the seventh day is a Sabbath of Adonai your God: you shall not do any work" (Exodus 20:9–10; Deuteronomy 5:13–14).

Although the meaning of this commandment seems clear, the Rabbis who actually tried to apply the commandment found that neither Exodus 20 nor Deuteronomy 5 was specific about the kinds of work forbidden on Shabbat.

Source: Rabbi Mark Dov Shapiro, ed., *Gates of Shabbat: A Guide for Observing Shabbat* (New York: CCAR Press, 2016), 100.

What is Shabbat Rest?

That is not to say that the Torah and the rest of the Bible are silent about activities that violate Shabbat. Kindling a flame (Exodus 35:3), plowing, harvesting, and reaping (Exodus 34:21), gathering wood (Numbers 15:32–35), baking and cooking (Exodus 16:22), carrying a burden or carrying something out of the house (Jeremiah 17:21–22; Nehemiah 13:19), and buying and selling (Nehemiah 13:15–17) are all prohibited on Shabbat.

Despite this, the desire to elaborate on the specific meaning of the term *m'lachah* led the Rabbis to develop a system in the Mishnah and Talmud consisting of no fewer than thirty-nine categories of work plus innumerable secondary categories derived from them. In addition, other kinds of activities were to be avoided because they were not in the spirit of Shabbat.

The source of the thirty-nine major categories lies in the Torah's juxtaposition of some laws regarding Shabbat (Exodus 35:1–3) with the description of the construction of the portable sanctuary begun at Mount Sinai. The fact that the Shabbat laws immediately precede the construction suggested to the Rabbis that the term *m'lachah* should cover the kinds of activities performed in constructing this sanctuary (Talmud, *Shabbat* 49b; *M'chilta Shabbat* 2 to Exodus 35:1).

These activities included work in the field (plowing, sowing, reaping, threshing, and so on), preparation of food (grinding, kneading, baking, slaughtering, hunting), preparation of clothing (sheepshearing, dyeing, spinning, sewing), and writing.

Basing itself on the Talmud, later Jewish legal literature has continued to define the meaning of work on Shabbat. In modern times, this has involved dealing with such matters as the use of electricity and the automobile.

Why does the Reform approach to Shabbat work and rest differ from that of traditional Judaism?

Reform Jews depart from the traditional definitions of work and rest because we believe that they do not represent the final word on Jewish practice. We maintain that the Talmudic Sages and their successors only developed definitions of work and rest in response to the specific historical needs of the Jews they knew. The Sages themselves even acknowledged that much of their Shabbat legislation was only loosely related to the Torah (*Mishnah Chagigah* 1:8). Nevertheless, they continued refining their ideas of Shabbat because the biblical Shabbat had to be clarified and elucidated if it was to be followed in their postbiblical world.

The same holds true for us today. We are "commanded," as it were, to continue what Jews have done for centuries. We must develop definitions of work and rest that resonate with the needs of contemporary Jews.

One caveat needs to be stated: In creating a contemporary approach to Shabbat, Reform Jews do not function in a vacuum. Although we may depart from ancient practices, we live with a sense of responsibility to the continuum of Jewish experience.

Therefore, we try to balance our creativity in practice with the desire to conserve and adapt what speaks to us from the past. We are free to be novel but proud as well to maintain as much as possible our connections with the best of the Jewish past.

Does Reform Judaism have a position on the specific matter of pursuing one's occupation on Shabbat?

Reform Jewish sources affirm the principle that a person should not pursue his or her gainful occupation on Shabbat. In the first edition of the *Shabbat Manual*, a precursor to this publication, Rabbi W. Gunther Plaut wrote, "Reform Judaism . . . upholds the principle that proper Shabbat observance calls for cessation from unnecessary work and business activity."

By the same token, Reform Judaism also accepts the reality that circumstances sometimes make it impossible for a person to avoid work. In such cases, you ought to participate in as many aspects of Shabbat as possible.

What does Reform Judaism say about scheduling or attending private or public events such as parties or school functions on Friday evenings and Saturdays?

Here life becomes complicated. As committed to Shabbat as you may become, you will undoubtedly have family, friends, and associates (Jewish and not Jewish) who do not include Shabbat in their lives. They do schedule events for Friday evenings and Saturdays. In an ideal world, observing Shabbat would mean not attending events like these that take you away from Shabbat. In the real world, that may prove to be difficult. As is the case with working or not working on Shabbat, you will need to find a balance between the Shabbat you value, the people you care about, and the larger world in which you conduct your life.

I'm the parent of two young children. Our weekends are packed with soccer, baseball, and ballet. How can we wedge Shabbat "rest" into such a hectic schedule?

Your challenge is very real. Even if you want to take back your time and create some quiet weekend moments, the odds seem to be against you. As was said in the opening chapter, we don't live in a world that is conducive to Shabbat. In a way, Shabbat is countercultural.

But the good news is that Shabbat is not an all-or-nothing enterprise. The models of the walker, museumgoer, and artist are theoretical. The image of the household gathered around a Friday evening table reciting all the blessings, eating a sumptuous meal, and then singing songs and talking with each other into the night is also an ideal. On some weekends some households do it all. Their Shabbat is total. On other weekends, many people do the best they can by bringing parts of the Shabbat spirit into what they are doing.

And that is okay. The perfect should not be the enemy of the good. Lighting candles over takeout pizza after the soccer game sometimes needs to be your Shabbat. Taking a moment for a family blessing in your car on the way to Saturday morning's ballet rehearsal may also suffice some weeks.

The narratives throughout this book—especially the final set of thirty-six at the end of this chapter—suggest that there are many ways to bring Shabbat into your weekend. The key is not to feel guilty for what you are not doing; the goal is to plan for making Shabbat as best you can in your real world.

Should life-cycle ceremonies be scheduled on Shabbat?

B'rit milah (the covenant of circumcision).

In Genesis (17:11–12), the Torah first mentions circumcision for Jewish male children. Because these verses so clearly link circumcision to the eighth day of the child's life, the *b'rit milah* ceremony takes place on the eighth day even if that day falls on Shabbat. Circumcision may be postponed for medical reasons, although it should be rescheduled as soon as the child is healthy. Since some modern covenant or baby-naming ceremonies for female children follow the model of *b'rit milah* by being connected to the eighth day, they should also be conducted on that day even if it is Shabbat.

Weddings and wedding preparations.
Weddings do not take place on Shabbat. Once again, however, complications arise when a wedding is scheduled on Saturday evening and final preparations need to be made during Shabbat. The key is to find that balance referred to above: the balance between the Shabbat you value and the larger world in which you conduct your life.

Funerals and mourning.
Funerals are not held on Shabbat, nor do people visit the cemetery. Although Shabbat does "count" as one of the days of shivah, mourners interrupt their mourning insofar as they do observe Shabbat at home and they do leave the house to attend synagogue services.

What do I do with my computer and cell phone on Shabbat?
It all depends. You may like the idea presented earlier in this book of welcoming Shabbat by connecting with distant friends or family via a cell phone, tablet, or laptop. Reaching out to strengthen or renew relationships seems like a perfect kind of Shabbat activity. It's something the museumgoer and the painter would almost certainly endorse.

Once your electronic device is on, however, your challenge may be to resist being drawn into the weekday habits of checking e-mails, sending messages, and spending a large part of your day with your face in front of a screen.

Think about what you do on Shabbat. Does the use of technology make it more or less likely that Shabbat will achieve a quality of *k'dushah* (holiness)? Does it give Shabbat a sense of liberation? Does it help cultivate a sense of wonder at God's creation?

The odds are that the technology doesn't accomplish these goals. That is why Rabbi Arthur Green writes that his bumpersticker slogan for Shabbat reads, "Visit people, not websites."

Some members of the Jewish community have called for "A National Day of Unplugging." They have done so in part because halachah calls for us to put aside electronics on Shabbat, but also because they believe Shabbat can best renew us by being a day when we are free from the ever-present glow of a screen.

Consider how you might complete the following sentence: "I unplug to . . ." Here are some possible completions that might engage your *n'shamah y'teirah* (additional soul): "I unplug to recharge, to hug, to escape, to remember what I did before the internet, to be mindful, to hear my thoughts, to *oneg*, to find my divine spark."

What other activities could I pursue on Shabbat afternoon?

Study a Jewish text.

Over the centuries, part of Shabbat afternoon was customarily set aside for study.

You and your family or a group of friends can continue this tradition of textual study. For example, start with *Pirkei Avot*, a tractate from the Mishnah that contains wonderfully relevant wisdom from early Common Era rabbis. (Hillel, who is referred to in the Haggadah, is among those quoted in *Pirkei Avot*. You may recognize Hillel's most famous saying from *Pirkei Avot* 1:14, "If I am not for myself, who will be for me? But if I am only for myself, what am I? And if not now, when?") Various translations and commentaries on *Pirkei Avot* are readily available. You can also access much of *Pirkei Avot* online.

Shabbat afternoon would also be a good time for turning to the Torah portion of the week. You can read and study the material using *The Torah: A Modern Commentary* or *The Torah: A Women's Commentary*. You can also go online through the website of the Union for Reform Judaism (www.reformjudaism.org) for a collection of commentaries on the weekly portion stretching over many years. There are many other online Torah commentaries to help you study as well.

You can also focus on other Jewish literature—nonfiction, fiction, or poetry. Exploring the world of Jewish music might also be interesting.

For more ideas that can make your seventh day special, consider the ideas presented in the next section, where a number of Reform Jews tell their Shabbat "story."

S'udah sh'lishit (the third meal of Shabbat).

As was mentioned above, the Rabbis of the Talmud mandated that the Jews of their time, who were used to eating only two meals a day, ought to distinguish Shabbat by making it a day on which they would eat three meals.

In the course of Jewish history the Friday evening and Shabbat noon meals were given special status that included the recitation of *Kiddush*. In contrast to this, the third meal was not associated with *Kiddush*. It developed into a simpler meal, somewhat of a snack, that was assigned to late afternoon on Shabbat. This simple meal was even given the straightforward name of *s'udah sh'lishit*, which translates literally as "third meal."

Approaching the end of Saturday afternoon, you may find *s'udah sh'lishit* to be a comfortable and relaxed way of concluding your Shabbat. Family and friends can come together for desserts or something light to eat. You can study together if you wish or simply enjoy each other's company. After that, the group can bring Shabbat to a close with the *Havdalah* service.

Source: Rabbi Mark Dov Shapiro, ed., *Gates of Shabbat: A Guide for Observing Shabbat* (New York: CCAR Press, 2016), 105 –107.

Thirty-Six More Ways
to Celebrate Shabbat

BASED ON MATERIALS DEVELOPED BY THE
UNION FOR REFORM JUDAISM AND THE
MEMBERS OF TEMPLE EMANU-EL IN DALLAS, TEXAS

Here are the voices of thirty-six more Reform Jews presenting their sense of Shabbat. Some options suit Friday evening only; many apply to Friday evening as well as Saturday morning and afternoon. Which might help you turn the seventh day into Shabbat?

"I don't open mail on Shabbat."

"The most profound change came when I turned off the TV. That suddenly transformed the whole Shabbat experience. It wasn't about the electricity; it had more to do with the noise, the intrusion of the mundane into the sacred."

"I don't do housework on Shabbat."

"Not wearing a watch on Shabbat reminds me that Shabbat is an island in time."

"On Friday night I turn off most of the lights and let the candles bring Shabbat light into my space. I like the physical symbolism of 'turning off' the week and 'turning on' Shabbat. After I bless the candles I take time to meditate and center myself."

"When my boys were young, I set aside two boxes of toys just for Shabbat. As they got older, they chose certain games they would only play on Shabbat."

"I save any new clothing for its first wearing on Shabbat."

"On Thursday evening, I set the table in the dining room with our best linens, dishes, silverware, and fresh flowers. When we return home on Friday from work, volunteering, or errands, the house already has an air of Shabbat about it."

"I listen to Shabbat music while driving home from work on Erev Shabbat."

"I try to observe a 'green' Shabbat, minimizing my detrimental impact on the earth. I do errands by bicycle rather than by car, eat vegetarian rather than meat meals, and refrain from using appliances (washers, dishwashers, etc.)."

"I live in New York City, and on the way to temple I give tzedakah *to someone who is homeless."*

"Over Shabbat, one member of our family takes dinner to an elderly neighbor who relies on Meals on Wheels during the week but does not receive them on weekends. She especially loves the home-baked goodies and looks forward to the companionship."

"I'm thirteen and recently became a bar mitzvah at our temple's alternative minyan that takes place parallel to the official sanctuary bar/bat mitzvah service. I've been participating in this alternative service for half my life. It was fun to have the community there, supporting and celebrating with me! I didn't get nervous because I really knew the service and when I looked out I saw familiar faces. It was meaningful to have an aliyah *the week after my bar mitzvah."*

"Even though I am a newcomer to the synagogue, I feel connected to fellow congregants as we pray together. Perhaps this is the key. I find a sense of community each Shabbat. I feel centered that once again the week has cycled around and I see the same familiar faces."

"We have a Jewish storybook, and every Saturday morning my children and I read one story. It doesn't take a long time, and it helps make the day feel like Shabbat."

"I differentiate Shabbat by keeping kosher: no milk and meat together, no otherwise forbidden foods, etc."

"To highlight the joy of Shabbat, I have a special set of dishes and a unique coffee cup that I set aside to be used only on Shabbat."

"From Friday evening through Saturday night I wear a kippah.*"*

"Starting on Friday afternoon and continuing through Saturday we listen to Jewish music instead of the news or our regular music stations. It sets the mood."

"I began attending the Saturday morning Torah study to say Kaddish *for my husband. He enjoyed this Torah study, and I felt connected to him, in some sense, by attending. This group is smaller, more informal, and less couples-oriented than Friday night services, and it has provided a weekly oasis for me."*

"After Shabbat morning services at temple we spend the afternoon with two families, alternating homes. We study, raise questions about the Torah portion, eat, laugh, joke, talk, eat, and laugh some more."

"Shabbat afternoon is an excellent time for tikkun olam. *On different occasions, I have tutored a needy child and served at a local soup kitchen. I have also participated in a Habitat for Humanity program after services on Shabbat afternoon."*

"I get a weekly e-mail on the Torah portion. I bring something to the Friday evening table from whatever I've read in the e-mail."

"If we go out to dinner on Friday night we bring Shabbat with us: blessing the bread and the wine distinguishes this meal and day from the rest of the week. If friends join us, they become part of our Shabbat-away-fromhome tradition. Going to services after dinner is also part of our ritual."

"Even when we are out of town our family takes traveling candlesticks with us and we say the blessings wherever we are."

"Vegetarianism is something I aspire to but, as yet, feel unable to maintain. But I do keep vegetarian for Shabbat—beginning with Friday night dinner. It helps heighten my awareness of Shabbat as a different and truly holy time."

"I like writing a letter (with real ink and paper!) to someone with whom I've lost contact. I also feel good calling someone I've meant to call but somehow never found the time."

"I linger at the Oneg *after services and make a new friend."*

"A few times a year, I sign up to read Torah or haftarah at services."

"For me, Shabbat is family time. I have had fun teaching my children to play the card game Hearts and to play chess as well. I made cupcakes with them too. I think finger-painting may be next on the agenda. Get messy."

"Shabbat is when I get my creative juices flowing. I have loved making time to embroider or cross-stitch a tablecloth for Shabbat dinners. I have a friend who likes to play her favorites on the piano. Another does the same on his flute."

"Once, I wrote a note to my child's teacher about something he had done that I really appreciated."

"Host a potluck Shabbat lunch."

"I think it's important to welcome newcomers to the community by hosting them for Shabbat dinner."

"I enjoy reading some of the beautiful poetry in our prayer book, Mishkan T'filah."

"A friend was going through a rough patch. I invited him for coffee on a Saturday afternoon, just to be there for him."

————

I struggle to reconcile my secular world with a deep yearning for the sacred and the serenity that complete rest promises.

Observing Shabbat is not a black-and-white commandment for me; it is a whispered invitation that I strain to hear.

This is Shabbat for the Reform Jew—not simple; not prescribed; not obvious.

Yet like Jews everywhere, I do hear the invitation and find myself pulled toward the sweetness that Shabbat offers.

—Michelle Shapiro Abraham

Source: Rabbi Mark Dov Shapiro, ed., *Gates of Shabbat: A Guide for Observing Shabbat* (New York: CCAR Press, 2016), 114–117.

The *Yamim Noraim* (High Holy Days): The Days of Awe

Source Texts

Leviticus 23:23–32

²³The Eternal One spoke to Moses, saying: ²⁴Speak to the Israelite people thus: In the seventh month, on the first day of the month, you shall observe complete rest, a sacred occasion commemorated with loud blasts. ²⁵You shall not work at your occupations, and you shall bring an offering by fire to the Eternal. ²⁶The Eternal One spoke to Moses, saying: ²⁷Mark, the tenth day of this seventh month is the Day of Atonement. It shall be a sacred occasion for you: you shall practice self-denial, and you shall bring an offering by fire to the Eternal; ²⁸you shall do no work throughout that day. For it is a Day of Atonement, on which expiation is made on your behalf before the Eternal your God. ²⁹Indeed, any person who does not practice self-denial throughout that day shall be cut off from kin; ³⁰and whoever does any work throughout that day, I will cause that person to perish from among the people. ³¹Do no work whatever; it is a law for all time, throughout the ages in all your settlements. ³²It shall be a Sabbath of complete rest for you, and you shall practice self-denial; on the ninth day of the month at evening, from evening to evening, you shall observe this your Sabbath.

.

Jonah 3:1–10

¹ And the word of the Eternal came unto Jonah the second time, saying, ² Arise, go unto Nineveh, that great city, and preach unto it the preaching that I bid thee. ³ So Jonah arose, and went unto Nineveh, according to the word of the Lord. Now Nineveh was an exceeding great city of three days' journey. ⁴ And Jonah began to enter into the city a day's journey, and he cried, and said, Yet forty days, and Nineveh shall be overthrown. ⁵ So the people of Nineveh believed God, and proclaimed a fast, and put on sackcloth, from the greatest of them even to the least of them. ⁶ For word came unto the king of Nineveh, and he arose from his throne,

and he laid his robe from him, and covered him with sackcloth, and sat in ashes. [7] And he caused it to be proclaimed and published through Nineveh by the decree of the king and his nobles, saying, Let neither human nor beast, herd nor flock, taste any thing: let them not feed, nor drink water: [8] But let human and beast be covered with sackcloth, and cry mightily unto God: let them turn every one from their evil way, and from the violence that is in their hands. [9] Who can tell if God will turn and repent, and turn away from God's fierce anger, that we perish not? [10] And God saw their works, that they turned from their evil way; and God repented of the evil, that God had said that would be done unto them; and God did not.

Babylonian Talmud, *Rosh HaShanah* 1: Mishnah 1 & 2

There are four New Years: The first of Nisan is New Year for (the ascension of) kings and for (the regular rotation of) festivals; the first of Elul is New Year for the cattle-tithe, but according to R. Eliezer and R. Simeon, it is on the first of Tishrei. The first of Tishrei is New Year's day, for reckoning of years, and for Sabbatical years and Jubilees; and also for the planting of trees and for herbs. On the first day of Sh'vat is the New Year for trees, according to the school of Shammai; but the school of Hillel says it is on the fifteenth of the same month.... At four periods in each year the world is judged: on Passover, in respect to the growth of grain; on Shavuot, in respect to the fruit of trees; on Rosh HaShanah all human beings pass before God as sheep before a shepherd, as it is written [Psalm 33:15]: "The One who has fashioned all their hearts understands all their works"; and on Sukkot judgment is given in regard to water (rain).

P'sikta Rabbati, 40

The Holy One, Blessed be God, said to the people of Israel: "Repent during these ten days between Rosh HasHanah and Yom Kippur and I shall acquit you in judgment and create you anew. . . . If you repent during these days and stand before Me on Yom Kippur, then even if your transgressions extend from the earth to the heavens, I shall whiten them as snow."

Moses Maimonides, Mishneh Torah, Laws of Repentance 2:2

What constitutes repentance? That the sinner should abandon their transgression, remove it from their thoughts, and resolve in their heart not to repeat it . . . also, they must regret what they have done.

On *S'lichot*

Study: Modern Era

*I want to make a confession, to give an accounting to myself, and to God.
In other words, to measure my life and actions against the lofty ideals
I've set for myself. To compare that which should have been with that
which was. . . .*

—Hana Senesh (1921–1944),
diary entry of October 11, 1940

Before I go to the market, I like to make lists. I look in the cupboards, see what
is missing, in short supply, or might add some delight to our family's life. Once
in the market, I find my list helps me to avoid overlooking anything and being
distracted by attractions on every side.

In Elul, the month preceding Rosh HaShanah, I do the same thing. I take
out my pocket calendar, look through every day of the waning year, and reflect
on each day's events—where did I fall short, what was missing in my actions,
on what good qualities was I running low? What new actions would add some
holiness to my life?

I bring the list to *S'lichot*, and to services on Rosh HaShanah and Yom
Kippur, and compare its items to the specific sins in *Al Cheit*. I remember
the circumstances of each *cheit*, each mark I missed; each *avon*, each time I
twisted the path God set before me; each *pesha*, each time I outwardly rebelled
against what I knew was right. I think, too, about having composed my solitary
list of sins by myself, when the *Al Cheit* phrase says, "the sin which we have
sinned before You." It is an important reminder that I am part of a company
of listcheckers; the ruefulness and shame I feel are shared by others. We all

stand *l'fanecha*, "before You." We can face God with this list. God does not turn away, and we do not have to either.

—Rabbi Richard N. Levy (b. 1937)

AL CHEIT. The public confession of wrongdoing, recited at the *S'lichot* (forgiveness) service on the Saturday night preceding Rosh HaShanah, and multiple times on Yom Kippur.

CHEIT, AVON, PESHA. Three biblical terms for wrongdoing, each connoting a different type of misdeed. The Talmud (*Yoma* 36b) identifies these as follows: a *cheit* is an error—a wrong act committed unintentionally or inadvertently; an *avon* is a deliberate misdeed; a *pesha* is an act whose purpose is to defy God and flout divine teaching. Rabbi Levy defines the terms somewhat differently here, drawing on the meaning of the Hebrew root of each word: *cheit* (from the verb "to miss the mark"), *avon* (from the verb "to twist"), *pesha* ("to rebel").

Source: Rabbi Edwin Goldberg, Rabbi Janet Marder, Rabbi Sheldon Marder, and Rabbi Leon Morris, eds., *Mishkan HaNefesh: Machzor for the Days of Awe*, vol. 1, Rosh HaShanah (New York: CCAR Press, 2015), 118.

Approaching the High Holy Days

RABBI ELAINE ZECHER

The world can be a very scary place. The uncertainty—over there, around the corner, under here, somewhere, everywhere—has created a disease, a disequilibrium, a dissatisfaction, a disintegration in every direction. Where should we turn?

Fortunately, Judaism provides us with a sanctuary within the sanctuary of the synagogue, a moment of repose to collect ourselves, to turn in so that we might turn out, not to escape but to contemplate and prepare ourselves to face the world. That refuge comes in the form of the High Holy Days. Judaism invites us to engage and to use these days for introspection, evaluation, and motivation. As we make our way from the first days of the Hebrew month of Elul to the prayers of *S'lichot* on the Saturday night before the first of Tishrei, to the sound of the shofar on Rosh HaShanah, to the path of the intervening days leading up to Yom Kippur eve with the *Kol Nidrei* melody, to the final, long blast of the shofar to mark the end of *N'ilah*, Jewish tradition offers us a great gift.

These days afford us the opportunity to reflect on our past, to discover our authentic selves again, to be present in this moment, and then to look forward and toward the future. As we experience these days, we visit, revisit, transfix, and transform what has happened, how it is happening, and what will happen.

Our lives spiral and circle back again. We open ourselves to creating a vision of our own future based on our understanding of the past and the present. Not all of our past is perfect. Some of it is even traumatic. We also know the future will arrive no matter what we do. How we regard it all and what we do with it, however, is in our control.

In Judaism, we move in a circular motion. Defining *t'shuvah* as "repentance" does not do it justice. Moses Maimonides called *t'shuvah* a positive commandment. It means the act of turning. It means coming around again in a constant state of remembering, applying wisdom and experience, to transform our behavior, our outlook, our lives. *T'shuvah* enables us to perceive the way we view the world differently. *T'shuvah*, the act of turning, returning, reviewing, re-collecting, recasting, and reframing our understanding has the power to transform the way we respond now and the way we will construct our respective futures.

Have you ever played back a conversation in your head, interacting as if you could push the replay button? You are not acting in that previous moment. You are using the present with its transformed understanding to inform your reaction to that situation. You have already processed the past and integrated it into the present. Hindsight is 20/20.

So is looking forward, potentially. The Talmud (BT *M'nachot* 29b) has multiple tales that are not factual but reveal truths nonetheless. In one story, when Moses went up on high to receive the Torah, he found the Holy One sitting and embellishing each letter with calligraphic marks. He said to the Holy One, "Ruler of the universe, why do You need to add these marks?" The Holy One answered, "There is a man who will appear at the end of several generations and Akiva the son of Joseph is his name, and he will need these crowns, because from each and every calligraphic mark above the letter he will derive scores and scores of laws." Moses implored, "Ruler of the universe, show this man to me." The Holy One said, "Turn around!"

So, Moses went and sat in the back of Rabbi Akiva's class, the very Rabbi Akiva who lived in the first century CE, in other words, several millennia after Moses lived. Moses had no idea what they were saying with regard to Torah passages. It sounded nothing like what he was receiving from Sinai. He did not understand their interpretation and became weak and disoriented. Soon the class reached an issue and a student asked, "Rabbi Akiva, what's your source for this ruling?" He said, "It's a law of Moses from Sinai." Ah, the past recalled in order to inform a moment in the future. Moses was relieved.

At the precise moment when Moses went up on the mountain for those forty days and forty nights, he "went back to the future." The story is wildly imaginative. God surely did not take pen to parchment and literally serve as calligrapher—scribe, but the message is clear. Embedded in the Torah scroll itself, these crowns, as they are called, adorn the letters as a sacred reminder that the Torah contains not only the past and the present but the future as well.

Why should this be important? As Alan Lew teaches, "when we reach the point of awareness, everything in time—everything in the year, everything in our life—conspires to help us. Everything becomes the instrument of our redemption," our own promise for the potential of what is to come. This is the essence of these Days of Awe. They inspire us to aspire to our better, higher selves. As time circles around us, we can acknowledge the truth of our own lives in the fullness of our individual and collective past, present, and future.

Hashiveinu v'nashuvah k'kedem are the words that conclude the Book of Lamentations, "Return to us and we will return to You, as in the beginning" (Lamentations 5:21).

On these High Holy Days, we can go back to the beginning—like a fresh place, a time to contemplate what paths our lives will take from these days forth, not simply a reflection of all the days that have passed behind us. How will we plot a future course? How might we open our hearts, search our soul to turn around and look ahead with greater clarity and purpose?

Every single one of us was once a child. There is no escaping it. You can't be here if you weren't there, and yet does that experience need to remain solely in the past? From a child's point of view, the world is a great wonder. The fascination is unspoiled. Our minds were facile, elastic, plastic, and open to the new and different (except food with weird texture or that was green or that touched anything else on the plate). We were not yet tainted by so many disappointments, hesitant to the potential of failure, frightened by all that is wrong or by the fact that unexpected tragedies happen to good people all the time, even people we know and love. Think of a picture of yourself as a child. Her face is sweet. His expression sparkles. What do you want to tell that little human being? Watch out? Be careful? No, we want to share hope and potential. Rather than limit them, we express excitement for the future. Their future! We want them to know that there are many paths that they may choose. It is not about perfection but possibility. Failure and disappointment are also their teachers. You can't warn that child. You can only celebrate him. You can only rejoice for her. Remember her. Remember him. Let that memory inspire you, in the sanctuary of the High Holy Days, even now to go forward.

On these holy days of the year, we invoke our communal memory for God, taking note of our ancestors, of God remembering the covenant, of God paying attention. And though we may not feel we are direct recipients of God's focus, we are. This day tells each of us, "You matter!" The Talmud (BT *Rosh HaShanah* 16a) states that on this day we pass before God like sheep passing before a shepherd who wants to make sure each one is counted. The ancient metaphor makes its point. You can't blend into the crowd. We are not alone in our own isolated universe. Like the voice on the phone that tells us that our call is being monitored for training purposes, here, in a "meta-spiritual" way, we are noticed.

The whole universe is paying attention to us. Our tradition conveys this idea in the Torah. When Moses makes his final poetic speech to the Israelites as they stand perched preparing to enter into their future, into the Land, he uses the following image: "Give ear, O heavens, let me speak; let the earth hear the words I utter!" (Deuteronomy 32:1). Heaven and earth are aware of our presence. On Yom Kippur when we hear the words from Deuteronomy 30:19, "I call heaven and earth to witness," we are reminded again. Heaven and earth are watching. We matter. By mattering, we connect to a larger purpose with meaning. Not only *who* we are and *that* we are matters, but what we do has unmatched significance.

Rabbi Bernard Bamberger, a prominent Reform rabbi of the twentieth century, takes this idea to an even higher level. He says: It matters what each of us does with our lives, our talents and powers, our resources and opportunities. No person's behavior is just private enterprise. What we do, what we try to do and to be makes a difference not only to ourselves and to those around us but to humanity, to the universe, and to God.

And this impacts the future at every moment.

Bachya ibn Pakuda taught: Your life is like a scroll; write on it what you want remembered. We project into the future what will become our past.

On the High Holy Days we ask God, *Zochreinu l'chayim*, "Remember us toward life." It is all we have. Life and living it.

Yes, the world is a scary place. Uncertainty pervades. But this we know: from the first moments of Elul to the longest blast of the shofar ending Yom Kippur, these holy days provide the opening to ponder what we can do to harness all of the positive, creative, compassionate, and sacred obligations we are capable of. We can choose a more optimistic future for ourselves, for those who come after us, and yes, for the world, too. Let us use these days and this sacred time and the swirling, rotational pull of the life that surrounds us to harvest hope for a broken world waiting to be redeemed.

Source: Rabbi Elaine Zecher, "Approaching the High Holy Days," in *Mishkan Moeid: A Guide to the Jewish Seasons*, ed. Rabbi Peter S. Knobel (New York: CCAR Press, 2013), 110–114.

Aseret Y'mei T'shuvah
(The Ten Days of Repentance)

The ten-day period from Rosh HaShanah through Yom Kippur is known as *Aseret Y'mei T'shuvah*, the Ten Days of Repentance.

On Rosh HaShanah we take the first steps toward atonement. But this initial recognition of wrongdoing with its accompanying remorse requires further steps to complete the process of repentance.

Activities during this period should be directed toward the sacred goal of reconciliation with both God and other human beings. Jewish tradition teaches that Yom Kippur makes atonement only for those sins that we commit against God, but it does not atone for those sins that we commit against other human beings unless we first attempt to make amends and seek their forgiveness.

The mood of Rosh HaShanah and Yom Kippur permeates these days. A high point during this period is Shabbat Shuvah, the "Sabbath of Return." Turning toward God and toward other people is the purpose of these days.

The Mitzvah of Self-Examination

It is a mitzvah to reflect upon our behavior during the ten-day period beginning with Rosh HaShanah and concluding with Yom Kippur and to determine how to improve ourselves in the new year. This process of self-examination is known as *cheshbon hanefesh*. During these intervening days we are encouraged to set aside a period each day for reflection and self-examination.

The Mitzvah of Reconciliation

It is a mitzvah to seek reconciliation during the Ten Days of Repentance with those whom we may have hurt or harmed during the past year. Our tradition teaches, "For transgressions against God, the Day of Atonement atones; but for transgressions of one human being against another, the Day of Atonement does not atone until they have made peace with one another." It is appropriate to approach any person whom we might have offended in order to bring about reconciliation.

The Mitzvah of Forgiveness

It is a mitzvah to forgive a person who has wronged you during the past year and who seeks your forgiveness. The Talmud states, "A person should be as pliant as a reed and not hard like a cedar in granting forgiveness." Bearing a grudge is destructive to both parties and subverts the purpose of the Ten Days of Repentance.

Visiting Graves of Relatives

Many observe the custom of visiting the graves of relatives during this period and reciting prayers in their memory.

Shabbat Shuvah

The Shabbat between Rosh HaShanah and Yom Kippur is known as Shabbat Shuvah. Its name is derived from the first word of the haftarah, Hosea 14:2–10, which begins with the words *Shuvah Yisrael*, Return, O Israel. Attending Shabbat Shuvah services to hear the reading of this haftarah provides an important introspective prelude to Yom Kippur.

Source: Rabbi Peter S. Knobel, ed., *Mishkan Moeid: A Guide to the Jewish Seasons* (New York: CCAR Press, 2013), 36–37.

New Fruits and Old Crumbs
for Rosh HaShanah

ELLEN ZIMMERMAN

My husband and I experimented with a CSA (community-supported agriculture) this year for the first time. It was like getting a surprise box every week. In our second CSA, we pulled out something we'd never seen before.

The next time I Skyped with our grandsons, I told them, "We got a mystery vegetable in our box this week! We have no idea what it is."

Our 4-year-old, puzzled, asked, "Not even Grandpa?"

Well, there's a world in that answer! Surely, Grandpa knows *everything*. Even *he* doesn't know what it is?

Turned out, it was kohlrabi, a turnip cabbage and we really liked it.

In the end-of-summer/early fall seasons, it is a tradition to eat a fruit that you haven't had yet. On the second night of Rosh Hashanah, families can tap into this love children have for discovery and *ahha* moments but making a journey out of finding something new. You can elevate the excitement of the journey by going to a farmers market, but a grocery store is a fine excursion, as well. Many people choose pomegranates for this tradition, because is said to contain 613 seeds, the exact number of commandments in the Torah. By eating a pomegranate, then, we show our wish to perform all the *mitzvot* (commandments). But don't be limited by the pomegranate. Haven't had pears yet this year? Or figs? Or cherries? Invite your child to create a platter or bowl with your new find. Then he or she can own the *tada* moment when you say the blessing over the new fruit:

Baruch atah Adonai, Eloheinu melech ha-olam, borei p'ri ha-eitz.

We praise You, Eternal God, Sovereign of the Universe, Creator of the fruit of the tree.

Another Rosh HaShanah custom is *tashlich*, the tradition of throwing bread-crumbs into a body of water as a means of symbolically casting away one's sins or wrongdoings. Many synagogues hold *tashlich* services the afternoon of Rosh Hashanah (find a congregation near you), but you can embrace this tradition your own way, too. All you really need is a flowing body of water and some breadcrumbs.

The word *tashlich* comes from the Hebrew "to cast," because we cast away our sins—in the form of bread crumbs—into a flowing body of water. Jewish author Anita Diamant suggests taking a bag of stale bread to a duck pond. In *Living a Jewish Life*, she writes,

> Some families use this time to apologize to one another for the wrongs of the past year and promise to try to be more patient and kinder in the year ahead.

I have been to a variety of *tashlich* services—both self-created and with syna-gogue groups—where we assembled near a body of moving water, recited poetry, danced the *mayim* (water) dance, and shared we were going to work harder on next year. In all cases, we threw our stale bread crumbs (or, once, Dorito crumbs!) into the water and watched them float downstream.

How do you celebrate the Jewish new year and make it your own?

Rosh HaShanah

In the seventh month, on the first day of the month, you shall observe complete rest, a sacred occasion commemorated with loud blasts.

—LEVITICUS 23:24

In the seventh month, on the first day of the month, you shall observe a sacred occasion: you shall not work at your occupations. You shall observe it as a day when the horn is sounded.

—NUMBERS 29:1

On the first day of the seventh month, Ezra the priest brought the Teaching before the congregation, men and women and all who could listen with under-standing. He read from it, facing the square before the Water Gate, from the first light until midday.

—NEHEMIAH 8:2–3

Rosh HaShanah, which falls on the first of the Hebrew month of Tishrei, marks the beginning of the new year. It is, however, far more than the first day of the calendar year. It is the beginning of a ten-day period of rigorous introspection and self-examination that continues through Yom Kippur. So important did the Rabbis consider this period, that they proclaimed the whole of the preceding month of Elul as a period of preparation.

The Torah designates the first of Tishrei as "a sacred occasion commemo-rated with loud blasts" (Leviticus 23:24; see also Numbers 29:1). For Jews the sound of the shofar became a multifaceted symbol recalling past events, looking to the messianic future—a time of universal peace and prosperity, proclaiming divine sovereignty—and much more.[4] The sound of the shofar is a call to hearken to the divine summons, to examine our hearts, and to plead our case before the Eternal Judge.

Rabbinic tradition identifies Rosh HaShanah as Yom HaDin, "Judgment Day." In this spirit, a Talmudic parable pictures God as sitting in judgment of the world as a whole, as well as each individual on Rosh HaShanah. The image of God as Judge, about to inscribe human beings according to their deeds in the appropriate Book of Life, underscores the Jewish concept of human beings as moral free agents responsible for the choices that they make. We are further encouraged to believe that our fate, and indeed the fate of the entire world, depend upon our every act.

Following from the theme of divine judgment is the concept of making amends for the past and beginning the year with a clean slate. According to Jewish tradition, "repentance, prayer, and charity [*t'shuvah, t'filah,* and *tzedakah*] temper judgment's severe decree." Through these mitzvot, Jews seek to reestablish their relationship with God and with other human beings and accomplish reconciliation with both. This is also the opportunity to forgive ourselves for wrongdoings committed during the past year. While we cannot determine our fate, how we respond to the exigencies of life is under our control, and these three mitzvot help us to persevere in spite of the inevitable vicissitudes of life.

The theme of Rosh HaShanah is that in spite of human weakness, "the gates of repentance are always open." The struggle for righteousness never ceases. The mitzvot and customs of Rosh HaShanah are designed to help Jews enter into the new year with a new spirit so that they might be inscribed in the Book of Life and Blessing.

The Month of Elul

It is a mitzvah to prepare for the Days of Awe during the preceding month of Elul. Special penitential prayers called *S'lichot* are added to the daily liturgy, and many congregations have a late-night *S'lichot* service, usually on the Saturday night before Rosh HaShanah. Some congregations follow the custom of blowing the shofar each weekday during the month of Elul as a reminder of the approaching season of atonement.

Since proper preparation includes serious reflection and self–examination, it is important to set aside regular periods of time for contemplation and study.

It is customary to visit the graves of relatives during the month of Elul and during the Ten Days of Repentance. Through these visits, links to preceding generations are reinforced, and by contemplating the virtues of the deceased and their devotion to faith and people, we find strength and inspiration.

The Mitzvah of Observing Rosh HaShanah

It is a mitzvah to observe Rosh HaShanah on the first of Tishrei. As the Torah teaches, "In the seventh month, on the first day of the month, you shall observe a sacred occasion: you shall not work at your occupations. You shall observe it as a day when the horn is sounded" (Numbers 29:1).

The Mitzvah of Repentance

It is a mitzvah to express one's personal repentance (*t'shuvah*) on Rosh HaShanah. Through repentance (*t'shuvah*), prayer (*t'filah*), and charity (*tzedakah*), one begins moving toward reconciliation with God, other human beings, and oneself. This process reaches its climax on Yom Kippur.

Repentance begins with the recognition of one's faults, failures, and weaknesses and the commitment to change and sincere efforts to rectify impaired relationships. Through discussion with friends and family, one seeks understanding and forgiveness and, where appropriate, to offer compensation to right the wrong that one has inflicted. The reciting of confessional prayers opens the heart to repentance. The goal of repentance is to turn (לָשׁוּב, *lashuv*) the individual and the community toward each other and toward God and for the individual to become a new person.

Tashlich (literally, "you shall cast off") is an annual ceremony of symbolically casting off the sins of the past year. The Hebrew root *shin-lamed-kaf* means "to throw away." It takes place on Rosh HaShanah afternoon, unless the first day is Shabbat, in which case it takes place on the second day in congregations that observe two days of Rosh HaShanah. This ceremony became popular among Ashkenazic Jews in the Middle Ages and has become a beloved portion of the High Holy Day cycle in many communities.

The custom seems to be derived from the following verses from the Book of Micah:

> Who is a God like You, pardoning iniquity and passing over the transgression of the remnant of Your possession? God does not retain anger forever, because God delights in showing clemency. God will again have compassion upon us; our iniquities will be tread underfoot. You will cast all our sins into the depths of the sea.
>
> —Micah 7:18–20

The custom of *Tashlich* involves going to a body of water and symbolically casting off one's sins by throwing small pieces of bread into the water while reciting a very brief liturgy. Its meaningful symbolism is explained by Rabbi Moses Isserles, who added glosses to Joseph Caro's work, the *Shulchan Aruch* (the "code of Jewish law"), who wrote: "The depths of the sea saw the genesis of Creation; therefore to throw bread into the sea on New Year's Day, the anniversary of Creation, is an appropriate tribute to the Creator" (*Torat HaOlah* 3:56).

The Mitzvah of *Tzedakah*

It is always a mitzvah to give *tzedakah*, but on Rosh HaShanah, this mitzvah takes on added significance. *Tzedakah* is one of the mitzvot that tempers judgment's "severe decree." Through direct aid to the needy and to the institutions that serve those in need, and through aid to synagogues and other institutions that support the spiritual and cultural life of the Jewish community, we exemplify our obligation as human beings to share the bounty of the earth with others. The period immediately before Rosh HaShanah is an especially appropriate time to fulfill this mitzvah.

In many homes, it is the custom to deposit money in the *tzedakah* box as one comes to the table for the lighting of the candles before the festive meal.

The Mitzvot of the Holy Day

Shabbat observance is the model for the observance of Rosh HaShanah and all other major festivals. The following mitzvot are common to both Shabbat and Rosh HaShanah:
1. preparation
2. including guests at the festive table
3. lighting candles
4. *Kiddush*
5. *HaMotzi*
6. Blessing after Eating

Some of the blessings and prayers differ from those on Shabbat.

Apples and Honey

It is customary to dip a piece of apple in honey and to eat it after reciting the appropriate blessing. The apple and honey symbolize hope for a good and sweet year. The text of the prayer is as follows:

בָּרוּךְ אַתָּה, יְיָ אֱלֹהֵינוּ,   *Baruch atah, Adonai Eloheinu,*

מֶלֶךְ הָעוֹלָם,   *Melech haolam,*

בּוֹרֵא פְּרִי הָעֵץ.   *borei p'ri ha-eitz.*

Praise to You, Adonai our God, Sovereign of the universe, Creator of the fruit of the tree.

יְהִי רָצוֹן מִלְּפָנֶיךָ,   *Y'hi ratzon milfanecha,*

יְיָ אֱלֹהֵינוּ   *Adonai Eloheinu*

וֵאלֹהֵי אֲבוֹתֵינוּ וְאִמּוֹתֵינוּ,   *velohei avoteinu v'imoteinu,*

שֶׁתְּחַדֵּשׁ עָלֵינוּ   *shet'chadeish aleinu*

שָׁנָה טוֹבָה וּמְתָקָה.   *shanah tovah um'tukah.*

Our God and God of our people, may the new year be good for us, and sweet.

The Mitzvah of Congregational Worship

It is a mitzvah to join the congregation in worship on Rosh HaShanah. As members of the Jewish people, we have personal and communal responsibilities. Participation in the congregational worship service is one such communal obligation, but our attendance at services is more than a matter of obligation. The public celebration of Rosh HaShanah through prayer, song, and Torah study is the heart of the Rosh HaShanah experience. Rosh HaShanah worship draws us into the circle of the community, strengthening our ties to one another and to our historical values. If illness prevents attendance at services, Rosh HaShanah prayers should be recited at home. Some synagogues offer live streaming of their services as well, for those who are not able to leave the house.

The Mitzvah of Hearing the Shofar

Hearing the sound of the shofar on Rosh HaShanah is a mitzvah, as the Torah teaches, "You shall observe it as a day when the horn is sounded" (Numbers 29:1). Jewish tradition is rich with explanations for the meaning of the shofar.[20] The liturgy of the Shofar Service emphasizes the themes of God's sovereignty (*Malchuyot*), reminiscences of encounters between God and Israel (*Zichronot*), and God's promise of redemption (*Shofarot*). As the shofar is sounded, we are invited to concentrate on its meaning and hearken to its call.[21] Provisions should be made so that those unable to attend the synagogue because of illness or infirmity may hear the sound of the shofar.

The Mitzvah of Refraining from Work on Rosh HaShanah

It is a mitzvah to refrain from work on Rosh HaShanah. As the Torah teaches, "In the seventh month, on the first day of the month, you shall observe complete rest" (Leviticus 23:24). For the purpose of observing the holiday, children and university students are encouraged to refrain from attending classes, and all who are able should attend synagogue services.

Greetings on Rosh HaShanah

It is a time-honored tradition to greet friends and neighbors during the Days of Awe, especially on Rosh HaShanah, by expressing the wish that they be blessed with a good year. The traditional words of blessing, whether uttered personally or sent through the mail or the internet, are *L'shanah tovah tikateivu*, May you be inscribed [in the Book of Life] for a good year. After Rosh HaShanah one might say, *G'mar chatimah tovah*, May the final decree be good; or *L'shanah tovah teichateimu*, May you be sealed [in the Book of Life] for a good year.

Visiting with Friends and Relatives

On Rosh HaShanah it is customary to visit with friends and relatives, to wish them well. Such visits are part of *simchah*, the joy of the festival.

The Second Day of Rosh HaShanah

Although early Reform Judaism adopted the biblical practice of observing Rosh HaShanah for only one day, as is specified in the Torah (Leviticus 23:21; Numbers 29:1), currently Reform Judaism follows the calendar of the Land of Israel, with increasing numbers of congregations observing two days.

Mourning on Rosh HaShanah

Formal mourning (i.e., the observance of shivah) is suspended for the observance of Rosh HaShanah, at which time the mourners attend services and observe the customs of the day. The Talmud prescribes the complete termination of formal mourning when a festival intervenes. Although Reform Judaism agrees to the suspension of formal mourning for the holy day itself, it is left to the family and their rabbi to decide whether or not to resume shivah after a festival, particularly when the festival falls within a day or two of the death.

The Mitzvah of *Havdalah*

At the conclusion of Rosh HaShanah, it is a mitzvah to recite *Havdalah* prayers separating the holy from the ordinary—Rosh HaShanah from the other days of the year.

Source: Rabbi Peter S. Knobel, ed., *Mishkan Moeid: A Guide to the Jewish Seasons* (New York: CCAR Press, 2013), 28–35.

How to Harness the Healing Power of Forgiveness and Repentance

Aron Hirt-Manheimer

Dr. Solomon Schimmel is professor of Jewish education and psychology at Hebrew College, Newton, Massachusetts, and the author of three books on religion and psychology, including *Wounds Not Healed by Time: The Power of Repentance and Forgiveness* (Oxford University Press).

ReformJudaism.org: Why is it so hard to forgive someone who has hurt us?
We all want to be treated justly and with dignity, so when someone mistreats us without justification or doesn't take us seriously, our self-dignity is affronted. And it's even more difficult to forgive when the perpetrator doesn't show remorse, offer an apology, or provide restitution.

So how does one begin the process of forgiveness?
In approaching forgiveness, it's useful to differentiate two types. In the first type of forgiveness, you have been emotionally injured, but in the interest of peace, harmony, or to give the perpetrator an opportunity to reconstruct his or her life, you forego your legal or moral claim. For example, a wife whose husband has cheated on her gives him another chance. The second kind of forgiveness centers on assuaging one's own inner feelings of anger at the offender. Such forgiveness can be useful to individuals who are stymied from leading a constructive life because they are trapped in a web of hatred and resentment.

Does Jewish tradition offer any biblical models of forgiveness?

Joseph forgave his brothers for selling him into slavery once it becomes clear to him that they had changed their ways. His act of forgiveness is reflected in the Talmudic teaching that, in most cases, we should forgive perpetrators who sincerely admit their wrongs.

From a Jewish perspective, are you obligated to forgive someone who has caused you harm?

The great Jewish scholar, Maimonides (1135–1204), wrote that a victim of injury is required to forgive someone who repents through actions such as apologizing and asking the victim for forgiveness. We can infer from his position that in the absence of repentance, there is no obligation to forgive.

Why are some people better able to forgive than others?

Empathetic people who are able to discern extenuating circumstances that might have led to the perpetrator's action are more likely to be able to let go of their grievances. However, there is a danger in being too empathetic and forgiving. A perpetrator who is "let off the hook" too easily might repeat the offense and injure other people. In addition, if forgiveness is granted "cheaply," the offender might not feel obligated to repent, as often happens in cases of spousal abuse. For this reason, an abused spouse should never be pressured to forgive and not hold the perpetrator accountable.

What does Judaism teach us about how to seek forgiveness from someone we have wronged?

First, we must recognize we've wronged another human being. Second, we should try, whenever possible, to apologize to the person whom we've injured. It is not enough to apologize with words, because words can be cheap. It's very important that the apology also includes, where possible, actions of reparation (repairing the hurt) and restitution (restoring the situation to where it was before the misdeed). For example, if we have caused financial loss, we have to be willing to pay compensation.

The highest form of repentance requires a fundamental transformation of one's values and behavior. For example, a person who has lived his or her life narcissistically may need to realize there is more to life than just satisfying the self. He or she may then resolve to focus on helping others. Judaism, we refer to a shift of such magnitude as *t'shuvah*, literally a returning to Jewish values.

What if, after all this, the victim still refuses to forgive?
Then you have the right to say, "I've done everything I can. I don't have to go on with this guilt. I feel bad that the victim is not forgiving me, but there is nothing more that I can do. I forgive myself." In such cases, the process of self-forgiveness is very therapeutic.

Can there be forgiveness without reconciliation?
You can forgive somebody and not want to be reconciled. For example, if you've been in an abusive marriage, you might take pity on your abusive partner and be willing to forgive, but not necessarily want to continue living with that person.

Is there a prescribed period of penitence on the Jewish calendar?
Our tradition specifies that we do *t'shuvah* during the 10 days between Rosh HaShanah and Yom Kippur, but not only on those days. We are supposed to be engaged in this process every day, every minute, asking ourselves, "How can I improve myself?"

This teaching is reflected in the rabbinic aphorism: "One should always repent the day before one dies." Not knowing when that will be, we are obliged to repent every day.

Source: Aron Hirt-Manheimer, "How to Harness the Healing Power of Forgiveness and Repentance," ReformJudaism.org blog, September 19, 2016, http://www.reformjudaism.org/blog/2016/09/19/how-harness-healing-power-forgiveness-and-repentance.

Shofar's Voice:

A POEM FOR THE HIGH HOLIDAYS

STACEY ZISOOK ROBINSON

What is the voice of the shofar?
I hear its call.

It resonates
somewhere deep
in my bones,
in my blood,
that flows through
my body,
Through my fingers
and heart and
my arms that have
Known weight
and tenderness
and empty
and weary.
And I carry its sound

In the broken notes
that stutter,
Resounding
in the still air
That shatters my
complacency.

For a moment,
For an endless moment,
That is the voice:
When my steps
Stutter
and are caught
And I hear.

Source: Stacey Zisook Robinson, "Shofar's Voice: A Poem for the High Holidays," ReformJudaism.org blog, September 9, 2015, http://www.reformjudaism.org/blog/2015/09/09/shofars-voice-poem-high-holidays.

Yom Kippur

For on this day atonement shall be made for you to purify you of all your sins; you shall be pure before the Eternal. It shall be a sabbath of complete rest for you and you shall practice self-denial; it is a law for all time.

—LEVITICUS 16:30–31

Mark, the tenth day of this seventh month is the Day of Atonement. . . . For it is a Day of Atonement, on which expiation is made on your behalf before the Eternal your God. . . . Do no work whatever; it is a law for all time, throughout the ages in all your settlements. It shall be a sabbath of complete rest for you, and you shall practice self-denial; on the ninth day of the month at evening, from evening to evening, you shall observe this your sabbath.

—LEVITICUS 23:27–28, 31–32

On the tenth day of the same seventh month you shall observe a sacred occasion when you shall practice selfdenial.

—NUMBERS 29:7

Yom Kippur, the Day of Atonement, occurs on the tenth of Tishrei (Leviticus 23:27). It is the culmination of the Ten Days of Repentance. It alone of all the Jewish holidays is the equivalent of Shabbat in sanctity. Its mood is reflective and introspective—a day devoted totally to personal and communal self-examination, confession, and atonement. Yom Kippur provides us with the opportunity to alter our conduct, readjust our values, and set things right in our lives. The day demands absolute honesty as we confess our wrongdoings: "We have gone astray, we have sinned, we have transgressed."[33] The grandeur of the liturgy and music adds to the drama and seriousness of the day. From *Kol Nidrei*, the eve of Yom Kippur, to the last triumphant note of the shofar at the conclusion of the *N'ilah* service, its purpose is to move us toward reconciliation with God and our fellow human beings and to aid us to do better in the coming year.

Primary among the Yom Kippur mitzvot is fasting. The Torah says three times, "And this shall be to you a law for all time: In the seventh month, on the tenth day of the month, you shall practice self-denial" (Leviticus 16:29, 23:27; Numbers 29:7). The Mishnah interprets "self-denial" to include not eating, drinking, engaging in sexual activity, bathing for pleasure, anointing, and the wearing of leather shoes.

The threefold repetition of this mitzvah in the Torah has suggested three reasons for fasting, as described in our prayer book:

> Judaism calls for self-discipline. When we control our appetites on Yom Kippur, we remember that on other days, too, we can be masters, not slaves, of our desires.
>
> Judaism calls for empathy. When we consciously experience hunger, we are more likely to consider the millions who need no Yom Kippur in order to suffer hunger. For some, most days are days without food enough for themselves and their children.
>
> Judaism calls for penitence. The confession we make with our lips is a beginning. The penance we inflict upon our bodies through fasting leads us along further still toward the acknowledgment that we have sinned against ourselves and others. (*Gates of Repentance*, page 229)

Yom Kippur is a day of concentration on the past so that the future may be better for us as individuals, as a community, and as part of the human family. Despite its solemnity, Yom Kippur is also a day of joy, when the truly penitent person begins gradually to feel at one with God and humankind. Reconciliation and change are the goals of the day's prayers and fast. When the final blast of the shofar is heard at the end of *N'ilah*, those who have observed the day with sincerity should feel that they have been inscribed and sealed in the Book of Life.

The Mitzvah of Observing Yom Kippur

It is a mitzvah to observe Yom Kippur on the tenth of the Hebrew month of Tishrei. As the Torah says, "Mark, the tenth day of this seventh month is the Day of Atonement. It shall be a sacred occasion for you. . . . For it is a Day of

Atonement, on which expiation is made on your behalf before the Eternal your God" (Leviticus 23:27–28).

The Mitzvah of Repentance

It is a mitzvah to repent on Yom Kippur. As the intense ten-day period of self-examination, reflection, and reconciliation initiated on Rosh HaShanah reaches its climax, the recitation of confessional prayers brings into sharp focus our shortcomings and failures and initiates a process of change and transformation.

It is through repentance (*t'shuvah*) that we return to God and find God returning to us.

The Mitzvah of Reconciliation

It is a mitzvah for each of us to seek reconciliation with members of our family and with all those we might have offended before the onset of Yom Kippur. We should enter into the sacred day having made sincere efforts at personal reconciliation.

The Mitzvah of *Tzedakah*

It is always a mitzvah to give *tzedakah*. However, *tzedakah* (charity)—along with *t'filah* (prayer) and *t'shuvah* (repentance)—is an integral part of Yom Kippur observance.

There is an old custom of setting aside money (referred to as *kaparah*, atonement money) before sunset on the eve of Yom Kippur. Implicit in this act of *kaparah* is the idea that this charity money serves as an atonement for one's sins. Therefore, it is especially appropriate before the onset of the day to perform specific acts of *tzedakah* that will improve the spiritual and material well-being of the community.

The Meal on Erev Yom Kippur

Unlike the meal held on the eves of Shabbat and other festivals, there are no special rituals connected with the Erev Yom Kippur meal, because it is eaten before the sacred day begins. The mitzvot of *HaMotzi* and *Birkat HaMazon* are observed, as at any meal. This meal, which is called *s'udah mafseket* (the concluding meal before a fast), should begin early so that it is completed before the onset of the holy day. It should be noted that *Kiddush* is not recited at this meal, which must be completed before the onset of Yom Kippur. Since the *Kiddush* usually sets aside the festival as holy and may not be recited before the beginning of the festival, and since the *Kiddush* is normally recited over either wine or bread (neither of which may be consumed on Yom Kippur), *Kiddush* is not recited at the *s'udah mafseket*.

The Mitzvah of Kindling Yom Kippur Lights

Unlike on Shabbat and the other festivals, Yom Kippur candles are lit *after* the meal, because the lighting of the candles marks the formal beginning of Yom Kippur and therefore the beginning of the fast. Before lighting the Yom Kippur candles, it is customary to light a memorial candle, which will burn throughout the holy day. A single candle may be used for all who are to be remembered.

It is a mitzvah to light and recite the appropriate blessing over the Yom Kippur lights after the meal and before leaving for the synagogue:

בָּרוּךְ אַתָּה, יְיָ אֱלֹהֵינוּ,
מֶלֶךְ הָעוֹלָם, אֲשֶׁר קִדְּשָׁנוּ
בְּמִצְוֹתָיו וְצִוָּנוּ,
לְהַדְלִיק נֵר שֶׁל
יוֹם הַכִּפּוּרִים.

Baruch atah, Adonai Eloheinu,
Melech haolam, asher kid'shanu,
b'mitzvotav v'tzivanu,
l'hadlik ner shel
Yom HaKippurim.

Blessed are You, Adonai our God, Sovereign of the universe, who hallows us with mitzvot, commanding us to kindle the lights of the Day of Atonement.

The Mitzvah of Blessing Children

It is a mitzvah for parents to bless their children before leaving for the synagogue. Families may establish their own ritual or use the traditional words

The Mitzvah of Fasting

It is a mitzvah to fast (*tzom*) throughout Yom Kippur. The Torah (Leviticus 16:29, 23:27) designates Yom Kippur as a day of self-denial or, more literally, affliction of the soul. Fasting requires self-discipline and is an attempt to control one's physical needs in order to concentrate on the spiritual. By symbolically denying the most basic biological necessity that humans share with all animals, we focus on that aspect of human nature that we share with God.

Children below the age of bar/bat mitzvah should be taught to fast by beginning with a few hours' fast and increasing the number of hours each year until at thirteen they fast throughout Yom Kippur. A person who is ill or pregnant should follow the advice of a physician on fasting.

The fast begins with the kindling of Yom Kippur candles and concludes with the sounding of the shofar at the end of *N'ilah* and *Havdalah*.

The Mitzvah of Congregational Worship

It is a mitzvah to join the congregation in worship by attending the *Kol Nidrei* service on Yom Kippur night and the several services on Yom Kippur day until the sounding of the shofar at the end of *N'ilah* and recitation of *Havdalah*. As members of the Jewish people, we have personal and communal responsibilities. Participation in the congregational worship service is one such communal obligation, but our attendance at services goes beyond obligation. The public celebration of Yom Kippur through prayer, song, and Torah study is the heart of the Yom Kippur experience. Yom Kippur worship draws us into the circle of the community, strengthening our ties to one another and to the historical values that we Jews hold dear. If illness prevents attendance at services, Yom Kippur prayers should be recited at home.

The Mitzvah of *Yizkor* (Memorial Service)

It is a mitzvah to recite *Yizkor* on Yom Kippur. In some communities, it is a custom that everyone remains for *Yizkor* even if one's parents are alive since *Yizkor* is a service of remembrance for the martyrs of our people as well as for our own relatives and friends.

The Mitzvah of Refraining from Work

It is a mitzvah to refrain from work on Yom Kippur. As the Torah states, "You shall do no work throughout that day. . . . It shall be a sabbath of complete rest for you" (Leviticus 23:28, 32). The same concepts that apply to Shabbat apply to Yom Kippur, known as the Sabbath of Sabbaths.

The Mitzvah of *Havdalah*

At the conclusion of Yom Kippur it is a mitzvah to recite *Havdalah*, separating the holy from the ordinary, and Yom Kippur from the other days of the year.

Beginning the Sukkah after Yom Kippur

Immediately after *Havdalah*, it is customary to make a symbolic start on the suk-kah—by putting up one board or driving one nail. In this manner we conclude the Ten Days of Repentance and turn at once to the performance of a mitzvah.

Breaking the Fast

The meal following Yom Kippur should be a particularly joyous one. There is a feeling of exhilaration and relief that comes from having experienced a day of introspection and prayer in addition to a sense of divine forgiveness. "Go your way, and eat your food with joy, and drink your wine, for God has already accepted your deeds." It is especially appropriate to seek out those in the synagogue who are alone and invite them to join in breaking the fast.

Source: Rabbi Peter S. Knobel, ed., *Mishkan Moeid: A Guide to the Jewish Seasons* (New York: CCAR Press, 2013), 38–44.

Fasting on Yom Kippur

Yom Kippur is a day set apart by the Torah for us to "practice self-denial" (Leviticus 23:27). The "self-denial" that seems to be most expressive of Yom Kippur is fasting, abstaining from food and drink for the entire day.

Fasting is an opportunity for each of us to observe Yom Kippur in a most personal way. It is a day of intense self-searching and earnest communication with the Almighty. This search requires an internal calm that derives from slowing down our biological rhythm. Fasting on Yom Kippur provides the key to our inner awakening.

On Yom Kippur we seek reconciliation with God and humanity. Repentance (*t'shuvah*) involves a critical self-assessment of the past year and the resolve to avoid lapses in sensitivity in the future. *T'shuvah* requires discipline. Our fasting on Yom Kippur demonstrates our willingness to submit to discipline. How can we atone for our excesses toward others unless we can curb appetites that depend on no one but ourselves? To set boundaries for our own conduct in this very private matter is to begin the path toward controlling our public behavior.

The fast of Yom Kippur reaches beyond our inner spiritual awakening and discipline into our ethical behavior. In the Yom Kippur morning haftarah, we read of the prophet Isaiah providing us with the ultimate goal of our fast—to unlock the shackles of injustice, to undo the fetters of bondage, to let the oppressed go free, to share bread with the hungry (Isaiah 58:1–14).

Finally, to fast on the Day of Atonement is an act of solidarity with the suffering of the Jewish people. Through fasting we are drawn closer to all who live lives of deprivation. Our faith demands more of us than twenty-four hours of abstinence from food. It demands that upon the completion of our fast we will turn back to the world prepared to act with love and compassion. In this way fasting touches the biological as well as the spiritual aspects of our being.

Source: Rabbi Peter S. Knobel, ed., *Mishkan Moeid: A Guide to the Jewish Seasons* (New York: CCAR Press, 2013), 123.

Indulging in the Physical?
No, Not on Yom Kippur

BY JANE E. HERMAN

"When we refrain from indulging our physical appetites for a limited period, in order to devote ourselves for a time more exclusively to demands that rank higher in our hierarchy of values, we are not denying the physical appetites their just place in life; we are simply recognizing the need of putting them in their place."

Rabbi Mordecai Kaplan

Three mornings each week, fighting the urge to hit the snooze button, I join a friend in my building's basement gym, stretch my muscles, and walk briskly on the treadmill for 30 minutes. During that time, it's all about my body: the ache in my calves as I trek uphill, the increase in my heart rate, and the sweat that drips from my brow and trickles down my back, soaking through my T-shirt.

On Yom Kippur, I'll skip this physical workout for a spiritual one instead. In fact, Yom Kippur is all about getting beyond our physical selves so we can focus solely on doing the difficult, sacred work the High Holidays demand of us, free from the distractions of our bodies and their needs.

Although many Jews expect to fast on Yom Kippur, to help ensure we devote ourselves to a most accurate *cheshbon hanefesh* (accounting of the soul), it is customary to refrain from five specific activities related to our bodies throughout the holiest day of the Jewish year:

1. **Eating and drinking**: The majority of our lives take place in our physical selves, which require sustenance to function optimally. In an effort to get beyond our corporeal body on this day, we forego food and drink. Of course, you should only do what your body can manage in a healthy way. Those who are sick, pregnant, elderly, or otherwise unable to fast should not do so or should do so only in a modified way.

2. **Wearing leather**: In an earlier era, leather shoes often were among our most comfortable. If we're focused on our personal comfort, we can't also be fully attentive to our spiritual selves. For this reason, you may notice clergy or other worshippers sporting canvas sneakers in lieu of leather shoes on Yom Kippur.

3. **Bathing and shaving**: Because we are engaging with our souls on this day, cleaning and grooming our bodies can take a backseat on Yom Kippur.

4. **Anointing ourselves with oil**, cream, cologne, perfume, or other balms and salves for physical pleasure diverts our attention from the spiritual reckoning for which Yom Kippur is intended. Thus using lotions and the like also is an activity from which we abstain on this sacred day.

5. **Sexual relations**: For all the reasons noted above, refraining from sexual relations on Yom Kippur turns our attention away from our bodies, centering it instead on our actions and misdeeds of the past year.

By abstaining from these activities for the day, we set ourselves up to truly examine our innermost, intimate beings in a most meaningful way, giving ourselves an opportunity to explore what we can do differently in the coming year to tip the balance toward good.

When the sun sets on the Sabbath of Sabbaths, we slowly ease back into our physical selves – returned, revived, refreshed. *Mishkan HaNefesh*, the new Reform *machzor* (High Holiday prayer book), eloquently petitions:

May this long day of fasting and self-denial inspire acts of creativity, generosity, and joy. May we go from strength to strength.

Yes, throughout the coming year and beyond, may it be our bodies that feed the hungry, comfort the bereaved, clothe the naked, and bring justice and humanity to the places they are needed most.

Source: Jane E. Herman, aka JantheWriter, is the senior writer and editor at the Union for Reform Judaism. http://reformjudaism.org/blog/2016/10/11/indulging-physical-no-not-yom-kippur

The Three Festivals
(Sukkot, Pesach, and Shavuot),
Chanukah, Purim, and More

Source Texts

Exodus 12:15–20

[15]Seven days you shall eat unleavened bread; on the very first day you shall remove leaven from your houses, for whoever eats leavened bread from the first day to the seventh day, that person shall be cut off from Israel. [16]You shall celebrate a sacred occasion on the first day, a sacred occasion on the seventh day; no work at all shall be done on them; only what every person is to eat, that alone may be prepared for you. [17]You shall observe the [Feast of] Unleavened Bread, for on this very day I brought your ranks out of the land of Egypt; you shall observe this day throughout the ages as an institution for all time. [18]On the first month, from the fourteenth day of the month at evening, you shall eat unleavened bread until the twenty-first day of the month at evening. [19]No leaven shall be found in your houses for seven days. For whoever eats what is leavened, that person—whether a stranger or a citizen of the country—shall be cut off from the community of Israel. [20]You shall eat nothing leavened; in all your settlements you shall eat unleavened bread.

Exodus 23:15-16

[15]You shall observe the Feast of Unleavened Bread—eating unleavened bread for seven days as I have commanded you—at the set time in the month of Aviv, for in it you went forth from Egypt; and none shall appear before Me empty-handed; [16]and the Feast of the Harvest, of the first fruits of your work, of what you sow in the field; and the Feast of Ingathering at the end of the year, when you gather in the results of your work from the field.

Leviticus 23:4-8

[4]These are the set times of the Eternal, the sacred occasions, which you shall celebrate each at its appointed time: [5]In the first month, on the fourteenth day

of the month, at twilight, there shall be a Passover offering to the Eternal, [6]and on the fifteenth day of that month the Eternal's Feast of Unleavened Bread. [7]On the first day you shall celebrate a sacred occasion: you shall not work at your occupations. [8]Seven days you shall make offerings by fire to the Eternal. The seventh day shall be a sacred occasion; you shall not work at your occupations.

Leviticus 23:39-44

[39]Mark, on the fifteenth day of the seventh month, when you have gathered in the yield of your land, you shall observe the festival of the Eternal to last seven days: a complete rest on the first day, and a complete rest on the eighth day. [40]On the first day you shall take the product of *hadar* trees, branches of palm trees, boughs of leafy trees, and willows of the brook, and you shall rejoice before the Eternal your God seven days. [41]You shall observe it as a festival of God for seven days in the year; you shall observe it in the seventh month as a law for all time, throughout the ages. [42]You shall live in booths seven days; all citizens in Israel shall live in booths, [43]in order that future generations may know that I made the Israelite people live in booths when I brought them out of the land of Egypt, I the Eternal your God. [44]So Moses declared to the Israelites the set times of the Lord.

Deuteronomy 16:9-11

[9]You shall count off seven weeks; start to count the seven weeks when the sickle is first put to the standing grain. [10]Then you shall observe the Feast of Weeks for the Eternal your God, offering your freewill contribution according as Adonai your God has blessed you. [11]You shall rejoice before the Eternal your God with your son and daughter, your male and female slave, the Levite in your communities, and the stranger, the fatherless, and the widow in your midst, at the place where Adonai your God will choose to establish God's name.

Ecclesiastes 3:1–8

1. To every thing there is a season, and a time to every purpose under the heaven:
2. A time to be born, and a time to die; a time to plant, and a time to pluck up that which is planted;

3. A time to kill, and a time to heal; a time to break down, and a time to build up;

4. A time to weep, and a time to laugh; a time to mourn, and a time to dance;

5. A time to cast away stones, and a time to gather stones together; a time to embrace, and a time to refrain from embracing;

6. A time to get, and a time to lose; a time to keep, and a time to cast away;

7. A time to rend, and a time to sew; a time to keep silence, and a time to speak;

8. A time to love, and a time to hate; a time of war, and a time of peace.

Mishnah P'sachim 10:4 (Source of the Four Questions)

They then mix him the second cup. And here the son asks his father (and if the son has not enough understanding his father instructs him how to ask), "Why is this night different from other nights? For on other nights we eat seasoned food once, but this night twice; on other nights we eat leavened or unleavened bread, but this night all is unleavened; on other nights we eat meat roasted, stewed, or cooked, but this night is all roasted. And according to the understanding of the son his father instructs him…"

Vayikra Rabbah 30:12 & 30:14

Another explanation: "The fruit of a beautiful tree"—these are [referring to] Israel. Just like this citron (*etrog*), which has taste and has smell, so too Israel has among them people that have Torah and have good deeds. "The branches of a date palm"—these are [referring to] Israel. Just like this date, which has taste and has no smell, so too Israel has among them those that have Torah but do not have good deeds. "And a branch of a braided tree (a myrtle)"—these are [referring to] Israel. Just like this myrtle, which has smell and has no taste, so too Israel has among them those that have good deeds but do not have Torah. "And brook willows"—these are [referring to] Israel. Just like this willow, which has no smell and has no taste, so too Israel has among them people that have no Torah and have no good deeds. And what does the Holy One, Blessed Be, do to them? To destroy them is impossible, but rather the Holy One, Blessed Be, said "Bind them all together [into] one grouping and these will atone for those." And if you will have done that, I will be elevated at that time. This is [the meaning of] what is written (Amos 9:6), "The One who built the upper chambers in the heavens" (indicating God's elevation). And when is God elevated? When they make one grouping, as it is stated (ibid.), "and established God's grouping on the earth." … Rabbi Mani opined, "'All of my bones shall say, "Adonai, who is like You?"'" (Psalms 35:10). This verse was only stated for the sake of the *lulav* (the four species). The spine of the palm branch is similar to the spine of person. And the myrtle is similar to the eye. And the willow is similar to the mouth. And the *etrog* (citron), is similar to the heart. David said, 'In all of the limbs, there are no greater ones than these, as they are compared to the entire body.' This is [what is meant] by 'All of my bones shall say.'"

Moses Maimonides, *Mishneh Torah,*
Laws of Sanctification of the New Month 5:4

As long as the Sanhedrin functioned and the new month was designated according to the sighting [of the new moon], the people of Israel and in locations close by, whom the Tishrei messengers reached quickly, would observe only one day of Yom Tov. Those who dwelt far away [from Israel], whom the Tishrei messengers did not reach in time, would therefore keep two days out of doubt, for they were not certain which day the people of Israel had determined as the new moon.

The Pilgrimage Festivals
(*Shalosh R'galim*)

Three times a year you shall hold a festival for Me. You shall observe the Feast of Unleavened Bread—eating unleavened bread for seven days as I have commanded you—at the set time in the month of Aviv, for in it you went forth from Egypt; and none shall appear before Me empty-handed; and the Feast of the Harvest, of the first fruits of your work, of what you sow in the field; and the Feast of Ingathering at the end of the year when you gather in the results of your work from the field.

—EXODUS 23:14–16

Three times a year—on the Feast of Unleavened Bread, on the Feast of Weeks, and on the Feast of Booths—all your males shall appear before the Eternal your God in the place that [God] will choose.

—DEUTERONOMY 16:16

Then Solomon offered up burnt offerings to the Eternal upon the altar . . . as the duty of each day required . . . and the annual feasts—the Feast of Unleavened Bread, the Feast of Weeks, and the Feast of Booths.

—II CHRONICLES 8:12–13

Pesach, Shavuot, and Sukkot are collectively known as the *Shalosh R'galim*, the Three Pilgrimage Festivals. During the existence of the Temple, they were the three annual occasions for pilgrimage to Jerusalem with offerings of thanksgiving for the bountiful harvest (Exodus 23:14). The day following Sukkot, Sh'mini Atzeret–Simchat Torah, although a separate festival, is considered part of the Sukkot holiday. Although the origins of the Festivals are bound up with the seasonal changes and the agricultural cycle of ancient Israel, each also commemorates an important event in the history of the Jewish people: Pesach—the Exodus from Egypt; Shavuot—the giving of the Torah at Mount Sinai; and Sukkot—the forty-year journey through the wilderness. Through these historical associations, the Festivals have remained significant in the life of the Jewish people even when they lived in the Diaspora, far from the Land of Israel and its natural rhythms. Wherever Jews live they are able to celebrate liberation, Revelation, and the journey toward the promised future.

The dates for celebrating the Festivals depend on the seasons as they occur in the Land of Israel. Thus, through the celebration of the Festivals, Jews, no matter where they live, feel a connection to the Land of Israel. The reestablishment of the State of Israel has helped renew the original agricultural significance of the Festivals for Jews throughout the world.

Rejoicing is characteristic of the Festivals, for they are opportunities to enrich our lives by renewing our commitment to the Jewish ideals of redemption, responsibility, and hope. Through the performance of the unique mitzvot of the Festivals, we participate in the continuing drama of sacred history, and through our celebration, we reaffirm our identity as part of the Jewish people.

The festivals have certain mitzvot in common, and others that are unique to each festival. For the sake of clarity, the mitzvot common to all festivals are listed first in a preliminary section, followed by the mitzvot of the particular festivals.

The Mitzvah of Observing the Festivals

It is a mitzvah to observe the Festivals, as the Torah says, "Three times a year you shall hold a festival for Me" (Exodus 23:14). The Festivals are Pesach, Shavuot, and Sukkot (including Sh'mini Atzeret–Simchat Torah).

The Mitzvah of Rejoicing (*Simchah*) on the Festivals

It is a mitzvah to rejoice on the Festivals. The Torah teaches, "You shall rejoice in your festival" (Deuteronomy 16:14). This mitzvah sets the tone and mood of the Festivals.

Special liturgy, special ceremonial objects, and special foods make each celebration distinctive. Our joy is also derived from our recalling the decisive moments in the history of the Jewish people that helped shape the ideals of Judaism. Through the reaffirmation of our commitment to those ideals and by joining together with other Jews in the ongoing task of working to repair the world (*tikkun olam*), our lives take on renewed significance.

The Mitzvot of the Festivals

Shabbat observance provides the paradigm for the observance of the Festivals. The following mitzvot are common to both Shabbat and the Festivals: (1) preparation (2) including guests at the festive table; (3) lighting candles ; (4) *Kiddush*; (5) blessing of children); (6) *HaMotzi*; and (7) concluding the meal with *Birkat HaMazon*. Several of the blessings for the Festivals differ from those for Shabbat. The text of these prayers can be found in *Mishkan T'filah: A Reform Siddur*.

It is customary for the mealtime conversation to reflect the joy and holiness of the occasion and talk can be interspersed with *z'mirot* (table songs). The festival table is a particularly appropriate place to discuss the meaning of the festival.

Weddings on the Festivals

Jewish tradition holds that Shabbat and the Festivals are days on which weddings may not be held. The reason is twofold: first, the signing of the *ketubah* and the exchange of rings are derived from contract law and fall into the category of a business transaction; second, since Shabbat and the Festivals are already days of joy and holiness, prohibiting weddings on Shabbat and the Festivals emphasizes the special joy and holiness of the wedding, according to the concept *ein m'ar'vin simchah b'simchah*, not to mix two happy occasions together.

The Mitzvah of *Havdalah*

It is a mitzvah to recite *Havdalah* at the conclusion of the Festivals. The blessing of separation is recited over wine and marks the end of the Festivals. As the formal beginning of a festival is marked by blessings and the festival set apart and distinguished from ordinary days, the departure of the festival is similarly marked. Having both a formal beginning and formal conclusion helps us to hallow the festival and to savor the experience of the festival even after it is concluded.

Source: Rabbi Peter S. Knobel, ed., *Mishkan Moeid: A Guide to the Jewish Seasons* (New York: CCAR Press, 2013), 46–50.

The Three Pilgrimage Festivals

RABBI JOEL SISENWINE

In Exodus 23:14, God says, "Three times a year you shall hold a festival for Me." And ever since, so the Jewish people has done, gathering together to rejoice in God's presence. Early in our history, the festivals of Pesach, Shavuot, and Sukkot were largely agricultural in nature, revolving around the harvest and God's role within it. Later, as Jews moved away from the farms and into the cities, historical meanings prevailed, linking each festival with the biblical narrative of the Israelites' journey. Passover was no longer solely Chag HaAviv, the holiday celebrating the onset of spring, but now emphasized the Exodus from Egypt. Shavuot was no longer solely the Festival of First Fruits (Chag HaBikurim), or the Harvest Festival (Chag HaKatzir), but now *z'man matan Torateinu*, the day that the Jewish people received the Torah. Sukkot was no longer solely Chag HaAsif, the time to rejoice in the harvest and sleep in agricultural huts (sukkot), but also a time that reminded us of our desert wanderings.

"None shall appear before Me empty-handed," the Torah continues, exhorting the people to bring an offering to God (Exodus 23:15). In Temple times, these offerings came in the form of animal sacrifices and agricultural sacrifices, carefully described in the biblical text. Jews would travel from far and wide, making pilgrimage to the Temple, giving the festivals the collective name *Shalosh R'galim*, "the Three Pilgrimage Festivals" (*shalosh* for "three"—the three times of Passover, Shavuot, and Sukkot; and *r'galim* for "feet," a reference to the necessary walking that pilgrimage requires). But soon another type of sacrifice came to dominate Jewish observance, the sacrifice of the heart, *avodah shebalev*, otherwise known as prayer.

Source: Rabbi Joel Sisenwine, "The Festival and Holy Day Liturgy of *Mishkan T'filah*," in *Mishkan Moeid: A Guide to the Jewish Seasons*, ed. Rabbi Peter S. Knobel (New York: CCAR Press, 2013), 115.

Sukkot

(Including Sh'mini Atzeret–Simchat Torah)

On the fifteenth day of this seventh month there shall be the Feast of Booths to the Eternal, [to last] seven days.

—LEVITICUS 23:34

After the ingathering from your threshing floor and your vat, you shall hold the Feast of Booths for seven days.

—DEUTERONOMY 16:13

On the eighth day you shall observe a sacred occasion.

—LEVITICUS 23:36

Sukkot begins on the fifteenth of the Hebrew month of Tishrei and concludes on the twenty-second with Sh'mini Atzeret–Simchat Torah. Sukkot is the fall harvest festival. The eighth day, Sh'mini Atzeret, functions as the conclusion of Sukkot but is also a separate festival. Since Reform Jews follow the calendar of the Land of Israel and do not add a ninth day to the festival, we celebrate Simchat Torah and Sh'mini Atzeret on the same day.

More than any other of the Pilgrimage Festivals, Sukkot, also known as *He-Chag*, has retained its agricultural character. However, Sukkot is also the commemoration of a significant event in the life of the Jewish people: the journey through the wilderness toward the Land of Israel. The Torah identifies the sukkah (booth) with the temporary dwellings in which the Israelites lived during that journey (Leviticus 23:42).

The mood of Sukkot is particularly joyous. Its beautiful symbolism of the successful harvest provides a welcome change of religious pace from the solemn days of prayer and introspection of Rosh HaShanah and Yom Kippur. While all of the Three Pilgrimage Festivals are times of rejoicing, Sukkot is specifically designated as *z'man simchateinu*, "the season of our rejoicing." Even while we rejoice, the sukkah's temporary and fragile structure reminds us how precarious life can be.

Through the use of the *lulav* and *etrog*, we acknowledge our dependence on God for the food we eat. Living in an urban environment, it is easy to forget that both human labor and divine blessing make the world fruitful. On Sukkot our thoughts turn to the wonder and beauty of the world, to our responsibilities as its caretakers, and to our obligation to share, for God is the true owner of the land and its produce.

Sh'mini Atzeret–Simchat Torah is the day on which we finish reading the last verses of Deuteronomy and immediately begin again with the first verses of Genesis. The Torah scrolls are removed from the ark and carried around the synagogue. The celebration is one of unbridled joy as we express our happiness at having lived to complete the reading of the Torah yet another time and to begin reading it again.

The Mitzvah of Observing Sukkot

It is a mitzvah to observe Sukkot for seven days, from the fifteenth of the Hebrew month of Tishrei, and to conclude on the twentysecond (the eighth day) with the observance of Sh'mini Atzeret– Simchat Torah, as the Torah says, "On the fifteenth day of the seventh month there shall be the Feast of Booths to the Eternal, [to last] seven days. . . . On the eighth day you shall observe a sacred occasion" (Leviticus 23:34, 36).

The Mitzvah of Rejoicing

It is a mitzvah to rejoice on Sukkot, as the Torah teaches, "You shall rejoice on your festival . . . for the Eternal your God will bless all your crops and all your undertakings, and you shall have nothing but joy" (Deuteronomy 16:14–15). While rejoicing is a mitzvah on all of the Three Pilgrimage Festivals, it is characteristic of the observance of Sukkot—so much so that the tradition has designated it as *z'man simchateinu*, "the season of our rejoicing."

The Mitzvah of *Tzedakah*

It is always a mitzvah to give *tzedakah*. However, since on Sukkot we give thanks for the harvest, all the more should we feel obliged to share with those who are less fortunate.

The Mitzvah of Building a Sukkah

It is a mitzvah for every Jew to dwell in the sukkah, though today that generally means spending time in the sukkah rather than actually living in it. It is a custom to begin the construction of the sukkah immediately after the conclusion of Yom Kippur services followed by decorating it. The sukkah may be built in a yard or on a roof or balcony. Those who live in apartments or other locations where the construction of a sukkah is not feasible can help in the building or decorating of the sukkah at the synagogue, the community center, or the home of friends—and spend time within it.

The Mitzvah of *Lulav* and *Etrog*

It is a mitzvah to take up the *lulav* and *etrog* and recite the appropriate blessing at any time during the whole day of Sukkot.

בָּרוּךְ אַתָּה, יְיָ אֱלֹהֵינוּ,   *Baruch atah, Adonai Eloheinu,*

מֶלֶךְ הָעוֹלָם,   *Melech haolam, asher kid'shanu*

אֲשֶׁר קִדְּשָׁנוּ בְּמִצְוֹתָיו   *b'mitzvotav v'tzivanu*

וְצִוָּנוּ עַל נְטִילַת לוּלָב.   *al n'tilat lulav.*

Praise to You, Adonai, Sovereign of all, who hallows us with mitzvot, commanding us to take up the *lulav*.

By taking up the *lulav* and *etrog* and waving them in all directions, we symbolically acknowledge the sovereignty of God over all nature.

The *lulav* and *etrog* are two of the four species (*arbaah minim*). They consist of *etrog* (citron), *lulav* (palm), *hadas* (myrtle), and *aravah* (willow). The identification of the four species is based on the interpretation of Leviticus 23:40, "On the first day you shall take the product of the *hadar* trees, branches of palm trees, boughs of leafy trees, and willows of the brook."

The *etrog* has maintained a separate identity. Two willow branches and three myrtle branches are bound together around one palm branch and are called the *lulav*.

It is desirable to acquire a *lulav* and *etrog*, and it is preferable, where possible, to select one's own set. By selecting a beautiful *lulav* and *etrog*, we enhance the performance of the mitzvah. The palm, myrtle, and willow should be fresh and green. It is customary to take special care in selecting the *etrog*. It should be yellow, with no discoloration on its skin. The tip (*pitom*) should not be broken.

The Mitzvah of Celebrating in the Sukkah

It is a mitzvah to celebrate in the sukkah. The Torah says, "You shall live in booths seven days; all citizens of Israel shall live in booths, in order that the future generations may know that I made the Israelite people live in booths when I brought them out of the land of Egypt" (Leviticus 23:42–43).

The Torah speaks of living in the sukkah for seven days. Where climate and circumstances permit, some will want to do so. However, others will prefer to fulfill this mitzvah by eating in the sukkah (either a whole meal or a symbolic meal or by making *Kiddush* there). When eating or reciting *Kiddush* in the sukkah, an additional blessing is recited:

בָּרוּךְ אַתָּה, יְיָ אֱלֹהֵינוּ,
מֶלֶךְ הָעוֹלָם, אֲשֶׁר קִדְּשָׁנוּ
בְּמִצְוֹתָיו וְצִוָּנוּ
לֵישֵׁב בַּסֻּכָּה.

Baruch atah, Adonai Eloheinu,
Melech haolam, asher kid'shanu
b'mitzvotav v'tzivanu
leisheiv basukkah.

Praise to You, Adonai our God, Sovereign of the universe, who hallows us with Your mitzvot, commanding us to dwell in the sukkah.

When circumstances do not permit one to fulfill this mitzvah in one's own sukkah, one should seek out the sukkah at the synagogue, at the community center, or at the home of friends.

The Mitzvah of Hospitality

As part of the mitzvah of hospitality, we are urged to share our meals in gratitude for God's gifts. There is a ceremony of welcoming guests known as *ushpizin*, which evokes the presence of the Patriarchs and Matriarchs as our spiritual companions in the sukkah.

Reading of *Kohelet*

The Book of *Kohelet* (Ecclesiastes) is read on the Shabbat during Sukkot. Like the sukkah, it reminds us of the transitory nature of life.

Chol Hamoeid

The intermediate days of Sukkot are known as *chol hamoeid*. The mitzvot of celebrating in the sukkah and blessing the *lulav* can be performed during this time. Each day can be an opportunity for rejoicing and for preserving the festival atmosphere.

Sh'mini Atzeret–Simchat Torah

Sh'mini Atzeret–Simchat Torah follows the seventh day of Sukkot and is celebrated as a day of rejoicing. The mitzvot that are common to all the other festivals are observed on Sh'mini Atzeret–Simchat Torah.

The Mitzvah of Completing and Beginning the Torah Cycle on Sh'mini Atzeret–Simchat Torah

It is a mitzvah to participate in the *hakafah* (Torah procession) honoring the completion and beginning of the Torah-reading cycle and to hear the reading of the end of Deuteronomy and the beginning of Genesis. The Torah is divided into weekly portions that are read throughout the entire year, from beginning to end. The completion of the reading of the Torah is a time of rejoicing and an opportunity to express love for Torah. Immediately after completing the reading of the last verses of Deuteronomy, the first verses of Genesis are read to indicate that the study of Torah never ends. It symbolizes our obligation to observe the mitzvah of *talmud Torah* constantly.

The Mitzvah of *Yizkor*

Yizkor services take place on Sh'mini Atzeret–Simchat Torah. It is a mitzvah to join with the congregation in reciting *Yizkor*. It memorializes our deceased relatives and friends as well as the martyrs of our generation and previous generations.

Consecration

Since Simchat Torah is a joyful affirmation of the mitzvah of Torah study, some congregations hold a special ceremony for children entering religious school for the first time. The ceremony, called consecration, emphasizes the importance and joy of *talmud Torah* in Jewish tradition. It is also the custom at consecration to give the children something sweet so that they may look upon the learning of Torah as sweet. In addition, many congregations present the children with miniature Torah scrolls, which the children then keep in a special place.

Source: Rabbi Peter S. Knobel, ed., *Mishkan Moeid: A Guide to the Jewish Seasons* (New York: CCAR Press, 2013), 64–70.

Dwelling in Safety on Sukkot:

A PRAYER FOR REFUGEES

Rabbi Michael Adam Latz

We pray to you
Creator of the Universe,
who causes the winds to blow
and the seas to rage…

For the weary and the heart shattered
refugees
escaping violence and bloodshed and war

Who step into raging waters
with an impossible prayer
it is safer than the ground on which they stand
clasping the hands of their children
desperate for life
without the horror of bombs and bloodshed and rape.

We build our sukkah—
Tall enough to stand underneath
Wide enough to fit a table to eat
and to feast
and to gaze up and see the stars.

Protected.
Stable.
Portable.
Enduring.

As we hammer the nails into our sukkah,
We meditate on the mitzvah—*leysheiv ba-sukkah*—
to dwell in the sukkah.

We are blessed for
when it rains
or is too cold
or inconvenient
we go inside and dry ourselves,
warmed by the illusions of our contentment.

But too many of our sisters and brothers fleeing war in Syria have
No such shelter
No safety
No prayer for dwelling in safety.

If the sukkah stands for anything at all,
let it be a shelter for our Divine empathy,
That we hear the cries of the oppressed
and do God's work to walk with them to freedom
To provide shelter—
Warmth and food and—

Who
like our ancestors,
set out on an epic journey
to freedom.

If our sukkah stands for anything at all,
It must call each of us to conscience—
We were slaves
And now we are free

To serve God.
And walk with the oppressed
To freedom.

Jewish tradition calls upon us to invite
ancient guests
into our sukkah.

The Jewish conscience demands we welcome
Refugees—
living, breathing, aching, hurting people—
into the sukkah of our nation:
Ibrahim
Mariam
Ya'qub
Nuri
Abdul
Rasha
Dawud

Come in.
Welcome.

Source: Rabbi Michael Adam Latz, "Dwelling in Safety on Sukkot: A Prayer for Refugees," ReformJudaism.org blog, September 25, 2015, http://www.reformjudaism.org/blog/2015/09/25/dwelling-safety-sukkot-prayer-refugees.

Pesach

You shall observe the [Feast of] Unleavened Bread, for on this very day
I brought your ranks out of the land of Egypt; you shall observe this day
throughout the ages as an institution for all time. In the first month,
from the fourteenth day of the month at evening, you shall eat unleavened bread until the twenty-first day of the month at evening.

—EXODUS 12:17–18

You shall observe this as an institution for all time, for you and your descendants. . . . And when your children ask you, "What do you mean by
this rite?" you shall say, "It is the passover sacrifice to the Eternal, who
passed over the houses of the Israelites in Egypt when smiting the Egyptians, but saved our houses."

—EXODUS 12:24, 26–2 7

You shall observe the Feast of Unleavened Bread—eating unleavened
bread for seven days, as I have commanded you—at the set time of the
month of Aviv, for in the month of Aviv you went forth from Egypt.

—EXODUS 34:18

Pesach, which begins on the fifteenth of the Hebrew month of Nisan and lasts for
seven days, commemorates the Exodus from Egypt. In the Torah, it is designated
by several names: Chag HaAviv (based on Deuteronomy 16:1), the Spring Festival; Chag HaMatzot (based on Exodus 12:20), the Festival of Unleavened Bread;
and Chag HaPesach (based on Exodus 12:21), the Festival of the Paschal Lamb.

While current Pesach observance draws some of its symbolism from the agricultural and pastoral origins of the festival, it is primarily a celebration of the
Exodus from Egypt.

The liberation of the Jewish people from Egyptian bondage has become a powerful symbol of redemption—not only the redemption of the Jewish people, but the redemption of the entire world. The Haggadah, reflecting the historical experience of the Jewish people, recognizes that slavery is not limited to physical bondage, but that spiritual slavery and social degradation are no less potent methods of depriving human beings of liberty.

The highlight of Pesach observance is the seder, with its many symbolic foods and its elaborate liturgy, the Haggadah. The seder is designed to re-create the events of redemption:

> In every generation, each of us should feel as though we ourselves had gone forth from Egypt, as it is written: "And you shall explain to your child on that day, it is because of what the Eternal did for me when I, myself, went forth from Egypt."

As *z'man cheiruteinu*, "the season of our freedom," Pesach is a constant reminder of our responsibility to those who are oppressed or enslaved physically, intellectually, or ideologically. On Pesach we express our solidarity with other members of the Jewish community who are unable to celebrate Passover in freedom. The experience of redemption in the Passover celebration inspires us all to assist in the future redemption of humanity. As the midrash teaches, just as the Sea of Reeds did not split until the Israelites stepped into it, so redemption cannot come unless we take the first step.

The Mitzvah of Observing Pesach

It is a mitzvah to observe Pesach for seven days, beginning on the eve of the fifteenth of Nisan, as the Torah says, "In the first month, from the fourteenth day of the month at evening, you shall eat unleavened bread until the twenty-first day of the month at evening" (Exodus 12:18).

The Mitzvah of Removing Leaven

It is a mitzvah to remove leaven from our homes prior to the beginning of Pesach. Leaven refers to products made from wheat, barley, rye, oats, and spelt that have been permitted to leaven. Ashkenazi custom adds rice, millet, corn, and legumes (e.g., peas, beans), referred to as *kitniyot*. The removal of leaven is based on the biblical injunction found in Exodus 12:15: "On the very first day you shall remove leaven from your houses." Some will choose to remove all leaven from their homes. Others may choose to put all the leaven in a specially marked cabinet or closet that is appropriately marked, as a constant reminder of the special dietary elements of Pesach. Still others use this as an opportunity to donate food to a local food bank or soup kitchen.

Searching for leaven, *b'dikat chameitz*, on the night before the first seder is a Pesach custom that adds a wonderful dimension to Pesach preparation. After the house has been cleaned for Pesach, a symbolic search for the last remains of leaven is made. At various places in the home, pieces of leaven are hidden. Then children and adults, with flashlights or other illumination, search them out in the dark. Often a wooden spoon and a candle are used. When the leaven is found, it is scooped onto the wooden spoon with a feather. The leaven is gathered in a bag and burned or disposed of the next morning at which time we recite the following blessing:

בָּרוּךְ אַתָּה, יְיָ אֱלֹהֵינוּ,
מֶלֶךְ הָעוֹלָם, אֲשֶׁר קִדְּשָׁנוּ
בְּמִצְוֹתָיו וְצִוָּנוּ,
עַל בִּעוּר חָמֵץ.

Baruch atah, Adonai Eloheinu,
Melech haolam, asher kid'shanu
b'mitzvotav v'tzivanu,
al biur chameitz.

Blessed are You, Eternal our God, Sovereign of the universe, who sanctifies us with Your commandments and calls upon us to remove leaven.

Since leaven has been removed, refraining from eating bread after breakfast on the day before the seder is part of the preparation for the observance of Pesach. To heighten the appetite for matzah at the seder itself, it is a custom not to eat matzah at least a full day before the seder.

The Mitzvah of Abstaining from Eating Leaven

It is a mitzvah to abstain from eating leaven during the entire seven days of Pesach, as the Torah states, "You shall eat nothing leavened" (Exodus 12:20). Abstaining from leaven may take many forms—from not eating those foods that obviously contain leaven, such as bread or cake, to avoidance and examination of all ingredients in a particular foodstuff. By consciously making a choice to abstain during the whole week of Pesach, we are constantly aware of the festival and of our Jewish identity.

The Mitzvah of Preparing a Seder

The word *seder* means "order." The seder is an ordered table service, using a Haggadah, of fourteen (or in some interpretations, fifteen) steps that lead from slavery to freedom. It is a mitzvah for everyone to participate in the preparation for the seder—cooking, cleaning, and setting the festive table. The leader of the seder has the special obligation to review the Haggadah in advance and decide which passages will be included. The experience of the seder is enhanced when all the participants are provided with the same Haggadah.

The Central Conference of American Rabbis offers several different Haggadot. The well-known classic is *A Passover Haggadah*, edited by Rabbi Herbert Bronstein and illustrated by Leonard Baskin, with essays by Rabbis Lawrence A. Hoffman and W. Gunther Plaut. An innovative Haggadah with many readings and songs from around the Jewish world is *The Open Door*, edited by Rabbi Sue Levi Elwell and drawings by Ruth Weisberg. Another wonderful option is *Sharing the Journey: The Haggadah for the Contemporary Jewish Family*, written by Alan Yoffie and illustrated by Mark Podwal, with an inclusive, welcoming text that is a great introduction for first-time seder participants. This Haggadah offers a track list of seder songs for download, as well as a step-by-step leader's guide. CCAR also publishes a Haggadah for children, *A Children's Haggadah*, with text by Rabbis Howard Bogot and Robert Orkand and illustrated by Devis Grebu.

In addition, the tradition encourages the use of beautiful ritual items to increase our enjoyment of the mitzvot.

Although Reform Jews do not officially celebrate the second day of Pesach as a holiday, many people have a second seder. Sometimes they join in a congregational seder or gather with relatives and friends who attended other first-night sedarim. The second seder may follow the same pattern as the first or may have another focus. A second seder may provide the opportunity for additional reflection that was omitted on the first night.

The Mitzvah of Hospitality (*Hachnasat Or'chim*)

It is a mitzvah to invite guests to join in the seder. So important is it that the invitation is included in the text of the Haggadah, "Let all who are hungry come and eat. Let all who are in want share the hope of Passover." Arrangements should be made to see that no one has to celebrate Passover alone. Many communities make special arrangements for those who are alone, including the elderly and college students who are away from home. One might also invite non-Jewish friends and family to join in this important celebration of human freedom. It is an excellent way for people to learn about Judaism in an engaging and enjoyable manner.

It is a mitzvah to give *tzedakah* before the beginning of Passover. Tradition encourages the solicitation of מָעוֹת חִטִּין (*ma-ot chitin*), special funds, to provide a proper seder for the poor.

The Mitzvah of Participating in the Seder and Reciting the Haggadah

It is a mitzvah for every Jew to participate in the recitation of the Haggadah, which recalls the Exodus from Egypt. The text of the Haggadah teaches that we should look upon ourselves as having personally experienced the Exodus. "In every generation, each of us should feel as though we ourselves had gone forth from Egypt, as it is written: 'And you shall explain to your child on that day, it is because of what the Eternal did for me when I, *myself*, went forth from Egypt.'"[27]

The Seder Plate

* Not included on
every seder plate.

In front of the leader or in front of each participant, a special seder plate is set. The following are arranged on it: three separate pieces of matzah—two pieces represent the two traditional loaves (*lechem mishneh*) set out in the ancient Temple during Sabbaths and festivals, and the third matzah is symbolic of Passover; a roasted shank bone (*z'roa*), burned or scorched, representing the ancient Passover sacrifice; parsley or green herbs (*karpas*), symbolizing the growth of springtime, the green of hope and renewal; the top part of horseradish root (*maror*) or other bitter herbs, symbolic of the bitterness that our ancestors experienced in Egypt and, in a contemporary sense, the lot of all who are enslaved; (*charoset*), representing the mortar that our ancestors used for Pharaoh's labor; a roasted egg (*beitzah*), representing the (*chagigah*), or festival offering, a symbol of life itself, the triumph of life over death. Some seder plates also include a place for additional bitter greens like romaine lettuce (*chazeret*), and some also include salt water. In recent years, a new tradition has developed of placing an orange on the seder plate, as a symbol of gay and lesbian inclusion. This is meant to represent the additional fruitfulness of a society that welcomes and includes all people.

The Cup of Elijah

A special cup filled with wine is placed prominently on the table. In popular legend the prophet Elijah (herald of redemption) visits every Jewish home at some time during the seder. Therefore, one cup of wine is set aside for him. After the meal, one of the participants, usually a young child, opens the door for Elijah. This is a moment filled with hope and anticipation.

The Cup of Miriam

A recent addition to the seder table is a ceremonial cup for the prophetess Miriam, who led the Jewish people in song and dance after the crossing of the Reed Sea (Exodus 15:20–21). According to legend, a special well called Miriam's well traveled with the Israelites as they journeyed through the desert. Miriam's cup represents the lifegiving waters.

The Mitzvah of Eating Unleavened Bread

By eating matzah we recall that the dough prepared by our people had no time to rise before the final act of redemption: "And they baked unleavened cakes of the dough since they had been driven out of Egypt and could not delay, nor had they prepared provisions for themselves."

It is a mitzvah to eat matzah during the seder and to recite the appropriate blessings.

בָּרוּךְ אַתָּה, יְיָ אֱלֹהֵינוּ,
מֶלֶךְ הָעוֹלָם,
הַמּוֹצִיא לֶחֶם מִן הָאָרֶץ.

Baruch atah, Adonai Eloheinu,
Melech haolam,
hamotzi lechem min haaretz.

Blessed are You, Eternal our God, Sovereign of the universe, who brings forth bread from the earth.

בָּרוּךְ אַתָּה, יְיָ אֱלֹהֵינוּ,
מֶלֶךְ הָעוֹלָם, אֲשֶׁר קִדְּשָׁנוּ
בְּמִצְוֹתָיו וְצִוָּנוּ,
עַל אֲכִילַת מַצָּה.

Baruch atah, Adonai Eloheinu,
Melech haolam, asher kid'shanu
b'mitzvotav v'tzivanu
al achilat matzah.

Blessed are You, Eternal our God, Sovereign of the universe, who has sanctified us with Your commandments and has commanded us concerning the eating of unleavened bread.

The Mitzvah of Eating Bitter Herbs

Maror is eaten to remind us that the Egyptians embittered the lives of our people, as it is written: "With hard labor at mortar and brick and in all sorts of work in the field, with all the tasks ruthlessly imposed upon them."

It is a mitzvah to eat *maror*, the bitter herbs, with the appropriate blessing.

בָּרוּךְ אַתָּה, יְיָ אֱלֹהֵינוּ,
מֶלֶךְ הָעוֹלָם, אֲשֶׁר קִדְּשָׁנוּ
בְּמִצְוֹתָיו וְצִוָּנוּ,
עַל אֲכִילַת מָרוֹר.

Baruch atah, Adonai Eloheinu,
Melech haolam, asher kid'shanu
b'mitzvotav v'tzivanu
al achilat maror.

Blessed are You, Eternal our God, Sovereign of the universe, who has sanctified us with Your commandments and has commanded us concerning the eating of bitter herbs.

The Mitzvah of Four Cups

It is a mitzvah to drink four cups of wine or grape juice during the seder.

The Four Questions

It is customary for the youngest participant or participants to recite the Four Questions. These questions point to the unusual features of the seder meal and provide an opportunity to teach the lesson of Passover.

Reclining

It is the custom to simulate a reclining position while eating by propping oneself up with cushions. Reclining at the seder is symbolic of being free people who are able to eat wth leisure.

Afikoman

The *afikoman* is the half matzah that is set aside during the breaking of the matzah early in the seder. An old tradition held that the group could not leave the seder table unless all had tasted of the *afikoman*. In connection with this, and in order to arouse and maintain the interest of the children and to provide some entertainment for them, a practice developed of hiding and searching for the *afikoman*. Sometime during the meal, the leader hides the *afikoman*, trying to elude the watchful observance of the children, whose endeavor it is to search out its hiding place. Prizes might be awarded to all who participated, with a special gift to the one who actually finds it. In some households, it is the custom for children to "steal" the *afikoman* in order to hide it and hold it for "ransom," since the meal cannot conclude without it.

Chol HaMoeid

The intermediate days, between the first and the seventh days, are known as *chol hamoeid*. During this period no leaven is eaten, but many people enjoy cooking and eating special Passover foods. Every effort is made to preserve the holiday mood.

The Song of Songs

On the Shabbat during Pesach, the Song of Songs (*Shir HaShirim*) is read. The Song of Songs refers to springtime and thus befits the Festival. In addition,

Jewish tradition has interpreted Song of Songs as an allegory of the love of God for Israel. The experiences of hope and redemption, which characterize Pesach, make the Song of Songs particularly appropriate to this season.

The Mitzvah of *Yizkor*

It is a mitzvah to recite *Yizkor* on the seventh day of Pesach. It memorializes our relatives and our friends, as well as the martyrs of our generation and previous generations.

The Study of *Pirkei Avot*

Beginning with the first Shabbat after Pesach, it is customary to study one of the chapters of *Pirkei Avot* (Ethics of the Ancestors) each Shabbat afternoon until Shavuot. *Pirkei Avot* is devoted to the ethical religious maxims of the Rabbis. The study of this material is part of the preparation for Shavuot. As we complete each weekly study session, we are one week closer to Shavuot and the recollection of (*matan Torah*), the giving of the Torah at Sinai.

Source: Rabbi Peter S. Knobel, ed., *Mishkan Moeid: A Guide to the Jewish Seasons* (New York: CCAR Press, 2013), 50–60.

Passover Kashrut

A REFORM APPROACH

RABBI MARY L. ZAMORE

This day shall be to you one of remembrance: you shall celebrate it as a festival to the Eternal throughout the ages; you shall celebrate it as an institution for all time. Seven days you shall eat unleavened bread; on the very first day you shall remove leaven from your houses, for whoever eats leavened bread from the first day to the seventh day, that person shall be cut off from Israel. You shall celebrate a sacred occasion on the first day, and a sacred occasion on the seventh day; no work at all shall be done on them; only what every person is to eat, that alone may be prepared for you. You shall observe the [Feast of] Unleavened Bread, for on this very day I brought your ranks out of the land of Egypt; you shall observe this day throughout the ages as an institution for all time. In the first month, from the fourteenth day of the month at evening, you shall eat unleavened bread until the twenty-first day of the month at evening. No leaven shall be found in your houses for seven days. For whoever eats what is leavened, that person— whether a stranger or a citizen of the country—shall be cut off from the community of Israel. You shall eat nothing leavened; in all your settlements you shall eat unleavened bread.

—Exodus 12:14–20

These verses establish the holiday of Passover and command that we should eat matzah and refrain from eating *chameitz*, leavened bread, during the seven days. The Rabbis define *chameitz* as five grains—wheat, barley, spelt, rye, and oats (BT *P'sachim* 35a)—that are exposed to water for more than eighteen minutes. This time frame is counted from the minute the water touches the flour to the time it is fully baked. Although the time frame was debated through the development of this law, eighteen minutes is considered the boundary between matzah and *chameitz* (BT *P'sachim* 46a; *Shulchan Aruch, Orach Chayim* 459). Therefore, matzah is produced from start to finish in under eighteen minutes. Kosher-for-Passover foods that contain these grains (e.g., cookies, cakes, crackers, pasta) are usually made from matzah meal (finely ground matzah) rather than flour to ensure that there is no *chameitz* in the product.

In the strictest observance of Passover, the entire household is thoroughly cleaned. All dishes, pots, and utensils are switched to sets reserved for Passover use. All food products containing any morsel of *chameitz* are used up before the holiday or are removed from use and stored away. Then, these forbidden foods are symbolically sold (see CCAR Responsum 5756.9). All food brought into the cleaned home must be certified kosher for Passover. This level of observance may be overwhelming to Jews who did not grow up with these practices; it may seem unnecessary to others.

Therefore, the following approach is for those who are just beginning to keep Passover and those seeking a simpler way to keep Passover. It can also be used as a paradigm as to how to teach Passover kashrut within the liberal community. Clearly, this can be adjusted to incorporate more or fewer observances; it can be adjusted according to the age and knowledge levels of the students.

A Simple Model for Keeping Passover Kashrut

Clean your kitchen and eating areas to remove crumbs, etc. (If you eat in your car, you may want to vacuum it.)

1. Go through your pantries, refrigerator, and freezer, removing all obvious *chameitz*. (*Kitniyot* are discussed CCAR responsum 5756.9.) Children love to sort things; engage their help. It will help them learn the laws of Passover and excite them about the holiday.

2. Store away nonperishable foods in closed bags, boxes, or cabinets, so they are not a temptation. Many people mistakenly believe that Jews must throw out all of their unused food before Passover. This is not true and would be wasteful. However, if you can afford it, Passover cleaning provides a wonderful opportunity to donate unused food to a local food pantry. It is also a good time to support your local kosher food pantry so that other Jews can celebrate Passover.

3. If you have an extra refrigerator and/or freezer, put perishable foods in it and tape it shut. If you have only one refrigerator/freezer, designate a particular drawer or shelf for *chameitz*. Place *chameitz* in black plastic bags and then place in the refrigerator/freezer. It is easier to keep the holiday if you are not looking at *chameitz*.

4. Go shopping, buying lots of delicious foods. If you are short on time, consider what is easy to prepare. You do not need to limit yourself to the Passover aisle. There are plenty of foods found throughout the store that are good for the holiday. You can either buy foods that are certified for Passover or read labels to stay away from the five grains. Consider allowing a few treats like sugary Passover cereal if that helps motivate your family. Also, remember that fresh fruits and vegetables are all kosher for Passover, making Passover a great time to return to a back-to-basics diet, avoiding commercially processed foods.

As you feel comfortable with your level of observance, you can evaluate and adjust your practices, adding more rituals as you see fit.

Source: Rabbi Peter S. Knobel, ed., *Mishkan Moeid: A Guide to the Jewish Seasons* (New York: CCAR Press, 2013), 154–156.

Next Year, May We All Be Free

CHARLIE ARNOWITZ

When I was little, I would practice the Four Questions for hours on end before the seder began, ensuring that I pronounced every Hebrew word correctly and hit every musical note. When I finally would recite them shortly after the seder began, I was so nervous I could barely think about anything else. Afterward, my family would applaud and tell me how good a job I had done, and I would be so excited and relieved that I usually paid little attention the next part of the service. But this part, though I did not know it at the time, was the crucial answer to my four questions:

> We were slaves to Pharaoh in Egypt and Adonai our God took us out from there with a strong hand and with an outstretched arm. If the Holy One, blessed be He, had not taken our ancestors out of Egypt, then we, our children and our children's children would have remained enslaved to Pharaoh in Egypt. And even if all of us were wise, all of us understanding, all of us knowledgeable in the Torah, we would still be obligated to tell the story of the Exodus from Egypt.

Because we ourselves may have been slaves, we are obligated to tell the story of the Exodus: to remind ourselves of how lucky we are, but never to forget what it is to be in bondage. It is this drive, this distant memory of our slavery in Egypt that inspires our commitment to telling this story and to working toward society free of all sorts of bondage.

The main theme of Passover is this celebration of our journey from bondage to freedom, but around the globe and here at home, there are many who have

162

yet to fully experience freedom. From poverty and inequality to discrimination in areas like employment, voting, the criminal justice system, wages, or legal status, we still have yet to fully realize the promise of our Exodus. At Pesach, the Haggaddah tells us, we are obligated to tell this story of the Exodus, to remind us of the fact that we were slaves. But we should also tell it to remind ourselves that our society is full of injustices, and that like Moses who led the Israelites out of Egypt, we have the potential to do something about it.

At the end of the seder, we stand and open the door, hoping for redemption, as have Jews for centuries on this night. Pesach is fundamentally about looking forward, even as we examine this crucial chapter in our own people's history. This year, at the end of the seder, as we look back and then look forward to the year ahead, let us think about what we can each do to make this a better world.

Source: Charlie Arnowitz, "Next Year, May We All Be Free," ReformJudaism.org blog, April 7, 2014, http://www.reformjudaism.org/blog/2014/04/07/nextyear-may-we-all-be-free.

Counting the Omer

RABBI A. BRIAN. STOLLER

From the day on which you bring the omer of elevation offering— the day after the Sabbath—you shall count off seven weeks. They must be complete: you must count until the day after the seventh week— fifty days; then you shall bring an offering of new grain to Adonai.

—Leviticus 23:15–16

Just as all the crops are ripening during these days [of counting], so too is the life of man revealed [during this time]. For all of it is but an allusion to the way of the inner life.

—S'fat Emet

No fraction of time ... should slip through the fingers, left unexploited; for eternity may depend upon the brief moment.

—Rabbi Joseph Soloveitchik

Counting the Omer,[1] the traditional practice of counting the forty-nine days between Passover and Shavuot, is making a comeback in Reform Judaism. Once virtually ignored as an ancient custom that had lost its religious significance,

1 On the *halachot* of *S'firat HaOmer*, see Leviticus 23:9–21; *Mishneh Torah, Hilchot T'midim uMusafim* 7:3–25; *Sefer HaChinuch*, commandments 302–306 (*Parashat Emor*); and *Shulchan Aruch, Orach Chayim* 489:1. The requirements for Counting the Omer outlined in this introduction are drawn from these sources, unless otherwise noted.

S'firat HaOmer (as it is known in Hebrew) is now increasingly regarded among Reform Jews as a meaningful way to mark time, express gratitude, refocus priorities, and contemplate deeply the meaning and purpose of our existence.

Rabbi Karyn D. Kedar, one of the Reform Movement's most inspiring authors and composers of creative liturgy, introduced the practice to her community in Deerfield, Illinois, several years ago by e-mailing her congregants a short reading or prayer each day of the Omer and inviting them to reflect on it. Their responses were thoughtful and deeply emotional. Congregants wrote heartfelt notes about how the daily messages had touched their lives and provided a spark of inspiration in the middle of their busy days, they circulated the e-mails to their friends and family, and soon an entire congregation of Reform Jews who previously had never heard of Counting the Omer came to regard it as one of the most meaningful spiritual events of the year.

This book, which is a continuation of Rabbi Kedar's initial project, aims to help the broader Reform community similarly experience the power of *S'firat HaOmer*. In some sense it is like a prayer book: just as a prayer book gives us the vocabulary to pray, this book gives us a vocabulary to count the Omer through daily meditation on contemporary poetry and prose, both Jewish and secular. Before we can begin counting the days and contemplating these texts, however, we need to understand the basics of *S'firat HaOmer* and some of the key spiritual insights that emerge from Jewish interpretation of this practice.

Spiritual Dimensions of S'firat HaOmer

The Nature and Purpose of Wealth

The period from the second day of Passover to Shavuot coincides with the spring harvest in *Eretz Yisrael* (the Land of Israel). The rituals prescribed in the Torah structure the time and activity of this season so as to elevate consciousness of and inspire gratitude for God's role as the source of the bounty. To sanctify the harvest's beginning, the biblical Jew was commanded to bring to the Jerusalem Temple an omer offering of barley, the first fruit to ripen during the season. Giving God the first and best of the new crop, in a measure amounting to "sufficient food for a person for one day,"[2] meant putting God before one's own person al needs and satisfaction. Indeed, a person was not permitted to eat anything from the harvest until he had brought the omer offering—an acknowledgment that,

---

2 Rabbi Samson Raphael Hirsch, comment to Leviticus 23:10, in *The Hirsch Chumash: Sefer Vayikra—Part 2*. transl. Daniel Haberman (Jerusalem: Feldheim, 2008), 783.

without God, his abundance and sustenance would not be possible. The counting of the Omer commenced immediately thereafter, numbering the days until Shavuot, which ritually marked the end of the harvest season.

Though most Reform Jews today (especially outside *Eretz Yisrael*) do not live in farming societies, these agricultural themes are eminently relevant to modern Jewish life. Broadly understood, the "harvest season" is when we reap the fruits of our labors, whether on the farm, in commerce, or wherever we earn our livelihood. This is the time when instinct and societal norms tell us finally to relax and enjoy the abundance we have sown. But as Rabbi Samson Raphael Hirsch points out, this moment when others stop counting is precisely the moment when Jews *begin* to count,[3] affirming the connection between our God-given freedom to produce (symbolized in Passover) and our responsibility to dedicate what we reap to the service of God (embodied in Shavuot). *S'firat HaOmer* thus teaches us that wealth is not an end unto itself, but rather, as Hirsch writes, that "material prosperity has meaning only insofar as it helps attain and maintain right and morality."[4] The act of counting reminds us to view our wealth with gratitude to the One who made it possible and inspires us to see it as a blessing that God has entrusted to us so that we can serve God's purposes in the world.

The Power of the Moment

In contrast to other instances of halachically mandated day-counting, we may not simply keep track of the Omer period in our heads;[5] rather, we are commanded to count the days and weeks of the Omer in a formal ritual manner, orally and while standing, in part because doing so draws our attention to the spiritual significance of time.[6] We begin counting each night by reciting the following blessing:

3 See Hirsch, comment to Leviticus 23:15
4 Hirsch, comment to Deuteronomy 16:9, in *The Hirsch Chumash: Sefer Devarim*, trans. Daniel Haberman (Jerusalem: Feldheim, J179 2009), 358.
5 Nachmanides (comment to Leviticus 23:15) notes that in cases where a person has an emission, he/she must count seven days to himself (*lo*)/herself (*lah*) before becoming pure (see Leviticus 15:13 and 15:28)—i.e., the person is required simply to keep track of the days, but not to count them aloud. The command to count the Omer, by contrast, is stated as *us' fartem lachem* ("for yourselves" in the plural), which, according to Nachmanides, indicates that the obligation is for each individual person to count the Omer orally.
6 See Rabbi Michael Rosensweig, quoted in David Shapiro, *Rabbi Joseph B. Soloveitchik on Pesach*, Sefirat ha-Omer *and Shavu'ot* (Brookline, MA: Rabbi Joseph B. Soloveitchik Institute, 2005), 149.

בָּרוּךְ אַתָּה,
יְיָ אֱלֹהֵינוּ,
מֶלֶךְ הָעוֹלָם, אֲשֶׁר קִדְּשָׁנוּ
בְּמִצְוֹתָיו וְצִוָּנוּ, עַל סְפִירַת הָעוֹמֶר.

Baruch atah,
Adonai Eloheinu,
Melech haolam, asher kid'shanu
b'mitzvotav v'tzivanu, al s'firat haomer.

Our praise to You, Adonai our God, Sovereign of all, who hallows us with mitz-vot, commanding us to count the Omer.[7]

During the first six days of counting, one should say: Today is the (first / second / . . . sixth) day of the Omer.

From the seventh day onward, one should take care to mention both the days and the weeks,[8] in the following manner:

Today is the fifteenth day—two weeks and one day of the Omer.

Rabbi Joseph Soloveitchik teaches that this practice of verbally counting days and weeks makes us aware both of where we have been and where we are going, thus evoking a sense of movement from one state of being to another.[9] Time, in the Jewish consciousness, is purposeful and directed, ripe with potential, and filled with meaning. Yet even as we look toward the future, counting each day forces us to acknowledge and appreciate the significance of the moment. Every day presents us with the choice to stay where we are, to revert to where we have been, or to progress toward fulfilling our destiny. The classical law codes instruct us to count the Omer at night (when a Hebrew calendar day begins) so that each day is counted *in full*. This halachic requirement evokes an essential lesson of *S'firat HaOmer*: that every moment of our lives is consequential, that every moment counts.

Spiritual Purification and Preparation

Counting the days from the Exodus to Sinai establishes a philosophical link between the two events, reminding us that freedom comes with responsibility: God redeemed us from Egyptian slavery not merely so we could be free, but rather

---

7 The liturgy for *S'firat HaOmer* is found in *Mishkan T'filah*, ed. Elyse D. Frishman (New York: CCAR Press, 2007), 570. This translation comes from *Mishkan T'filah;* throughout the rest of this volume an original, alternate translation is used for the same Hebrew.
8 Shapiro, *Rabbi Joseph B. Soloveitchik on Pesach*, Sefirat ha-Omer *and Shavu'ot*, 151–52.
9 Shapiro, *Rabbi Joseph B. Soloveitchik on Pesach*, Sefirat ha-Omer *and Shavu'ot*, 151–52.

so we would serve God and live by God's Torah. Because fulfilling the Torah is the purpose of a Jew's life, we should glorify the day on which Torah was given by counting the days in eager anticipation "as is done by one who waits for the coming of the human being he loves best and counts the days and hours."[10]

Just as a bride is given time to prepare for her wedding day by adorning herself in jewels,[11] so too the Jewish people were given the Omer period to ready themselves to receive the Torah. The *Zohar*, the central text of Kabbalah, teaches that while they were slaves in Egypt, the Israelites were under the evil influence of the "other side" (*sitra achra*), which rendered them spiritually impure. Although God liberated them from these dark forces on Passover, they still required time to purify themselves before becoming fit to receive the Torah. Pointing to a halachic principle that a ritually impure person must complete a period of seven days before becoming pure again,[12] Kabbalah scholar Isaiah Tishby explains that "the seven weeks of Counting the Omer are seen as the seven 'clean' intervals necessary before Israel can be purified from the remains of the uncleanness in Egypt."[13]

Modern life continues to be, as the Rabbis understood it, a perpetual struggle between *yetzer hara* (the evil inclination) and *yetzer hatov* (the good inclination). Occasionally the dark forces of the other side tempt us astray; like our ancestors, we too need to be purified. Fortunately, Judaism offers a way back into the light. The Chasidic master S'fat Emet teaches that "the doorway to redemption is opened in Nisan [at Passover]," but in order to walk through it, we first must do the difficult work of cleansing ourselves of spiritual impurity. The Omer is a "clarifying period" during which we have the opportunity to focus intently on strengthening our good character attributes, tempering our negative ones, improving our actions, and realigning our priorities.[14] In so doing, we prepare ourselves intellectually, emotionally, and spiritually to stand again at Sinai and renew our covenant with God each year at Shavuot.

In the kabbalistic tradition, this purification is achieved through daily contemplation of the seven lower *s'firot*, which, as Lawrence Kushner and Nehemiah Polen explain, constitute seven "dimensions of the divine psyche":

10 Moses Maimonides, *Guide of the Perplexed* 3:43, trans. Shlomo Pines (Chicago: University of Chicago Press, 1963), 2:571.
11 See mishnah at Babylonian Talmud, *K'tubot* 57a and Rashi ad loc.
12 See note 5 above.
13 Isaiah Tishby, *The Wisdom of the Zohar: An Anthology of Texts* (Portland, OR: Littman Library of Jewish Civilization, 1989), 3:1241–42.
14 S'fat Emet, in *Likkut mi-Sifrei ha-Gaon ha-Kodesh Ba'al ha-"S' fat Emet" al Seder haT'filah* (Hebrew) (Jerusalem, 5767), 2:190.

1. *Chesed*, "love," means unlimited expansion and inclusiveness.
2. *G'vurah*, "rigor," means the setting of boundaries.
3. *Tiferet*, "beauty," means balance or harmony.
4. *Netzach*, "victory," means commitment, eternity, and showing up.
5. *Hod*, "splendor," means the reverberation that comes from making definitions, as these definitions ripple outward throughout our perception of the world.
6. *Y'sod*, "foundation," means the joy of creation, the (almost) orgiastic pleasure that is the foundational moment in every project.
7. *Malchut*, "kingdom," means receptivity to take in the blessing that is given.[15]

According to kabbalistic theory, all seven *s'firot* continuously act and react upon each other, creating dynamic spiritual energy within God. Because we are made in God's image, the same spiritual dynamism exists within us as well. To help us tap into it, kabbalistic practice sets each of the seven *s'firot* as the theme of one of the Omer's seven weeks: the first week's theme is *Chesed*, the second week's theme is *G'vurah*, and so on. On each day of the *Chesed* week, for example, we contemplate *Chesed* together with one of these seven *s'firot*, progressing from one *s'firah* to the next in the order enumerated above:

- On the second day, we consider *Chesed* in combination with *G'vurah* (rigor): Why would I need to set boundaries on love? How do I know where those boundaries are, and how do I set them in practice? What happens if my boundaries are too loose or too firm?
- On the third day, we contemplate *Chesed* in combination with *Tiferet* (beauty): What makes love beautiful? How can love bring balance and harmony into my life and into the lives of others? Is it possible for love to create imbalance?

This method of reflection continues throughout the remainder of the forty-nine-day Omer period. Rabbi Laibl Wolf, a contemporary Chasidic writer and lecturer, teaches that these forty-nine combinations within the divine psyche correspond to forty-nine shades of emotions in the human personality.[16] To

---

15 Adapted from Lawrence Kushner and Nehemiah Polen, "Chasidic and Mystical Perspectives," in *My People's Prayer Book: Traditional Prayers, Modern Commentaries*, vol. 9, *Welcoming the Night*, ed. Lawrence A. Hoffman (Woodstock, VT: Jewish Lights, 2005), 169.
16 I heard Rabbi Wolf discuss these ideas at a Jewish Learning Institute Lecture in Skokie, Illinois, on August 26, 2012.

count the Omer using the kabbalistic method, therefore, is to engage in intense exploration of our own mind, character, and spirit in order to strengthen and elevate them.

Purifying ourselves spiritually during the Omer period raises us to a new level of holiness and enables us to commune with God on Shavuot.[17] As discussed above, the ancient omer offering that was brought at the beginning of the counting period was a sacrifice of barley; the Shavuot sacrifice marking the end of the Omer, by contrast, was a gift of wheat. These agricultural practices have profound spiritual meaning, as Hirsch explains:

> The omer is brought from barley flour. Barley, however, is not a primary food of man, but food for animals (see b. Sotah 14a). The omer, then, represents merely physical existence. . . . Only on the fiftieth day, after struggling to purification and freedom while counting the days and weeks; only on the day that commemorates the giving of the Torah, does Israel approach God's altar with wheat bread—which is designed for man.[18]

In short, Counting the Omer inspires us to do the hard work of spiritual purification—work that elevates us above an earthly, animallike existence and helps us become more fully human.

Evolving Attitudes, Evolving Practices

Classical Concerns: The Temple, Mourning Rituals, and Lag BaOmer

Although the omer sacrifice can no longer be offered in the absence of the Temple, the commandment of S'firat HaOmer remains obligatory as a *zeicher laMikdash*, an act performed in remembrance of the Temple's destruction.[19] As

---

17 See S'fat Emet, s.v. *us' fartem lachem* (*Emor*, 652), 188, where he interprets the two loaves of bread that are commanded to be brought as a Shavuot offering (Leviticus 23:17) as an allusion to the fusion of divine and human spiritual forces on that festival.
18 Hirsch, comment to Leviticus 23:17. *The Hirsch Chumash: Sefer Vayikra*, 794.
19 Rabbi Joseph Soloveitchik teaches that there are two types of *zeicher laMikdash* (a ritual performed in remembrance of the Temple): One type of *zeicher laMikdash* recalls the glory and splendor of the Temple while it stood. This type, which includes the commandments to take the *lulav* on Sukkot and to blow the shofar on Rosh HaShanah, is a joyous kind of remembrance; for that reason, we say the *Shehecheyanu* blessing before performing these commandments. The second type of *zeicher laMikdash* recalls the Temple's destruction and, in contrast to the first type, has a mournful connotation. Soloveitchik contends that because the Sages did not ordain that we should say *Shehecheyanu* before counting the Omer, we can conclude that they understood the mitzvah of S'firat HaOmer in our time to be a *zeicher laMikdash* of the second, mournful type. For an extended discussion of this issue, see Shapiro, *Rabbi Joseph B. Soloveitchik on Pesach*, Sefirat ha-Omer *and Shavu'ot*, 135–37.

such, the Omer period, which was originally tied to the bounty of the harvest, has in the post-Temple era taken on a sad and somber character that, due to historical events, has deepened over time. According to the Talmud, thousands of Rabbi Akiva's disciples died during the days of the Omer of a plague brought on because they acted disrespectfully toward one another.[20] Other Jewish national tragedies have similarly occurred during the counting period, including massacres of German Jews by the Crusaders and the Nazi deportation of Hungarian Jews.[21] The halachah gives expression to this somber mood by requiring abstention from haircuts, weddings, and other joyous events from the beginning of the Omer until the thirty-third day (known as Lag BaOmer), since according to tradition, the suffering of Rabbi Akiva's disciples halted on that day.[22] Thus it is common for observant Jews to celebrate Lag BaOmer by having weddings, holding festive bonfires, and cutting their hair. Rabbi Isaac Klein adds that in modern times, Yom HaAtzma-ut (Israel's Independence Day), which occurs on the twentieth day of the Omer (5 Iyar), provides another festive interruption during the counting period. These days present opportunities for modern Reform Jews to celebrate and reflect on the themes of freedom, independence, and responsibility.

Reform Attitudes and Practice: Then and Now

Reform Judaism, in the main, has abandoned the mourning practices associated with the Omer. An 1871 synod of early European Reform leaders formally abrogated the halachic ban on weddings during the Omer, and a 1913 American Reform responsum asserted that the prohibition was no longer religiously significant in light of scholarship demonstrating it to "have [its] parallel in ancient

---

20 See Babylonian Talmud, *Y'vamot* 62b.

21 See Isaac Klein, *A Guide to Jewish Religious Practice* (New York: Ktav, 1992), 142–43.

22 See *Shulchan Aruch, Orach Chayim* 493:1–3. Rabbi Moses Isserles notes that weddings are permitted from Lag BaOmer through the end of the Omer period (493:1). Rabbi Joseph Caro holds that haircutting is prohibited through the end of Lag BaOmer, until the morning of the thirty-fourth day (493:2), but Isserles explains that in Ashkenazic lands, it is permitted to cut one's hair on Lag BaOmer itself (ad loc.). Isserles adds, however, that customs regarding haircutting vary from place to place: in some locales, people are accustomed to cutting their hair on the first of Iyar, whereas in other places, haircutting is prohibited until Lag BaOmer, but permitted thereafter (gloss to 493:3). Isaac Klein likewise notes variation in the mourning customs practiced during this period and explains that "in Ashkenazic communities, the most widespread custom has been to observe mourning from Pesah [*sic*] until three days before Shavuot. Exceptions are made on Rosh Hodesh Sivan, Rosh Hodesh Iyar, and Lag Ba'Omer" (Klein, *A Guide to Jewish Religious Practice*, 143).

Roman superstition, or rather mythology."[23] Beyond this, Reform literature is largely silent as to why Counting the Omer fell out of practice. Liturgy for *S'firat HaOmer* is omitted without explanation from CCAR Reform prayer books prior to *Mishkan T'filah*, and *Gates of the Seasons: A Guide to the Jewish Year* likewise contains no mention of the practice. One possible reason is that in its original biblical context, there is no indication that Counting the Omer had any purpose other than to ensure that the Shavuot festival, marking the harvest's end, would be celebrated on the proper day. For this reason, explained Rabbi Mark Washofsky in 2001, "Reform Judaism has [in the past] generally regarded this 'counting' as a regulation of the calendar"—that is, a utilitarian activity without spiritual significance—and thus concluded that "there is no need . . . to count the days in a ritual manner."[24]

But we are in a new era of our Movement, in which it is common for Reform congregations and individuals to reclaim traditional practices once discarded by previous generations for whom they lacked resonance. Reform Judaism is defined by its commitment to change, and as some of our Movement's leading voices have put it, "Nothing would, therefore, hinder us as Reform Jews from readopting customs once omitted if a new generationfindsthemmeaningfuland-usefulinitspracticeof Judaism."[25] Movement in this direction is already evident: the newest CCAR prayer book, *Mishkan T'filah*, published in 2007, includes liturgy for Counting the Omer, as does *Mishkan Moeid: A Guide to the Jewish Seasons* (2013), which is meant to replace *Gates of the Seasons*.[26] In this proud tradition of change, Rabbi Kedar aims to help us rediscover and reinvent *S'firat HaOmer* ina way thatembodies the contemporary Reformspirit. Taking inspiration from Chasidic tradition, which sees these days between Passover and Shavuot as "good days [*yamim tovim*], like *chol hamo-eid* [the intermediate days of a festival], because there is holiness before them and after them,"[27] she gives us access to *S'firat Ha-Omer* as a modern spiritual practice, focused not on sadness and mourning, but rather on contemplation and reflection, inner exploration, and spiritual growth.

Source: Rabbi A. Brian Stoller, *Introduction, Omer: A Counting*, by Rabbi Karyn D. Kedar (New York: CCAR Press, 2014), xi–xxiii.

23 K. Kohler and D. Neumark, "Times When Weddings Should Not Take Place," in *American Reform Responsa*, ed. Walter Jacob (New York: CCAR Press, 1983), 410.
24 Mark Washofsky, *Jewish Living: A Guide to Contemporary Reform Practice* (New York: URJ Press, 2001), 110. In the 2010 edition of his book (p. 109), Washofsky notes the inclusion of *S'firat HaOmer* in the new CCAR prayer book *Mishkan T'filah*, indicating that this previous Reform attitude has begun to change.
25 Walter Jacob et al., "Discarded Practices," in *American Reform Responsa*, 4.
26 See note 7 above.
27 S'fat Emet, s.v., *us' fartem lachem* (Emor, 642), 187.

Shavuot

You shall observe the Feast of Weeks, of the first fruits of the wheat harvest.

—EXODUS 34:22

On the day of the first fruits, your Feast of Weeks, when you bring an offering of new grain to the Eternal, you shall observe a sacred occasion.

—NUMBERS 28:26

You shall count off seven weeks; start to count the seven weeks when the sickle is first put to the standing grain. Then you shall observe the Feast of Weeks for the Eternal your God, offering your freewill contribution according as the Eternal your God has blessed you.

—DEUTERONOMY 16:9–10

Shavuot occurs on the sixth of the Hebrew month of Sivan. The name Shavuot (meaning "weeks") derives from its celebration seven weeks (a week of weeks) after Pesach.[43] In the Torah it is also designated by the names Chag HaKatzir, the Harvest Festival (Exodus 23:16), and Chag HaBikurim, the Festival of First Fruits (Exodus 34:22). It is also know as *z'man matan torateinu*, the time of the giving of the Torah.

Current observance is based on the Talmudic identification of Shavuot with the events at Sinai. Therefore it is called *z'man matan Torateinu*, "the season of the giving of the Torah." On Shavuot, we celebrate our covenantal relationship with God and reaffirm our commitment to a Jewish life of study (*talmud Torah*) and practice (mitzvah). The significance of the events at Sinai derives not only from the receiving of mitzvot but also from their acceptance, as is illustrated in Israel's response, *Naaseh v'nishma*, "We will faithfully do" (Exodus 24:7). Sinai represents a constant effort to confront life and history in light of this covenantal relationship. The ceremony of confirmation (*Kabbalat Torah*) is a Reform innovation and has added a new dimension to the meaning of the festival. It provides an opportunity for students of post–bar/bat mitzvah age to affirm their relationship to Judaism and the Jewish people.

The Mitzvah of Observing Shavuot

It is a mitzvah to observe Shavuot seven weeks after Passover, on the sixth of Sivan, as it is said, "From the day on which you bring the sheaf of elevation offering—the day after the Sabbath [understood by the Rabbis to mean the first day of Passover]—you shall count off seven weeks. They must be complete: you must count until the day after the seventh week—fifty days. . . . On that same day you shall hold a celebration; it shall be a sacred occasion for you" (Leviticus 23:15–16, 23:21).

Decorating the Home and Synagogue

It is customary to decorate one's home and the synagogue with greens and fresh flowers on Shavuot. The greenery is a reminder of the ancient practice of bringing first fruits (*bikurim*) to the Temple in Jerusalem. It also calls to mind our hopes for an abundant harvest.

The Mitzvah of Reaffirming the Covenant

It is a mitzvah to reaffirm the covenant on Shavuot. Through the reading of the Ten Commandments at services, which recalls the establishment of the covenant and the contemplation of the importance of Torah and its lifelong study, (*talmud Torah*), we renew our commitment to being part of the covenant people, (*am b'rit*). As part of the celebration of Shavuot, many congregations practice the custom of studying Torah late into Shavuot night. This Torah vigil is called (*Tikkun Leil Shavuot*).

Attending Confirmation Service

The ceremony of confirmation is one of the highlights of Shavuot observance in many synagogues. When the Temple stood, Jews brought offerings of first fruits, *bikurim*, to the Temple on Shavuot. Today, parents bring their children to participate in confirmation. These young people are the first fruits of each year's harvest. They represent the hope and promise of tomorrow. During the service, the confirmands reaffirm their commitment to the covenant. "[The confirmation's] purpose is to encourage the intellectual and spiritual growth of young people, to strengthen the bonds between them and the Israelites who received the Torah at Sinai (Exodus 19:3–8 and Deuteronomy 29:9–14), and to stimulate their love for God and the Jewish people" (*Gates of Mitzvah*, page 22, E-8).

Reading of the Book of Ruth

The Book of Ruth (*M'gilat Rut*) is read on Shavuot. The story of Ruth takes place during the barley harvest at the Shavuot season. More important, Rabbinic tradition sees a parallel between Ruth's willing acceptance of Judaism and the Jewish people's acceptance of Torah.

Special Foods

It is customary to eat dairy dishes on Shavuot. Rabbinic tradition draws an analogy between the sweetness and physical nourishment the Jew receives from milk and honey and the sweetness and spiritual nourishment of the words of Torah.

Yizkor on Shavuot

Yizkor is recited on Shavuot. It is a mitzvah to join with the congregation in reciting *Yizkor*. It memorializes our deceased relatives and friends as well as the martyrs of our generation and previous generations. The text for the *Yizkor* service can be found in *Mishkan T'filah: A Reform Siddur*, pages 574–583.)

Source: Rabbi Peter S. Knobel, ed., *Mishkan Moeid: A Guide to the Jewish Seasons* (New York: CCAR Press, 2013), 61–64.

What Are the Numbers of Shavuot?

ELLEN ZIMMERMAN

This year, Shavuot starts at sundown on June 3rd. Aside from what happens in synagogue, your home celebrations can take so many forms — decorating with fresh greens and flowers, making special foods, and so much more. I thought it would also be fun to think about various numbers that are meaningful during Shavuot. (Anyone else see a home trivia game here?!) Play along and add even more numbers.

#1: *Bikurim*, or first fruits, are key symbols of Shavuot. These first fruits—including some of the Seven Species crops—were carried in a basket of gold or silver to the Temple in Jerusalem.

#2: Moses received two forms of Torah on Mount Sinai—the written law and the oral law.

#3: Shavuot is one of the three pilgrimage festivals, along with Sukkot and Passover, during which the Israelites trekked to Jerusalem to bring offerings to the Temple.

#6: Shavuot comes on the sixth day of the month of Sivan.

#7: There are seven weeks between the end of Passover and the beginning of Shavuot, during which we Count the Omer.

#10 According to the Talmud, God gave the Ten Commandments to the Jews on Shavuot.

#40: So why do we eat dairy products on Shavuot? There are lots of explanations. Here's one that's new to me: the *gematria* (numerology) of the Hebrew word for milk, *chalav*, is 40, corresponding to the 40 days and 40 nights that Moses spent on Mt. Sinai before descending with the Torah.

#90: Many congregations read a 90-line poem written in Aramaic, called *Akdamut*, on the first day of Shavuot praising the greatness of God, Torah and Israel.

#613: Sephardic Jews do not read *Akdamut*. Instead, they sing a poem called *Azharot* which mentions the 613 Biblical commandments.

What numbers can you add for Shavuot?

Source: Ellen Zimmerman, "What Are the Numbers of Shavuot?," ReformJudaism.org blog, May 13, 2014, http://www.reformjudaism.org/blog/2014/05/13/what-are-numbers-shavuot.

Purim
Source Texts

Esther 9:20–28

[20] Mordecai recorded these events. And he sent dispatches to all the Jews through-out the provinces of King Ahasuerus, near and far,[21] charging them to observe the fourteenth and fifteenth days of Adar, every year—[22] the same days on which the Jews enjoyed relief from their foes and the same month which had been transformed for them from one of grief and mourning to one of festive joy. They were to observe them as days of feasting and merrymaking, and as an occasion for sending gifts to one another and presents to the poor. [23] The Jews accord-ingly assumed as an obligation that which they had begun to practice and which Mordecai prescribed for them. [24] For Haman son of Hammedatha the Agagite, the foe of all the Jews, had plotted to destroy the Jews, and had cast *pur* — that is, the lot — with intent to crush and exterminate them. [25] But when [Esther] came before the king, he commanded: "With the promulgation of this decree, let the evil plot, which he devised against the Jews, recoil on his own head!" So they impaled him and his sons on the stake. [26] For that reason these days were named Purim, after pur. In view, then, of all the instructions in the said letter and of what they had experienced in that matter and what had befallen them, [27] the Jews undertook and irrevocably obligated themselves and their descendants, and all who might join them, to observe these two days in the manner prescribed and at the proper time each year. [28] Consequently, these days are recalled and observed in every generation: by every family, every province, and every city. And these days of Purim shall never cease among the Jews, and the memory of them shall never perish among their descendants.

Purim

> The rest of the Jews, those in the king's provinces, likewise mustered and fought for their lives. . . . That was on the thirteenth day of the month of Adar; and they rested on the fourteenth day and made it a day of feasting and merrymaking. (But the Jews in Shushan mustered on both the thirteenth and fourteenth days, and so rested on the fifteenth, and made it a day of feasting and merrymaking.) That is why village Jews, who live in unwalled towns, observe the fourteenth day of the month of Adar and make it a day of merrymaking and feasting, and as a holiday and an occasion for sending gifts to one another.
>
> —ESTHER 9:16–19

Purim, which occurs on the fourteenth of the Hebrew month of Adar (or in Jerusalem, on the fifteenth), is a celebration of the events described in the Scroll of Esther (*M'gilat Esther*). The holiday, with its joyous carnival-like atmosphere, focuses on one of the main themes in Jewish history—the survival of the Jewish people despite the attempts of their enemies to destroy them. According to the Scroll of Esther, the name Purim is derived from the lot (*pur*) cast by Haman to determine the day on which the Jews would be exterminated (Esther 3:7).

The story of Purim is about hunger for power and about hatred born of the Jews' refusal to assimilate and their unwillingness to compromise religious principles by bowing before the secular authority. It is an old story. However, it has been repeated many times, making it both an ancient and modern tale.

In the story, it is related that Mordecai, Esther's cousin, refuses to prostrate himself before Haman, the vizier of King Ahasuerus. So infuriated is Haman that he seeks the annihilation of the Jewish people. Haman's accusation against the Jewish people has become the paradigm for all anti-Semites: "There is a certain people, scattered abroad and dispersed among the peoples . . . their laws are different from those of other people, they do not obey the king's law, and the king should not tolerate them" (Esther 3:8). The prudent actions of Mordecai and the courage of Esther avert tragedy.

Purim recalls the dangers of minority status. Hatred of the foreigner and the stranger is still prevalent throughout the world. Anti-Semitism has not disappeared, but despite everything, the Jewish people has survived. Purim, however, is most of all a happy story—a story of survival and triumph over evil.

The Mitzvah of Observing Purim

It is a mitzvah to observe Purim on the fourteenth of Adar. This is based on the statement "Village Jews, who live in unwalled towns, observe the fourteenth day of the month of Adar and make it a day of merrymaking and feasting, and as a holiday and an occasion for sending gifts to one another" (Esther 9:19). However, in walled cities like Shushan, Purim was observed on the fifteenth day (Esther 9:18). Even though the walls of Jerusalem had been destroyed at this time, the Rabbis designated Jerusalem the status of a walled city.

The Mitzvah of Reading the Scroll of Esther (M'gilat Esther)

It is a mitzvah to read the biblical Scroll of Esther (M'gilat Esther; commonly, the M'gilah) and to celebrate the holiday with the congregation. As part of the M'gilah reading, it is customary for the listeners to attempt to drown out the sound of Haman's name by shouting or using gragers (raashanim—special noisemakers).

Rejoicing and Feasting

The almost unrestrained merriment that pervades the celebration of Purim makes it unique among the Jewish holidays. Adults and children are encouraged to wear costumes. Synagogues and communities stage Purim plays, hold carnivals, and serve festive communal meals. All these activities are an expression of great joy at having survived Haman and countless other enemies.

Special Foods

Hamantaschen (Haman's pockets), or oznei Haman in Hebrew (Haman's ears), are three-cornered cookies filled with poppy seeds or other fruits served on Purim.

The Sending of Portions *(Mishlo-ach Manot)*

Traditionally Purim is a time for exchanging gifts. It is customary to send gifts of food or pastries to friends and family. The sending of these gifts is called *mishlo-ach manot*, "the sending of portions" (Esther 9:22). (This custom is often called *shalachmanos*.)

The Mitzvah of Sending Gifts to the Poor

It is a mitzvah to send gifts to the poor on Purim. The sending of gifts to the poor is an act of *tzedakah* that is especially connected with Purim.

Source: Rabbi Peter S. Knobel, ed., *Mishkan Moeid: A Guide to the Jewish Seasons* (New York: CCAR Press, 2013), 76–79.

An Adult Look at the Less-Than-Savory Truths of Purim

Rabbi Sari Laufer

Oh, once there was a wicked wicked man, and Haman was his name, sir.
He lied and lied about the Jews, though they were not to blame, sir.

Wait, *hold up!*

Now, my husband would tell you that I have a knack for imagining I learned song lyrics differently from others (until my last breath, I really believe we used to sing: "Little Bunny Foo Foo, I don't like your attitude.") Perhaps I'm not the most trustworthy on song lyrics, but trust me when I say that, growing up, our lyrics were a little different:

Oh, once there was a wicked, wicked man, and Haman was his name, sir.
He would have murdered all the Jews, though they were not to blame, sir.

Now, as the parent of young children, I appreciate the pivot. I understand age-appropriate learning, and I'm thankful I don't need to explain genocide to my 3-year-old just yet. Purim is, and should be, a joyous holiday, a raucous holiday, a time for fun and frivolity.

But there's also a dark side to the Purim story, and I think it's time we let the grownups in on some truths. I don't want to be the one to burst your bubble, but there are a couple of things you might not have known about the Purim story... and this list is by no means exhaustive.

1. Vashti probably didn't head off to an exotic island.

The story begins with the king's first wife, Vashti, who has become a feminist hero for her refusal to parade and dance naked in front of the king and his cronies. It was not just her refusal that incensed the king, but the fear that she might incite a *Lysistrata*-esque resistance amongst the women of the land (#neverthelessshepersisted).

While our standard telling of the tale suggests a no-fault divorce of some kind, the rabbinic tradition is far less kind to Vashti. *Midrashim* (rabbinic stories) imagine banishment at best, beheading at worst. Imagine what we could teach our sons and daughters about their bodies, and about consent, as it became appropriate for them to learn about what really happened to Vashti.

2. Queen Esther did not enter the Miss America pageant.

In our attempt to pretty up Purim and make it palatable for our littlest learners, we've set the story in an innocent beauty pageant, the stuff of pretty dresses and sparkly jewels. In reality, as I recently read,

"the voiceless, virginal Esther is delivered, by whom we're not told), to the king's harem. There she spends a year, 'six months with oil of myrrh and six months with perfumes and feminine cosmetics' (Esther 2:12), under the tutelage of seven court-appointed handmaidens, preparing for a sexual liaison with Ahasuerus. If she fails to win the king's favor and become the queen, she faces a lifetime sentence as a royal concubine."

Then, as now, women's bodies were seen as commodities, as something to barter and trade. We cannot ignore it then, as we cannot ignore it now.

3. At the end of the story, we did not just "nosh some hamantaschen."

Growing up in religious school, I can remember loudly singing "Oh, today we'll merry merry be," as I happily grabbed the poppy seed hamantaschen (I'm a purist, and no one else wanted them). Even today, as I tell the story to the under-5 crowd, we end with a vague: "Then the Jews were saved, and we all lived happily ever after!" – all of us, that is, except for Haman, his 10 sons, and about 75,000 other people who were killed by the Jews of Shushan in a revenge-fantasy/ surprise ending to the tale.

It's ugly, it's bloody, and it's the way the story *actually* ends. It's difficult to find a silver lining to this ending – and maybe we're not meant to. Maybe we're meant to understand the impulse, of a people persecuted and targeted, to rise up against their oppressors. Maybe we're meant to see our own impulse to extremism, in order that we not succumb to it, even in our darkest hours.

Far from being a pediatric holiday or a Jewish Halloween, there's also a grownup side to Purim—and we don't just mean the beverages. There's a dark side, and we shouldn't shy away from that, at least not as adults.

There are plenty of terrible texts in our tradition—texts that challenge the stories we've been told, texts that challenge our values, texts that challenge our visions of what Judaism is and should be. From the moment we become a people, though, we are *b'nai Yisrael*, the children of Israel—the ones who wrestle. We teach our children to question, to explore, to grapple with holding hard truths and competing narratives.

Underneath and in the midst of the costume parades and funny shpiels, Purim carries with it significant lessons—about sovereignty and oppression, about identity and pride, and about speaking truth to power, even when it is hard and scary. They are lessons for the young and the young at heart, just packaged differently. I do not expect to tell my 3-year-old all the dirty details of the King and his cronies. But us grownups? We can handle it. And nosh some hamantaschen.

Source: Rabbi Sari Laufer, http://reformjudaism.org/jewish-holidays/purim/adult-look-less-savory-truths-purim.

Chanukah
Source Texts

Babylonian Talmud, *Shabbat* 21b

Our Rabbis taught: The commandment of Chanukah requires one light per household; the zealous kindle a light for each member of the household; and the extremely zealous—Beit Shammai maintain: On the first day eight lights are lit and thereafter they are gradually reduced [by one each day]; but Beit Hillel say: On the first day one is lit and thereafter they are progressively increased. Ulla said: In the West [Eretz Yisrael] two amoraim, R. Jose b. Abin and

R. Jose b. Zebida, differ concerning this: one maintains, the reasoning of Beit Shammai is that it should correspond to the days still to come, and that of Beit Hillel is that it shall correspond to the days that are gone. But another maintains: Beit Shammai's reason is that it shall correspond to the bullocks of the Festival [of Tabernacles; i.e. Sukkot], while Beit Hillel's reason is that we increase in matters of sanctity but do not reduce.… Our Rabbis taught: It is incumbent to place the Chanukah lamp by the door of one's house on the outside; if one dwells in an upper chamber, place it at the window nearest the street. But in times of danger it is sufficient to place it on the table. Raba said: Another lamp is required for its light to be used, yet if there is a blazing fire it is unnecessary. But in the case of an important person, even if there is a blazing fire another lamp is required.

What is the reason for Chanukah? As our Rabbis taught: On the twenty-fifth day of Kislev, the eight days of Chanukah begin, during which it is forbidden to eulogize the dead or to fast. When the Greeks entered the sanctuary of the Temple, they defiled all of the oil. When the Hasmoneans overpowered them and were victorious, they searched but could find only one cruse of oil that was intact with the seal of the High Priest. It contained only sufficient oil [to kindle the menorah] for one day, but a miracle occurred, and they were able to light

185

with it for eight days. The next year, they designated these days as a festival with the recitation of hymns of praise and thanksgiving.

Jerusalem Talmud, *Taanit* 2:12

Though all other festivals be abolished, Chanukah and Purim will never be annulled.

Chanukah

Now on the twenty-fifth day of the ninth month, which is called the month of Kislev, in the 148th year, they rose up in the morning and offered sacrifice according to the law upon the new altar of burnt offerings, which they had made. At the very season and on the very day that the gentiles had profaned it, it was dedicated with songs, citterns, harps, and cymbals. . . . And so they kept the dedication of the altar eight days. . . . Moreover Judah and his brethren, with the whole congregation of Israel, ordained that the days of the dedication of the altar should be kept in their season from year to year for eight days, from the twenty-fifth day of the month Kislev, with mirth and gladness.

—I MACCABEES 4:52–59

What is Chanukah? For the Rabbis have taught: Commencing with the twenty-fifth day of the month of Kislev, there are eight days upon which there shall be neither mourning nor fasting. For when the Hellenists entered the Temple, they defiled all the oil that was there. It was when the might of the Hasmonean dynasty overcame and vanquished them that, upon search, only a single cruse of undefiled oil, sealed by the High Priest, was found. In it was oil enough for the needs of a single day. A miracle was wrought and it burned eight days. The next year they ordained these days a holiday with songs and praises.

—BABYLONIAN TALMUD, *Shabbat 21b*

Chanukah begins on the twenty-fifth day of the Hebrew month of Kislev and lasts for eight days. It commemorates the victory of Judah Maccabee and his followers over the forces of the GrecoSyrian tyrant Antiochus Ephiphanes and the rededication of the Temple in Jerusalem, which the Syrians had profaned. Chanukah celebrates more than the end of an unsuccessful attempt by an outside power to destroy Judaism. The threat to Judaism was both internal and external. The assimilation to Hellenistic culture was so great that certain elements within Jewish society sought to become fully assimilated, to be accepted as Greek citizens, and to participate in Greek culture at the expense of their own unique Judaic culture. The resistance of the Maccabees and their allies to the blandishments of assimilation preserved Judaism. The story of Chanukah is the age-old struggle of the Jewish people to remain Jewish in a non-Jewish world.

To celebrate their victory and to rededicate the Temple, the Maccabees proclaimed an eight-day festival, which was to be observed annually. According to the Talmudic legend, when the Hasmoneans recaptured and cleansed the Temple, they were able to find only a single cruse of oil with the seal of the High Priest, sufficient for one day's lighting of the menorah. But, as the story goes, a miracle occurred, and it burned for eight days.

The nightly kindling of the menorah with its increasingly brighter light has become a symbol for both our physical and spiritual resistance to tyranny and assimilation. Jewish tradition has preserved this twofold concept of resistance. The heroic Maccabean triumph is counterbalanced by the words of the prophet Zechariah: "Not by might, nor by power, but by My Spirit, says the God of heaven's hosts" (Zechariah 4:6).

The Mitzvah of Observing Chanukah

It is a mitzvah to observe Chanukah for eight days. The Rabbis taught, "Commencing with the twenty-fifth of Kislev, there are eight days upon which there shall be neither mourning nor fasting."

The Mitzvah of Kindling Chanukah Lights

It is a mitzvah to kindle the Chanukah lights at home with the appropriate blessing. Some people choose to use oil lamps instead of candles to strengthen the connection to the rekindling of the menorah in the Temple:

בָּרוּךְ אַתָּה, יְיָ אֱלֹהֵינוּ,
מֶלֶךְ הָעוֹלָם,
אֲשֶׁר קִדְּשָׁנוּ בְּמִצְוֹתָיו
וְצִוָּנוּ לְהַדְלִיק נֵר שֶׁל חֲנֻכָּה.

Baruch atah, Adonai Eloheinu,
Melech haolam, asher kid'shanu
b'mitzvotav v'tzivanu
l'hadlik ner shel Chanukah.

Blessed are You, Adonai our God, Sovereign of all, who hallows us with mitzvot, commanding us to kindle the Chanukah lights.

בָּרוּךְ אַתָּה, יְיָ אֱלֹהֵינוּ,
מֶלֶךְ הָעוֹלָם, שֶׁעָשָׂה נִסִּים
לַאֲבוֹתֵנוּ וְאִמּוֹתֵנוּ
בַּיָּמִים הָהֵם
בַּזְּמַן הַזֶּה.

Baruch atah, Adonai Eloheinu,
Melech haolam, she-asah nisim
laavoteinu v'imoteinu
bayamim haheim
baz'man hazeh.

Blessed are You, Adonai our God, Sovereign of all, who performed wondrous deeds for our ancestors in days of old at this season.

FOR FIRST NIGHT ONLY:

בָּרוּךְ אַתָּה, יְיָ אֱלֹהֵינוּ,
מֶלֶךְ הָעוֹלָם, שֶׁהֶחֱיָנוּ
וְקִיְּמָנוּ וְהִגִּיעָנוּ
לַזְּמַן הַזֶּה.

Baruch atah, Adonai Eloheinu,
Melech haolam, shehecheyanu
v'kiy'manu v'higianu
laz'man hazeh.

Blessed are You, Adonai our God, Sovereign of all, for giving us life, for sustaining us, and for enabling us to reach this season.

One candle is lit for each night. The candle for the first night is placed on the right side of the special eight-branched (menorah) (or *chanukiyah*). On each subsequent night, an additional candle is placed to the left of the preceding night's candle. The lighting proceeds from left to right so that the new candle is kindled first. No practical use may be made of the Chanukah lights, such as illuminating the room. Therefore, according to Jewish tradition, a special candle known as the (*shamash*) is used to light the others and to provide light.

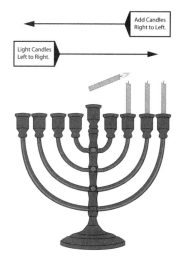

On Friday night the Chanukah lights are lit before Shabbat candles, and on Saturday night they are lit after *Havdalah*.

Displaying the (*Chanukiyah*)
(*Persumei HaNeis*—Publicizing the Miracle)

It is an old custom to place the *chanukiyah* where its lights will be visible from the outside. The public proclamation of the miracle of Chanukah (of the cruse of oil and of our survival against the external enemy Antiochus and the internal threat of assimilation) is part of the observance of the holiday. Displaying the *chanukiyah* is a demonstration of Jewish pride and an affirmation of Jewish identity.

Special Foods

The food customs of Chanukah include eating dairy dishes, as well as foods cooked in oil. Among Ashkenazi Jews, the most frequently served dish is potato latkes. Some communities also make sweet cheese latkes. The Israeli custom of serving *sufganiyot* (jelly doughnuts) has been adopted around the Jewish world. The eating of special foods adds to the enjoyment of the holiday.

Dreidel

Playing games has long been associated with Chanukah. The most popular is the game of dreidel (or *s'vivon*.) A dreidel is a four-sided top with the Hebrew letters *nun*, *gimel*, *hei*, and *shin* inscribed on its sides. The letters have been popularly identified as a mnemonic for *Neis gadol hayah sham*, "A great miracle happened there." Dreidels in Israel use the letters נ (*nun*), ג (*gimel*), ה (*hei*), and פ (*pei*), standing for *Neis gadol hayah po*, "A great miracle happened *here*."

Chanukah Gifts

Many people exchange gifts during Chanukah or give small sums of money to children. These practices are part of Chanukah's special appeal during what has become a time of almost universal gift giving. While this practice can add to the enjoyment of the holiday, undue emphasis should not be placed upon the giving and receiving of gifts. When money is given, children can be encouraged to use some of it for *tzedakah*. In any case, it is important to stress the real message of Chanukah—the struggle of the Jewish people to remain distinctive in a non-Jewish world.

Source: Rabbi Peter S. Knobel, ed., *Mishkan Moeid: A Guide to the Jewish Seasons* (New York: CCAR Press, 2013), 72–76.

Tu Bish'vat (Fifteenth of Sh'vat)

The fifteenth day of Sh'vat (Chamishah-Asar BiSh'vat or Tu BiSh'vat) is designated by the Mishnah as the New Year for Trees. While it is a minor holiday without many prescribed observances, it is customary to eat fruits grown in Israel, especially the fruit of the carob tree (*bokser*). Among the kabbalists, a seder modeled on Pesach developed that highlighted the seven biblical species found in the Land of Israel. These are wheat, barley, olives, pomegranate, honey (most likely from dates), figs, and grapes.

Two options for Tu Bish'vat seders can be found in *Seder Tu Bishevat*, by Adam Fisher (CCAR Press, 1989).

Since the resettling of Israel, the day has been observed as a time for planting trees as a part of the reclamation of the land. Many Reform religious schools arrange special programs aimed at raising funds for the Jewish National Fund and celebrating the gradual awakening of the land from the grip of winter. Because there are no special mitzvot associated with Tu BiSh'vat, its observances vary from place to place, and new celebrations are emerging.

Source: Rabbi Peter S. Knobel, ed., *Mishkan Moeid: A Guide to the Jewish Seasons* (New York: CCAR Press, 2013), 86–87

The Festival of the Trees

With new buds formed and new rains falling, Tu BiSh'vat was the new year for tithing fruit which the trees would soon bear. A tenth of the produce was brought to the Temple, and every third year it was given to the poor. It was given in recognition that God is the source of all blessings:

> "Every year, you shall set aside a tenth part of the yield, so that you may learn to revere your God forever."

> (Deuteronomy 14:22-23)

Four New Years

The Rabbis taught that there were four new years. The first of Nidan, in the spring, is the new year for kings and feasts—Passover is the first festival. The first of Elul, in late summer, is the new year for tithing animals born that year. The first of Tishri, our Rosh HaShanah, is the new year for counting the passage of years. The fifteenth of Sh'vat, Tu BiSh'vat, is the new year for tithing the first fruit of fruit trees.

> (Mishnah Rosh HaShanah 1.1)

Why The Trees' New Year is in Sh'vat

What is the reason that the New Year for tithing trees in in Sh'vat? By then, most of the rainy season has passed and the sap has risen; but the time of ripening has not yet begun.

> (Rosh HaShanah 14a with Rashi)

Names for tu BiSh'vat
TuBiSh'vat is shorthand for the Hebrew Chamishah Asar BiSh'vat, the fifteenth of Sh'vat. This day is also called "Chag Hallanot, Festival of Trees" and "Chag Hapeirot, Festival of Fruit."

The New Year for Trees
All Year
They have kept a careful record
Of everything
The waters of the moon
The slow descent
Of every sun
All Year
They have charted the course
of every comet
Eyes drawn to the center
To the star that supports
The planet
The beam that holds up every arch
The line that continues into the future
Unbroken
Unchanged.

But tonight
As the light descends into sleep
The trees
All lift their branches to the sky
Cradling the moon
That shines through the night
Like blossoms of the almond
That have already appeared
To announce
That all fruit that follows
Belongs to the new year
To come.

(Howard Schwartz)

Sephardic Customs

Sephardic Jews call this day "Frutas, the Feast of Fruits: or Rosasano dos Arbores, Rosh HaShanah of the Trees." In Morocco, the rich invite the poor to fill their hats with fruit. In Safed the Kabbalists celebrated a special seder.

Modern Israel

Since our people have returned to the land we have drained the swamps and planted forests on the mountains, grain in the valleys and flowers in the desert. On Tu BiSh'vat, Israel celebrates by planting trees.

(*When many children are present:*)
Tu BiSh'vat is a birthday
Every person has a birthday.
Every year has a birthday—Rosh HaShanah.
Every tree has a birthday too.

Today is the birthday for trees.
This day is called Tu BiSh'vat.

It is still cold outside
but now, after their winter rest,
the trees begin to grow again.
They draw water from the ground
into their roots
and sap begins to flow
into their branches.
In a few weeks
we will see their leaves and flowers.
In a few months they will give us their fruit.

Today we celebrate their birthday.
Today is the birthday for trees.

Winter Air
A small green spruce
struggles through gray brush,
near the shadow

of a winter-dead oak,
and suns itself
while gently swaying
to the air of God's love.

(Adam Fisher)

Fifteenth of Sh'vat

On the fifteenth of Sh'vat
when spring comes,
an angel descends, ledger in hand,
and enters each bud, each twig, each tree,
and all our garden flowers.
From town to town, from village to village
he makes his winged way,
searching the valleys, inspecting the hills,
Flying over the desert
and returns to heaven.
And when the ledger will be full
of trees and blossoms and shrubs,
when the desert is turned into a meadow
and all our land is a watered garden,
the messiah will appear.

(Sh. Shalom)

Song of Songs

Arise my love, my fair one,
and come away;
for lo, the winter is past.
Flowers appear on the earth,
the time for singing is here.
The song of the dove
is heard in our land.
Let us go down to the vineyards
to see if the vines have budded.
There will I give you my love.

(Song of Songs 2.10–12; 7.12)

Nitzanim Niru

Nit-sa-nim nir-u va-a-rets
eit za-mir hi-gi-a, eit za-mir. (2x)
Ki hi-nei se-tav a-var,
se-tav cha-laf ha-lach lo
ha-ge-fa-nim se-ma-dar
na-te-nu na-te-nu rei-cham.

Buds are seen in the land
the time of singing has come.
Fall has passed; the vines are blooming,
giving their scent.

(Song of Songs 2)

Source: Adam Fisher, *Seder Tu Bishevat: The Festival of the Trees* (New York: CCAR Press, 1989)

Tishah B'av (Ninth of Av)

Tishah B'Av (the Ninth of Av) has been the traditional day of mourning that commemorates major tragic events of the past—the destruction of the First Temple by the Babylonians in 587 BCE and of the Second Temple by the Romans in 70 CE, and the expulsion from Spain in 1492. Tradition has assigned additional subsequent major tragedies to the ninth of Av. The special liturgy of the day, which has developed from the biblical Book of Lamentations, recalls the pain and suffering of the Jewish people.

Although many Jews have abandoned Tishah B'Av, in part because of the reestablishment of the State of Israel, others continue to observe it by attending special services or by fasting, or both.

It is suggested that weddings not be scheduled for Tishah B'Av. Many Reform Jews do not, however, observe the traditional strictures of avoiding weddings during certain periods before Tishah B'Av.

Source: Rabbi Peter S. Knobel, ed., *Mishkan Moeid: A Guide to the Jewish Seasons* (New York: CCAR Press, 2013), 86.

Unit III

The Cycle of Jewish Life

Creating a Jewish Home and Life

Source Texts

Leviticus 19:18

You shall not take vengeance or bear a grudge against your countrymen. Love your fellow as yourself: I am Adonai.

Deuteronomy 14:3–21

[3] You shall not eat anything abhorrent. [4] These are the animals that you may eat: the ox, the sheep, and the goat; [5] the deer, the gazelle, the roebuck, the wild goat, the ibex, the antelope, the mountain sheep, [6] and any other animal that has true hoofs which are cleft in two and brings up the cud—such you may eat. [7] But the following, which do bring up the cud or have true hoofs which are cleft through, you may not eat: the camel, the hare, and the daman—for although they bring up the cud, they have no true hoofs—they are unclean for you; [8] also the swine—for although it has true hoofs, it does not bring up the cud—is unclean for you. You shall not eat of their flesh or touch their carcasses. [9] These you may eat of all that live in water: you may eat anything that has fins and scales. [10] But you may not eat anything that has no fins and scales: it is unclean for you. [11] You may eat any clean bird. [12] The following you may not eat: the eagle, the vulture, and the black vulture; [13] the kite, the falcon, and the buzzard of any variety; [14] every variety of raven; [15] the ostrich, the nighthawk, the sea gull, and the hawk of any variety; [16] the little owl, the great owl, and the white owl; [17] the pelican, the bustard, and the cormorant; [18] the stork, any variety of heron, the hoopoe, and the bat. [19] All winged swarming things are unclean for you: they may not be eaten. [20] You may eat only clean winged creatures. [21] You shall not eat anything that has died a natural death; give it to the stranger in your community to eat, or you may sell

it to a foreigner. For you are a people consecrated to the Eternal your God. You shall not boil a kid in its mother's milk.

Deuteronomy 16:20

Justice, justice shall you pursue, that you may thrive and occupy the land that the Eternal your God is giving you.

Micah 6:8

God has told you, O human, what is good, and what Adonai requires of you: Only to do justice and to love goodness, and to walk modestly with your God.

The Jewish Home

FROM THE PHYSICAL TO THE SPIRITUAL

RABBI JOUI M. HESSEL, RJE

As children, we find joy and peace within our bedrooms; we play make-believe, build forts with bedsheets, and read books with flashlights late into the night. As parents, we seek to transform a house into a home, taking it from the profane and the ordinary to the sacred and extraordinary. We infuse each room with our love for those who live within the walls, and we build memories to last a lifetime by celebrating holidays, cooking delicious Shabbat dinners, and nurturing special moments for our family.

Why is our home so special? What makes it a sacred space in which we can find serenity and peace, joy and laughter? To find the answer, we must go back in history thousands of years. At that time, the place where God dwelled was thought to be the Temple, the *Beit HaMikdash*, in Jerusalem. There, the High Priests on behalf of the Israelites offered sacrifices, as a way to communicate with God and to receive blessings. When the Romans destroyed the Temple in 70 CE, the Rabbis were forced to consider whether God would continue to reside with the Jewish people. And the answer was, yes. Having decided that, the question was then where that would take place without the central Temple available to God. At that time it was believed, as we do today, that God would continue to be with the Jewish people, but as they transitioned into a world without the Temple in Jerusalem, God's presence would be found in two places: the synagogue and the home. The home, therefore, became a small sanctuary—a *mikdash m'at*, where God's presence would be felt and the space itself would become holy.

According to the Talmud (BT *M'gilah* 29a), God will dwell in the holy spaces we create, for those creations are the Temple in miniature. How do we transform our homes into small sanctuaries? Perhaps it begins with shifting our viewpoint of our homes as places for storing material possessions to places for restoring spiritual connections. Instead of using an architect's blueprints, we are to use the blueprints found within the Torah, the mitzvot commanded us to make our homes physically, emotionally, and spiritually safe. Our homes should strive to be places of extreme hospitality, following our forefather Abraham's example in Genesis. Our homes should become places of gathering where friends come together for holiday celebration and ritual observance. Our homes should be locales of worship, not in lieu of synagogues but in addition to, where children can recite the words of *Sh'ma* at bedtime or roommates can share in the recitation of blessings at the table. Our homes should be places where we can meditate, communicate with God, and offer thanks for life's blessings we experience each day. Our homes should be places of study, whereby its residents become scholars of Jewish text.

The daily study of Jewish text is a fundamental part of Jewish living. The Rabbis long ago taught that each Jew was to study every day: "One should always divide his years into three parts, devoting one-third to the study of Scripture, one-third to the study of Mishnah [Oral Law], and one-third to the study of Talmud" (BT *Kiddushin* 30a). The Talmud thus concludes that the only certain way to fulfill this obligation is to do it daily. Early on (and still today in some communities), Jewish communities would study texts centered on sacrifices, viewing it as their own offerings, since their actual sacrifices were unable to be offered in the Temple once it had been destroyed. Today, Reform congregations recite a version of *Eilu D'varim*, which stems from the Talmudic passage in *Shabbat* 127a:

These are things that are limitless,
of which a person enjoys the fruit of the world,
while the principal remains in the world to come.
They are: honoring one's father and mother,
engaging in deeds of compassion,
arriving early for study, morning and evening,
dealing graciously with guests, visiting the sick,
providing for the wedding couple,
accompanying the dead for burial,
being devoted in prayer,

and making peace among people.

But the study of Torah encompasses them all.

Therefore, study in the home is a central part of modern Judaism and it is not just reserved for the synagogue any longer. *Shabbat* 127a teaches us about the obligations we have as Jews. But it is much more than an obligation, as the joy of helping others provides us with rewards that are beyond measure. The significance of the study of Torah (or of any Jewish text) being equal to any of these obligations underscores the importance of the value of *talmud Torah*, Jewish learning.

From *talmud Torah* to hospitality to guests, from honoring our parents to creating opportunities to fulfill deeds of compassion for others in our midst, all of these mitzvot stem from how we choose to live our lives and nurture others' lives within the home.

A Jewish home is recognized immediately upon gazing on the mezuzah, placed on the outer doorpost. The mezuzah contains a scroll of parchment within its casing, where the words of the *Sh'ma* are found painstakingly written in perfect calligraphy. These words recall the mitzvah from Deuteronomy 6 that speaks of writing these words and posting them on the doorposts of our house and on our gates. Traditionally, when we enter such a house, we lift our fingers and gingerly touch the mezuzah, recognizing its symbolism with a touch, and then we bring our fingers to our lips, allowing the words to become a part of us—a recognition of these ancient words becoming relevant to the modern day, reminding us of how we are to live ethically and morally, guided by the words of Torah.

Inside of the home, there are surely artifacts and treasures that reflect a sense of the Jewish calendar through ritual objects displayed in cabinets and on counters. Challah platters and seder plates, Shabbat candlesticks and Chanukah menorahs (*chanukiyot*), dreidels and groggers, and *tzedakah* boxes can be found in addition to Jewish books that serve as resources and guides to our daily questions that arise. The usage of these ritual objects and the synthesis of ritual with commandment is what transforms Judaism from a religion of learning to a religion of doing. And it is in *doing* that we actively participate in Jewish life with those around us, beginning in our homes.

But it is not only through ritual that a Jewish home exemplifies a *mikdash m'at*, a small sanctuary. Indeed, Judaism is lived not only through the physical space and the use of physical object, but also in the spiritual realm through the adherence to Jewish values, *midot*. For it is the way in which we treat our loved ones with whom we share living space that illustrates the synthesis of *talmud Torah*, the study of Torah, with that of practice. The Jewish philosopher Martin Buber taught that we should each strive to move from an I-It relationship of superficial objectification to the true deep connection of I-Thou. Recognizing the holiness that exists within each of us is how we are able to make that transition from text to reality, from ancient words to modern actions. The relationships and the Jewish values that serve as each relationship's foundation is what the prophet Micah (6:8) commands of us—to do justly, to love mercy, and to walk humbly with our God.

> May our homes be filled with the light of Torah.
> May our homes be overflowing with words and deeds of love.
> May our homes be complete with the blessings of family and of friendship.

Source: Rabbi Joui M. Hessel, RJE, "The Jewish Home: From the Physical to the Spiritual," in *Navigating the Journey: The Essential Guide to the Jewish Life Cycle*, ed. Rabbi Peter Knobel (New York: CCAR Press, 2017).

Consecration of a House

For the ceremony of consecration, a mezuzah, a Bible, wine or grape juice, Challah, and salt are required Members of the household and guests participate in the ritual

To affix a mezuzah to a room (the house having already been consecrated), begin on page 212.

In the spirit of our Jewish faith, we consecrate this house with prayers of thanksgiving and invoke upon it God's blessing,

שְׁמַע יִשְׂרָאֵל יְהֹוָה אֱלֹהֵינוּ יְהֹוָה אֶחָד.

Sh'ma Yisrael, Adonai Eloheinu, Adonai Echad.
Hear O Israel, Adonai is our God, Adonai is One.

בָּרוּךְ שֵׁם כְּבוֹד מַלְכוּתוֹ לְעוֹלָם וָעֶד.

Baruch shem k'vod malchuto l'olam va-ed.
Blessed is God's glorious majesty forever and ever.

וְאָהַבְתָּ אֵת יְיָ אֱלֹהֶיךָ
בְּכָל לְבָבְךָ וּבְכָל נַפְשְׁךָ
וּבְכָל מְאֹדֶךָ. וְהָיוּ הַדְּבָרִים
הָאֵלֶּה אֲשֶׁר אָנֹכִי
מְצַוְּךָ הַיּוֹם עַל לְבָבֶךָ.
וְשִׁנַּנְתָּם לְבָנֶיךָ וְדִבַּרְתָּ
בָּם בְּשִׁבְתְּךָ בְּבֵיתֶךָ וּבְלֶכְתְּךָ
בַדֶּרֶךְ וּבְשָׁכְבְּךָ וּבְקוּמֶךָ
וּקְשַׁרְתָּם לְאוֹת עַל יָדֶךָ וְהָיוּ
לְטֹטָפֹת בֵּין עֵינֶיךָ וּכְתַבְתָּם
עַל מְזֻזוֹת בֵּיתֶךָ וּבִשְׁעָרֶיךָ.

*V'ahavta et Adonal Elohecha,
b'chol l'vav'cha uv'chol nafsh'cha
uv'chol m'odecha, V'hayu had'varim
ha-eileh asher anochi
m'tzav'cha hayom al l'vavecha,
V'shinantam l'vanecha v'dibarta
barn b'shivt'cha b'veitecha uv'lecht'cha
vaderech uv'shochb'cha uv'kumecha,
Uk'shartam l'ot al yadecha v'hayu
l'totafot bein einecha, Uch'tavtam
al m'zuzot beitecha uvish'arecha.*

209

You shall love Adonai your God with all your heart, with all your soul, and with all your might. Take to heart these instructions with which I charge you this day. Impress them upon your children. Recite them when you stay at home and when you are away, when you lie down and when you get up. Bind them as a sign on your hand and let them serve as a symbol on your forehead; inscribe them on the doorposts of your house and on your gates.

לְמַעַן תִּזְכְּרוּ וַעֲשִׂיתֶם אֶת
כָּל מִצְוֹתָי וִהְיִיתֶם קְדֹשִׁים
לֵאלֹהֵיכֶם. אֲנִי יְיָ אֱלֹהֵיכֶם
אֲשֶׁר הוֹצֵאתִי אֶתְכֶם מֵאֶרֶץ
מִצְרַיִם לִהְיוֹת לָכֶם לֵאלֹהִים
אֲנִי יְיָ אֱלֹהֵיכֶם.

L'maan tizk'ru vaasitem et
kol mitzvotai vih'yitem k'doshim
l'Eloheichem. Ani Adonai Eloheichem
asher hotzeiti et-chem mei-eretz
Mitzrayim lih'yot lachem l'Elohim
ani Adonai Eloheichem.

Thus you shall remember to observe all My commandmenrs and to be holy to your God. I am Adonai, your God, who brought you out of the land of Egypt to be your God: I am Adonai your God.

Our homes have always been the dwelling place of the Jewish spirit. Our tables have been altars of faith and love. It *is* written: "When words of Torah pass between us, the Divine Presence is in our midst." Our doors have been open to the stranger and the needy. May this home we now consecrate keep alive the beauty of our heritage.

Challah is dipped in salt and distributed.

בָּרוּךְ אַתָּה, יְיָ אֱלֹהֵנוּ,
מֶלֶךְ הָעוֹלָם,
הַמּוֹצִיא לֶחֶם מִן הָאָרֶץ.

Baruch atah, Adonai Eloheinu,
Melech haolam,
hamotzi lechem min haaretz.

Our praise to You, Adonai our God, Sovereign of the universe, who brings fotth bread from the earth.

Wine or grape juice is gjven to each guest.
Wine and grape juice are equally "fruit of the vine."

בָּרוּךְ אַתָּה, יְיָ אֱלֹהֵינוּ,
מֶלֶךְ הָעוֹלָם, בּוֹרֵא פְּרִי הַגָּפֶן.

Baruch atah, Adonai Eloheinu,
Melech haolam,
borei p'ri hagafen.

Praise to You, Adonai our God, Sovereign of the universe, Creator of the fruit of the vine.

The open Bible is raised.

The Torah has been our life; it has taught us how to live. May this home be a place for learning and doing. May the hearts of all who dwell here be filled with a love of Torah and its teachings.

בָּרוּךְ אַתָּה יְיָ
אֱלֹהֵינוּ מֶלֶךְ הָעוֹלָם,
אֲשֶׁר קִדְּשָׁנוּ בְּמִצְוֹתָיו
וְצִוָּנוּ לַעֲסוֹק בְּדִבְרֵי תוֹרָה.

Baruch atah, Adonai
Eloheinu, Melech haolam,
asher kid'shanu b'mitzvotav
v'tzivanu laasok b'divrei Torah.

Blessed are You, Adonai our God, Sovereign of the universe, who hallows us with mitzvot, commanding us to engage with words of Torah.

יְיָ מִי־יָגוּר בְּאָהֳלֶךְ?
מִי־יִשְׁכֹּן בְּהַר קָדְשֶׁךָ?
הוֹלֵךְ תָּמִים וּפֹעֵל צֶדֶק,
וְדֹבֵר אֱמֶת בִּלְבָבוֹ.
לֹא־רָגַל עַל־לְשֹׁנוֹ,
לֹא־עָשָׂה לְרֵעֵהוּ רָעָה,
וְחֶרְפָּה לֹא־נָשָׂא עַל־קְרֹבוֹ.
נִשְׁבַּע לְהָרַע וְלֹא יָמִיר,
כַּסְפּוֹ לֹא־נָתַן בְּנֶשֶׁךְ,
וְשֹׁחַד עַל־נָקִי לֹא לָקָח.
עֹשֵׂה־אֵלֶּה לֹא יִמּוֹט לְעוֹלָם.

Adonai mi-yagur b'oholecha?
Mi yishkon b'har kodshecha?
Holeich tamim ufo-eil tzedek,
v'doveir emet bil'vavo.
Lo ragal al l'shono,
lo asah l'rei-eihu raah,
v'cherpah lo-nasa al k'rovo.
Nishba l'hara v'lo yamir,
kaspo lo-natan b'neshech,
v'shochad al-naki lo lakach.
Oseih eileh lo yimot l'olam.

Eternal God:
Who may abide in Your house?
Who may dwell in Your holy mountain?
Those who are uptight; who do justly,

all whose hearts are true.
Who do not slander others, nor wrong them,
nor bring shame upon their kin.
Who give their word and, come what may, do not retract it.
Who do not exploit others, who never take bribes.
Those who live in this way shall never be shaken.

An additional scriptural passage, such as I Kings 8:54-61, might be read here.

The mezuzah is raised.

This ancient symbol speaks to us of our need to live by the words of Adonai.
We affix the mezuzah to the doorposts of this house with the hope that it will
always remind us of our duties to one another as members of the Household of
Israel. May the divine spirit fill this house—the spirit of love and kindness and
consideration fur all people.

בָּרוּךְ אַתָּה יְיָ
אֱלֹהֵינוּ מֶלֶךְ הָעוֹלָם,
אֲשֶׁר קִדְּשָׁנוּ בְּמִצְוֹתָיו
וְצִוָּנוּ לִקְבּוֹעַ מְזוּזָה.

*Baruch atah, Adonai
Eloheinu, Melech haolam,
asher kid'shanu b'mitzvotav
v'tzivanu likboa m'zuzah.*

Praise to You, Adonai our God, Sovereign of the universe,
who hallows us with mitzvot, commanding us to affix the mezuzah.

*The mezuzah, its top inclining inward, is affixed to the upper part of the doorpost on the
right, as one enters the house. If desired, a mezuzah may be affixed to the right doorpost
of the principal rooms.*

בָּרוּךְ אַתָּה יְיָ
אֱלֹהֵינוּ מֶלֶךְ הָעוֹלָם,
שֶׁהֶחֱיָנוּ וְקִיְּמָנוּ
וְהִגִּיעָנוּ לַזְּמַן הַזֶּה.

*Baruch atah, Adonai Eloheinu,
Melech haolam,
shehecheyanu v'kiy'manu
v'higianu laz'man hazeh.*

Praise to You, Adonai our God, Sovereign of the universe,
fur giving us life, sustaining us, and enabling us to reach this season.

אִם יְיָ לֹא יִבְנֶה בַיִת שָׁוְא עָמְלוּ בּוֹנָיו בּוֹ.

Im Adonai lo yivneh vayit, shav amlu bonav bo.

Unless Adonai builds the house, its builders labor in vain.

In this awareness we pray that our home be blessed by the sense of God's presence.

We offer thanksgiving for the promise of security and contentment this home represents, and express our resolve to make it a temple dedicated to godliness. Let it be filled with the beauty of holiness and the warmth of love. May the guest and stranger find within it welcome and friendship. So will it ever merit the praise: "How lovely are your tents, O Jacob, your dwelling places, O Israel!"

For all who are assembled here, and for all who will enter these doors, we invoke God's blessing:

יְיָ יִשְׁמָר צֵאתְךָ וּבוֹאֶךָ מֵעַתָּה וְעַד עוֹלָם.

Adonai yishmor tzeit'cha u'vo-echa mei-atah v'ad olam.

May Adonai guard your going out and your coming in, now and always. Amen.

Source: Rabbi Chaim Stern, ed., *On the Doorposts of Your House: Prayers and Ceremonies for the Jewish Home*, rev. ed. (New York: CCAR Press, 2010), 155–159.

The People of the Food

TINA WASSERMAN

The chicken cooking in the pot with the usual onion, carrot, and celery, and the addition of the turnip and mandatory fresh dill, created an aroma that at once recalled my mother, Pesach, Shabbat, and home. But this soup wasn't to be eaten. Instead, frozen into two gallon-sized freezer bags, it was schlepped through Canadian customs to the URJ Biennial in Toronto—where it also wasn't consumed. It wasn't intended for consumption but rather for evoking memory. Brought to a simmer in a slow cooker and placed right by the door to the assembly room, over two hundred people walked past the soup and subliminally were primed for my talk about historical Jewish cuisine.

Instead of being called "the people of the book," I often feel we should be called "the people of the food," for food has played a pivotal role in our identity. Food sets us apart from others, thus serving historically as a survival technique, and also brings us together as a community. This sense of community has sustained us throughout time and our dispersion. It has allowed us to sometimes thrive but always survive in the face of insurmountable odds.

What makes food Jewish? First and foremost two laws: the laws of kashrut and the laws of Shabbat. The laws of kashrut were designed to separate us from the non-Jew. The command "You shall not boil a kid in its mother's milk" (Deuteronomy 14:21) refers to the culinary practice, in ancient times, of boiling meat in milk to tenderize it. Prohibiting a cooking technique that was commonly followed served to separate the ancients into those who followed the laws of the Torah and those who didn't. Later, the sharing of common food practices served as a way to keep the Jewish community united, separate from the people among whom they lived. Jewish travelers could thus find a welcoming community to whom they were connected through a shared food culture.

A side benefit of observing Shabbat was the establishment of many Jewish communities in remote places. The ninth-century Jewish traders known as Radanites, who found themselves on the road to and from the Far East when Shabbat was nearing, often looked for a home that followed kashrut observance or for an inn that had a separate pot put aside for the Jew. If their skill or trade was lacking in that community, the Jewish traveler often put down roots, and the beginnings of a Jewish community were formed.

One of the most iconic Ashkenazic Shabbat dishes is gefilte fish. Fish was traditionally served for Shabbat and actually was a necessity, since the resourceful, albeit often poor, Jewish cook had already stretched one chicken to provide as many dishes as possible. The classic Shabbat meal readily shows this resourcefulness; one chicken provided the meat, the soup, the fat to spread on the challah, the neck skin to be stuffed, and the liver for the pate. The Rabbis, however, deemed that taking bones out of fish was work, and therefore fish could not be eaten on Shabbat. Our ancestral cooks got around that decree by taking the fish meat out of its carcass, deboning it, and then placing the seasoned chopped fish back into the carcass to be poached in a large pot of water with a few meager vegetables. *Gefilte* literally means "stuffed"! Over time recipes were modernized to accommodate the time allotted to cooking and the newer equipment available. The whole stuffed fish morphed into balls of ground, seasoned fish steamed on top of the fish carcass with a few vegetables poached in water, broth, or white wine or baked in a loaf.

The tales and myths of our heritage lent many opportunities for creative interpretation in the foods we prepared for specific holidays. The kreplach that swim in our bowl of golden chicken soup during the High Holy Days, and most specifically for Erev Yom Kippur, can be traced to the medieval custom of writing one's wish for the new year on a piece of paper, tucking it into the center of a piece of dough, and wearing it around one's neck as an amulet. Although there is no proof, I suggest that a frugal housewife decided not to waste good milled flour on an amulet, and the symbol of being "sealed" in the Book of Life for the coming year wound up in our soup!

Chanukah, for most of the Jewish world, is associated with fried foods and the tale of the vial of oil lasting for eight days instead of one. The question is, which came first, the story that needed a recipe to commemorate itself or the daily affairs of the Jews that easily lent themselves to the creation of a tale?

The establishment of the Chanukah celebration in late fall coincided with the "harvest" of the geese that had been methodically fattened for the previous three months. The down and feathers were used for warmth, the meat was preserved as a confit to be eaten throughout the winter months ahead, and the fat was rendered to provide cooking oil for the next year. With the newly rendered fat readily available, the Jewish cook could always find some potatoes and onion, and a simple preparation was transformed into a culinary legend.

Centuries ago a large portion of the Jewish world occupied the Middle East and Orient, where they created a culinary legend around the story of Judith that is associated with Chanukah. As the story goes, Judith avoided annihilation of her community at the hands of General Holofernes and his army by daring to go into his tent and seducing him with cheese and wine. After Judith plied him with salty cheese and copious amounts of wine, the general got drunk and fell asleep. Judith, according to legend, cut off his head, placed it on a staff, came out of the tent, and scared off the general's troops and saved the Jews of her village. Because of this legend, it became a custom to eat dairy foods on Chanukah. The story of one person craftily saving an entire village was very popular in the Sephardic Jewish community in Holland as well, so much so that in the sixteenth century the Jewish community celebrated the defeat of the invading Spanish army at the hands of a small band of soldiers by adopting and adapting the recipe for a stew that was left simmering in the deserted camp when they fled.

Haman's physiognomy was the culinary basis for enacting his defeat. Italians would pinch thin strips of dough together and fry them to resemble Haman's misshapen ears. French Jews served palmiers to commemorate Haman's aural appendage. German Jews would often bite off the head of the ubiquitous gingerbread man in order to display their disgust for the villain. But, the most iconic food for Purim are the hamantaschen, "Haman's pockets." This pastry was originally adapted from the non-Jewish food customs of Bavaria. Filled with poppy seed, the *mohntaschen* (poppy seed pockets) sounded like *hamantaschen*, and the seeds paralleled the promise of God in Genesis 22:17 to make the seed of the offspring of Abraham as extensive as the sands on the seashore. In the eighteenth century, a Bavarian prune merchant named David Brandeis was accused of poisoning a magistrate and was scheduled to be hanged (an odd parallel to Purim). At the last minute the *povidl*, or prune, merchant was acquitted, and the townspeople celebrated by making their hamantaschen with prune filling that year, starting a new tradition that has endured to this day.

Matzah is one of the few foods actually prescribed in the Torah as a commandment. Any other food associated with a holiday is based on custom. *Charoset* is made to resemble the mortar that held the bricks together on the pyramids built by Jewish slaves. Preferably dark and brownish in color, the mixture itself often gave clues to its origin. Contains apples? Must be an Ashkenazic recipe from lands where apples were a mainstay. Bananas and oranges? From the Maghreb region, where Romans planted orange trees all along the shores of the Mediterranean before the empire fell. The trees' cultivation was renewed when the Moors conquered Spain. Dates? From the Middle East. Walnuts? From Georgia and Eastern Europe. Pecans? Why, the southern United States, of course!

As you make your way through the culinary traditions of our heritage, may you hear and taste the stories of the survival and perseverance of our people. The recipes are stories, and the stories are recipes.

Eat in good health! B'tei-avon!

Source: Tina Wasserman, "The People of the Food," in *Mishkan Moeid: A Guide to the Jewish Seasons*, ed. Rabbi Peter S. Knobel (New York: CCAR Press, 2013), 141–144.

Eating Our Values

Rabbi Mary L. Zamore

At the holidays, we break out of our normal patterns to appreciate the time and season. Often we celebrate by bringing out our best: a new dress, fresh flowers, grandma's china, home cooking. In many ways, we strive to live during holidays in the manner we aspire to live every day. However, as we clean our homes, gather family around us, and invite guests over, we should be polishing not only our silver but also our values. Since our Jewish holidays are frequently centered on food, these moments are wonderful times to live out the food values that we wish to incorporate every day. Integrating Jewish ethical and spiritual food values into our holiday celebrations will only deepen the significance of these special times for our families and communities. Eight values central to Jewish eating are outlined in alphabetical order below. With limitless applications, each of these values represents a rich opportunity to infuse holiday celebrations with meaning. Holiday eating can be a beginning to living these values every day.

Bal Tashchit—Environmentalism

While the Rabbinic term *bal tashchit* literally means "do not destroy," it is rooted in the biblical commandment *lo tashchit* (Deuteronomy 20:19–20), meaning the same. *Bal tashchit* is often used synonymously with *shomrei adamah*, "guardians of the earth," a term that describes humanity's relationship to the earth. Both terms become the heading under which environmental issues are addressed. The application of the value of environmentalism to Jewish eating is boundless. It can be invoked as an argument in favor of reducing meat consumption through Jewish vegetarianism or meat minimalism; it can support the call for reduced packaging of kosher food and minimal use of disposable items at Jewish communal meals.

Rather than being on vacation from our values, we must uphold our commitment to the environment, especially at holidays. Since festive meals are usually planned well in advance, we have the opportunity to think ahead about how to reduce our dependency on disposable serving pieces (e.g., cups, plates, tablecloths, forks).

We can borrow items from family and guests to reduce the use of disposables, which merely become landfill after one meal; we can organize volunteers to wash dishes in order to share the burden of reusable dishes.

The choice of our food can also have an impact on the environment. Many Jews are reducing the role of meat, especially red meat, in their diets. Reconsider the amount of meat served at holiday meals. While some Jews cling to the Talmudic statement "There could be no joy without meat," many are learning that meat does not need to be the center of every holiday meal. The meat course can be one choice among many other dishes, or a festive, completely vegetarian menu can be created. Eating seasonal and local food is also good for the environment, as this reduces the impact of transport, also known as the carbon footprint, of our food. Choosing a fruit or vegetable that is in season and grown locally is a better choice than picking one that has been transported across the world. A bonus is that seasonal and local produce usually tastes better.

B'rachot—Blessing

While it is a mitzvah to recite *b'rachot*, blessings, every time we eat, this may not be part of our individual daily practice. However, holidays are a wonderful time to sanctify our food and table by reciting *Kiddush*, the blessing over wine, *HaMotzi*, the blessing over bread, and *Birkat HaMazon*, the blessing after we eat. These blessings allow us to pause before we eat and to reflect gratefully on the gifts of food and company. We connect to God through this contemplative practice. We set the mood at our holiday table, reminding ourselves why this meal is different from all other meals.

These blessings can be recited according to our ability. For example, while there are long versions of the evening *Kiddush* specifically for the Festivals, if no one knows the full blessing, it is fine to sing the part you do know in Hebrew and then read the rest in English or sing along with a recording, online video, or app. The same can be applied to *Birkat HaMazon*, the blessing after we eat.

It should be noted that one does not require a challah in order to say *HaMotzi*, the blessing over any type of bread. Before you recite these prayers, you can add some personal, spontaneous prayers that are tailored to the specific holiday and people around the table.

Kashrut—Kosher Food and Wine

If kashrut is an unfamiliar practice, it need not seem foreign or intimidating, for ultimately kashrut is our Jewish relationship with food. Any time we allow Jewish law and values to inform our food choices, we are keeping Jewish dietary laws. Therefore, when we eat matzah on Passover, fruits and vegetables on Tu BiSh'vat, or we fast on Yom Kippur, we allow our rich tradition to shape our food choices. When Jewish dietary laws influence our eating habits, we affirm our Jewish identities and connect to our greater Jewish community, our sacred tradition, and God.

Traditional Jewish holiday recipes reflect kashrut, the Jewish dietary laws, by excluding nonkosher foods like pork, shellfish, and nonkosher meats and by separating milk from meat foods and their related products. While you may or may not keep kosher during the rest of the year, you can sanctify your holiday table by following some or all of the Jewish dietary laws. Making a kosher-style meal is a good place to start for Jews who do not regularly keep kosher. For example, you can avoid mixing milk and meat by using oil and oil-based margarine in recipes, by not serving glasses of milk, and by skipping cream or cheese sauces at a meat meal. Keeping some or all of the laws of kashrut will distinguish your Jewish holiday table from the other daily and festive meals you serve throughout the year, it will connect your home to Jews throughout the world, and it will model living Judaism for your family.

Another way to bring kashrut to your table is to use kosher wine. While it is acceptable from a Reform Jewish outlook to say *kiddush* over any wine, Jewish holidays are wonderful times to try kosher wine. While some Jews look forward to the unique taste of kosher wine labeled "heavy Concord grape," others will appreciate the wonderful variety of fine kosher wines now available. In particular, Israel produces an amazing variety of kosher wines in many different price ranges. You can take the opportunity to connect to and support Israel by making a point to buy Israeli kosher wine.

Kesher—Connection through Food

Eating together creates connection among people. The value of *hachnasat or'chim*, welcoming guests, teaches us to gather friends and family around our tables. We should especially try to remember those who may be alone or do not have the means to make a holiday meal. While entertaining can add extra work to already full lives, it is a great joy to nurture family and friends, especially on a holiday, and to draw them closer to us and each other over good food. As hosts, we bond with our families and friends, but we also connect to our food through our meal preparation. During the regular week, we often cook on autopilot, depending on a rotation of familiar and fast recipes or, even more often, prepared foods. Holidays bring a fresh inspiration to our menus and give us an opportunity to prepare food from scratch.

In planning and preparing our holiday meals, we can connect to our food and through food to the Source of our food. The Torah teaches us, "God Eternal took the man, placing him in the Garden of Eden to work it and keep it" (Genesis 2:15). Recalling our ancient connection to the soil, we can also encounter God in the garden. However, gardener or not, we all have the blessing of rejoicing in the beauty, variety, and miracle of food. As we prepare and cook our holiday meal, we can pause to reflect on the food before us, appreciating the beautiful partnership that is intrinsic to cooking. Food preparation offers an awesome intersection among Creator—God, the Source of our nourishment; food workers—those who toil to bring food to our markets; and cooks—we who draw upon communal human history and knowledge to prepare the food. As we shape our menus, we also connect to our personal histories when we select recipes handed down through our families or cultural traditions. When we cook, we can acknowledge the spirituality that infuses food preparation. We can know that we are not simply alone with our pots and pans.

Oshek—Worker's Rights

Oshek, the oppression of a worker, is expressly forbidden in the Torah. The Torah instructs, "You shall not defraud your fellow. You shall not commit robbery. The wages of a laborer shall not remain with you until morning" (Leviticus 19:13–14). In addition, "You shall not abuse a needy and destitute laborer, whether a fellow Israelite or a stranger. . . . You must pay out the wages due on the same day" (Deuteronomy 24:14–15). In a modern context, the concept *oshek* is readily applied to the workers who produce and help serve our food. We must treat and pay our help fairly, whether they work in our Jewish institutions or homes. Being clear about work duties, hours, and pay is important. Making sure those who work for us have a safe way of getting home, especially at night, is also vital. Thanking our employees privately and publicly is also respectful of their role in creating a beautiful holiday.

When we buy our food, whether prepared or unprepared, we can look for certifications that assure that agricultural and food workers involved in its production have been fairly paid. There are a growing number of secular and specifically Jewish certifications that attest to food workers' conditions. These include Fair Trade, a secular agency that certifies the payment of living wages to workers, especially in the notorious coffee, tea, chocolate, and nut industries; Magen Tzedek (originally named Hechsher Tzedek), which was created by Rabbi Morris Allen through the Conservative Movement to certify that kosher products adhere to additional ethical guidelines, including *oshek*; the Israeli Orthodox social justice organization Bema'aglei Tzedek's *Tav Chevrati*, a seal of approval granted free of charge to restaurants and other businesses that respect the legally mandated rights of their employees;" and the American Orthodox social justice organization Uri L'Tzedek's *Tav haYosher*, which seeks to certify kosher restaurants that uphold "the right to fair pay, the right to fair time, and the right to a safe work environment." While it is extremely difficult to find a large range of food products with these certifications, we can support this value by seeking out such products, especially when we buy coffee, tea, and chocolate.

Sh'mirat HaGuf—Preserving Our Health

Sh'mirat haguf, the value of caring for our bodies, is rooted in the concept that we were created *b'tzelem Elohim*, "in the image of God" (Genesis 1:27). To honor God is to care for God's handiwork. *Sh'mirat haguf* commands us to tend to our own bodies, but also to feel responsible for our fellow beings. Therefore, if the food we eat is produced with chemicals that can harm the agricultural workers, we should have two concerns—the effect of the chemicals on our health and on the workers' health. Emphasizing organically produced foods will benefit our health, the workers' health, and the environment.

Holidays can be a time of great indulgence. While some treats are certainly called for, it is possible to lighten the health impact of our festive meals by choosing lighter versions of our favorite recipes, emphasizing fruits and vegetables in our menus, and avoiding the subtle (and sometimes not so subtle) message that everyone has to become members of the clean plate club. Urging family and friends to eat too much or to eat foods that may harm their health is not considerate or loving. A kind host will inquire about guests' allergies, dietary needs, and do the best to accommodate them. If particular guests' diets are too complicated, it is perfectly fine to politely explain the situation and invite them to bring their own food.

Tzaar Baalei Chayim—Animal Rights

Tzaar baalei chayim, "the prevention of suffering to animals," is considered to be a biblical commandment, based on the verse "When you see the ass of your enemy lying under its burden and would refrain from raising it, you must nevertheless help raise it" (Exodus 23:5). While a good part of the laws under this heading have to do with the treatment of work animals, the treatment of food source animals is reflected in the traditional dietary laws, kashrut. For example, in ritual kashrut, the separation of milk and meat are based on the thrice repeated command "You shall not boil a kid [young goat] in its mother's milk" (Exodus 23:19, 34:26; Deuteronomy 14:21). While this verse is widely used to support the ritual practice of separating milk and meat, its ethical dimension is frequently recognized for teaching the humane treatment of animals. In our daily and holiday eating, we can live this value by reducing the role of meat in our diets or by choosing sources for our meat, dairy, and eggs that are dedicated to the humane treatment of animals. We can also shun foods, like veal and foie gras, that are technically kosher yet violate the value of *tzaar baalei chayim.*

Tzedakah and Tzedek—Charity and Social Justice

The work of *tzedek* (social justice), including the concern for the oppressed and hungry, can be expressed through many of the values discussed, as it is intrinsic to Judaism's daily observance. Nutritious food is not a privilege, but a right. Judaism also considers the joy of celebrating holidays as a right deserved by all Jews. Some people do not have the financial means to make a proper holiday; others do not have family and friends. We can open our homes to community members who may find themselves alone at the holidays. Your rabbi can help make a match if you are not sure who may need support. If you are not in a position to invite acquaintances or strangers to your home, you can buy gift cards at local grocery stores and let your rabbi distribute them without you or the recipient knowing each other (a modern twist on Maimonides's ladder of *tzedekah*). Better yet, lead your synagogue in organizing a collection of gift cards or holiday foods to be anonymously distributed. Many grocery stores give away turkeys (and other foods) at certain holiday seasons. If you are not using yours, claim it anyway and donate it. Include a foil pan and nonperishable side dishes to ensure the recipient has the means to cook the meal. Again, this can be a community-wide collection.

When we celebrate holidays, we can remember the poor of our communities by volunteering at local soup kitchens, food pantries, or meals-on-wheels programs. Clearly, these acts of kindness do not have to be done on the actual holiday, although they often can be. Giving a donation to your favorite feeding program is also an appropriate way to sanctify your holiday. Finally, when you are planning your festive meal, think about the leftovers. Distributing the leftovers in a meaningful way should always be on your checklist of hosting responsibilities. Many local feeding programs will take fresh leftovers. Just make sure that you are giving away something that you are willing to eat yourself.

Where to Start

Each of these values is worthy in its own right; many intersect in their practical application. Do not get overwhelmed by trying to incorporate every value to its fullest extent into your holiday meals. Start with the ones that speak to you and are easy to achieve. Make sure you have a good mix of the spiritual and ethical, as these reinforce one another. Then, build from there, adding as you can. Most of all, enjoy your holiday table, fill it with good food, and surround yourself with family and friends.

For more information about Jewish food ethics, see The Sacred Table: Creating a Jewish Food Ethic, *edited by Mary L. Zamore (New York: CCAR Press, 2011).*

Notes
1. BT *P'sachim* 109a.
2. Fair Trade USA, http://www.transfairusa.org/.
3. Magen Tzedek, http://magentzedek.org/.
4. Bema'aglei Tzedek, http://www.mtzedek.org.il/english/TavChevrati.asp.
5. Uri L'Tzedek, http://www.utzedek.org/tavhayosher.html.
6. BT *Bava M'tzia* 32a-b.

Source: Rabbi Mary L. Zamore, "Eating Our Values," in *Mishkan Moeid: A Guide to the Jewish Seasons*, ed. Rabbi Peter S. Knobel (New York: CCAR Press, 2013), 145–152.

Marriage, Partnership, and More

Source Texts

Mishnah Kiddushin 1:1

A woman is acquired in one of three ways . . . by money, written deed, or inter-course. How much money? Beit Shammai says by a *dinar* or its equivalent. Beit Hillel says by a *perutah* or its equivalent.

Babylonian Talmud, *Y'vamot 62b*

Rabbi Tanchum said in the name of Rabbi Chanilai: A man who has no wife dwells without joy, without blessing, without goodness. . . . "Without goodness" as it is written: "It is not good for a person to be alone." (Genesis 2:18).

Babylonian Talmud, *Gittin 57a*

At the birth of a girl, a cypress tree is planted, and at the birth of a boy, a cedar tree is planted. When a couple is married, they stand under a *chuppah* made from wood from the trees planted at their birth.

From the Baal Shem Tov

From every human being there rises a light that reaches straight to heaven. And when two souls that are destined to be together find each other, their streams of light flow together, and a single brighter light goes forth from their united being.

Reform Jewish Sexual Values

CENTRAL CONFERENCE OF AMERICAN RABBIS AD HOC COMMITTEE ON HUMAN SEXUALITY

RABBI SELIG SALKOWITZ, DMIN

Jewish religious values are predicated upon the unity of God and the integrity of the world and its inhabitants as Divine creations. These values identify *sh'leimut* as a fundamental goal of human experience. The Hebrew root *sh-l-m* expresses the ideal of wholeness, completeness, unity, and peace. Sexuality and sexual expression are integral and powerful elements in the potential wholeness of human beings. Our tradition commands us to sanctify the basic elements of the human being through values that express the Divine in every person and in every relationship. Each Jew should seek to conduct his/her sexual life in a manner that elicits the intrinsic holiness within the person and the relationship. Thus can *sh'leimut* be realized. The specific values that follow are contemporary interpretations of human *sh'leimut*:

1. *B'tzelem Elohim* ("in the image of God"). This fundamental Jewish idea, articulated in Genesis 1:27, "And God created humankind in the Divine image—male and female," is at the core of all Jewish values. *B'tzelem Elohim* underscores the inherent dignity of every person, woman and man, with the equal honor and respect due to each individual's integrity and sexual identity. *B'tzelem Elohim* requires each of us to value one's self and one's sexual partner and to be sensitive to his/her needs. Thus do we affirm that consensuality and mutuality are among the values necessary to validate a sexual relationship as spiritual and ethical and, therefore, "in the image of God."

2. *Emet* ("truth"). Authentic and ethical human relationships should be grounded in both truth and honesty. "These are the things you are to do: speak the truth to one another, render true and perfect justice in your gates" (Zech. 8:16). People can only truly know each other and appreciate the Divine in all people when they come to each other openly and honestly. Both partners in an intimate relationship should strive to communicate lovingly. They should tell each other what gives them pleasure and what does not, and should honestly share their love as well as the challenges that their relationship presents. However, honesty that is destructive of the relationship lacks the quality of rachamim, "mercy." "Mercy and truth shall meet, justice and peace shall embrace" (Ps. 85:11). For that reason, intimate partners should be mindful that there might be moments when they are better served by not being totally candid with each other. In addition, falsehood that manipulates is sinful. Dating partners must not lie to each other in order to mislead the other into a sexual relationship. Neither partner should use the other as a sexual object. Finally, parents should learn how to teach their children both the facts and the physical, emotional, and spiritual consequences of sexual behavior. Parents should then use that teaching to help their children face the realities of the contemporary world.

3. *B'riut* ("health"). Our tradition enjoins upon us the responsibility to rejoice in and to maximize our physical, emotional, and spiritual health. "Blessed is our Eternal God, Creator of the Universe, who has made our bodies with wisdom, combining veins, arteries, and vital organs into a finely balanced network" (*Gates of Prayer*, p. 284). Reform Judaism encourages adults of all ages and physical and mental capabilities to develop expressions of their sexuality that are both responsible and joyful. The abuse of human sexuality can be destructive to our emotional, spiritual, and physical health. We have a duty to engage only in those sexual behaviors that do not put others or ourselves at risk. In our age of HIV/AIDS and epidemic sexually transmitted diseases, irresponsible sexual behavior can put our lives and the lives of others at risk. We must act upon the knowledge that our sexual behavior is linked to our physical health.

4. *Mishpat* ("justice"). Judaism enjoins upon us the mandate to reach out and care for others, to treat all those created in the image of God with respect and dignity, to strive to create equality and justice wherever people are treated unfairly, to help meet the needs of the less fortunate, and to engage in *tikkun olam*, "the repair of God's creation." The prophet Amos exhorts us to "let justice well up as waters, righteousness as a mighty stream" (Amos 5:24). As a people who have historically suffered at the hands of the powerful, we must be especially sensitive to any abuse of power and victimization of other human beings. According to the sages, *yetzer hara*, through its sexual component, may sometimes lead to destructive behavior and sin. All forms of sexual harassment, incest, child molestation, and rape violate the value of *mishpat*. Our pursuit of *mishpat* should inspire

us to eradicate prejudice, inequality, and discrimination based upon gender or sexual orientation.

5, *Mishpachah* ("family"). The family is a cornerstone of Jewish life. The Torah, through the first mitzvah, *p'ru ur'vu*, "be fruitful and multiply" (Gen. 1:28), emphasizes the obligation of bringing children into the world through the institution of the family. In our age, the traditional notion of family as being two parents and children (and perhaps older generations) living in the same household is in the process of being redefined. Men and women of various ages living together, singles, gay and lesbian couples, single-parent households, and the like, may all be understood as families in the wider, if not traditional, sense. "Family" also has multiple meanings in an age of increasingly complex biotechnology and choice. Although pro-creation and family are especially important as guarantors of the survival of the Jewish people, all Jews have a responsibility to raise and nurture the next generation of our people. The importance of family, whether biologically or relationally based, remains the foundation of meaningful human existence.

6. *Tz'niut* ("modesty"). Nachmanides' classic *Igeret HaKodesh*, "The Holy Letter," sets forth the Jewish view that the Holy One did not create anything that is not beautiful and potentially good. The human body in itself is never to be considered an object of shame or embarrassment. Instead, "it is the manner and context in which it [i.e., the body] is utilized, the ends to which it is used, which determine condemnation or praise." Our behavior should never reduce the human body to an object. Dress, language, and behavior should reflect a sensitivity to the Jewish respect for modesty and privacy. As Jews we acknowledge and celebrate the differences between public, private, and holy time as well as the differences between public, private, and holy places.

7. *B'rit* ("covenantal relationship"). For sexual expression in human relation-ships to reach the fullness of its potential, it should be grounded in fidelity and the intention of permanence. This grounding mirrors the historic Jewish ideal of the relationship between God and the people Israel, with its mutual responsibilities and its assumption of constancy. The prophet Hosea wrote, "I will betroth you to Me forever; I will betroth you to Me in righteousness and justice, in love and compassion; I will betroth you to Me in everlasting faithfulness" (Hos. 2:21–22). A sexual relationship is covenantal when it is stable and enduring and includes mutual esteem, trust, and faithfulness.

8. *Simchah* ("joy"). Human sexuality, as a powerful force in our lives, has the potential for physical closeness and pleasure, emotional intimacy and communication. The experience of sexual pleasure and orgasm, both in relationships and individually, can greatly delight women and men. Our

tradition teaches that procreation is not the sole purpose of sexual intimacy; it not only recognizes but also rejoices in the gratification that our sexuality can bring to us. As an expression of love, the physical release and relaxation, the enjoyment of sensuality and playfulness that responsible sexual activity can provide are encouraged by our Jewish tradition. The sages teach that the *Shechinah*, the "Divine Presence," joins with people when they unite in love, but add that if there is no joy between them, the *Shechinah* will not be present (*Shabbat* 30b, *Zohar* 1). Judaism insists that the simchah of human sexual activity should be experienced only in healthy and responsible human relationships.

9. *Ahavah* ("love"). The mitzvah from Leviticus 19:18, "You shall love your neighbor as yourself; I am Adonai," serves as an essential maxim of all human relationships. The same Hebrew value term, ahavah, is used to describe the ideal relationship between God and humanity as well as that between people. The Jewish marriage ceremony speaks of "*ahavah v'achavah, shalom v'reiyut*," "love and affection, wholeness and friendship," as ideals that should undergird holy relationships. For Jews, ahavah is not only a feeling or emotion, but also the concrete behaviors we display toward God and our fellow humans. *Ahavah* implies "self-esteem," the internal conviction that each of us should appear worthy in our own eyes. To be loved, one must consider oneself lovable; without regard for self, one can hardly care for others. *Ahavah* forbids any abuse or violence in sexual or any aspect of human relationships. *Ahavah* should be expressed through behavior that displays caring, support, and empathy.

10. *K'dushah* ("holiness"). This value comes from the meaning of the Hebrew root *k-d-sh*, "distinct from all others, unique, set apart for an elevated purpose." The Torah instructs us: "You shall be holy, for I, Adonai your God, am holy" (Lev. 19:2). Holiness is not simply a state of being; rather, it is a continuing process of human striving for increasingly higher levels of moral living. In a Reform Jewish context, a relationship may attain a measure of *k'dushah* when both partners voluntarily set themselves apart exclusively for each other, thereby finding unique emotional, sexual, and spiritual intimacy.

Our Torah teaches that, on the eve of Jacob's meeting and reconciliation with his brother Esau, he wrestled with a manifestation of Divinity and was wounded. The text continues: "*vayavo Yaakov shaleim*," "and Jacob arrived shaleim" following his struggles with himself and others. Thus did he become known as Yisrael, the one who wrestles with God. We, too, as *B'nei/B'not Yisrael*, the spiritual descendants of Jacob, as human beings and as liberal Jews, wrestle with ourselves and our lives to achieve a measure of *sh'leimut*. It is hoped that the sexual values described in this statement serve as a source of guidance that leads us to a life of holiness.

Source: Central Conference of American Rabbis Ad Hoc Committee on Human Sexuality (Rabbi Selig Salkowitz, DMin), "Reform Jewish Sexual Values," in *The Sacred Encounter: Jewish Perspectives on Sexuality*, ed. Rabbi Lisa J. Grushcow (New York: CCAR Press, 2014), 241–246; originally published in CCAR Journal 48, no. 4 (Fall 2001): 9–13.

Resolution on State Restrictions on Access to Reproductive Health Services

ADOPTED BY THE 119TH ANNUAL CONVENTION OF
THE CENTRAL CONFERENCE OF AMERICAN RABBIS
CINCINNATI, OHIO APRIL, 2008

Background

For decades, the Reform Jewish Movement has supported and defended a woman's right to control her own reproductive health decisions and has advocated that all people be equipped with the information they need to make healthy choices and the tools to implement those choices. We believe that both American law and Jewish tradition entrust patients with autonomy in making health care decisions, free from government interference, and we assert that in a diverse democracy each person has the liberty to draw upon his or her own faith for guidance, and not be subject to the religious views of others. As the Central Conference of American Rabbis noted in its 1975 resolution on Abortion, with respect to traditional Judaism's own limited approval of abortion: "as we would not impose the historic position of Jewish teaching upon individuals nor legislate it as normative for society at large, so we would not wish the position of any other group imposed upon the Jewish community or the general population."

Difference in opinion between religions regarding health care options is inevitable and occurs daily. Since the landmark 1973 case, *Roe v. Wade*, recognized a woman's right to terminate a pregnancy, many organizations, religious groups and elected and appointed officials have tried to restrict, if not eliminate, the ability to exercise this right, effectively codifying their own beliefs. More recently, these groups and individuals have focused on state-level initiatives to incrementally chip away at reproductive rights, from curtailing access to abortion services and birth control to imposing an abstinence-only sexuality education curriculum that has not only been proven ineffective, but often misrepresents scientific truths and blatantly asserts a particular moral and religious agenda.

These laws and programs intrude upon a woman's reproductive rights and infringe upon the our country's guarantee of religious freedom and personal liberty. State Legislatures are no more suited than Congress to make reproductive health decisions for women. Government should not, at any level, interfere with personal health choices or intrude upon the confidential decision-making process a woman engages in with her doctor and clergy.

Abortion Services

Over the past decade, individual states have considered and adopted hundreds of pieces of legislation that restrict access to important reproductive health services. As of the beginning of 2008, four states have "trigger" laws that would impose near-total criminal bans on abortion that would go into effect if the Supreme Court overturned *Roe v. Wade*. Forty-seven states and the District of Columbia currently allow certain entities or individuals associated with the provision of health care to deny a woman specific reproductive health services, information or even referrals. Forty-four states prohibit certain qualified health care professionals from performing abortions, subjecting providers of this service to burdensome restrictions not applied to other medical professionals, and twenty-five of these states restrict the provision of abortion care to hospitals or other specialized facilities. These laws have no medical basis and are solely designed to make it harder for women to consider or even learn about abortion as an option, creating a *de facto* ban in those regions.

Forty-three states mandate parental notification or consent before a young woman is allowed to terminate her pregnancy, but only twenty nine of these states' laws include a medical exception and only 14 include an exception for cases of rape or incest. While all of these states include the option of obtaining a judicial bypass, many judges refuse to grant bypasses to minors; young women without their parents' help too often do not have access to the qualified legal counsel necessary to put forth a compelling case, making this alternative a non-viable option for those young women. Additionally, because the earlier an abortion is performed, the safer it is, the time required to go through legal process only endangers the patient.

Parental notification and consent laws serve only to force young women already in a terrifying position into further danger and seek to address a problem that does not really exist. The great majority of young women faced with unwanted pregnancy turn to their families for guidance and help, regardless of the law. However, there are too many unfortunate young women who are denied a supportive family and for whom disclosure of a pregnancy may result in abandonment or even physical harm. In some cases, the person whose consent a young woman must secure is the very person who placed her in that situation. These laws only serve to further burden the young women who are least equipped to confront these issues.

Recently, some states have considered laws that would require publication of statistics on judges who grant judicial bypasses to young women seeking abortion care without parental notification or consent. These laws would compromise the necessary confidentiality of the judicial bypass process, are intended to discourage judges from granting warranted bypasses, and could foster violence against judges who act in accordance with the law.

Women with low incomes also have been disproportionately affected by restrictions. Seventeen states prohibit insurance plans for public and/or private employees from covering abortion services. Nineteen states prohibit some or all state employees or organizations that receive state funds from providing counseling or referrals for women for abortion services. Because of the Hyde Amendment, passed in 1976, no federal funding is available for abortion counseling or services either, forcing women in these states, particularly including those who rely on Medicaid, Medicare, the State Children's Health Insurance Program, Indian Health Service clients, and clients of the District of Columbia's public health care programs for health care to risk their health by delaying the procedure as they seek private funds, or leaving them entirely unable to afford abortion services. Unwanted pregnancy creates an additional burden for poor women, who may not have the resources to afford pre-natal medical care, or be able to take time off from work to visit their doctor, stay on bed-rest if prescribed or recuperate from their delivery.

Thirty-one states further meddle with women's reproductive health by subjecting women seeking abortions to biased counseling requirements and/ or mandatory delays. Some require doctors or nurses to inform all women seeking an abortion of the pain their fetus could endure during the procedure, despite the lack of any compelling scientific evidence proving this is true before the seventh month, while other states require women to wait twenty-four hours after mandated counseling to undergo the procedure. These laws force women to take an additional day off from work for the paternalistic purpose of insisting that women further agonize over their choice, as if they had not yet already sufficiently considered their decision.

Only ten percent of counties in the United States have abortion service providers, many of whom only work part time at each of several clinics. The laws discussed above impede safe reproductive health services and chip away personal rights, creating a *de facto*, if not legal, abortion ban in many regions of the country. However, research shows that banning abortion does not reduce the number of procedures performed; it only reduces the number of *safe* procedures. Allowing states to restrict access to reproductive health services condemns desperate women to seek illegal, unsafe abortions that all too often end in the woman's injury or death.

Family Planning

The United States has one of the highest rates of unintended pregnancy among Western nations. Each year, half of the more than 6 million pregnancies in this country are unintended, and nearly half of those end in abortion. Access to family planning services significantly reduces the number of unintended pregnancies. While many states have, thankfully, expanded access to these services, including birth control, others have restricted access.

Recently, a new trend has emerged, with pharmacists refusing to dispense Emergency Contraception (EC) or prescription birth control because of their own religious beliefs. Emergency Contraception is essentially a high dose of birth control medication taken within seventy-two hours of unprotected sex to prevent pregnancy. Though some confuse Emergency Contraception with medication that induces abortion, in fact, EC does not interrupt an existing pregnancy, but rather prevents pregnancy from occurring. In August 2006, the Food and Drug Administration approved the sale of Plan B (the brandname of the only approved Emergency Contraception medication) without a prescription for people over 18 and with a prescription for those under 18. Plan B is kept behind the pharmacy counter and, even for those who do not need a prescription, can only be purchased from a licensed pharmacist. This allows pharmacists the power to refuse to supply patients with Emergency Contraception, just as they can refuse to dispense a birth control prescription.

When a health care provider objects on religious grounds to filling a valid prescription, a conflict arises between the rights of the provider and the rights of the patient. Under Title VII of the Civil Rights Act, employers with 15 or more employees must accommodate the religious beliefs of their employees, provided such accommodations do not impose more than a minimal burden on the employer. But the provider's religious liberty, with which the CCAR is also particularly concerned, must be balanced by the patient's right to make his or her own health care decisions. There are thirteen states that currently permit health care providers to refuse to provide contraceptive services and four states have existing laws or regulations that explicitly permit pharmacists to refuse to dispense contraception. None of these statutes protect the patient by requiring that the prescription be filled on the premises without undue delay by another pharmacist without a religious objection. It is our belief, as well as that of the American Civil Liberties Union and the Religious Coalition for Reproductive Choice that pharmacies can accommodate both concerns without placing undue burdens on the patient, such as an unreasonable delay or forcing the patient to travel to other pharmacy locations.

In addition, some states have enacted laws that prohibit Medicaid family planning funds to be allocated to entities that also provide abortions, even if they do so with private funds. At the same time, these and similar laws set aside significant percentages of federal family planning funds, which pass through the States, for Federally Qualified Health Centers, which may be outstanding health care providers but are not necessarily the best qualified to provide family planning services. Moreover, these laws cynically misdirect a percentage of federal family planning funds to "Crisis Pregnancy Centers," which provide no birth control services whatsoever.

Care for Victims of Rape and Incest

At some hospitals, information about Emergency Contraception is not provided to victims of sexual assault. While such a policy may be in line with the protected religious expression of the hospital, it is highly problematic, for the traumatized victim, who may not know such options exist and may face the added trauma of a pregnancy resulting from a sexual assault. In some jurisdictions, government funds for treating sexual assault victims are allocated to hospitals that do not provide Emergency Contraception or any information about it.

Sexual and Reproductive Education

Comprehensive, medically accurate sexuality education in schools has repeatedly been shown to significantly reduce unintended pregnancy and sexually transmitted infection rates among students. In contrast, the government's own reviews of the federally funded abstinence-only-until-marriage programs have shown that such programs do not significantly delay sexual debut or reduce rates of unintended pregnancy or sexually transmitted diseases when compared to students receiving no sexuality education. The CCAR stated in 2001 that modern Judaism "views sexuality, and its ultimate goal of a healthy and committed relationship, a matter of religious concern" and resolved to urge the inclusion of comprehensive sex education in public schools from grade school through high school.

The content of educational curricula is determined at the state and local levels and it is up to each state to decide whether or not to accept federal funds that are restricted for abstinence-only sex education programs. It is our belief that allocating money to these programs not only diverts funds from the more effective comprehensive programs, but also provides government endorsement of ineffective and misleading curricula laden with false gender stereotypes and unhelpful moralizing.

THEREFORE, the Central Conference of American Rabbis resolves to:

1. Affirm the legal right of a family or a woman to determine on the basis of their or her own religious and moral values whether or not to terminate a particular pregnancy, free from government interference; the right of all women to access the birth control; and the right of all people to receive comprehensive and medically accurate sexuality education;

2. Urge the broad liberalization of abortion laws in the various states;

3. Oppose laws that require a minor to obtain parental consent or notification before she is legally able to terminate her pregnancy that do not include:
    a. An exception for pregnancies that endanger the life or health of the pregnant woman and pregnancies resulting from sexual crimes including rape, statutory rape, and incest; and
    b. A judicial bypass alternative, taking into account the difficulty minors may experience in their attempt to navigate the court system without the help, consent or knowledge of their parents.

4. Oppose any law or process that seeks to publicize the records of or target judges who have granted bypasses to minors, in an attempt to direct public pressure toward such judges;

5. Oppose conditions placed on the allocation of federal or state funds for family planning that restrict the provision of counseling or abortion services;

6. Oppose measures that require women seeking abortions to be counseled with misleading, incorrect, or unscientific information regarding the abortion procedure;

7. Oppose laws that mandate a waiting period before a woman may undergo an abortion procedure;

8. Support pharmacy policies that recognize both the religious liberty of providers and a woman's right to obtain contraceptives in a timely manner by guaranteeing that:

   a. Patients at a pharmacy receive contraceptives without delay caused by a staff member who has a religious objection to dispensing them;

   b. When an employee of a pharmacy objects to providing contraceptives on religious grounds, the pharmacy accommodates that employee in a manner that provides the patient timely access to contraceptives without requiring the patient to go to another pharmacy or return to that same pharmacy at another time; and

   c. Pharmacy staff members provide all medications absent advance notice to their employers of their religious objection to dispensing a particular type of medication, thereby giving the employer the opportunity to make appropriate arrangements;

9. Encourage hospitals and other emergency care facilities that cannot, because of religious principle, provide Emergency Contraception to direct victims of sexual assault to other facilities, wherever available; Facilities that provide care for sexual assault victims utilizing governmental funds should be required to provide information about emergency contraception to all female patients who are not clearly pre-pubescent.

10. Recognize that it is up to individual parents to imbue their children with their specific moral and religious values and that no government funds should go to any program that promotes a particular religious view;

11. Encourage states to refuse federal funding directed specifically for abstinence-only-until-marriage sexuality education programs; and

12. Urge states to implement comprehensive, medically accurate sexuality education curricula that inform all students about their bodies, how to make healthy decisions and negotiate with their partners, thus equipping them with the information they need to make intelligent decisions for

themselves, to avoid unwanted pregnancy and sexually transmitted diseases and to better ensure good health throughout their lives.

Source: "Resolution on State Restrictions on Access to Reproductive Health Services, Adopted by the 119th Annual Convention of the Central Conference of American Rabbis Cincinnati, Ohio, April, 2008," CCAR, http://ccarnet.org/rabbis-speak/resolutions/all/state-restrictions-on-access-to-reproductive-health-services/.

Working Together to
Create a Holy Context

RABBI NANCY H. WIENER

The root of the word *kiddushin*, the most common term used for a Jewish wedding, means to take someone or something that others might see as ordinary and to separate it out, to distinguish it, to elevate it for a holy purpose. For most other people, your beloved is just another person. But for you, that is far from the case. In your eyes, in your heart, in your life, this seemingly ordinary individual is like no other you have ever known. And the relationship that you have with each other is also like no other. For some time now, in ways large and small, you have been setting each other apart and treating each other in ways that demonstrate the love, concern, and commitment that have been growing between you. A wedding day offers you many opportunities to articulate the distinctiveness this relationship has for each of you and the special place each of you will have in the other's life, to celebrate the unique fusion of emotional, spiritual, and sexual intimacy you have created. In truth, the only thing the two of you are bringing to each other is yourselves. That is what you and your guests will be celebrating—each of you freely offering your whole being to the other.

With that in mind, how can you navigate the entire planning process and not lose sight of this? How can you create a holy context for your relationship and the ritual that celebrates it?

As you begin your wedding planning process, take ample time, even before you discuss details with family and friends, to take a step back and think:

241

1. What does your relationship mean to you?
2. What about your relationship is distinctive?
3. What about your relationship is worthy of celebration and recognition?
4. What are your shared values?

Source: Rabbi Nancy H. Wiener, *Beyond Breaking the Glass: A Spiritual Guide to Your Jewish Wedding*, rev. ed. (New York: CCAR Press, 2012), 1.

The Ceremony

Rabbi Nancy H. Wiener

Most Jews, in large or small measure, still adhere to the ritual structure adopted by Jewish communities in the Middle Ages. The form of the ceremony begins with greetings and blessings, builds to your sharing vows and receiving more blessings, and ends with a joyous *mazal tov* from all in attendance. The words, symbols, and gestures create a coherent whole with consistent messages.

A practical consideration: Hebrew is a gender-based language in which all nouns, verbs, and adjectives indicate gender. Therefore, all prayers and documents in Hebrew have traditionally referenced the genders of the members of the couple. In recent decades new versions of older prayers have been written to reflect sensitivity to egalitarian, feminist, and gender-related concerns. Some of these variations include gender-ambiguous or alternating gender references to God. Others intentionally reference the members of the couple with gender-ambiguous language.

The Wedding Canopy: Chuppah

At a Jewish ceremony, it is under the chuppah, the nuptial canopy, that the extraordinary transformation marked by *kiddushin* traditionally occurs. Originally, a bride's arrival under the chuppah symbolized her entrance into her husband's domain and becoming a member of her husband's household. In the grand scheme of Jewish history, the central place of the portable chuppah at a Jewish wedding is fairly recent, dating only from sometime in the sixteenth century. Nonetheless, today in America, most Jews and many non-Jews recognize the chuppah as one of the most distinctive and enduring ritual objects and symbols of a Jewish wedding. As we explore some of the meanings that the chuppah has had and some of the forms that it has taken, perhaps you will be inspired to look at the chuppah in new and meaningful ways.

Chuppah literally means "covering." This covering demarcates the holy space in which a Jewish couple affirms the sanctity of their relationship. In earlier times, when Jews often held weddings on market days, the chuppah was a physical means of distinguishing the special area in which the wedding ceremony occurred from the surrounding hubbub. In a very real sense, no matter where your wedding takes place, there will be inherent distractions for all who are present; the chuppah continues to focus attention upon you and the holy space in which your lives together will be transformed.

Chuppot (the plural) have taken a wide variety of forms, from the canopied couches for brides and grooms of medieval Central Europe, to an embroidered *parochet*, or ark cover, to simple but luxurious cloths, such as silks and velvets suspended on poles or draped over a couple's shoulders. In some Jewish communities in Asia, a tallit was placed over the heads of the couple until after the *Sheva B'rachot*, when it was removed. In other communities, the bride's family bought the groom a new tallit, which both sets of parents placed on their children's heads at the start of the ceremony. Standing under a bower of flowers also has a long history. Unlike the case for many other Jewish ritual objects, there are no requirements for chuppot.

Today, from an egalitarian perspective, the chuppah is most commonly understood as a symbol of the new home that you are establishing together through your *kiddushin*. As such, your chuppah can convey some of the qualities you hope to enjoy in your future life together.

A large chuppah is reminiscent of the nomadic tents used long ago by our Jewish ancestors. Such a tent roof with no walls might seem to lack form and strength, much like the new family and the new home you are establishing. However, such a tent is also flexible; it can adapt to variable circumstances and withstand harsh, abrupt changes that a more rigid structure might not. Your new home can be filled with acts of love and kindness, a place in which guests are always welcome, as they were in the tents of our ancestors Abraham and Sarah. Like the chuppah, your new home will be inhabited by you, surrounded by your family and friends, honored by representatives of the many communities to which you belong, and protected by the sheltering presence of God.

Four styles of chuppot.

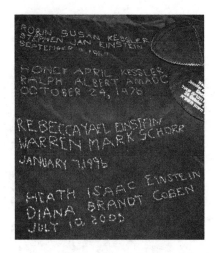

Above: Embroidery of names of couples married under chuppah.

Your chuppah may be of any size, so it is up to you to decide whether it will cover only you, you and the rabbi, you and your immediate families, or you and your entire wedding party. The options are numerous, as are the meanings you are choosing to convey. To help figure out the right size for you, ask yourselves: what is the relationship between you and your new home, you and your family, you and your community? Agreeing on answers to these questions can serve as a practical guide to your decision regarding the size of your chuppah.

In some communities it is customary for the chuppah to be freestanding; in others, it is handheld by members of the wedding party. In either case, it is considered an honor to be a chuppah holder, whether the task is real or symbolic. Some communities own chuppot that members can rent or borrow. In areas with sizeable Jewish communities, florists have chuppot that they use or make. Alternatively, many couples choose to make or buy their own, or they ask family or friends to join in creating one for (or with) them. As a ceremonial object, it is intended to heighten the beauty of your marriage cerecmony.

Source: Rabbi Nancy H. Wiener, *Beyond Breaking the Glass: A Spiritual Guide to Your Jewish Wedding*, rev. ed. (New York: CCAR Press, 2012), 25–28.

Circling

RABBI NANCY H. WIENER

Peoples all around the world and from every era of history have believed that circles have magical powers. Many Jewish folk customs, including those connected to weddings, reinforce this belief. One custom, whose original form and meaning have been lost, has the bride circling the space that she and her husband will inhabit. Among the Jews of rural Muslim Africa, the bride, seated on an animal, was led from the *mikveh*, the ritual bath, to the house of her husband-to-be; prior to the wedding blessings and feast, she was led in circles around the house. The number of circles she made varied from community to community.

Bride and groom circling each other.   *Bride circling groom.*

Among most Western Jews, the practice of circling has become incorporated into the public ceremony of *kiddushin* and now takes place at the couple's symbolic home, the chuppah. Law codes and writings from various Jewish communities and eras mention differing numbers of circles, three and seven being most common. In most descriptions of this custom, the bride is not alone as she circles her husband; she is led around him by her mother, the rabbi, or another significant member of the community.

Over the centuries, rabbis have attempted to find biblical and legal bases for this custom. Some trace it to a passage from the Book of Jeremiah (31:22), in which Jeremiah suggests that in a future messianic time, relationships between men and women will be radically different. The image that he uses to express this is "A woman will court a man," rather than the reverse. Because the Hebrew verb for "courting" can also mean "to go around," it became customary for the woman literally "to go around" the man. Another tradition locates the biblical basis for a woman's circling in the Song of Songs (8:9–10), which likens a woman to a wall; various commentators believed that the wife's circling created a protective wall around her husband, keeping him from external temptation. Yet another explanation offered in communities in which three circles are the norm is that each circle represents one of the three obligations a husband must fulfill toward his wife: sustenance, clothing, and sexual relations. Jewish mystics, kabbalists, associate the number seven with wholeness or completion. As the earth revolved around the sun seven times to complete Creation, so a bride revolves around her husband seven times to show that their marriage symbolically re-enacts Creation.

Early Reform practice dispensed with this ritual altogether, viewing it as superstitious, non-egalitarian, and inessential. However, today some couples are again choosing to include the tradition of circling in their ceremonies, reinterpreting it and refocusing it with modern understandings. Some couples choose to ascribe meanings to the circles by having biblical or poetic verses read as each circle is made. One popular choice is from Hosea (2:21–22), which says: "I will betroth you to me forever; and I will betroth you to me in righteousness and justice, and in loyal love, and in mercy. And I will betroth you to me in faithfulness."

> Emily and Jeff found the notion of defining a protective circle around each other appealing. Marie circled her husband as an act of empowerment, through which she delineated the sacred space of the union. Camille and Karen chose to share the circling, with each one of them circling the other an equal number of times, and then walking together to create a final circle. Jason and Miriam chose to have each circle represent an emotion they brought into the safe and sacred space that they created through their union; with each circle, they acted out a different emotion.

It is up to you to decide whether or not you want to include this custom; if you do, feel free to be creative in your adaptation of its symbolism.

Source: Rabbi Nancy H. Wiener, *Beyond Breaking the Glass: A Spiritual Guide to Your Jewish Wedding*, rev. ed. (New York: CCAR Press, 2012), 33–35.

The *Ketubah*

Rabbi Nancy H. Wiener

Ketubah means "written document." Though it can refer to any written Jewish legal document, over time *ketubah* has come to be associated with a document signed immediately prior to or during a Jewish wedding. The text of a *ketubah* was originally prepared and signed by the fathers or agents of the brideand groom-to-be. The document was traditionally written in Aramaic (the lingua franca of Jews, and therefore the language of business transactions and literature for many centuries, beginning in the late biblical period). It attested to the bride's virginity and stated the value that the groom or his family would pay for the bride, the amount of the dowry, the responsibilities of the husband for his wife's maintenance and welfare, the amount the bride would receive in the event of a divorce, and the fact that the ceremony would be in accordance with strict Jewish law and witnessed by two "kosher" males. The bride played no part in its preparation, and she did not sign it. To this day, some Jewish communities use the same Aramaic *ketubah* described above, and their religious courts continue to recognize it as legally binding.

Finding the economic aspects of this signed agreement objectionable, the first Reform rabbis did not require such a *ketubah* for the *kiddushin* they performed. They introduced a *ketubah* written in the vernacular, so that both members of the couple and all those in attendance could understand it. As an expression of their commitment to egalitarianism, they allowed either male or female witnesses to sign it. References to the virginity of the bride were removed from the text, as were all references to money. It simply attested to the fact that a binding religious ceremony had occurred.

Some Reform rabbis felt that it was unnecessary to have a specific Jewish marriage document at all. They reasoned that since Jews needed to register their marriages with the state, the civil license was sufficient to attest to the validity of the marriage. By the middle of the twentieth century, therefore, many Jews in the United States did not include a traditional Aramaic *ketubah* or any Jewish document in their wedding ceremony. Those that did had them written in English.

In recent years, the decision to include a *ketubah* has again become a common practice across the Jewish spectrum. For many contemporary Jews, the *ketubah* is an expression of the couple's personal pledges to each other, as well as a values statement, and is often made into a beautiful piece of art. Most rabbis today expect a couple to have a *ketubah*, though its form and content are not fixed.

Ketubot usually contain information affirming that the *kiddushin* took place on a specific date, in a specific place, and for a specific couple. They identify the members of the couple by their English and/or their Hebrew names. Hebrew names do not include surnames; they identify people as the sons or daughters of their parents. The traditional form is [first name(s)] *ben* (son of) / *bat* (daughter of) [father's first name(s)]; for example, *Yosef ben Avraham* or *Miriam bat Moshe Mendel*. However, many contemporary Jews construct their Hebrew names using both parents' names. The form for this option is [first name(s)] *ben* (son of) / *bat* (daughter of) [father's first name(s) and mother's first name(s)]; for example, *Yosef ben Avraham u-Devorah* or *Miriam bat Moshe Mendel v'Chayah*. Some also indicate relationships with non-legally-recognized parental figures who helped raise or nurture them.

Source: Rabbi Nancy H. Wiener, *Beyond Breaking the Glass: A Spiritual Guide to Your Jewish Wedding*, rev. ed. (New York: CCAR Press, 2012), 40–41.

Rings and Vows

RABBI NANCY H. WIENER

A groom giving a the bride a valuable token while saying prescribed words in the presence of witnesses has been a mainstay of weddings for millennia. In a Jewish ceremony, the groom placed a ring on the bride's index finger, and said in Aramaic, "Behold, you are consecrated to me with this ring, according to the laws of Moses and Israel." Until the modern period, the words and actions were unilateral; the bride did not give the groom a token and did not make a verbal pledge.

Nevertheless, some of the most extraordinary pieces of Jewish ritual art are rings designed for weddings. In parts of medieval Europe, grooms placed a large silver ring, intricately designed in the shape of a house, on the bride's index finger. In some communities, one highly stylized ring was used during the ceremony, and another ring was worn on the ring finger as a permanent marriage token.

During the past thousand years or more, any ring that the husband owned, made of a solid piece of precious metal, whose weight and value could be determined (remember, this was in part a business transaction), would have been deemed "kosher" at any Jewish wedding in any part of Central, Eastern, or Western Europe.

Using a solid metal without a stone was understood as a reminder that (1) the relationship had no beginning and no end and (2) a woman should not equate herself with a precious stone, which can be lost. Many communities no longer adhere to these requirements. Over the centuries, both the ring style and the finger upon which the ring is placed have varied. Some communities maintain the custom of placing the ring on the bride's index finger to make it visible to

*Jewish wedding ring,
19th century.*

all. In many contemporary Jewish circles, the ring is placed directly onto the ring finger. Some couples who wish to use rings that are family heirlooms during the cermony place them on the index finger and wear other rings following the ceremony.

Replace the ring with a piece of cloth, expensive spices, a coin, or other articles of specific value and you could be in a Jewish community from Asia, the Indian subcontinent, the Middle East, or Africa in the same time period. As the groom handed her the agreed-upon item and recited words that identified it as a token of marriage in accordance with Jewish law, they were married.

Since so many contemporary Jewish communities no longer recognize *kiddushin* as a business transaction, contemporary *kiddushin* rituals allow for several variations in this part of the ceremony. For one thing, both partners can choose to give each other a token. Also, the choice of tokens has broadened considerably. Some rabbis will require that couples use a ring of one solid piece of metal, while others will accept any style of ring or any other object as the official token. The only limits are set by your imaginations, tastes, and the customs of your communities, so be sure to consult with your rabbi.

The token given is only a symbol, a material pledge for the promises, colloquially known as vows, you say. The traditional formulaic declaration is:

הֲרֵי אַתְּ מְקֻדֶּשֶׁת לִי בְּטַבַּעַת זוֹ כְּדַת מֹשֶׁה וְיִשְׂרָאֵל.

Harei at m'kudeshet li b'tabaat zo k'dat Moshe v'Yisrael.

This literally means:

> Behold, you are consecrated for/to me, with this ring, according to the religion/tradition of Moses and Israel.

Originally, it was only the man who said this. However, today in modern, egalitarian *kiddushin*, both members of the couple make this declaration. Since Hebrew is a gender-based language, with most words (including nouns, pronouns, adjectives, and verbs) indicating gender and number, the traditional phrase above must be modified if it is to be said to a man:

הֲרֵי אַתָּה מְקֻדָּשׁ לִי בְּטַבַּעַת זוֹ כְּדַת מֹשֶׁה וְיִשְׂרָאֵל.

Harei atah m'kudash li b'tabaat zo k'dat Moshe v'Yisrael.

Notice that the changes are made to indicate the person being *spoken to*, not the person *speaking*. Your rabbi will ensure that you say the correct form if these are the words you plan to use. If you choose to exchange tokens other than rings, you will also need to make sure that your words reflect the substitution. For those of you who are transgender, you will need to work closely with the rabbi to make sure the language you use is comfortable for you and your beloved.

Let us take a few moments to consider the import of these words. *Harei at/atah* means "Behold! [Or, 'Pay attention!'] Don't make a mistake. Take a look." It is as if each member of the couple turns to the other and affirms, "You are the one to whom I am speaking." *M'kudeshet/mikudash li* comes from the same root as *kiddushin*. With these words you are saying to each other, in front of witnesses, "I am setting this relationship, and you, apart from all others, for myself.

I will treat you differently from all others. I will see you as no others see you. And I will treat our relationship as holy." How does this happen? How can we be sure that this is your intent? *B'tabaat zo*, "with this ring" (substitute the appropriate token if rings are not used) that you give. And lest anyone think that this is not a serious matter, that it is not valid and binding, the declaration ends with the words, *k'dat Moshe v'Yisrael*, "in accordance with the tradition of the

Jews," referred to in shorthand by invoking "Moses and Israel." Pretty powerful statements!

This is the traditional formula. Some rabbis require it; others may be open to varying degrees of innovation and creativity. The words you choose can link you to age-old traditions, or they can intentionally distance you from aspects of the tradition with which you are not comfortable or to which you cannot easily relate. They can be in Hebrew or English or both, or in any language that is meaningful to you and/or those celebrating with you. Be sure to discuss your desires and concerns with your rabbi so that together you can decide what you want to say and how you want to say it.

As you plan your vows, consider also the people you will be inviting to your *kiddushin* and the message you want to convey to them. You may choose to use the traditional vows so that people familiar with the formula will recognize your ceremony as authentically Jewish. In truth, depending on who attends your ceremony, any words in Hebrew may have the same effect. Or you may choose to communicate your own thoughts, promises, and hopes for your relationship in a more personal form—a letter, a poem, a song, a picture—and share these in addition or instead.

Source: Rabbi Nancy H. Wiener, *Beyond Breaking the Glass: A Spiritual Guide to Your Jewish Wedding*, rev. ed. (New York: CCAR Press, 2012), 47–50.

The Wedding Address,
the *Sheva B'rachot*,
and Breaking a Glass

RABBI NANCY H. WIENER

The Wedding Address

At some time during the ceremony, the officiant will speak directly to the two of you for a few minutes. Some speak generally of the meaning and responsibilities of marriage, interspersing their remarks with personal comments, based on personal memories of you and/ or the discussions they have had with you during your premarital meetings. Some focus on the particular themes that dominated your premarital discussions. Others draw on themes and messages of nearby Jewish holidays or the weekly Torah portion. Ask your rabbi about the approach she/he generally takes in order to get a better sense of this part of the ceremony.

Seven Blessings: Sheva B'rachot

The earliest ritual for marriage (*nisuin*) consisted of the recitation of a series of blessings, and nothing more. These blessings were said not under the chuppah, but rather at a large feast. Since the fusion of the ceremonies in the Middle Ages, these blessings, known in Hebrew as the *Sheva B'rachot* (literally "Seven Blessings"), have been a part of the ceremony itself. Here again, as with the circling, Jewish-mystics attribute special significance to the number seven, seeing it as representing completion, creation, and wholeness.

The traditional *Sheva B'rachot* use metaphors that were readily understood by earlier generations of Jews, based on imagery from the Bible and customs from late antiquity. They found in them their own associations of marriage with heterosexuality and procreativity. Since its inception, the Reform Movement has created wedding rituals that modified this section, altering language and providing different numbers of blessings to be included. For many contemporary Jews, the language and imagery of the traditional *Sheva B'rachot* seem unintelligible. Yet, if we look beneath the images and metaphors, their overarching themes offer enduring and powerful messages you may want to express at your *kiddushin*:

1. The human capacity to express joy, embodied in the symbol of wine
2. The wonder of Creation
3. The creative and procreative power of humanity
4. The extraordinary nature of being human, imbued with a capacity to strive toward the divine
5. The healing and restorative capacity of meaningful relationships, both for the people involved and for the whole world
6. The joy we experience when celebrating the loving commitment of two people to each other
7. The joy that those two people find in each other

There are many ways to incorporate these themes into your ceremony. During the past few decades, couples have begun to invite friends and family to draw on these themes and offer their own personal blessings as well as or instead of the traditional ones. Some couples choose to have the traditional blessings, or a reworked version of them, chanted during their *kiddushin*, followed either by a modern interpretive rendition in English or by personal blessings offered by guests. Some couples choose to have the traditional blessings chanted at the ceremony and for friends to offer their own blessings at the meal that follows. Others choose not to use the traditional blessings at all, but instead ask friends or family members to prepare personal blessings on a pre-assigned theme. Sometimes the rabbi will give a brief explanation of the custom of offering blessings and then invite the guests to think of the blessings they hope you will enjoy together as the blessings are chanted in Hebrew. This is a wonderful opportunity to involve friends and family and to underscore the heightened sense of being blessed that you are likely to feel on the day of your *kiddushin*. Many rabbis are willing to alter both the Hebrew and the English liturgical texts of the *Sheva B'rachot* in a variety of ways.

Finally, as an extension of the original custom, in many Jewish communities the *Sheva B'rachot* are chanted at the wedding reception or wedding meal as well as at the ceremony itself. They customarily follow the recitation of *Birkat HaMazon*, the Blessing after Meals.

Breaking a Glass

Of all the customs associated with Jewish weddings in contemporary America, the breaking of the glass is probably the best known. In some communities, the groom breaks the glass under his foot; in others, he breaks it by throwing it against a wall. The origins of this convention are unclear. Some anthropologists believe that this represents a symbolic rupturing of the bride's hymen; others point to a practice, shared by many cultures, of breaking a glass or a plate upon agreeing to a contract, in order to chase away or deceive evil spirits. The most widely known traditional interpretation of this custom at Jewish weddings, which can be dated only back to the fourteenth century, is that even amidst joy, we must remember and mourn the destruction of the Temple. (For more information about the destruction of the Temple and its impact on Jewish wedding practices, see "Collective Mourning Periods," p. 99.) In some Moroccan Jewish villages, the custom of breaking the glass was understood as a way of enacting the saying "A difficult beginning is a good sign" (after the verse "All beginnings are difficult" [*P'sikta Zutarta, Sh'mot* 19:5]).

Source: Rabbi Nancy H. Wiener, *Beyond Breaking the Glass: A Spiritual Guide to Your Jewish Wedding*, rev. ed. (New York: CCAR Press, 2012), 54–56.

What Weddings Can Teach Us about Community

RABBI LARRY KAROL

These elements comprise the essence of every life event, both joyous celebrations and times of sorrow. They are the ingredients of our most treasured relationships; they lie at the foundation of any community.

Family, holiness, and love were present in large measure in my son Adam's birth ceremony, consecration, bar mitzvah, and confirmation, and even in his graduations from elementary school, middle school, high school, and college.

All of the same elements were present when Adam got married this year, too, but it was different, somehow.

It was deeper.

It was unique.

All of those other life events are significant landmarks along the path of life, bringing both sides of a family together. A wedding, though, is a moment of creation, when two families become one through the union of the couple standing under the chuppah (wedding canopy). Weddings also define which friends have become family-by-choice, not just through their presence on the guest list but through the connection they feel to the couple and the future events by which a shared history will unfold. *Mishpachah*, family, is a tree of generations, a web of connections, a story of how all of those bonds came to be and will continue to grow.

All religious and secular life events include specific rituals that set them apart from other moments, giving those times a dimension of *k'dushah*, holiness. A

Jewish wedding typically includes: the *chuppah*, the canopy that represents the couple's first home; rings that illustrate their union as they form a circle of two; wine as a symbol of joy; and the breaking of a glass at the end of a wedding ceremony. With the shout of "*Mazal tov!*" this final tradition offers the culmination of a holy celebration often called *kiddushin* (taken from the root word for holiness).

Adam and Juli's sacred ceremony was linked with weekly sacred Jewish time. We welcomed Shabbat with selected prayers before the rehearsal dinner, participating with Juli's parents. The next night, we recited Havdalah together before the signing of the *ketubah* (marriage contract), and then we moved into the wedding itself. We entered the holy space of *kiddushin* having marked the beginning and end of Shabbat, of which it has been said, "More than the Jewish people have kept Shabbat, Shabbat has kept the Jewish people." I know, that Shabbat will define a regular part of life for Adam and Juli, not only in time but in its underlying values of creation and working for freedom and liberation for all people. Those principles reflect a *k'dushah* all their own.

Ahavah, love, is central to what Rabbi Akiba called the "fundamental principle of the Torah": Love your neighbor as yourself. It is, of course, all-important in a marriage, in family relationships and friendships, and in the interconnections of community that we have the opportunity to create together.

As I looked around at those assembled for Adam and Juli's wedding, I could see the love in their eyes for the couple. I could hear the depth of the bonds between each of the rabbis and the bride and groom. I could sense the spirit that flowed between the parents standing on either side of the *chuppah* and the two people who were about to merge their life stories into one. Throughout the weekend, as I looked around at those present, I thought about how so many of them were a part of my own story, including my wife's and my shared journey.

Yes, there was *mishpachah*, family. Yes, there was *k'dushah*, holiness, because of the uniqueness of the tales we have spun through shared experiences. And there was *ahavah*, love—not only among family, but among friends, as well. Such love can be a powerful source of joy, inspiration, and hope. As I picked up Adam's high school friends at the train station, I was reminded of the love and friendship that exists between them—and what a joy it is to behold.

Now, a young woman new to our family calls my wife "Mom" and me "Dad"; our son will call her parents the same. *Mishpachah*, *k'dushah*, and *ahavah* will guide us in strengthening newly formed ties that we will always cherish.

We know that this can happen in any type of community, if we see each other as part of the same family, if we are willing to recognize that what brings us together is unique and special, and if we allow the love of our neighbor and the love of God to embrace and engulf our souls. Then we will know what it truly means to be one.

Source: Rabbi Larry Karol, "What Weddings Teach Us about Community," *Rabbi Larry Karol* (blog), http:// rabbilarrykarol.blogspot.com/2015/02/what-weddings-teachus-about-community. html.

Divorce and Remarriage

What is the Jewish view of divorce?

Judaism has allowed divorce since earliest times,[1] often on quite liberal grounds. However, because the sanctity of home and family are central principles of Judaism, divorce in the Jewish community was relatively rare and until recent times and was historically considered a necessary misfortune.[2]

Today divorce is as common in the Jewish community as it is in society as a whole. Couples who are experiencing difficulty in their relationship may seek the input of rabbis, who will generally recommend professional counseling along with rabbinic support. A frank reappraisal of the strengths and weaknesses of a marriage under professional guidance can sometimes bring together alienated people and reestablish a marriage on more solid, possibly more sacred, foundations. But Jewish tradition acknowledges that divorce is sometimes the best solution, enabling each member of the couple to go on to live a more fulfilling and satisfying life.

What is a *get*?

While historically Judaism requires the obtaining of a religious divorce decree (a *get*) before a divorced person may remarry,[3] Reform rabbis will generally accept

---

1 The earliest laws of divorce in Judaism can be found in the Torah (Deuteronomy 24:1–4) and in the Talmudic tractate on divorce, *Gittin*.

2 The Talmudic tractate on divorce, after ninety folios covering all its legal ramifications, concludes with the following words: "If a man divorces his first wife, even the altar sheds tears" (BT *Gittin* 90b).

3 In traditional Judaism a person who has only a civil but not a religious divorce (*get*) is not considered divorced. Subsequent remarriage by such a person and the legitimacy of the children of such a remarriage will be questioned wherever traditional law is binding (as, for example, in Israel).

The traditional process for acquiring a *get* is complex and requires the convening of a rabbinical court (*beit din*) and the services of a scribe (*sofer*). A *get* is usually issued by a rabbinical court only after a civil divorce has been granted. Because a traditional *get* involves the husband agreeing to grant his wife a divorce and is thus inherently not egalitarian in nature, Reform

a civil divorce as sufficient. The decision as to whether it is advisable to obtain a *get* before remarriage should be made in consultation with your rabbi. Lawyers involved in a divorce should be advised to familiarize themselves with the procedures related to obtaining a *get* in order to counsel their clients more fully.

After receiving a civil divorce, the couple or individuals might consider whether a religious ritual might be appropriate to mark their new status. There are many contemporary rituals that have been created to help couples transition out of a marriage.

What is the Jewish view on remarriage?

Judaism, with its emphasis on love and companionship, has historically been supportive of remarriage after divorce or death of a spouse. While someone who has been divorced or widowed is encouraged to date and enter a new relationship that could possibly lead to marriage, it is important to go through a meaningful period of emotional growth or mourning and not rush too quickly into a new relationship. Once a remarriage is being planned, it is appropriate to consider a role for the children at the wedding while also taking into account their potentially complicated feelings about the marriage.

Source: Rabbi Peter S. Knobel, ed., *Navigating the Journey: The Essential Guide to the Jewish Life Cycle* (New York: CCAR Press, 2017).

---

rabbis do not typically require one. However, the CCAR provides a contemporary, egalitarian *get*, called "A Document of Separation and Release," which serves as a symbolic Jewish way to acknowledge the end of a marriage.

Mourning a Marriage

During the traditional *get* ceremony,
I began to feel released—still I needed a
ritual through which I could release myself.

RABBI LAURA GELLER

"When a man divorces the wife of his youth, even the altar of God sheds tears."

—(*Gittin* 90b)

In most divorces, God is not the only one to shed tears. Divorce is not only the end of a marriage, but also a kind of death that must be mourned before one can go on to create new dreams.

As a Reform rabbi, I had worked over the years with many individuals who were going through divorces. I thought I understood their pain, their shame, their anger, and their grief. I had often seen that civil divorce wasn't sufficient to help people separate emotionally as well as financially and physically. I thought I understood the need for Jewish ritual to help them move through their loss to a place where they could begin again. I thought I understood that divinity needed to be present as a marriage ended just as it is present under the *huppah*, the marriage canopy, when a marriage begins. I thought I understood it all, but it wasn't until my marriage ended after twelve years, two children, and a thousand shattered dreams that I really began to understand.

I know full well that a traditional *get* (divorce document) is a patriarchal ritual in which a man releases his wife, and his wife is released. Therefore, I was surprised to discover that I wanted a *get*. It was not for political reasons—i.e., so that no one would even question the status of any children that might come from a subsequent marriage—for I was already forty; there was little chance of other children. My reason was personal, not political. I felt I needed to be released, to be set free from the commitments and the promises I had made to this marriage and to the man I had loved since I was twenty years old. I needed to face him one last time, and to hear him acknowledge through ancient words that our dreams had been shattered and that the sacred bonds that had connected us had been destroyed. I didn't want the ritual that ended our marriage to be easy or pleasant; I wanted it to reflect the pain and dislocation that I felt. I somehow believed that only by facing the pain could I begin to reconnect with the holiness in my life.

Because I knew the ritual would be difficult, I asked my friend Ruth to come with me for support. The ceremony was to take place at the home of the head of the Orthodox *beit din* (religious court). She and I arrived at the rabbi's home in the middle of the afternoon. I was invited to sit at a long table at the front of the living room; Ruth sat on the sofa in the back. When my ex-husband arrived, he joined me at the table, across from the rabbi, the two witnesses, and the scribe—all Orthodox men. After asking to see the front page of our civil divorce, our *ketubah* (Jewish marriage document), and our driver's licenses, the rabbi asked both of us to give our Hebrew names, our nicknames, and any other names we have ever used. All this was to ensure that the information on the *get* would identify us properly.

Then the rabbi turned to my ex-husband and asked: "Do you, Michael, the son of Abraham, give this *get* of your own free will without duress and compulsion?" Even after the affirmative answer, question after question followed to determine that Michael was freely choosing to give this *get*. Satisfied, the rabbi asked Michael to recite: "Hear ye witnesses: in your presence I declare null and void any previous declaration that I may have made which may invalidate this *get*."

I sat silently as the scribe presented to Michael the pen, the paper, and the ink he would use to write the *get*. Michael lifted them up to show he had acquired them, and returned them to the scribe as he read a statement ordering the scribe to write a *get* for him to divorce me—for him exclusively, for me exclusively, and for the purpose of a *get* exclusively—to write even a hundred *gittin* until one valid *get* was written.

We sat in silence as the scribe wrote out the *get*. We were only required to remain in the room while the first line was being written, but neither of us moved. The only sound was the scratching of the quill pen, a sound that evoked the unraveling of dreams.

We were lucky. The scribe completed a perfect *get* on the first attempt. We had only waited about twenty minutes. The scribe held it up for the witnesses to see. They both agreed it was very beautiful. Before the witnesses signed it, they asked each other to confirm that this was the *get* Michael had asked them to witness in order to divorce me.

Then the rabbi held up the *get* and turned to the scribe. "Is this the *get* you have written?" In the questions that followed, he determined that this was indeed the *get* that the scribe had written for Michael for the express purpose of divorcing me. He asked again whether Michael was giving this *get* freely and instructed him to disavow any statement he might have made to invalidate the *get*.

As the rabbi turned to me, I asked if I could see the *get*. The rabbi seemed surprised that a woman would ask to see her *get*. It was beautiful; perfectly formed Hebrew letters on twelve lines. Asking to see the *get* gave me a sense of power.

Then the rabbi asked me a series of questions similar to those he had asked Michael, questions about my willingness to accept the *get*. I too declared null and void any statements that might have nullified the *get*.

The rabbi folded the *get* in half and then in thirds; the folded *get* looked like a collar. He asked each of us to stand and face the other. I took off all jewelry from my hands as the rabbi handed the *get* to Michael. Michael dropped it into my cupped hands and said: "This is your *get* and with it be you divorced from this time forth so that you may become the wife of any man." I took my *get*, lifted it over my head to indicate that I had acquired it, put it in my pocket, and walked out of the room. At that moment, I felt that I could finally begin again.

Those few moments facing the man I had once loved and walking away from him transformed me. Although we had been separated for two years and divorced by civil law for six months, it was not until that moment that I began to feel released. The knot was finally untying.

I returned to the table with my *get*. The rabbi opened it to determine again that it was in fact the very *get* written for this specific occasion. Then he refolded it and cut it with scissors like I had cut out paper snowflakes as a child.

There was something ancient and powerful about the ritual. All this attention to create a beautiful and perfect document—only to have it cut apart. It seemed like a good way to mark the end of a marriage that began with hope but ended in pieces.

The rabbi kept the *get* and gave each of us a document *(petur)* certifying that we had ended our marriage with a *get*. He and the witnesses wished us both well. Then Ruth took me out for High Tea at a wonderful restaurant to celebrate the beginning of the rest of my life.

The *get* ceremony, though powerful, was insufficient. I needed a ritual in which I was the actor, not the one acted upon—a ritual through which I could release myself. At first, I thought about saying *kaddish* for my marriage, but I was beyond that stage. I was ready to end the mourning. The image that came to mind was returning from an unveiling, lifting the veil from a period of intense mourning, and signaling to the mourner and the community that the mourner was ready to "go forth in peace to life." After a funeral, the friends bring food and take care of the mourner. After an unveiling, the mourner's status changes; now she can feed those who took care of her. I wanted to thank my friends for taking care of me during the darkest time of my life.

On the evening after my traditional *get*, eleven women friends joined me at my home to help me create a new ceremony. It was the fifth night of Chanukah.

We began in darkness, sitting in a circle around the *chanukiyah* (candelabra). I had asked each woman to come prepared to share a story about a journey from darkness to light. After each had shared her story, I thanked them all for helping me move from darkness to light. Then we lit the *chanukiyah* and sang *"Shehechiyanu"*—"Thank you God, for having kept us in life, sustained us, and brought us to this time."

Ruth described the *get* ritual she had witnessed, and I read a new version of the *get*, one that I had written. It, too, had twelve lines, but this time I was the one releasing myself. After I read it aloud, all of my friends signed it as witnesses.

Then we went in to the backyard and stood near the trees I had planted at the *b'rit* (covenant ceremony) of my son and daughter. Just as I had planted my son's foreskin and my daughter's umbilical cord, so we planted my version of the *get* under a new tree that my friends had given me as a present. As we buried it, I asked each of my friends to voice everything they hoped I would bury from my marriage and divorce.

We returned to the house and I served the best dinner I could cook. After all the months of their feeding and caring for me, I was finally ready to give something back. I placed a present at each table setting to thank my friends for all their gifts of love.

We ended the evening with singing, laughing, and some tears.

When people divorce, it is not only God who sheds tears. My divorce rituals taught me that while it is good to cry, there will come a time when the crying will end. These rituals helped me understand that I could begin again, grateful for the blessings that had come from my marriage and ready to learn from its mistakes.

Source: Rabbi Laura Geller, "Mourning a Marriage," *Reform Judaism* 28, no. 3 (Spring 2000): 54, 56–57.

Birth and Raising Up
the Next Generation,
and the Wisdom of Adulthood

Source Texts

Genesis 1:28

[28]God then blessed them, and God said to them, "Be fruitful and multiply; fill the earth and tame it; hold sway over the fish of the sea and the birds of the sky, and over every animal that creeps on the earth.

Genesis 17:9-13

[9]God then said to Abraham, "As for you, observe My covenant—you and your descendants after you—in all your generations. [10]This is my covenant that you and your descendants after you are to observe: let every male among you be circumcised. [11]When the flesh of your foreskin has been circumcised, it shall become a sign of the covenant between us. [12]And in all your generations let every eight-day-old boy among you be circumcised, [whether it be] a homeborn slave or bought from foreigners, not of your own descent. [13]Let your homeborn slave and the one you buy be circumcised, so that My covenant may be in your flesh as an everlasting covenant.

Mishnah Nidah 5:6

The vows of a girl of age eleven years and one day must be examined. The vows of a girl of age twelve years and one day are valid. . . . The vows of a boy of age twelve years and one day must be examined. The vows of a boy of age thirteen years and one day are valid.

Moshe Isserles, Gloss on *Shulchan Aruch, Orach Chayim* 225:2

There are those who rule that one whose son has become bar mitzvah should recite the following blessing: "Blessed are You . . . Who has absolved me [*shep'tarani*] from responsibility for this one."

Birth and Childhood

God created the human being in [the divine] image . . . creating them male and female. God then blessed them.

—Genesis 1:27–28

Be fruitful and multiply. A people and a host of peoples shall come from you.

— Genesis 35:11

Take to heart these instructions with which I charge you this day. Impress them upon your children.

—Deuteronomy 6:6–7

The first commandment in the Torah is *p'ru ur'vu,* "Be fruitful and multiply" (Genesis 1:28). Historically, Judaism regards children as a blessing from God and the procreation of children as a mitzvah. Jews have seen their progeny as evidence of their love and as assurance of the continued existence of the Jewish people. Raising a Jewish family is also a way of proudly asserting one's Jewish heritage and identity in the face of current and past historical and demographic realities that threaten the vitality of Jewish communities around the world.

The Bible teaches that each birth is an event blessed by God. In Genesis we read that God says to Abraham, "I will bless her [Sarah] and, too, I will give you a son through her" (17:16). Since earliest times Jews have felt that there is an element of the sacred in each birth, that is, that procreation, no matter how a family looks or defines itself, involves far more than sexual intercourse and conception. The Bible is not vague or evasive as to the biological preconditions for birth—"The man now was intimate with his wife; she became pregnant and gave birth to Cain"—but when Eve gives Cain his name, she acknowledges, "Both I and the Eternal have made a man" (Genesis 4:1). In the biblical tradition, God is always present as the essential partner in the process of procreation.

Modern Jews, too, believe that there are spiritual dimensions to the birth of a child and that the blessing of parenthood should be shared with the entire community. Every child born of a Jewish parent is a part of the Jewish community, and the community shares in the responsibility of raising the child.[1] There are no greater communal joys than the *b'rit* and the baby naming, for every Jewish child bears the seed of continuing Jewish presence and life in the world.

It is a fundamental principle of Judaism that every child is created pure, in the divine image.[2] The first chapters of Genesis state repeatedly that the human being is fashioned "in the image of God" (1:26, 1:27, 5:1, 5:3, 9:6), implying that the child is born with the potential of growth toward ideal love, creativity, justice, and mercy. Jewish parents have the amazing power to instill in their children the values that have guided our people for generations so that they will be able to make wise and moral choices.

Judaism has developed certain traditions surrounding the birth of a child and the formative years, helping us to take note of and mark the sacred milestones and moments that punctuate everyday life.

1 The Talmud is quite specific in a number of instances about the responsibility of the community for the proper raising and educating of a child. Of course, the primary responsibility rests with the child's parents, but when there are no parents or when the parents are incapable, the responsibility rests with the Jewish community. The Talmud (BT *Bava Batra* 21a) points out that there was a time when children without parents were not educated. How did the Rabbis learn that it is a mitzvah for the community to educate such children? From the verse "And you shall teach them to your children" (Deuteronomy 11:19), laying the emphasis on the word "you" (plural). In the earlier, better-known passage in Deuteronomy, the text reads "and you [singular] shall teach them" (6:7). Thus, we learn that the primary responsibility rests on the parent and the secondary responsibility on the community.

2 The doctrine is set forth explicitly in the Talmud and midrash in many places, e.g., "As God is pure, so also the soul is pure" (BT *B'rachot* 10a); "As the spirit was given to you pure, so return it pure" (BT *Shabbat* 152b). That this doctrine of innate purity is very much a part of Reform Jewish belief may be attested by the fact that the ancient Talmudic prayer thanking God for the purity of the soul ("My God, the soul that You placed within me is pure. You fashioned it; You breathed it into me; You sustain it within me; and You will one day take it from me" [BT *B'rachot* 60b]) was preserved in the old *Union Prayer Book* (page 101), in *Gates of Prayer* (e.g., page 53), and in *Mishkan T'filah* (e.g., pages 34–35), as it is in all traditional Jewish prayer books.

Birth

What does Judaism say about having children?

It is a mitzvah for a married couple (heterosexual or same-sex) to recognize the sanctity of life and the sanctity of the marriage partnership by bringing children into the world. While great medical advances have increased the possibility of procreation for many couples who previouslycould not have children, the problem of infertility is real and painful In vitro fertilization and surrogacy have enabled both heterosexual and same-sex couples to have biological children. For some people, this mitzvah of parenting and creating the next generation of Jews is so important that they may choose to have or adopt children on their own, without a partner. All children, those of married parents of all genders and those of single parents, biological or adopted, are welcomed equally and with joy into the Jewish community.

There are people who, for a variety of reasons, do not become parents. Those who do not choose to become parents or who are unable to do so are considered no less Jewish. For some, supporting children in the community or in their extended families, whether financially, as a teacher or volunteer mentor, or through other means, is a way to fulfill this mitzvah without having children of their own.

What is the Jewish view on adoption?

Adoption is a mitzvah equal to that of procreation.[3] All of the mitzvot and traditions that apply to biological children apply equally to adopted children. The innovative leadership of the Reform

Movement has created new and special rituals surrounding adoption as well. Ask your community's rabbi for support to frame your adoption through Jewish ritual.

Is birth control allowed in Judaism?

Reform Judaism respects the right of parents to determine how many children they should have. In considering family size, parents might reflect on the relatively small size of the worldwide Jewish population and on the Talmudic interpretation of *p'ru ur'vu* (be fruitful and multiply) as suggesting a minimum of two children. In addition, the tragic decimation of our people during the Shoah has caused some to think about a larger family to ensure Jewish survival. All of

---

3 BT *Sanhedrin* 19b: "Whoever raises an orphan in his home, Scripture considers him as if he were the natural parent."

these thoughts aside, the most important consideration is how many children a couple or an individual feels able to care for and raise.

The use of birth control also supports other values important to Reform Judaism, such as women's reproductive rights and, in regard to the use of condoms as part of the practice of safe sex, the importance of caring for one's health.

What is the Jewish view on abortion?

Judaism has since ancient times permitted and even prescribed abortion in cases where the life or the physical or emotional health of the mother is in danger. Judaism affirms the right of a woman, after due regard to the sanctity of life and in accordance with the principles of Jewish morality, to determine whether she can continue the pregnancy to term. Abortion may be medically indicated in cases where genetic disease or malformation of the fetus is probable. While Judaism affirms the right of woman to determine what is best for her, it is recommended that in all such cases the couple jointly seek medical and rabbinical counseling. On a national legislative level, Reform Judaism has long and unequivocally supported women's right to choose.

What is the Jewish way to mark childbirth?

It is a mitzvah for parents to join in a prayer of gratitude for the health of the mother and the joy of new life as soon as possible after the child's birth. Science alone cannot comprehend the mystery of human birth and the wonder of parenthood. Witnessing childbirth and the miracle that is human life allows us to transcend the mundane and tap into a reality greater than ourselves. In addition to recognizing the sanctity of life, Jewish tradition provides a prayer for moments like these. The *Shehecheyanu* creates a moment and space for us to bask in the wonder and awe of childbirth—a pause in time to express our gratitude and deep appreciate for life.[4]

Shehecheyanu

The prayer *Shehecheyanu* is particularly appropriate:

Baruch atah, Adonai Eloheinu, Melech haolam, shehecheyanu v'kiy'manu v'higianu laz'man hazeh.

---

4 Procreation, in the traditional Jewish view, requires not only a man and a woman, but the presence of God as an equal creative partner. Thus, the act of procreation is sanctified and spiritualized. As the midrash teaches, "Man [does not fulfill his destiny] without woman, nor woman without man, nor the two of them together without the Divine Presence" (*B'reishit Rabbah* 8:9).

Praise to You, Adonai our God, Sovereign of the universe, for giving us life, sustaining us, and enabling us to reach this season.

Other prayers for parents and grandparents can be found in *On the Doorposts of Your House*, pages 127–128, as well as in *L'chol Z'man v'Eit: The CCAR Life-Cycle Guide*.

Tzedakah

It is a mitzvah to make a gift of *tzedakah* in honor of the birth of one's child. Giving *tzedakah* allows us to cultivate a practice of generosity and appreciation. Through doing so we mark a special moment in time while also thinking of those in need. A gift to the synagogue and particularly to the religious school might be particularly appropriate. In keeping with the ancient tradition of planting trees to celebrate the birth of children,[5] the purchase of trees in Israel is alsoa common practice.

Entering the Covenant

How does a child join the Jewish community?
It is a mitzvah for every Jewish child to be brought into the covenant community with prayer and appropriate ritual.

B'rit

The Jewish people is a covenant (*b'rit*) community, as we read in the Torah: "'If you will obey Me faithfully and keep My covenant, you shall be My treasured possession among all the peoples. Indeed, all the world is Mine, but you shall be to Me a kingdom of priests and a holy nation.' . . . All the people answered as one, saying, 'All that the Eternal has spoken, we will do!'" (Exodus 19:5–8).

Jewish tradition is specific about the fact that both men *and* women entered into the covenant at Mount Sinai with God.[6] And so, even though the word *b'rit*

---

5 BT *Gittin* 57a: "It was the custom when a boy was born to plant a cedar tree and when a girl was born to plant a pine tree, and when they married the tree was cut down and a canopy made of the branches."

6 See Deuteronomy 29:9–14. The midrash takes the poetic parallelism of Exodus 19:3 to prove that the revelation at Sinai and the consequent covenant were participated in equally by the men and the women of Israel. "'Thus shall you say to the house of Jacob'—this refers to the women; . . . 'and declare to the children of Israel'—this refers to the men."

has come to be associated with the circumcision of Jewish male children since the days of Abraham (Genesis 17:9–14), it should be understood that every child born into the Jewish people, male or female, is a part of the *b'rit.*

The Mitzvah of Circumcision

B'rit Milah

Ancient tradition prescribes the method by which a male child is brought into the covenant, as we read in the Torah: "God said to Abraham: 'As for you, you shall keep My covenant [*b'rit*]— you and your descendants after you—in all your generations. This is My covenant that you and your descendants after you are to observe: let every male among you be circumcised'" (Genesis 17:9–10). The act of circumcision, therefore, serves as a building block for the creation of an intentional Jewish community in which the distinction between public and private spheres is blurred in recognition of a sacred and timeless act. It is a mitzvah to bring a male child into the covenant through the rite of circumcision—*b'rit milah.* There has been much discussion about *b'rit milah* in recent years. Where families have particular concerns, the rabbi may be a helpful resource for conversation and information.

B'rit milah is, however, more than a surgical procedure. It is a symbolic binding of one's son to the covenant community. Circumcision alone, performed as a medical procedure without the appropriate prayers, does not constitute entrance into the covenant. The *b'rit milah* service can be found in *On the Doorposts of Your House,* pages 129–132, as well as in *L'chol Z'man v'Eit: The CCAR Life-Cycle Guide.*

The Mitzvah of Circumcision on the Eighth Day

It is a mitzvah to circumcise a male child on the eighth day, as we read in the Torah: "In all your generations let every eight-day-old boy among you be circumcised" (Genesis 17:12). So significant is the mitzvah of circumcision on the *eighth* day that tradition requires the performance of the ceremony on that day even if it falls on Shabbat or Yom Kippur. In cases where this is not possible, the rabbi should be consulted.

While there is a strong preference that *b'rit milah* take place on the eighth day, the health of the baby is primary, and circumcision may be postponed for medical reasons. If postponed, it should be held as soon as possible consistent with the health of the child. In the case of hemophilia or any other medical contraindication, circumcision may be indefinitely postponed or contraindicated. In such cases, parents can arrange for appropriate prayers initiating their son into the covenant community. Such an uncircumcised Jewish male is considered a full member of the Jewish people and a participant in the *b'rit*.

The Joy of the Mitzvah

Parents are encouraged to share the joy of the *b'rit milah* service with family and friends.[7] This service is held most appropriately in the home but may also be held in the synagogue or in the hospital, depending on the wishes of the family and the facilities available.

The Officiant at *B'rit Milah*

Mohel/Mohelet

In keeping with the sacred nature of *b'rit milah*, parents are encouraged to consult with the rabbi about the ceremony. Whenever possible, *b'rit milah* should be performed by a *mohel/mohelet*, somone specially trained, both religiously and medically, in this procedure,[8] If a *mohel/mohelet* is not available or if the parents prefer that a doctor perform the procedure, it is preferable to select one who is Jewish and familiar with the ritual of *b'rit milah* and who will perform the surgical procedure with due regard for the sanctity of the occasion.

When neither a *mohel/mohelet* nor a Jewish doctor is available, a non-Jewish doctor may perform the circumcision with the understanding that it is being performed for religious reasons, and a rabbi or another knowledgeable Jew should be invited to recite the appropriate payers.

A B'rit *Service for Girls*

It is a mitzvah to bring daughters as well as sons into the *b'rit*. Reform Judaism is committed to the equality of all people, and in consonance with this principle, parents should arrange a *b'rit* service for girls either at home or in the synagogue.

---

7 The *Shulchan Aruch* prescribes a feast for circumcision, following the passage in the Talmud (BT *Shabbat* 130a): "Every precept which [Israel] accepted with joy, e.g., circumcision . . . they still observe with joy." While it is preferable to perform a *b'rit milah* in the company of friends and family, a minyan is not required.

8 The term *mohel* (ritual circumciser) is derived from *milah* (circumcision). Commenting on who is allowed to perform a circumcision, Maimonides ruled, "All are permitted to circumcise," including a woman or a non-Jew when there is no *mohel* available (*Mishneh Torah, Hilchot Milah* 2:1). Noam is an organization of certified medical professionals who are specially trained in ritual circumcision. They can be found at http://www.reformjudaism.org/mohel-search.

New rituals have emerged for bringing girls into the covenant and giving them Hebrew names. Options for *b'rit* services and naming ceremonies for girls can be found in *On the Doorposts of Your House*, pages 133–136, as well as in *L'chol Z'man v'Eit: The CCAR Life-Cycle Guide*.

Parents' Role in the B'rit

The responsibility for bringing a child into the *b'rit* rests upon its parents. Historically, it was the father who was required to circumcise his son or to present him to the *mohel* for circumcision. In Reform Judaism, parents share the responsibility for bringing their sons and daughters into the *b'rit*, and both mothers and fathers are involved in the ceremonies. The parents' declarations and prayers can be found in *On the Doorposts of Your House*, pages 129–136, as well as in *L'chol Z'man v'Eit: The CCAR Life-Cycle Guide*.

Additional B'rit Customs

Several customs involving grandparents and/or honored friends have evolved over the Several customs involving grandparents and/or honored friends have evolved over the centuries and become a part of the *b'rit* ceremony in various communities. One of these is the appointment of a *sandak* (the person who is given the honor of holding the child during the procedure); another is the appointment of a *kvater* and a *kvaterin* (godfather and godmother) to present the child to the *mohel/mohelet*.[9] There are many ways to include close friends and relatives in the ceremony. The rabbi can assist the parents in determining how to include family members and friends in the ceremony.

---

9 These customs and the definition of these roles varied from one Jewish community to another through the centuries. The role of *sandak* was unknown before the medieval period but became second in importance to the *mohel* in traditional communities. Usually the *sandak* holds the infant on his knees while the *mohel* performs the circumcision. The *kvater* (derived from the medieval German *Gevatter*, meaning "godfather") and the *kvaterin* (feminine form) traditionally carried the infant from the nursery to the *sandak*. This honor was often given to a childless couple, who thereby assumed a share of the responsibility for raising the child.

Another and an earlier custom is the chair of Elijah (*kisei shel Eliyahu*), a chair usually kept in the synagogue and taken to homes for circumcisions in order to symbolize the presence of Elijah. The source of this custom is probably the reference to Elijah in Malachi 3:1 as "the messenger of the covenant." Since Elijah was the messenger of the *b'rit*, it was only proper that he be present for the occasion.

There are also many local customs regarding foods to be served at the circumcision meal. All of these are in the realm of custom and may be observed or not as the family desires.

Naming the Child

How, and why, does a child get a Hebrew name?

It is a mitzvah to give a child a Hebrew name.[10] The Hebrew name is given at the *b'rit* ceremony. It is also appropriate to announce the name and bless the child in the synagogue, though many choose to do so at a ceremony at home, among family and friends. Bringing the child to the synagogue to announce the name and have the child blessed usually takes place at a regular Shabbat or daily service at the earliest time after the birth of the child when parents and baby can attend, though it may happen at any time.

Ben, Bat

Every aspect of the *b'rit* ritual serves to connect new life with thousands of years of tradition, forming an everlasting bond between Jewish individuals and communities through time and space. In this spirit it was customary to link the name of the child with that of the father through the connecting Hebrew words *ben* (son of) or *bat* (daughter of), for example, Yosef *ben* Daniel. Reform Jewish practice links the name of the child with both parents, for example, Yosef *ben* Rachel *v'*Daniel or Sarah *bat* Rachel v'Daniel.

The Choice of a Hebrew or Jewish Name

For a more complete discussion of the naming of Jewish children from ancient to modern times, see B. Kaganoff, *A Dictionary of Jewish Names and Their History* (Northvale, NJ: Jason Aronson, 1996). Different communities follow various customs as to the propriety of naming a child after a living relative or, if after a deceased relative, which one. There is no objection in Reform Judaism to naming a child after a living person.[11] Such decisions should be left to the parents; controversy over the choice of names should not be allowed to mar the joy of the naming.

---

10 Jewish tradition ascribes special merit to those who preserve their heritage through the bestowing and retention of Hebrew names. The midrash states that one of the reasons why the Children of Israel deserved to be redeemed from Egyptian bondage was that "they did not change [i.e., Egyptianize] their names; as Reuben and Simeon they descended [Genesis 46] and as Reuben and Simeon they departed [Exodus 1]" (*Vayikra Rabbah* 32:5). The custom of bestowing both a Hebrew and a non-Hebrew name upon a person goes back to the Bible, e.g., Esther/Hadassah (Esther 2:7) and Daniel/Belteshazzar (Daniel 1:7).

11 Among Jews of Middle European and Eastern European origin (i.e., Ashkenazim), it is considered proper to name children after deceased relatives. However, among Jews of the Mediterranean or Eastern countries, (i.e., Sephardic or Mizrachi Jews), it is common to name children after living grandparents. And so parents should not be deterred from naming a child after a loved one, living or deceased, because it is "against Jewish custom." We are heir to many different customs in the area of naming.

However, a name should be chosen with sensitivity and with the realization that the child will generally have to carry it through life.[12] Parents should realize that the choice of a name is often symbolic of one's aspirations for the child, whether by naming the child after a particularly beloved or praiseworthy person or by the choice of a name with a particular meaning. In some families there are Yiddish rather than Hebrew names that are precious. In such cases these names may be included as well. The parents may want to consult the rabbi to help them choose a Hebrew/Jewish name.

How else is the birth of a new baby celebrated?

Kiddush / Oneg Shabbat

One way for parents to share their joy on the occasion of the naming of a child is to host a *Kiddush* or an *Oneg Shabbat* for the congregation following the service and naming ceremony.[13]

Pidyon haben

The ritual of *pidyon haben* (redemption of the firstborn son)[14] is generally not observed in Reform congregations. However, the birth of the first child, boy or

---

12 Children are sometimes given names that are in inappropriate or even embarrassing in adulthood. And while Jewish tradition has always ascribed special merit to those who strengthened the Jewish heritage by bestowing and carrying Jewish names (see note 15), it must be mentioned that as far back as the Bible, some Jewish parents gave children "non-Jewish" names, i.e., names typical of the country in which they lived. Moses is an Egyptian name; many of the rabbis of the Mishnah had Greek and Roman names; Saadyah and Maimonides bore names typical of their Arab environment. The Talmud admits ruefully that "the majority of Jews in the Diaspora have names similar to their heathen neighbors" (BT *Gittin* 11b). Though we cannot accept the biblical idea that "like his name, so he is" (I Samuel 25:25) as a general rule, surely the name that a person carries through life is of importance and should be chosenthoughtfully. "Every person has three names: the one given by his father and mother, the one that others call him, and the one he acquires for himself" (*Kohelet Rabbah* 7:1).
13 It is a custom of long standing to prepare a *s'udat mitzvah* (a mitzvah feast) to celebrate joyous occasions such as the birth of a child, a circumcision, and so on. The traditional literature refers to many such opportunities to share one's joy with the community, e.g., *s'udat bar mitzvah* (a feast in honor of a bar mitzvah), *s'udat chatanim* (a feast in honor of bride and groom), *s'udat mazal tov* (lit. "a good luck feast," given in honor of the birth of a daughter after her naming). The earliest such feast in honor of a child in Jewish tradition can be found in Genesis 21:8: "On Isaac's weaning day, Abraham held a great feast."
14 *Pidyon haben* is based on Exodus 13:2 and 13:11–15, where Israel is commanded to redeem all male issue who "breach the womb," i.e., who are firstborn to the mother. These firstborn sons are "redeemed" from the priesthood through a ritual in which a *kohein* (descendant of Aaron the priest) is given five shekels. Firstborn sons of priests or Levites are exempt from this ritual, which derives from the ancient custom of dedicating firstborn sons to the priesthood. Since

girl, in a family is a unique event that deserves special celebration. The Reform Movement has created a ceremony called *kiddush peter rechem* (sanctification of the firstborn) to celebrate the profound joy of having a first child. The ceremony can be found in *L'chol Z'man v'Eit: The CCAR Life-Cycle Guide*.

B'rit and Naming in the Case of Adoption

What rituals are followed in the case of adoption?

An adopted son should be named and entered into the *b'rit* as soon as the initial legal procedures for adoption have been completed.[15] If a male child is not an infant, the rabbi and a doctor should be consulted about the circumcision. If the adopted son or daughter was born of non-Jewish or undetermined parents, the rabbi should also be consulted so that the child can be formally welcomed into the Jewish people and the Jewish community. This may involve taking the child to the mikveh, which is a joyous, symbolic covenantal act.

Source: Rabbi Peter S. Knobel, ed., *Navigating the Journey: The Essential Guide to the Jewish Life Cycle* (New York: CCAR Press, 2017).

Reform Judaism does not recognize a hereditary priesthood and does not believe that firstborn sons should be differentiated in any way from daughters or other sons, this ceremony is generally considered incongruous for Reform Jews.

15 According to most current statutes on adoption in the United States and Canada, adoptive parents have the right to circumcise their child as soon as the initial order of temporary custody has been issued by the court. It is not necessary to wait for the order of permanent custody, which is generally issued six months later. In all such cases, one should consult with legal authorities before proceeding.

RESOLUTION ADOPTED BY THE CCAR
THE STATUS OF CHILDREN OF MIXED MARRIAGES

Following is the final text of the Report of the Committee on
Patrilineal Descent adopted on March 15, 1983

The purpose of this document is to establish the Jewish status of the children of
mixed marriages in the Reform Jewish community of North America.

One of the most pressing human issues for the North American Jewish community is mixed marriage, with all its attendant implications. For our purpose,
mixed marriage is defined as a union between a Jew and a non-Jew. A non-Jew
who joins the Jewish people through conversion is recognized as a Jew in every
respect. We deal here only with the Jewish identity of children which one parent
is Jewish and the other parent is non-Jewish.

This issue arises from the social forces set in motion by the Enlightenment
and the Emancipation. They are the roots of our current struggle with mixed
marriage. "Social change so drastic and far reaching could not but affect on several levels the psychology of being Jewish.... The result of Emancipation was to
make Jewish identity a private commitment rather than a legal status, leaving it a
complex mix of destiny and choice" (Robert Seltzer, *Jewish People, Jewish Thought*,
p. 544). Since the Napoleonic Assembly of Notables of 1806, the Jewish community has struggled with the tension between modernity and tradition. This
tension is now a major challenge, and it is within this specific context that the
Reform Movement chooses to respond. Wherever there is ground to do so, our
response seeks to establish Jewish identity of the children of mixed marriages.

According to the Halachah as interpreted by traditional Jews over many centuries, the offspring of a Jewish mother and a non-Jewish father is recognized as

a Jew, while the offspring of a non-Jewish mother and a Jewish father is considered a non-Jew. To become a Jew, the child of a non-Jewish mother and a Jewish father must undergo conversion.

As a Reform community, the process of determining an appropriate response has taken us to an examination of the tradition, our own earlier responses, and the most current considerations. In doing so, we seek to be sensitive to the human dimensions of this issue.

Both the Biblical and the Rabbinical traditions take for granted that ordinarily the paternal line is decisive in the tracing of descent within the Jewish people. The Biblical genealogies in Genesis and elsewhere in the Bible attest to this point. In intertribal marriage in ancient Israel, paternal descent was decisive. Numbers 1:2, etc., says: "By their families, by their fathers' houses" (*lemishpechotam leveit avotam*), which for the Rabbis means, "The line [literally: 'family'] of the father is recognized; the line of the mother is not" (*Mishpachat av keruya mishpachah; mishpachat em einah keruya mishpachah; Bava Batra* 109b, *Y'vamot* 54b; cf. *Yad, Nachalot* 1.6).

In the Rabbinic tradition, this tradition remains in force. The offspring of a male *Kohen* who marries a Levite or Israelite is considered a *Kohen*, and the child of an Israelite who marries a *Kohenet* is an Israelite. Thus: *yichus*, lineage, regards the male line as absolutely dominant. This ruling is stated succinctly in Mishna Kiddushin 3.12 that when *kiddushin* (marriage) is licit and no transgression (*ein avera* is involved, the line follows the father. Furthermore, the most important *parental* responsibility to teach Torah rested with the father (*Kiddushin* 29a; cf. *Shulchan Aruch, Yoreh Dei-a* 245.1).

When, in the tradition, the marriage was considered not to be licit, the child of that marriage followed the status of the mother (*Mishnah Kiddushin* 3.12, *havalad kemotah*). The decision of our ancestors thus to link the child inseparably to the mother, which makes the child of a Jewish mother Jewish and the child of a non-Jewish mother non-Jewish, regardless of the father, was based upon the fact that the woman with her child had no recourse but to return to her own people. A Jewish woman could not marry a non-Jewish man (cf. *Shulchan Aruch, Even Ha-ezer* 4.19, *la tafsei kiddushin*). A Jewish man could not marry a non-Jewish woman. The only recourse in Rabbinic law for the woman in either case was to return to her own community and people.

Since Emancipation, Jews have faced the problem of mixed marriage and the status of the offspring of mixed marriage. The Reform Movement responded to the issue. In 1947 the CCAR adopted a proposal made by the Committee on Mixed Marriage and Intermarriage:

With regard to infants, the declaration of the parents to raise them as Jews shall be deemed sufficient for conversion. This could apply, for example, to adopted children. This decision is in line with the traditional procedure in which, according to the Talmud, the parents bring young children (the Talmud speaks of children earlier than the age of three) to be converted, and the Talmud comments that although an infant cannot give its consent, it is permissible to benefit somebody without his consent (or presence). On the same page the Talmud also speaks of a father bringing his children for conversion, and says that the children will be satisfied with the action of their father. If the parents therefore will make a declaration to the rabbi that it is their intention to raise the child as a Jew, the child may, for the sake of impressive formality, be recorded in the Cradle-Roll of the religious school and thus be considered converted.

Children of religious school age should likewise not be required to undergo a special ceremony of conversion but should receive instruction as regular students in the school. The ceremony of Confirmation at the end of the school course shall be considered in lieu of a conversion ceremony.

Children older than confirmation age should not be converted without their own consent. The Talmudic law likewise gives the child who is converted in infancy by the court the right to reject the conversion when it becomes of religious age. Therefore the child above religious school age, if he or she consents sincerely to conversion, should receive regular instruction for that purpose and be converted in the regular conversion ceremony. (*CCAR Yearbook*, Vol. 57)

This issue was again addressed in the 1961 edition of the *Rabbi's Manual*:

Jewish law recognizes a person as Jewish if his mother was Jewish, even though the father was not a Jew. One born of such mixed parentage may be admitted to membership in the synagogue and enter into a marital relationship with a Jew, provided he has not been reared in or formally admitted into some other faith. The child of a Jewish father and a non-Jewish mother, according to traditional law, is a Gentile; such a person would have to be formally converted in order to marry a Jew or become a synagogue member.

Reform Judaism, however, accepts such a child as Jewish withouta formal conversion, if he attends a Jewish school and follows a course of studies leading to Confirmation. Such procedure is regarded as sufficient evidence that the parents and the child himself intend that he shall live as a Jew. (*Rabbi's Manual*, p. 112)

We face today an unprecedented situation due to the changed conditions in which decisions concerning the status of the child of a mixed marriage are to be made.

There are tens of thousands of mixed marriages. In a vast majority of these cases the non-Jewish extended family is a functioning part of the child's world, and may be decisive in shaping the life of the child. It can no longer be assumed *a priori*, therefore, that the child of a Jewish mother will be Jewish any more than that the child of a non-Jewish mother will not be.

This leads us to the conclusion that the same requirements must be applied to establish the status of a child of a mixed marriage, regardless of whether the mother or the father is Jewish.

Therefore:

The Central Conference of American Rabbis declares that the child of one Jewish parent is under the presumption of Jewish descent. This presumption of the Jewish status of the offspring of any mixed marriage is to be established through appropriate and timely public and formal acts of identification with the Jewish faith and people. The performance of these *mitzvot* serves to commit those who participate in them, both parent and child, to Jewish life.

Depending on circumstances,[1] *mitzvot* leading toward a positive and exclusive Jewish identity will include entry into the covenant, acquisition of a Hebrew name, Torah study, Bar/Bat Mitzvah, and *Kabbalat Torah* (Confirmation).[2] For those beyond childhood claiming Jewish identity, other public acts or declarations may be added or substituted after consultation with their rabbi.

Notes

1. According to the age or setting, parents should consult a rabbi to determine the specific *mitzvot* which are necessary.

2. A full description of these and other *mitzvot* can be found in *Shaarei Mitzvah*.

Source: "Resolution Adopted by the CCAR: The Status of Children of Mixed Marriages; Report of the Committee on Patrilineal Descent, Adopted March 15, 1983," CCAR, http://ccarnet.org/rabbis-speak/resolutions/all/status-of-children-of-mixed-marriages-1983/.

CONTEMPORARY AMERICAN REFORM RESPONSA

61. A Child Raised in Two Religious Traditions

QUESTION: A couple in which the wife is Jewish and the husband is Christian were married by a priest and a rabbi. Their child has been baptized and circumcised. During the early years of the boy's life, he went to religious school sporadically, but now the parents wish to enroll him in Hebrew classes as well as regular religious school class in preparation for Bar Mitzvah. Further probing shows that they also intend to have him prepared for First Communion. What is the status of this child? Should he be enrolled in the Bar Mitzvah program? Would the answer to the question be different if the mother were Christian and the father Jewish? (M. K., St. Louis, MO).

ANSWER: The status of a Jewish child, according to tradition, is determined by the Jewishness of the mother. We, as Reform Jews, changed this through a resolution passed by the Central Conference of American Rabbis, in 1983, which stated:

"The Central Conference of American Rabbis declares that the child of one Jewish parent is under the presumption of Jewish descent. This presumption of the Jewish status of the offspring of any mixed marriage is to be established through appropriate and timely public and formal acts of identification with the Jewish faith and people. The performance of these mitzvot serves to commit those who participate in them, both parents and child, to Jewish life.

"Depending on circumstances, mitzvot leading toward a positive and exclusive Jewish identity will include entry into the covenant, acquisition of a Hebrew name, Torah study, Bar/Bat Mitzvah, and *Kabbalat Torah* (Confirmation). For those beyond childhood claiming Jewish identity, other public acts or declarations may be added or substituted after consultation with their rabbi."

This means that the child of a Jewish mother or a Jewish father is potentially Jewish if the parents act to assure the Jewish identity of the child through education, appropriate ceremonies, etc. Here, of course, the parents have done that, but have also, and at the same time, provided the youngster with a Christian identity. Furthermore, we are faced with two religious traditions which place exclusive claims upon a child. Traditional Judaism would insist that this child, by virtue of its Jewish mother, remains Jewish regardless of any actions which may be taken on its behalf or which the child may take. He would be considered an apostate because he is affiliated with Christianity, but he would always be welcome to return to Judaism with a minimum of ceremony. On the other hand, Catholicism places a similarly exclusive claim on the child by virtue of his baptism, although this need not concern us.

We would say to the parents that although their family life thus far has followed a dual path, they have now come to a juncture at which a decision must be made. It would have been much simpler if such a decision had been made at the time of their marriage, then some of these problems would not have arisen. Now, however, the child must follow one religious tradition or another. We cannot in good conscience prepare a child for Bar Mitzvah with the knowledge that at the same time he is being prepared for First Communion. Furthermore, the child will not be helped by this equivocal stand of the parents, for he will merely be confused, both now and in the future when his status will remain a puzzle to him. This matter must be settled at this moment, and we must insist on a decision for this child. The rabbi and the congregation should be absolutely certain that the path upon which the parents agree will be followed and should ask for such an agreement in writing.

September 1983

Source: "CCAR Responsa: 61. A Child Raised in Two Religious Traditions," September 1983, CCAR, http://ccarnet.org/responsa/carr-98-99/.

Raising and Educating a Jewish Child

What is a parent's responsibility in raising a Jewish child?

The Mitzvah of Talmud Torah

The mitzvah of *Talmud Torah*, that is, ongoing Jewish learning, is a lifelong pursuit. The words of the daily morning service in the prayer book teach us:

> These are the things that are limitless, of which a person enjoys the fruit of the world, while the principal remains in the world to come. They are: honoring one's father and mother, engaging in deeds of compassion, arriving early for study, morning and evening, dealing graciously with guests, visiting the sick, providing for the wedding couple, accompanying the dead for burial, being devoted in prayer, and making peace among people. But the study of Torah [*talmud Torah*] encompasses them all.

All these behaviors are important parts of living a Jewish life steeped in the practice of mitzvot.

It is a parent's responsibility to teach one's child the traditions and beliefs of Judaism, as it says in the Torah: "Take to heart these instructions with which I charge you this day. Impress them upon your children. Recite them when you stay at home and when you are away" (Deuteronomy 6:6–7). Parents are a child's most important role model. Even parents who feel they don't know much about Judaism or who weren't brought up Jewish themselves can fulfill the mitzvah of *talmud Torah* by learning as they teach. When a parent approaches Judaism with a sense of joy, the child learns that Judaism is both something positive and important.

The Partnership of Synagogue and Home

In the raising of a Jewish child, responsibility is shared by the family and the Jewish community. The family and the community can partner together to create a culture of learning and love for Judaism in which a child can immerse himor herself and thrive. Working together, parents and the community can provide children with both formal and informal learning experiences that will help build and bolster young Jewish identities and practices. It is important to find or help create a Jewish community that is an appropriate fit for the values of each individual family. It is also therefore important to support the community and its institutions so that it can fulfill its role in providing education, worship, acts of *tikkun olam* (social justice), and life-cycle mitzvot for its members.

How can a parent create a Jewish home?

The best way for parents to strengthen the connection between Jewish practice and regular ritual is to live and celebrate their Judaism at home[1] as well as in the synagogue. In this way parents become role models for their children and impress upon them their own commitment to Judaism and the Jewish people. This commitment involves active membership in a congregation, prayer, discussion of topics of Jewish concern, *tzedakah*, the purchase of Jewish books and periodicals, participation in acts of *tikkun olam*, enrollment in synagogue adult classes, and other means of involvement in the life of the Jewish community.

How can a parent serve as a Jewish role model for the child?

Tzedakah literally means "righteous giving." It is understood to be a basic obligation, in contrast to the English word "charity," which is more optional. The giving of *tzedakah* is one of the foundations of a Jewish life—all people are expected to help those less fortunate. Parents can model this behavior for children, incorporating the giving of *tzedakah* into regular family ritual in a myriad of creative ways. Children learn not only by seeing but by doing. Many families use birthday celebrations as means to do *tzedekah*—for example, by limiting the number of gifts a child receives and having the participants in the celebration take part in activities that benefit others but are also enjoyable to children, such as baking cookies for a local soup kitchen. The possibilities are endless, and the lessons learned can be applied throughout one's life.

The Mitzvah of Congregational Prayer

Congregational prayer is central to Jewish life. Sharing congregational prayer with one's children is an important part of a positive familial spiritual experience.

---

[1] There are scores of deeply meaningful and beautiful home ceremonies that are a part of the life of the observant Reform Jew. Most of these revolve around the holy days of Judaism. It is strongly recommended that parents keep copies of *On the Doorposts of Your House*, *Gates of Shabbat*, *Mishkan Moeid: A Guide to the Jewish Seasons*, and other books on the festivals in their homes for ready reference.

Parents can help to ensure that their congregation provides a proper and inspiring environment for Jewish worship and education and to immerse children in the life of the congregation. Whenever possible, parents and children should participate in worship together. In this way, parents and children can create a joint experience that enhances the meaning and function of prayer in their lives. Most congregations offer family or children's services. Attending services together can be a vehicle for encouraging families to begin creating their own rituals to be used at home.

What is Jewish religious education, and why does it matter?
There are a number of settings in which Jewish education occurs, some formal and some informal. Jewish summer camps, early childhood programs, congregational religious schools, and day schools all offer significant opportunities for learning. Ideally, each of these provides children with an environment that cultivates a deep love for Jewish tradition and knowledge in a nurturing setting surrounded by Jewish peers and role models. Through providing children with an opportunity to learn about and experiment with prayer, Hebrew, and Jewish history and values, religious education can serve as the cornerstone for a strong Jewish identity. Many congregations mark the beginning of religious education through a ceremony on Simchat Torah or some other time, often called consecration, designed to impress the child with the joy and importance of entrance into his or her Jewish education.

At times when children have a myriad of supplementary and after-school activities, it is crucial for parents to emphasize their own commitment to the importance of religious education. Supplementary religious education can sometimes be challenge. After a long day of school and on weekends, children have many competing activities and concerns. Parents who themselves participate in adult or family Jewish studies, worship, and activities can help their children see Jewish education as a positive and important mitzvah. Religious education can be a family activity, one that both strengthens Jewish identity and deepens the connections among family members.

How can I help support education within my community?
So important is the place of learning within Jewish tradition that just as it is a mitzvah to teach the beliefs and traditions of Judaism to one's own children, it is equally a mitzvah to teach Judaism to the children of the community. Illustrating

the importance of this mitzvah, the Talmud teaches, "Teaching Torah to the child of another is the same as giving the child life" (BT *Sanhedrin* 19b).

What is the role of Hebrew in raising a Jewish child?

Hebrew is called *l'shon kodesh* (the holy language).[2] Its revival in Israel as a modern spoken language is a great miracle unprecedented in Jewish history. Most of our basic literary and legal texts were originally written in Hebrew, and we are fortunate to live at a time when so many of them are available in translation. But the ability to access the Hebrew directly possesses a certain magic and connects us to the totality of Jewish history and the worldwide Jewish community. Hebrew is a language of depth and beauty, a language that renders letters and punctuation infinitely meaningful, a language that articulates the soul of the Jewish people. It is a mitzvah to learn and teach the Hebrew language. It is the key to a deeper understanding of the Torah and the other classical sources of Judaism.

What is bar/bat mitzvah?

It is a mitzvah to be called to the reading of the Torah and to recite the appropriate blessings.[3] This is called an *aliyah* (lit. "going up") and takes place for the first time when the child reaches the age of thirteen and thus becomes a bar mitzvah or a bat mitzvah.[4] An *aliyah* may also be used to mark a special occasion or to honor a member of the community.

The bar/bat mitzvah ceremony is a meaningful and traditional way to mark the beginning of puberty, the accomplishment of a degree of Hebrew and prayer proficiency, and the entering of a new phase in a young person's relationship to

---

2 Hebrew is referred to in Jewish tradition as *l'shon hakodesh*—the holy language. The Talmud goes so far as to promise the blessings of "the world-to-come" to those who speak Hebrew (JT *Shabbat* 1:3).

3 The Torah blessings can be found in the Reform prayer book *Mishkan T'filah*, page 368, in Hebrew, English, and transliteration.

4 The meaning of bar mitzvah is "one who is responsible for the performance of mitzvot." The Mishnah refers to a thirteen-year-old as responsible for the fulfillment of mitzvot (*Avot* 5:21); elsewhere the Mishnah specifies that a thirteen-year-old is responsible for his own oaths (*Nidah* 5:6). Rabbi Asher ben Yechiel (the most authoritative Jewish legal authority of the thirteenth and fourteenth centuries) in his responsa established the thirteenth birthday as a basic part of Judaism by asserting, "It is a law given to Moses at Sinai that a male must take responsibility for his transgressions [*bar onshin*] at the age of thirteen and a girl at twelve." Since Reform Judaism believes in the value of equality between the sexes, in Reform congregations, both boys and girls become bar or bat mitzvah at age thirteen. Those who observe the tradition of *t'fillin* (phylacteries; see Deuteronomy 6:8) begin at age thirteen also.

his or her Jewish identity as an emerging adult. The worship service emphasizes the sanctity of the occasion and introduces the new and unique responsibilities the bar/bat mitzvah will be able to take on. By placing emphasis on the customary *Kiddush* and the sharing of a festive meal (*s'udat mitzvah*),[5] parents preserve the beauty and meaning of the ritual. The party following the worship service and *Kiddush* can be an opportunity for not only further celebration but also a meaningful act of *tzedakah* in honor of the occasion. At the same time, an act of *tzedakah* connected to the occasion is an important way to recall our responsibilities to neighbors and fellow human beings.

While the goal of Hebrew language study extends beyond becoming bar/bat mitzvah, this ceremony generally includes recitation of prayers, the reading of passages from the Torah and haftarah, and the delivery of a *d'var Torah* (a commentary on the Torah portion). However, congregations generally customize the requirements based on the ability of each individual student and adjust the requirements as necessary for those with special needs. While a milestone in the life of a young Jewish person, becoming a bar/bat mitzvah is really only the beginning of a full Jewish education. When a child has reached a certain intellectual maturity, students are prepared for a higher level of study. By encouraging their child to continue Jewish education through *Kabbalat Torah* (confirmation) and through high school, parents can help their children understand that the richness and vastness of the Jewish heritage can best be experienced through the same sophisticated lens that will inform their secular education.

What is confirmation?

The mitzvah of confirmation, or *Kabbalat Torah* as it's sometimes known, is to be confirmed in the Jewish religion as a member of the Jewish people. Originally, the ceremony of confirmation was established by the Reform Movement as a means of educating young women equally with young men and keeping students involved in the process of Jewish education beyond the age of thirteen. In fact in some synagogues, confirmation replaced bar and bat mitzvah for some time.

---

5 It is a custom of long standing to prepare a *s'udat mitzvah* (a mitzvah feast) to celebrate joyous occasions such as the birth of a child, a circumcision, and so on. The traditional literature refers to many such opportunities to share one's joy with the community, e.g., *s'udat bar mitzvah* (a feast in honor of a bar mitzvah), *s'udat chatanim* (a feast in honor of bride and groom), *s'udat mazal tov* (lit. "a good luck feast," given in honor of the birth of a daughter after her naming). The earliest such feast in honor of a child in Jewish tradition can be found in Genesis 21:8: "On Isaac's weaning day, Abraham held a great feast."

In many synagogues today, the confirmation class guides young adults in their transition from religious school students to active leaders within their respective Jewish communities. In recent years confirmation is being renamed as *Kabbalat Torah* (receiving Torah) in some communities, signifying that as our ancestors stood at Sinai and affirmed their place in the covenant community, so do these young adults affirm their place as members of the Jewish community.

The age for *Kabbalat Torah* varies in different congregations, from the end of tenth grade to the end of high school, but at whatever age it is held, it should leave participants with the tools and passion to pursue ongoing Jewish education. Its purpose is to encourage the intellectual and spiritual growth of young people, to strengthen the bonds between them and the Israelites who received the Torah at Sinai (Exodus 19:3–8 and Deuteronomy 29:9–14), and to stimulate their love for God and the Jewish people.

Source: Rabbi Peter S. Knobel, ed., *Navigating the Journey: The Essential Guide to the Jewish Life Cycle* (New York: CCAR Press, 2017).

Go and Learn from Abraham and Sarah

JEWISH RESPONSES TO FACING INFERTILITY

Daniel Kirzane and Rabbi Julie Pelc Adler

God, in love, creates the world.[1]

Then, in love, God shares the power of creation with human beings. Indeed, the Creator even commands them, "Be fruitful and multiply" (Gen. 1:28, 9:1, 9:7). God's intention is clear: just as God has brought life into the world, so should human beings.[2]

Before the first couple is able to fulfill this obligation, they eat of the fruit of the Tree of All Knowledge, prompting their expulsion from the Garden of Eden. Their sexuality awakened, they then can embark on their journey of adult responsibility. The man and the woman come together sexually, giving birth to the world's first baby. Eve declares, "I have made a man with the Eternal" (Gen. 4:1). This appears to be the proper course of life. Our God-given sexuality allows us to fulfill our God-given responsibility to populate the next generation.

But what happens when things don't go according to plan?

Despite God's apparent design that human beings should give birth to children, the progenitors of the people of Israel all struggle with infertility. The tragic irony of our story surrounds God's promise to Abraham that he will become "a great nation" (Gen. 12:2). Despite God's assurances of abundance, Abraham and Sarah and generations of their descendants struggle for years to bear children. We are forced to ask: If fertility is the most basic seed of God's covenant with Israel, why are so many matriarchs and patriarchs, heroes of our tradition, plagued with a compromised ability to bear children? And what can we learn from them in our own similar struggles?

Classical Approaches to infertility

In trying to answer these self-imposed questions, Jewish tradition offers several models for how we might understand the meaning of infertility.

First, there's the challenge model: God puts challenges in our way so that we may overcome them. This is not the same as the prevalent platitude "God doesn't give us anything we can't handle." Rather, this is a teaching that inspires us to find new motivation in our lives, given the difficulties we face. We can see this model at work in the story of Rachel, who is described as "barren" (Gen. 29:31). Her inability to bear children weighs heavily on her, and for years she struggles contentiously with her prodigiously fertile sister (see, e.g., Gen. 30:8). Ever active, Rachel attempts to overcome her situation first by offering her maidservant as her surrogate and later by bargaining for Leah's dudaim ("mandrakes," understood by Ibn Ezra as a fertility aid) (Gen. 30:14–16). At last, God "remembers" Rachel and "listens to" her (Gen. 30:22), allowing her to bear a son, Joseph. Having struggled so hard through this challenge, Rachel now catalyzes a major turning point in her family's life. Immediately after Joseph is born, Jacob chooses to leave Haran, inaugurating the next chapter in the history of the people of Israel. The way that Rachel overcomes the challenge of infertility teaches that facing life's trials with fortitude can open up new doors that could not have been imagined before.

There's also the piety model. Not dissimilar from the challenge model, this portrayal suggests that God causes the affliction of infertility in order to inspire a more spiritual life, to urge turning toward the Eternal One with sincere hope of the heart. This is explained in *B'reishit Rabbah* 45:4:

> Why were the matriarchs barren? Rabbi Levi said in R. Shila's name and Rabbi Chelbo in Rabbi Yochanan's name: Because the Holy Blessed One yearns for their prayers and supplications. [Thus it is written,] "O my dove, in the cranny of the rocks [hidden by the cliff]" (Song of Songs 2:14). Why did I make you barren? In order that [you would] "show me your face [and] let me hear your voice" (ibid.).

This is made even more explicit in the midrashic collection *Yalkut Shimoni*:[3]

> Once I [Mar Zutra] was going from one place to another, and I found an old man. He said to me, "Rabbi, why is it that certain heads of households in Israel are prevented from having children of their own?" I said to him, "My son, because the Holy Blessed One loves them with a complete love and rejoices in them and refines them in order that they should supplicate before God. Go and learn from Abraham and Sarah: that they were childless of Isaac for seventy-five years, and they supplicated until Isaac came, and they rejoiced in him. Go and learn from Rebekah: that she was barren for twenty years, and she supplicated until Jacob came, and they rejoiced in him. Go and learn from Rachel: that she was barren fourteen years from her two children [Joseph and Benjamin], and she supplicated until the two of them came, and she rejoiced in them. Go and learn from Hannah: that she was barren for nineteen years and six months until Samuel came, and she rejoiced in him."

These midrashim teach us that God yearns to hear the prayers of those struggling to bring new life into the world. God creates infertility with *ahavah g'murah*, "complete love," in order to inspire heartfelt prayer. In the biblical narrative, we see this model at work especially with Hannah, whose womb God had "shut" (I Sam. 1:5), and of Isaac, whose wife was "barren" (Gen. 25:21) and who is understood by the Rabbis to have been barren himself (Babylonian Talmud, *Y'vamot* 64a). Both of these ancestors turned to God in supplication (I Sam. 1:10–11; Gen. 25:21), and God was pleased by their actions, ultimately granting them children. The Rabbis see both of these figures as emblematic of Jewish prayer: Hannah's prayer serves as the model for *T'filah*, the central component of Jewish worship (Babylonian Talmud, *B'rachot* 31a–b), and Isaac is credited with the creation of Minchah, the afternoon prayer (Babylonian Talmud, *B'rachot* 26b), which includes in it the day's most fervent supplications to God. These figures, then, show us that from the agony of childlessness can emerge tremendous religious creativity and spiritual meaning.

A third paradigm for understanding the meaning of infertility is the retribution model, wherein infertility is a punishment for a crime. In this approach, God is recognized not only as the One who can provide children to those who are infertile but also as the One who has the power to afflict infertility on those who otherwise would give birth. Thus, Leviticus 20:20–21 decrees that the consequence for certain unethical sexual relations is to die "childless," a reversal of the intended natural order. Narratively, we see God punish the entire household of Abimelech, who took Sarah away from her husband, by "shutting" their wombs (Gen. 20:18). As well, God may be seen to curse Michal after she criticizes her husband, King David; for after her insult, Michal "had no child until the day of her death" (II Sam. 6:23). The implication in each of these cases is that fulfilling the commandment to "be fruitful and multiply" is a privilege, not a right, and it can be taken away for grievous misconduct. The retribution model is a common explanation in today's world even though it contradicts contemporary Jews' understanding of God's role in humans' lives. The ancient roots of this approach lend it a sense of authority, and it is not surprising that many who struggle with infertility struggle also with this message.

Those facing infertility today will likely find in these three interpretations neither satisfaction nor succor. Indeed, we may wonder whether even our biblical forebears themselves would have been consoled by the Rabbis' attempts to explain their suffering. Like our ancestors, those who struggle with infertility feel inadequate, inauthentic, unfulfilled. Complicated questions arise in conversation with Jewish tradition. The Psalmist describes God's partnership with human beings to make life: "For you have made my inner parts; you fashioned me in my mother's womb" (Psalm 139:13); why can't I participate in this marvelous act? God has charged, "Impress [My commandments] upon your children" (Deut. 6:7); why can't I pass on my traditions to my own descendants? God has promised that our people would be blessed with fruitfulness, that we would be "a numerous people" (Gen. 50:20); why am I excluded from this promise? No simple response can fully answer these questions, nor can an easy answer assuage the ache of infertility.

Alternative Approaches in Jewish Tradition

Jewish tradition reaches out to us in our pain. In searching for answers to these profound questions, we may turn to Jewish wisdom to open up what God actually means in commanding, "Be fruitful and multiply." Rabbinic literature offers several ways that individuals can fulfill this mitzvah that are alternatives to childbearing.

A key figure in this conversation is Shimon ben Azai, the rabbi who asserted that the greatest principle of Torah is Genesis 5:1–2, "On the day that God created human beings, they were made in the likeness of God—male and female God created them."[4] In the Babylonian Talmud, Y'vamot 63b, Ben Azai recalls this essential doctrine when he teaches that "a person who does not engage in being fruitful and multiplying" is like one who diminishes his or her inborn likeness of God and, indeed, is even like one who sheds blood. Ben Azai clearly avows the central significance of childbearing in Judaism. However, Ben Azai's disciples immediately retort to him, "You give a pleasant sermon, but you don't fulfill your own words!" From this we learn that Ben Azai himself had not fathered any children.[5] Ben Azai replies to them, "What can I do, [seeing] that my soul loves Torah? It is possible for the world to be sustained by others." Ben Azai, childless, knows that others will have to propagate new generations. His role will be to teach them Torah so that the world will continue to bear witness to the "likeness of God" that shines forth in the wise and proper conduct of the people of Israel.

This parallel between teaching and parenting is made clear only a few pages earlier in the Talmud. In *Y'vamot* 62a–b, the Rabbis struggle to determine whether one generation of offspring is sufficient to satisfy the commandment to "be fruitful and multiply" or whether those children must also have children. In this context, Rabbi Akiva concludes that the verse from Ecclesiastes 11:6, "In the morning, sow your seed," applies both to having children and to having disciples. Immediately thereafter, we are told that during one period of time, a tragedy befell Akiva's many thousands of disciples and that the world was "desolate" or "empty" (shameim) until he was able to train more students. We may infer from this exposition that Akiva—as well as his student, Ben Azai—considered disciples to be as important as children.

Indeed, the Rabbinic tradition is explicit on this count: teaching Torah can substitute for having children. Rabbi Yonatan teaches, "Everyone who teaches Torah to the child of his fellow, Scripture credits him as if it were his own child" (Babylonian Talmud, *Sanhedrin* 19b). This is derived from Numbers 3:1, in which Moses is identified as a forebear of his brother's children. How could this be? As Rashi explains in his commentary on the verse, "Since he taught them Torah." Similarly, Reish Lakish ties this principle to Genesis 12:5, concluding that Abraham and Sarah taught Torah to multitudes, and these disciples counted as their offspring while they were unable to bear children biologically (Babylonian Talmud, *Sanhedrin* 99b). Thus, Jewish tradition affirms that the education of the next generation is the same kind of activity and fulfills the same obligations as giving birth to the next generation. Just as we commonly acknowledge that an author can be "prolific" or a class can be "productive," we assert as well that a teacher can be "fruitful." Just as Rabbi Akiva increased the number of his disciples, so can teachers "multiply" their students. Thus, the commandment "Be fruitful and multiply" is not off-limits to those who cannot bear children.

This applies as well to adoption. In *Tanach*, Sarah, Rebekah, and Rachel all struggle with infertility and agree to adopt the biological children that their husbands bear through their handmaidens.[6] As well, it was mentioned above that

Michal, wife of King David, "had no child until the day of her death." Nevertheless, II Samuel 21:8 reports that Michal bears five children with Adriel the Meholathite. Since this same Adriel is identified as the husband of Michal's sister, Merab (I Sam. 18:19), Rabbi Y'hoshua ben Korchah concludes that Merab is the biological mother of these children but that Michal raised them (Babylonian Talmud, *Sanhedrin* 19b).[7] Since Michal is their adoptive mother, they carry her name and are counted as her own children. Likewise, Naomi, beyond her childbearing years with no living children,[8] adopts the son of her daughter-in-law, Ruth: "Naomi took the child and held it to her bosom, and she became his foster mother. Her neighbors gave him a name, saying, 'A son is born to Naomi!'" (Ruth 4:16–17). From these examples, the Rabbis conclude that one who adopts a child, raising it as her own, "Scripture credits her as if it were her own child" (Babylonian Talmud, *Sanhedrin* 19b). Indeed, "the one who raises [a child] is a parent, not one who gives birth" (*B'midbar Rabbah* 46:5). Adoption, therefore, is another way of fulfilling the obligation to nurture the next generation.

Jewish tradition thus offers at least three ways that a person may fulfill the commandment to "be fruitful and multiply." One may bear biological children, one may teach Torah to children, or one may adopt as one's own someone else's biological child. We honor the heroes of our tradition who have fulfilled this commandment in all of these ways, including Eve, Shimon ben Azai, and Naomi. Although contemporary Jewish and North American cultures suggest that biological children are the only fulfillment of this central commandment, classical Jewish texts challenge us to consider other possibilities.

The Role of Sexuality

This leads to fundamental questions about sexuality. Our initial reading of the creation of humankind was that their sexuality was created so that they may "be fruitful and multiply." If this commandment does not refer only to having children, we must ask: how can we understand our sexuality outside the context of bearing children? *Tanach* bears witness that sexual relations between Abraham and Sarah and between Isaac and Rebekah were both "pleasurable" (Gen. 18:12) and "fun" (Gen. 26:8) while both of these couples were classically troubled with infertility. Rachel Adler reminds us that the Rabbis permitted sexual intercourse "when women are pregnant or menopausal, when male semen is insufficiently numerous or active to enable procreation, and, in certain cases, when procreation is intentionally prevented."[9] Rabbinic approval of non-procreative sex has also been applied to same-sex sexuality, affirming the value and importance of every individual's sexuality outside the scope of having children. The understanding of sexuality as encompassing more than procreative potential has held true from antiquity through today; sexuality does not exist merely for fertility. What, then, is it for?

We turn once again to Shimon ben Azai, recalling his suggestion for the greatest principle in the Torah: "On the day that God created human beings, they were made in the likeness of God—male and female God created them" (Gen. 5:1–2). This recalls Genesis 1:27, "God created humanity in God's image; in the image of God did God create it. Male and female God created them." Rachel Adler suggests that our sexuality—represented here as "male" and "female"—is "a metaphor for some element of the divine nature."[10] Whatever our sexuality is, we share it on some level with the Holy One.

According to Genesis 2:18, God declares that it is "not good for a person to be alone." Classically, this has been understood as a proof text for the foundational value of lifelong companionship. In short, the Genesis account teaches us that God made human beings with an inherent longing for relationship. Likewise, God longs to be in relationship with us. Our liturgy proclaims, "You love us with abundant love." The Psalmist declares, "I know that You delight in me" (Ps. 41:12). God cries out, "Return to Me" (Isa. 44:22), and we reply, "Return us to You, O Eternal, and we shall return" (Lam. 5:21).[11] Our God is a God of relationship, and we, God's people, embody that yearning for connection.

Nowhere is this clearer than in the Song of Songs. This majestic love song follows the stormy and steamy relationship of a pair of young lovers. Each of the two protagonists proclaims love for the other, describing in erotic and fantastic detail what attracts them to one another. Sexuality infuses the entire text, both explicitly and metaphorically, though the principal characters never consummate their relationship physically. The Rabbis classically understand this text to be a symbol for Israel's relationship with the Eternal, illustrating God as one who yearns for human connection and depicting human beings as people who long for their Creator. At the same time, it is impossible to overlook the poem's focus on human relationship, both exalted and celebrated. Song of Songs is a climactic Jewish text that sanctifies sexuality, honoring it as a divine quality that is rooted in the body while not tethered to physical contact.

Sexuality, therefore, is a holy essence of humanity, reflective of the divine spark in every person. This sexuality is a symbol for attraction toward others, and like God's own relationship with Creation, it can be understood in a wide variety of ways. Relationships with life companions, sexual partners, close friends, dear teachers, and respected students are all emanations of the divine drive to establish lasting relationships and to grow through connection with others.

Seeking Comfort and Understanding

In the face of this focus on relationship, we cannot forget that every person at one time or another faces tragic loss in this realm of sexuality. We are frustrated in our desire to find a life partner, we find ourselves seeking a friend we can trust, or we miss terribly the loved ones who have passed away. And among all these sufferings, one of the most painful is the experience of infertility. We ask why these unfulfilled consummations fill our lives, why God would have created infertility in the first place if God wanted us to "be fruitful and multiply." Jews throughout the ages have spent years, perhaps their entire lives, in the midst of this painful question. And for generations, they have turned for inspiration and support to people and stories held as treasures to the heart.

As we have seen, the sacred texts of Judaism affirm that there are many ways to follow God's commandment "Be fruitful and multiply." *Tanach*, Rabbinic wisdom, and Jewish liturgy all teach that a variety of productive relationships in our lives can fulfill this fundamental mitzvah. They remind us that our sexuality is a profound part of our human nature, reflective of God's own desire to be in relationship. Those who struggle with infertility may turn to our earliest forebears, drawing support from the company of our ancestors who have felt the same pain. We seek the comfort of a renewed understanding of fruitfulness as we take to heart God's promise:

> I will look with favor upon you.
> I will make you fruitful, and I will help you to multiply.
> I will maintain My covenant with you.
> You shall eat old grain long stored,
> And you shall have to clear out the old to make room for the new.

> —*(Leviticus 26:9–10)*

NOTES

1. *Chesed* can be understood as God's loving relationship with God's creations. Several sources affirm that God created the world with chesed, e.g., *Avot D'Rabbi Natan* 1:37, and *T'hillim Rabbah* on Ps. 119:138. Psalm 89:3 affirms *olam chesed yibaneh*, "Your steadfast love is confirmed

forever." These words have been understood through the lens of Kabbalah to mean "the world is built with chesed," that God creates through love. Rabbi Jonathan Sacks affirms in various writings and speeches that God "created all in love" (invocation for United States Senate, Nov. 2, 2011) and writes, "[God] creates the world out of no compulsion but as a free act of love" (*To Heal a Fractured World: The Ethics of Responsibility* [New York: Random House, 2007], 136).

2. *Mishnah Y'vamot* 6:6 teaches, "The man is commanded concerning being fruitful and multiplying but not the woman." The Gemara of *Y'vamot* 65b–66a records debate among several rabbis as to whether this reading is accurate or whether this commandment also applies to women. Maimonides, in *Mishneh Torah, Hilchot Ishut* 15:2, confirms that only men and not women are obligated concerning "being fruitful and multiplying." A responsum of the Central Conference of American Rabbis Responsa Committee rejects this distinction between men and women ("Jewish Marriage without Children," 1979).

3. 247:78, commenting on I Samuel 1:20.

4. *Sifra, K'doshim* 2:4.

5. This passage is often understood as indication that Ben Azai was not married. However, the Babylonian Talmud, *K'tubot* 63a, reports that Rabbi Akiva's daughter was engaged to Ben Azai, and the text presumes that they later married. *Sotah* 4b reflects the prevailing attitude that Akiva was unmarried but proposes as well that he may have been married and later divorced. These accounts suggest that Ben Azai may not have been intentionally celibate. Regardless of his marital status, which ultimately is ambiguous, there are no records of Ben Azai having children.

6. Sarah famously abrogates this commitment in Gen. 21:10. After giving birth to Isaac, she says to her husband, "Throw this slave girl and *her* son out. The son of this slave girl is not going to share in the inheritance with *my* son Isaac!" (italics added).

7. Rabbi Y'hoshua ben Korchah holds that it is appropriate for Michal to raise Merab's children because the marriage between Merab and Adriel was a "marriage in error" (Babylonian Talmud, *Sanhedrin* 19b).

8. See above, Babylonian Talmud, *Y'vamot* 62a–b, in which most rabbis conclude that one's children must survive and bear children of their own in order to fulfill the obligation to "be fruitful and multiply."

9. Rachel Adler, *Engendering Judaism* (Boston: Beacon Press, 1999), 131. Adler refers here to David M. Feldman, *Marital Relations, Birth Control and Abortion in Jewish Law* (New York: Schocken, 1987), 81–105.

10. Adler, *Engendering Judaism*, 118.

11. The Masoretic tradition reads *v'nashuvah*, "And let us return." This translation follows the written text *v'nashuv*, "And we shall return."

Source: Daniel Kirzane and Rabbi Julie Pelc Adler, "Go and Learn from Abraham and Sarah: Jewish Responses to Facing Infertility," in *The Sacred Encounter: Jewish Perspectives on Sexuality*, ed. Rabbi Lisa J. Grushcow (New York: CCAR Press, 2014), 491–501.

Jewish Genetic Diseases

Adopted by the 117th Annual Convention of the
Central Conference of American Rabbis

San Diego, CA
June, 2006

Background:

In 1975, at its 86th Annual Convention, the CCAR adopted a Resolution on Jewish Genetic Diseases, namely Tay-Sachs. In 1997, at its 108th Annual Convention, the CCAR adopted a Resolution on Breast Cancer, Genetic Testing, and Health Insurance Discrimination. Concurrently, at the 1997 UAHC Biennial in Dallas, the Union adopted a nearly identical position supporting continued research for prevention, early detection, and treatment of genetic disorders, promoting education about genetic testing, and supporting legislation that outlaws genetic discrimination by insurance carriers and mandates privacy of personal genetic information. Additionally, the URJ Department of Family Concerns published a Bioethics study guide #12 in 2001 that focuses on genetic testing. We urge our members to review this guide for a detailed understanding of issues raised in this resolution.

Over the past three decades, significant advances in our understanding of genetic conditions have enabled us to screen and test for a variety of serious genetic disorders. Whereas prenatal and preconception screening for Tay-Sachs has been available to individuals of Ashkenazi Jewish descent for several decades, even in the decade since our last resolution carrier testing for a host of other autosomal recessive genetic disorders have become available to members of the Jewish community. A couple or pregnancy is not "at-risk" for an affected child unless both members of a couple carry a copy of an alteration in the same gene. About 1 in 4 Ashkenazi Jews are carriers of one of a number of genetic conditions, yet testing for most couples is most often done in the context of an ongoing pregnancy. This means that a pregnant woman may not learn of her carrier status until well into a pregnancy, leading to high levels of anxiety while waiting for her partner's results. Even more disconcerting is learning during an ongoing pregnancy, that both members of the couple are, in fact, carriers of the same genetic condition. This leads to very difficult discussions and emotional decisions about prenatal diagnosis for the fetus and what to do if the fetus is found to be affected. Pre-conception screening could avert these hurried decisions for an at-risk couple. Furthermore, with advances in assisted reproductive technologies, some couples may be able to avert prenatal diagnosis altogether by taking advantage of preimplantation genetic diagnosis, but only if they are both known, in advance, to be carriers of the same genetic condition.

While the list of conditions for which carrier testing is now available is growing steadily, there are 11 that represent the current panel of conditions that may be offered to individuals of Ashkenazi descent. These include: Tay-Sachs Disease, Canavan Disease, Gaucher Disease, Familial Dysautonomia, Cystic Fibrosis, Bloom Syndrome, Fanconi Anemia type C, Niemann-Pick type A, Mucolipidosis type IV, Glycogen Storage Disease type 1a and Maple Syrup Urine Disease. Although most of these conditions also occur in the non-Jewish population (but at a lower frequency), carrier screening for mutations in individuals of Ashkenazi ancestry is far easier because of common lineage and a limited number of gene changes in this population. There are more disorders being added to the testing panel as our knowledge expands in this field. However, the underlying principles are essentially unchanged: Carrier screening can lead to prevention of disease in future offspring. Knowing more about these serious genetic conditions, as well as the availability of screening for these disorders, would empower young adults in the Jewish community to become proactive in their family planning and may avert the anxiety surrounding prenatal carrier screening or the need to make a potentially heart-wrenching decision during pregnancy.

Therefore, the CCAR Resolves:

1. To urge its members to include in pre-marital counseling for all marriages at which we are asked to officiate for couples of child-bearing age:
    a. Discussion of the possibility that the couple may be carriers of one or more Jewish Genetic Diseases.
    b. Detailed information on the specific Jewish Genetic Diseases for which there is testing.
    c. Encouragement to seek genetic counseling to learn of the implications and options available to them to have healthy children.
    d. Information regarding local genetic counseling centers.

2. To support legislation banning potential discrimination by health insurance carriers arising from genetic information and inherited characteristics, including the use of such information in determining denial, limits, or increased premiums on coverage.

3. To ask the Union for Reform Judaism's Department of Family Concerns to join the CCAR, ACC, and HUC-JIR, to work in concert with the Jewish Genetic Disease Consortium (www.jewishgeneticdiseases.org) to build on the 2001 JFC manual in creating educational resources for Rabbis, Cantors, future Rabbis and Cantors, and the communities we serve, and particularly to engage colleagues who work with college students and young couples approaching marriage.

Source: "Resolution Adopted by the CCAR: Jewish Genetic Diseases; Adopted by the 117th Annual Convention of the Central Conference of American Rabbis, San Diego, CA, June, 2006," CCAR, http://ccarnet.org/rabbis-speak/resolutions/2006/genetic-diseases-jewish/.

Contemporary American Reform Responsa

16. WHEN IS ABORTION PERMITTED?*

QUESTION: Assuming that abortion is halachically permitted, is there a time span in which abortion may take place according to tradition? (Rabbi A. Klausner, Yonkers, NY)

ANSWER: Let us begin by looking at this assumption. There is currently considerable difference of opinion among Orthodox authorities about the permissibility of abortion, as well as circumstances and time when it would be permitted. The laws have been analyzed by a growing number of scholars (V. Aptowitzer in the *Jewish Quarterly Review* [New Series], Vol. 15, pp. 83 ff; David M. Feldman, *Birth* Control in Jewish Law; Robert Kirschner, "The Halakhic Status of the Fetus with Respect to Abortion," *Conservative Judaism*, Vol. 34, No. 6, pp. 3 ff; Solomon B. Freehof, "Abortion" in W. Jacob *American Reform Responsa*, #171; *Noam*, Vols. 6 and 7, etc.). The fetus is not considered to be a person (*nefesh*) until it is born. Up to that time it is considered a part of the mother's body, although it does possess certain characteristics of a person and some status. During the first forty days after conception, it is considered "mere fluid" (Yeb. 69b; Nid. 3.7, 30b; M. Ker. 1.1).

The Jewish view of the nature of the fetus is based upon a statement in Exodus which dealt with a miscarriage caused by men fighting and pushing a pregnant woman. The individual responsible for the miscarriage was fined, but was not tried for murder (Ex. 21.22 f). We learn from the commentaries that payment was made for the loss of the fetus and for any injury done to the woman. Obviously no fatal injury occurred to her. This was the line of reasoning of the various codes (*Yad* Hil. *Hovel Umazik* 4.1; *Shulhan Aruch Hoshen Mishpat* 423.1;

sekr Meirat Enayim Hoshen Mishpat 425.8). If this case had been considered as murder, the Biblical and rabbinic penalties for murder would have been invoked.

The second source on the nature of the fetus is found in the Mishnah, which stated that it was permissible to kill a fetus if a woman's life is endangered by it during the process of giving birth. However, if a greater part of the fetus had emerged, or if the head had emerged, then the fetus possesses the status of a person and cannot be dismembered, as one may not take one life in order to save another (*M. Ohalot* 7.6). This view considers the unemerged fetus entirely part of the woman's body; as any of her limbs could be amputated to save her life, so may the fetus be destroyed. The same point of view was taken in another section of the Mishnah, which discussed the execution of a pregnant woman for a crime. The authorities would not wait for her to give birth even if that process had already begun (Arackh. 7a). The statement from *Ohalot* is contradicted by San. 72b and led to controversy in recent centuries (Akiba Eger and *Tos.* to *M. Ohalot* 7.6; Epstein, *Aruk Hashulhan* 425.7, etc.)

A *tosefot* to another section simply stated that it was permissible to kill an unborn fetus; this passage, which stands in isolation, is taken seriously by some authorities, while others say that it represents an error (Nid. 44b) and is contradicted elsewhere (San. 59a; Hul. 33a).

The Mishnaic statement in *Ohalot* was based on two Biblical verses. In them the fetus was portrayed "in pursuit" (*rodef*) of the mother, and therefore, has endangered her life (Deut. 25.11 f; Lev. 19.16; *Yad* Hil. *Rotzeah Ushemirat Hanefesh* 1.9; *Shulhan Arukh Hoshen Mishpat* 425.2). Maimonides, who did recognize the fetus as possessing some status, and Caro were willing to use either drugs or surgery in order to save the life of the mother.

Modern rabbinic authorities have felt that the variety of attitudes toward the fetus and embryo in the Talmud also point to potential restrictions in the matter of abortion. When we review the discussion of fetus and embryo, as it arose in various situations, we see that it was not treated consistently. Different criteria were applied when dealing with slaves, the problems of animal sacrifice and issues of inheritance. No uniform definition from Talmudic sources can be achieved (see Robert Kirschner, *op. cit.* for a full discussion).

Some recent scholars have felt that only the argument of "pursuit" provides the proper basis for abortion when the mother's life is endangered. They reason that although the fetus is not a person (*nefesh*), it still possesses a special status, and therefore, should not be treated as nothing or destroyed for no good reason (Jacob Emden, *Responsa Sheelat Yavetz*, 1.43; Yair Bacharach, *Havat Yair*, #31;

Eliezer Waldenberg, *Tzitz Eliezer*, Vol. #273, 9; *Noam* Vol. 6, pp. 1 ff). Others have felt a fetus may be aborted whenever there is any danger to a mother, as the status of a newborn child less than full term is in doubt until thirty days have elapsed, although it is, of course, considered a *nefesh* (Maharam Schick, *Responsa Yoreh Deah* #155; David Hoffmann, *Melamed Lehoil Yoreh Deah* #69).

On the other hand, a line of reasoning which dealt with the mother's psychological state has been based on *Arakhin* 7a; it would permit abortion for such reasons or for the anguish caused to the mother by a child's potential deformity or other problems. So, Ben Zion Uziel permits abortion when deafness is indicated in the fetus (*Mishpetei Uziel, Hoshen Mishpat*, #46). Uziel Weinberg permits it when rubella occurs in early pregnancy (*Seridei Esh* III, No. 727). Eliezer Waldenberg does so for Tay-Sachs disease and other serious abnormalities (*Tzitz Eliezer*, Vol. 9, #236).

Other traditional rabbis have been very reluctant to permit abortion on the grounds that one is not permitted to inflict a wound on one's self (Joseph Trani, *Responsa* Maharit 1.99; Zweig, "*Al Hapalah Melahutit*," *Noam*, Vol. 7, pp. 36 ff). Rabbi Unterman has argued against abortion as tradition permits the desecration of the *shabbat* in order to save an unborn fetus (Ramban to Nid. 44b); this would prove that the fetus possesses human status. An unborn child, although not yet a human being, is a potential human being, and abortion is "akin to murder" (I. Y. Unterman, "*Be-inyan Piquah Nefesh Shel Ubar*", *Noam*, Vol. 6, pp. 1 ff). Others have followed this line of reasoning. Unterman, however, also reluctantly permits abortion under some circumstances (*Ibid*. 52; *Shevet Miyehudah*, I, 29).

In summary, we see that there are some who agree with Rabbi Unterman and reluctantly permit abortion to save the mother's life. Others permit abortion when the mother faces a wider array of life-threatening situations, such as potential suicides, insanity, etc. Both of these groups would permit abortion only for serious life threatening dangers.

Those authorities who do not consider abortion "akin to murder" are more lenient, but would not permit an abortion lightly either (Solomon Skola, *Bet Shelomo, Hoshen Mishpat* 132). They would permit it for rape (Yehuda Perlman, *Responsa Or Gadol*, #31) or to avoid undue pain (Jacob Emden, *Sheelat Yavetz*, #43), but not in the case of a woman who seeks an abortion after adultery (Yair Hayim Bachrach, *Havot Yair*, #31). This group also permits abortion when there is serious danger to the mother's mental health (Mordechai Winkler, *Levushei Mordekhai, Hoshen Mishpat* #39), or when serious fetal impairment has been discovered in the first three months (Eliezer Waldenberg, *Tzitz Eliezer*, Vol. 9, #327).

We can see from the recent discussion that there is some hesitancy to permit abortion. A number of authorities readily permit it if the mother's life has been endangered, or if there is potentially serious illness, either physical or psychological. Others are permissive in cases of incest or rape. A lesser number permit it when a seriously impaired fetus is known to exist not for the sake of the fetus, but due to the anguish felt by the mother.

The Reform Movement has had a long history of liberalism on many social and family matters. We feel that the pattern of tradition, until the most recent generation, has demonstrated a liberal approach to abortion and has definitely permitted it in case of any danger to the life of the mother. That danger may be physical or psychological. When this occurs at any time during the pregnancy, we would not hesitate to permit an abortion. This would also include cases of incest and rape if the mother wishes to have an abortion.

Twentieth century medicine has brought a greater understanding of the fetus, and it is now possible to discover major problems in the fetus quite early in the pregnancy. Some genetic defects can be discovered shortly after conception and more research will make such techniques widely available. It is, of course, equally true that modern medicine has presented ways of keeping babies with very serious problems alive, frequently in a vegetative state, which brings great misery to the family involved. Such problems, as those caused by Tay-Sachs and other degenerative or permanent conditions which seriously endanger the life of the child and potentially the mental health of the mother, are indications for permitting an abortion.

We agree with the traditional authorities that abortions should be approached cautiously throughout the life of the fetus. Most authorities would be least hesitant during the first forty days of the fetus' life (Yeb. 69b; Nid. 30b; M. Ker. 1.1; *Shulḥan Arukh Hoshen Mishpat*, 210.2; Solomon Skola, *Bet Shelomo, Hoshen Mishpat* 132; Joseph Trani, *Responsa Maharit*, 1.99; Weinberg, *Noam*, 9, pp. 213 ff, etc.) Even the strict Unterman permits non-Jews to perform abortions within the forty day periods (Unterman, *op. cit.*, pp. 8 ff).

From forty days until twenty-seven weeks, the fetus possesses some status, but its future remains doubtful (*goses biydei* adam; San. 78a; Nid. 44b and commentaries) as we are not sure of its viability. We must, therefore, be more certain of our grounds for abortion, but would still permit it.

It is clear from all of this that traditional authorities would be most lenient with abortions within the first forty days. After that time, there is a difference of opinion. Those who are within the broadest range of permissibility permit abortion at any time before birth, if there is a serious danger to the health of the mother or the child. We would be in agreement with that liberal stance. We do not encourage abortion, nor favor it for trivial reasons, or sanction it "on demand."

January 1985

Source: "CCAR Responsa: 16. When Is Abortion Permitted?" (January 1985), CCAR, http://ccarnet.org/responsa/ carr-23-27/.

On Our Humanity

Rabbi Sue Levi Elwell

1

Like life itself, being created in God's image is both a gift and a responsibility. This essential Jewish concept is a *prozdor*, "an entryway," to Jewish life and Jewish practice. God created humans not to duplicate or replace the One who is unique, but to extend God's reach through righteous, just, and compassionate action. When we sing, *Ein k'Eloheinu*—"There is none like our God," we are celebrating God's singularity. Like human twins, or parents and their biological offspring, individuals may share many similarities. But each individual is, finally, unique. So it is with us, created in God's image, yet other, reaching always toward our uniquely human potential to "be like God." As creatures of flesh and blood, we are created from dust (Genesis 2:7), and we will return to dust.

Judaism invites us, every day, to reach beyond our humble beginnings and to enter into conversation with God. Prayer offers us tools for expressing what the writer Anne Lamott calls "Help, Thanks, Wow" (Lamott, *Help, Thanks, Wow*), providing language for petition, gratitude, and praise. Jewish prayer reveals God's attributes and invites us to partner with God in imagining, building, and nurturing a more just and equitable world. When we sing *Nasim shalom*—"Let us make peace," we take our place as God's partners, created in God's image, striving to realize in this world God's goodness, God's generosity, and God's loving-kindness (*tovah, chein, chesed v'rachamim*).

A first step toward realizing these goals is by seeing ourselves in God's image. For some of us, this is the work of a lifetime. Because we are dynamic and ever-evolving individuals, we return, again and again, to this goal: seeing ourselves as God's partners. And just as we work toward seeing ourselves as reflections of holiness, our perspective on the world changes when we begin to consider every individual, every human being, as created in God's image. Our tradition gives us language to express our amazement when we encounter the Divine Presence in every soul: "You are Blessed, Holy One, who has such creatures in the world! You are Blessed, Holy One, who varies Creation!" When we see ourselves, and every other, as a mirror of the Blessed Holy One, we may glimpse what the world looks like through God's eyes. This is our gift, our sacred opportunity.

2

We are living at a time of amazing discoveries about the beauty and the mystery of human creation. Most of us were educated to see human beings as a binary universe, divided up neatly into male and female. The first question asked when a new soul enters the world is often, "Is it a boy or a girl?" Myriad assumptions follow when the infant's sex is announced. But sexual assignment, that is, immediately apparent physiological characteristics, does not always correlate with gender, the social roles and behaviors that are most natural, comfortable, and life-affirming for each individual.

Jewish tradition has long understood that the categories of male and female are insufficient descriptors of all people. The Mishnah introduces the categories of *androgynos*, someone with both male and female sexual characteristics; *tumtum*, an individual with neither fully developed male or female genitals; *aylonit*, an individual who was assigned female gender at birth but later developed male characteristics; and *saris*, an individual who was assigned male gender at birth but lacks male genitals, either since birth or due to a medical intervention.

Our ancestors understood that gender is more complex than male and female and that each of us may carry characteristics that are dominant and recessive. Until the middle of the last century, however serious Jewish study and teaching, as well as community leadership and representation, were the sole province of men and those who were accorded male privilege. Thankfully, that has begun to change in most corners of the Jewish world. It is nevertheless important to listen to the voices of the past to mark our progress—or lack thereof—in ensuring equal access to Jewish life, Jewish text, Jewish community.

In 1912, Bertha Pappenheim, a German Jewish social justice pioneer and historian, wrote,

> The house of study—the home and nursery of specifically Jewish culture—has ever been closed to the woman . . . thus, not only in the past, have we been referred always to the male concept of the Torah, the commentaries, and the tradition. . . . We Jewish women must take, unquestioningly, praise and blame, admiration and condemnation of the sex, as we get it scattered through the vast masses of literature, through the spectacles of male scholars, who read into Jewish literature their own personal opinion and personal experiences. (Pappenheim, "The Jewish Woman in Religious Life," 160)

One hundred years later, we must ensure that our Jewish study includes the voices, the interpretations, and the wisdom of women and men, of transgender individuals, and of those who identify as gay, lesbian, and bisexual. We are all created in God's image. Each of us must be a full partner in the conversation about what it means to be fully human and fully Jewish.

3

We named our first born Hana in gratitude to God's graciousness in bringing this infant into the world and to express our amazement at the grace that emanated from and surrounded this perfect being. In the Torah, and in contemporary Hebrew usage, the phrase *limtzo chein*, "to find grace or favor," is used when referring to individuals finding favor in God's eyes, people being received by one another with grace or favor, and God ensuring that the Israelites will be welcomed and treated fairly by other peoples. Our behavior and our interchanges with others shimmer with energy and purpose when we become conscious of reaching toward or mirroring God's *chein*. And when we regard one another as if looking through God's eyes, everyone we encounter becomes surrounded by the light of *chein*.

Y'shuah is more than physical rescue. Particularly in the language of Psalms, *y'shuah* is divine deliverance. While contemporary Jews may not say, "I've been saved, delivered, rescued," we may feel that an intervention we might attribute to a higher power has helped us from slipping away into despair or depression. We may see the kindness of another as God's hand reaching out to us when we had abandoned hope. *Y'shuah* invites deep conversation about the timing of events, encounters, and opportunities in our lives.

The *Sh'ma* is often the first prayer that Jewish parents teach to their children. After declaring that God is One, we continue with *V'ahavta*, "And you shall love." This prayer, which occurs twice in the daily liturgy, commands us to love God. We may be surprised and challenged by this directive. How can we be commanded to love? By introducing our children to Judaism with these words, repeated as a bedtime ritual, *V'ahavta* becomes an expression of the love and care that young children associate with the safety and security of parental protection and home. Interestingly, our tradition teaches that while we are commanded *to love* God, we are commanded *to respect* our parents. Because our parents are, like us, fragile human beings, they, or we, may not be able to feel or express love. *V'ahavta* welcomes each of us to discover a love that transcends human frailty, passion, and desire, a love that is more powerful than even the love of a mortal parent, a love that is more powerful than death.

4

I was born into a loving family, and I remember my dad saying the *Sh'ma* with me every night when I was a child. My ritual continued, "God bless Mommy, God bless Daddy . . . ," adding everyone in my family and extending the list as long as I could to make sure that Dad would stay in my bedroom as long as possible. I remember the night I realized that my father's father was *dead*. It hit me hard. How could my father be in the world when his father, my grandfather, was *dead*? I still remember my sense of disbelief, incomprehension, and fear.

I am now a grandmother myself. And my dear father, who cared for each of us with such intention and devotion, is no longer living. Yet my father lives in me and in each of us who were privileged to know him. When we remembered him at a simple memorial service and as we gathered each night for a week of *shivah* services, we shared stories and memories and anecdotes of a life well lived. And now, a year later, each of my father's children and especially my mom, my father's devoted partner of sixty-five years, carries him in our hearts every day, as we go about our lives, interacting with others, using words that we learned from him, making decisions that are influenced by his choices, his values, his deep commitments, his Judaism.

My father's soul lives on through the worldviews of each of us who were privileged to learn from him. We, his heirs, bear the most precious legacy: his words, his deeds, his admonitions, his hopes.

I believe that God's mind is an endless vault filled with memory banks that will never be erased. We mortals are challenged: *zachor—remember* those who have come before us. I am trained as a historian; we must sometimes spend months and years archiving the past to discover parts of the truth that happened before our own day. But no truths are ever completely lost; no souls are ever truly gone. God holds all our stories, all our secrets, all our loves, all our joys. Those who love us may access some of the stories, some of the truths. But in the end, each moment has meaning, even when we ourselves cannot parse that meaning. God collects those moments, and savors them, and saves them. The Holy One, whose presence transcends time, will keep our souls for all eternity.

Source: Rabbi Sue Levi Elwell, in *Lights in the Forest: Rabbis Respond to Twelve Essential Jewish Questions*, ed. Rabbi Paul Citrin (New York: CCAR Press, 2014), 116–121.

Talmud Torah: A Lifelong Pursuit

The mitzvah of *talmud Torah*, that is, ongoing Jewish learning, is a lifelong pursuit. The words of the daily morning service in the prayer book teach us:

> These are the things that are limitless, of which a person enjoys the fruit of the world, while the principal remains in the world to come. They are: honoring one's father and mother, engaging in deeds of compassion, arriving early for study, morning and evening, dealing graciously with guests, visiting the sick, providing for the wedding couple, accompanying the dead for burial, being devoted in prayer, and making peace among people. But the study of Torah [*talmud Torah*] encompasses them all.

All these behaviors are important parts of living a Jewish life steeped in the practice of mitzvot.

Adult Education

What kind of Jewish study opportunities are available for adults?

The Mitzvah of Study for Adults

Learning is central to the life of a Jew. Which is why every Jew, no matter his or her age, is expected to engage in *talmud Torah*, Jewish education. One of our tradition's most well-loved principles for living is ""Make yourself a teacher" (Ethics of the Sages, *Pirkei Avot)*. Temples, Jewish Community Centers, and Jewish Studies programs nearby are likely to offer some combination of study opportunities for adults. Whether or not one acquired a Jewish education as a child, we all have access to the knowledge and wisdom the tradition teaches. For those who are not Jewish but are raising Jewish children, engaging in Jewish education and sharing with your children what you learn allows you to lead by example.

Adult Bar/Bat Mitzvah and Confirmation

It is always possible to celebrate the joyous mitzvot of bar/bat mitzvah and confirmation, no matter your age. Adults who have not celebrated their own bar/bat mitzvah or confirmation but who are interested in strengthening their Jewish knowledge and experiencing these traditions should seek out opportunities for further study within their communities.

Family Talmud Torah

The essential mitzvot of *talmud Torah* for children and for adults may be observed most powerfully when they are interlinked, for example, when parents bring their children to religious school and then attend adult classes or lectures, when parents and children attend a Shabbat service, program, or weekend retreat together, or when the family sets aside a regular hour for Jewish study together in the home. In the same way that parents can be models of Jewish living for their children, raising children can bring new meaning and understanding to Jewish rituals and values for parents. A commitment to learning about and experiencing rituals and texts with family fosters a connection to Judaism and ensures that both parents and children will not let their Jewish practices and identities stagnate.

Source: Rabbi Peter S. Knobel, ed., *Navigating the Journey: The Essential Guide to the Jewish Life Cycle* (New York: CCAR Press, 2017).

Lech L'cha, Go Forth

AGING AS AN INVITATION TO GAINING WISDOM

RABBI LAURA GELLER

In *Pirkei Avot* (5:21) we read, "At five years old, you begin Torah. At ten, Mishnah. At J323
thirteen, you are responsible for mitzvot. At fifteen, for Talmud. At eighteen, you get married. At twenty, you are ready to pursue a career. At thirty, for strength. At forty, for understanding. At fifty, for advice. At sixty, for *ziknah*."

Ziknah is hard to translate. Old age? Maturity? Some commentaries read the word as an acronym for *zeh sh'kanah chochmah*, "one who has acquired wisdom."

The stages of a life are measured differently now than in the days of *Pirkei Avot*. In the middle of the twentieth century the stages were childhood, adolescence (invented in the early twentieth century), midlife (when the task was the building of career and family), and then old age. Now there is a new stage between midlife and old age. This stage, where people realize that there is less time ahead than behind, heightens people's longing for meaning and purpose.

One way Judaism teaches about meaning and purpose, and acquiring wisdom, is through ritual. Ritual marks the important moments where a culture both wants to reflect and to teach what is important to its members. What messages do we want our tradition to teach about this new stage? What are the moments that ought to be noticed, marked, and celebrated that could both reflect and teach what is important?

Some moments relate to significant birthdays; others to transitions like retirement, becoming a grandparent, taking off a wedding ring after the death of a spouse. Some relate to moments of joy; others to difficult times that might lie ahead. The messages embedded in marking these moments through ritual remind us that divinity is present at every stage of our life and that growing older presents opportunities as well as challenges. This view disrupts the vision of aging as just one of decline and pushes back against the ageism and negative stereotypes about aging that are so deeply rooted in our culture.

An example: Not long ago, I got a call from a congregant on her way with her sister to clean out her mother's home after having moved her mother to an assisted-living facility. She asked, "Rabbi, what is the prayer you say when you begin to close up the home you grew up in?" I thought, "Yes, there should be a prayer!" I found one online, by Rabbi Jack Reimer, which we adapted slightly:

> Holy One, as we enter the home of our beloved mother at this moment of transition in her life, please guide our actions to be in accordance with Jewish tradition as well as in accordance with her wishes.
>
> Help us to move through her home, which so enriched our lives, in a manner that is a tribute to her teachings and her values. May we perform this poignant duty with reverence and with dignity.
>
> May we do so with generosity to others in the family, acknowledging their desire for some of these mementos, and with generosity to others in the community who might benefit from these possessions.
>
> *Kein y'hi ratzon*—May this be Your will.

They said this prayer before they began the work, and it helped them experience their task as a sacred one. And it made the ritual of putting up a mezuzah in their mother's new home much more meaningful for all of them.

Another more personal example is related to what could be called "the sacred conversation," that difficult conversation about what we want at the end of our life. My husband and I brought our children together and shared with them a document we had prepared called "The Five Wishes." It asks five questions: Who is the person or who are the people I want to make care decisions for me when I can't? What kind of medical treatment do I want or don't want? How comfortable do I want to be? How do I want people to treat me? What do I want my loved ones to know?

Some of what we each wanted is the same; some of it is different. If I were in a situation close to death and life-support treatment would only delay the moment of my death, I don't want that treatment. My husband would want it if his doctor thought it could help.

The kids asked lots of questions: "What if you change your minds? Would the situation be different if this happens before you get really old?" The kids and their partners talked about their grandparents' deaths and their feelings about how they had died. And then they asked for blank copies of "The Five Wishes," because they realized it would be good for them to think about these questions for themselves.

The hardest part for me, surprisingly, was the wish for what we wanted our loved ones to know. My husband was clear that he wanted his family, friends, and others to know that he has forgiven them for when they may have hurt him in life. I am not yet ready to issue a blanket statement on forgiving everyone who has hurt me, which led us gently into a conversation about forgiveness and reminded me that I have a bit more work to do around the issue. We also talked about organ donation, and burial versus cremation, and whether the children thought "visiting" a cemetery where we were buried would be important to them. And we talked about how we would want to be remembered. Finally, we talked about Alzheimer's and dementia. We told our kids that if one of us no longer could recognize the other, our understanding of love meant that we would want the healthy partner to be free to live a full life.

Later in the week, just before we lit the Shabbat candles, we turned "the sacred conversation" into a short ritual. We read out loud our *B'rit Ahuvim*, the promises we made to each other when we married. And then we added a new provision to our covenant:

> Now, ten years after we first entered into our *B'rit Ahuvim*, we reaffirm the commitments we made then, and, in the presence of our children, we add another:
>
> We declare that if one of us should become ill with such serious dementia or Alzheimer's disease that it becomes impossible to recognize our partner, and that this condition is attested to by two doctors and one rabbi, the other one of us should feel free to live as full a life as possible, including having other intimate relationships. That freedom in no way compromises the promise we have made to honor and to care for each other physically and financially as we grow older. We make this declaration because each of us believes that loving each other includes granting this freedom to pursue new intimate relationships even as we honor our commitment to be present to each other as we age.

Then we lit Shabbat candles as we do each week—one for each of our children and their partners, along with the traditional two. And then we blessed our children, not in absentia as we do each week, but in their presence, our hands on their heads, whispering the blessing that each of them is to us both.

Thinking about new ritual for this new stage of life evokes the story of God's call to Avram and Sarai, which is in fact the beginning of the Jewish narrative, in the Torah portion called *Lech L'cha*. They too were older adults, called by God to go forth (*lech l'cha*) from their safe and familiar place to a place where God would send them, with the promise that this new journey would lead to their becoming a blessing. After God calls to Avram and Sarai, three important things happen. The first is that their names are changed by adding the letter *hei*, one of the names of God. Avram becomes Avraham; Sarai becomes Sarah. The second is that they make a covenant, a new promise to God. And the third is that they offer a sacrifice. These actions suggest questions that can help us think about creating new rituals for this new stage.

First, in what way are our names changing as we transition to the new stage? From mother to mother-in-law? From parent to grandparent? From full-time professional to retired? From salaried employee to volunteer? From spouse to widow or widower? From child to orphan? From adult to elder? In a classic text about *t'shuvah*, Maimonides teaches, "Among the paths of repentance [*t'shuvah*], is for the person to change his name, as if to say 'I am becoming a different person now.'"[1] In what ways might we be becoming different people now? Who do we want to become? How could the ritual we create reflect those changes?

Second, is there a new covenant, a new promise, that we want to make at this stage of our lives? For Abraham and Sarah it was a covenant with God that clarified their life purpose. This is a moment to try to be clear about ours. The only way to get clear is to look back, understand what we have achieved and where we've made mistakes, and think about how we want to do things differently. This might suggest a commitment to renew our wedding vows, or to reappropriate the long-standing Jewish tradition of writing an ethical will, a letter to our children and their children, about how we want to be remembered and what we hope our legacy will be.

Finally, at the end of the story, Abraham (and Sarah) offer a kind of sacrifice to seal their covenant. The Hebrew word for sacrifice (*l'hakriv*) comes from a root that means both "coming close" and "letting go." Therefore, preparing for the ritual as we enter this stage suggests that we think about what we are ready to let go of and to what we want to draw close.

What might rituals that evoke this familiar biblical story look like? Is it public, in a synagogue, like an adult bar or bat mitzvah? Is it a celebration with family and friends, like a wedding or a ceremony where we consciously declare that we have become an elder? Or is it a private family gathering, where we explain the

---

1 Maimonides, *Mishneh Torah, Hilchot T'shuvah* 2:4.

process that led us to this moment, introduce the new names we are adding to ours, and read our ethical will out loud? Perhaps it is even more private, with us working through these questions in our own journal or with a spiritual director and marked, for example, by a visit to a local *mikveh*.

However we choose to mark the transition, the important steps are to become clearer about the new "names" we are acquiring, the promises to we want to make, and what we want to let go of and to what we want to draw close. Framing these questions within the Jewish narrative can bring us closer to Judaism and direct us to do the spiritual work we need to do to become the very old people we would like someday to become—openhearted, grateful, and connected to other people both young and old.

Using these questions as the basis for creating new Jewish ritual, as individuals and as communities, can unlock the potential of this new stage to teach us to look forward and give back. Through this work, we hope not only to leave a legacy but also to live our legacy. Maybe that is what it means to acquire wisdom.

Source: Rabbi Laura Geller, "*Lech L'cha*, Go Forth: Aging as an Invitation to Gaining Wisdom," in *Navigating the Journey: The Essential Guide to the Jewish Life Cycle*, ed. Rabbi Peter S. Knobel (New York: CCAR Press, 2017).

End of Life,
Death, and Mourning

Source Texts

Numbers 20:28–29

[28]Moses stripped Aaron of his vestments and put them on his son Eleazar, and Aaron died there on the summit of the mountain. When Moses and Eleazar came down from the mountain, [29]the whole community knew that Aaron had breathed his last. All the house of Israel bewailed Aaron thirty days.

Babylonian Talmud, *K'tubot* 104a

On the day when Rabbi [Yehudah HaNasi] died, the rabbis decreed a public fast and offered prayers for heavenly mercy. They, furthermore, announced that whoever said Rabbi was dead would be stabbed with a sword. Rabbi's handmaid ascended to the roof and prayed, 'The immortals desire Rabbi [to join them] and the mortals desire Rabbi [to remain with us]; may it be the will [of God] that the mortals may overpower the immortals." When, however, she saw how often he resorted to the privy, painfully taking off his ritual garb and putting it back on again, she prayed: "May it be the will [of God] that the immortals may overpower the mortals." As the rabbis continued incessantly continued their prayers for [heavenly] mercy, she picked up a jar and threw it from the roof to the ground. [For a moment] they ceased praying, and the soul of Rabbi departed to its eternal rest.

Moses Maimonides (12th century), from "Moses Maimonides: Two Treatises on the Regimen of Health," American Philosophical Society 54 (1964)

The physician, because he is a physician, must give information on the conduct of a beneficial regimen, be it [Jewishly] unlawful or permissible, and *the sick have the opportunity to act or not to act.* . . . It is manifest that the [Jewish] Law commands whatever is of benefit and prohibits whatever is harmful in the next world, while the physician gives information about what benefits the body and warns against whatever harms it in this world.

Yosef Karo, *Shulchan Aruch, Yoreh Dei-ah* 376

The comforters are not permitted to say anything until the mourner speaks first . . . when the mourner gestures with his head in a manner that suggests that he would like them to leave, they are not permitted to stay any longer.

Yosef Karo, *Shulchan Aruch, Yoreh Dei-ah* 380

These are the things that are forbidden to the mourner: he is forbidden to engage in work, to wash, to anoint, to wear shoes [of leather], or to engage in marital relations. He is also forbidden to read from the Scriptures, to extend greetings, or to launder his clothing . . . he is further forbidden to press his clothing, to cut his hair, to rejoice, or to restitch the tear during the entire thirty day period of mourning.

Arukh HaShulchan 339:1, 19th century Jewish Law Code

It is forbidden to do anything to a *goseis* [actively dying] that would hasten his death . . . and despite the fact that we see that he is suffering greatly during the dying process, and he would be better off dead, it is still forbidden to do anything to hasten his death for *the world and all that is in it are God's*, and that is His will.

Death, and Mourning

Though I walk through the valley
of the shadow of death,
I shall fear no evil,
for You are with me.

—Psalm 23:4

They are like grass that renews itself;
in the morning it flourishes anew;
in the evening it withers and dries up. . . .
Teach us to count our days rightly,
that we may obtain a wise heart.

—Psalm 90:5–6, 90:12

Naked I came from my mother's womb,
and naked shall I return there.
The Eternal gave and the Eternal has taken away;
blessed be the name of the Eternal.

—Job 1:21

"Judaism teaches us to understand death as part of the divine pattern of the universe. . . . Mortality is the tax we pay for the privilege of love, thought and creative work."[1] Thus, Judaism has developed numerous mitzvot and customs relating to death and mourning, to help the mourners cope with their loss and their grief. Jewish tradition encourages a realistic acceptance of the inevitability of death and teaches the sacredness of grief, sympathy, and memory.

1. Joshua Loth Liebman, as quoted in *Gates of Prayer: The New Union Prayerbook* (New York: CCAR Press, 1975), p. 625.

The mitzvot related to death and mourning are governed by four principles. The first concerns the process of grieving. Jewish tradition established the various periods of mourning in order to allow and encourage the expression of grief. But these periods were also meant to provide limits to mourning. The grieving process is complex, and while everyone mourns differently, the traditional mourning periods are meant to prevent the bereaved from indulging in elaborate, painful, and lengthy periods of mourning that would interfere with the ability to live a full life. With the Jewish emphasis on life, the tradition teaches, "We must not mourn for the dead excessively."[2]

The second principle is the recognition of the reality of death.[3] Tradition prescribes certain conduct at the bedside of a dying person, in the preparation of the body for burial, at the funeral, and in the house of mourning. These rituals are designed to help mourners accept their loss and express their grief, so that the pain might be eased gradually and the mourners adjust to life without their loved one.

A third principle is respect for the dead (k'vod hameit). Since biblical times, Judaism has established the principle that every dead person, even the basest criminal, must be accorded the honor of proper burial (Deuteronomy 21:22–23). The body, which is the house of the soul, is to be treated with dignity. Historically, if there was no family, the mitzvah was incumbent upon the Jewish community, every member of which was expected to assist at the burial of the dead[4] and the comforting of mourners.

And the fourth principle is equality in death; "the small and great are there alike, and the servant is free of his master" (Job 3:19). Time and again in the traditional texts of Judaism we see evidence of the sensitivity of the Rabbis toward the poor, but nowhere is this more marked than in the meticulously spelled out

---

2 *Shulchan Aruch, Yoreh Dei-ah* 394. The Talmud imposes clear limits on the various periods of grief and suggests that God says to those who choose to mourn excessively, "You should not be more compassionate to the dead than I am" (BT *Mo-eid Katan* 27b).

3 Jewish tradition prescribes a multitude of acts, from the bedside vigil to shoveling earth into the grave, that are meant to help us accept the reality of death. Modern psychotherapists confirm the wisdom of such funeral and mourning procedures, emphasizing "the deeper psychological and spiritual wisdom inherent in mourning observances, and [in] Jewish teachings about life after death" (S. P. Raphael, "Grief and Bereavement," in Dayle A. Friedman, ed., *Jewish Pastoral Care* [Woodstock, VT: Jewish Lights, 2005], 401).

4 "Where there is no one to attend to the burial of a corpse, it is called a *meit mitzvah* [a dead person whose burial is a commandment], that is to say, a corpse whose burial is obligatory upon every person" (Maimonides, *Sefer HaMitzvot*, Positive #231). Maimonides derives this mitzvah from Deuteronomy 21:23, "You shall surely bury him."

funeral procedures, where we find a deep compassion for the mourners, as well as an understanding of their vulnerability.[5]

It is the spirit of these time-hallowed principles that underlie the mitzvot and customs of death and mourning in Judaism.

Source: Rabbi Peter S. Knobel, ed., *Navigating the Journey: The Essential Guide to the Jewish Life Cycle* (New York: CCAR Press, 2017).

---

5 Commenting on the Mishnaic rule that food should not be brought to a house of mourning on trays or salvers or in fancy baskets, but rather in plain baskets, the Talmud says:

> Formerly they would bring food to the house of mourning, the rich in silver and gold baskets and the poor in baskets of willow twigs, and the poor felt shamed. They therefore instituted that all should bring food in baskets of willow twigs, out of deference to the poor. . . .
>
> Formerly they would bring out the rich for burial on stately beds and the poor on plain biers, and the poor felt shamed. They therefore instituted that all should be brought out on plain biers, out of deference to the poor. . . .
>
> Formerly the expense of burying the dead was a greater blow to the family than the death itself, so that the dead person's kin would abandon him. Finally, Rabban Gamliel came forward and, disregarding his own dignity, gave orders that he [himself] be buried in plain linen garments. Thereafter the people followed his example and all were buried in linen garments." (BT *Mo-eid Katan* 27a–b)

For the Mourner

הַמָּקוֹם יְנַחֵם אֶתְכֶם.

"May you be comforted among all who mourn."

Grief is universal. But death strikes us as individuals, leaving pain and loneliness in its wake. You need not live through it alone. Jewish tradition provides for others to accompany you back from the darkness of deep sadness to the light of fresh promise. As your mourning progresses, may you feel as if an outstretched hand that is greater than yourself is moving you toward hope and possibility.

Jewish mourning customs are rooted in antiquity and enriched by the experience of numerous generations around the globe. Individual mourners of many times and places have adopted and adapted them to their circumstances. As you do the same, consult with your rabbi or cantor, who can suggest what may best comfort you in your time of sorrow.

Shivah

As soon as you leave the cemetery, you begin shivah ("seven"), a period of up to seven days when you will receive visitors.

- Some families place a pitcher of water outside their door, allowing visitors to wash their hands as a symbolic separation between death and life, between cemetery and home.
- As a visible symbol of heartrending bereavement, a torn garment or torn ribbon (*k'riah*) is customarily worn by the deceased's immediate relatives—generally, sons and daughters, spouses/partners, siblings, and parents. Some follow a custom of wearing the cut mourning ribbon on a specific side of their clothing—left side for one's parents and right side for other close relatives. This may already have been done before the funeral.

- A memorial candle is lit to honor the deceased and to indicate God's presence, for we say that God, too, visits those in mourning. As you light the candle, you may want to offer these words (or your own), to sanctify the moment:

Grant me/us strength to endure what cannot be escaped, And courage to continue
   with no bitterness or despair.
Let me/us find You, God,
   In the love of friends and family,
   In the deep recesses of my/our being,
   In hearts that open to me/us, when it seems that love has vanished.
May this candle rekindle in me/us strength and hope.
May this light shine with the certainty of Your Presence, O God,
   Here and now,
   In this home and at this hour,
As I/we remember [name].

בָּרוּךְ אַתָּה, יְיָ, נֹטֵעַ בְּתוֹכֵינוּ חַיֵּי עוֹלָם.

Baruch atah Adonai, notei-a b'tocheinu chayei olam.
Blessed is the Eternal One, who has implanted within us eternal life.

Shivah is the time for you to express your grief in the comforting presence of friends and family who come with nothing in mind but to be present for you. Jewish wisdom encourages you

   not to be overly concerned with your appearance,
   not to engage in mundane tasks,
   not to concern yourself with what you see in the mirror,
   not to go to work,
   not to run errands, and
   not to attend celebrations that conflict with the need to mourn.

Public signs of shivah are temporarily halted for Shabbat, and shivah ends at the start of any Jewish holiday. Mourners attend services in synagogue to say Kaddish on Shabbat.

As visitors come and go, you are not expected to serve as host. Ask a friend or relative to handle all details of arranging for your shivah, including the ordering and serving of food. It is customary to leave the front door ajar so that visitors can enter without you having to greet them. Some mourners choose to sit low to the ground on wooden boxes or stools. You are not expected to rise to receive those who visit you.

Tellingly, the first meal back home from the cemetery is called *s'udat havraah*, meaning "a meal of healing." Some choose to serve round foods such as hard-boiled eggs or lentils, which symbolize the circle of life.

Saying *Kaddish*

The miracle of memory is a sacred gift. Each day of shivah, your memory deepens with the recitation of the Kaddish ("sanctification"), words of praise and blessing that conclude each worship service. Except for Shabbat, friends and family may join you in your home for a service where you recite this prayer in tribute to the person(s) whose loss you are mourning. This prayerbook includes the afternoon and evening prayer services.

- It is preferable to recite the *Kaddish* in the presence of a minyan, a quorum of ten or more people beyond the age of bar/bat mitzvah.
- In the absence of a minyan, you may say the *Kaddish* anyway—even alone, if it gives you comfort.
- It is a mitzvah (sacred obligation) to recount stories of the deceased as a personal introduction to the *Kaddish*.
- Children are encouraged to participate according to their parents' discretion.

Concluding Shivah

The rule in sitting shivah is that any part of a day counts as a whole one. You therefore count the day of the funeral as day one, and you may conclude the final day of shivah any time past the first hour that you are awake.

It is customary to go for a short walk outdoors to symbolize your reengagement with the world.

You may wish to end shivah with a personal prayer of your own or with the one that follows:

God of comfort and of hope:
As I/we have walked through the valley of the shadow of death,
Lead me/us back toward the light of life.
Lift me/us once again to the heights of possibility, And grant me/us certain knowledge
Of the blessed bond of memory that links us all to eternity.
Blessed is the Eternal One, who lifts up the fallen.
Baruch atah Adonai, someich noflim.

Extended Mourning Periods: Thirty Days (*Sh'loshim*) and a Year

The grief of a loss does not magically vanish when shivah ends. In addition, while the mitzvah "to remember" applies to all our immediate relatives, an additional obligation "to honor" applies to parents. Over time, therefore, it has become customary, in the case of a parent who dies, to continue saying *Kaddish* for eleven months, not just the period of shivah. Reform practice has extended the obligation to a full year.

Jewish tradition also recognizes a thirty-day mourning period called *sh'loshim*—more than shivah but less than an entire year. The end of thirty days marks the time to concentrate on transitioning back into life.

The path of mourning may take many turns. But you need not walk alone. We pray that the prayers, blessings, and poems contained within this prayer book will help you find solace in your grief.

For the Visitor to a House of Mourning

"Comforting the mourner is an act of loving-kindness."

In all of Judaism, there is no greater mitzvah (sacred obligation) than comforting the bereaved. Your presence offers profound solace and support to those facing the sadness and devastation of the death of a loved one. Both law and custom provide guidance for comforting mourners. Here is a guide of what you may experience in a house of mourning. No particular family will necessarily follow all of these practices, but you are likely to see some of them. As one who has come to comfort, you are invited to take part in these customs and are welcome to ask questions about them.

The most intense stage of mourning is called shivah ("seven"), a period that begins at burial and continues up to seven days. Families generally "sit shivah" from three to seven days. During shivah, mourners receive visitors who offer condolences, comfort, and support. During this time, your presence ensures that mourners do not suffer grief alone.

What You May See

If visiting the house immediately after the funeral, you may see a pitcher of water and a basin set outside the door. This is for those who choose to wash their hands before entering, as a symbolic separation between death and life, between cemetery and home. The door may be unlocked, a welcoming gesture that invites guests to enter without bothering the mourners with the need to greet you. Inside, a lit candle serves as a memorial to the deceased and a reminder of God's presence.

Mourners observe certain customs to signify their status and to express their grief. They may sit on stools or boxes low to the ground and may wear a torn piece of clothing or a torn ribbon to represent their "torn heart." Since they focus on their loss, they are discouraged from being overly concerned with physical appearance; they may even cover the mirrors in their home. Visitors customarily bring food to feed the mourners and their many guests. Mourners themselves are not expected to act as hosts or even to have to worry about their own sustenance.

What You May Experience

During your visit, a short worship service may take place. This provides a moment of quiet sanctity when mourners may experience God's comforting presence. The service culminates in a mourner's prayer called the *Kaddish* ("sanctification"). To the extent that you feel comfortable, you are welcome to participate as a worshiper.

Nothing can adequately express the importance of your visit to a house of mourning. You may wonder what to say to express condolences. Do not be too concerned with finding the right words. (Remember, however, that attempts to justify the death or lessen the blow can be unintentionally hurtful.) Instead, you can follow the mourner's lead in conversation, encourage a discussion of the deceased person's life, or just listen—listening alone brings great comfort.

You are encouraged to make a donation in memory of the deceased. You may ask whether the mourner has designated a particular charity as the preferred beneficiary of your gift.

Please know how much your presence makes a difference. As a traditional Jewish teaching reminds us, "Comforting the mourner is an act of loving-kindness toward both the living and the dead."

Related Resources published by the CCAR:

On the Doorposts of Your House: Prayers and Ceremonies for the Jewish Home, Revised Edition, edited by Chaim Stern (2010).
The Gates of Healing: A Message of Comfort and Hope, edited by Hirshel L. Jaffe and H. Leonard Poller (1988).

Gates of Mitzvah: A Guide to the Jewish Life Cycle, edited by Simeon J. Maslin (1979).

Rabbi Hara E. Person and Rabbi Elaine Zecher, eds., *Mishkan T'filah for the House of Mourning* (New York: CCAR Press, 2010), viii–xii.

Yizkor

One of the most moving portions of the Yom Kippur and Festival worship services is the Memorial Service (*Hazkarat N'shamot*). Popularly known as *Yizkor*, after the opening words of the silent devotion *Yizkor Elohim* ("May God remember [the soul of] . . ."), this service is generally recited in Reform synagogues on Yom Kippur and on the last day of Pesach, on Shavuot, and on Sh'mini Atzeret–Simchat Torah. *Yizkor* emphasizes the transience of life, our yearning for eternity, and the inspiration provided by the memory of the deceased. The service reminds us that time moves swiftly forward and bids us "to number our days that we may grow wise in heart" (Psalm 90:12).

Memory is a precious gift, for it transforms the discrete moments of our lives and events in history into an unfolding narrative. We become acutely aware of being a part of an eternal people that began a spiritual journey in the distant past with its goal to be realized in the remote future. Through the words and music of the service, we become conscious not only of our own mortality, but also of the sacred opportunity that we have in our brief lives to perform acts of sanctification that may improve our lot and the lot of humanity generally.

The life of the Jewish people is composed of sacred moments that, when recalled, inspire us to live our lives according to certain Jewish values. For example, the bitter experience of slavery is tasted in the eating of *maror* on Pesach. By re-creating the sense of physical and spiritual bondage, we commit ourselves to an ethical system that teaches us that freedom is essential for human development. How we act toward others must be judged in the light of the verse "We were slaves to Pharaoh in Egypt" (Deuteronomy 6:21).

On Shavuot, when we hear the Ten Commandments read, we are transported backward to Mount Sinai and utter in our hearts the ancient formula of commitment *Naaseh v'nishma*, "We will faithfully do" (Exodus 24:7). The ancient covenant is renewed through memory. By observing the mitzvot of Shavuot, our individual memory becomes part of the collective memory of the Jewish people.

For Jews, the inspiring figures in both the remote and recent past remain as constant companions and role models. They teach by precept and example. Their story is our story. Their courage, wisdom, and goodness are a permanent challenge.

Memory roots us firmly in the past. The fertile soil of more than four thousand years of history nurtures us, providing us with a clear sense of who we are. Our lives add new branches to the tree of the Jewish people. A living past provides for a meaningful present and hope for the future.

As we recite the *Yizkor* prayer, we mention in our hearts the names of all who were close to us—grandparents, parents, friends, and relatives. By preserving the memory of those who were our teachers, we are encouraged to continue the tasks they bequeathed to us. The memorial service is an act of faith that proclaims that goodness does not die with a person but exists in the memory of those who remain alive.

Our thoughts also turn to those of our people who sought, through their lives and through their deaths, to testify to the undying spirit of the Jewish people and its mission as a holy nation. In the past, custom dictated that only those whose parents were deceased attended the Memorial Service. But recognizing that so many who died in the Shoah have no one to recite *Kaddish* for them, and realizing that memory helps to forge a chain of solidarity and continuity between our generation and the past, all are encouraged to participate.

The words of the memorial prayer *El Malei Rachamim* ("Fully compassionate God") is a petition for the repose of the deceased and an expression of our faith in the ultimate sacredness of humankind.

Death removes our loved ones from their earthly abode, yet Jewish tradition affirms the faith that the divine spark in every human soul has a permanent dwelling place with the Eternal. The mystery of what lies beyond the grave is shrouded by an impenetrable veil, yet within our hearts is planted the hope for eternity. Memory is the sacred link between past and future and between time and eternity.

Immortality is a word that we can associate only with God, but the blessing of memory and the blessedness of the memory of the righteous can be guaranteed by our devoted recall. The mitzvah of *Yizkor* is a door that opens on eternity, making the present more significant by allowing us to combine memory and hope.

Source: Rabbi Peter S. Knobel, ed., *Mishkan Moeid: A Guide to the Jewish Seasons* (New York: CCAR Press, 2013), 120–122.

Organ Donation

It is praiseworthy for an individual to donate tissue and organs for the purpose of medical transplantation upon his or her death. This does not violate the traditional prohibition against deriving benefit from a corpse (*hanaah min hamet*), nor is it an example of disgraceful treatment of the body (*nivul hamet*). It is, rather, an act of respect for the dead, allowing them to become a source of healing to others even when their own lives have come to an end (*ARR*, nos. 85–86, pp. 104–21; *RR21*, vol. 2, no. 5763.2, sec. 1, pp. 144–46).

Source: Rabbi Don Goor, ed., *L'chol Z'man V'Eit: For Sacred Moments;* The CCAR Life-Cycle Guide (New York: CCAR Press, 2015), 27–28.

On Our Humanity

Rabbi Stephen Lewis Fuchs

In recent decades we Jews—Reform Jews in particular—have submerged mention of the afterlife to the degree that many Jews frame the question to me as an assumption: "We don't believe in life after death, do we, Rabbi?"

I would respond, "Yes, we do!"

For Jews, attaining the reward in *olam haba*, "the world-to-come," does not depend on what we believe. It depends on how we live our lives.

My belief in life after death has two parts: what I hope and what I know.

I hope, and in my heart I believe, that good people receive in some way rewards from God in a realm beyond the grave. I hope that they are reunited with loved ones and live on with them in a realm free of the pain and debilitation that might have marked the latter stages of their earthly life.

My father died at age fifty-seven, and my mother, who never remarried, died at age eighty-eight. She was a widow for more years than she was married. My fondest hope since her death is that they are together again.

I cannot, of course, prove that any of this is true. Yet I cling tenaciously to my hope.

But there is also an aspect of afterlife of which I am absolutely sure. Our loved ones live on in our memories, and those memories can surely inspire us to lead better lives.

At the beginning of Noah Gordon's marvelous novel *The Rabbi*, the protagonist, Rabbi Michael Kind, thinks of his beloved grandfather, who died when he was a teenager, and recalls a Jewish legend that teaches, "When the living think of the dead, in paradise the dead know that they are loved and they rejoice" (Gordon, *The Rabbi*, 1).

Each time we do something worthy because of their teaching or example, our deceased loved ones come alive. If we listen, we can hear them call to us as God called to Abraham in establishing the sacred covenant of our faith: Be a blessing (Genesis 12:2)!

Source: Rabbi Stephen Lewis Fuchs, in *Lights in the Forest: Rabbis Respond to Twelve Essential Jewish Questions*, ed. Rabbi Paul Citrin, (New York: CCAR Press, 2014), 101–102.

Unit IV

CREATING A JEWISH THEOLOGY

Different Understandings
of God

Source Texts

Genesis 9:17

[8]And God said to Noah and to his sons with him, [9] "I now establish My covenant with you and your offspring to come, [10]and with every living thing that is with you -birds, cattle, and every wild beast as well -all that have come out of the ark, every living thing on earth. [11]I will maintain My covenant with you: never again shall all flesh be cut off by the waters of a flood, and never again shall there be a flood to destroy the earth." [12]God further said, "This is the sign that I set for the covenant between Me and you, and every living creature with you, for all ages to come. [13]I have set My bow in the clouds, and it shall serve as a sign of the covenant between Me and the earth. [14]When I bring clouds over the earth, and the bow appears in the clouds, [15]I will remember My covenant between Me and you and every living creature among all flesh, so that the waters shall never again become a flood to destroy all flesh. [16]When the bow is in the clouds, I will see it and remember the everlasting covenant between God and all living creatures, all flesh that is on earth. [17]And God said to Noah, "This is the sign of the covenant that I have established between Me and all who live upon the earth.

Exodus 19:5-6

[5]" 'Now then, if you will obey Me faithfully and keep My covenant, you shall be My treasured possession among the peoples. Indeed, all the earth is Mine, [6]but you shall be to Me a kingdom of priests and a holy nation.' These are the words that you shall speak to the Children of Israel."

Leviticus 19:1-2 (Holiness Code)

[1]The Eternal One spoke to Moses, saying: [2]Speak to the whole Israelite community, and say the them: You shall be holy, for I, the Eternal your God, am holy.

Deuteronomy 7:6

⁶For you are a people consecrated to the Eternal your God: of all the peoples on earth the Eternal God chose you to be God's treasured people.

Maimonides's Thirteen Principles of Faith

1. God exists; God is perfect in every way, eternal and the cause of all that exists. All other beings depend upon God for their existence.
2. God has absolute and unparalleled unity.
3. God is incorporeal—without a body.
4. God existed prior to all else.
5. God should be the only object of worship and praise. One should not appeal to intermediaries, but should pray directly to God.
6. Prophets and prophecy exist.
7. Moses was the greatest prophet who ever lived. No prophet who lived or will live could comprehend God more than Moses.
8. The Torah is from heaven. The Torah we have today is the Torah that God gave to Moses at Sinai.
9. The Torah will never be abrogated, nothing will be added to it or subtracted from it; God will never give another Law.
10. God knows the actions of humans and is not neglectful of them.
11. God rewards those who obey the commands of the Torah and punishes those who violate its prohibitions.
12. The days of the Messiah will come.
13. The dead will be resurrected.

On God

RABBI KENNETH CHASEN

As a teenager, I couldn't make much sense of the God-images that had been most frequently presented to me as a child. The God I learned about in religious school was anthropomorphic and omnipotent, and I just didn't see God operating as an almighty human being in the world. A further complication was that I, like so many, had been hung up on the literal meanings of the Jewish prayers. As I grew into young adulthood and began applying my critical thinking skills to the siddur, I grew uncomfortable with the notion of a God who intercedes to grant healing, bestow abundance, and free captives. There were just too many worthy people praying for those blessings and others but not receiving them. I concluded that I couldn't believe in a God who would listen to the penitent yearnings of some while rejecting the desperation of others. If I was going to be a believer, I needed a concept in which I could believe.

I found that concept during my college years, when I began to study the writings of Rabbi Abraham Joshua Heschel. I can still recall the specific teaching that reintroduced God to me in a way that I could understand:

> When in doubt, we raise questions. When in wonder, we do not even know how to ask a question. . . . Under the running sea of our theories and scientific explanations lies the aboriginal abyss of radical amazement. Radical amazement has a wider scope than any other act of man. While any act of perception or cognition has as its object a selected segment of reality, radical amazement refers to all of reality; not only to what we see, but also to the very act of seeing as well as to our own selves, to the selves that see and are amazed at their ability to see. (Heschel, *Man Is Not Alone*, 13)

When I first discovered these words, I remember feeling as though they practically proved God's existence. Suddenly, I sensed a horizon of knowledge that was wondrously beyond my view and my control as a human being. God wasn't some non-corporeal Santa Claus, deliberating over human requests. God was where the unknowable was known, and in relation with that God, my job was—and still is—to demonstrate both humility and gratitude in the face of a bounty of blessings I can hope neither to produce nor explain.

Source: Rabbi Kenneth Chasen, in *Lights in the Forest: Rabbis Respond to Twelve Essential Jewish Questions*, ed. Rabbi Paul Citrin (New York: CCAR Press, 2014), 3–4.

Women and Contemporary Revelation

ELLEN M. UMANSKY

In Hebrew, there is no single word for revelation. Rather, revelation is described as both *matan Torah* (the giving of Torah) and *kabbalat Torah* (the receiving of Torah). Revelation occurs when these two intersect and the voice of God is heard, directly or indirectly. Drawing on Deuteronomy 30:12 (in which Moses states that the Torah is "not in the heavens that you should say: 'Who among us can go up can go up to the heavens and get it for us and impart it for us . . . ' "), later rabbinic sages asserted that the will of God, as represented in the Torah, was no longer in Heaven but is entrusted to human interpreters (BT *Bava M'tzia* 59b). In the rabbinic context this meant that the community could discern God's voice by wrestling with the text, that is, by intensely engaging with Torah. Thus, Torah study replaced prophecy as the source of revelation.

Even when women were exempt (or excluded) from Torah study, the Rabbis did not exclude women as bearers of revelation. They acknowledged that in ancient Israel, God spoke to female prophets as well as male prophets, who consequently served as divine messengers. Indeed, whereas the Bible identifies by name only four female prophets (see at Deuteronomy 13:2), the Rabbis expand this list considerably. According to one source, seven women were prophets. Acknowledging Miriam (Exodus 15:20), Deborah (Judges 4:4), and Huldah (II Kings 22:14), but ignoring Noadiah (Nehemiah 6:14), rabbinic sages add Sarah (Genesis 11–25), Hannah (I Samuel 1–2), Abigail (I Samuel 25), and Esther (BT *M'gillah* 14a). The Midrash also emphasizes the prophetic qualities of all four matriarchs (Sarah, Rebecca, Rachel, and Leah; *Breishit Rabbah* 67.9; 72.6) and maintains that "just as sixty myriads of male prophets arose for Israel, so there arose for them sixty myriads of female prophets" *(Shir HaShirim Rabbah* 4.11).

Who hears the divine voice? The rabbinic sages did not understand one's relationship to God as connected primarily to gender, but rather, as Barry Holtz notes, to "talent, inclination and strength" *(Finding Our Way*, 1990, p. 102). For example, one midrash enjoins its readers, "Come and see how the voice [of God] went forth [at Sinai]— coming to each Israelite according to his individual strength—to the old, according to their strength; to the young according to their strength; to the children according to their strength; to the infants according to their strength; *and to the women according to their strength*" *(Shmot Rabbah* 5.9, emphasis added).

New and challenging scholarly theories in the 19th century about the historical formation of the Bible led Reform Jews, and later Conservative and Reconstructionist Jews, to rethink the concept of divine revelation and to reevaluate women's religious roles. This created new opportunities for women to see themselves as bearers of revelation. Reform Judaism's notion of progressive revelation particularly encouraged women and men to recognize the many ways in which one could hear God's voice. In a sermon delivered in 1918, Lily Montagu, founder of the Liberal Jewish movement in England and of the World Union for Progressive Judaism, maintained that "we [Liberal Jews] are no longer worried by the claims of tradition when these clash with our conception of truth. We have boldly enunciated our belief in progressive revelation, and this faith has quickened our hope for the future and intensified our reverence for the past" ("Kinship With God," in Ellen M. Umansky, ed., *Lily H. Montagu*, 1985, p. 113).

In line with this new understanding, Reform Judaism made religious education equally available to girls and boys, and the ceremony of confirmation, which initially replaced bar mitzvah, marked the end of one's formal Jewish studies. Unlike the celebration of one's becoming a bar or bat mitzvah, which is usually held on or soon after one's 13th birthday, confirmation is held on Shavuot, the holiday traditionally marking the revelation at Sinai. Confirmation was at first an individual or small group ceremony, with girls confirmed at a temple in Berlin as early as 1817. In the U.S., confirmation became a group or class celebration, taking place at the end of 10th grade. Becoming a confirmand on Shavuot serves as a reminder of the centrality of the Torah (whether equated with God's moral teachings or including ritual observance as well); it also reenacts symbolically for each person the receiving of the Torah and living in covenantal relationship with God. By the 20th century, the notion of continuing revelation—the idea that God continues to speak to each and every generation—was largely accepted. Indeed, for many if not most Jews today, the concept of Torah has expanded to mean Jewish learning or learning in general.

In his 1955 book *God in Search of Man*, Rabbi Abraham Joshua Heschel asked, "How did Israel know that what their eye and ear perceived in the desert of Sinai was not a phantom? Was it truly a moment of revelation, or was such a perception only an illusion? "*What* we see, he concluded, "may be an illusion; *that* we see can never be questioned (p. 196). Speaking before members of the Central Conference of American Rabbis in 1986, Reform rabbi Laura Geller similarly emphasized the importance of lived experience. Describing revelation as a moment of connection with God, she, like Heschel, emphasized the transformative nature of this moment. Yet moving beyond what he identified as Torah, she came to realize that although she had not noticed, God is always present. She asserted:

> I wasn't looking, or perhaps I was looking in the wrong places. . . . I needed to listen to the gentle whisper, the still small voice, the Presence one encounters by diving deep and surfacing. . . . I suddenly realized that my experience is Jewish experience. There is a Torah of our lives as well as the Torah that was written down. Both need to be listened to and wrestled with: both unfold through interactive commentary (*Four Centuries of Jewish Womens Spirituality: A Sourcebook*, 1992, pp. 244–45).

Like Geller, Judith Plaskow advocates expanding our understanding of Torah to include not just the first five books of the Hebrew Bible and traditional Jewish learning, "but women's words, teachings, and actions hitherto unseen. Plaskow asserts that Jewish feminists must "reclaim Torah as our own in order to make visible the "presence, experience, and deeds of women erased in traditional sources, telling the "stories of women's encounters with God and captur[ing] the texture of their religious experience." She also insists upon reconstructing history to include women's history, not by changing the past, but by altering the shape of Jewish memory (*Standing Again at Sinai: Judaism from a Feminist Perspective*, 1990, p. 28).

Rachel Adler has identified such efforts as "engendering Judaism." She also calls for models of thinking about and practicing Judaism in a way that enables both women and men to "recreate and renew together as equals" (*Engendering Judaism: An Inclusive Theology and Ethics*, 1998, p. xiv). In so doing, Adler draws heavily on narrative as a tool of critique and vision, while advocating among liberal or progressive Jews the re-appropriation of halachah (the traditional authoritative legal tradition) as a source of meaning, rather than one of power. This means, among other things, retaining those laws that remain grounded in the practice of the progressive Jewish community while adding new laws, grounded in new stories, that reflect new communal practices.

In "We All Stood Together," poet Merle Feld reenvisions both women and men at Mt. Sinai, ready to receive the words of God. In her creative remembering, her brother kept a journal of what he saw and heard while she, always holding a baby, was never able to write anything down. Consequently, she came to forget the particulars of this revelatory moment, until she was left with nothing but the feeling that something important had occurred. At the poem's conclusion, she writes that if Jews could somehow remember that moment at Sinai as it was experienced by men *and women*, that sacred moment could be recreated (see *Yitro,* Voices, p. 425).

In this *Commentary*, the section called Contemporary Reflection contains responses by women who, in a variety of ways, explore the continuing meanings of the revelation of Torah. Written by Jewish professionals from a variety of fields, these pieces represent new, individual wrestlings with the biblical text. Explicitly or implicitly revealing an awareness of both biblical and post-biblical interpretations, the brief essays reflect a contemporary, often feminist, perspective. They not only focus on women's roles and concerns, but also attempt to draw on women's lived experiences (what Geller describes as "the Torah of our lives") in order to create to recreate Jewish memory (as articulated by Plaskow and Feld) and, in the process, engender Judaism (as suggested by Adler).

Many of the topics explored in these reflections are identical to those found in other sections of this *Commentary*, including notions of covenant, peoplehood, religious leadership, free will, social justice, purity, pollution, sacrifice, forgiveness, and mercy. Yet instead of reading the text within a postbiblical or early rabbinic context, these reflections offer readings that are clearly in the present and have implications for the future. Some underscore the contemporary relevance of the Torah's teachings, like Noa Kushner's reflection on *parashat P'kudei* and God's earthly presence, and Alice Shalvi's on *parashat KiTavo* and the Israelites' setding in the land of Israel. Others, like Suzanne Singer's reflection on the hardening of Pharaoh's heart in *parashat Bo*, suggest reading against the text— creating counter-narratives that provoke new theological questions and problems. Many of the pieces move beyond the text altogether, using words, phrases, or concepts within a particular *parashah* as a means of exploring issues and ideas that are of particular interest to contemporary readers, including women. Judith Plaskow, for example, draws on the priestly evaluation of sexual behavior in *parashat Acharei Mot* to discuss the persistence of homophobia, as well as sexual and family violence in today's society; in my reflection on *parashat Hazinu*, I reject the text's imagery of God as Rock and Warrior, and instead offer new images that, in my view, better convey the love and justice of God. Writing more personally, Zoe Klein, in her reflection on *parashat Ki Tisa*, draws upon similarities to her husband's proposing marriage to her at Mount Sinai and God's continual revelation to Israel there, using one to view the other as moments of "eternal, loving joining," while Blu Greenberg explores the impact of sudden loss, as she grapples with *parashat Sh'mini*.

The importance of the Contemporary Reflection sections of this *Commentary* is that they enable us to hear women's voices that reckon with divine revelation. The reflections in this *Commentary* represent different attitudes toward the Torah and the many ways in which its teachings can be appropriated into our lives. While some authors defend its teachings, others challenge them. Yet each essay shows the significance of Torah as a record of God's revelation to Israel: it is a repository of Jewish memory, however incomplete, from which we, as individuals and as members of contemporary Jewish communities, can attempt to hear and understand the voice of God.

Source: Ellen M. Umansky, "Women and Contemporary Revelation," in *The Torah: A Women's Commentary*, ed. Tamara Cohn Eskenazi and Andrea L. Weiss (New York: URJ Press, 2008; Reform Judaism Publishing/CCAR Press, 2015), lvi–lix.

On God

RABBI PAUL KIPNES

God is not a being; God is a verb. Jewish tradition understands God's four-letter name as a meaningful combination of three verbs: *hei-vav-hei*, or *hoveh*, signifying the present tense and meaning "is"; *hei-yod-hei*, or *hayah*, meaning "was"; and *yodhei-yod-hei*, or *yih'yeh*, meaning "will be." God is that which was, is, and will be forevermore. As we sing in the prayer *Adon Olam*, God is the sum total of existence. The issue is not whether we believe in God. It does not matter. Because God just Is–Was–Will Be. The question, instead, should be whether we are willing to open our eyes, our minds, and our hearts to the continuously sacred flow of Existence.

God is found everywhere in every moment. That's why the ancient Rabbis knew God as *HaMakom*, "The Place," meaning God is in every place, everywhere. God is here, over there, up there (pointing skyward), down there (pointing earthward), in there (pointing inside you and me). Wherever we can stop focusing on ourselves and our own material needs and open our eyes to the reality and beauty surrounding us, we might find God. The kabbalists knew God as *Ein Sof*, "No End," because God is everywhere, the Essence that is without end. Moses found God on a mountaintop, and so can we. Miriam encountered God at the shores of the sea, and so can we. The Levites—originally ritual singer/musicians—heard God in the sweet multi-instrument musicals they played and sang, and so can we. And the prophet Elijah experienced God in the still small voice within that spoke to him, and so can we.

My relationship with God is always in flux. Sometimes I feel closer to the Holy One; sometimes farther away. There have been times when I have felt estranged from God. During my "rationalist" phase, God was an idea, an ideal. During my "non-rationalist" period, the Source of Life was in each relationship, à la philosopher Martin Buber's "I-Thou." Sometimes the Maker of Peace is in my meditative breath. Other times the Almighty is the recipient of my anger. Yes, I have yelled at God, but that's okay; God can take it. How I view God changes year by year, and sometimes day by day. Nonetheless, God's reality has been and remains a constant in my life.

Source: Rabbi Paul Kipnes, in *Lights in the Forest: Rabbis Respond to Twelve Essential Jewish Questions*, ed. Rabbi Paul Citrin (New York: CCAR Press, 2014), 13–14.

On the Jewish People

RABBI JOSHUA STANTON

Both covenant and commandment rely on history. They are responses on the part of Jews as a group to the significance of their shared history. Derived from the sacred narrative of Torah, they are applied retrospectively to events either that happened in actuality or that Jews adopted as sacred memories, which can feel every bit as real as historical events themselves.

Following the lead of Mordecai Kaplan, I believe that "a people is prior to its religion" (Eugene Borowitz, *Choices in Modern Jewish Thought*, 103). The Jewish people existed before the Torah was given, as is affirmed within the narrative arc of the Torah itself: Abraham was Jewish before Moses went up Mount Sinai. The experiences of the Jewish people existed before they were recast and described within the Torah.

The two concepts of covenant and commandment are significant insofar as they demonstrate the sacred inspiration that exists within people to derive principles from historical narratives. Covenant and commandment shape principles that define the Jews in the present and the future.

What makes the ideas of covenant and commandment significant is the extent to which they manifest the sacred impulse on the part of Jewish human beings to care for the group of which they are a part and take personal responsibility for actions that can contribute to a just society. In relating individual and group, justice and personal accountability, both concepts transcend time and enable Jews to connect to their sacred purpose as people and a people that pursues righteousness.

Source: Rabbi Joshua Stanton, in *Lights in the Forest: Rabbis Respond to Twelve Essential Jewish Questions*, ed. Rabbi Paul Citrin (New York: CCAR Press, 2014), 207–208.

On the Jewish People

RABBI BRUCE KADDEN

As a Reform Jew, I affirm that the *b'rit*), "covenant," that God first made with Abraham (Genesis 12) and extended to the entire people Israel at Mount Sinai (Exodus 19–20) continues to define my relationship to the Jewish people and the relationship of the Jewish people to God. When I affirm that I am part of this covenant, I commit myself to supporting *K'lal Yisrael*, "the greater community of Israel," which also embraces this covenant. I also commit myself to maintaining a relationship with the Divine through study and wrestling with Torah.

The Torah is sacred because it was created through our earliest ancestors' encounters with the Divine and with each other. Their experiences were passed on orally until written down and reshaped over a number of generations, before taking form as the text we read today. Through studying the written Torah in subsequent generations, our people has produced an Oral Torah, which attempts to understand and apply the teachings of the text in an ever-changing Jewish world. This Oral Torah includes Mishnah and Talmud, midrash, responsa, commentaries, and codes of law, but also philosophical works, poetry, novels, and our own discussions that draw their inspiration from the text.

The Torah is the primary source for mitzvot (sacred obligations). By wrestling with Torah and its interpretations throughout the ages, we come to understand that some mitzvot are incumbent upon all human beings (the Noahide Laws), and some mitzvot are incumbent on every Jew (such as studying Torah, visiting the sick, and observing Shabbat). In addition, each person will determine how to fulfill the mitzvot he or she finds compelling and meaningful as an individual, a member of a family, and/or a member of a Jewish community.

Many of these mitzvot have been observed by our people throughout the ages. Other mitzvot may be contemporary interpretations of classical mitzvot. Still other mitzvot may be radically new observances or obligations that we derive through studying Torah and creating communities with our fellow Jews. As we continue to wrestle with Torah, our understanding of the *b'rit* and mitzvot evolves. Through this process, we together create the Judaism of today and tomorrow.

Source: Rabbi Bruce Kadden, in *Lights in the Forest: Rabbis Respond to Twelve Essential Jewish Questions*, ed. Rabbi Paul Citrin (New York: CCAR Press, 2014), 185–186.

On Holiness

Chapters 18–20 of Leviticus [known as the Holiness Code] give a clear account of holiness in life. The prime emphasis is ethical. And the moral laws of these chapters are not mere injunctions of conformity. They call for just, humane, and sensitive treatment of others. The aged, the handicapped, and the poor are to receive consideration and courtesy. The laborer is to be promptly paid. The stranger is to be accorded the same love we give our fellow citizens. The law is concerned not only with overt behavior, but also with motive; vengefulness and the bearing of grudges are condemned. . . .

In holy living, the ethical factor is primary, but it is not the only one. In combining moral and ceremonial commandments, the authors of the Holiness Code displayed sound understanding.

Such are the components of the way of life called *kadosh* (holy). Leviticus 19 begins with the startling declaration that by these means we can and should try to be holy like God. The same Torah that stresses the distance between God's sublime perfection and our earthly limitations urges us to strive to reduce that distance. The task is endless, but it is infinitely rewarding. Rabbi Tarfon said: "Do not avoid an undertaking that has no limit or a task that cannot be completed. It is like the case of a fellow who was hired to take water from the sea and pour it out on the land. But, as the sea was not emptied out nor the land filled with water, he became downhearted. Then someone said to him, 'Fool! Why should you be downhearted as long as you receive a dinar of gold every day as your wage?'" (*Avot d'Rabbi Natan* 27) The pursuit of the unattainable can be a means of fulfillment.

The Law of Holiness is not addressed to selected individuals. It is addressed to the entire community of Israel. Its objective is not to produce a few saints withdrawn from the world in contemplative or ascetic practices. Rather, the Torah aims to create a holy people which displays its consecration to God's service in the normal day-to-day relations of farming, commerce, family living, and communal affairs.

—Rabbi Bernard Bamberger (1904–1980)

For Reflection

As I consider the most fulfilling activities of my life, in what ways do they provide me with opportunities to strive for holiness?

Have I created a spiritual practice that includes ethical and ritual elements?

What might be preventing me from developing a richer practice that encourages "holy living"?

N'kadeish et shimcha baolam,	נְקַדֵּשׁ אֶת שִׁמְךָ בָּעוֹלָם,
k'shem shemakdishim oto	כְּשֵׁם שֶׁמַּקְדִּישִׁים אוֹתוֹ
bishmei marom;	בִּשְׁמֵי מָרוֹם,
kakatuv al yad n'vi·echa:	כַּכָּתוּב עַל יַד נְבִיאֶךָ׃
V'kara zeh el-zeh v'amar:	וְקָרָא זֶה אֶל זֶה וְאָמַר׃

"Kadosh, kadosh, kadosh Adonai tz'vaot,	קָדוֹשׁ, קָדוֹשׁ, קָדוֹשׁ יְיָ צְבָאוֹת,
m'lo chol-haaretz k'vodo."	מְלֹא כָל הָאָרֶץ כְּבוֹדוֹ.
Adir adireinu, Adonai adoneinu —	אַדִּיר אַדִּירֵנוּ, יְיָ אֲדֹנֵינוּ--
mah-adir shimcha b'chol haaretz.	מָה אַדִּיר שִׁמְךָ בְּכָל הָאָרֶץ.
"Baruch k'vod-Adonai mim'komo."	בָּרוּךְ כְּבוֹד יְיָ מִמְּקוֹמוֹ.
"Echod hu elohinu, hu Avinu"	אֶחָד הוּא אֱלֹהֵינוּ, הוּא אָבִינוּ,
hu malkeinu, hu moshi·einu —	הוּא מַלְכֵּנוּ. הוּא מוֹשִׁיעֵנוּ --
v'hu yashmi·einu b'rachamav	וְהוּא יַשְׁמִיעֵנוּ בְּרַחֲמָיו
l'einei kol chai:	לְעֵינֵי כָּל חָי׃
"Ani Adonai Eloheichem."	אֲנִי יְיָ אֱלֹהֵיכֶם.

We sanctify Your name in the world,
as celestial song sanctifies You in realms beyond our world,
in the words of Your prophet:

Holy Holy Holy is the God of heaven's hosts.
The fullness of the whole earth is God's glory.

God of Strength who gives us strength,
God of Might who gives us might —
how magnificent the signs of Your Being throughout the earth.
Blessed is the God of eternity who comes forth in splendor.

Our God is one —
Avinu and *Malkeinu*, sovereign Source of life and liberation —
revealing with mercy to all who live: "I am Adonai your God."

K'dushat HaShem: The Blessing of Holiness

נְקַדֵּשׁ אֶת שִׁמְךָ בָּעוֹלָם.

N'kadeish et shimcha baolam . . .
Let us sanctify Your name in this world
as celestial song sanctifies Your name on high.

Asked the *Chofetz Chayim*:
Is it not presumptuous for us to compare ourselves to angels?
One might think it is like a pauper dressed in rags who appears before the king,
pretending to be one of the royal ministers!

And he answered:
In truth, we have as much right to stand before God as the angels. For it is written in the Torah:
"God blew into Adam's nostrils the breath of life, and he became a living soul."
Holy One, You breathed into the human soul something of Yourself;
a spark of You is within us, yearning to rise up and unite with its Source.

And so we hunger for holiness;
we long to lift up mundane acts and make them beautiful.
Let us re-imagine our tables as holy altars where each day we offer up our best—
through blessings and mindful eating,
thoughtful conversation and care for one another. Let us make marriages that
are truly *kiddushin*—holy partnerships of intimacy, faithfulness, and love.
Let us sanctify time, preserve and remember Shabbat, and keep the holy days
of our people.

In a world that can be cruel, let us create holy communities—oases of
compassion.

The Torah teaches:
"Do not profane My holy name—
that I may be sanctified amidst the people of Israel."

We sanctify Your name in this world
when we bring Your spirit into all our deeds.

The Chofetz Chayim. Yisrael Meir Kagan Poupko (1838–1933) was a Lithuanian rabbi popularly known by the title of his most famous work, *Chofetz Chayim* (The One Who Desires Life), a discussion of the laws of gossip and ethical speech.

God blew into Adam's nostrils, Genesis 2:7.

Holy One, You breathed. Adapted from the *Zohar* ("Splendor" or "Radiance"), the central text of Jewish mysticism.

Let us re-imagine our tables. See Talmud *B'rachot* 55a.

Do not profane My holy name, Leviticus 22:32.

Source: Rabbi Edwin Goldberg, Rabbi Janet Marder, Rabbi Sheldon Marder, and Rabbi Leon Morris, eds., *Mishkan HaNefesh: Machzor for the Days of Awe*, vol. 2, *Yom Kippur* (New York: CCAR Press, 2015), 367–369.

What Is a Mitzvah?

The word mitzvah is used many times throughout this volume. Mitzvah is a complicated concept, one with which Jews have long wrestled. As you notice, we have made a deliberate choice to not translate mitzvah. The word mitzvah derives from the Hebrew root *tzadi-vav-hei*, which means "to command," and is used throughout the Torah. The simplest way to translate the word mitzvah would then be "commandment," but that the leads to a number of important questions. What is the source of the commandments? God? If so, how did God communicate the commandments? And as Reform Jews we have to ask: If God is not the sole author of the material in the Torah, then how do we understand the meaning of mitzvah? Perhaps the source of the commandments is the historical experience of the Jewish people. Perhaps the source of the commandments is the lived interaction with our environment and the wisdom we have gained to create a better world. Or perhaps the only thing we can truly call a commandment is ethical behavior, where we treat others with the respect and dignity that is implied in the concept that each human being is created in the image of God.

Rather than defining this complex term mitzvah, we share with you the thoughts of prominent Jewish thinkers from past and current generations. Perhaps in reading their thoughts on the meaning of mitzvah, you will be able to shape your own sense of what it means to live in relationship with the commandments as a Jew.

In *Gates of Mitzvah*, a companion volume to this publication, there are four essays by leading rabbinic scholars of the past generation who explored each of these possibilities from their own perspective. Each essay, excerpted here, provides a different perspective on mitzvah. Following these are excerpts from more contemporary rabbis.

Rabbi Herman E. Schaalman (*z"l*) affirms the divine authority of the mitzvah. He writes:

A mitzvah—commandment—comes from a *M'tzaveh*, a Commander. In our case, indisputably, that Commander was God, first by way of Moses and then by way of prophets and rabbis, the spiritual descendants of Moses. . . .

What do we mean by stating that God is Commander, *M'tzaveh*? How does God command? Does God "speak"? How did Moses or others "hear"? Why these commandments as found in Torah and later tradition and not others?

Revelation, for that is what we are talking about, is a mystery. The character of a mystery, its very essence, precludes our ability to describe and analyze it with precision, in clearly stated detail. If we could so understand and describe it, it would no longer be a mystery. There is something impenetrable about a mystery, something that ultimately defies our human efforts at understanding in ordinary, day-to-day terms. . . .

Language is the problem here. We use terms such as "speaks" and "hears" when talking of God in the same manner as we do when talking of humans. We apply them to the mystery of encounter with God, to the unique and rare moments when a given person and the Divine Presence "meet," without making due allowance for the essentially different use and meaning of these words when they are applied to the mystery of revelation.

God becomes the "Speaker," the "Commander," the *M'tzaveh*, because Moses, in his extraordinary nearness to God, thus understood, thus interpreted, thus "heard," the impact and meaning of God's Presence. God is *M'tzaveh*— Commander—because Moses experienced himself as *m'tzuveh* —commanded, summoned, directed. And this is why Moses transmitted what he "heard," why he expressed the meaning of God's Presence in the mitzvot, the commandments to the people at Sinai and to their descendants ever after. This is why the Torah is both *Torat Adonai*, God's Torah, and *Torat Mosheh*, Moses's Torah.

This is why the Talmud can say, *Dibra Torah bilshon b'nei adam*, "Torah speaks human language." . . .

Why do we do mitzvot? Why should we do mitzvot? Because we are the descendants of those ancestors, the children of those parents who said at Sinai, *Naaseh v'nishma*, "We shall do and we shall hear" (Exodus 24:7). All authentic Judaism until now has so understood itself, has so acted, and so handed it on to hitherto faithful new generations.

Thus the Divine Presence waits for us, and we for It. Thus the commandment comes to us in our time, asking to be heard, understood, and done. . . .

It is built into the very definition and basic assumption of a mitzvah that it is the human response to the "Commanding Presence of God." That response is not, and cannot be, invariably the same. It depends on circumstances. It is not automatic. That response to the commanding God should never be altogether unthinking, routine. To be a genuine response of the person to God, it needs to take account of the condition, capacity, responsiveness, of the commanded one, that is, me.

Rabbi David Polish (*z"l*) asserts that the historical experience of the Jewish people is the source of the mitzvot. He writes:

The observance of mitzvot reflects a Jewish conception of history. This conception is composed of two elements. The first consists of historical events of which we are reminded by specific practices. The second consists of an outlook upon human events and the world that is embodied in a system of conduct and discipline, individual as well as corporate.

Mitzvot are related to historic experiences in which the Jewish people sought to apprehend God's nature and God's will. They are to be observed not because they are divine fiats, but because something happened between God and Israel, and the same something continues to happen in every age and land. Note the words of blessing preceding the performance of a mitzvah: *asher kid'shanu b'mitzvotav, v'tzivanu . . .* , "who has sanctified us through mitzvot and has commanded us. . . ." Mitzvot sanctify the Jewish people because they mark points of encounter by the Jewish people with God. They are enjoined upon us, because through them we perpetuate memories of the encounters and are sustained by those memories. Since they are so indigenous to us, they are incumbent primarily upon us, the Jewish people, and they constitute the singularity of the Jewish religion. . . .

Mitzvot are "signs" of the covenant, affirmed and reaffirmed through the ages at various turning points in which Jewish existence stood in the balance. Out of these turning points came hallowed insights, pointing to the pivotal moment and fashioning the mitzvah marking it. Thus, the Chanukah lights, marking Israel's rededication after near extinction. Thus, *milah* (circumcision), which began with Abraham and which was invoked with special intensity during critical periods in Jewish history. . . . Moments in the life of the individual Jew are intimately related to Israel's historic career. . . .

It cannot be stressed too strongly that the observance of any particular mitzvah is a symbol of, and points to, a higher truth. Some symbols, because of their overpowering hold on us, endure; others change. Some fall into desuetude; new ones come into being. . . .

Finally, the mitzvah enabled the Jewish people to live creatively.

Rabbi Roland B. Gittelsohn (*z"l*) was a religious naturalist. He writes:

What is a religious naturalist? Briefly, he or she is a person who believes in God, but asserts that God inheres within nature and operates through natural law. A religious naturalist perceives God to be the Spiritual Energy, Essence, Core, or Thrust of the universe, not a discrete Supernatural Being. . . .

Mitzvah, by its very definition, must be cosmically grounded; it must possess empyreal significance. For the religious naturalist, as for all believing, practicing Jews, in order to have mitzvah—that which has been commanded—there must be a *m'tzaveh*, a commander. That commander, moreover, needs to be more than human ingenuity or convenience. . . .

But how can an Energy or Essence, a Core or a Thrust, command? For the religious naturalist, who is the *m'tzaveh*? Answer: reality itself. Or, more precisely, the physical and spiritual laws that govern reality. Mitzvot must be observed because only by recognizing and conforming to the nature of their environment can human beings increase the probability of their survival in any meaningful way. Mitzvot are not human-made; they inhere within the universe. . . .

Most of the mitzvot spelled out in this guide, however, deal with ritual observance rather than physical law or ethics. Are they, too, related to cosmic reality? In a less obvious but equally binding sense than the physical or moral imperatives suggested above, yes. Human nature is such that we need to express our emotions and ideals with our whole bodies, not just our tongues. We need also to be visually and kinetically reminded of our noblest values and stimulated to pursue them. As otherwise lonely and frightened individuals, we need common practices and observances that bind us into meaningful and supportive groups. All of which adds up to the fact that we need ritual as something more than social luxury or convenience. For us as Reform Jews, a particular ritual may not be mitzvah. But the need for a pattern of such rituals, this—because it grows out of and satisfies our very basic nature as human beings—is mitzvah. And this we desperately need. . . .

The seder means no less, however, to the religiously naturalistic Jew, who rejects miracles. Plugging into centuries of our people's tradition as well as its unique pursuit of freedom, we visually, audibly, and dramatically commemorate that pursuit and rededicate ourself to it. Our *m'tzaveh* is triune: our very special human need to be free, both as a person and a Jew; our equally human need to augment speech with memory and motion in reinforcement of our highest values; and our specifically Jewish need to identify with our people's destiny.

Rabbi Arthur J. Lelyveld (z"l) reminds us that as Reform Jews we are deeply committed to ethics and social justice. He writes:

We liberal Jews read Scripture not as the literal word of God, but as the work of members of the people of Israel seeking to understand the demand of God. Once we approach our Bible within that frame of reference, we necessarily become selective, for there are points in Scripture at which humans have broken through to an understanding of the highest, while there are also points that preserve primitive practices, anachronisms, or injunctions that long ago became obsolete.

The solution of our difficulty lies in the very fact that we use the word mitzvah in two distinct ways. We talk about specific mitzvot, and we also speak of mitzvah in a more generalized sense, as enjoining upon us a certain attitude toward our fellows. . . .

"Small-m" mitzvot—the performance of ritual acts—have an aesthetic and affective function. They both beautify and enhance by religious drama the moral values and the ideals of our heritage. They become a structure on which the preservation of our people's tradition and its continuity may rest. We select the mitzvot we will perform, we shape our folkways, change our music, revise our prayers, eliminate customs, and add other and new customs. But mitzvah is not the product of our human social engineering. Mitzvah is

God's demand issuing in moral and spiritual values. Ceremonial mitzvot with their folk associations, their customs, and their symbolic objects and actions are the carrier of the values, the structural framework for the people's task of transmission. But "large-M" Mitzvah is the enduring essence to which the structure of small-m testifies and pays obeisance. . . .

In the last analysis, liberalism cannot escape its commitment to the supreme right and obligation of decision that is reserved to the individual soul. It is true that this makes the individual the ultimate authority as to what is Mitzvah and what is not Mitzvah.

Contemporary Reform Jews continue to study and think about the meaning of mitzvah in our lives. The following statements represent further ideas on this subject, both from some of today's Reform rabbinic leaders and from the up-and-coming next generation of rabbinic leadership.

Rabbi Herbert Bronstein writes about mitzvah as part of the relationship to the Divine Other outside the self:

No one knowledgeable about Judaism will deny that these terms, Torah and mitzvah, are central to its lexicon. They are integral with the overreaching metaphor of the relationship between God and the community of Israel: the covenant (*b'rit*). No metaphor for the relationship between God and the people of Israel has been more pervasive in the Jewish religious outlook. This has been the case from the stories of the ancestors, through the prophetic literature, the later codes of law, and rabbinic discourse, to the theological expositions of our own day. The covenant relationship, whether conceived of as a partnership, alliance, or bond with God, or as engagement with God, can be actualized on the human side only through mitzvot, that is, deeds, actions, observances, and practices.

This interrelated cluster of terms (Torah, mitzvah, *b'rit*) implies a spiritual mind-set that assumes an authority that transcends the individual ego, a sense of obligation, an "ought" to the Other beyond the individual self. Furthermore, after Sinai, the covenant with God is with the entire community of Israel as a group. All of these constructs—Torah, mitzvah, *b'rit*—therefore imply not only a strong sense of obligation to God but also a communal consciousness, a sense of "we" that transcends the "me" or ego. This is clearly manifest in the communal stance of Jewish worship, of communal Jewish confession, of communal moral obligation, all of which have long been recognized as characteristics of historic Jewish identity.

Rabbi Elaine Zecher offers the idea of mitzvah as the quintessential Jewish action:

Our tradition guides us with this teaching: "*Eilu d'varim she-ein lahem shiur:* These are things that are limitless, of which a person enjoys the fruit of this world, while the principal remains in the world to come. They are: honoring one's father and mother; engaging in deeds of compassion; arriving early for study, morning and evening; dealing graciously with guests; visiting the sick; providing for the wedding couple; accompanying the dead for burial; being devoted in prayer; and making peace among people."

These are mitzvot, deeds that have the potential to bring enhanced meaning to our lives and to those of others through conscious, mindful choices. Being present in our choices, being conscious in our decisions, draws us nearer to Judaism.

What does it mean to "to do a mitzvah" for us as liberal Jews? For one thing, mitzvot teach us how to regard our lives, how to "measure our days."

Tradition has it that 613 mitzvot exist in the Torah. There are 248 positive ones, like "honor your father and mother" (Exodus 20:12) and "remember the Sabbath day and keep it holy" (Exodus 20:8). There are 365 negative mitzvot, such as "do not murder" (Exodus 20:13) or "do not boil a calf in its mother's milk" (Exodus 23:19). A poetic interpretation of the numerical value of the division provides us with a great metaphor for the purpose of mitzvot. What if the 365 represented the number of days in the solar year, and what if 248 corresponded to the number of parts of the human body, modern scientific knowledge notwithstanding? Couldn't these numbers remind us that our tradition provides us with a way to live our lives every day with our whole being?

A mitzvah is a quintessential Jewish action, whether it is ethical or ritual, rational or irrational. Infused with a mindfulness of action, it has the potential to take on a variety of meanings. Consider the mitzvot related to keeping kosher, for example. We could spend hours analyzing them anthropologically, sociologically, or even politically. No matter how hard we try, however, we will never truly understand why some animals are kosher and others aren't. Understanding the essence of the mitzvah is another story. Could keeping kosher help to raise our consciousness about the food we eat? Could it help teach us how precious food is and how others might be hungry while we feast? The mitzvah of kashrut may raise our awareness about the issues of this world, like hunger or pollution or the sanctity of our own tables.

The divisions of ethical mitzvot and ritual mitzvot, or rational and irrational, are modem interpretations. All are inextricably intertwined. Abraham Joshua Heschel, one of the greatest modern-day theologians, saw no difference between different kinds of mitzvot. When he marched in Selma, Alabama, beside Dr. Martin Luther King, in the fight for civil rights, he returned home and described what he did. He said, "I felt my legs were praying" (*Moral Grandeur and Spiritual Audacity* by Abraham Joshua Heschel, p. viii). Heschel took the daily obligation of prayer and transformed it. The action spoke for itself. Heschel never wavered in his sense of purpose and mission. Mitzvot motivated him. They can motivate us as well, even when we are not sure we are able to take action.

Rabbi Elyse Frishman sees mitzvah as a way that we can find meaning and seek a connection with God:

> Covenant can be understood in two ways: as obligation and as relationship. If one has little sense of relationship, covenant feels like a burdensome obligation. When one is embraced in relationship, the responsibilities of upholding it seem reasonable and necessary.
>
> Reform Judaism is based on voluntary covenant: We choose to live Jewishly. It is crucial to base our theology in Torah. Torah is the starting point of all things Jewish. No matter what an individual believes, if it's not rooted in Torah, it's not Jewish; it is merely personal opinion. Torah has been commented upon, interpreted, even challenged; but all Judaism grows from it.
>
> When we listen to Torah, we are listening to God's voice. But this is not necessarily what God speaks; it reflects what we hear. Dialogue between two people grows not from what is said but from what is heard. . . .
>
> Tradition holds that God gave us mitzvot, that God commands certain behaviors. These commands were given to us in Torah. We consider the dialogue of Torah as God speaking to us. But, what if, instead, we consider that the language of Torah is not necessarily God's; it's a record of how we heard God. . . .
>
> So why follow God's directions? Because they are compelling and infuse our lives with meaning. This is why liberal Jews observe and uphold the ritual and ethical guidelines. . . .
>
> Perhaps the extensive comfort and security possessed by American Jewry frees us to hear God's voice differently from the way a persecuted community might. Indeed, freedom is our reality. The current trend toward spiritual life reflects the desire for more than personal fulfillment. We want to be of something greater than our individual selves. We yearn for true community. We seek God. And God's voice need not be heard as stern and commanding. God is the blessed Holy One: loving, caring, and seeking relationship with us.

Rabbi Richard Levy writes about mitzvah as an act of love:

> Mitzvah means "command." But to understand Torah as a call suggests that the call comes in a manner befitting the relationship we have with God. Two of the important ways in which Jews have traditionally related to God are as a child to a parent and as a lover with a spouse. . . . From human relationships we know that a child relates most closely with a parent and a lover relates most closely with the beloved, in hearing not a demand, but a request: As my wife puts it, "This is something I want you to do that is very important to me." One may say "No" to such requests—but the act of saying "No," or as Rosenzweig put it, "Not yet," also is a response.
>
> In all these cases, heeding the call of a mitzvah becomes an act of love, responding to the call *V'ahavta et Adonai Elohecha,* "You shall love Adonai your God," just as, two prayers earlier, *Ahavah rabbah ahavtanu,* "A great love has God loved us."

How is that love most profoundly manifest? The *Ahavah Rabbah* asks that the God who taught our ancestors the laws of life might also show how much God loves us, however unworthy we may be, by teaching us Torah, as well (*t'choneinu ut'lamdeinu*). We are encouraged, when we study Torah, to feel ourselves invited to sit at God's study table, while the Author of the universe says, in a tone pitched differently for each of us, "This is a law that will help you live out more fully the direction of your life. This is a mitzvah by which you can further the harmony of the universe. I would like you very much to do it."

Mitzvah as loving request reminds us again of Franz Rosenzweig's distinction between the two kinds of Torah—the entire tradition that has a claim on us all and the individual mitzvah that speaks to each of us differently, at different times, out of the darkness. But it is not we who choose—it is the text, and the God behind it, who chooses us. This is a text study that asks, "What do you hear in this mitzvah?" This is an encounter with a text that says, "Listen to the self in you that stood at Sinai when you first heard this mitzvah: What do you hear that self saying to you?

What does your self today hear in it?"

Rabbi Evan Moffic defines mitzvah as that which creates the boundaries of a community, understood through studying and living in an ongoing encounter with God:

> In a seminal essay, my late mentor and teacher Arnold Jacob Wolf argued that "there is no Judaism but Orthodoxy and all Jews are Reform." For Rabbi Wolf, and for me, Judaism cannot be understood outside of a system of commandments, of mitzvot, given by God. Yet, neither can it be understood without recognizing that the nature of those mitzvot changes over time, and that we have a choice as to the way we follow them. There is no Judaism without mitzvah, and there is no Judaism without autonomy. Mitzvot are what create the boundaries that define our community. Yet, the boundaries are different for every synagogue, every community, every individual. This core tension may seem to lead to anarchy and confusion. Yet, it is a tension that has stood at the heart of Jewish life since the onset of modernity and that is not inconsistent with building communities of study, worship, and action. The tension is resolved only when we, as Franz Rosenzweig put it, "enter into life."
>
> In my life, God is the partner in the covenant with Israel established in the Torah and explicated through Torah. We discover what God demands of us by studying Torah and by living within communities dedicated to living by its teachings. That is what it means to be part of the covenant. We do not discover God's will by hearing a voice from on high or by memorizing a book of laws. Each of us learns it by studying and living. We discover what God demands of us only by studying the texts that reflect our people's ongoing encounter with God.

Rabbi Rachel Timoner envisions mitzvah as an opportunity to create a set of values by which to live:

> The question of whether liberal Jews should live by a halachah (a set of mitzvot) is not whether we should have rules. We already follow many norms and expectations absorbed from our surrounding culture. The question is whether the rules by which we are already living will get us where we need to go. Will they make us who we want to be? Do they allow us to respond effectively to the moral and existential crises of our times? If the answer to these questions is no, then what rules would enable us to be who we are meant to be in the world?
>
> One might say that Judaism is a three-thousand-year-old yearning on this very question: given the commanding presence of God, how should we live? The halachic conversation, as preserved in Rabbinic texts, demonstrates a creative and courageous approach to the question of how Jews ought to live. Halachah was originally designed to respond to the changing circumstances of the changing world, to be reinterpreted and adapted by each generation. Unfortunately, halachah became constricted to a narrow range of topics and ideas over the centuries, leaving important areas of Jewish life and significant portions of the Jewish people unaddressed. Even with the responsa system, halachah has not expanded or adapted enough to speak to the changing demands of our world, the changing challenges facing Jewish life, and the changing consciousness and values of the Jewish people.
>
> Increasing numbers of Reform and liberal Jews are seeking a Jewish path by which to live spiritually and responsibly in this time. Perhaps this is the time to shape a liberal halachah. Perhaps this is the time for liberal Jews to collectively live out our values through our actions, to commit to a set of mitzvot that would bridge the world we live in to the world as it should be. (Inspired by "Here Comes Skotsl: Renewing Halakhah" from *Engendering Judaism: An Inclusive Theology and Ethics* by Rabbi Dr. Rachel Adler.)

Rabbi Jeff Goldwasser proposes that mitzvot are part of our heritage, to be studied and argued with and reinterpreted, and to ultimately be woven into who we are as Jews:

> In 1885, Reform Judaism declared, "We accept as binding only [Torah's] moral laws." The Pittsburg Platform stated that Reform Jews would accept the parts of Torah that conformed with "modern civilization" and reject the rituals and superstitions that did not.
>
> The division, to me, seems arrogant. I do not believe that I have the authority to run an editor's red pen through Torah. It is the transcendent teaching that guides us toward sanctity. How can the preferences of "modern civilization" overrule it?
>
> The problem, I think, is the way we fundamentally understand Torah and the mitzvot. If you think of mitzvot as rules of behavior—what to do and what

not to do—then it makes sense to pick and choose. We choose to observe "love your neighbor," but not putting people to death for insulting their parents. That makes sense.

However, Jewish tradition has never viewed Torah as just a checklist of dos and don'ts. To do so is to see only the external garment and ignore what lies beneath. The Rabbis of the Talmud did not kill people for insulting their parents any more than we do. They read the Torah as they saw it—a wedding present from God given on the day we were married at Mount Sinai. It is not to be accepted or rejected; it is to be loved.

Reform Judaism today should recapture that relationship. The work of the ancient Rabbis is not complete; it is our job to continue to search Torah for its timeless truths. We do not need to reject anything in Torah to make it live within us.

Reform Jews today probe the dietary laws to find ways to dignify our lives by eating ethical food. We rediscover tallit and *t'fillin*, not to tie ourselves to empty obligation, but to brighten our spiritual dimension. Yes, we should argue and struggle with Torah, but we should never ignore or reject it.

The challenge for our times, as it has been for all times, is to read Torah actively so as to interpret it. We linger over the words to find treasures, even in the difficult parts.

Rabbi Jason Rosenberg approaches a definition of mitzvah by describing the relationship between mitzvah and habit:

Franz Rosenzweig teaches that performing an act can, over time, lead to that act becoming a mitzvah—a commandment. For me, it's easiest to explain with an example.

I started keeping kosher almost by accident. I was living with some more observant Jews in Jerusalem for a semester, and keeping kosher was an almost default behavior; I did it because that's how we ate. I was deeply surprised when, a few months into the semester, someone offered me some pork and I turned it down. I couldn't say why, exactly. I just realized, suddenly, that keeping kosher had become something—a habit, maybe, or maybe more than that. I wasn't ready to commit to it, but I wasn't ready to stop, either. So, I committed to trying it and—this was the key— learning more about it.

And so, learn I did. I learned theories of the origins of kashrut. I learned modern interpretations. And, I learned through the practice, as well. I learned what it felt like to have Judaism be a regular part of my day, not something with which I engaged only sporadically. I learned about taking a mundane part of my life and treating it like a sacred one instead.

And, I learned that the more I kept kosher, and the more that I learned about and thought about it, the more it meant to me.

Somewhere along the way, I had a realization—I couldn't stop keeping kosher. Not without a penalty. Not a penalty in the form of divine punishment, of course. But, I had spent so much time engaged with this one set of mitzvot that, if I *did* stop, it would hurt me. I would lose something. My regular, thoughtful practice had turned into something that I loved to do and needed to keep doing. My habit had become a mitzvah.

Rabbi Ariana Silverman suggests that a commandment is divine unless proved otherwise:

> The easiest answer for why one should observe the commandments is that they come from God. But in the Reform Movement we do not have the luxury of such certainty. Many of us are unsure what we believe about God and God's role in the writing of the Torah. So I start from the premise that there is a God, and that the Torah's commandments reflect God's divinity, unless and until a commandment is inconsistent with a central tenet of our faith. Many commandments fall into the latter category. But many remain, and we do not get to discard them simply because they are inconvenient or complicated.
>
> Sometimes, we need to observe them precisely *because* they are inconvenient or complicated. Part of living a life of holiness is feeling obligated and feeling limited. Observing some kind of dietary restriction reminds us that we cannot have an insatiable appetite for the earth's resources. Developing a Shabbat practice keeps our obsession with productivity in check. We do not get to do whatever we want.
>
> And we cannot simply choose to observe the "ethical" commandments. As Rabbi Arnold Jacob Wolf (*z"l*) taught us, "Distinctions between 'ethical' and 'ritual' commandments are invariably premature if not downright useless" (Arnold Jacob Wolf, *Unfinished Rabbi* [Chicago: Ivan R. Dee, 1998], page 21). The commandments cited above are technically ritual commandments, but they have clear ethical implications.
>
> When asked if I observe a particular commandment, I often reply, "Not yet." If I believe that it violates a major tenet of my life as a Jew, I say no. But if not, I presume the positive. My Jewish practice is evolving, and I am constantly prioritizing which obligations I wish to assume—not based on whether they are convenient, but based on serious study and reflection.

The question remains: do we really need to know the source of a mitzvah to determine whether to perform it? While belief and theology are important, Judaism teaches us that theology and belief are derived from doing, not the other way around. There is a famous quotation from the Talmud where God says, "Would that my people would abandon Me and observe My Torah, for then they would find Me." One other way to think about mitzvah is as a sacred opportunity. By observing a mitzvah, we have the potential to enhance the spiritual quality of our lives, connect to the Jewish people, perform acts of *tikkun olam*, and encounter the Divine.

While in this volume we sketch out what we believe are the key mitzvot to sanctifying time, *Mishkan Moeid* is not a recipe book where if one ingredient is omitted the whole dish is spoiled. Reform Jewish observance is not an all-or-nothing approach. It is about entering into observance as a dialogue between oneself and the traditions of the Jewish people. Our approach to observance is pluralistic, as is demonstrated in *The Sacred Table* (2011), our publication on ethical eating. The goal is to make good choices about how best to incorporate Jewish observance into our lives. Some will decide to take a comprehensive approach and observe many or all of the mitzvot in this book. Others will decide just to stick their toe into the fountain of observance. During the course of our lives, depending on many factors, our pattern of observance may change. That which was most important may become less important, and that which seemed insignificant can take on new meaning. As one explores the mitzvot that create sacred time and enhance the Jewish cycle of the year, it is helpful to find an empathetic and wise teacher and a supportive community. Each day is an opportunity to add another mitzvah. The real key to observance is to begin.

Source: Rabbi Peter S. Knobel, ed., *Mishkan Moeid: A Guide to the Jewish Seasons* (New York: CCAR Press, 2013), 90–106.

On Halachah and Reform Judaism

RABBI MARK WASHOVSKY

To date, the Responsa Committee of the CCAR has issued approximately thirteen hundred opinions, a collection that constitutes the largest body of Reform halachic writing and, for that matter, the single largest collection of Reform Jewish writing of any kind on the subject of religious practice and observance.

This record of writing and publication may surprise the reader. One might well ask: isn't halachah, a word that has various meanings but that here will stand for "traditional Jewish law," contradictory to the spirit of Reform Judaism? Do we not define ourselves as a "non-halachic" or "post-halachic" movement? Reform Jews, it is often said, do not tend to consult traditional Jewish law when making their religious decisions. And even when they do, they are likely to find its conclusions and methodologies strange and off-putting. Halachah, after all, is rooted in ancient texts like the Bible and the Talmud and is elaborated in countless medieval codes, commentaries, and responsa. It therefore reflects the values of those bygone days and proceeds from a set of cultural assumptions that can hardly be called "modern." This places it sharply at odds with the world in which Reform Jews live and enthusiastically participate. The very notion of legal discipline, moreover, conflicts with the cherished Reform doctrine of autonomy, which asserts the freedom of the individual and the local community to make their own choices in matters of ritual and ethical practice. Given these objections, it might seem reasonable for Reform Jews to reject halachah as an element foreign to our religious lives and the concept "Reform halachah" as an oxymoron.

Some in our movement do draw that conclusion. In their teaching and writing about Reform Judaism, they assign very little importance to the two-thousand-year-old tradition of Jewish legal thought. In making that choice, however, they shoulder a weighty burden of explanation: if halachah is so irrelevant to the religious experience of the Reform Jew, how do we account for the production of so much Reform halachic literature? Why are there so many articles, guidebooks, and responsa? It will not do to dismiss this outpouring of writing as the quaint intellectual pastime of a handful of exceptional—or eccentric—scholars. The list of those who have composed this extensive body of Reform halachic literature includes a large number of names, indeed, some of the most illustrious names in the history of North American Reform Judaism.[2] Reform halachah, it turns out, is a preoccupation of the mainstream—and not simply the margins—of our supposedly non-halachic movement.

The fact is that, despite all claims to the contrary, Reform Judaism is very much a "halachic" movement. Indeed, halachah is central to any adequate description of Reform Jewish life. Were we to remove halachah from Reform Judaism, we would be unable to render anything approaching an adequate account of our actual religious practice. To illustrate, let's consider the contours of that practice. When we Reform Jews gather for worship, we recite a liturgy and perform synagogue rituals that, even allowing for all the changes we have introduced into them, follow structures set down in the traditional halachic literature: the Talmud and the legal codes. Our Shabbat and Festival observances—the lighting of candles, *Kiddush*, the festive meal, the reading of the Torah, the ceremony of *Havdalah*, the Passover seder and the foods associated with the holiday, the sounding of the shofar, fasting on Yom Kippur, the building of and the dwelling in the sukkah, the waving of the *etrog* and *lulav*, the lighting of the Chanukah menorah, the recitation of *Hallel*, and so many others—are all halachic institutions, defined in the Rabbinic halachic sources and given shape by the discourse of Jewish law. Our life-cycle ceremonies—the rituals with which we mark birth, the stages of life, marriage, and death— are set forth, constructed, characterized, and developed in the Talmud and subsequent Jewish legal writing. The same is true when we turn our gaze outward, beyond the walls of the synagogue and the confines of our ritual observance. Our Jewish conversation on issues of personal morality and social justice, in which we attempt to apply Jewish values to construct our responses to the challenges we encounter in the marketplace, in medicine, in politics, and in world affairs, is based upon a discourse that is anchored in the Rabbinic literature and is suffused with references to halachic texts. Halachah, it turns out, is all around us in Reform Judaism, giving structure, meaning, and context to our community's ritual practice and our religious life.

Such, indeed, was the insight of our teacher Rabbi Solomon B. Freehof, of blessed memory, who chaired the CCAR Responsa Committee for many years and whose eight published volumes of Reform responsa did much to define the nature of this style of Reform halachic writing. In his introduction to the first of those volumes,[3] Rabbi Freehof points to the effort, characteristic of early Reform Judaism, to draw a clear theological line of distinction between the Bible and subsequent Jewish literature. The early Reformers sought to distance their movement from "the authority of the old rabbinate," which included the literary sources—"the rabbinical literature, the Talmud and the codes"—upon which that authority was based. In place of this vast literary corpus, the Reformers wanted to make the Bible the sole foundation of their religious worldview. In this, however, they failed. As Rabbi Freehof writes:

> The weakness of the position was primarily that the self-description of Reform as being solely Biblical was simply not true. All of Reform Jewish life in all its observances was actually post-Biblical in origin. None of the arrangements of worship, the hours of service, the text of the prayers, no matter how rewritten, was primarily Biblical. The whole of Jewish liturgy is an achievement of post-Biblical times. The religious calendar, based indeed on Scripture, was elaborated in post-Biblical times. Marriage ceremonies and burial rites were all post-Biblical. The Bible, of course, was the source of ethical ideas, but the actual religious life was rabbinic. Early Reform may have rejected contemporary rabbinic authority, but it could not avoid the constructs that lived in the pageantry of the Jewish mode of life.

That last sentence makes a critical distinction between the "authority" of the halachah and the halachah itself. Reform Jewish individuals and communities do not consider themselves bound to adhere to the legal rulings found in our sacred texts or in the decisions of leading rabbinical authorities past and present. Reform Judaism does not accept the notion that a particular observance or action is either obligatory or forbidden *solely* because some book or set of books—the Bible, the Talmud, or a code of halachah—says so. This, perhaps, is what some Reform Jews really mean when they describe our movement as "non-halachic." But even if we do not accept the law's binding authority upon us, it would be incorrect to say that we reject the relevance of those books—which is to say our sacred texts—in wholesale or systematic fashion. To do that, to reject the substance of the halachah, the forms, patterns, and content of the Rabbinic legal tradition, would be to turn our backs on all that is recognizably *Jewish* in what Rabbi Freehof terms "the Jewish mode of life." And, as Rabbi Freehof points out and as the evidence of our eyes confirms, Reform Judaism has never done that. None of this means, of course, that we are forbidden to depart from the traditional structures of Jewish religious observance, to reshape them or to create new ones. Ritual innovation has always been a hallmark of the Reform Jewish consciousness. The point, rather, is that our innovations have historically taken place within a context of practice that is inextricably rooted in the traditional rabbinical literature. We often say that the readiness to embrace change is central to the idea of Reform Judaism, and that is true. But so is the desire to live in continuity with the religious heritage of the Jewish people. To ignore or to minimize the importance of either of these aspirations is to distort the history of Reform Judaism and to render an inadequate account of our particular version of the Jewish religious experience.

To put this another way: halachah is the foundation of all Jewish religious practice, the authentic home of our Reform ritual and ethical observance. By "authentic," I mean simply that the discussions and debates that we Jews have conducted for centuries over the proper form and structure of our religious life take place within the parameters of traditional Rabbinic law. Therefore, if the question we are addressing has anything to do with Jewish religious practice, with sacred action, then Jews have historically found the answer or answers to that question in the texts and discourse of the halachah. And this, in turn, helps to explain why Reform rabbis have produced such an extensive halachic literature. Since we Reform Jews have sought to ground our own observance in the historical Jewish tradition, it is no surprise that we have learned to express ourselves in the very language with which the tradition has created and developed that observance.

To call halachah a "language" is to say that it is more than simply a collection of rules and directives, of thou-shalts and thou-shalt-nots imposed upon the Jew. Halachah is better understood as a discourse, a way of speaking, a conversation carried on through history by the students of Jewish tradition. It is the medium of communication through which Jews for more than fifteen centuries have analyzed and explored, discussed and debated how they should answer the myriad manifestations of the central question of Jewish life: what is it that God wants us to do? We might summarize the nature of this discourse in the words "interpretation" and "argument." By "interpretation" I mean a claim of meaning that a reader or readers make upon a text, which serves as the object of interpretation. In halachic language, the object of interpretation is Torah, specifically the body of sacred texts historically and collectively recognized as the literary source[4] of Jewish religious practice. The halachist interprets these texts in order to determine "the practice they are to follow" (Exod. 18:20), that is, how Torah would have us act. At times, it is not difficult at all to arrive at the "right" answer to a question of Jewish practice. Halachah knows of many easy cases, issues upon which there is widespread consensus, questions for which virtually every student of Jewish law would arrive at the identical answer. At other times, the matter is not so simple. These are the hard cases, the questions for which the texts and sources do not offer a single, obviously correct answer, when textual interpretation yields two or more plausible solutions to the problem.[5] In those cases, how do we know which of the available answers is the best one? We don't; at any rate, we can't identify it with any degree of precision. Halachah, like disciplines such as law, ethics, and theology, is not a hard science; there is no formula by which to distinguish the "right" from the "wrong" answers to controversial questions of Jewish law.[6] And here is where "argument" comes in. Since one cannot *deduce* the answer to a question of Jewish practice as though it were a problem in mathematics, one must *argue* that a suggested answer is correct or, at least, that it is better than the other answers that might reasonably be adopted. That argument will draw upon the body of texts and techniques that make up the language of halachah, that for centuries have supplied the intellectual resources for scholarly interpretation and debate. The argument succeeds to the extent that a consensus forms around it, a consensus that takes shape when the halachist persuades the intended audience, the particular community of interpretation to which he or she[7] addresses the argument, that *this* answer represents the best reading of the texts and sources of Torah as they relate to the question at hand.

The responsa literature, by far the largest body of rabbinical legal writing,[8] occupies a central position in this culture of halachic argument. The word "responsa" is a Latinate translation of the Hebrew term *sh'eilot ut'shuvot*, "questions and answers." The typical responsum (*t'shuvah*, "answer") conveys the opinion of its author on a submitted question (*sh'eilah*) of Jewish law or practice. Like the opinion written by a judge,[9] a responsum does more than merely report a decision; it *argues* for it, offering reasons to justify the decision as correct. This does not guarantee that its decision is in fact "correct," any more than we would say that a judge's ruling is automatically correct merely because she writes an opinion in support of it. The argument may fail to achieve its objective. The members of its intended audience may find its reasoning and evidence unconvincing; they may prefer a different interpretation of the texts and sources. The point is that the responsum *is* an argument, a written effort to persuade its readers that "*this* is what Torah says, *this* is how we should read the tradition, and for *these* reasons." What if the readers disagree? In that case they can and frequently do offer counterarguments, reasons of their own that explain their disagreement and that would support a different decision. It is through just this sort of dialectic and debate, this ongoing clash of interpretations, that the Torah has developed over the centuries, that its meanings and understandings have been clarified, adjusted, reshaped, and altered to meet the challenge of the constantly changing times.

Reform responsa are our contribution to this prodigious, historic genre of Jewish legal writing. They are literary embodiments of halachic argument, written by Reform rabbis and addressed primarily, though not exclusively,[10] to a Reform Jewish audience or community of interpretation. The specifically Reform context of this writing helps to account for two distinctive features of the Reform halachic enterprise. First, Reform responsa will often read the halachah in ways that differ from the decisions reached by Orthodox rabbis. This difference of opinion, we believe, is as it should be. All too often, we hear assertions that identify the halachah with the consensus opinion among the contemporary Orthodox rabbinate. We disagree. Halachah, as we have noted, is a discourse, a language, a way of arguing about matters of Jewish practice as well as the historical record of such arguments. Differences of opinion and conflicts of interpretation are inevitable in this sort of discourse. They are also legitimate. The existence of a large and variegated Reform halachic literature is testimony to our determination to state *our* opinion, to take *our* place as Reform Jews within this history of Jewish legal interpretation and argument. Second, as we have seen, Reform Judaism does not recognize the absolute binding authority of a rabbinical ruling on a question of practice or, for that matter, a question of belief or doctrine. No Reform rabbi or committee of rabbis enjoys the status of the *g'dolei hador*, the "great sages of the generation" whose halachic decisions determine the practice of Orthodox Jews. No Reform Jew is obligated to adopt a responsum's conclusion if he or she disagrees with it. Reform responsa are "authoritative" if and only if they are persuasive, to the degree that they convince their readers that *this* particular answer, this particular application of Torah corresponds to the readers' own conception of Judaism.

NOTES

2. For example, the chairpersons of the CCAR Responsa Committee have included such leading Reform rabbis as Kaufman Kohler, Jacob Lauterbach, Jacob Mann, Israel Bettan, Solomon B. Freehof, Walter Jacob, and W. Gunther Plaut. Committee responsa published during the late 1970s and early 1980s and included in the volume *American Reform Responsa* (New York: CCAR Press, 1983) are signed by the members of the Committee, including Leonard Kravitz,

Eugene Lipman, Simeon Maslin, Stephen Passamaneck, Harry Roth, Herman Schaalman, Rav Soloff, Sheldon Zimmerman, and Bernard Zlotowitz, in addition to committee chair Walter Jacob See as well the acknowledgments to this volume for a list of those rabbis who served on the Committee from 1996 to 2007 and participated in the writing of the responsa included herein.

3. Solomon B. Freehof, *Reform Responsa* (Cincinnati: Hebrew Union College Press, 1960), pp. 15–16.

4. As opposed to another type of "source." For example, legal theorists speak of a law's "historical source," the social, political, or economic conditions that led to the creation of a particular legal institution or to the adoption of a particular legal interpretation. "Literary source" refers to the written text or texts in which the law is to be found or from which the legal authorities are expected to derive their decisions and interpretations.

5. On the distinction between "easy" and "hard" cases, see *Reform Responsa for the Twenty-first Century*, no. 5758.12, vol. 1, pp. 10–11, at notes 1 and 2.

6. Mention should be made here of the traditional "rules of decision making" *(k'lalei p'sak)* that we find in the Talmud and subsequent halachic literature, rules such as "the law follows the majority opinion," "the law follows the anonymous opinion in the mishnah," "the law follows the ruling laid down by the latest authorities," "Sephardic Jews are obliged to adopt the ruling of R. Yosef Karo in the *Shulchan Aruch*," and so forth. These rules are frequently cited by halachists, but they do not always resolve legal controversies. In fact, the rules themselves are often the subject of controversy, since not all authorities accept them in all cases. Moreover, in any given case they are likely to clash with other such rules that would lead to a different decision in the instant case. At best, these rules serve as "rules of thumb," arguments in favor of a particular decision, rather than as guarantees that a particular decision is objectively correct.

7. The active participation of women in the conversation is one of the most obvious factors that distinguish our liberal community of halachic interpretation from others.

8. The response literature "contains the preponderance of the material on Jewish law produced in the post-Talmudic period" (Menachem Elon, *Jewish Law: History, Sources, Principles* [Philadelphia: Jewish Publication Society, 1994], p. 1462). How large is this "preponderance"? Elon cites the estimate of three hundred thousand extant responsa, contained in more than three thousand separate volumes.

9. Like most analogies, this one is not exact. The responsum differs from the judicial opinion for the simple reason that the author of the responsum does not ordinarily act as a judge sitting on a case. Unlike most judges, the responsum's author does not exercise the power to enforce the ruling. In this sense, the rabbinical responsum more closely resembles the advisory opinion issued by the attorney general in the American legal system than it does the judicial opinion. See Solomon B. Freehof, *The Responsa Literature* (Philadelphia: Jewish Publication Society, 1955), p. 16. Historically speaking, the rabbinical *t'shuvah* has much in common with the *responsa prudentium* (hence the word "responsa" as the accepted translation of the Hebrew term) of ancient Roman law. Like the rabbinical variety, the Roman responsa were learned opinions authored by legal scholars *(iuris prudetttes)* who wrote them in order to advise judges *(iudices)* as to the correct law in a particular case. The roles, however, were distinct: it was the judge, and not the author of the responsum, who actually ruled on the case.

10. Many of the statements, deductions, inferences, and interpretations contained in a Reform responsum are "nonsectarian" in nature: that is, they would be just as much at home in a similar communication written by an Orthodox or Conservative rabbi. Torah is something that all Jews share in common, and it should not be impossible for us to converse and to argue productively across denominational lines.

Source: Mark Washofsky, ed., *Reform Responsa for the Twenty-First Century*, vol. 1 (New York: CCAR Press, 2010), xv–xxiii.

On Our Humanity

RABBI MICAH CITRIN

Too often we worry about our inclination to anthropomorphize God. But perhaps we have it wrong. It is not God who has human characteristics, but we who have godly characteristics. We are a dim reflection of the Creator here on earth, "little less than divine," as the Psalmist suggests (Psalm 8:6). We possess transcendent, holy attributes even as we are limited by mortality and the flaws each of us struggles to subdue, accept, and overcome during the course of our lifetime.

A fundamental source of our divine reflection radiates from one of the few dogmas Jews embrace about God: *Sh'ma Yisrael, Adonai Eloheinu, Adonai Echad*, "Hear O, Israel, *Adonai* is our God, *Adonai Echad*." When we declare God *Echad*, One, it goes beyond a statement of quantity, that there is only One God. We cannot quantify the Infinite. Rather, *Echad* means wholly unique, holy in otherness and distinction, complete in unity. God is the complete Oneness that pervades existence, singular in being, whose essence is quality, not quantity.

Like God, each of us is unique, a singular being. Even though we are born from our parents and carry the traits of our family gene pool, we each exist as a unique manifestation of life. The Talmud illustrates this divine gift in a story that seeks to explain the distinctive nature of each person.

Adam, the first human, was created alone, according to the Rabbis, in order to proclaim the greatness of God. The story continues, "Our Rabbis taught that if a person mints coins from the same mold, they all turn out alike. Yet, God fashioned each human being from the same mold, Adam, but not one person is alike" (Babylonian Talmud, *Sanhedrin* 38a).

More than just the stamp of a common humanity, we are stamped with the image of God. Every human being shares this commonality, yet in God's image we are each unique, completely different from anyone who has ever lived or who ever will live. We each exist as one of a kind, experiencing God's world, and contributing to it, in our own way. This is God's promise to us, the spark of the Holy One within us, and it lends us the overwhelming sense of the precious nature of our lives. Humanity becomes the vessel through which *Echad* is projected into this world. Our task is to live with this awareness and conduct ourselves in a manner that is worthy of this image.

Source: Rabbi Micah Citrin, in *Lights in the Forest: Rabbis Respond to Twelve Essential Jewish Questions*, ed. Rabbi Paul Citrin (New York: CCAR Press, 2014), 80–81.

Our Role in the World

RABBI ARIANA SILVERMAN

Why be Jewish? Why stay Jewish? Why live Jewishly? Our ancestors probably had little choice in the matter. Their identity was fixed, unchangeable. Ghetto walls and social intolerance confined them. But that is not the case for us.

Leon Wieseltier said, "To be a Jew is not to be an American or a Westerner or a New Yorker. It is its own category, its own autonomous way of moving through the world" (quoted in Pogrebin, *Stars of David*, 159).

The Jewish people still exists because in every generation there have been Jews who believed that our existence as a people and what we bring to the world *matters*. By all odds, we should have disappeared long ago, as many other peoples did. But we are here because we know that Judaism brings something essential to our lives—something that we cannot get anywhere else, something that animates and drives and comforts us. No matter the struggles or the successes, Judaism asserts that at the end of the day what we do with our time on earth matters. And it helps us determine how best to use that time.

Abraham Joshua Heschel put it best: "We are God's stake in human history" (quoted in *Time*, March 14, 1969). I don't think that statement is hyperbole. *Tikkun olam*, the Jewish duty to repair our broken world, arises from the observation that the world is fundamentally out of order; that everything is *not* okay. Despite their pervasiveness, corruption, inequality, and violence are each a divine injustice, a serious breach in the way God intended things.

Visitors to the Anne Frank Haus in Amsterdam are greeted with an excerpt from Anne's writings: "Who knows, maybe our religion will teach the world and all the people in it about goodness, and that's the reason, the only reason, we have to suffer. We can never just be Dutch, or just English, or whatever; we will always be Jews as well. And we'll have to keep on being Jews, but then, we'll want to be."

As Rabbi Jerry Davidson said, "[We are] a people that have endured [and], in spite of everything, have never failed to hope and to dream" (excerpted from *Temple Beth-El of Great Neck Bulletin*, September 1988). That is our unique role in the world. And that endurance, that hope, will inspire us to create the messianic world of our dreams.

Source: Rabbi Ariana Silverman, in *Lights in the Forest: Rabbis Respond to Twelve Essential Jewish Questions*, ed. Rabbi Paul Citrin (New York: CCAR Press, 2014), 166–167.

Where is the Spiritual Action?

RABBI MIKE COMINS

1

"If to believe in God means to be able to talk about him in the third person, then I do not believe in God. If to believe in him means to able to talk to him, then I believe in God" (Schlipp and Friedman, *Philosophy of Martin Buber*, 24). It was only after ordination, at age forty, that I internalized this teaching from Martin Buber. You don't *think* God; you *meet* God. You don't *reason* God; you *perceive* God. God is not in a concept; God is in a moment.

I feel most "spiritual" in the most "material" places, like in nature or in the bedroom, and closest to God when hiking, praying, conversing, creating art, making music, or practicing the Taoist moving meditation, qigong. But in my upbringing, abstract thinking about God replaced explicit instruction on how to meet God in the world and what that might look like.

When I think of a religion, I ask: Where is the spiritual action? For Buddhism, it is in the mind; for Christianity, in the afterlife. Jewish practice is well grounded in everyday life, but the spiritual action, I was taught—the divine target of Jewish prayer and ritual—was always in some intangible, non-physical dimension accessed through speculative (and to me, unbelievable) arguments and ideas. Despite a wealth of God-moments, for most of my life, I was a wannabe when it came to belief in God.

What changed? Buber, through I-Thou relation, and Rabbi Abraham Joshua Heschel, through awe and wonder, taught me that one gets to God not by taking a mental turn around the physical world, but by engaging with it as deeply as possible.

Rabbi Lawrence Kushner's works made Jewish mysticism plausible for me. When I was taught qigong, based on the same Chinese medicine that brings us acupuncture and other healing therapies, I immediately felt the energy called *chi*. I realized that a central claim of Jewish mysticism is true. *Chiyut*, a Chasidic term meaning "divine lifeforce," and derived from *chayim*, "life," flows through the world, and I can tap into it most anytime I try through deep listening, meditative awareness, and prayer. I embraced the *Zohar*'s description of God (through Kushner) as the River of Light.

Most important, I feel *chiyut* in my body. Once I paid attention to the *feel* of connecting to godliness, my body became a thermometer to measure and guide my Jewish practice. I have learned which activities and spiritual practices, readily and reliably, bring me into God's presence.

Even the most mystical, sublime, "spiritual" moment is experienced in a body. Would it not make more *sense*, and give people the realistic, achievable expectation of meeting God in the everyday fabric of their lives, if we acknowledge that we encounter God, and that we best gain knowledge of the Divine, not through abstract, unprovable speculation, but through the experience of our bodies in transcendent moments?

2

Heschel writes, "This is the most important experience in the life of every human being: something is asked of me. Every human being has had a moment in which he sensed a mysterious waiting in him. Meaning is found in responding to the demand, meaning is found in sensing the demand" (Heschel, *Who Is Man?*, 107–8).

As long as I can remember, I have felt the call to the right and the good. When Heschel explained this to me as a manifestation of the Divine, my intuition was validated.

An all-good, all-powerful God could not let drunk drivers kill innocents, let alone allow the Holocaust. When Harold Kushner suggested that God is not all-powerful (or chooses not to be all-powerful), my intuition was validated.

I do not believe God operates like a super event planner according to a master plan, or that God is an idea, or that God can be reduced to an interior psychological state. Rather, I know that *chiyut* is always running through me, in dialogue with the world. Just as the divine flow influences me, I influence it, through thought and action. When I pray for someone's healing, I don't believe that I'm petitioning a God who makes human-like decisions as to who will live and who will die. But I know how to build *chiyut*, the divine life-force, within me through meditation and movement, and I know how to send it toward other people through prayer, and I know that it has an effect.

* * *

Life could not have evolved without the rotation of the earth and the motion of continents that create hurricanes, earthquakes, and tsunamis. Human acts of malice are optional, but disease and natural disasters are as necessary as the air we breathe. Since I don't believe God personally decides when and where disease hits, when my mother died of cancer before her time, I didn't ask, "Why her?"

All that sufficed until I experienced the long, slow, painful death of my father due to Lewy body dementia. Then I knew the anger of Job in the face of random, unbearable, undeserved suffering. I cried out in protest—to the God I don't believe in!

I am baffled and offended by the depths of human suffering and human evil in God's good world. Nothing alleviates or justifies the pain.

And nothing makes truth, justice, beauty, and love less noble and extraordinary.

Every day, I say thanks to God for the privilege of living in this marvelous world. When I can't, I stand with Aaron and Job before the mystery, in silence.

3

When an infant cries in your arms, what the child needs becomes your command. When my spouse suffers, what she needs is my response-ability. Buber located I-Thou moments of transcendence, in which we are in dialogue with the world around us from a posture of communion and empathy, as the source of ethics. This prompted Buber to understand that God is present in every moment of genuine dialogue.

For me, God's role in I-Thou is the hardest part of Buber's thought to fathom. Rabbi Eugene Borowitz helped me to understand. God permeates transcendent moments of I-Thou as an inexplicable but real sense of "quality" (Borowitz, *Renewing the Covenant*, 101). We feel the call mentioned above by Heschel. We are lured beyond self-interest and moral mediocrity.

I believe God's presence is real in ethical moments because I am not reasoning, projecting, or inventing this invitation/demand that I act my best. I am reacting to it. I-Thou doesn't reinforce my habits, assumptions, and predispositions; it shatters them. I am called, attracted, and pulled to the right and the good by meeting God's transcendent quality, an experience available to me every day.

Does recognizing God as the source of ethics in moments of transcendence make a difference in our lives? As practicing Jews, we are called to do *t'shuvah*, "repentance," particularly on Yom Kippur.

Most of my life, I dutifully dwelt on my shame and guilt. I thought about self-change and didn't change much. Now the transcendent, right-brain God-moments of a fruitful Jewish, spiritual practice draw me out of my neurotic thoughts and show me what is possible. I am pulled forward, by light and hope.

4

Based on Enlightenment philosophy, modern thinkers compartmentalized science and religion into neat cubicles—science reveals facts; religion generates meaning. Postmodernism emerged as this and similar value/fact dichotomies were proved false.

Science cannot explain everything, and during the previous century it constantly overreached, especially in the social sciences. But when it deals with what it can competently explain, no source of truth is more certain, not to mention more noble, effective, and fruitful, than scientific method.

Truth is not optional for the spiritual seeker. We cannot base Jewish belief and practice on wishful thinking. Maimonides's great philosophical work *Guide for the Perplexed* explicitly integrated the science of the time, neo-Aristotelian thought, with Judaism. It never would have occurred to him, or any other Jewish thinker of note, to ignore or deny the best knowledge available. Otherwise, Judaism becomes distorted or, worse, trivial. We ignore science at the price of irrelevance. Good religious thinking draws on all sources of truth, especially science, for if God did not "create" the world, God certainly operates in the world. (Personally, I think God creates the world every day.)

I would go further. The deeper our encounter with the world, scientific and not scientific, the better our religious thinking. It is no coincidence that Buber begins *I and Thou* by describing his encounter with a tree, or that Heschel develops the components of radical amazement—awe and wonder—to reinterpret and renew the Jewish relationship with God.

The spiritual action is right here.

Source: Rabbi Mike Comins, in *Lights in the Forest: Rabbis Respond to Twelve Essential Jewish Questions*, ed. Rabbi Paul Citrin (New York: CCAR Press, 2014), 8–12.

Jewish Faith

Rabbi Paul Citrin

Many Jews today wonder or even explicitly ask, "What is Jewish faith? What does it mean to me, in my life?" So too, those considering Judaism want to know about Jewish faith and how they could partake in it. The beginning of a wide variety of responses comes with understanding the meaning of the Hebrew word for faith, *emunah*. *Emunah* means confidence and trust. *Emunah* does not refer to blind belief, assent to reason-denying principles, or accepting bequeathed dogma.

A person of *emunah* has confidence that the universe is undergirded by a life-sustaining, unifying force that is the source of moral insight and ethical imperative. One who possesses *emunah*, according to Jewish understanding, trusts in the goodness of life and its blessings. That trust includes a radical conviction that salvation—repairing ourselves and human society—is an eternal summons and possibility that is built into the fabric of the cosmos.

Emunah flows from a searching heart, a heart of openness and yearning. At the same time, we enhance and strengthen *emunah* in our world by becoming, each one of us, persons who embody trust, confidence, loyalty, and integrity. *Emunah*, then, is more than a personal philosophy. It is a religious stance or attitude. It must, perforce, demonstrate its living reality and power in our interpersonal relations, our *tzedakah*, our compassionate deeds, our honest self-reflection.

Source: Rabbi Paul Citrin, ed., preface to *Lights in the Forest: Rabbis Respond to Twelve Essential Jewish Questions* (New York: CCAR Press, 2014), ix.

The Synagogue

About the Sanctuary

- **Bimah:** In the main sanctuary the bimah is the raised area from which the service is conducted and the Torah is read.
- *Aron Hakodesh*: This is the Holy Ark, the "closet" that houses the Torah scrolls of the congregation.
- *Ner Tamid:* This is the Eternal Light that hangs over the Ark in every synagogue to remind us of God's eternal presence. The *Ner Tamid* in the main sanctuary is solar powered.
- **Torah Scroll:** The Torah consists of the Five Books of Moses. Each scroll is handwritten on parchment by a trained professional called a *sofer*, or scribe.
- **Torah Ornaments:** Torah ornaments include: the mantle (cover): a silver breastplate depicting the insignias of the Twelve Tribes of Israel: two silver finials or a single silver crown; and a *yad* (hand), or pointer, which the reader uses to avoid touching the parchment.
- **Artistic Symbolism:** Within the stained glass windows are various symbols of Jewish tradition including the lions of Judah, the crowns of Torah, the hands of the Priestly Benediction, and the tents of Jacob.
- **Flags:** As loyal American citizens, we display the American flag on our bimah. Because of our strong ties to the State of Israel, we also display the Israeli flag.

Source: Union Temple of Brooklyn, http://uniontemple.org/worship/ our-services/.

The *Tallit*

Rabbi Harvey J. Fields

בָּרוּךְ אַתָּה, יְיָ אֱלֹהֵינוּ, מֶלֶךְ הָעוֹלָם, אֲשֶׁר קִדְּשָׁנוּ בְּמִצְוֹתָיו וְצִוָּנוּ לְהִתְעַטֵּף בַּצִּיצִית.

We praise You, Eternal God, Sovereign of the universe: You hallow us with Your mitzvot and teach us to wrap ourselves in fringed *tallit*.

COMMENTARY

The *tallit*, prayer shawl, with its *tzitzit*, or fringes, has been worn by Jews since biblical times. Today, many Jews continue to wear the *tallit*. Among Reform Jews the wearing of a *tallit* at worship is optional. The commandment to wear the *tallit* is found in the Torah, in the Book of Numbers:

> The Eternal spoke to Moses saying: Speak to the Israelite people and instruct them to make for themselves fringes on the corners of their garment through-out the ages. . . . Look at it and recall all the Eternal' commandments and observe them, so that you do not follow your heart and eyes to do evil.
>
> —*Numbers 15:37-39*

Why?

Why have Jews worn the *tallit* from biblical times until today?

We know that dress has always played an important part in the way people relate to one another. The Native American headdress, for instance, indicates the tribal position of the person wearing it. The uniform a soldier wears tells us his or her rank in the army. A Catholic priest is known by the white collar he wears.

Dress is also associated with various kinds of rituals. There is the white dress of the bride, the robes of the priest, and the animal masks worn by some Native American tribes at special festive occasions.

Often ancient people wore special garments or charms because they believed this practice would protect them from evil spirits or be pleasing to the gods. Today, many people still wear what they call "good luck" charms, believing that the charms will bring them safety, good health, success in their sport, or even protection from harm.

Originally the Hebrews, like other peoples, may have worn the *tallit* for protection from evil or for good luck. The Torah, however, transformed these superstitious practices and gave them a higher, spiritual meaning. The Torah teaches that the *tallitot* were meant to help us recall all the Eternal's command-ments. The Hebrew word for "commandment" is mitzvah. A mitzvah is a Jewish responsibility. The word *mitzvot* is also used for any good deed or act of piety or kindness. Later on we will discuss the variety of different *mitzvot* in Jewish tradition.

The *Tallit* and Prayer

The *mitzvah* of prayer is one of the most important responsibilities of the Jew. Prayer is our opportunity to share our Jewish faith, to express our love of God and humanity, to judge our actions and relationships with others, and to seek ways of improving ourselves and the world in which we live.

Putting on the *tallit* with its *tzitzit* is the way some Jews "dress up" for prayer. Wearing this helps many Jews get into the mood for worship. When we put on the *tallit*, we do something that Jews have done for centuries when they prayed.

Rebbe Nachman of Breslov, a great-grandson of the Baal Shem Tov, taught that "it is a *mitzvah* to be properly dressed for prayer." Would you agree with him? You may wish to arrange a discussion or debate on what is "proper dress" for prayer. Should you have such a discussion, be sure to include the *tallit* and the wearing of the *kippah*, *yarmulke* or skullcap, and *t'fillin*, phylacteries. You may also wish to discuss if "proper dress" includes the kinds of clothes we choose to wear to services. Are there certain outfits that add to or detract from our ability to pray? Do you think that there should be standards for what "proper dress" means in the synagogue? Why or why not? If "yes," what would some of these standards be?

Who Wears the *Tallit?*

For many centuries, only the men wore the *tallit* and *kippah* when they came to synagogue. The reason may have been that only the men were obligated to pray three times a day: *Shacharit*, morning; *Minchah*, afternoon; and *Maariv*, evening. Because of the duties of the home and the rearing of children, women were not expected to be at the synagogue at the special assigned times for prayer. This may explain why it became a custom for only men to wear the *tallit*.

When you attend services today, however, you may notice that things are very different. While you will see many men who are wearing *tallit* and *kippah* to pray, you may see that some choose to worship without tallit and kippah. You will also find that the tallit and kippah are now worn by women as well as men. There is nothing in Jewish law that prohibits a woman from wearing *tallit* or *kippah*, and more and more women are choosing to wear them when they pray. At Conservative, Reform, and Reconstructionist synagogues today, you are *likely* to see female rabbis, female cantors, and female worshipers wearing *tallit* and *kippah*.

What do you think? Should "dress up" for worship include wearing a *tallit*, *kippah*, or *tefillin*? Why or why not? Do you find it meaningful to wear your best clothes to synagogue? Is there a benefit to "dressing up" for special occasions? Are there certain clothes that are not appropriate to wear in the synagogue? Discuss some of these questions with friends, with the rabbi and cantor, and with adults in your congregation. The differences in opinion might make an interesting debate.

Looking at the *Tallit*

If you look carefully at each of the four corners of the *tallit*, you will notice a long fringe. It is made in a very special way out of four threads.

The four threads are drawn through a small hole at the corner of the *tallit* and tied in a double knot. Then one of the threads, called the *shamash*, or serving thread, is wound around the others seven times and knotted; and then eight times and knotted. Then it is wound another eleven times and tied; and finally another thirteen times and tied.

Why is the long fringe tied in such an elaborate way? Because it is a symbol. A symbol is an object that represents a special meaning. When we look at it, it reminds us of an idea, hope, or great truth. For instance, the flag of our nation is a symbol. When we look at it, we are reminded of our country and of our responsibilities as citizens.

The long fringe of the *tallit* is a symbol. The special way in which it is tied reminds us of an important teaching of Judaism.

The *Tallit Katan*

Traditional Jews wear the *tzitzit* not only on a *tallit* at times of prayer, they wear them as a special garment at all times!

The garment used for this purpose is called a *tallit katan*, "small *tallit*," or *arba kanfot*, "four corners." It is similar to an undershirt with four corners.

As on the *tallit*, there are fringes on each of the four corners. Usually the fringes are left to hang out so that the wearer may see them and be reminded of the commandments of the Torah and that God is One.

Wearing a *Kippah*

Through Jewish history, our people have dressed in many different styles, usually choosing clothing like those living around them. We are not sure just where and when Jewish men began wearing the *kippah*, or *yarmulke* in Yiddish, as a head covering. We are not even certain when some Jews declared it necessary for Jewish men to be wearing a head covering for prayer or when it became expected that every male wear a *kippah* at all times, whether at work or at prayer.

What is clear from the study of Jewish customs is that the Torah does not command the wearing of a *kippah* and that there were many Jewish communities where men did not cover their heads for prayer. The leading Jewish teacher of the twelfth century, Moses Maimonides, declared that covering the head was a way of demonstrating respect for God. Later, others argued that by wearing a *kippah*, a man proudly acknowledged himself as a Jew. In other words, the *kippah* became a badge of Jewish identity.

In nineteenth-century Germany and America, many within the developing movement of Reform Judaism discarded the wearing of *tallit* and *kippah*.

Sensitive to the dress customs of non-Jews who actually removed their hats as a sign of reverence to God when they entered their churches, they chose to copy them within their synagogues.

Over the course of the last decades, however, Reform Jews have been making different choices. More males are choosing to wear a *kippah* while in prayer, study, or in the fulfillment of *mitzvah*. And what is true of males is also true of females. Increasing numbers of Reform, Conservative, and Reconstructionist Jewish women are also wearing *kippot*.

Why is this so? Why are so many Jews, men and women, choosing **to** wear a *tallit* and *kippah*? Ask some of the adult members of your congregation. Find out whether they wear their *kippah* at home, at work, just when they are celebrating a Jewish ritual, or only at synagogue. Ask how many carry a *kippah* with them in their pocket or purse. What can such a survey teach us about Jewish celebration and the way Jews identify with their people today?

Source: Rabbi Harvey J. Fields, *B'chol L'vavcha*, rev. ed. (New York: URJ Press, 2001; Reform Judaism Publishing/CCAR Press, 2015), 2–6.

Prayer

Source Texts

Genesis 28:10–18

[10]And Jacob left Beersheba and set out for Haran. [11]Coming upon a [certain] place, he passed the night there, for the sun was setting; taking one of the stones of the place, he made it his head-rest as he lay down in that place. [12]He dreamed, and lo—a ladder was set on the ground, with its top reaching to heaven, and lo—angels of God going up and coming down on it. [13]And lo—the Eternal stood up above it, and said, "I, the Eternal, am the God of your father Abraham and God of Isaac: the land on which you are lying I will give to you and your descendants. [14]And your descendants shall be like the dust of the earth, and you shall spread out to the west and the east and the north and the south. Through you and your descendants all the families of the earth shall find blessing. [15]And here I am, with you: I will watch over you wherever you go, and I will bring you back to this soil. I will not let go of you as long as I have yet to do what I have promised you."

[16]Waking from his sleep, Jacob said, "Truly, the Eternal is in this place, and I did not know it!" [17]He was awestruck, and said, "How awe-inspiring is this place! This is none other than the house of God, and this is the gate of heaven!"

[18]Rising early that morning, Jacob took the stone that he had put under his head and set it up as a monument. He then poured oil on its top.

Numbers 15:38–41

[38]Speak to the Israelite people and instruct them to make for themselves fringes on the corner of their garments throughout the ages; let them attach a cord of blue to the fringe at each corner. [39]That shall be your fringe; look at it and re-call all the commandments of the Eternal and observe them, so that you do not

follow your heart and eyes in your lustful urge. [40]Thus you shall be reminded to observe all My commandments and be holy to your God. [41]I the Eternal am your God, who brought you out of the land of Egypt to be your God: I, the Eternal your God.

Deuteronomy 6:4–7

[4]Hear, O Israel! The Eternal is our God, the Eternal alone. [5]You shall love the Eternal your God with all your heart, with all your soul, and with all your might. [6]Take to heart these instructions with which I charge you this day. [7]Impress them upon your children. Rwcite them when you stay at home and when you are away, when you lie down and when you get up.

I Samuel 1:1–18

[1]There was a certain man from Ramathaim, a Zuphite[a] from the hill country of Ephraim, whose name was Elkanah son of Jeroham, the son of Elihu, the son of Tohu, the son of Zuph, an Ephraimite. [2] He had two wives; one was called Hannah and the other Peninnah. Peninnah had children, but Hannah had none.[3]Year after year this man went up from his town to worship and sacrifice to God Almighty at Shiloh, where Hophni and Phinehas, the two sons of Eli, were priests of the Eternal. [4] Whenever the day came for Elkanah to sacrifice, he would give portions of the meat to his wife Peninnah and to all her sons and daughters. [5]But to Hannah he gave a double portion because he loved her, and Adonai had closed her womb. [6] Because Adonai had closed Hannah's womb, her rival kept provoking her in order to irritate her. [7] This went on year after year. Whenever Hannah went up to the house of the Eternal, her rival provoked her till she wept and would not eat. [8] Her husband Elkanah would say to her, "Hannah, why are you weeping? Why don't you eat? Why are you downhearted? Don't I mean more to you than ten sons?"[9] Once when they had finished eating and drinking in Shiloh, Hannah stood up. Now Eli the priest was sitting on his chair by the doorpost of God's house. [10] In her deep anguish Hannah prayed to God, weeping bitterly. [11] And she made a vow, saying, "God Almighty, if you will only look on your servant's misery and remember me, and not forget your servant but give her a son, then I will give him to Adonai for all the days of his life, and no razor will ever be used on his head."[12] As she kept on praying to God, Eli observed her mouth. [13] Hannah was praying in her heart, and her lips were moving but her voice was not heard. Eli thought she was drunk [14] and said to her, "How long

are you going to stay drunk? Put away your wine."[15] "Not so, my lord," Hannah replied, "I am a woman who is deeply troubled. I have not been drinking wine or beer; I was pouring out my soul to Adonai. [16] Do not take your servant for a wicked woman; I have been praying here out of my great anguish and grief." [17]Eli answered, "Go in peace, and may the God of Israel grant you what you have asked."[18] She said, "May your servant find favor in your eyes." Then she went her way and ate something, and her face was no longer downcast.

Mishnah B'rachot 1:2-3

From what time in the morning may the *Sh'ma* be recited? So soon as one can distinguish between blue and white. R. Eliezer says: Between blue and green. And it should be finished before sunrise. R. Joshua says: Before the third hour: for so is it the way of kings, to rise up at the third hour. He that recites it from that time onward suffers no loss and is like to one that reads in the Law.

The school of Shammai say: In the evening all should recline when they re-cite *Sh'ma*, but in the morning they should stand up, as it is written, *And when you lie down and when you rise up* (Deut. 6:7). But the School of Hillel say: They may recite it every one in their own way, as it is written, *And when you walk by the way* (Deuteronomy 6:7). Why then is it written, *And when you lie down and when you rise up?* [It means] the time when people usually lie down and the time when people usually rise up. . . .

Babylonian Talmud, *Taanit* 2a

"Love Adonai your God and serve God with all your heart and soul" (Deuter-onomy 11:13). What is the service of the heart? This is prayer.

Rashi on Numbers 15:39

The tzitzit reminds us of all of the commandments because the *g'matria* [numeri-cal value] of the word tzitzit is 600. In addition, there are 8 threads and 5 knots, which all together comprise 613.

Shulchan Aruch, Orach Chayim 98:1

One who prays needs to concentrate on the words he expressing, imagine that the Divine Presence is opposite him, and remove from his mind all distracting thoughts, so that he has a clear concentration and *kavanah*. As he would speak before an earthly king, organizing his words and considering them well, lest he stumble, how much more should he do this when standing before the King of kings, the Holy One, blessed be God, who probes all of our thoughts.

Jewish Music and Worship

Cantor Rosalie Boxt

It must certainly be the case that a Jewish worship service has existed—somewhere in time—without music. But we would be hard-pressed to imagine it. Every part of the service—even breathing, meditation, and reflection—is couched in music. The way Jews pray, even with an inexperienced musical leader, or even someone who does not have an "ear" or "voice," almost always has chanting, davening, a sing-song way of engaging the prayers of the liturgy. On any given Shabbat one can attend two different congregations and hear different melodies at each one, or be part of the same congregation week after week and hear significant variations in the repertoire. This musical diversity in our prayer service is truly a gift to us as a pray-ing people, for it provides us with rich opportunities for growth of soul and spirit.

New compositions, not just in current days, but through all time, are really a reflection of people who have had unique experiences of prayer and worship. They felt that the current repertory didn't express their own response to a given liturgical text. As a result, there are hundreds of settings to every liturgy (not the least of which Shabbat), as well as Psalms, wedding ceremonies, biblical and Talmudic sayings, and more. Just as with texts it makes intellectual sense to have so many different books on political leaders, or on child rearing, why not express our deep yearnings when we seek to connect with the Divine in multiple ways? As humans and individuals we each have "unique" experiences, view points, and ways of identifying with the world around us. Why not even more so for prayer, which is challenging on just about every level for most people? We are challenged in prayer if we aren't sure to What (if Anything) we are praying. Hebrew is not the native language for many Jews, and so we wonder what it all means or how the historical events described in worship fit in with our daily lives. Does it surprise us that Jews (and people of other faith backgrounds) have tried for generations to express their own prayer questions and feelings through new musical settings? Music has always been a natural response to deep questioning—a form of expression when conventional methods of inquisition are insufficient. Classical composers, folk singers, and pop performers frequently have the deep questions of life and the universe, of love and war at the center of their compositional motivation, if not actually articulated in a text. The creation of liturgical music is similar. If we can't imagine what the Exodus might have felt like, because it actually seems beyond our grasp, musical settings can express what we hope the experience might have felt like, which may be easier than explaining our theology of redemption. The spoken word can lock us into a commitment of belief, whereas music is more nuanced in the way it expresses the way we may or may not be feeling. When we sing, or experience music set to prayers or texts that are challenging, the ideas become more palatable, more relatable. This is not to say that music should become a cover for theological questioning. Rather, our liturgy is often set to music because, just as the music is diverse, so too is the invitation that our theologies, our yearnings, our confusion, our hopes can be diverse.

New settings are written not to replace, but to add, and thereby acknowledge that every person's experience is unique. Yes it is true that in a given service, we all sing along to one melody at a given moment, but sometimes the shifts that occur, the diversity of musical settings over repeated attendance, tap into more possible expressions of a prayer that speaks to us, that we didn't know we felt, until a particular music setting opens that part of our spirit-self that hadn't been opened before. To be sure, we cannot sing every setting of a single prayer in a given service, but the beauty of music in worship is that it expresses an experience that might not be ours alone in a given moment but that might be someone else's. This kind of openness can be powerful—someone else's experience can in fact be our own. The richness of these settings allows us a window into the soul of others with whom we walk the journey of Jewish life.

While this constant evolution of repertoire and an ever growing canon is not unique to Reform Judaism, it is in and of itself in line with the essence of Reform Judaism. For part of the richness of this way of living a Jewish life is how it connects us to the history and traditions, and weaves them into our search for meaningful expression. Therefore, when we share a liturgical text that is part of our canon, one that Jews in other communities also recite, but with a different melody, we are articulating this unique idea that there is not a singular expression, path, doorway into a religious life. Cantors are constantly asked if there are so many melodies because the cantor is bored; but if you ask any members of a worshiping community which setting of a certain powerful text (a prayer for peace, the joy of celebrating Shabbat) they are drawn to, all will have a different opinion—and perhaps a different idea depending upon how they felt on the given Shabbat at which they attended services. Each melody provides a window into a possible liturgical experience—be it a connection to the Divine, or to the community, or to joy, or through hope. The hope is that new melodies continue to help each person in our communities move even deeper into their own sense of prayer and spirit through worship.

The music that comes from different parts of the world, as well as repertoire that is rooted in different musical genres, helps people already rooted in a given community appreciate the diversity of the Jewish world at large, and perhaps even the diversity within our own communal midst. Much of this music has reached us from across the Diaspora, when Jews from other lands have immigrated to America. These styles are specific to the cultures in which those Jews lived previous to their move to North America and cultural relationships created in those countries of origin (such as *Mizrachi*, or Middle Eastern sounds – influenced by North Africa and Iraq, or Latin American sounds and rhythms). Melodies like *Ein "K'Eloheinu/Non Komo Muestro Dio"* (with Hebrew and Ladino) and or *"Et Dodim"* from Israel, brought by many Argentinian and Israeli cantors and musicians, or *"Elohei Oz"* (a healing song) from Bagdad via Calcutta, have opened our ears and our bodies to new syncopations, non-Western counting forms, and different harmonization. By expressing this international diversity in the liturgical selections within worship, we are reminded that the story of the Jewish people is not linear, monolithic, and singular of experience, but instead one that has traveled many streams and offshoots, becoming part of the tapestry of who we (all) are. When texts which we often imagine must be *miSinai* (from Sinai itself) are paired with a melody that seems wholly foreign, it might seem surprising in the moment, but at the same time, it illuminates and connects us to the generations of Jews all over the world who sang the same songs of freedom, of yearning, of Torah but with utterly different tonality, rhythm, and sensibility. We are no longer a completely Ashkenazic Jewry, here in North America—we may know this intellectually to be sure. To be faced with it, or, more specifically, to hear it in the words and music of our liturgy, we are reminded anew of our brethren from all corners of the globe.

The Jews and Jewish music that have influenced our repertory have not only come from lands across the seas, they have come from within these North American borders as well. Jews of color, Jews by choice, and non-Jews alike who have rich musical and prayer traditions to share have brought the soundtracks of their lives into our synagogues and communities, adding to the rich tapestry of the music we have to choose from for worship moments.

All this music opens doorways to those who are just beginning to step over the threshold. As many seekers, or those searching for a spiritual home, usually attend worship in order to figure out what a given congregation is about, the music in worship can say a lot about who prays there and what prayer means to that group. Music that expresses the richness of different cultures and different styles serves to welcome and invite those who maybe do not see themselves as the antiquated, stereotypical model of "Jewish." This growing cohort includes Jews of color, Jews from the Middle East, as well as those who were not born Jewish. When people hear the music of their ancestors or their upbringing in the context of worship and prayer, which is already very challenging, perhaps they are more willing to take further steps to learn and explore their own spirituality. But if the service and music does not remind them of their own experience, or does not seem to say "you are part of the story that we are telling," they are less likely to want to continue to write their story with us.

Our synagogue communities encourage participation from all kinds of individuals. For decades we have invited, encouraged, even sought families where one partner is not Jewish, and as other authors in this volume have noted, this has had a real positive impact on our Reform community. And yet, if the music, chanting, expression of our prayers was held firm in all Hebrew or a musical mode that was familiar or accessible only to those raised Jewish and who grew up attending synagogue, I suspect a significant portion of our communities would truly struggle. Rabbi Rick Jacobs, the President of the Union for Reform Judaism, has shown time and time again, when gathering a group of synagogue presidents, that the majority of them were not Reform Jews before adulthood. They were from other faith backgrounds or came from Conservative, or Orthodox, or unaffiliated congregations. If our presidents, the most active and committed members of our synagogues, did not grow up knowing the same "traditional" (read, 1950s melody) tunes, why would we imagine that our congregations are made up solely of folks who come from similar "traditionally Reform" upbringing?

The challenge for our congregations and worship leaders is of making a connection between the changing nature of the members of our community, with the changing nature of the music they might experience in worship. The influence of rhythm instruments, of English, of melodies that come from a hymnal or an African American spiritual of freedom, is not the invention of music leaders! Instead, it is a response to, and influence of, the growing diversity of our Reform community. There is something very powerful in witnessing the relaxing of features, or slight movement of bodily engagement when a member of the congregation recognizes a melody of *his* childhood. When someone hears the story of *her* people being expressed in the musical style of a prayer that until then she couldn't quite understand or find her way into, the communal worship is made richer and the individual's prayer life made more meaningful.

New melodies are being written every day. Composers, pray-ers, members of congregations are continually inspired by our texts and by their experiences to create new settings to share new ideas. The more Jewish music is seen as integral to the worship experience, the more people who experience it are subsequently moved to compose. In the last decade plus, hundreds of people, young and old, have been setting liturgy in new ways. We have new compositions that blend Hebrew and new English interpretations, or storytelling, or spoken word/rap within. Some music is composed with oud or mandolin or slide-guitar. We have acapella groups writing liturgy and teens finding their voice through the expression of new music, to "old" prayers. With access to technology, new music can be recorded and shared instantly—which creates fast access, and sometimes an overwhelming volume of new music. Only twenty years ago we had to wait for a publishing company to make a CD or a songbook to learn what the new sounds were. Now we have instant access. Some melodies may move one person and never move another. Some melodies may move all of us at one time or another, but never at the same moment. Liturgical music can evolve as we evolve—as each of us experiences prayer anew each day, each week—so too can the melodies of those prayers express those ever shifting emotions.

At the core of this discussion of music and worship, is the prayer service. The values of the community, why members of a given group pray the way they do, and how the worship leaders and community agree to embark on this prayer business together are central. Decisions about music used for liturgical expression, to elevate a moment, or to highlight a text have to be based in a clear vision of what the point of a given prayer moment is at a given time in a service.

Communicating values and ideas is central to Reform Judaism and our religious practice. We have shown a passionate commitment, most significantly through the publication of new prayer books, to being intentional (and constantly growing, making mistakes, and growing again) about language and inclusion, about engaging our sacred texts in living dialogue. How much the more so should our music do the same! Why would our texts evolve, and our liturgy adapt as we recognize an ever changing communal makeup—and our music not grow and struggle right along with it?

Some worship leaders may consider "diversity" of music style to mean the creating of intentionally "eclectic" services, which show in their attention to many modalities (Cantor Benjie Ellen Schiller taught us to consider the four 'M's of prayer: meditation, majesty, memory, meeting) that prayer can and should express multiple yearnings of the soul. For example, music of meeting will allow the congregation to connect to each other, through communal singing accessible to all, whereas music of majesty takes our hearts away from the interpersonal and toward the Universe beyond our knowing, which we might experience with a soaring piece of music, or a spoken word/music underscore moment. Music of memory may be the "traditional" or "old war horse" tunes, and music of meditation are moments that lend themselves to quieting the breath, reflection, and peace. And these moments should all find their place in the prayer life of a community. But perhaps each form might not need to exist in every service. We run the risk of getting stuck in a fragmented worship experience if we attempt to ensure that the Jew from abroad, the Jew of color, the person of another faith background, and the Orthodox-raised Jew all have a "moment" in the service. This serves neither the worship nor the worshipper. While as individuals we might hope that every moment speaks to us personally, the joy and tension of communal prayer is giving over some of the desire for expected comfort in all moments, to the knowledge that those around us are moved by what they are experiencing.

The need for an expansive sense of how our Jewish musical repertory can be used need not be prescriptive; each community will create its own soundtrack to prayer. The richness of our musical tradition is that there are so many settings to evoke so many aspects of prayer. We can intentionally widen our understanding of Jewish music and prayer to include the sounds of our community that we may not have always considered, particularly as some within our community still consider themselves (if not intentionally, in language) "Ashkenazi." Our worship music repertoire now contains the rhythms and sounds of Argentinian Jews (part of our story for many years), Yemenite Jews, and Jews of color, as well as the influences they bring from cultural or communal pieces of their identity, melodies rooted in the secular or Christian musical traditions, Ladino, contemporary Israeli … the list goes on. Worship leaders are now able to create an environment where not only can their community be exposed to and enriched by the prayer expression from other communities or new voices, but those within our own communities, or who perhaps stand in the doorway peeking in, believing they can hear, feel, and sense that they too belong.

Source: Cantor Rosalie Boxt, "Jewish Music and Worship," from *A Life of Meaning: Embracing Reform Judaism's Sacred Path* (New York: CCAR Press, 2018)

The Order of Prayer

RABBI HARVEY J. FIELDS

Birchot HaShachar and *P'sukei D'zimrah*
Benedictions of Praise
Elohai N'shamah: The Soul That You Have Given
Nisim B'chol Yom: Miracles Every Day Of Courage and Truthfulness
Baruch She-amar: Praised Be the Eternal One and Praised Be Them Who
Praise the Eternal One
Psalms 100 and 135
Nishmat: The Soul of Everything That Lives

Sh'ma
Bar'chu: The Call to Worship *Yotzer:* Creator of Light
Ahavah Rabbah: Deep Love *Sh'ma:* Hear, O Israel
V'ahavta: You Shall Love *G'ulah:* Redemption

Amidah
Avot: Ancestors *G'vurot:* God's Power
K'dushah: Sactification
K'dushat HaYom: Sanctification of the Day
Avodah: Worship
Hodaah: Thanksgiving
Birkat Shalom: Blessing of Peace
Elohai N'tzor

K'riat HaTorah
  At the Ark
  Taking the Torah from the Ark
  The *Aliyah* and the Torah Service
  The Haftarah Blessings
  The New Month
  Honoring the Torah

Siyum HaAvodah
  The *Aleinu*
  The *Kaddish*
  Adon Olam
  Ein Keiloheinu
  Yigdal
  Kiddush for Shabbat Day

Source: Rabbi Harvey J. Fields, *B'chol L'vavcha*, rev. ed. (New York: URJ Press, 2001; Reform Judaism Publishing/CCAR Press, 2015), xxii.

Praying With Others

RABBI JEFFREY W. GOLDWASSER

A religious and faithful Jew is one who lives in *yirat shamayim*, "Reverence for Heaven," and *ahavat HaShem*, "Love of God." A faithful Jew is one whose deepest loyalty is in the eternal values of our tradition and one who finds greatest fulfillment in a connection to the source of our being.

There are things we do to affirm that internal experience through external action. One of the most obvious is prayer.

When we pray, we attempt to put our experience of life's ultimate meaning into words. The only prayer that cannot work is one that is made with an empty heart. As our tradition teaches, "If a person makes prayer a merely rote recitation, it is not a true entreaty to God" (*Mishnah B'rachot* 4:4).

In Jewish tradition, the ideal way to pray is with others. The experience of praying together reminds us that our relationship to God is communal. By connecting to God as a community, we rediscover that being "religious" is something that we can all share, regardless of our individual choices, beliefs, and observance.

Source: Rabbi Jeffrey W. Goldwasser, in *Lights in the Forest: Rabbis Respond to Twelve Essential Jewish Questions*, ed. Rabbi Paul Citron (New York: CCAR Press 2014), 176.

Building a Holy Network

RABBI EVAN MOFFIC

In Judaism, it does not make sense to say, "I have faith in God." Rather, it makes sense to say, "I live with faithfulness to God." Judaism is not a set of propositions. It is a way of life. To be religious is to follow, as best one can, the way of life set forth in the Torah and lived by hundreds of generations of the Jewish people.

Prayer is one of the ways we live out the Jewish way of life. First, it is a statement of principles. Reciting the Pledge of Allegiance or singing the national anthem is a way we express a dedication to American ideals. Similarly, praying is a way we express a commitment to Jewish tradition. Second, it is a concrete way of expressing our faithfulness to the Jewish way of life. We pray not only to find comfort. We pray not only to express gratitude. We pray because it is part of the definition of Jewish living set forth in Torah and Jewish tradition. This approach to prayer helps us understand why it is imperative to pray as part of a community. We cannot be Jewish all alone.

Consider this teaching from Maimonides: "The prayer of the community is always heard. . . . Hence a person must join with the community, and should not pray alone so long as one is able to pray with the community" (*Mishneh Torah*, Laws of Prayer 8:1).

This may seem rather strange at first. Why should God care whether a person is praying alone or as part of a larger group? Does the number of people change the nature or content of one's prayer?

My sense is that the number of people may not concern God, but it should concern us. When we worship as part of a larger group, we feel part of something larger. Our words connect us to those around us, helping us understand our interdependence and our responsibility to our community.

Several years ago, Rabbi Larry Kushner wrote a beautiful book called *Invisible Lines of Connection*. When I pray and look around at the community that surrounds me, I imagine all of those invisible lines of connection that link us to one another and to God. Those threads build a holy network and lift each of us a little higher.

Source: Rabbi Evan Moffic, in *Lights in the Forest: Rabbis Respond to Twelve Essential Jewish Questions*, ed. Rabbi Paul Citron (New York: CCAR Press, 2014), 198–199.

Communal Prayer

Rabbi Rachel S. Mikva

When I was a congregational rabbi, I used to take fifth graders and their families away on retreat in the spring. Frequently the weekly Torah reading was *K'doshim* which contains the charge "You shall be holy, for I, *YHVH* your God, am holy" (Leviticus 19:2)—and before we read the text, I asked participants to describe a holy person. Invariably, they responded with models they knew from Christian contexts: monastics who leave mainstream society to live out their days in prayer and contemplation or who dedicate themselves to lives of poverty in their service to the suffering. After reading parts of Leviticus 19, however, they revised their portrait: ordinary people who honor their parents, make Shabbat, generously share their blessings, are scrupulous in business, model profound integrity and a capacity for forgiveness, are careful not to speak ill of others, guard the rights of the laborer and the stranger, and so forth.

Torah transformed their expectations by offering a model of Jewish religiosity that invests the details of our daily lives with the potential for holiness. Most important is the idea that the person of faith is not "someone else," not the person who does religion professionally, not the more observant Jew, not the evangelical Christian who talks about God all the time—but you.

Ritual and ethical in form, conscious and unconscious in execution, every time you respond to the call of the covenant you are a person of faith. In theory, it does not require communal prayer any more than other avenues of response. But I can tell you this: I struggled with finding a spiritual home once I entered academia, so after twenty years of a regular prayer life, I now daven relatively infrequently. I still study sacred texts and teach them in religious contexts; I still

419

observe Shabbat and festivals, keep kosher, and work for social justice; I still try with every decision I make to become the human being God created me to be. But my relationship with God and with the Jewish community, my capacities for critique of self and empathy for others, the depth of my *kavanah*, "intention," and my commitment—all have become attenuated. Communal prayer is the spiritual discipline that develops religious muscles and sharpens the vision of faith.

Source: Rabbi Rachel S. Mikva, in *Lights in the Forest: Rabbis Respond to Twelve Essential Jewish Questions*, ed. Rabbi Paul Citrin (New York: CCAR Press, 2014), 193–194.

Creating New Prayers-
A Controversy: Old and New

RABBI HARVEY J. FIELDS

Should we use prayers written by others or only those we have composed ourselves? Should we use a prayer book that gives us a fixed order for prayer or create
our own order of worship each time we wish to pray?

Can a congregation exist without some order of service that it uses each time
it comes together for prayer? Does a congregation need its own special fixed
prayers, as a nation needs its own special anthems, in order to express feelings
of unity and common concern?

Which is better, fixed or spontaneous prayer?

These are not new questions. The issue of whether prayers should be fixed or
spontaneous was hotly debated by the Rabbis of the Talmud over two thousand
years ago. And the debate was never really resolved. In almost every age the controversy has continued between those who wanted a fixed prayer book and those
who preferred newly created prayers.

Today, the debate is as alive as ever. All you have to do is ask a group of
people which they prefer, fixed or spontaneous prayer, and the side will quickly
be drawn. Below are some of the arguments on each side of the debate. In other
places on the next pages you will find quotations from Jewish sources that record
the variety of opinions on the issue. How do you think we can resolve the debate
within our own congregation? What rules ought to be followed in our debate
and why? How shall we make change and preserve our congregation?

Arguments for Fixed Prayer

1. We are a congregation, and in order for us to feel a sense of unity with one another, we need to use the same words. The more we share, the closer we will feel.

2. If we wait until we feel like composing a prayer, we might never pray or we might lose the ability to pray. Prayer demands the discipline of regular practice and the same words if we are to be successful at it.

TWO THOUGHTS

Change not the fixed form in which the Sages wrote the prayers.

—Talmud

Be not rash with your mouth, and let your heart not be hasty to utter a word before God.

—Ecclesiastes 5:1

---

3. Not all of us are great poets or writers. It is silly not to make use of the outstanding poetry and prayers of our tradition that have been tested by time and many generations. They can express our feelings better than we ourselves can.

4. When we use prayers composed by Jews throughout our history, we identify ourselves with the traditions and generations of our people. When we pray with the same prayers used by Jews throughout the world, we feel at one with our people no matter where they are. Fixed prayer insures the unity of the Jewish people.

5. Often when an individual composes a prayer, it is self-centered and expresses only selfish concerns. Fixed Jewish prayer is concerned with the welfare of the community and has been carefully written so as to avoid selfish, fleeting needs.

6. The Rabbis teach us that a person should not be hasty to utter a word before God. That temptation is eliminated by fixed prayer. Spontaneous prayer is often hastily and carelessly composed. Prayer ought to be written with concentration by individuals possessing great skill. Fixed prayer fulfills this requirement.

7. Spontaneous prayer causes confusion among the worshipers. The talmudic sage Rabbi Zeira once said: "Every time I added new words to my prayers, I became confused and lost my place." Such confusion takes away from the beauty and meaning of the prayer experience. A fixed order of worship solves this problem.

8. Beautiful prayers, like great poetry, never lose their meaning through repetition. The more we read them with open minds and hearts, the more meanings we can discover. The cure for dull prayer experiences is in us, not in the creation of new prayers.

Arguments for Spontaneous Prayer

1. While the fixed prayers may be beautiful, after you have said them over and over again, they become dull and repetitive, and they lose their meaning. The Rabbis recognized this, and in the Mishnah they tell us: "Do not let your prayers be a matter of fixed routine but rather heartfelt expressions."

2. Spontaneous prayer allows us to express our feelings, hopes, and concerns. If we are bound by a fixed text, we are prevented from making our worship as personally meaningful as it should be. The Bratzlaver Rebbe, a leading teacher of Chasidism, once said to his students: "You must feel your words of prayer in all your bones, in all your limbs, and in all your nerves." When we use our own prayers, we feel deeply about that for which we are praying.

3. We are not machines, and we can't be programmed to be in the same mood as everyone else at the same time. Spontaneous prayer allows us the freedom to express our true feelings in the moment we pray.

4. We should not forget that the fixed prayers of tradition were once spontaneous expressions of individuals and their communities. Throughout Jewish history, Jews have been composing new prayers and adding them to the prayer book. We need to continue that creative process, for it has helped keep Jewish prayer meaningful and even added to the survival of Judaism.

5. In every generation our people has faced new problems and challenges. These should be expressed in our prayers. Obviously, if we are bound to a fixed text or style of prayer, we cannot include contemporary issues or forms in our worship.

Rabbinic Opinions

Only that person's prayer is answered who lifts his hands with his heart in them.

—*BT Taanit 8a*

Rabbi Eliezer said: If a person prays only according to the exact fixed prayer and adds nothing from his own mind, that prayer is not considered proper.

—*BT B'rachot 28a*

Rabbi Abahu would add a new prayer to his worship every day.

Rabbi Acha in the name of Rabbi Yosei said: It is necessary to add new words to the fixed prayers each time they are recited.

—*BT B'rachot 4a*

Creating New Prayers

The controversy over fixed and spontaneous prayer continues in our own day. There are those who oppose any changes either in the order of Jewish worship or in any of the traditionaJ prayers. Others favor innovation and the creation of new prayers and worship experiences. *B'chol L'vavcha* attempts to compromise between the two positions. It combines the order and prayers of our tradition with new prayers and invites us to create our own expressions.

Source: Rabbi Harvey J. Fields, *B'chol L'vavcha*, rev. ed. (New York: URJ Press, 2001; Reform Judaism Publishing/CCAR Press, 2015), 7–9.

Sacred Texts

Source Texts

Mishnah Avot 1:1

Moses received the Torah from Sinai and committed it to Joshua, and Joshua to the elders, and the elders to the prophets; and the prophets committed it to the men of the Great Synagogue. They said three things: Be deliberate in judgment, raise up many disciples, and make a fence around the Torah.

Source: Rabbi Bernard J. Bamberger, "The Torah and the Jewish People," in *The Torah: A Modern Commentary*, rev. ed., ed. Rabbi W. Gunther Plaut (New York: URJ Press, 2005; Reform Judaism Publishing/CCAR Press, 2015), li.

Jewish Sacred Texts Timeline

TORAH (FIVE BOOKS OF MOSES)	Canonized 450 BCE	
	Canonized 440 BCE	N'VIIM
KETUVIM	Canonized 100 BCE	
	Compiled 220 CE	MISHNAH
JERUSALEM TALMUD	Canonized 400 CE	
	Canonized 620 CE	BABYLONIAN TALMUD
MIDRASH AND AGGADAH	Written from 400 CE onward	
	From 650 CE onward	RESPONSA
RASHI'S COMMENTARIES	Written 11th–12th Century CE	
	Written 12th–13th Century CE	TOSAFOT
MAIMONIDES' MISHNEH TORAH AND GUIDE TO THE PERPLEXED	Written 12th Century CE	
	First Appearance 13th Century CE	THE ZOHAR
SHULKAN ARUKH— JOSEPH CARO (WITH COMMENTARY BY MOSES ISSERLES)	Written 1565 CE	

The Torah and the Jewish People

RABBI BERNARD J. BAMBERGER

The Torah was always the possession of all Israel. It was addressed to the entire people, who were to learn its contents and teach them diligently to their children. A number of biblical passages, in particular Psalms 19 and 119, testify to the love that the Torah evoked and the widespread concern of the people with its teachings.

The Book of Nehemiah (chs. 8-10) reports a public reading of the Torah in Jerusalem, probably in the year 444 B.C.E. This reading was conducted by Ezra the Scribe, with the aid of assistants who were to make sure that all those present heard and understood what was read to them. A few days later, the entire people entered into a solemn undertaking to obey the Torah; and this agreement was ratified in writing by the leaders. From the traditional standpoint, this incident was a reaffirmation of the covenant at Sinai. But many modern scholars explain the event as marking the completion of the written Torah in substantially its present form and its adoption as the official "constitution" of the Jewish community.

The Torah and the Synagogue

We do not know exactly where, how, or when the synagogue came into existence; it must have been some time between 500 and 200 B.C.E. From the start, one of the principal activities of the synagogue was the public reading and exposition of the Torah. A portion was read every Sabbath. But there were farmers who lived in scattered communities, too for from a synagogue to travel to it on the Sabbath. That they might not be deprived of hearing the sacred word, a Torah passage was read in the synagogues each Monday and Thursday— the market days when the country-folk came to town to sell their produce. This custom survives to the present in the traditional synagogues.

The reading of the Torah portion in Hebrew was often followed by a translation, in Greek or Aramaic, for the benefit of those who did not understand the original. It is out of such translation or paraphrase, in all probability, that the sermon arose. This explains why the sermon was normally based on the Torah reading of the week.

From an early date, the instruction of children was associated with the synagogue. The effectiveness of its educational program, for young and old, was fully recognized by the enemies of Judaism. When the Syrian King Antiochus IV wished to break down Jewish solidarity and hasten the assimilation of Jews into Hellenistic society, he not only forbade the practice of Jewish ritual but also prohibited the reading and teaching of the Torah, on pain of death. But the decrees could not be enforced.

Similarly, the Roman Emperor Hadrian, after he finally put down the Jewish revolt in 135 C.E., proscribed all those who persisted in teaching the Torah. It was then that the aged Rabbi Akiba defied the edict and suffered death by torture. The Torah, he declared in a famous talmudic parable, is Israel's natural element, as water is the natural element of the fish. In water the fish is exposed to many dangers, but out of water it is sure to perish at once (Ber. 1b).

The Oral Torah

Thus far we have used the word Torah with reference to the Five Books. But some kind of commentary was always needed. A sacred text, and especially one containing laws and commandments, must be interpreted and applied to the concrete situations of life. Those who proposed to make the Torah the rule of their life found many provisions that required more exact definition. The Torah, for example, forbids work on Sabbath; but what precisely constitutes work, and what activities are permissible? Again, the Torah speaks of divorce (Deut. 24:1 ff.) but does not make clear the grounds for divorce. And on many important subjects—the method of contracting a marriage, real estate law, the prayers in the synagogue, to name a few—the written Torah gives no guidance at all.

Such problems generated the concept of the oral Torah, in part explanation and elaboration of the written Torah, in part supplement to the latter. This oral Torah was not created consciously to meet the need of a certain time. Much of it was no doubt derived from established legal precedents and from popular custom and tradition. Once, however, the process of applying the law to new situations was undertaken in earnest, the material grew rapidly.

For a long time this was literally oral Torah; it was deemed improper to put down in writing what Moses had not written down at God's command. Only much later was it found necessary to compile this material in the Mishnah and other works of talmudic literature. But it was generally agreed that the entire body of oral Torah was also given to Moses at Sinai. It was to learn this vast corpus of teaching that Moses remained on the mountain forty days and nights.

The teachers of the oral Torah were drawn chiefly from the laity (that is, non-priests) who are known to us as the Pharisees. From about the year 100 C.E. on, accredited teachers bore the title of rabbi. These teachers were opposed by a conservative party, made up mostly of priests, known as the Sadducees. They denied the validity of oral tradition and regarded the written text alone as authoritative. They interpreted the commandments in a strict literalist fashion. Perhaps it was this opposition that led the Pharisees to devise the method of midrash, in order to find some support in Scripture for their oral teachings. The Midrash uses a free, creative, and—let us admit—often farfetched method of biblical interpretation. In expounding legal passages—what the Rabbis called halachah—the teachers were subject to some rules and restrictions in the use of midrash. But it was applied with virtually unlimited freedom to non-legal materials—to the ethical, theological, and folkloristic subject matter known as *aggadah* or *haggadah*. Many beautiful examples of midrash are to be found in this commentary, especially in the sections headed "Gleanings." (The word "midrash" is used in three ways: to apply to a method in general, to a single instance of the method, and to literary works in which the method is employed.)

For rabbinic Jews, the written Torah was understood in accordance with the interpretation of the oral Torah, just as in modern law a written statute means what the courts interpret it to mean. The commandment "eye for eye, tooth for tooth" (Exod. 21:24) meant that one who injures another must pay money damages to the victim. "You shall not boil a kid in its mother's milk" (Exod. 23:19) was taken to prohibit the cooking or eating of any kind of meat with milk or milk products. Similarly, people did not always differentiate between biblical stories and their aggadic elaborations.

Though the growth of the oral Torah, later written down in the Talmud, obscured the plain sense of Scripture in many instances, it was a force for progress that enriched Judaism. Beginning in the 8th century C.E., a countertrend appeared in Persia and spread widely. The rebels against talmudic Judaism were called Karaites (Scripturalists). Returning to the Sadducean position, they proposed to live strictly by the simple word of the written Torah. But this program was not easy to carry out. The Karaites disputed bitterly among themselves as to the proper interpretation of many commandments. Moreover, many rabbinic modifications of scriptural law were both reasonable and humane, and to reject them meant turning the clock back—always a futile undertaking.

Christian and Moslem Views

The Christian apostle Paul, himself a Jew by birth, proposed in his writings a new view of the Torah. Its innumerable commandments, he held, constitute an overwhelming burden; no one can ever fulfill them properly. The "Law," in fact, was given by God to make us conscious of our sinfulness, that we may despair of attaining salvation by our own strivings. Now, Paul taught, salvation is available through faith in the crucified and risen Jesus; the "Law" has served its purpose, and, for Christian believers, it is abrogated (Romans 7:8; Galatians 2:15-3:14). This view has profoundly influenced Christian thought, though the churches rarely adopted Paul's teaching in its radical form and usually asserted the validity of the ethical laws of the Pentateuch (cf. Matthew 5:17-20; 19:18 f.).

In contrast to, and perhaps in reply to, the Pauline doctrine, Jewish teachers insisted on the continuing authority of the Torah and on its beneficent character. "The blessed Holy One desired to confer merit on Israel; that is why they were given a voluminous Torah and many commandments" (Mishnah Makkot, end). Failure to obey the Torah fully does not result in damnation; rather it calls for repentance (return) and a fresh start.

Christian teachers through the centuries found in the Torah—and indeed the entire Hebrew Bible—many passages that they interpreted as prophecies of the career and the messianic (or divine) character of Jesus of Nazareth. In the past, Jewish spokesmen had to devote much time and effort to refuting these christological interpretations. Today, however, such views have been discarded by competent Christian scholars.

Centuries later, Mohammed, founder of the third monotheistic religion, was to call the Jews also "the people of the Book" because their religion was founded on Scripture. He did not know the book at first hand, or even in translation, for he never learned to read, but in his contacts with Jews and Christians he acquired a sketchy knowledge of biblical narratives with their aggadic embellishments.

To these stories he occasionally alludes in the Koran (some selections will be found in the Gleanings). The Koran, which records the revelations received by the prophet, holds a position in Islam similar to that of the Torah in Judaism. It is supplemented by a tradition analogous to the oral Torah.[1]

The Middle Ages

In its wanderings, Judaism encountered many new constellations of ideas. Sometimes these novelties were rejected by Jewish thinkers; but often they were accepted as compatible with Judaism. In such cases an effort was made to show that these ideas were already suggested in Scripture.

The first exemplar using this method was Philo of Alexandria, who lived at the beginning of the Christian era. A devout Jew, Philo was deeply influenced by Plato and the Stoics; and so he was led to "discover" the ideas of the philosophers in the text of the Torah. For Philo, the biblical word veiled deeper meanings and had to be explained allegorically. (For instance, Sarah symbolizes divine wisdom, her handmaid Hagar typifies secular learning.) The Jewish philosophers of the Middle Ages also employed allegorical interpretations, though with more restraint. They used this method to deal with Bible passages that appeared to contradict reason or morality, especially those describing God in human terms. Such authors as Saadia, Maimonides, and Ibn Ezra frequently found sophisticated philosophic concepts in the biblical text.

Still more extreme were the methods of the mystics. "We possess an authentic tradition," wrote Rabbi Moses ben Nachman (Nachmanides), "that the entire Torah consists of the names of God, in that the words may be redivided to yield a different sense, consisting of the names." In general, the Kabbalists found cryptic meanings in the words and letters of Scripture, without any reference to the meaning of the text as a coherent whole. The Zohar, the chief work of the Kabbalah, is a vast mystical midrash on the Torah; and many Kabbalists, and later on Chasidim, wrote their mystical treatises in the form of commentaries on the Pentateuch.

Ultimately the view emerged that there are four ways to expound the Torah, each valid in its own area: the rabbinic midrash, the philosophical implication (*remez*), and the mystical arcanum (*sod*), in addition to the plain meaning (*p'shat*).[2]

In the Middle Ages, in fact, Jews recovered an awareness of the literal meaning of Scripture. This trend away from midrash to a simpler exegesis may have been stimulated by the Karaite revolt. The first great exponent of the *p'shat* was Rav Saadia Gaon, the outstanding critic of Karaism. He was followed by a distinguished school of grammarians and commentators in Moslem Spain, who developed a genuinely scientific approach to the Hebrew language and to textual studies. These scholars wrote chiefly in Arabic; their findings were made accessible to the Hebrew-reading public by Abraham ibn Ezra, who hailed from Spain, and the Provencal Hebraists Joseph and David Kimchi.

Meanwhile another school of biblical scholars appeared independently in northern France; they were more traditionalist, less systematic and philosophic than the Spaniards, but they displayed a keen sense for niceties of language and for the spirit of the Bible. The outstanding production of this school is the Torah commentary of Rashi (Rabbi Solomon Itzchaki of Troyes), the most popular commentary ever written in Hebrew. Its popularity was due both to the clarity of Rashi's style and to the fact that he combined the exposition of the plain sense with a judicious selection of attractive midrashim, legal and nonlegal. His successors, however, concentrated more and more on the *p'shat*.

The last of the great medieval expositors, Moses ben Nachman, despite his mystical tendencies, also offered original and independent comments on the plain sense. He and his predecessors had no difficulty with the fact that their simple exegesis sometimes contradicted biblical interpretations given in talmudic literature. In nonlegal matters there was no problem, since the aggadists gave many diverse explanations of the same verse. On halachic matters, these writers accepted the talmudic expositions for practical legal purposes but noted that, according to the rules of grammar, a given verse might be understood differently.

These medieval exegetes (and others we have not mentioned) made a permanently valuable contribution to the understanding of the biblical text. Though many other Hebrew commentaries on the Torah were written between the 14th and 19th centuries, they added little that was new. Only in the last two hundred years have new resources been available to broaden our understanding of Scripture; at the same time, new problems have arisen for the modern Bible reader.

The Torah Scroll

By the 7th century C.E., Hebrew manuscripts, including portions of the Bible, were being written in the form of books—that is, a number of pages fastened together along one edge. We have many manuscripts of the Hebrew Bible of this sort; they are usually provided with vowel signs and with the punctuation indicating both sentence structure and the traditional chant. It is on such vocalized manuscripts that our printed Hebrew Bibles are based.

For ceremonial use in the synagogue, however, Jews have continued to employ Torah manuscripts in the more ancient scroll form. Each scroll is made up of numerous sheets of parchment, stitched together to make a continuous document, which is attached at either end to a wooden roller. The public reading of the Torah, to this day, is from such a scroll *(Sefer Torah)*, containing only the consonantal text, without vowel points or punctuation, written on parchment with a vivid black ink. Tradition prescribes many details concerning the Sefer Torah—the beginning and end of paragraphs, the arrangement of certain poetic passages in broken instead of solid lines, the care of the scroll, the correction of mistakes, even the spiritual preparation of the scribe.

A synagogue usually possesses several scrolls. In ancient times they were kept in a chest (Hebrew *tevah* or *aron)*, which was placed by the wall of the synagogue, generally on the side nearest Jerusalem. In many early synagogues this "ark" stood in a niche, before which, in some cases, a curtain was hung. In modern synagogues the ark is usually a built-in recess, with a shelf for the scrolls; it is closed either by a curtain or by ornamental doors of wood or metal.

The removal of the scroll from the ark to the pulpit for reading and its return to the ark after the reading constitute a ceremony of considerable pomp, including the singing of processional melodies and demonstrations of respect and affection on the part of the congregants. When the ark is opened, and especially when the Sefer Torah is carried in procession, everyone stands.

The reverence and love evoked by the scroll is expressed in its outward adornments. Eastern ("Oriental") and Sephardic Jews generally keep the scroll in a hinged metal or wooden case, often handsomely painted or carved, from which the ends of the rollers project. The scroll remains upright in the case while it is open on the reading desk, and it may be rolled to a new passage without removing it from this receptacle. When it is closed, the upper rollers are often adorned with artistic metal finials (called *rimonim*, "pomegranates"). In most European and American congregations, however, the scroll, after being fastened with a band of some woven material, is covered with a robe of silk or velvet, through which the top rollers protrude. It may be decorated with a silver (or other metal) breastplate *(tas)* as well as with *rimonim*. Sometimes a single crown covers both wooden uprights. Eastern and Western Jews alike use a pointer *(yad,* literally "hand"), most often of silver, which the reader uses to track the place in the scroll.

Some congregations, chiefly Sephardic, attach a silk or other woven strip to the outside of the parchment, which is rolled with the scroll to provide additional protection.

The Public Reading

It is customary to read from the scroll during every Sabbath and festival morning service, as well as on Monday and Thursday mornings. At the Saturday afternoon service *(minchah)*, part of the following week's portion is read. There is no Torah reading on holy day afternoons, with the exception of the Day of Atonement and certain other fast days.

For centuries dating back to ancient times, the Jews of the Levant completed the reading of the entire Torah twice in seven years.[3] (This is commonly referred to—somewhat inaccurately—as a "triennial" cycle.) We know, for the most part, how the text was divided into sections for this purpose; but scholars disagree as to when in the year the Levantine cycle began and ended.

Babylonian-influenced congregations, however, adapted the older cycle in order to read through the entire Torah each year, and their custom ultimately became standard. It was the Babylonian Jews who created the festival of Simchat Torah, rejoicing over the Torah. On this day, all the scrolls of the congregation are carried around the synagogue in joyous procession; the closing section of Deuteronomy is read from one *sefer*, and then the first section of Genesis is read from another.

For the annual cycle, the Torah is divided into fifty-four sections, called *s'darot*. They are read consecutively, starting with the Sabbath following Simchat Torah. To complete the reading in a year, two sections must be read on certain Sabbaths, except when a leap year adds an additional month. Each *sidrah* is known by its first (or first distinctive) Hebrew word. For each holiday, a suitable selection has been designated, apart from the weekly series. On holidays and certain special Sabbaths, an additional passage is read from a second scroll, according to traditional practice.

Each *sidrah* is divided into seven subsections. It is customary to "call up" seven worshipers to take part in reading the several subsections. (The number of participants varies on holidays, weekdays, etc.) Originally each person called up was expected to read a passage with the correct chant.

The participants who were insufficiently familiar with the text recited the benedictions and someone else read the portion for them. This was embarrassing to the unlearned; so it became customary long ago to assign the reading to one qualified person (the *ba'al k'riah*), and those "called up," no matter how learned, recited only the benedictions.

In many traditional congregations, the lengthy period of the Torah reading became a disorderly part of the service. Those who had the honor of participating were expected to make contributions, which were duly acknowledged in the prayer (*Mi Shebeirach)* recited on behalf of the donor or the donor's dear ones. Others present might also have recited special prayers of thanks or petition. On important holidays, moreover, the honors were sold at auction before the Torah service was conducted.

In reaction against such practices, Reform synagogues abolished the entire system of honors and limited participation to the ministry and to the congregational officers on the pulpit. Many temples later reintroduced participation from the membership, but continued the approach of eliminating the old abuses.

In order to shorten the weekly reading, some of the early Reformers proposed a return to the so-called triennial cycle; but the suggestion met with little favor. So Reform congregations follow the annual cycle, but instead they usually read only one subsection of each *sidrah.* In some congregations, the text is chanted, and in others the reader translates it into the vernacular after reading it, or even sentence by sentence.

The Torah and Modernity

The last three centuries have seen a great upheaval in the religious thinking of the West, in general, and of the Jew, in particular. The development of natural science has undermined belief in the supernatural and miraculous and, thus, brought into question the authority of all sacred scriptures. Further, the champions of religion could no longer follow the method of Philo, who read into the Torah the ideas of Plato, or of Maimonides, who understood the same texts in terms of Aristotelian thought. We cannot claim to discover the findings of Darwin or Einstein in the Torah, for modern methods of Bible study preclude such an approach. Philological analysis and historical criticism make it impossible to "explain away" errors of fact and, to us, unacceptable theological apprehensions and moral injunctions. All of these must be understood in their own context and their own time. Furthermore, the rediscovery of the rich culture and literature of the ancient Near East revealed many similarities between biblical and non-Israelite writings, and even some cases in which the biblical authors borrowed from their pagan neighbors.

These new methods and discoveries have added enormously to our understanding of the biblical world. But they raise basic and difficult questions. Can the informed Jew of today regard the Torah as the word of God? And, if so, to what extent and in what sense? This commentary is an attempt to grapple with such questions. (See above, General Introduction to the Torah.) The readers are urged to base their judgments on a thoughtful reading of the Torah itself, with the aid of the comments in this volume. But a few suggestions are offered here:

1] We learn from the Torah how the Jewish people has understood its own character and destiny. For this reason the Torah is indispensable for our own self-understanding. It is our foundation document, whether or not it is factual. Indeed, modern scholarship (literary and archeological) indicates that the Torah's narratives are not historical. Thus, the accounts of even its most basic episodes and leading figures are to be read symbolically and ideologically. (History neither confirms or denies religious commitment. Acknowledging that Martin Luther was a historical figure does not make us Lutherans; denying the historicity of Moses does not preclude our fervor as Jews.)

2] Comparison reveals similarities between biblical writings and other old Near Eastern sources, but it also reveals striking dissimilarities. Despite the many parallels between biblical and Mesopotamian law, for example, only Israel claimed that its laws were divine in origin—thus endowing them with ultimate, rather than royal, authority. More important, it was through the Torah (and the Bible as a whole) that the highest ethical principles of the ancient Near East—such as society's obligation to protect its most defenseless—were transmitted through the millennia.

3] The historical approach evokes our awe in another way. We see the vast distance between the more primitive elements of the Torah and its most sublime and advanced passages; and we marvel that such great progress occurred in a few centuries. At the same time, we no longer feel the need to rationalize or justify those things in the Torah that intellect forbids us to accept as true or conscience will not let us defend. No satisfactory explanation has ever been given in terms of climatic, geographical, economic, and political factors for the unique religio-ethical development in Israel. It is thus not unreasonable to discern revelation *within* the historical processes.

4] Though the Torah contains chapters that are, at most, of historical interest only, it also contains much that is relevant and vital today. If it sometimes expresses moral judgments we have discarded as unsatisfactory, it also challenges us with ideals we are far from having attained. Moreover, for us as for our ancestors, the line between written and oral Torah cannot be drawn over-sharply. We too read the text in the light of the experiences and associations that have become attached to it. Every great classic suggests or reveals new insights to each succeeding generation. And the Torah is the classic of classics.

Source: Rabbi Bernard J. Bamberger, "The Torah and the Jewish People," in *The Torah: A Modern Commentary*, rev. ed., ed. Rabbi W. Gunther Plaut (New York: URJ Press, 2005; Reform Judaism Publishing/CCAR Press, 2015) xlv–li.

Women and
Interpretation of the Torah

DR. TAMARA COHN ESKENAZI AND RABBI ANDREA L. WEISS

The word *torah*, or "teaching," can mean different things in different contexts. In Proverbs 6:20, which states "do not forsake your mother's *torah*," the term denotes human wisdom in general. Elsewhere in the Bible, the word refers to particular divine precepts (see Exodus 13:9), certain priestly instructions (see at Leviticus 6:2), or the core of the book of Deuteronomy (see at Deuteronomy 31:9).

While in the Bible the word *torah* (translated variously as "Teaching," "Instruction," "ritual," or "Law") refers to a number of different kinds of teachings, in time "*the* Torah" came to mean the books of Genesis, Exodus, Leviticus, Numbers, and Deuteronomy (in Hebrew: *B'reishit, Sh'mot, Vayikra, B'midbar,* and *D'varim).* Together, those five books constitute the first of the three parts of the Jewish Scriptures, or the Hebrew Bible, namely: Torah, Prophets, and Writings (or *Torah, N'viim,* and *K'tuvim,* which combine to produce an acronym that is pronounced *Tanach).* A common Jewish name for any published volume of the Torah is *Chumash,* which is related to the Hebrew word for "five." The term "Pentateuch" (from the Greek word for "five") is commonly used as well, especially in scholarly circles.

The word "Torah," then, refers to the foundation of authoritative teachings in Judaism and the repository of God's teachings for Israel. From antiquity, Jewish (and subsequently Christian) traditions typically considered the Torah—in the sense of the first five books of the Bible—to have been written by Moses and to represent a record of God's words to Moses; hence the customary reference to "the Five Books of Moses." However, this title is misleading, because nothing in the Torah claims that Moses wrote the entire collection. Genesis and Exodus mention no author; and although most of Leviticus and major parts of Exodus and Numbers purport to represent God's words to Moses or Israel, only Deuteronomy claims to quote Moses extensively and states that he wrote those sections.

Some Rabbis noted early on that certain statements in the Torah could not have been written by Moses (such as the report about his death in Deuteronomy 34). Nevertheless, a widespread presumption that Moses wrote the whole Torah at God's dictation prevailed until the modern era.

In the modern era, academic scholars began to challenge the view of the Torah as the unified work of Moses. The theory that became most widely accepted in scholarly circles, beginning in the 19th century, claims that the Torah is composed of four major sources that were combined gradually over many centuries. In general, this "Documentary Hypothesis" (associated with the German biblical scholar Julius Wellhausen) posits that the source labeled "J" (or "Yahwist," marked by the prominence of God's name, *YHVH*) was the earliest (10th or 9th century B.C.E.) and represented the interests and traditions of the kingdom of Judah. (Prior to that time traditions were transmitted orally.) Source "E" (or "Elohist," distinguished by its preference for referring to God as Elohim) represented northern traditions, that is, the kingdom of Israel, from about a century later. Source "D " (or "Deuteronomist") refers primarily to the book of Deuteronomy, a work that becomes influential in the 7th century B.C.E. Finally, the "P" (or "Priestly") source represented the concerns of the priests from the period when Israel was exiled in Babylon or shortly after, in the post-exilic period of the 6th to 5th centuries B.C.E.

Proponents of the Documentary Hypothesis describe the particular literary characteristics and concerns of each source; and some have sought to identify the actual authors as well. Harold Bloom and David Rosenberg speculated that the author of J was in fact a woman living in King David's court *(The Book of J*, 1990), an idea that Richard Friedman first proposed in *Who Wrote the Bible?* (1987, p. 86). However, the speculation that J was a woman has not been widely accepted for a number of reasons. First, while the idea that women had a role in the composition of the Torah (or other parts of the Bible) remains theoretically possible, the very notion of a single individual author of J is no longer accepted. Second, Bloom's criteria for what he identifies as a woman's voice are highly flawed (even sexist). Third, as scholars in a variety of fields demonstrate, identifying the gender of an author even in a modern setting is extremely difficult; how much more so in an ancient setting when we have no supporting evidence! Therefore, most scholars question our ability to recover such precise information about the origins of the sources.

The Documentary Hypothesis maintains that the entire Torah as we know it only came into being in the 5th century B.C.E. with the work of Ezra the priest and scribe. Nehemiah 8 depicts the dramatic moment when Ezra reads the book of the Torah (sefer ha-torah) in Jerusalem in the presence of all the people, "men and women and all who could listen with understanding" (8:2). Some regard the enthusiastic affirmation of the Torah by the entire community at the time of Ezra as a "second Sinai." For many scholars, this moment represents the time that the Torah was finally complete.

Many aspects of the Documentary Hypothesis no longer represent scholarly consensus; others remain influential. Its enduring contribution is the claim that the Torah is the fruit of a long process and contains diverse sources, often shaped by responses to new crises. This conclusion continues to be important and often guides scholarly interpretation, but along lines that differ from the Documentary Hypothesis itself. Moreover, two of the sources, J and E, no longer seem to be widely recognized. References to P, the distinctive priesdy traditions, remain useful insofar as such material has a coherent world view (as in Genesis 1) and often focuses on the sanctuary and its personnel, as well as on genealogies. But some scholars now distinguish between two types of priestly writings: one priestly school labeled "P" and another whose work is referred to as "H."

Source: Dr. Tamara Cohn Eskenazi and Rabbi Andrea L. Weiss, "Women and Interpretation of the Torah," *The Torah: A Women's Commentary*, ed. Dr. Tamara Cohn Eskenazi and Rabbi Andrea L. Weiss (New York: URJ Press, 2008; Reform Judaism Publishing/CCAR Press, 2015), xxxvi–xxxvii.

Women and Post-biblical Commentary

DR. JUDITH R. BASKIN

Jews have traditionally believed that each of the books that comprise the Hebrew Bible reflects God's word in some way. As a "religion of the book," Judaism has looked to these revealed writings for guidance in every aspect of human life. Yet a religion based upon static texts, however holy, cannot easily adjust to the ever-varying conditions of human life. That Judaism has endured is due, in large part, to our traditions of biblical interpretation. In every generation, expositors of the divine message have discovered new meanings in the Hebrew Scriptures and demonstrated their relevance to an ever-evolving Jewish community.

For each parashah, *The Torah: A Women's Commentary* includes a section titled Post-biblical Interpretations. Rabbinic biblical commentaries, written from the 3rd through the 19th centuries, have played a central role in shaping how Jews have understood the Torah. Like *The Torah: A Women's Commentary*, these interpretations endeavored to keep biblical teachings alive, relevant, and compelling. The authors of our Post-biblical Interpretations have chosen from this vast treasury those passages that they believe will illuminate our contemporary understandings of biblical texts. Wherever possible, these selections focus on female characters and larger issues concerning women in Jewish law and Jewish life.

This essay presents an historical overview of the Jewish commentaries and commentators cited in the Post-biblical Interpretations sections.

Written Torah and Oral Torah

Jewish biblical interpretation is already present in the Bible, since later biblical books often (directly or indirectly) interpret earlier writings. Following the destruction of the Second Temple (70 C.E.), textual scholars and interpreters, generally referred to as "the Rabbis, emerged as Jewish spiritual leaders. During the rabbinic period (from the beginning of the Common Era to the end of the 6th century), much of their intellectual endeavors concentrated on recording, preserving, and expanding the biblical interpretations that they deemed essential for the conduct of day-to-day Jewish life.

The word "*torah*" can be understood broadly as "teaching" or "revelation." Rabbinic teachers enlarged the meaning of Torah itself to include the entire body of rabbinic interpretive literature. Thus, "Written Torah" came to refer to the Bible, and "Oral Torah" became a designation for the voluminous rabbinic texts that grew up around the Bible. The oral tradition of Torah interpretation assumed the sanctity and inviolability of the written word. The Rabbis taught that both components of divine revelation were delivered to the people of Israel at Mt. Sinai and subsequently passed down through later prophets and other recognized authoritative figures (Mishnah *Avot* 1).

Rabbinic interpretation begins with the premise that Torah in all of its parts, both written and oral, is of divine origin and authority. Sometimes God's will is evident in the plain sense of the words, what is called the *p'shat*. This term refers to the contextual meaning of a biblical passage that is evident through a straight-forward reading of a text. More frequently, the Rabbis believed, the actual import of biblical words can be discerned only by those who know how to penetrate to the *drash*, the deeper sense that lies beneath the surface. They sought to discover and elucidate those inner meanings, and in this way they maintained continuity with the past while adapting law to the changing conditions of the present and the needs of the future.

Rabbinic Literature

The rabbinic method of biblical interpretation is called *midrash*, frequently translated as "exposition" or "elucidation." There are two types of midrash, legal and non-legal. Legal midrash contains a composite of ceremonial ordinances, ritual teachings, ethical rulings, and civil, criminal, and domestic laws that generally find their origin in a biblical statement or commandment. Since biblical laws are often vague or incomplete, rabbinic elaboration provides the details to allow for their implementation in a variety of particular situations. As later generations sought to follow the laws and teaching of the Bible, many topics required elucidation, such as the proper way of keeping Shabbat or how to solemnize a marriage or write a bill of divorce. Thus, rabbinic law enlarged and clarified the biblical text, applying scriptural principles and contemporary practices to an ever-broader variety of cases, while also considering a greater number of contingencies. The other type of rabbinic biblical interpretation is non-legal in nature and includes expansions of biblical narratives, folktales, and anecdotes about the Rabbis themselves. These rabbinic writings also contain homilies (sermons) that teach religious beliefs and ethical behavior, and that comfort the downcast of Israel with promises of future redemption. Convinced that biblical texts contained neither contradiction nor repetition, the Rabbis creatively exercised their interpretive powers to demonstrate that this was so. Most of the biblical interpretations in this volume focus on this second type of interpretation, known as *midrash aggadah*.

Eventually, the Rabbis collected what is known as the "Oral Torah" into compilations that preserve competing interpretations and opinions; while majority views are generally honored, minority opinions are recorded as well. These complex texts interweave traditions, motifs, and influences from a variety of sources, time periods, and diverse environments, reflective of the extended duration of their composition and editing. Those texts from the Land of Israel incorporated and responded to Greco-Roman and early Christian cultural influences. Other texts were shaped in the very different world of mostly pre-Islamic Iraq, known in Jewish tradition as Babylon. The main collections are the Mishnah and the Talmud (usually cited as BT or JT, see below for details).

Women in Rabbinic Writings

The shapers and expositors of rabbinic Judaism were men, and the ideal human society that they imagined was decidedly oriented towards men. Nevertheless, women were a part of these men's lives and a number of rabbinic writings address issues involving women. An entire division of the key rabbinic texts, the Mishnah and Talmuds, is entitled *Nashim* ("Women"), and its seven tractates deal with women in their legal relationships to men in matters of betrothal, marriage, levirate marriage, divorce, suspected adultery, and women's limited ability to make vows of various kinds. Another section, *Niddah* ("The Menstruating Woman"), one of the twelve tractates in the division *Tohorot* ("Ritual Purity"), is mainly concerned with strict definitions of female impurity during and after menstruation and following childbirth, in order to prevent communication of this ritual impurity to men.

With few exceptions, female voices are not heard in rabbinic literature. When they are, they are usually mediated through rabbinic assumptions about women's lesser intellectual, spiritual, and moral capacities, reflecting set views of women's appropriate roles in life, which were believed to differ from those of men. Rabbinic texts do not grant women a significant role in any aspect of rabbinic Judaism's communal life of leadership, study, and worship. Neither women's religious rituals—which undoubtedly existed—nor female understandings of their lives, experiences, and spirituality are retrievable in any significant way from rabbinic Judaism's androcentric writings that became so central to a millennium-and-a-half of Jewish existence. From rabbinic literature alone, a reader would never know, for example, that in various parts of the Roman Empire, some Jewish women held leadership roles in synagogue life and other public arenas. (Archeological evidence shows that such was the case in the first six or seven centuries of the Common Era. Some of the women involved, who appear to have been independent and wealthy, may have been converts to Judaism. See Bernadette Brooten, *Women Leaders in the Ancient Synagogue*, 1982.)

In their interpretive writings, the Rabbis praised biblical women who played central roles in the destiny of the people of Israel, including the matriarchs (*imahot*). According to the Babylonian Talmud (abbreviated as BT), Sarah, Miriam, Deborah, Hannah, Abigail, Huldah, and Esther have the status of prophets (*M'gillah* 14a); and the midrash collection *Breishit Rabbah* declared that all four mothers of Israel were prophets (67.9 and 72.6). The Rabbis also lauded the women whose supportive roles in the domestic realm enabled husbands and sons to participate in public worship and communal study. For example, they extol Rachel, wife of Rabbi Akiva, as an exemplary woman who sacrificed her own comfort for her husband's scholarship (Judith Baskin, *Midrashic Women*, 2002, pp. 101–3). On the other hand, the Rabbis condemned as immodest women who appeared unveiled in public or gathered in groups with other women, or those whose voices the Rabbis considered too strident. Similarly, some sages criticized women who asserted themselves as public leaders. Thus, the Babylonian Talmud goes on to denigrate the judge Deborah as a hornet and the prophet Hulda as a weasel (the meaning of their respective names), since they held powerful positions usually associated with men (*M'gillah* 14b; Baskin, *Midrashic Women*, 2002, pp. 31–32, 109–14, 140–54).

The *midrash* about Rahab the harlot is a good example of the creative and transformative powers of rabbinic commentary when applied positively to a biblical woman. Rahab appears in Joshua 2 as a prostitute who lived independently in the city of Jericho. She is a righteous woman who hides Joshua's two spies in her house and saves them from capture. According to Joshua 2:9-11, Rahab recognizes the overwhelming power of God and foresees the future victory of Israel.

The Rabbis taught that Rahab became a convert to Judaism; and her statement of faith in Joshua 2:11 earned her the highest place among all biblical proselytes (*M'chilta Amalek 3*; *Dvarim Rabbah* 2.26–27). A midrash recounts that she became the ancestor of priests and prophets in Israel (*B'midbar Rabbah* 8.9). According to the Rabbis, Joshua himself married her. Thus, his illustrious descendants were also hers (BT *M'gillah* 14b). (On how priests and prophets could be descended from a non-Israelite prostitute, see *Sifrei B'midbar* 78 and the discussion in Baskin, *Midrashic Women*, 2002, pp. 154–60.) Her rabbinic rehabilitation as a wife and mother demonstrates how the Rabbis preferred to imagine women, even as it provides a firm precedent for our own contemporary reconstructions of biblical women and men in ways that reveal meanings from the ancient text that speak to our own lives and concerns.

Rabbinic literature also preserves anecdotes about contemporaneous admirable women. These include Imma Shalom (1st century C.E.), whose husband was Rabbi Eliezer ben Hyrcanus and whose brother was the Patriarch Gamliel II (BT *Shabbat* 116a, BT *Bava M'tzia* 59b); she mediated a bitter quarrel between those two men. Traditions associated with Beruriah (2nd century C.E.), whose father and husband were rabbis, acknowledge the possibility of a learned female. A number of passages depict Beruriah as having a profound knowledge of rabbinic biblical exegesis and outstanding intelligence (for instance, BT *P'sachim* 62b, BT *B'rachot* 10a, and BT *Eiruvin* 53b–54a). However, beyond one very early attribution , which is repeated nowhere else, no actual legal rulings are ever credited to her (Tosefta *Keilim, Bava M'tzia* 1:6). Moreover, Beruriah's reputed scholarly expertise became a problem for rabbinic Judaism. In a medieval reference, which may reflect earlier sources, she reaps the tragic consequences of the "light-mindedness" supposedly inherent in women. Rashi (see below) relates a tradition that Beruriah was seduced by one of her husband's students and subsequently committed suicide (Rashi's commentary on BT *Avodah Zarah* 18b; Baskin, *Midrashic Women*, 2002, pp. 81–83).

Seven aggadic narratives in the Babylonian Talmud discuss Yalta, an aristocratic Jewish woman of notable learning who exercised significant communal authority in the Jewish community in Babylon. Clearly, the Rabbis were aware of women like Yalta whose strong personalities, control of significant financial resources, and exalted lineage afforded them far more communal respect and power than ordinary women could imagine. While several of the stories about Yalta report her ability to act independently against Jewish rabbinic and political rulings when necessary, at least two of the anecdotes (BT *Kiddushin* 70a–b and BT *B'rachot* 51b) demonstrate a rabbinic desire to curtail such female pretensions to independence and power (Baskin, *Midrashic Women*, 2002, pp. 83–87).

Why Rabbinic Literature Is Included Here

The Rabbis adapted the Hebrew Bible to their own circumstances and attitudes, but always with the conviction that they were proceeding with divine authority. The traditions they established about the inappropriateness of women's presence in the communal domains of worship, study, and leadership were continued, with few exceptions, in medieval and early modern Judaism. They persist in some Jewish communities up to the present day. Although the patriarchal approach toward women that is typical of rabbinic and medieval biblical commentary was never unique to the Jewish community, the consequences of this attitude have been long lasting in stifling female intellectual, spiritual, and leadership roles in Judaism. Contemporary women may well ask what this androcentric literature, written and transmitted by men, has to offer and why they should read it. Why have we included "Post-biblical Interpretations" in this volume at all?

For one thing, this complex and multifaceted literature is a rich part of our Jewish heritage. The Rabbis and later exegetes were profoundly immersed in biblical literature and had considered deeply its wide range of meanings and possible applications. The many dimensions they read into and out of the biblical text over the centuries have shaped the course of Jewish intellectual and spiritual history— and continue to amaze and enlighten us today. Moreover, rabbinic exegesis has always been sensitive to the multilayered and multivocal qualities of the Hebrew Scriptures. While the majority of exegetical teachings about women's intellectual capacities and public roles tend to be negative, differing points of view have also been preserved. One example that acknowledges the injustice of arbitrary limitations on female roles appears in the midrash collection *Sifrei Numbers* 133, in a discussion of the redoubtable daughters of Zelophehad (Numbers 26): "The compassion of God is not like human compassion. Human rulers favor males over females but the One who spoke and brought the world into being is not like that. Rather, God shows mercy to every living thing (see *parashat Pinchas*, p. 984). Thus, our commentary includes "Post-biblical Interpretations" because they are part of our legacy of Oral Torah, because they have a great deal to teach us about biblical writings, and because they represent the diverse points of view that have always been a part of the way Jews read the Torah.

When thinking about women, it is especially important that we pay attention to this immense body of post-biblical interpretive literature which is a central part of Jewish tradition. Contemporary interpretations of Jewish texts have played a leading role in bringing about positive changes in women's status in Judaism and in the larger world, and in enlarging women's access to the realms of Jewish learning. Indeed, the many scholars who have contributed "Post-biblical Interpretations" to this volume demonstrate that women are now expert in rabbinic writings. As educated women and men advocate for a Judaism that is egalitarian and forward looking, it is essential that we become knowledgeable about all aspects of our heritage and build on those teachings of the past.

Documents of Rabbinic Judaism

The Mishnah is the earliest written document of rabbinic Judaism. It is a legal compilation based on biblical law, actual practice, and spiritual vision. This work, edited in the early 3rd century C.E., is written in Hebrew and is organized according to six subject divisions, which are further separated into a total of sixty-three tractates. The Tosefta, generally held to be a slightly later collection of legal rulings, follows the order of the Mishnah and supplements it. These works are attributed to the rabbinic sages from the 1st to 3rd centuries C.E. In the following centuries, rabbinic scholars in the land of Israel and in Babylonia (today's Iraq) produced extensive commentaries on the Mishnah, known as Gemara. Much of the Gemara is written in Aramaic, a language close to Hebrew that was dominant in Western Asia in that period. In the 6th century C.E., the Mishnah and this more extensive Gemara were combined and edited by several generations of Rabbis to form the Babylonian Talmud (cited here as BT). This work became the definitive compilation of Jewish law and tradition for many centuries to come. The Talmud of the Land of Israel (cited here as JT), completed at the end of the 4th century C.E., although less comprehensive than the Babylonian Talmud, also became an important part of the larger body of rabbinic literature.

Parallel to the Mishnah, Tosefta, and Talmuds are midrash collections that either provide a running commentary on a specific biblical book or are organized according to cycles of scriptural readings. These midrash compilations, typically named after biblical books (for example, *B'reishit Rabbah*, also known as *Genesis Rabbah*), are mainly in Hebrew and share numerous interpretations and rulings in common with the Mishnah and Talmuds. The dates of composition for these midrashic documents extend from the period of the Mishnah into the early Middle Ages and are often difficult to determine with any exactitude.

Medieval Biblical Interpretation

During the medieval period (from 600 C.E. to 1500 C.E.), many important biblical commentaries were written by scholars throughout the Jewish world. Several of these exegetes are cited in the "Postbiblical Interpretations entries in this volume. The most famous medieval commentator is Rabbi Solomon ben Isaac (known by the acronym Rashi), who lived in France between 1040 and 1105. Best known for his commentaries on both the Babylonian Talmud and most of the biblical books, Rashi's exegesis has long been admired for its clarity and for his attention to the *p'shat* or contextual meaning of a biblical passage. Only after he had explicated the plain sense of a text as he understood it, did Rashi turn to *drash*, using *midrash aggadah* to expand his readers' understanding of the Bible. Rashi had only daughters and they were apparently well educated. Most of his grandsons became important interpreters of Jewish texts.

Rabbi Abraham Ibn Ezra (died 1165), a native of Spain whose first language was Arabic, is often considered the most original of medieval Jewish biblical interpreters. He composed commentaries on all the biblical books, as well as Hebrew poetry and works on astronomy and science. As a scientist and philosopher, Ibn Ezra used his knowledge of Hebrew and Arabic grammar to demonstrate the contextual meaning (*p'shat*) of biblical words and phrases; he had little interest in the elaborations of *midrash aggadah* that appealed so much to Rashi. His approach to the Bible is in many ways a precursor to modern biblical scholarship. Another important Spanish exegete was Rabbi Moses ben Nachman (1194-1270), also known as Nachmanides or by his acronym, Ramban. He lived most of his life near Barcelona, spending his final days in the Land of Israel. He is well known for his commentary on the five books of the Torah and for the strong influence from Jewish mysticism that infuses his interpretation.

The *Mikraot G'dolot* ("Rabbinic Bible") became a popular repository of medieval biblical commentary for later generations. Published with the vocalized text of the Bible, an Aramaic translation, and selected Masoretic notes, the typical volume of *Mikraot G'dolot* contains the commentaries of Rashi; Rabbi Samuel ben Meir (1085-1158), one of Rashi's grandsons who is also known as Rashbam; Abraham ibn Ezra; Nachmanides; and Obadiah Sforno (1475-1550), an Italian rabbi, physician, and commentator.

Pre-modern Jewish Women and Hebrew Scriptures

Most Jewish women in rabbinic and medieval times lacked access to the Torah and interpretive writings, since very few women learned to read Hebrew. The greatest Jewish philosopher of the Middle Ages, Moses Maimonides (1135-1204), who was born in Spain and spent most of his life in Cairo, discouraged girls' education in traditional texts, on the grounds that women had no halachic obligation to study. He also believed that women were deficient in the mental skills required for serious Torah learning. In his famous law code the *Mishneh Torah*, Maimonides wrote, "Our sages said: 'Whoever teaches his daughter Torah, it is as if he taught her frivolity [or: lasciviousness]' (Mishnah *Sotah* 3:4). This all refers to the Oral Torah. However, regarding the Written Torah he should not set out to teach her; but, if he does teach her, it is not considered as if he taught her frivolity" (*Mishneh Torah*, Study of Torah 1:13). The French scholar Moses of Coucy (early 13th century) explained that although "a woman is exempt from both the commandment to learn Torah and to teach her son, even so, if she aids her son and husband in their efforts to learn [by supporting them financially], she shares their reward for the fulfillment of that commandment" (*Sefer Mitzvot Gadol*, Positive Commandment 12). The invention of printing in the 15th century and the spread of printed works in vernacular languages transformed Jewish women's educational opportunities. Most rabbinic leaders agreed with Maimonides that the rabbinic injunctions against female study applied to the Talmud but not to the Bible or the legal rulings necessary for women's everyday activities. It is no accident that translations and paraphrases of portions of the Bible into Yiddish were among the first printed Jewish books intended for a female audience. (These were also important works for the large number of Jewish men who also lacked a good understanding of Hebrew.) Particularly popular were the *Taytsh-khumesh* ("Yiddish Five Books of Moses") by Sheftl Hurwitz of Prague and first published in 1590, and the *Tsenerene* (or *Tzenah U'renah*, "Go Out and See"), by Rabbi Yaakov son of Isaac Ashkenazi. Both of these biblical paraphrases included homilies on the weekly biblical readings from the Torah and Prophets, as well as stories, legends, and parables from rabbinic literature, the *Zohar*, and other mystical texts. The *Tsenerene* was particularly popular and appeared in more than three hundred editions. As Chava Weissler has written, "Women read it for inspiration and catharsis, often weeping over the text, as a regular part of their Sabbath afternoon activities (*Voices of the Matriarchs*, 1998, p. 6). In this way, for the first time, large numbers of women became familiar with the Torah and haftarah portions of the week, a wide variety of *midrash aggadah*, and the teachings of the best-known commentators. Aspects of this knowledge, particularly about biblical women, was also incorporated contemporaneously into women's vernacular supplicatory prayers (*tkhines*), at least some of which were composed by women (see *Voices of the Matriarchs*). Thus, a new technology in the larger culture (namely, printing) transformed the piety and possibilities of Jewish women, just as the technological and social changes of the past hundred years have profoundly altered the opportunities available for Jewish women at the beginning of the 21st century.

Source: Dr. Judith R. Baskin, "Women and Post-biblical Commentary," in *The Torah: A Women's Commentary*, eds. Dr. Tamara Cohn Eskenazi and Rabbi Andrea L. Weiss (New York: URJ Press, 2008; Reform Judaism Publishing/CCAR Press, 2015), xlix–lv.

Our Tree of Life

RABBI AMY SCHEINERMAN

We are all searchers. As we travel through life, we seek purpose and meaning, a sense of deep belonging, a path to lives of integrity and decency, and a way to leave a positive mark on the world. Jewish tradition has always held that the key to purpose, meaning, belonging, wisdom, morality, and immortality is our sacred books. The precious teachings of Torah and its rewards are unlocked by study. This is reflected in the many dynamic, exciting, and inspiring Torah study groups fostered by Reform congregations. Study requires intellectual skills and emotional openness, and preferably a social venue (with one partner or as a member of a class) but it is, fundamentally, the quintessential Jewish spiritual practice. Happily, Jewish tradition is brimming with literary gems.

Torah is our *Eitz Chayim*, our Tree of Life. Lying at the core of Jewish identity, Torah roots us historically and religiously. It is the glue that binds Jews together across time and space. Our customs and traditions vary significantly from place to place and from century to century, but we all hold sacred a set of texts that we identify as "holy books." Studying, interpreting, and reinterpreting Torah (both the Written Torah, the Five Books of Moses, and the Oral Torah, the Talmud)—complete with disagreements, debates, and differing interpretations—have been the mainstay of Jewish life throughout the centuries. What is more, Torah has served as the sounding board and reflective window for Jews to examine their own live and situations; Torah study has been a means of examining the big, thorny questions of life, something off of which to bounce new, even radical ideas, in the quest for insight. Through Torah study, each generation has found wisdom and meaning in our sacred texts. As an outgrowth of study, each generation has promulgated its own understandings and interpretations of Torah, adding new branches to the growing, life-giving tree that sustains the Jewish people. The understandings we glean are gifts we give our contemporaries and a heritage we leave the generations to come. The *Eitz Chayim* is not so much one tree as it is an ever-expanding forest.

Talmud, which tradition holds is Oral Torah, affirms this in a teaching that inspired one of our morning prayers: "These are the obligations without measure, whose reward, too, is without measure: To honor father and mother; to perform acts of love and kindness; to attend the house of study daily; to welcome the stranger; to visit the sick; to rejoice with bride and groom; to console the bereaved; to pray with sincerity; to make peace where there is strife. And the study of Torah is equal to them all, because it leads to them all."[1] Talmud Torah—Torah study—surpasses other mitzvot (Jewish obligations, practices, and traditions) because it teaches the student of Torah how to live as a Jew and inspires him or her to become immersed in Jewish life and live by the moral values cherished throughout our generations. Torah study, more than any other aspect of Jewish life and practice, combines our spiritual and intellectual proclivities, and our obligations to better ourselves, nurture our families, improve our communities and repair the world.

Reform Judaism has always affirmed the value and centrality of Torah study, no less now than at any time in the past, and perhaps more in recent decades as we rekindle our relationship with a wider sense of what constitutes Torah: Talmud, midrash, Kabbalah, Musar literature, and chasidut are all the products of Torah study that are thus Torah themselves. From the 1885 Pittsburgh Platform to the Pittsburgh Platform of 1999, we have acknowledged Torah as our guide and Torah study as a fundamental obligation of committed Jewish living. In 1885, the leaders of Reform Judaism asserted the centrality of our *Eitz Chayim* to our essential purpose as a people: "We recognize in the Bible the record of the consecration of the Jewish people to its mission as the priest of the one God, and value it as the most potent instrument of religious and moral instruction."[2]

In time, our vision of Torah grew. In 1999, the second Pittsburgh Platform stated:

"We affirm that Torah is the foundation of Jewish life. We cherish the truths revealed in Torah, God's ongoing revelation to our people and the record of our

---

1 See Mishnah *Pei-ah* 1:1 and Babylonian Talmud, *Shabbat* 127a.
2 "The Pittsburgh Platform" (1885). http://ccarnet.org/rabbis-speak/platforms/declaration-principles/.

people's ongoing relationship with God. We affirm that Torah is a manifestation of (*ahavat olam*), God's eternal love for the Jewish people and for all humanity… We are called by Torah to lifelong study in the home, in the synagogue and in every place where Jews gather to learn and teach."[3]

With time, our horizons have been broadened and we are rewarded when we engage with sparkling, spiritual texts that speak to the mind, the heart, and the soul. What is more, Torah study brings us together with other Jews, forming communities of learning and forging relationships we might not otherwise enjoy.

Reform Judaism is uniquely positioned to extend Torah learning in new directions, due to its historical respect for the full spectrum of academic and intellectual fields and methods the secular world offers. (These range from sciences such as physical cosmology and quantum physics, to social sciences such as anthropology, psychology, and economics, to the gifts of the humanities, including comparative literature, philosophy, and semiotics.) The tools and insights of the many academic disciplines help us shed light on the contextual meaning of our sacred texts. They also offer new ways to read traditional texts and extract their wisdom and meaning, obtaining direction for our lives. Where the academic wishes to understand the author's intent—and that can help us appreciate the text in new ways—the goal of Torah study as a spiritual practice is to find interpretations that speak to us not only on an intellectual level, but on a religious and spiritual level. We prize the spiritual meaning our sacred texts impart when we allow them to speak to us and the lives we live. As liberal Jews, we appreciate both the historical, rational view of the texts, as well as the spiritual nurturing and succor we derive from the texts.

Bridging the worlds of the modern intellectual study of our sacred texts and traditional spiritual searching for wisdom and meaning can be challenging. What is "true"? What is "real"? Here, I have found the spiritual development theory of philosopher Paul Ricoeur helpful. Ricoeur describes three steps of spiritual interpretation. The first, which he terms "the first naiveté," is the literal interpretation of Scripture, accepting it on faith, at face value. Once rationalism (the second stage) entered the world, Scripture was subjected to rational scrutiny and analysis, and the narratives and laws once accepted as "true" came to be regarded as "myth." In the third stage, "the second naiveté," we learn how to engage the text without insisting upon a literal reading and without jettisoning rationalism.

---

3. "A Statement of Principles for Reform Judaism" (May 1999), https:/ccarnet.org/rabbis-speak/platforms/statement-principles-reform-judaism/.

In the third stage, we recognize symbol and metaphorical constructs that bespeak values dear to us, uplift us, and address the core questions of life. For Reform Jews, Ricoeur offers the best of all possible worlds: we retain our sacred texts as bridges to the Divine and view them through all the intellectual and spiritual lenses that help us draw out their wisdom.

As much as Reform Judaism respects the choices of the individual concerning religious and spiritual life, we nonetheless affirm that Torah study is an obligation. I would hope that all Reform Jews would recognize the value of committing ourselves to Torah learning for our own sake, to the benefit of our children (for whom we are behavioral role models), toward the strengthening of the broader community who will benefit from our insights and ideas, and as a gift to future generations who will look to those who came before them for insight.

We should aim to make Torah study a central facet of our communal life, with room and opportunity for a wide variety of learners. Paraphrasing the cultural Zionist Achad HaAm, who wrote about Shabbat observance, as much as the Jews preserve Torah, Torah study preserves the Jews. Rabbi Shlomo Ephraim (1550–1619) of Lunschitz, Poland, in his popular commentary on Torah, *Kli Yakar*, identifies Torah study as *minchah chadashah* ("**new** meal offering") of Leviticus 23:15–16. He writes, "The Torah must be new for each person every day as the day that it was received on Mount Sinai.... For, in truth, you are commanded to derive novelty each and every day."

The only way for Torah to be new is for us to explore it through study so that we might find new interpretations that speak to us concerning the lives we are living. Rabbi Lunschitz goes beyond inviting us in to learn; he considers study and the generation of new interpretations an obligation. I am in total agreement. Torah, our *Eitz Chayim*, emits life-sustaining oxygen, but we must actively breathe it in deeply. Gerald Bruns put it this way: "What is at stake with respect to the Scripture is not what lies behind the text in the form of an original meaning, but what lies in front of it where the interpreter stands. The Bible always addresses itself to the time of interpretation: one cannot understand it except by appropriating it anew."[4]

Talmud tells an intriguing tale about Moses at the moment God gave him the Torah. Standing atop Mount Sinai, Moses is eager and impatient for God to reveal the Torah to him. He sees that God is busily tying *tagin* (decorative crowns) on

---

4 Gerald L. Bruns, "Midrash and Allegory: The Beginnings of Scriptural Interpretation," in *The Literary Guide to the Bible*, ed. Robert Alter and Frank Kermode (Cambridge, MA: Harvard University Press, 1987), 627–8.

some of the Hebrew letters of the text. Impatiently, Moses asks why God delays giving the Torah in order to finish what seem inconsequential aesthetic flourishes. God responds that these *tagin* will help ensure that novel interpretations of Torah enter the world when R. Akiba learns and teaches Torah. Moses is astonished. If God has someone like R. Akiba who can interpret Torah with such skill and virtuosity, what need has God for Moses? God's response is to transport Moses some fourteen centuries into the future. Moses finds himself sitting in the back row of R. Akiba's classroom. He listens, comprehends nothing R. Akiba says. Finally, another student asks the source of the law R. Akiba is expounding, and Moses hears him say, "*Halachah l'Moshe mi-Sinai* / It is a law transmitted to Moses at Sinai." Moses' Torah is the Torah of the words on the scroll; R. Akiba's Torah includes the myriad laws and lessons he derives from the *tagin*. The Rabbis who craft this story are keenly aware that the historical R. Akiba's hermeneutics and halakhic exegesis form the foundation of Rabbinic Judaism. Moses gave Israel the Written Torah (the Five Books of Moses), but R. Akiba made possible and thereby *gave* to Israel the Oral Torah (Talmud). We, too, can join the interpretive conversation. The Rabbis view R. Akiba as a Second Moses, giver of the Oral Torah. We can find another layer to the story: It is not that Moses is incapable of grasping the ideas propounded by R. Akiba. Rather, Torah is a living, breathing text tradition, and it will grow and change with each generation in ways that we cannot foresee. There will be extraordinary minds whose imprint on Torah tradition is groundbreaking, formative, and eternal— R. Akiba is a prime example—but each generation will generate a wealth of novel interpretations, *Kli Yakar's minchah chadashah* ("new meal offering").

When we come together to study Torah, or share our insights and interpretations, we will not always agree with one another. That, too, is Torah. Talmud is filled with disagreement and arguments. One of the most valuable outcomes of learning Torah with others is learning how to agree to disagree—and remain civil and friendly. Our Sages sometimes found this challenging, no less than we do today. Mishnah teaches:

> "An argument that is in the name of Heaven shall in the end lead to a permanent result; but every controversy that is not in the name of Heaven, shall not lead to a permanent result. Which controversy was that which was in the name of heaven? Such was the controversy of Hillel and Shammai. And that which was not in the name of Heaven? Such was the controversy of Korah and all his company. (*Pirkei Avot* 5:2)

This teaching is more than about how to hold a civil argument. It's about what builds community and what destroys community. The mishnah references

Numbers 16–17. Korach and his minions attempt to undermine Moses's leadership. Korach, jealous of Moses's authority and seeking Moses's power, equipped with an appealing ideology and supported by followers, foments a self-aggrandizing rebellion. He does not have the needs of the entire community in mind, but only his own narrow interests.

The Rabbis contrasted Korach with our feisty and spirited sages Hillel and Shammai, who agreed on very little and disputed virtually every morsel of Jewish practice, theology, and philosophy. They did not argue for their narrow interests or reputations, however, but rather for religious and spiritual truth as they understood it. During one of their disputes, recounted in the Babylonian Talmud (*Eiruvin* 13b), we are told that Beit Hillel (the School of Hillel) and Beit Shammai (the School of Shammai) were so deeply divided that heaven intervened. A *bat kol* (heavenly voice) declared in the hearing of all: *Eilu v'eilu divrei Elohim chayim*, "Both the words of the one and the words of the other are the words of the living God." The story of their vociferous disagreement and God's assertion that differing opinions can both hold divine valence is valuable enough, but the story doesn't end there. It goes on to say that nonetheless, the *halachah* more often follows the opinions of Beit Hillel. But neither is that the end of the story. The climax concerns *why* Beit Hillel was given predominance. Talmud explains: it is because they were *nochin v'aluvin* (kind and humble), they would study the teachings of their rival, Beit Shammai, and what is more, they would mention the opinions of Beit Shammai before their own. The medieval Talmudist Rabbi Menachem Meiri elucidates the Talmud's intention even further: a *machloket l'shem shamayim* is a dispute in which one party challenges the other not merely to provoke or to seek victory but rather out of a sincere desire to know truth. This is a profound lesson about managing a *machloket l'shem shamayim*, a conflict for the sake of heaven. The Sages are teaching us that Torah study rests on a foundation of respecting the views of others when their intentions are noble, a value that transcends the hours we spend studying Torah and informs our relationships and interactions with others on every level. At the same time that the Talmud affirms the legitimacy of diverse views concerning Jewish practice and interpretation, it elevates kindness and humility to the level of crowning moral achievements. Torah study not only brings us together in the common pursuit of wisdom and meaning, but teaches us—nay, demands of us—civility and mutual respect.

Torah study is a lifelong process. As a community, we read Torah (the Five Books of Moses) annually, and those who dive into its waters know that although we return to it year after year, it is never the same twice, because each time we come to the text we are different. This is why, when we finish a book, we acknowledge its power to support and strengthen us by reciting together, *Chazak chazak v'nitchazeik*, *"Strengthen us, strengthen us, and we will be strong."*

A parable from the Chasidic master Rebbe Nachman of Bratzlav is as germane to our lives as it was to his followers' lives in the Ukraine early in the nineteenth century: A Jewish man named Isaac dreamed that priceless treasure lay buried under a bridge far from his home. He set out and traveled for many days to uncover and lay claim to the treasure. When he reached the bridge that had appeared in his dream he began to dig. A soldier approached him and asked, "What are you doing?" He described his dream to the soldier, who laughed heartily and replied "What a crazy old man you are! Why, if I believed my dreams, I would travel at once to the town you come from and dig in the cellar of somebody named Isaac, where a great treasure is to be found." Isaac quietly put away his shovel, returned home, and climbed down into his cellar, where he found a great treasure.

We have a wonderful treasure right here at home. We are blessed with a wide variety of jewels, holy books to challenge our intellect and refine our *n'shamah*, rewarding both mind and soul. And we are fortunate to have such a rich and bountiful library of choices so each of us can follow our interests and inclinations, nourished, enlarged, and enriched by the traditional Jewish spiritual practice of Jewish learning.

Source: Rabbi Amy Scheinerman, "Our Tree of Life, " from *A Life of Meaning: Embracing Reform Judaism's Sacred Path*, ed. Rabbi Dana Evan Kaplan (New York: CCAR Press, 2018).

Why Should Reform Jews
Study Talmud?

Rabbi Dvora E. Weisberg, Ph.D.

Fifteen years ago, soon after I accepted a job teaching Rabbinic literature on the Los Angeles campus of Hebrew Union College-Jewish Institute of Religion, I participated in a conference call with two of my new colleagues. They wanted to help me think about what I would teach during my first semester of the introductory Talmud course required of all rabbinical students. The Talmud is a massive compilation that has been at the center of Jewish study and has served as one of the bases for Jewish law and practice since the early Middle Ages; it is characterized by debate and rhetorical discussions. I could not expect my students to be enthusiastic about studying Talmud, my colleagues told me. They recommended that I teach only passages about festival observance—fasting on Yom Kippur, lighting Hanukkah candles, the Passover Seder—since the more "relevant" the material, the more likely my students would respond positively.

Fast forward ten or twelve years. I am teaching an adult education class at a Reform congregation in Southern California where the rabbi is one of my former students. The topic for my session is "Why Reform Jews Should Study Talmud." After the session, a woman comes up to me. She introduces herself as the daughter of a Reform rabbi and a regular participant in the temple's adult education program. "I wasn't sure about coming today," she said, "because I didn't think Talmud was important for Reform Jews."

These stories have what we would call happy endings. My HUC-JIR students over the years have, for the most part, enjoyed their study of Talmud, and the woman assured me that she had enjoyed the class. At the same time, these occurrences underscore the challenge of arguing that Talmud study should be part of Reform Judaism. Reform Jews, be they committed laypeople or future Jewish professionals, do not take it for granted that Talmud study fits into their self-understanding. We tend to associate Talmud with *halachah*, traditional Jewish law, and with Orthodox Judaism. Even as adult education programs have flourished in our congregations, Reform Jews avoid studying Talmud. There are several reasons for this.

We are, as our platform statements and history remind us, a prophetic movement. Our vision of the world is built on the Bible, specifically that portion of the Hebrew Bible known as *Nevi'im*, the books of the Prophets. Reform Jews have traditionally defined themselves by their commitment to the ethical ideals of Isaiah and Amos, two of the biblical prophets whose calls for justice continue to inspire us today, not the laws of either Moses or the Rabbis. Even our sustained study of Torah, now a regular feature of many Reform congregations, is a relatively new feature. But Torah study seems a natural step for us to take. After all, the Torah is the text that resides in the ark in our sanctuary. It is read every week during our Shabbat services. It is, together with the other sections of the *Tanakh*, the Hebrew Bible the basis of Judaism. And, of course, Torah is an accessible text. It is available in beautiful English translations and with excellent commentaries. The narrative parts are great, and the legal sections are usually thought provoking.

Contrasted with the Torah, the Talmud feels alien. Its language is terse, its use of technical and legal terminology unfamiliar to the novice. While there are now English translations of the Talmud, they cannot be easily picked up and read the way the Torah can, for the Talmud is a highly edited and stylized document; some students find it difficult at first to make sense of its structure. The Rabbis' thinking, while undoubtedly logical to them, often seems less reasonable to us: why give the weakest answer first, why ask so many questions about a subject and then offer no definitive answer, why spend all this time on a ritual no longer practiced?

The inaccessibility of the Talmud is an issue for many Jews, Reform, Conservative, and even Orthodox. In the past two decades, two new English translations of the Talmud have been published, largely to make Talmud accessible to a wider readership. But as Reform Jews, we face another obstacle when we try to imagine ourselves studying Talmud. We are the heirs of a movement that, on some level, dismissed Rabbinic Judaism and turned for its guidance and inspiration back to the prophets. In its early phases, our movement also expressed minimal interest in—and even distaste for—ritual. We are often told or assume that the Talmud is first and foremost a legal text, the early Rabbis' expansion on the laws of the Torah. Therefore for us, the possibility of Talmud study raises the question of relevance or applicability. Why should we, as modern, liberal Jews, spend any time on Talmud, particularly those parts of the Talmud that deal with law?

So why should Reform Jews study Talmud? I could argue that all forms of Judaism build on earlier Judaisms. When you read early documents of Reform Judaism, you can see that the founders of Reform were struggling with Rabbinic Judaism, the Judaism represented in and shaped by the Talmud. Today, as we explore the role of ritual in Reform Judaism, we are considering the role Rabbinic practice and theology will have in shaping our Judaism. As important as the Bible is to Jewish tradition, we are Rabbinic Jews in our practice and in the way we approach the Bible.

Consider, for instance, our celebration of Jewish holidays. One of the holidays most commonly observed by Reform Jews is Hanukkah. But Hanukkah is not a biblical festival. It has its origins in the second century before the Common Era, when the Jews of Judea rebelled against religious persecution and triumphed, rededicating the Temple in Jerusalem. If you read the books written closest to the Maccabean Revolt, their descriptions of Hanukkah focus on battles and on cleansing and dedicating the Jerusalem temple; the eight-day observance that we now know as Hanukkah commemorates the rededication of the temple or the belated observance of Sukkot that occurred after the temple was rededicated. Observance of Hanukkah through kindling lights and our common explanation of the reason for the holiday are first set forth in the Talmud.

> What is [the reason for the festival of] Hanukkah? Our rabbis taught: From the twenty-fifth day of Kislev are the days of Hanukkah, which are eight, on which eulogies and fasting are forbidden. When the Greeks entered the sanctuary, they defiled all the oil in it. But when the Hasmonean house grew strong and defeated them, they searched and found but a single cruse of oil that was sealed with the seal of the high priest. It contained sufficient oil for only one day. A miracle occurred, and they lit [the menorah] from it for eight days. The next year, they established them and made them festival days with Hallel and thanksgiving. (Babylonian Talmud, Shabbat 21b)

So when we celebrate Hanukkah today, we are following the practice set forth in the Talmud.

When we look at the discussion of Hanukkah that precedes the story of the miracle, we learn something else that makes the Talmud a valuable resource for

Reform Jews. The Talmud is *not* a code of Jewish law, but discussion of ritual practice is a major feature of the Talmud. The Talmudic discussion of lighting Hanukkah candles underscores both the ways that Judaism today reflects the Judaism of centuries before and the ways that it has evolved.

> Our rabbis taught: The commandment of Hanukkah is [to light] one [lamp] per household. Those who are more exacting [light] one [lamp] for each and every person [in the house]. And those who are the most exacting—the House of Shammai say: On the first day one should light eight; from then on, he reduces [the number of lights] as the holiday progresses. But the House of Hillel say: On the first day one should light one; from then on, he adds [to the number of lights] as the holiday progresses....

This passage reflects something about Judaism that is crucial to the project of the Reform Movement: Judaism is not static. Between the Maccabean Revolt and the institution of Hanukkah in the second century BCE, and the compilation of the Talmud seven hundred years later, there were several stages in the development of the ritual created to mark the holiday. First, every household lit a single lamp to commemorate the miracle. Then some people decided they wanted to make a bigger deal over Hanukkah (and I suspect they were also people with money to burn – pardon the pun), so each person in the household had his or her own Hanukkah lamp. Then others decided to go a step further and light multiple lamps on a given night. This version of the ritual became the focus of a debate between the followers of Shammai and the followers of Hillel. Our current practice reflects the view of the Hillelites, with some of us also honoring the practice of the first set of "exacting" folks by giving each member of the family his or her own *hanukkiyah*.

Another passage that teaches us about the evolution of Jewish practice, while also offering us an insight into rabbinic disputes and leadership, deals with sounding the *shofar*, the ram's horn, on Rosh Hashanah that coincides with Shabbat.

> When Rosh Hashanah fell on Shabbat, the *shofar* was sounded in the Temple but not around the country. When the Temple was destroyed, Rabban Yohanan ben Zakkai decreed that the *shofar* could be sounded [on Shabbat] any place where there was a court.
> Our rabbis taught: It once happened that Rosh Hashanah fell on the Sabbath. Everyone came together. Rabban Yohanan ben Zakkai said to the sons of Beterah, "Let us sound the *shofar*." They said to him, "Let us discuss the matter." He said to them, "Let us first sound the *shofar* and then discuss the matter." After they sounded the *shofar*, they said to him, "Now let us discuss the matter." He said to them, "The *shofar* has already been sounded in Yavneh,

and one does not undo that which has been done." (Babylonian Talmud, *Rosh Hashanah* 29b)

Again, we see a ritual evolving, this time in response to external events. According to the Mishnah, the earliest compilation of rabbinic law (3rd century Common Era) and the starting point for the Talmud, when Rosh Hashanah fell on Shabbat, the *shofar* was sounded only in the Jerusalem Temple. We learn from Talmudic discussions on sounding the *shofar* that the Rabbis believed it was forbidden to sound the *shofar* on Shabbat due to concern lest a person carry the *shofar* through the streets to reach the synagogue (Rabbinic tradition forbids carrying objects more than a few feet through public spaces on the Sabbath). This type of secondary prohibition did not apply to the Temple, so the *shofar* could be sounded there. After the destruction of the Temple, Yohanan ben Zakkai wanted to allow the sounding of the *shofar* on Shabbat in many places.

The Talmud's story offers the back story for Yohanan ben Zakkai's decree. It asks us to imagine what might have been the first time after the destruction of the Temple that Rosh Hashanah fell on Shabbat. According to some readings of the Talmud, many people gathered together in Yavneh, presumably hoping to hear the *shofar*. Yohanan is prepared to sound the *shofar*, but his colleagues want to debate the subject first. Unwilling to wait—or perhaps unwilling to risk losing the argument – Yohanan tricks his colleagues. After sounding the *shofar*, he argues that a discussion would be counterproductive, insofar as it might lead the sages to undermine something that they had already done.

At first glance, this passage validates contemporary Reform practice. But a look at other Talmudic passages about *shofar* indicates that Yohanan ben Zakkai's ruse did not lead to ongoing sounding of *shofar* on Shabbat. The Talmud simultaneously provides a basis for our ritual practice while indicating that another practice, the custom of not sounding the *shofar* on Shabbat, remained the norm.

Beyond teaching about the evolution of a ritual practice, this story asks us to consider the way we make decisions. We might ask ourselves: Why did Yohanan's view carry the day, but fail to pass the test of time? Was the reason for his Pyrrhic victory his disregard for process or his treatment of his colleagues?

A third example of the evolution of ritual over time can be found in Tractate *Pesahim*, a tractate that focuses on the observance of Passover. The tenth chapter of Mishnah *Pesahim* discusses the Seder; parts of this text appear word for word in the Haggadah. Early rabbinic literature—Mishnah, Babylonian Talmud, and Palestinian Talmud—reveal multiple versions of what we know as the Four Questions. Study of this material indicates that during Late Antiquity, the number of questions grew from three to four and several of the questions underwent changes, with one falling into disuse as another came into existence. In this way, the study of Talmud allows us not only to see the connections between our liturgy and the liturgy of Jews who lived close to two thousand years ago, but to see how liturgy and ritual first came into being, then changed in response to changing circumstances.

While the passages I cited above focus on ritual, the Talmud is also a repository for Jewish ethics. The rabbis whose words fill the Talmud saw no distinction between ritual and ethical imperatives; both derived from Torah and expressed the will of God for the people of Israel. The Talmud teaches us how to treat each other in a complex world. Through a combination of law and story, the Talmud offers guidance for human and humane interactions.

> Some porters broke wine jars belonging to Rabbah bar bar Hana. He confiscated their cloaks [to pay for the damage they had caused]. They went and complained to Rav. Rav said to Rabbah bar bar Hana, "Give them their cloaks." Rabbah bar bar Hana said to Rav, "Is this the law?" Rav said to him, "[Yes,] 'Follow the way of the good' (Proverbs 2:20)." So he gave them their cloaks. They said to him, "We are poor men, and we worked hard all day and we have nothing to show for our labor." Rav said to him, "Give them their wages." Rabbah bar bar Hana said to him, "Is this the law?" He said to him, "[Yes,] 'And keep to the paths of the just' (Proverbs 2:20)." (Babylonian Talmud, *Baba M'tsia* 83a)

This story comes at the end of a discussion of the laws regulating the conduct of employers and employees. The law teaches that workers, if they are negligent, are responsible for damage to goods they had been hired to convey from one place to another, a ruling that anyone who has ever hired a long-distance moving company can appreciate. The story speaks of just such a case; Rabbah bar bar Hana hires porters to transport wine and the wine is lost through their carelessness. Yet when Rabbah seeks compensation for his loss by confiscating the porters' outer garments—perhaps hoping to hold them until he receives payment for the damages—the porters sue him! Moreover, his colleague Rav rules in favor of the porters, not only forcing Rabbah to return their cloaks but also compelling him to pay their wages. Rabbah is understandably annoyed; he is also surprised, since he thought the law supported him. When he asks Rav, "Is this the law," Rav responds with a quote from Proverbs. The verse from Proverbs says nothing about employer-employee law; rather it counsels us to do that which is right and just. Some versions of the Talmud add the word "Yes" to Rav's response, while other versions omit the word. In either case, it seems clear that what Rav is telling Rabbah is that even with the law on his side, in this situation he should not use the law against the workers. Rav calls upon Rabbah to go beyond the letter of the law and forgo his legal rights, in consideration of the porters' poverty. In placing this story at the end of the legal discussion about workers, the Talmud reminds us that a just society is not only a society based on law; it must be a society that refuses to use the law to harm others.

So far, I have made a case for studying material from the Talmud. In this day and age, English translations and on-line resources make it very easy to extract material on almost any topic from the Talmud. Because of this, Jews with no background in Talmud study and with no knowledge of Aramaic can be exposed to what we might call "the wisdom of the Talmud." However, I want to make a more sweeping argument, namely that Reform Jews should consider studying Talmud itself, rather than being satisfied with snippets of Talmud.

Why should Reform Jews study Talmud? I actually believe the question should be: Why *wouldn't* Reform Jews study Talmud? Although the study of Talmud is most widely embraced by Orthodox Jews, it is liberal Jews who ought to most appreciate the Talmud. Almost every page of the Babylonian Talmud contains disputes. One of the most noticeable (and, for the beginning student, often the most frustrating) characteristics of a talmudic discussion is a high degree of tolerance for difference of opinion. In fact, the Talmud delights in debate and is eager to consider every side of an argument. The editors of the Talmud were willing to devote considerable space and energy considering the most "preposterous" solutions to a problem. Answers—especially definitive *halachic* answers—are secondary or even irrelevant to many talmudic discussions. One of the hallmarks of Reform Judaism is its adherence to the principle of informed choice, the belief that every Jew should learn about Judaism in order to decide which aspects of Jewish ritual could guide and enrich his or her life, then Talmud is the very model of what it means to be a liberal Jew, a Jew who engages in study not to find a particular "right" answer but to think deeply about the enterprise of constructing a Judaism that speaks to us.

It is important to acknowledge that we will not like everything that we encounter in the Talmud. The Talmud is a product of a different world, of rabbis whose worldview and cultural assumptions are often foreign to us. The Talmud takes for granted the existence of slavery, the absence of women from the house of study and the synagogue, and the superiority of the Jewish people. Some of its theological positions are disturbing to many modern Jews. But to be Jewish is to engage with Torah in its broad sense, to struggle to find new meaning in old traditions, and sometimes to acknowledge that what spoke to Jews centuries ago does not speak to us with the same force. It is with that understanding that we can study Talmud and find value in much of what it offers.

I would argue that the best reason to study Talmud is that Talmud is our *y'rushah*, our inheritance as Jews. If we are going to transmit any kind of Judaism, we need to be firmly rooted in Judaism. We are entitled to react to any talmudic passage with enthusiasm or amazement or even horror, but we need to be in dialogue with these texts if our Judaism is to be part of the tradition stretching back to Sinai. In the years that I have studied Talmud, I have found it a deeply satisfying endeavor, both intellectually and spiritually. When we turn to the classic texts of Jewish tradition, we find more than instructions on the proper way to put Hanukkah candles into the menorah or drink four cups of wine at a Seder. We find the words of individuals who were deeply committed to living full Jewish lives, infusing the values of the Torah and the prophets into every moment of the day. Additionally, we enter into a conversation that has been going on for thousands of years and become active participants in that conversation about what it means to be Jewish. The study of Talmud, then, is not simply an intellectual or educational project. It is a religious activity through which we not only explore the Jewish past but become part of shaping the Jewish present and future.

Source: Rabbi Dvora E. Weisberg, PhD. "Why Should Reform Jews Study Talmud?" from *A Life of Meaning: Embracing Reform Judaism's Sacred Path*, ed. Rabbi Dana Evan Kaplan (New York: CCAR Press, 2018).

Responsa

Rabbi Mark Washofsky

Responsa, as a genre of rabbinical writing, have been around for a long time, and for most of that time, they have been the product of individual authors. It was not always thus. For example, we find traces of the responsa literature in the Talmud, which was redacted between 500–700 c.e., and the evidence there suggests plural authorship: "*Shal'chu* (*They* sent) the following answer to so-and-so." During the Geonic period, dated roughly from the eighth to the eleventh-twelfth centuries c.e., it was the *gaon*, the head of the Torah academy, who officially issued and signed the responsa that answered questions concerning religious practice. He did so, however, after having consulted his colleagues and discussing the queries with them. Yet during the many centuries since that time, the general custom has been for the correspondent or community to address their question (*sh'elah*) to a particular scholar, whose response (*t'shuvah*) expresses his own interpretation and application of Torah and halachah.

Some of our published Reform responsa (to say nothing of answers communicated through private correspondence) follow this pattern. They are clearly the work of a single author, conveying that individual's opinion on the question at hand. In general, though, we as a movement have sought to reinstitute the earlier custom.

Source: Rabbi Mark Washofsky, *Reform Responsa for the Twenty-First Century*, vol. 1 (New York: CCAR Press, 2010), ix.

Unit V

THE JEWISH STORY

The World of the Bible and the
Rabbis, and the Jewish World
through the Enlightenment

Jewish History Timeline

LIVES OF THE PATRIARCHS AND MATRIARCHS	1900-1700 BCE	
	1250 BCE	THE EXODUS FROM EGYPT AND FORTY YEARS IN THE DESERT
ENTERING THE LAND— BOOK OF JOSHUA	1200 BCE	
	1200-1025 BCE	TIME OF THE JUDGES
UNITED MONARCHIES OF SAUL, DAVID, AND SOLOMON	1025-928 BCE	
	950 BCE	CONSTRUCTION OF THE FIRST TEMPLE
DIVIDED MONARCHIES OF THE NORTH (ISRAEL) AND SOUTH (JUDAH)	928-722 BCE	
	722 BCE	DESTRUCTION OF THE NORTHERN KINGDOM (ISRAEL) BY THE ASSYRIAN EMPIRE
DESTRUCTION OF THE SOUTHERN KINGDOM (JUDAH) BY THE BABYLONIAN EMPIRE	586 BCE	
	586-539 BCE	THE BABYLONIAN EXILE
DECREE BY PERSIAN EMPEROR CYRUS II FREEING THE JUDEANS TO RETURN TO JERUSALEM	539 BCE	
	515 BCE	CONSTRUCTION OF THE SECOND TEMPLE IN JERUSALEM
CANONIZATION OF THE TORAH—BOOKS OF EZRA AND NEHEMIAH	450 BCE	
	333 BCE	ALEXANDER THE GREAT CONQUERS THE LAND OF ISRAEL FROM THE PERSIAN EMPIRE
MACCABEAN (HASMONEAN) REVOLT AGAINST THE GREEKS	166-160 BCE	
	152 - 63 BCE	HASMONEAN DYNASTY RULES OVER THE LAND OF ISRAEL
ISRAEL FALLS TO ROMAN RULE	60 BCE	
	30 BCE- 20 BCE	DEBATES BETWEEN THE HOUSES OF HILLEL AND SHAMMAI
JEWISH REVOLT AGAINST ROME	66-73 CE	
	70 CE	2ND TEMPLE DESTROYED
EARLY RABBINIC ("TANNAITIC") PERIOD	70–22 CE	
	80 CE–132 CE	ESTABLISHMENT OF YAVNEH
BAR KOCHBA REVOLT	132–135 CE	
	200–220 CE	COMPILATION OF THE MISHNAH— JUDAH HANASI
MIDDLE RABBINIC ("AMORAIC") PERIOD	220–500 CE	

	200–670 CE	BABYLONIAN AND JERUSALEM ACADEMIES DEVELOP THE TALMUD
LATE RABBINIC ("SAVORAIC") PERIOD	550–620 CE	
	620–800 CE	AGE OF THE GEONIM
GOLDEN AGE OF SPANISH JEWRY	700–1100 CE	
	1040–1105 CE	RASHI WRITES HIS BIBLICAL AND MIDRASHIC COMMENTARIES
MAIMONIDES WRITES THE MISHNEH TORAH AND GUIDE FOR THE PERPLEXED	1135–1204 CE	
	12TH CENTURY CE	INQUISITION
FIRST APPEARANCE OF THE ZOHAR	13TH CENTURY CE	
	1516–1948 CE	AGE OF THE EUROPEAN GHETTOS
EXPULSION FROM SPAIN	1492 CE	
	1700–1760 CE	BAAL SHEM TOV —HASIDISM
SETTLEMENTS IN AMERICA	1654 CE	
	1810–1840 CE	GERMAN REFORMERS
EUROPEAN EMANCIPATION	1791–1871 CE	
	1860–1904	HERZL/ZIONISM
RUSSIAN HASKALAH	1800–1860 CE	
	1948	STATE OF ISRAEL ESTABLISHED
SHOAH	1941–1945	

Four Exiles and
Four Spiritual Revolutions

Dr. Joel M. Hoffman

Some 3,000 years ago, according to historical and archaeological evidence, a Semitic group in Jerusalem who would later be called "the Jews" began an experiment in what they thought was a better way of living. Their experiment is ongoing and still thriving today, despite four potentially devastating exiles, because each exile was followed by a period of spiritual revolution that reinvented Judaism.

Though the early Jews (or, technically, Israelites) are primarily known now for advocating monotheism, they actually gave four things to the world: monotheism, the weekend (Shabbat), the alphabet, and the concept of human rights. These have all worked in tandem, and continue to do so to this day.

Shabbat seems like an obvious way to end a week, but that's actually looking at it backwards. The only reason for the *week* is to have the weekend, to have Shabbat. That is, unlike other common calendrical units, the week was invented for social purposes: A day is one rotation of the earth, a month one revolution of the moon around the earth, and a year one revolution of the earth around the sun. A week, though, doesn't correspond to anything in nature. Its purpose is not to mark a natural phenomenon but to create a social one based in a belief that people shouldn't spend their whole lives working.

Next is the alphabet, which the Jews created by modifying a pre-alphabetic consonantal system used by the Phoenicians. It proved so popular that 3,000 years later it still forms the basis of almost all of the world's communication, whether the Roman alphabet used in the Americas and Western Europe or the Cyrillic alphabet used in Eastern Europe, whether the Middle East's Hebrew and Arabic or the writing from the subcontinent of India; Chinese is written with a non-alphabetic system, but even it is often entered into a computer using an alphabet.

The Jews needed their alphabet for two important reasons. First, they hoped to record and thus preserve the guidelines of their experiment for future generations, in the form of written Scriptures. (Writing had never been used this way before, so its success was not guaranteed, though we now know, of course, that it worked). Second, the alphabet was crucial to making sure that all Jews could stay abreast of what was going on. The Jews were all expected to learn to read and write. (Archaeological confirmation of widespread Jewish literacy surfaced in 2016.)

So the alphabet was a distribution system for transmitting information to Jews of the day and to Jews of future generations. And the information that was transmitted included the novel idea that people should not spend their whole lives working ("Shabbat"). The reason people should not spend their whole lives working, the early Jews said, is that every person has value. Though this outlook lies at the core of Western thought, it is rare across the world and throughout history. The more widespread pattern is for people to be the property of a local monarch, whether a king, some other king-like ruler, or a dictatorial government. In antiquity, certainly, most people belonged to the king.

By contrast, the Jews decided that every person—rich or poor, man or woman, peasant or aristocrat, inept or talented, local denizen or visitor—was more than mere property and had certain basic human rights. Among these was the right to a day off every so often. Also among these was the right to due process of law. This is why the Torah commands that neither the rich nor the poor be favored in courts, and why the Torah specifically legislates that the rich cannot buy their way out of a death sentence.

To emphasize this new way of looking at humanity, the Jews reframed a familiar motif. Whereas in other cultures people belonged to the king, in the Jewish communities both the people and the king belonged to God. And this is where monotheism comes in.

Indeed, Genesis bravely declares that Adam and Eve—meant to represent all of humankind—were created in the image of God. And lest there be any confusion, the text is clear that both "men" and "women" are in God's image. Every person, then, is godlike and God's property, not to be coopted by human masters.

Taken in whole, then, we find an early Jewish agenda focused on universal human rights, including rights to due process, equality before the law, and a day off from work at least every seven days. The details of the day off from work were encoded in Shabbat, for which the Jews needed the week. The details of human rights more generally were tied to a single God, who was master over every human. And to let people know about the new program of human rights, the Jews needed mass communication: the alphabet.

The whole endeavor relied on various other institutions for support. A professional class of priests was tasked with maintaining the system. Because their job demanded their full-time attention, others had to provide for their sustenance. Sacrifices filled that need. To house those sacrifices as well as promote the centrality of God, the Jews built the impressive First Temple in Jerusalem.

Before long, the Temple and its city came to represent the validity and success of the Jewish experiment. This is why the traumatic exile of 586 BCE, when Nebuchadnezzar sent the Jews to Babylon (or Babylonia; roughly modern Iraq) might have marked the end of Judaism. For nearly half a millennium, Jerusalem had served as the center of Judaism, while the great Temple had served both as the physical manifestation of the people's connection to God and as the home for the priests who oversaw Judaism.

These most visible symbols of God's approval were more than mere aspects of Judaism. They were the embodiment of Judaism. Serving God meant sacrificing at the Temple, and God showed approval of the sacrifices—and approval more generally—by granting the Jews ongoing prosperity in Jerusalem.

A year of two of drought could be dismissed as a temporary sign that the Jews had made some minor error or be discounted as a minor setback in a larger pattern of success. Exile, though, from the very land that had birthed and then sustained Judaism for hundreds of years, pointed to one terrifying, tragic conclusion: There was no God.

The Bible even records the misery and confusion of exile, for example, in Psalm 137: "By the waters of Babylon, we sat down and wept," because "how can we sing God's song in a foreign land."

In the midst of this potentially devastating exile, the prophets step in and save Judaism. Facing a population increasingly worried that there was no God, the great prophets turn things around, pointing to the exile itself as proof that God exists. "Who do you think exiled you?" the prophets ask rhetorically. God, they say.

And the prophets explain that God exiled the Jews because they weren't taking good enough care of other peoples.

"You are just like the Ethiopians to me," Amos (9:7) quotes God as saying. The point is that Israel is no better than any other nation, and no more deserving of God's grace. Isaiah, for his part, demands equitable behavior in addition to ritual observance: "Is this the fast that I have chosen?" (Isaiah 58:6) Isaiah also opens Judaism to foreigners: "For My house shall be called a house of prayer for all peoples." (56:7) Micah goes so far as to reject sacrifice: "Will God be pleased with thousands of rams?.... Shall I offer my firstborn?" The implicit answer, Micah writes, is no, because "God has shown you" what is necessary; it is necessary to "act justly." (Micah 6:7–8) In other words, what God really wants isn't sacrifice but equitable behavior.

That is, the prophets explain that God demands more than ritual service. God has charged the Jews with taking care of other nations, a task at which the Jews have failed, bringing about their own exile.

What's amazing is that the prophets made this up. Not one line in the Five Books of Moses demands that the Jews do anything outside their own communities. While the Jews have a responsibility to foreigners visiting among them, they have no obligation to those same foreigners when they are in their own lands (with the possible exception of treating them equitably during war).

It is difficult now to appreciate just how revolutionary the prophets' revisionist understanding was because it has become part of mainstream Judaism.. It was this prophetic vision that, generations on, led Rabbi Stephen Wise to co-found the NAACP in 1914, for instance. More generally, it has led to our modern notion of *tikkun olam* and to the host of Jewish social-action projects that come with it. At the time, however, the prophets were completely reinventing Judaism—a fact all the more remarkable considering the prophets' relatively minor role before the exile.

This is a pattern we will see four times: a previously marginalized group steps in after an exile and remakes Judaism as part of a spiritual revolution. In this initial case, the prophets turn the Jewish eye outward, whereas formerly it had focused strictly inward on the Jews' own communities.

The next case will come about more than 500 years later, after the Second Exile (in 70 CE), when the Rabbis change Judaism even more.

The Second Exile was the culmination of a series of cascading events that began not too long after the First Exile ended. Around 515 BCE, the Temple was

rededicated as some Jews returned to Jerusalem. (Contrary to popular conception, most exiled Jews probably stayed in Babylonia).

For a while, the Jews again thrived in Jerusalem. Ezra started teaching Torah
in 458, and in 445, Nehemiah built new city walls. But 120 years later, Alexander
the Great died having conquered his known world but having neglected to put
in place a plan of succession. This unfortunate combination led to an ongoing
pattern that mixed chaos, temporary stability, and infighting among the families
that took over the territories Alexander had conquered. Jerusalem found herself
at the center of much of that turmoil.

One family that rose to power after Alexander died was named Seleucid. And
one Seleucid ruler in Syria, Antiochus IV (dubbed Antiochus the Insane), is well
known as the regent who sullied the Second Temple around 168 BCE. It's equally
well known that a family called the Maccabees repelled Antiochus IV a few years
later—events that are still commemorated by the holiday of Hannukah. Less well
known is the fact that the Maccabees were better at fighting than ruling, which
is why Jerusalem quickly descended into chaos in the final decades of the first
millennium BCE. Before long Rome would take over, the wicked Herod finding
himself in charge of Jerusalem. (It's ironic, perhaps, that Herod was eligible
to rule the Jewish city only because the Maccabees had forcibly converted his
grandfather to Judaism.)

Herod bequeathed Jerusalem to his son Archelaus, who took over in the
year 4 BCE. The younger ruler shared his father's cruelty but lacked his father's
ability, which is why the Roman ruler Augustus had to intervene in the year
6 CE, reorganizing the region of Jerusalem into a Roman province like any other.
Jerusalem, now a walking corpse, lasted only a few decades longer. Two years
after Nero's death in the year 68, Roman troops sacked the city and razed the
great Temple that had stood in one form or another for a thousand years. And
the Jews were exiled from their homeland for a second time.

Even more than Nebuchadnezzar's earlier banishment of the Jews in 586 BCE
, this new exile could have spelled the end of Judaism.

Instead, we find our pattern again: A previously marginalized group of people
stepped in to reinvent Judaism. This time it was the Rabbis, who would go on to
write the Talmud and the Midrash and generally give us most of what we now
think of as Judaism: worship services, Shabbat candle-lighting, fasting on Yom
Kippur, the laws of kashrut, and much more.

Amazingly, the Rabbis changed things even more than the prophets had. The
prophets advocated interest in and compassion for all peoples. But they didn't

eliminate any core aspects of Judaism. By contrast the Rabbis did nothing less than abandon the most central Jewish practice: sacrifice itself. And this after sacrifice had been the backbone of Judaism for fully 1,000 years.

A persistent rumor holds that sacrifice was impossible away from the great Temple in Jerusalem, and that, once exiled, the Jews has no choice but to abandon sacrifice. But we know that is not true. We know from the Dead Sea Scrolls that sacrifice was possible anywhere, with only the provision that people within a three-day walk of Jerusalem were supposed to sacrifice at the Temple. We also know that the First Exile to Babylonia didn't end sacrifice. Moreover, it surely would have been easiest, upon being exiled, to temporarily suspend any restrictions limiting sacrifice to the Temple.

The Second Exile, then, did not force an end to sacrifice. Rather, the Rabbis wanted an end to sacrifice, finding the practice to have outlived its usefulness. They wanted something new.

In place of sacrifice, the Rabbis instituted worship services, offering God words instead of food. And the Rabbis created an order for those words—what we now know as the liturgy—and rules for almost everything else, too.

We now call those rules *halachah*, or Jewish law. And though it currently lies at the heart of Judaism, the Rabbis' set of laws, like the prophetic innovation, was in its time a radical invention.

The Rabbis are the ones who give us, for instance, not just the tradition of putting Hanukkah candles into a Hanukkah menorah, but a right and wrong way to do so. (The right way is right to left.) There's also a right way to light those candles (left to right).

Similarly, there are rules about building a sukkah. The sukkah must have four, three, or two-and-a-half walls. It must be temporary, according to a wide variety of criteria. It must offer a partial view of the sky. It must be at least ten hand-breadths high (some three feet) but not more than about ten yards. These and other regulations are found in a book of the Talmud called *Sukkot*; and they were codified by the Rabbis in the centuries that followed the Second Exile.

Concerning the sukkah, the Talmud next asks whether an elephant can be used for one wall! The answer is no, because the elephant might walk away. What about a dead elephant? Yes, so long as the deceased pachyderm is at least ten hand-breadths tall.

This part of the discussion was obviously humorously intended. It highlights the way in which the Rabbis put the Judaism they had developed to use to enjoy being Jewish—something often lost in the modern quest merely to follow the laws.

At any rate, the Jews headed north, south, and east in the aftermath of the Second Exile (the Mediterranean Sea prevented direct movement west). Many Jews settled in Babyloni—modern-day Iraq—because of their ongoing connection to that area dating from the First Exile. "The" Talmud was in fact written by the Rabbis living in Babylonia. (There's also a lesser Talmud written by the Rabbis living in Jerusalem.) Other Jews moved south to Africa, then west across northern Africa, often settling somewhere on the way. Those who didn't stop eventually made their way to Morocco and, from there, across the Strait of Gibraltar to the Iberian Peninsula, southern Spain, where that locale's magic paved the way for what is now called the Golden Age of Spain.

Jews in the Iberian Peninsula were integrated into the newly formed Muslim empire, which had conquered the area in the 8th century. This fertile environment yielded such Jewish scholars as Abraham Ibn Ezra, the famed Bible commentator; Rabbi Yosef Karo, author of the authoritative *Shulchan Aruch*; Yehuda Halevi, a gifted poet, physician, and philosopher, and possiblely the first to write secular Hebrew poetry; Maimonides (Rambam), whose works seem to have come, Abraham Joshua Heschel once said, from an entire university rather than one man; and many more.

Jews thrived in non-religious ways, too, practicing law, medicine, and finance, and rising to positions of power in government. They spoke local languages (primarily Arabic) and assumed local names, as, for example, Hasdai Abu Yusuf ben Isaac ben Ezra ibn Shaprut, a 10th-century Jew who served as court physician to powerful caliph Abd al-Rachman III.

In fact, many 21st-century Jews living in the West will see their own circumstances mirrored in the Golden Age of Spain: success, general acceptance, and a balance between religious and secular life.

As it refers to the Jews, the term "Golden Age of Spain" is both ambiguous and contested. Some scholars date its start as early as the 8th-century's first decades, others two-hundred years later. Similarly, while its end is often pegged to 11th-century political upheavals, it was in 1492 that Jewish life in Spain came to a final end, a few months after the Christian Spanish army defeated the last remnants of Muslim power there. In March 1492, their Majesties Ferdinand and Isabella ordered every Jew to convert to Christianity or to leave by July 30. By July, 1492 the Golden Age of Spanish Jewry was over.

And this is the third time we find our recurring pattern of exile and spiritual revolution, again led by a previously marginalized group. In this case, however, the exile is not from Israel but rather to it. Among other destinations, the Spanish Jews arrived in a backwater city on a hill in northern Israel: Safed.

Not surprisingly, the Jews fled to many spots, but the destinations in which they would be most successful were those in the Ottoman Empire, including Safed. For unclear reasons, it was there that the previously marginalized adherents of a book called the *Zohar* thrived.

The *Zohar* was written in the 13th century in Spain by a man named Moses de Leon , though sacred myth attributes the book to Shimon ben Yohai of the 2nd century. According to the myth—promulgated by Moses de Leon himself—Moses's only involvement was as copyist. He only copied and distributed Shimon ben Yohai's much older original work, he said. But though the *Zohar* may incorporate older themes, all of the evidence points unequivocally in the direction of it being a 13th-century creation. Still, it's quite a creation.

The modern scholar and mystic Arthur Green aptly describes the *Zohar* as a work of "sacred fantasy" to "be considered the highest expression of Jewish literary imagination in the Middle Ages" and "one of the most important bodies of religious text of all times and places." He adds that it is "a lush garden of sacred eros." The work's "secret universe" is the center of Jewish mystical faith, or Kabbalah.

The Zohar's nearly unparalleled appeal in a context of practically fraudulent distribution meant that it met with immediate controversy and with only partial acceptance. Many Jews in 13th-century Spain loved it. Others hated it. The majority of Jews outside of Spain didn't care one way or the other.

Initially, followers of the *Zohar*'s teachings—the *Jewish mystics* or as they came to be known, the kabbalists—were like the prophets before the First Exile and like the Rabbis before the Second Exile, in that they envisioned great changes for Judaism, but their message fell largely on deaf ears. Then, after the 15th century, amid the upheavals in the aftermath of the Spanish Exile, the kabbalists both thrived and managed to become mainstream.

The kabbalists were the ones who insisted that Friday night services ought to differ significantly from services held on other nights, not just through the minor additions and changes that had previously marked the start of the Sabbath, but with new texts of joy and celebration. Friday night should be a wedding! Friday night was when God—separated during the week into male and female parts—came together in marriage to form a unified God, even consummating the marriage in ecstatic joy.

To mark these new ceremonial aspects of welcoming Shabbat, a man named Rabbi Shlomo Halevi wrote a poem in iambic tetrameter (a meter popular in classical Arabic) which may be the most perfect poem in our liturgy, perhaps in all of Judaism. He called it "*L'cha Dodi*." With text based almost entirely in Scripture, it is metrically perfect, brilliant in its imagery, and masterful in its kabbalistic allusions.

The poem's opening line, "Go forth my lover to meet the bride," reflects the revisioning of Shabbat as a wedding. (The line is often wrongly translated as "go forth my beloved," perhaps in an effort to downplay the sexual content.) The ten verses of the poem mirror a central organizing principle of Kabbalah, that of ten emanations of God—*sefirot*, in Hebrew.

The poem is among the most well-known texts in Judaism, and there is hardly a Jewish community that does not incorporate it into Friday evening worship services.

Yet for all its merit and ubiquity, "*L'cha Dodi*" is simply a poem that some guy wrote. It enjoys no Halakhic importance or mandate; the Talmud, obviously, doesn't mention it. Furthermore, Friday evening had never been a wedding. God had never had erotic male and female parts. And the world had never been Jewishly organized into ten emanations. More generally, mysticism in its broadest sense had never been part of mainstream Judaism.

But the kabbalists of Safed—though once marginalized in Spain—changed all this. Like the prophets who turned the Jewish eye outward after the First Exile, and like the Rabbis who substituted prayer and Halakhah for sacrifice after the Second Exile, the kabbalists in the aftermath of the Spanish Exile gave Judaism mysticism and the Friday evening *Kabbalat Shabbat* service.

We have one more exile and spiritual revolution. This last exile to date is much more modern, and, therefore, more immediately painful to modern readers, so it is harder to analyze with any sense of detachment. But it follows the same pattern of producing a spiritual revolution.

It is, of course, the Holocaust, or Shoah. During the 1940s, the Jews in Europe were slaughtered en masse, only the lucky ones escaping. A population of about 9.5 million European Jews—more than half of the world's total Jewish population—was cut to less than 4 million. By 1945, Europe was home to only about a third of the world's Jews (a number that has dropped to about 10% at the time of this writing).

And although Germany is most closely associated with the Holocaust, most of Europe's Jews in 1939—some 85%, in fact—lived in Eastern Europe (Poland, the former Soviet Union, and so on). Only about 200,000, or roughly 2%, lived in Germany. Or to put things in global context, about half of the world's Jews in 1939 lived in Eastern Europe; about 1% lived in Germany.

Yet it was Germany's Jews—once again, a previously marginalized group—who would lead the post-Holocaust spiritual revolution. In the early part of the 1800s, largely in response to Napoleon's message of an enlightened, modern Europe with emancipated Jews, some Jews in what would later become Germany started experimenting with an enlightened, modern Judaism. They wanted to leave the Jewish ghettos and live (then-) modern lives.

As early at the 18th century, Moses Mendelssohn (1729-1786) worked to integrate the enlightenment into Judaism, even translating the Torah into German. He argued for a rational, tolerant, modern, ethical religion. (Moses Mendelssohn's grandson, Felix Mendelssohn, is the famous composer.)

In response to this kind of thinking, a Hungarian rabbi named Moses Sofer, widely known as "the Chatam Sofer," began to argue that nothing in Judaism could be changed. He claimed that the Torah itself prohibits anything new. Ironically, though, the Chatam Sofer's argument was itself a new interpretation of an old text. He argued that "the new is forbidden by the Torah," quoting *Kiddushin* 38b in the Talmud. But in that phrase in the Talmud, "the new" specifically refers to "new" grain in certain circumstances. Sofer used the word "new" instead to denote the kind of new practices that Mendelssohn favored..

After reading Mendelssohn's writings, a man named Israel Jacobson (1768-1828) similarly began working to modernize Judaism. And having married the granddaughter of Philip Samson, founder of the prestigious center of Jewish education known as the Samson School, Jacobson was in a position of influence. He was also in a position to meet other influential people, including another future advocate for reforming Judaism, Leopold Zunz (1794-1886), who similarly attended the Samson School.

Likewise, a man named Abraham Geiger (1810-1874) sought to create a Judaism that welcomed secular fields like history and archeology, and, more generally, the then-new and growing *Wissenschaft* approach to the world that mirrors our modern notion of "science."

Geiger studied at the University of Bonn, where he met Samson Raphael Hirsch (1808-1888). Friends at first, Hirsch and Geiger became vehement opponents. Hirsch ended up founding a movement now called *Trennungsorthodoxy*, literally "Separation Orthodoxy" akin to today's Modern Orthodoxy. Hirsch disagreed with modernizers like Zunz and Geiger, but he also disagreed with the Chatam Sofer's radical opposition to change.

In many ways, Geiger is the founder of Reform Judaism, and Hirsch is the founder of Orthodox Judaism. Judaism's Conservative Movement was born in the United States in response to Eastern European immigration, but it traces much of its theology and approach to yet another German thinker, Zacharias Frankel (1801-1875). So the Reform and Orthodox movements began in 19th-century Germany as responses to modernity, and in a roundabout way the Conservative Movement did, too.

In the first half of the 19th century, these and other Jewish leaders, and their respective followers and supporters, battled over pivotal issues like organ music and sermonizing as part of a broader philosophical disagreement about the nature of Judaism in the face of modernity.

The fighting was both bitter and public. But the fights were largely limited to Germany. A few congregations beyond Germany—in the United States, for example—had been established in the spirit of the German movements. For the most part, though, the world's Jews were still in Eastern Europe, where they did not adhere to the schools of Jacobson, Geiger, Zunz, Hirsch, or the Chatam Sofer because they had never left the Ghetto, Napoleon never having conquered Eastern Europe. And certainly the Sephardic Jews of the Arab world (Yemen and Iraq, for example) didn't care about the German religious debates.

So as late as the start of the Holocaust, the vast majority of Jews were not Reform, Conservative, or Orthodox. All three were minority movements limited to Germany and a handful of other congregations.

Then, in the aftermath of the Holocaust—our fourth exile—we find the pattern we now recognize. A previously marginalized group reinvents Judaism in a fourth spiritual revolution. We naturally tend to focus on that group's internal divisions, because we ourselves are still in the fourth revolution. For instance, we devote attention to how Reform differs from Orthodoxy, to liturgical styles, and to cell phone use on Shabbat.

But such divisions mask the larger pattern. There was no Reform, no Conservative, and no Orthodox until 18th-century Germany, and only in the 20th century did any of the three become mainstream.

For political reasons, Orthodoxy's public platform emphasizes continuity, while Reform's emphasizes change. That difference makes it easy to imagine that only Reform was the product of a minority movement in Germany. But even a cursory look at history reveals a different story. We've already seen how even the most vehement opponent to new thinking based his argument in new thinking. More importantly, current Reform, Conservative, and Orthodox practices all evidence revoluation.

For instance, one modern battle-line is over the use of cell phones on Shabbat. Reform congregations allow it; Orthodox congregations do not. It is abundantly obvious, though, that the Jews of the 1800s, to say nothing of the Jews in the second century, had no policy for cell phones, just as they didn't have one for electricity.

Certain *Halachic* considerations do rein in particular uses of electricity on Shabbat. For example, the Talmud suggests that heating metal to the point that it glows is forbidden on Shabbat, and Maimonides explicitly says so. Since that is exactly how incandescent light bulbs work, there's good reason to think that turning on an incandescent light bulb should be considered a *Halachic* violation of Shabbat. But that reasoning doesn't extend directly to fluorescent or LED lights.

What *Halachah* might say about about cell phones is even more tenuous, and is based primarily on the (obviously modern) prohibition against using electricity in general on Shabbat. And here *Halachah* is anything but clear. What we seem to find is a desire among certain communities to prohibit electricity, and therefore cell phones and non-incandescent lights. But disagreement is rampant about how to achieve that prohibition. The earliest opinion—no longer highly regarded—was that using electricity, like spraying fragrance onto cloth, is creating something new (technically, *molid*), and that is a category of actions prohibited on Shabbat. Using electricity was later compared to other forbidden Shabbat activities: building, completing a project, creating sparks, burning (because additional fuel has to be burned at a power station to create the electricity), and more. The prominent Rabbi Shlomo Zalman Auerbach even wrote (Minchat Shlomo 74, 84) that there's no *Halachic* reason not to use electricity on Shabbat, but Jews still shouldn't do it!

So both the Reform practice of allowing cell phones on Shabbat and the Orhtodox practice of disallowing them are modern innovations.

A second modern battle-line is drawn over wearing a *kippah*. Through happenstance, the generally progressive practice of donning a *kippah* only for services has the most historical support. That's what Maimonides did in the 13th century. It was the post-Spanish Exile kabbalists who first suggested that Jews should always wear a *kippah*. So in this case, Reform and Orthdox practices draw on different historical opinions.

A third modern battle-line concerns kashrut and shows again how modernity challenges old ritual laws in surprising ways. In the case of kashrut, this is because the laws were created long before modern chemistry became involved in processing food. For example, is maltodextrin kosher for Passover? On one hand, maltodextrin is simply a polysaccharide, that is, a chain of glucose units. Glucose is kosher for Passover, so why wouldn't a chain of glucose units be kosher? On the other hand, maltodextrin can be made from corn (as is common in the U.S.) or wheat (the usual practice in Europe). The prevailing Orthodox opinion on wheat-based maltodextrin is that it is forbidden, because wheat is forbidden unless specially handled to avoid any rising, and to the extent that corn is forbidden, so too is corn-based maltodextrin. That's certainly reasonable. But it is not the only reasonable approach. Equally reasonable is the argument that two identical molecules ought to have the same kashrut status, wherever they might have come from.

Similarly, why should honey be kosher (though it is)? After all, honey comes from bees, bees are not kosher, and according to the Talmud (*B'chorot* 1a), anything that emerges from a non-kosher animal is not kosher. Camel milk, for instance, is forbidden because it comes from the non-kosher camel. So why is honey okay? The Talmudic answer (*B'chorot* 7b) is that bees don't produce honey the way camels produce milk. Bees only store honey, between the time they collect it from blossoms and the time they regurgitate it. But the Talmud was wrong. While bees do store nectar (in a special extra stomach, or *crop*), they also process the nectar while they are storing it. There are bee enzymes in honey The most common approach here is to ignore the (uncontested) modern scientific objections to the Rabbis, but an equally reasonable approach would be to introduce a long-overdue correction.

Our final example of kashrut comes from New York City tap water, which was discovered some years ago to contain tiny crustaceans related to shrimp called copepods.. Crustaceans are not kosher. And it's not just New York. Many public water supplies contain copepods. How can such water be kosher? Some rabbis ruled that it isn't. Others ruled that the laws of *kashrut* apply only to what we can see without a microscope. Once again, these are reasonable interpretations, but not the only reasonable interpretations.

In sum, the general pattern we see—with cell phones, with the *kippah*, with maltodextrin, and in many other instances—is that Reform Judaism tends toward less stringent practice while Orthodox Judaism tends toward more stringent practice, and both tendencies are modern reactions to the modern world. Modern

Jews tend to focus on the different outcomes, but these hide the common pattern: We are all recreating Judaism.

That is, we are living through only the fourth major spiritual revolution since the days of King David and our ancestors' original experiment in human rights and in a better way to live. We follow the pattern of the prophets, who moved from the periphery to the center and turned our eyes outward toward other peoples; the pattern of the Rabbis, who moved from the periphery to the center and created *Halakhah* even as they rejected traditional sacrifice; and the pattern of the Kabbalists, who moved from the periphery to the center and gave Judaism *Kabbalah* and *Kabbalat Shabbat*.

As participants in the revolution, we don't know how it will end. We don't know if the moderation of Reform or the intensification of Orthodoxy will ultimately triumph, though certainly the evidence so far suggests it will be a mixture heavily weighted toward moderation.

We do know that we are living through an extraordinary era. We are the modern guardians of an ancient dream of human dignity, joy, and honor. And we are the ones who will define Judaism not just for the coming decades, but for centuries and millennia. We are voicing the new prophetic vision, writing the new Talmud, living the new *Kabbalah*.

And what a privilege it is.

Source: Dr. Joel M. Hoffman, "Four Exiles and Four Spiritual Revolutions, from *A Life of Meaning: Embracing Reform Judaism's Sacred Path*, ed. Rabbi Dana Evan Kaplan (New York: CCAR Press, 2018).

Anti-Semitism and
the Shoah (Holocaust)

Yom HaShoah
(Holocaust Remembrance Day)

The 27th of the Hebrew month of Nisan, called Yom HaShoah, was set aside in 1951 as a day of remembrance for the victims of the Holocaust by the Knesset (the Israeli Parliament). The Central Conference of American Rabbis in June 1977 called for the annual commemoration of Yom HaShoah on this date.

Anti-Semitism and Nazism did not die with the end of World War II. The Shoah is a constant reminder of the potential for evil that lies below the veneer of civilization. The seeds of the Holocaust must not be allowed to find fertile soil again.

It is a mitzvah to remember the six million Jews who were murdered in the Shoah by attending special memorial services or programs at synagogues. Also, we should remember all of those who were singled out for death by the Nazis, such as Gypsies, handicapped people, and gays and lesbians. In addition we should remember and pay tribute to *chasidei umot haolam*, the righteous non-Jews who gave their lives in attempts to save members of the Jewish people.

To fulfill the mitzvah of remembrance, it is suggested that a memorial candle, often yellow, be lit, and relevant passages be read. Either as preparation or as part of the observance, one should spend time reviewing the events that led to the Shoah and discussing ways of preventing its recurrence.

In keeping with the spirit of Yom HaShoah as a day of mourning, weddings should not be scheduled. It is further suggested that one eat a very simple meal on the eve of Yom HaShoah as an act of identification and solidarity with those who were in the concentration camps and slowly starved to death. It is particularly important to provide a permanent memorial to the *K'doshim*, the holy ones who perished. Therefore, our *tzedakah* on Yom HaShoah should be directed to institutions that preserve their memory.

Source: Rabbi Peter S. Knobel, ed., *Mishkan Moeid: A Guide to the Jewish Seasons* (New York: CCAR Press, 2013), 83.

Yom HaShoah

Rabbi Joel Sisenwine

On April 12, 1951, Knesset member Mordecai Nurok approached the podium of the Knesset and exclaimed, "The heavens cry forth, the earth cries forth, and Israel is crying." With these words, Nurok introduced an impassioned plea to develop a common Holocaust observance. Until that time, there had been no common observance, because of the unique pain of the Holocaust and the diverse needs of the community. In order to balance secular Zionist and religious concerns, Nurok proposed the 27th of Nisan as "Holocaust and Ghetto Rebellion Memorial Day." Today, this date is most often referred to as Yom HaShoah. The 27th of Nisan represented a compromise date, acknowledging that the date could not be on the anniversary of the Warsaw Ghetto rebellion, April 19, as this fell on the eve of Passover, a time of celebration. Thus Nurok proposed 27 Nisan, as it was close enough to the rebellion date but fell within the period of the Omer, a traditional time of mourning.

Unlike *Gates of Prayer*, the prior Reform Movement prayer book, *Mishkan T'filah* includes its own service for Yom HaShoah. No longer grouped with Tishah B'Av (and the Rabbinic notion that the destruction of the Temples was caused by the sins of the Jewish people), the Yom HaShoah liturgy is one of remembrance. A modern observance, the Yom HaShoah liturgy does not maintain the prayer book structure of having the traditional liturgy on the right page and creative texts on the left. Rather, the Yom HaShoah liturgy is a collection of poetry and readings that call upon the reader to remember. It also provides the community for a way to say *Kaddish* for the many Jews who were killed in mass killings and whose dates of death are unknown.

Source: Rabbi Joel Sisenwine, "The Festival and Holy Day Liturgy of *Mishkan T'filah*," in *Mishkan Moeid: A Guide to the Jewish Seasons*, ed. Rabbi Peter S. Knobel (New York: CCAR Press, 2013), 119.

The 614th Commandment

RABBI SUZANNE SINGER

1

My mother was a survivor of Auschwitz. This reality has been the major driving force in my life. Overriding all that I do, think, and feel has been my struggle with the question: "Why?" When I was younger, I was torn between two poles. Either I was very angry at God or I could not believe in God at all. If God intervened to free us from slavery in Egypt, why had not God intervened during the Holocaust? Either God did not care what happened to human beings or, at best, God was impotent or nonexistent. And if one chose to blame the Holocaust on people and free will, then how could God have created a world in which such evil is possible? God's inaction during the Holocaust brooked no excuses.

Emil Fackenheim offered as a 614th commandment that we are forbidden from giving Hitler a posthumous victory by abandoning Judaism. In theological terms, that meant I could not give up on God. In my struggle to come to terms with God, I studied many different theologies. I slowly came to understand that God was not necessarily the equivalent of the old man with a white beard, sitting on a celestial throne and running the world like a puppeteer. This freed me from my narrow conception of God and allowed me to embrace a new understanding of the Divine.

I resonated most with Mordecai Kaplan's belief that God is the "power that makes for salvation," the power that allows us to achieve our full potential as human beings and that drives us to bring justice and truth to the world (Kaplan,

494

The Radical American Judaism of Mordecai Kaplan, 146). The God of the Bible is thus a metaphor. God is not a Being, but a Force; not a personal or providential God, but a Source from which to draw strength and inspiration. I realized that if I could open myself up to *this* God, I could become the person I was meant to be in the world. I no longer had to blame God for the Holocaust because that was no longer the kind of God I believed in or rejected. I understood that I was God's partner, co-responsible for perfecting the world.

Of course, there are still times that I revert to the notion of God as the old king in control, so I still get angry at Him on occasion. But who are we as Jews if not God-wrestlers, struggling to know and to respond to God, struggling to understand why we are here?

2

The suffering of so many innocent people in the world has troubled me my whole life, beginning with the experiences of my mother and her family, through the many holocausts that have continued to occur around the world, and the poverty and abuse to which so many are subjected. If God is the force for salvation, why are more people not saved? If God is only associated with the good, does that not let God off the hook? One of my greatest challenges has been to satisfactorily resolve the problem of theodicy—reconciling an all-good and allpowerful God with the existence of evil.

Eugene Borowitz and Harold Kushner have both suggested that God's power is limited, and it seems to me that this is the only possible resolution of this dilemma. The speeches from the whirlwind in the Book of Job illustrate this beautifully. In them, God gives Job a sweeping view of the universe's magnificence, making it clear that at best, God keeps the forces of evil—symbolized by Behemoth, the land monster, and Leviathan, the sea monster—at bay.

As intellectually satisfying as this solution has been to me, however, there are still times when my doubts take hold. Irving "Yitz" Greenberg has suggested that after Auschwitz, we must be able to defend our theology "in the presence of the burning children" (Greenberg, "Cloud of Smoke, Pillar of Fire," 23). I subscribe to Greenberg's understanding of "moment faiths"—times when we can believe in God's redeeming power, and times when we simply cannot. If there are no atheists in foxholes, there are atheists when confronted with the reality of devastated lives.

It is comforting to some to believe that God rewards us for our good deeds and punishes us for our transgressions. It gives people a sense of control over their lives. In my view, God does neither. We suffer either because of the consequences of our own actions or because God's redeeming power has not yet overcome the force of chaos. Several instances in our tradition feature God crying over the fate of God's people. The prophet Jeremiah quotes, "If you do not heed me, I will hide and I will weep because of your arrogance. I will cry and cry, My eyes will flow with tears because My flock has been taken into captivity" (Jeremiah 13:17). In a midrash on Lamentations, God cries twice over the destruction of the Jerusalem Temple (*Eichah Rabbah*, proem/*p'tichta* 24). When we suffer, I like to think that God is crying along with us.

Source: Rabbi Suzanne Singer, in *Lights in the Forest: Rabbis Respond to Twelve Essential Jewish Questions*, ed. Rabbi Paul Citrin (New York: CCAR Press, 2014), 36–38.

Love Letter to God

RABBI ZOE KLEIN

1

I imagine that God weeps at the sufferings of the whole disharmonious natural world. If God does weep with us, it is with a heart that we wrote into the story. We invented God's heart, our greatest contribution to God's tale.

I cannot know why suffering and evil exist. No work of fiction is free of it. It is the stuff of timeless story. However, our greatest spiritual resistance to suffering is metaphor and interpretation. To interpret is divine. God breathed that ability into us.

A traditional Jewish ritual response to nightmares is called "the Amelioration of a Dream" (Babylonian Talmud, *B'rachot* 55b). The ritual requires three friends to declare that the dream be interpreted for good. The text explains that all dreams have a hint of prophecy; however, all dreams can be interpreted positively. In fact, the prophecy of the dream lies partially in its interpretation. The dreamer says three times, *Adonai shamati v'yareiti*—God, I heard what You made me hear and I was frightened. Three friends respond with the prescribed words, "Choose life, for God has already approved your deeds. Repentance, prayer, and charity remove the evil of the decree."

We dream, but we are also dreamt. We are written, and within that story, we write. It is said in Torah and our liturgy: *U'vayom hash'vi-i shavat vayinafash*, "On the seventh day God 'rested.'" Translators struggle in translating *vayinafash*, suggesting, "On the seventh day God rested and was refreshed." *Vayinafash*,

497

however, literally means God "ensouled." On the seventh day God rested and created spirits. Out of God's dark, void chamber before Creation, God suddenly dreamed a dream/nightmare and based on that dream/nightmare, the world was sketched and animated in full color. We are the dream/ nightmare. We have little control over the outcome except to interpret it for the good.

A congregant had a double mastectomy and did not know how to love herself afterwards. She would stand before a mirror naked, seeing herself as grotesque. We sought a metaphor that would help her to see herself in a new light. We imagined her body as a sacred altar and that her breasts were the sacrifices that redeemed her life. Years later she told me that now when she stands before the mirror, she thinks "sacred altar" and has found a love for herself inside that she thought had disappeared. She reinterpreted her nightmare through metaphor.

2

I believe in God as Author of All Life, yet I live as if God is *Reader* of All Life. The difference is profound. We wake each morning to a pristine day, an open page, and our actions are stylus and papyrus.

Every day, our response to God's story is inked in heartbeats, lettered in breath, rolled into a perfumed scroll, and tucked into the crook of an ancient oak tree. The way I live my life is my narrative and commentary, tossed up into the vast, churning literature of conch shells and migrating birds and spiraling galaxies.

Many others believe that God is the Source of Ethical Values, the Moral Compass. I do not sense that our ethics come from some Outside Other. I think God is the Writer of this strange fiction in which we are the characters playing out our moral dramas. It is not that I think God doesn't *care*, although I hesitate to assign human emotions to that which I cannot comprehend. The most I can say is that the story God has written is of great interest to God. God studies the world, gazes upon God's reflection in it. Just as we try to emulate what we imagine is God's will (essentially our own fiction writing), God also tries to emulate us. In other words, our morality comes from inside of us. It is not God's rule; it is our gift to God. It is our rebellion against the cruelty of coldness of the violent, everbleeding natural world—that despite the constancy of death, despite the sword that hangs over my head, I will interpret this for good, and I will live my life as a love letter to God. I perform mitzvot, and they are a serenade to the Author. My religion is not to be believed; it is to be danced. Every life is a once-told tale. Your story is a scripture, and God is the Reader; therefore, we are swept up in a cosmic love affair, whether God cares or not. Despite the nightmare, I will interpret for good and seal this Book of Life with a kiss.

Source: Rabbi Zoe Klein, in *Lights in the Forest: Rabbis Respond to Twelve Essential Jewish Questions*, ed. Rabbi Paul Citrin (New York: CCAR Press, 2014), 20–22.

Where God Dwells

RABBI ANDREW VOGEL

No one can wave away the problem of God's coexistence with the presence of evil and suffering in our world. Human suffering is too great, too vast, too universal, too painful; the evil that we humans have wreaked upon each other is overwhelming in its scope and destruction. Who can bear to accept God's toleration of the murder, torture, and destruction we have brought into our world?

But much depends on how we think of God. If I hope God will swoop down with a mighty arm and change everything, I will be disappointed in God. All life, all experience, is a manifestation of God. Suffering, much like love and caring, is part of life. Suffering is not a punishment. God is not distinct from all Being, so blaming God for the evil done to me gets me nowhere; it is like blaming the ocean for its rough waves on a stormy day.

Yet, the evolutionary process has implanted within the human spirit an urge to resist evil and the will for life and good to triumph. Healing, emerging from suffering, and the struggle against evil, I believe, are all terms that are synonymous with the word "God." We Jews refer to God as the *rofeih chol basar umafli laasot*—roughly translated as "Healer of all creatures, who amazes us with unexpected deeds." If we are fortunate, surprising transformations can occur. Jewish tradition speaks of God as the possibility of healing and renewal, of hope: God is *mikveih Yisrael*, the Hope of Israel (Jeremiah 14:8). The Passover Haggadah reminds us that it is not just a myth, but rather very possible, for us to move from "slavery to freedom, from despair to joy, from mourning to celebration, from darkness to light, from enslavement to redemption" (Rabinowicz, *Passover Haggadah: Feast of Freedom*, 69).

Not every story ends happily with healing and celebration, of course. Suffering is a very real part of life, it is beyond our control, and often there seems to be no reason for it. What we can control, however, is our own religious attitude in the world, our response to suffering and evil. "Behold, I set before you this day life and good, death and evil. . . . Choose life, that you might live" (Deuteronomy 30:15, 30:19). Our choices, like many paths at a crossroads, lie before us. Through choosing compassion, strength, memory, and perseverance, we affirm life and its mysterious holiness, in which God dwells.

Source: Rabbi Andrew Vogel, in *Lights in the Forest: Rabbis Respond to Twelve Essential Jewish Questions*, ed. Rabbi Paul Citrin (New York: CCAR Press, 2014), 48–49.

Making Every Day a Blessing

RABBI KENNETH CHASEN

A congregant of mine who is struggling with lung cancer recently approached me for some spiritual counsel. She asked, "Can you help me figure out what to pray for? It is more than I can bear to pray for my cancer to clear. I just can't stand having too much false hope and ending up so disappointed." I told her that I understand her hesitancy to pray for a miraculous healing. She would have to think about what would be left of her emotionally and spiritually if her prayer should appear to go unanswered. However, that certainly doesn't mean that I told her to refrain from praying. I believe that the exercise of prayer itself possesses the power to produce some significant measure of the strength she most needs to face an uncertain future. Her prayers can also intensify her focus on making a blessing of each day, of each minute of her life, reminding her that none of what she had previously assumed to be "normal" about living is, in fact, to be taken for granted, nor is it permanent.

This is how I look at God's place in the experience of suffering. I do not believe in a God who selects certain children to be inflicted with leukemia, so neither can I believe in a God who selects certain children to be cured of leukemia. It is no accident that the overwhelming majority of traditional Jewish prayers are expressions of gratitude, not requests for intercession in our lives or world. The religious discipline of Judaism inspires a person to sense blessing in things that humans too often consider ordinary or expected—our breath, our freedom, our abundance, the many wonders of the universe. The goal is to engender the question "Why me?" in moments of good fortune, not just at times of suffering. If God's worth is to be evaluated solely on the basis of whether our wishes are granted when we pray, there is no humility in prayer. We are not seeking God; we are seeking to *be* God.

We will, of course, always yearn for a world without evil or suffering. However, it is the very existence of curse that enables us to recognize and hunger for blessing—and it is the existence of curse that will forever fuel our efforts to unleash more and more of God's light through our own actions.

Source: Rabbi Kenneth Chasen, in *Lights in the Forest: Rabbis Respond to Twelve Essential Jewish Questions*, ed. Rabbi Paul Citrin (New York: CCAR Press, 2014), 4–5.

Israel and Zionism

Source Texts

Psalm 126:1–2

¹ When Adonai restores the fortunes of Zion, we see it as in a dream.
² Our mouths shall be filled with laughter, our tongues, with songs of joy: then shall they say among the nations, "Adonai has done great things for them!"

Psalm 137:1–6

¹By the rivers of Babylon, there we sat down and we wept, when we remembered Zion. ² We hung our harps upon the willows in the midst thereof. ³ For there they that carried us away captive required of us a song; and they that wasted us required amusement, saying, "Sing us one of the songs of Zion." ⁴ How shall we sing the Eternal's song in a strange land? ⁵ If I forget you, O Jerusalem, let my right hand forget its cunning. ⁶ If I do not remember you, let my tongue cleave to the roof of my mouth; if I do not keep Jerusalem in memory even at my happiest hour.

Yehudah HaLevi (c. 1141)

My heart is in the east, and I in the uttermost west—My food has no taste. How shall it be sweet to me? How can I fulfill my vows and my bonds, while yet Zion lies beneath the fetter of Edom, and I in Arab chains. A light thing would it seem to me to leave all the good things of Spain—seeing how precious in mine eyes to behold the dust of the desolate sanctuary.

"Anat's Prayer for Israel" by Anat Hoffman, Director of the Israeli Religious Action Center (November 10, 2015)

My God, Eili

> In this sacred moment, give us hope for Israel and her future.
> Renew our wonder at the miracle of the Jewish State.

In the name of the pioneers who made the deserts bloom—give us the tools to cultivate a diversity of Jewish expression in Israel.

In the name of our fallen soldiers—give us courage to stand up to the words and ways of zealots. Those in our own midst and those among our neighbors.

In the name of Israeli inventors who have amazed the world with their innovations—help us apply the same ingenuity to finding a path to peace.

In the name of all these women and men—grant us the strength to conquer doubt and despair in Israel.

Replacing doubt with action.

Replacing despair with hope.

And let us say: Amen.

Hatikvah

כָּל עוֹד בַּלֵּבָב פְּנִימָה
נֶפֶשׁ יְהוּדִי הוֹמִיָּה
וּלְפַאֲתֵי מִזְרָח קָדִימָה
עַיִן לְצִיּוֹן צוֹפִיָּה.
עוֹד לֹא אָבְדָה תִּקְוָתֵנוּ
הַתִּקְוָה בַּת שְׁנוֹת אַלְפַּיִם
לִהְיוֹת עַם חָפְשִׁי בְּאַרְצֵנוּ
אֶרֶץ צִיּוֹן וִירוּשָׁלָיִם.

So long as within the inmost heart a Jewish spirit sings, so long as the eye looks
eastward, gazing toward Zion, our hope is not lost — the hope of two thousand
years: to be a free people in our land, the land of Zion and Jerusalem.

Source: Rabbi Elyse Frishman, ed., *Mishkan T'filah: A Reform Siddur* (New York: CCAR Press, 2007), 678.

Prayer for the State of Israel

Avinu shebashamayim,	אָבִינוּ שֶׁבַּשָּׁמַיִם,
Tzur Yisrael v'go·alo:	צוּר יִשְׂרָאֵל וְגוֹאֲלוֹ,
bareich et m'dinat Yisrael,	בָּרֵךְ אֶת מְדִינַת יִשְׂרָאֵל,
reishit tz'michat g'ulateinu.	רֵאשִׁית צְמִיחַת גְּאֻלָּתֵנוּ.
Hagein aleha b'evrat chasdecha;	הָגֵן עָלֶיהָ בְּאֶבְרַת חַסְדֶּךָ,
ufros aleha sukkat sh'lomecha.	וּפְרוֹס עָלֶיהָ סֻכַּת שְׁלוֹמֶךָ.
Ushlach orcha vaamit'cha l'rasheha,	וּשְׁלַח אוֹרְךָ וַאֲמִתְּךָ לְרָאשֶׁיהָ,
sareha, v'yo·atzeha;	שָׂרֶיהָ וְיוֹעֲצֶיהָ,
v'tak'neim b'eitzah tovah mil'fanecha.	וְתַקְּנֵם בְּעֵצָה טוֹבָה מִלְּפָנֶיךָ.
V'natata shalom baaretz,	וְנָתַתָּ שָׁלוֹם בָּאָרֶץ,
v'simchat olam l'yoshveha.	וְשִׂמְחַת עוֹלָם לְיוֹשְׁבֶיהָ.
V'nomar: Amen.	וְנֹאמַר: אָמֵן.

Avinu—You who are high above all nation-states and peoples—
Rock of Israel, the One who has saved us and preserved us in life,
bless the State of Israel, first flowering of our redemption.
Be her loving shield, a shelter of lasting peace.
Guide her leaders and advisors by Your light of truth;
instruct them with Your good counsel.
Strengthen the hands of those who build and protect our Holy Land.
Deliver them from danger; crown their efforts with success.
Grant peace to the land,
lasting joy to all of her people.
And together we say: *Amen.*

Prayer for Israel (continued)

Composed in honor of the birth of the State of Israel in 1948. This prayer is notable for its theological statement that the birth of the state was not just a political event in secular time, but "the first flowering of our redemption," a spiritual event in religious time. The return of Jews to the land of their ancestors in fulfillment of the vision of the prophets, their recovery of independence as a sovereign nation after two thousand years of dispersion and powerlessness, and their reaffirmation of life after the Holocaust: these form a new and epoch-making chapter in the narrative begun when Abraham and Sarah heeded God's call and set out on the journey "to the land that I will show you" (Genesis 12:1). (Rabbi Jonathan Sacks, b. 1948)

Source: Rabbi Edwin Goldberg, Rabbi Janet Marder, Rabbi Sheldon Marder, and Rabbi Leon Morris, eds., *Mishkan HaNefesh: Machzor for the Days of Awe*, vol. 1, Rosh HaShanah (New York: CCAR Press, 2015), 274.

CCAR Resolution Condemning the Boycott, Divestment, and Sanctions Campaign against Israel

February 18, 2016

Background:

Since its creation in 1948, The State of Israel has been attacked almost nonstop—by foreign armies, terrorists with bombs, rockets and now knives, and through economic warfare. In recent years, the movement to delegitimize the State of Israel and separate her from the community of nations has grown through a co-ordinated campaign of Boycott, Divestment, and Sanctions, known as BDS. The BDS movement does not recognize the right of Israel to exist as a Jewish state. Its leaders ignore the complexity of Israel's reality and fail to offer a reasonable path forward in resolving the Israeli-Palestinian conflict.

In singling out the Jewish State, BDS often opens the door to anti-Semitic rhetoric and activities and highlights modern anti-Semitic double standards. While the BDS movement is not explicitly anti-Semitic, BDS supporters and leaders have made anti-Semitic statements and anti-Semitic incidents have oc-curred alongside BDS campaigns.[1] Moreover, in its efforts to indict Zionism as a whole, the BDS movement seeks to deny Jews the right to our own homeland and therefore the ability to express our national identity.[2]

As Reform rabbis and liberal Zionists, we are deeply supportive of an Israeli society that not only tolerates but encourages critique and discourse. *Tochecha*, a critique made with care for the sake of correcting wrong behavior, is an im-portant Jewish value and one that should not only be accepted but encouraged by our community. As individual Reform rabbis and collectively as the Central Conference of American Rabbis, we often disagree with specific Israeli policies in the spirit of *machloket l'shem shamayim*, an argument conducted for the sake of heaven. Such critique is far from rejection and delegitimization of Israel as a whole. The BDS movement, with its sustained, coordinated effort to oppose Israel's existence, is flawed both in its spirit and in its execution.

Rather than bringing Israeli Jews closer together with Palestinians, both Muslim and Christian, BDS further divides us all. At a time when interactions between Israeli Jews and Palestinians are already scarce, economic, academic and cultural boycotts further lower prospects for coexistence. The "anti-normalization" movement, that calls for ending cooperation with Israelis and with Palestinians who do not support BDS, has the same deleterious effect.[3]

While exercising their own freedom of speech, BDS proponents deny that same freedom to others through academic and cultural boycotts. Such boycotts are intended only to further marginalize Israel.[4] Academic boycotts have rightfully earned widespread condemnation from organizations such as the American Association of University Professors and the Association of American Universities, as they interfere with partnerships between Israeli and international universities that underpin the shared pursuit of knowledge and the exercise of academic freedom.[5] Similarly, the increased pressure artists face to boycott Israeli cultural events impedes their ability to participate in open dialogue with members of Israel's diverse society.[6] Advocating for boycotts of universities or cultural institutions simply because they are Israeli punishes all who benefit from such ties, exposing the blatant disregard the BDS movement has for the Jewish State as a whole.

The BDS movement is also working to drive wedges between and within progressive communities in North America, recruiting others to its cause by narrowly applying the concept of "intersectionality." Intersectionality describes the ways in which multiple identities such as race, gender, nationality, sexuality, class, religion and others can overlap to produce unique experiences of power or the lack thereof.[7] While we recognize the importance of intersectionality as a concept that informs our social justice work, we are concerned that the BDS movement paints all forms of oppression with a broad brush and attempts to inject anti-Zionist ideology and tactics into other areas where they are irrelevant and counterproductive to the pursuit of social justice.[8] This puts progressive Zionists in the unacceptable position of having to deny the intersection between their Zionism and their progressivism and forces them to choose between the two. This is a false choice.

BDS is incapable of addressing the nuances of the Israeli-Palestinian conflict, exacting a disproportionate focus on Israel and ignoring horrific abuses of human rights worldwide. By using the term "apartheid" to describe Israel inaccurately with inflammatory language, BDS sheds more heat than light on the issues it addresses. By imposing demands on Israel that would make a two-state solution impossible, BDS rejects the one path forward that would ensure peace, security and national self-determination for both Israelis and Palestinians.[9] Ultimately, BDS fails to provide a realistic vision for peace in the Middle East, as it stands in the way of promising peace negotiations aimed at a two-state solution. Instead, BDS emboldens and empowers hard-liners on both sides of the conflict.

The BDS movement has made modest gains amongst church groups, labor unions and most notably on college campuses.[10] During the 2014-2015 school year, 19 campuses considered BDS resolutions, and 520 explicitly anti-Israel events were held on college campuses.[11] Campus debates have been particularly heated and divisive, leading at times to actions directed against pro-Israel students and in extreme cases, anti-Semitic incidents.[12] Pro-Israel students are deeply invested in addressing the challenges posed by the BDS movement, working closely with a number of organizations on strategies to oppose BDS and support Israel on campus.

Stringent opposition to BDS does not conflict with the deeply-held conviction that Israel must end virtually all settlement activity and the West Bank Occupation as we know it.[13] These ends can only be achieved through diplomacy—not boycotts, divestment, or sanctions.

THEREFORE, BE IT RESOLVED THAT the Central Conference of American Rabbis:

1. Denounces the global Boycott, Divestment, and Sanctions movement.
2. Urges all who support peace and reconciliation and the advancement of a two-state solution to join the efforts of like-minded organizations and to reject BDS in favor of a productive path toward a negotiated peace.
3. Encourages productive criticism, including *tochechah*, aimed at achieving peace for Israel and realizaion of the legitimate national aspirations of the Palestinian people.
4. Urges CCAR members and the communities we serve to create opportunities for healthy and robust discussions about Israel and her policies, based upon the fundamental tenet that the State of Israel must thrive as a Jewish and democratic State within secure and defensible borders.

5. Calls upon CCAR members to engage clergy of all faiths, government officials, and university leaders, who are increasingly bombarded by the BDS movement's biased and inaccurate information.

6. Pledges to support organized Jewish communities on college and university campuses, which are often on the front lines of the defense against the BDS campaign.

7. Affirms our ongoing commitment to overcoming those who seek the destruction of Israel by supporting peace and continuing to educate our communities about the importance of a two-state solution.

1. http://www.economist.com/blogs/democracyinamerica/2015/05/campus-politics
2. http://www.urj.org/blog/2014/06/19/rabbi-rick-jacobs-letter-delegates-presbyterian-churchusa-general-assembly
3. http://www.haaretz.com/jewish/the-jewish-thinker/.premium-1.664018
4. http://aaup.org/report/academic-boycotts
5. http://www.nytimes.com/2014/01/06/us/backlash-against-israel-boycott-throws-academicassociation-on-defensive.html?_r=0
6. http://www.theguardian.com/world/2015/oct/22/star-authors-jk-rowling-hilary-mantel-israelpalestinian-boycott-guardian-letter
7. https://www.washingtonpost.com/news/in-theory/wp/2015/09/21/intersectionality-aprimer/?tid=a_inl
8. https://www.washingtonpost.com/news/worldviews/wp/2015/10/15/the-growing-solidaritybetween-blacklivesmatter-and-palestinian-activists/
9. http://www.thedailybeast.com/articles/2013/02/08/why-bds-isn-t-compatible-with-twostates.html
10. http://www.nytimes.com/2015/05/10/us/campus-debates-on-israel-drives-a wedge-between-jews-and-minorities.html?_r=0
11. http://www.adl.org/israel-international/anti-israel-activity/c/bds-on-american-college-20142015.html
12. http://www.nytimes.com/2015/03/06/us/debate-on-a-jewish-student-at-ucla.html
13. *CCAR Declaration of Love and Support for the State of Israel and Its People*, 2015–16.

Source: "CCAR Resolution Condemning the Boycott, Divestment, and Sanctions Campaign against Israel," February 18, 2016, CCAR, http://ccarnet.org/rabbis-speak/ resolutions/2016/ccar-resolution-condemning-boycott-divestment-and-/.

Yom HaZikaron
(Israel Memorial Day)

The Israeli Knesset established the day before Yom HaAtzma-ut, Independence Day, as Memorial Day for soldiers who lost their lives fighting in the War of Independence and subsequent battles. Yom HaZikaron begins with an official ceremony at the Western Wall, as the flag of Israel is lowered to half-staff. Places of entertainment are closed by law. Radio and television stations play programs about Israel's military history and show programming that conveys the somber mood of the day.

As on Yom HaShoah, an air-raid siren is sounded twice during Yom HaZikaron. When the siren is heard, all activity, including traffic, immediately stops. People get out of their cars, freeze where they are, and stand at attention in memory of those who died defending Israel. The first siren marks the beginning of Memorial Day, and the second is sounded immediately prior to the public recitation of prayers in military cemeteries.

Numerous public ceremonies are held throughout Israel. There is a national ceremony at the military cemetery on Mount Herzl, where many of Israel's leaders and soldiers are buried. Many schools and public buildings have created memorials for those from their community who died in Israel's wars.

The day formally draws to a close at sundown with the official opening ceremony of Israel Independence Day on Mount Herzl, when the flag of Israel is returned to full staff. Scheduling Yom HaZikaron right before Yom HaAtzma-ut is intended to remind people of the sacrifice soldiers and their families and friends have made for Israel's independence and security. This transition shows the importance of this day among Israelis, most of whom have served in the armed forces or have a connection with people who were killed during military service.

Source: Rabbi Peter S. Knobel, ed., *Mishkan Moeid: A Guide to the Jewish Seasons* (New York: CCAR Press, 2013), 84.

Yom HaAtzma-ut
(Israel Independence Day)

On the fifth day of the Hebrew month of Iyar 5708 (May 14, 1948), Israel was reborn as a modern, independent state. Since that time Jews throughout the world have celebrated the day in commemoration and rejoicing. In response to the widespread observance of Yom HaAtzma-ut among Reform Jews, the Central Conference of American Rabbis, at its convention on Mount Scopus in 1970, proclaimed Israel Independence Day "a permanent annual festival in the religious calendar of Reform Judaism." In addition, the Reform Movement has provided special Torah and haftarah readings for the day.

The celebration of Yom HaAtzma-ut recognizes that a new era has dawned in the life of the Jewish people. It attests to the essential unity of the whole household of Israel and marks the cultural and spiritual renaissance that draws strength from the symbiotic relationship between Israel and world Jewry. The rebirth of Israel from the ashes of the Shoah is a symbol of hope against despair, of redemption against devastation.

It is a mitzvah for every Jew to mark Yom HaAtzma-ut by participation in public worship services or celebrations that affirm the bond between the Jews living in the Land of Israel and those living outside. Furthermore, a special act of *tzedakah* to an organization or institution that helps to strengthen the State of Israel is a significant way of affirming the unity of the Jewish people. Preparing a festive meal on Yom HaAtzma-ut that includes foods from Israel and Israeli songs is also an appropriate way to mark the day.

These three new commemorations, Yom HaShoah, Yom HaZikaron, and Yom HaAtzma-ut represent the effect of modern culture on the lengthy history of the Jewish people, being the firstadditions to the Jewish holiday calendar since antiquity. Together they function as a vital part of Israel's "civil religion," Yom

HaZikaron being a perfect example of a holiday whose commemoration and practice are uniquely Israeli while still being universally Jewish.

Source: Rabbi Peter S. Knobel, ed., *Mishkan Moeid: A Guide to the Jewish Seasons* (New York: CCAR Press, 2013), 85–86.

Restoring *Tikkun Olam* to Liberal Religious Zionist Activism

The first prophets and leaders of Zionism envisioned a future state that would rest on firm principles of justice, equality, and peace. Herzl's utopian vision was of a model, prosperous society, built on pillars of solidarity, support for the weakest members, equality, and morality—a testament of faith in the human spirit.[1]

Achad HaAm spoke about the critical *moral* role of prophetic truth and justice in the salvation of Jews through Zionism, a cause that would promote the most exalted and supreme moral values.[2] In his letter "Zionism and *Tikkun Olam*," Achad HaAm articulated the need for Zionism to solve not only the "Jewish" question but, by doing so, to also resolve the major social and economic questions for all. Universal *tikkun olam*, he claims, is central to the Zionist question.[3]

The Reform Movement, loyal to our values of justice, equality, and inclusivity, has been inspired particularly by these elements of the Zionist vision. For eighty years now, we have integrated the dream of peace and justice into our Zionist commitment and identity. The Columbus Platform, adopted in 1937 by the Central Conference of American Rabbis, includes the first official expression of support for Zionism by the Reform Movement. In this platform the movement embraced the Zionist enterprise as part of the effort to establish "the kingdom of God, of universal brotherhood, justice, truth and peace on earth."

The CCAR's Miami Platform on Reform Zionism, adopted in 1997, reiterates and expands on that commitment. It details a vision of Israel:

The Jewish State is therefore unlike all other states. Its obligation is to strive towards the attainment of the Jewish people's highest moral ideals to be a *mamlechet kohanim* [a kingdom of priests], a *goy kadosh* [a holy people], and *l'or goyim* [a light unto the nations] . . . the kind of society in which full civil, human, and religious rights exist for all its citizens. Ultimately, *M'dinat Yisrael* will be judged not on its military might but on its character. . . . We express the fervent hope that *M'dinat Yisrael*, living in peace with its neighbors, will hasten the redemption of *Am Yisrael*, and the fulfillment of our messianic dream of universal peace under the sovereignty of God.

In light of this inspiring and moving vision, we find ourselves faced not only with political challenges but with a crisis of faith as well. Twenty years after the Miami Platform was adopted we are further than ever from that vision: fifty years into the military occupation of the West Bank and Gaza (and with no end in sight); with the domestic democratic sphere shrinking and facing constant threats; with growing religious extremism in Israel affecting women and the LGBTQ community; with alarming racist militias violently targeting Arab citizens and residents; and with growing economic inequality.

When we discuss Israeli politics, we often elaborate on the progress that is constantly being made: more equality for the LGBTQ community, growing strength and recognition of Progressive Judaism, and technological and environmental innovation. This progress is indeed significant and encouraging. However, despite all this, we need to recognize the point of crisis in which we find ourselves.

Contemporary Israel is not the fulfilment of our Zionist vision when measured against our aspirational values of justice, peace, and brotherhood. Quite the opposite—on many moral questions the current situation in Israel is a profound disappointment.

As a religious movement, we need to provide the spiritual as well as the intellectual answers to how we cope with confronting this disappointment and find the strength to keep recruiting all of our creativity, energy, and faith in the struggle to fulfill our vision. We need to build our stamina as a movement for a long-term commitment to restoring *tikkun olam* a struggle that may take decades to complete and that will include multiple challenges even as we achieve certain successes.

In light of all this, I would like to suggest that the concept of *tikkun olam* is vitally necessary for us as a religious Zionist community. The concept of *tikkun olam* recognizes both the brokenness of our world and the fact that our role as partners with God in making the world more just is constant and ongoing. We are no longer envisioning a perfect moral society, but a society that is constantly (or at least for the foreseeable future) in need of urgent repair. Our role is not to eliminate deeply embedded problems, but to be constant partners in an ongoing work to improve an imperfect situation. I believe that this theological framework will work best to adapt our vision and build our capacity to deal with questions of justice in Israel.

The current discourse around Israel within Jewish communities around the world is dominated by two conflicting narratives: either a discourse that is promoted by the Israeli government that justifies every behavior and every policy with convoluted reasoning or a discourse that recognizes a profound moral crisis in Israel and offers a response in the form of boycott.

We, as a movement that is rooted both in Israel and around the world and that holds the concept of *tikkun olam* as a foundation of our faith can offer a third narrative: we recognize the profound moral crisis with all its intensity, but the response we offer is to engage more intensively with the issues. Our Movement—with powerful connections between Diaspora progressive Jews and Israeli progressive Jews—can put the emphasis on both understanding the issues *and* supporting change on the ground to address issues of justice and equality for all Israelis and for Palestinians.

The Israel Religious Action Center (IRAC) is a prime example of this kind of important work promoting *tikkun olam*. This response to the situation in contemporary Israel is exemplified in the stories of six leaders of our Israeli Reform Movement who work for *tikkun olam*. The work that they do with IRAC ties directly into their identity as Reform Jews.

Suzanne Cannon, a member of Congregation Kol Haneshama in Jerusalem, works for Bizchut—Israel's human rights center for people with disabilities. Bizchut was set up in 1992 as a special project for the Association for Civil Rights in Israel (ACRI). When Cannon began working there in 2001, it was a small organization with only six staff members; it has now grown to fourteen.

> It is a real *z'chut* [privilege] to be involved in an organization that is continuously at the forefront of changing the lives of people with disabilities in Israel. In contrast to other social issues, this is one where you can really succeed, where you can't with other human rights issues.

She described three anchors in her life: family, community, and the work that she does. She has high expectations of people and organizations around her. There are some values she takes for granted as a member of the Kol Haneshama community and has grown to expect them from other people. The Kol

Haneshama community is egalitarian and inclusive and believes in mutual responsibility.

Professor Galia Tsabar is the president of the Rupin Academic Center. She is extraordinary both in her academic achievements and in her leadership in the field of social change in Israel. She is a member of Congregation Beit Daniel in Tel Aviv and sits on the public council of the Israeli Reform Movement. She is on the board of the Hotline for Refugees and Migrant Workers and was very active in Jerusalem's Project AIDS, which built culturally sensitive programs for the prevention of HIV among Ethiopians, as well as for refugees and asylum seekers.

Professor Tsabar began working with Ethiopian Jews in Ethiopia in the 1980s, during which she learned about the many faces of the Jewish people.

> The Jewish experience I had then was different from anything I had known before. Their deep connection to Judaism, to Zion and Jerusalem, was so different from any Jewish experience I had ever encountered. Their journey was full of hope and difficulty on the one hand, and on the other hand a feeling of religious connection. For me, this was a formative experience in developing my pluralistic view, which is so meaningful in the Reform world. The voices I heard from Ethiopia were new voices that joined the different voices in the range of Judaism.

During her work with Ethiopian *olim* (immigrants) in Israel, she first encountered opacity, racism, and contempt—things that did not resonate with her at all within Judaism, the Zionist identity, or the State of Israel. When she saw the price the *olim* paid in Ethiopia and then the attitudes they encountered in Israel, she was shaken and her ties to Reform Judaism were strengthened.

This led her to research the religious space of refugees and migrants.

> As a Reform woman, I come with the view that the spiritual and religious experience is meaningful to one's daily conduct. With this view I encountered African migrants and asylum-seekers in Israel. I felt a strong connection to them. The fact that I knew how to identify these points of strength opened many doors for me that were closed for other researchers. Reform Judaism allowed the eye-to-eye connection (equal connection), a connection that every person knows. I invited many of my friends and members of the asylum-seeking community to Bet Daniel—there we had the opportunity to celebrate together, as equals, and share our religious-spiritual experience.

Rabbi Tamir Nir founded the Achva BaKerem (in Beit HaKerem, Jerusalem) congregation about a decade ago to do *tikkun*—to fix— the neighborhood socially, culturally, and physically. As time passed, these goals broadened to include people making changes in their lives, as well as a focus on the environment. His activities reached the people of the neighborhood, who subsequently became more active in city activities (including helping to elect him to the municipal government as the deputy mayor of Jerusalem). Today, because of this pattern of cooperation, there are over seventy community gardens throughout Jerusalem.

What is beautiful about community gardens is that they are a neutral space. Everyone who lives in the area is welcome to take part. The people who come create not only a garden, but also community leadership. It is a space not just for growing vegetables, but also for developing relationships and providing support to the community. It was from there that Rabbi Nir was elected to the city council and then served as deputy mayor in charge of transportation in Jerusalem.

In Israel, the tendency has been toward private cars, and Rabbi Nir believes that this is a basic mistake. We are on our way to a catastrophe, with traffic jams threatening the environment, freedom, and equality. To whom do the streets belong? And public space? How can we ensure that the streets are in fact for everyone? How do we ensure that public space is open to everyone equally, to those who can have five cars and those who have none? In order to promote equality, he envisions stricter regulation of parking, encouraging bike riding, creating spaces that are off-limits for cars, and expanding public transportation.

> I think that I am motivated/influenced by the Jewish values that are important to me: freedom, equality, responsibility, connection to and excitement from the world, prayer. Everything is expressed in action.

Rabbi Nir imagines an Israel in which Judaism is expressed in every aspect of society—not limited to separate religious spheres, but present in everything that we do, including the way we speak and create policy around the environment, transportation, and socioeconomic gaps.

Professor Rafi Walden is the deputy director of the Sheba Medical Center, the largest hospital in Israel. He is an active member of Congregation Beit Daniel in Tel Aviv and sits on the Public Committee of the Reform Movement in Israel. He is the chairperson of Physicians for Human Rights in Israel, an organization of health professionals committed to ensuring adequate medical services to all, including prisoners, the poor, the elderly, refugees and asylum seekers, Bedouin communities, and Palestinians in the Occupied Territories. Physicians for Human Rights provides essential medical services to tens of thousands of people annually.

He sees his pioneering work as rooted both in the Socratic oath and in Jewish values.

> In Judaism there is the obligation to treat the enemy's injured; as Maimonides says, we must treat everyone, so it is a Jewish obligation to treat and help all. My work is inspired by the Jewish value of life, and respect to all, as those apply in the medical world in Israel. We are responsible as Jews to not just help ourselves, but to help others, our neighbors in the area—that is *tikkun olam*.

Sarah Bernstein is also a member of Congregation Kol Haneshama. She serves as the director of the Jerusalem Center for Jewish-Christian Relations (JCJCR) and before that worked at the Interreligious Council. She has been working in the field of interfaith relations in Israel/Palestine for fifteen years.

The Jerusalem Center for Jewish-Christian Relations mainly focuses on educational work. Jewish-Christian relations are different in Israel than in the West because Israel is the only place in the world with a Jewish majority, and since the Christians here are also Arabs, the Israeli-Palestinian conflict plays into it. Recently the JCJCR has begun to do more work around different religions and is in the process of changing its name. It has expanded to do anti-racism work and teacher training.

We live in a situation of violent conflict, which creates its own dynamic of scarring and trauma. If we don't address this reality, we won't be able to move forward. The conflict becomes more intractable, and we now have generations of people who have never known peace, which affects the way we think of ourselves and of others. If we don't address and challenge our core beliefs, we are destined to many more years of violent conflict. It is not that the conflict is religious, it is political, but religion plays a more and more important role. Each side is bringing religious motifs to the conflict, and we are in danger that there could be a serious escalation of the conflict. It is extremely important to begin to address this conflict by working closely with various religious groupings and to take advantage of the influence that various religions can bring to bear to ease the tensions and to transform the conflict. We must learn to live together before the conflict evolves into a religious war.

Sarah Bernstein has stated:

> Over time my work has become my religious identity. I have come to believe that if we can't do this right, if we can't stop killing each other, none of the rest of it matters. I don't believe in a God that cares if I eat milk and meat together while we are killing each other. We have to learn to live with each other. This work very much ties in with everything that I do.

It also has very much impacted her prayer life. She changed some of the wording of the prayers that she struggles with, so that those texts are better integrated into her Jewish and community life.

> For me it's not for *tikkun olam*—it's more than that. It is the essence of what Zionism is about—I don't believe in the Jewish state just for the sake of having a Jewish state. I believe in having a Jewish state because the world is organized by nation-states and we need one too, as long as it serves the purpose of social justice and wider issues. It [*tikkun olam*] is right at the core of my Zionism—what it's all about. If Zionism isn't about that, then in my eyes there is no worth to it.

Each of the interviews above describes how individuals have focused on a specific cause within Israeli society and invested years, if not decades, in the effort to improve the conditions around the cause, viewing that as an ultimate expression of their liberal Judaism and an attempt to bring Jewish values to Israeli society.

In addition to the inspiring work of multiple Reform congregants toward *tikkun olam*, the Israel Religious Action Center is the body representing the Israeli movement, as well as all the Progressive and Reform Movements around the world in our political and legal work to make Israel live up to our Progressive Zionist values.

IRAC works on issues of society and religion: advocating for the end of the Orthodox monopoly on religious life in Israel, for gender equality, and against racism and Islamophobia. We believe our work is laying the essential foundations for our Progressive Zionist vision. It is crucial that we do this work as part of a Jewish religious movement (not only as human rights and civil liberties activists), because it expands the discourse on Progressive Jewish values in Israel.

Source: Rabbi Noa Sattath, "Restoring Tikkun Olam to Liberal Religious Zionist Activism," in *The Fragile Dialogue: New Voices of Liberal Zionism*, eds. Rabbi Stanley M. Davids and Rabbi Lawrence Englander, DHL (New York: CCAR Press, 2017).

The International Delegitimization Campaign against Israel and the Urgent Need of a Comprehensive, Two-State, End-of-Conflict Peace Agreement

JOHN L. ROSOVE

I decided to write this article because I have of late been asked questions from both Jews and non-Jews that until recently I had never heard before, questions that call into question the very legitimacy of the State of Israel. I have seen nothing in print that can serve as a comprehensive primer, fact sheet, briefing, and background paper that can assist rabbis, Jewish leaders, college and university students and faculty, and our friends in the interfaith community in dealing effectively with the complexities and nuances that underlie the growing international movement to delegitimize Israel.

I recently led a mission of my own synagogue leaders to Israel during which we met with more than a dozen political and security experts, journalists, settlers, peace and human rights activists, and Reform Movement leaders on the situation in which Israel and the Palestinians find themselves. Our very first speaker was Rabbi Danny Gordis, vice president of the Shalem Institute in Jerusalem, who said, "Israel today faces two external existential threats, a nuclear Iran and the international delegitimization movement." It was at that point that I realized that an article of this kind dealing comprehensively with the delegitimization movement is necessary.

I write this article from the perspective of Progressive Reform Zionism that affirms that in order for Israel to be a secure and great Jewish society reflecting authentic Jewish values, there can be no dichotomy between universalism and particularism. Progressive Reform Zionism affirms that Jewish nationalism must envision our people's national independence as a means of serving humanity as a whole, to be "a light to the nations" (Isa. 42:6). Progressive Reform Zionism therefore requires that social justice be applied to all the major issues confronting Israeli society including Palestinian rights, minority rights, immigrant worker rights, women's rights, poverty, education, and justice.

What Is the Delegitimization Movement and What Does It Seek to Do?

Since the establishment of the State of Israel in 1948, war has been waged against it in three forms: (1) conventional warfare, (2) terrorism at home and abroad, and (3) delegitimization.

Delegitimization is the most insidious of the three, for what has not been won on the battlefield or through terror is now being fought in diplomatic circles, academia, the international media, and polite society. Those waging it are a loosely coordinated group that includes the international Palestinian solidarity movement, left wing political activists, American and European academicians, and overt and covert anti-Semites.

Delegitimizers negate the right of the Jewish people to define itself as a self-sustaining, independent people in its own land and to manifest that definition into the creation of a Jewish state. Essentially, delegitimization is the denial of the right of the Jews to have their nation like all other peoples.

The delegitimization network aims to supersede the Zionist model of a Jewish democratic state with a one-state solution based on the "one person, one vote" principle. It claims that a two-state solution to the Israel-Palestinian conflict represents an inherent injustice to the Palestinians. Delegitimizers start from the joint premise that the existence of the State of Israel cannot be justified morally and that Israel therefore does not have the moral right to defend itself when it is attacked. They apply rules and standards of conduct to the government of Israel that they do not apply to other nations; they seek to turn Israel into a pariah state and advocate the same fate that befell the former apartheid South African regime through boycotts, divestments, and sanctions (i.e., the BDS movement).

While some delegitimizers are outright Holocaust deniers, others claim that the Palestinian people should not have to suffer because the Jews were victims of the Holocaust, an argument that is a gross oversimplification of a partial truth. Jews began populating Palestine long before the Holocaust and the Holocaust was not a factor in the development of the Zionist dream. That being said, it is beyond question that Jewish immigration to Palestine intensified in the 1930s after Hitler's rise to power, and the murder of the six million inspired sympathy for the Jewish people that led to the United Nations 1947 Partition resolution.

Delegitimization is based on a malicious misreading of and falsification of history and on ignorance and anti-Semitism. For example, in October 2010, Al-Mutawakel Taha, an Information Ministry official in the Palestinian Authority, speaking on behalf of the official position of the PA, published a paper that denies any Jewish connection to the Western Wall of the Second Temple known by Jews as the *Kotel*, saying that the so-called *Kotel* is an early twentieth century designation. They state that "the *Al Buraq* Wall is the western wall of *Al Aksa* and has no religious significance to Jews." Palestinian officials have often rejected claims of Jewish heritage in Jerusalem and claim that the "Wall" is part of "occupied" eastern Jerusalem.

In October 2010 UnESCO endorsed the Palestinian Authority's demands that Rachel's Tomb outside of Bethlehem, long a revered Jewish pilgrimage site, not only be removed from Israel's declared historic sites but actually be declared a mosque. Even Yasser Arafat did not make such a claim until 1996. UnESCO declared as well that Israel cannot claim the Cave of the *Machpelah* in Hebron, the traditional burial site of the biblical forebears of the Jewish nation (see Genesis 23), as a national heritage site.

The aim of delegitimizers is erasure of the Jewish connection with the biblical Land of Israel as the premise for the negating of the modern State of Israel's existence, despite volumes of biblical and written historical references and archaeological evidence. Delegitimizers consider Jewish immigration to what is now Israel only the result of nineteenth century European colonialism, thus inferring that Zionism is a falsehood. Jews, therefore, have no claim to the land and are thus seen as the oppressors of Palestinian Arabs living in Israel and the West Bank and the jailers of Palestinians living in the Gaza Strip.

Delegitimizers have advocated bringing charges of war crimes and genocide against Israel's politicians, diplomats, and officers of the Israel Defense Forces, and in some notable cases (e.g., former Prime Minister Ariel Sharon and former Foreign Minister Tzipi Livni) they have lodged arrest warrants in European capitals against Israeli leaders.

Delegitimizers have developed a narrative about what Zionism and Israel are in disregard of the facts, and they label Israel a murderous, brutal, and illegitimate entity whose very existence is unjust.

Why Israel Is Not an Apartheid State Despite Claims by the Delegitimization Network

Delegitimizers (especially the international Palestinian solidarity movement) equate the racist apartheid regime of the former South Africa with Israel in its policies towards Palestinians living in Israel and the West Bank. Even a cursory comparison between the old South African apartheid regime and the democratic State of Israel negates the equivalence.

In "An Open Letter to Archbishop Desmond Tutu" by Warren Goldstein, chief rabbi of South Africa, published in the *International Jerusalem Post*, Rabbi Goldstein writes,

> Israel has no Population Registration Act, no Group Areas Act, no Mixed Marriages and Immorality act, no Separate Representation of Voters Act, no Separate Amenities Act, no pass laws or any of the myriad apartheid laws. To the contrary, Israel is a vibrant liberal democracy and accords full political, religious and other human rights to all its peoples, including its more than one million Arab citizens, many of whom hold positions of authority including that of cabinet minister, Member of Parliament, and judge at every level, including that of the Supreme Court. All citizens vote on the same roll in regular, multiparty elections. There are Arab parties and Arab members of other parties in Israel's parliament. Arabs and Jews share all public facilities, including hospitals and malls, buses, cinemas and parks, universities and cultural [venues].[1]

Rabbi Goldstein's claims above are true, but it is not to say that Arab citizens of Israel enjoy the same benefits and rights that Israeli Jews enjoy, such as equal access to government funds and services and the right to live anywhere in the state of Israel. This, and the imperfections cited below, must be addressed if Israel is to maintain its democratic traditions.

Palestinian Arabs living in the West Bank, however, are not Israeli citizens as are those living on Israel's side of the Green Line (i.e., the 1949 armistice lines established after the War of Independence), and they do not enjoy the same protections as do those living in Israel. For them, their fight is and has always been one against occupation. We Jews may not like that claim, but it is a legitimate one born of a century of neglect by Arab and world powers who callously used the local Arab population as game pieces on a shifting board of changing geopolitical aims. While the case can be made that Israel's strong and often harsh security measures imposed on Palestinian Arabs living in the West Bank are a necessary evil in light of terrorism, we cannot ignore the fact that holding this territory for more than forty years and keeping the residents there under occupation has had a corrupting moral influence on Israeli troops who have served in the West Bank and upon Israel as a whole. Even David Ben Gurion recognized the dangers of occupation when he said in 1967: "Return [the captured territory] immediately, even if no one wants it back; return it."

The foundational Zionist dream as reflected in Israel's Declaration of Independence did not envision the Jewish people becoming military occupiers nor did they anticipate the corrosive effects that occupation would have both upon the Arabs and the Jews.

The United Nations General Assembly: The Central International Arena of Delegitimization Efforts

One might conclude after observing the United Nations' debates, reading its resolutions, and walking its halls (especially since 1967) that a principal purpose of the world body is to censure Israel. The campaign to demonize and delegitimize Israel in every UN and international forum was initiated by the Arab states together with the Soviet Union after the 1967 Six-Day War and supported by what has become known as an "automatic majority" of Third World member states. UN bias against Israel is overt in bodies such as the General Assembly, which each year passes numerous resolutions against Israel and almost none against most other member states, including the world's most repressive regimes.

While Israel has been the target of disproportional UN attention, a mere handful of the UN's other 191 countries have been cited only once. Since its creation in June 2006 the UN Human Rights Council (UNHRC) has criticized Israel on more than thirty occasions in resolutions that grant effective immunity to Hamas and Hezbollah and their state sponsors. In the first year of its existence, the Council failed to condemn human rights violations occurring in any of the world's other 191 countries. In its second year, the Council criticized one other country when it "deplored" the situation in Burma, but only after it censored out initial language containing the word "condemn." It even praised Sudan for its "cooperation" while it was conducting a genocidal campaign against the people of Darfur.

The UNHRC's fixation with Israel is not limited to resolutions. Israel is the only country listed on the Council's permanent agenda. Moreover, Israel is the only country subjected to an investigatory mandate that examines the actions of only one side and presumes those actions to be violations and therefore not subject to standard review.

Emergency Special Sessions of the United Nations General Assembly are rare. Whereas a number of such sessions have been called with respect to actions taken by Israel, between 1983 and 1998 no such session was convened with respect to the Chinese occupation of Tibet, the Indonesian occupation of East Timor, the Syrian occupation of Lebanon, the slaughters in Rwanda, the disappearances in Zaire, or the horrors of Bosnia.

Israel is the only member nation of the UN that is prohibited from serving on the UN Security Council.

Other Delegitimizing Actions

- **The UN Resolution on "Zionism as Racism"** was adopted on November 10, 1975, by a vote of 72 to 35 (with 32 abstentions), and determined that "Zionism is a form of racism and racial discrimination." The resolution is often referenced in debates of Zionism and racism. The resolution was eventually revoked by Resolution 46/86 on December 16, 1991, the only revocation in the history of the UN. However, the damage was done as language from the original resolution was introduced into school textbooks around the world and influenced the attitudes of millions of people thereby prejudicing them about the nature of the Zionist movement and the State of Israel.

- *The Protocols of the Elders of Zion.* The dissemination and promotion of the notorious nineteenth century anti-Semitic forgery (allegedly written by a cabal of Jews plotting to take over the world) is still widely published, distributed, and read in America and around the world.

- **Palestinian school textbooks.** The Palestinian Authority, despite promises to the contrary during the Oslo process, has failed to change school textbooks that overtly contain intolerant and prejudicial statements against Jews.

Official Palestinian maps do not include Israel.

- *The Israel Lobby.* This book by John Mearsheimer and Stephen Walt was published in 2006. The authors argue that no lobby in Washington, D.C., has managed to divert American foreign policy as far from the American national interest as has the American Jewish lobby. Mearsheimer and Walt use many classic anti-Semitic canards exaggerating Jewish power and theorizing conspiracy. The views of these two "scholars" (their areas of expertise are not in history or political science) are considered radioactive in virtually all reaches of the Jewish community.

- **Israel's security barrier.** Delegitimizers charge that the security barrier between Israel and the West Bank is a convenient excuse for Israel to grab Palestinian land with impunity and to unilaterally establish Israel's permanent border. Though it was built to stop suicide bombers and terrorists from entering Israel from the West Bank, the tragedy is that there is truth to the charge that the fence has caused disruption and injustice. It has torn up ancestral land plots, often cut off Palestinian villages from their fields, cut down olive groves (the main cash crop for Palestinian farmers), surrounded some villages making movement difficult, and brought added misery to the lives of Palestinians. The designers and builders of the fence say that they were ordered to build it with only one purpose in mind—to save Israeli lives. Since its effective completion, indeed, not one suicide bomber or terrorist has infiltrated Israel from the West Bank. In a meeting I had with the head of Military Administration that planned and established the fence from 2003–2006, retired Colonel Danny Tirza noted that he personally looked forward to being the one to begin tearing down this fence once a peace agreement is signed between Israel and the Palestinians. In response to delegitimizers and to pro-Israel critics of the fence, the only answer is "yes, the fence is awful, but it is necessary because it saves lives."

- **International boycott of Israel.** The delegitimization campaign successfully persuaded a number of international singers and artists to cancel their performances in Israel. They have also urged countries not to send their representatives to international meetings in Jerusalem.

- **Israel deemed the greatest threat to world peace.** Several years ago a poll taken in Europe found that Europeans believed that Israel is the greatest threat to world peace—ahead of Iran and north Korea.

- **The UN's Goldstone Report.** Fuel was added to the delegitimization effort by the publication of the UN's Goldstone Report following the Israel-Hamas War in Gaza. Israel refused to participate in this Un investigation because of the UN's historic antipathy and biases against Israel. Both Israel and Hamas were accused of war crimes and asked to investigate and show accountability. Israel was charged with deliberately targeting civilians in its campaign to attack Hamas fighters and military stockpiles. Because Hamas situated itself in civilian neighborhoods, Israel had no choice but to attack Hamas fighters where they were: in neighborhoods, schools, clinics, and mosques. The purpose of Israel's actions in the war was to stop the bombs (about eight thousand to date had targeted Israeli civilian towns and settlements over eight years). Innocent civilians had been killed and injured. The Israel Defense Forces investigated all charges and found some isolated criminal actions by individual soldiers. Hamas regarded the Goldstone Report as a victory and has, to date, not undertaken any investigations of its own. This report was used by the UNHRC to justify its position that Israel is a criminal state. It should be noted, however, that Judge Richard Goldstone had no intention of branding Israel as a criminal state. In truth, he is a Zionist Jew with deep respect and love for Israel. While we may find great fault with the Goldstone Report, we also can fault Israel for not participating, for had it done so the investigation would have given Israel the opportunity to disagree with its eventual conclusions, while pointing to Israel's openness and cooperation. Israel conducted a military review of its conduct of the war. Many friends of Israel and Israelis themselves argued that Israel should have set up an independent commission to investigate its own conduct as it did following the Yom Kippur War.

We Cannot Deny That Israel Is an Imperfect Democracy

Israel is an imperfect democracy, as is every democracy in the western world including the United States, Great Britain, Germany, France, and Italy. In the context of the Middle East, Israel is the only democracy—it has an independent judiciary, freedom of the press, the right to vote, free elections, and equality before the law of Jew and Arab alike. Since the 1967 Six-Day War when the Old City of Jerusalem passed from control by Jordan to Israel, Israel has protected and sustained all religious holy sites and allowed freedom of access. As Israel is an open society, more foreign reporters are based in Jerusalem than in any city in the world except new York and London, and there are eighty human rights organizations (including many Israeli nongovernmental organizations) that freely investigate alleged human rights violations without official Israeli interference or censorship.

Israel's challenges are nevertheless formidable and include increasingly high poverty rates and a widening discrepancy between the wealthy and poor; abuse of the rights of immigrant workers; inadequate policies concerning illegal immigration; often harsh treatment of Arabs living under occupation in the West Bank; unequal treatment of Israeli Arabs as Israeli citizens; discriminatory policies towards women; an ongoing sex slave industry, which Israeli authorities have not adequately confronted; the Orthodox rabbinate's monopoly of power over liberal Jewish religious streams; and an increasingly large population of ultra-Orthodox Jews who pay no taxes, do not serve in the military or in any national service, and are funded economically in the hundreds of millions of dollars by Israeli taxpayers but are not loyal to the State and are non-Zionist and/or anti-Zionist in their beliefs.

In addition, there are elements within the ruling coalition of the Israeli government that are extremist in outlook including Foreign Minister Avigdor Lieberman and his Russian-based Israel Bateinu party, which has called for the redrawing of the border between Israel and the West Bank so that Israel would include large Jewish settlement blocs and the Palestinian state would include large Arab-Israeli population centers. Though on its face this makes demographic sense, it would effectively transfer formerly loyal Arab-Israelis who have lived in Israel since the founding of the State of Israel. Lieberman has also called for the imposition of a loyalty oath by Israeli citizens with noncompliers losing their right to vote. And though this is a common practice around the world, the proposal is unnecessary given the democratic principles and values already stated in Israel's Declaration of Independence. The effect of this proposal is provocative in that it would demand that Arab citizens be loyal to a Jewish State rather than the State of Israel, thereby disenfranchising nonJewish Israeli citizens from the Israeli body politic by accentuating the Jewish religious and national character of the state.

There are problems as well regarding the status of Palestinian residents of East Jerusalem who are not citizens of the State of Israel. Though they have the vote over their own municipal concerns, they do not vote in Israeli national elections even though Jerusalem is treated by the State of Israel as unified.

The Settlements

The settlements constructed by Israel in the West Bank since the 1967 Six-Day War present problems regarding the ultimate disposition of the territories in an end-of-conflict agreement between Israel and the Palestinians, and some of the settlers themselves are a potentially violent resistant group that does not believe in or support a Palestinian state alongside Israel.

The settlement question for Israel is among the most difficult obstacles in the way of a resolution to this conflict. Israelis have argued, citing Camp David Accords and Israel's unilateral withdrawal from Gaza, that when Israel wishes to do so for the sake of peace, it will withdraw from settlements. However, we cannot deny that the original intent of the government and the settlers in the building up of the West Bank after the 1967 war was expansionist based in the view that "this is our land; this is our birthright; this is our inheritance." Today more than three hundred thousand Israelis live in the conquered territories. The issue isn't their right to do so. Rather, it is the wisdom of doing so.

The Israelis argue that not all settlements and settlers are similar. Essentially, they say that there are three categories: (1) the Jerusalem neighborhoods built after the 1967 Six-Day War in East Jerusalem forming a ring around Jerusalem and thereby expanding the city's borders; (2) the large settlement blocs (now small cities with more than twenty thousand residents), including Arielle, Efrat, and Maalei Adumim, as well as several others in the Gush Etzion bloc; and (3) the small settlements of a few dozen families spread out in large numbers over a wide area of the West Bank.

Yes, these three categories are different from each other. However, the creation of facts on the ground does not morally justify those facts. Regarding the Jerusalem neighborhoods, the vast number of apartment buildings has dramatically expanded the boundaries of the city of Jerusalem. And while Jews affirm that Jerusalem is the eternal capital of the Jewish people, we cannot claim the city as the exclusive inheritance of the Jewish people. It is also sacred to Christianity and Islam, and whether we like it or not, the Palestinians claim Jerusalem as their capital as well.

Given our people's experience during the nineteen years of Jordanian rule when the city was divided and Jews were not allowed access to our holy sites, no one can legitimately blame Israelis for insisting that the city remain unified and that overall security be in the hands of Israel. However, the status quo of exclusive rule is unsustainable and anyone thinking that there can be peace without appropriate sharing of the city is sorely mistaken.

Regarding the West Bank, there too we cannot deny that Israel's intent in the years after 1967 was to build settlements in order to expand Israel's borders. The Jewish state was and is small, and it is understandable that holding onto territory won in a war of selfdefense seems reasonable. But the Middle East is not like any other place, and for there to be peace Israel is going to have to be prepared to withdraw from many settlements, even the larger ones.

The Palestinians say repeatedly that they want their territory completely free of Jews. In principle, Israelis rightly ask why that is necessary since 1.2 million Arab Palestinians live in Israel as Israeli citizens. If peace is to be real, Israelis argue, why must a Palestinian state be *Judenrein?* If Jews wish to remain in their homes and live peacefully under Palestinian rule, why should they not be allowed to do so? However, as reasonable as this supposition seems, those settlements beyond the eventual border should be dismantled. In principle, this would also include the large population areas. Just because the cities are large does not justify them any more than one can justify the dozens of tiny settlements with only a few families each. Their presence is likely to be an impediment to reaching an accord, and if there were an accord without such dismantling, those settlements could become a continual source of friction undermining what is expected, at least for a while, to be a fragile peace. For all practical purposes, Jewish settlements on the Palestinian side and Palestinian villages on the Jewish side cannot be considered equivalent, at least for now.

B'tzelem (a leading Israeli Human Rights Organization) has documented many instances of settlements having illegally absorbed land owned by Palestinians and estimates that one-third of all Jewish settlements are built on privately owned Palestinian land. Settler groups, aided and supported by the Israeli government, are now also purchasing land in traditionally Arab neighborhoods of East Jerusalem (e.g., Silwan, Abu Dis, Sheik Jarah, and Jabel Mukaber) in order to establish a Jewish presence in all of Jerusalem and thereby make necessary compromises in an accord difficult.

Legitimate Criticism vs . Delegitimization: Embrace Loving Critics and Distance Delegitimizers

Much criticism of Israel is fair and accurate, and it is a mistake for Israel's friends to deny the existence of problems and injustices out of fear of being dismissed as "anti-Israel." Being a critic does not mean one is automatically anti-Israel. One can argue, as American Reform Jewish leaders did during the Civil Rights and Vietnam eras in the United States, that criticism from love is the highest form of patriotism. Indeed, Israelis themselves are among the most self-critical citizens of any nation in the world, and it is contrary to Jewish tradition to withhold legitimate criticism.

In recent years, the American Jewish community has become increasingly polarized in its views and relationship to Israel. This polarization has had a destructive impact on civil discourse within the American Jewish community and has resulted in the unfair demonizing of pro-Israel groups and individuals.

In the 2010 election, for the first time, long-time supporters of Israel in the Democratic Party were charged with being insufficiently pro-Israel by the Republican Jewish Coalition (RJC), a group of Jewish Republican funders and supporters. Representative Eric Cantor (R-VA and House Majority Leader) led the way in transforming support for right-wing policies vis à vis Israel into a political wedge issue for the first time since the establishment of the State of Israel. Israel has always benefited from nonpartisan support among Republicans and Democrats. It is hoped that the RJC will cease and desist from this short-sighted and dangerous politicization of Israel in American politics.

Since the emergence of J Street in 2007 as a pro-Israel, pro-peace, left-leaning lobby in Washington, D.C., right-wing forces in the American Jewish community and Israel including those in Israel's foreign ministry, have sought to characterize J Street as anti-Israel and "traitorous" based on policy positions it has taken that are different than those promoted by the American Israel Public Affairs Committee, even though J Street's positions enjoy significant support in Israel and among American Jews.

Although we American Jews appreciate that we are not on the frontlines and therefore must defer to Israelis to make the important decisions on such issues as security, peace, Jerusalem, the Palestinians, territorial boundaries, water, refugees, and the future of the Jewish State, it is also in the interest of the American Jewish community that Israel remain strong, secure, democratic, and Jewish, and so our perspective as pro-Israel friends must be respected and heard.

Jewish Organizational Perspectives:
Who Is Really In and Out of the Pro-Israel Camp

I present below the views of a number of American Jewish and Israeli organizations vis à vis Israel, the Palestinians, Zionism, and human rights. The list is not exhaustively inclusive. I offer this list because increasingly some Jewish leaders and groups dismiss others as outside the "Israel camp" because they disagree with them on the issues with which Israel and the Palestinians are struggling. I believe we have to be careful before narrowing the tent. not only is excluding actual pro-Israel Jews who disagree with us politically unwise, it is also contrary to Jewish tradition's historic commitment to honest and open debate.

I believe that all of the following organizations can be regarded as within the pro-Israel camp except The Jewish Voice for Peace. The descriptions of each are taken directly from the respective organization's mission statement. I have indicated where I believe each is on the American Jewish or Israeli political spectrum (i.e., left–center–right).

1. **Americans for Peace Now (APN)**. Established in 1981 to mobilize support for the Israeli peace movement, *Shalom Achshav* (Peace Now) has since developed into a prominent American Jewish and Zionist organization working to achieve a comprehensive political settlement to the Arab-Israeli conflict. APN is a leading voice of American Jews who support Israel and know that only peace will ensure Israel's security, prosperity, and continued viability as a Jewish, democratic state. APN and *Shalom Achshav* call for the evacuation of settlements in the West Bank and the creation of a viable Palestinian state. APN is a nonpartisan organization that supplies information and education, providing a pro-Israel, pro-peace, American Jewish perspective on issues and legislation, as well as engaging in grassroots political activism and outreach to the American Jewish and Arab American communities, opinion leaders, university students, and the public at large. APn is left on the political spectrum.

2. **American Israel Public Affairs Committee (AIPAC)** . Established in the 1950s, AIPAC is America's leading pro-Israel lobby working with both Democratic and Republican political leaders to enact public policy that strengthens the U.S.-Israel relationship. With the support of its members nationwide, AIPAC has worked with Congress and the Executive Branch on numerous initiatives from securing foreign aid for Israel to passing legislation aimed at stopping Iran's illicit nuclear program. It is judged by most observers as the most significant lobby representing the American Jewish community's concerns for Israel's security and survival in the nation's capital. AIPAC has historically supported whatever Israeli government was in office vis à vis Israeli security concerns. AIPAC is center-right on the political spectrum.

3. **American Jewish Committee (AJC).** Established in 1906 in response to pogroms aimed at Russian Jews, the AJC mission is to promote pluralistic and democratic societies where all minorities are protected. It serves as

an international think tank and advocacy organization identifying trends and problems early in order to take action. AJC's key areas of focus are to combat anti-Semitism and all forms of bigotry, promote pluralism and shared democratic values, support Israel's quest for peace and security, advocate for energy independence, and strengthen Jewish life. The AJC often works behind the scenes out of the public eye. The AJC is center-right on the political spectrum.

4. **Anti-Defamation League of B'nai B'rith (ADL).** Founded in 1913 "to stop the defamation of the Jewish people and to secure justice and fair treatment to all," the ADL is one of the nation's most significant civil rights/human relations agencies. Its mission is to fight anti-Semitism and all forms of bigotry, defend democratic ideals, and protect civil rights for all in the United States and abroad through information, education, legislation, and advocacy. It also serves as a resource for government, media, law enforcement, educators, and the public. The ADL is right on the political spectrum.

5. **Association of Reform Zionists of America (ARZA)**. Founded in 1978, the American Reform Movement's Zionist organization's mission "endeavors to make Israel fundamental to the sacred lives and Jewish identity of Reform Jews. As a Zionist organization, ARZA champions activities that further enhance Israel as a pluralistic, just and democratic Jewish state." Founded as an affiliate of the Union for Reform Judaism (at that time called the Union of American Hebrew Congregations), ARZA is associated with the Israel Movement for Progressive Judaism (IMPJ). While ARZA does work to impact Israeli society through advocacy, support for the Israel Religious Action Center (IRAC), a premier social justice advocacy organization in Israel, ARZA is not affiliated with any particular political party or platform in Israel. ARZA does take political stances regarding Israel based upon the resolutions of its board and various bodies within the Reform Movement such as the Union for Reform Judaism and the Central Conference of American Rabbis. However, ARZA is not affiliated with any political parties in the United States and works on its own and in partnerships to build consensus for strong support for Israel within the Reform Movement. ARZA is center-left on the political spectrum.

6. **B'nai B'rith Hillel Foundation.** Founded in 1923, Hillel is the largest Jewish campus organization in the world, providing opportunities for

Jewish students at more than five hundred colleges and universities to explore and celebrate their Jewish identity through its global network of regional centers, campus foundations, and student organizations. Hillel's mission is "to enrich the lives of Jewish undergraduate and graduate students. Hillel student leaders, professionals and lay leaders are dedicated to creating a pluralistic, welcoming and inclusive environment for Jewish college students . . . . Hillel is committed to the support of Israel as a Jewish and democratic state with secure and recognized borders and as a member of the family of free nations." Hillel is center on the political spectrum.

7. *B'tzelem* **(literally, "In God's image").** Established in 1989 by a group of prominent academics, attorneys, journalists, and Knesset members, the Israeli Information Center for Human Rights in the Occupied Territories endeavors to document and educate the Israeli public and policymakers about human rights violations in the occupied territories, combat denial of such violations prevalent in the mindset of the Israeli public, and help create a human rights culture in Israel. *B'tzelem* is left on the political spectrum.

8. **J Street.** Established in 2008, J Street is a new political action committee that gives political voice to mainstream American Jews and other supporters of Israel who, informed by their progressive and Jewish values, believe that a two-state solution to the Israeli-Palestinian conflict is essential to Israel's survival as the national home of the Jewish people and as a vibrant democracy. J Street's mission is twofold: to advocate for urgent American diplomatic leadership to achieve a two-state solution and a broader regional, comprehensive peace and, second, to ensure a broad debate on Israel and the Middle East in national politics and the American Jewish community. J Street represents Americans, primarily but not exclusively Jewish, who support Israel and its desire for security as the Jewish homeland, as well as the right of the Palestinians to a sovereign state of their own—two states living side-by-side in peace and security. J Street believes that ending the Israeli-Palestinian conflict is in the best interests of Israel, the United States, the Palestinians, and the region as a whole. J Street is left on the political spectrum.

9. **Jewish Community Relations Committee/Council (JCRC).** A consensus organization founded in the 1960s, the JCRCs seek to shape consensus on public issues, develop strategic responses, and work with

the media, elected officials, coalition partners, and others through public relations, advocacy, and lobbying. JCRCs customarily are concerned with international issues including Israel-U.S. relations, global anti-Semitism, the United Nations, the well-being of Jews in dangerous areas, and human rights. Its domestic concerns include anti-Semitism, social justice, poverty, education, public health, individual rights, and religious liberties including the preservation of the separation of church and state. JCRCs are nonpartisan and reflect the consensus views of its Jewish constituency groups. The JCRC is center on the political spectrum.

10. **Jewish Voice for Peace (JVP)** . Founded in 1996, JVP states that its goal is to "provide a voice for Jews and allies who believe that peace in the Middle East will be achieved through justice and full equality for both Palestinians and Israelis." JVP characterizes the Palestine-Israel conflict as a battle over territory and not based on conflicting cultures and religious and national identities. JVP begins with the premise that the creation of the State of Israel is an historic injustice to the Palestinian people. It has a strong Palestinian bias, though it includes Israelis and Jews in its membership. JVP has no opinion about whether there should be a Jewish State. It supports a complete suspension of American military aid to Israel suggesting either a cavalier or pernicious attitude toward Israel's survival. It is one of the key groups behind the BDS campaign directed against Israel. JVP is extreme left on the political spectrum and is outside the pro-Israel camp.

11. **New Israel Fund (NIF).** NIF is a leading organization committed to equality and democracy for all Israelis. It is a partnership of Israelis and supporters of Israel worldwide, dedicated to a vision of Israel as both the Jewish homeland and a shared society at peace with itself and its neighbors. NIF strengthens organizations and leaders that work to achieve equality for all civil and human rights for the citizens of Israel including its Palestinian citizens. It recognizes and reinforces the pluralism of Israeli society and strives to empower groups on the economic margins of Israeli society. The NIF is left on the political spectrum.

12. **Rabbis for Human Rights (RHR).** Established in 1988 with the purpose of giving voice to the Zionist ideal and the Jewish religious tradition of human rights, RHR has championed the cause of the poor in Israel, supported the rights of Israel's minorities and Palestinians, worked to stop the abuse of foreign workers, endeavored to guarantee the upkeep of

Israel's public health care system, promoted the equal status of women, helped Ethiopian Jews, battled trafficking in women, fought against human rights violations in Israel and in areas for which Israel has taken responsibility, and brought specific human rights grievances to the attention of the Israeli public while pressuring the appropriate authorities for their redress. RHR is left on the political spectrum.

13. **StandWithUs (SWU).** Founded in 2001 in response to the misinformation that often surrounds the Middle East conflict, and the inappropriate, often anti-Semitic language used about Israel and/or the Jewish people worldwide, SWU is an international education organization that ensures that Israel's side of the story is told in communities, campuses, libraries, the media, and churches through brochures, speakers, conferences, missions to Israel, and thousands of pages of Internet resources. SWU is right on the political spectrum.

14. **Zionist Organization of America (ZOA).** Founded in 1897, the ZOA is the oldest of all Zionists organizations in America, and "has been fighting for the Jewish people and the Land of Israel" ever since. It is currently the only mainstream American Zionist organization that is opposed to ceding territory to a Palestinian state in a two-state, end-of-conflict agreement. When it was founded, however, it was the organ of Israel's Labor Party. The ZOA is extreme right on the political spectrum.

Why Settling the Israeli-Palestinian Conflict Is Strategically and Morally Necessary Now Before It Is Too Late

It is in Israel's and America's strategic and moral interests to settle all issues between the State of Israel and the Palestinian Authority in a two-state, end-of-conflict agreement. As Zionists we cannot deny morally the right of self-determination for any other people, including the Palestinians.

In the context of an end-of-conflict settlement between Israel and the Palestinians it is essential also to Israel's and America's longterm interests that Israel establishes peace agreements with other Arab and Muslim nations. Such agreements will assure Israel's long-term security and peaceful coexistence with its neighbors, add stability to the nations of the Middle East, and further American geopolitical and strategic interests.

Though Israel will likely always have its detesters, an end-ofconflict settlement that resolves through compromise all of Palestinian and Israeli interests resulting in a two-state solution will be the greatest weapon against those who would strive to delegitimize Israel. With a comprehensive peace agreement, the issue of Jewish and Palestinian national rights will be settled and affirmed. Having said this, we should be under no illusions. Tragically, justice and fairness never fully can be addressed in the holy land. Our respective conflicting claims to the same territory can be accommodated but not fully resolved. And so, the goal of a two-state solution needs to not only affirm the legitimate national claims of both Jews and Palestinians, but also to reduce bloodshed and hostilities and develop a spirit of cooperation and mutual respect between our two peoples.

The current situation in which both Israel and the Palestinians find themselves is unsustainable. Unless there is a two-state agreement, Israel's democratic traditions and Jewish character will be diminished and the dreams of Israel's founders will never be realized.

What Do We Do Now?

The purpose of this article, as stated in the opening, is to offer a comprehensive primer, fact sheet, briefing, and background paper that can assist rabbis, Jewish leaders, college and university students and faculty, and interfaith leaders in confronting the delegitimization network in their communities, on campuses, in the media, and among their colleagues and friends.

It is not within the scope of this piece to offer specific actions to counter delegitimization efforts. Other organizations have already offered such guides, including AIPAC, Hillel, and StandWithUs, amongst others.

A word of caution: Many take the position that offense is the best defense, that showing any sign of weakness will signal defeat, that there is only one "true" narrative, the Jewish/Israeli narrative, and that the Palestinian "narrative" is inherently flawed and therefore should be dismissed. I believe that such thinking is not only wrong-headed and false, but cruel and counterproductive. Such a posture will never address the problem between our two peoples nor bring us closer to a peaceful resolution to the conflict.

The best strategy, and the one most likely to be effective, in my opinion, is that pro-Israel and pro-peace advocates (i.e., those who wish a two-state, end-of-conflict agreement) speak, write, and otherwise transmit the truth always, acknowledging the legitimate positions of Israelis and Palestinians alike. The "truth" means affirming first that there are, indeed, two narratives, Israeli and Palestinian, and second, that Israel has social problems and is an imperfect democracy relative to its national ideals expressed in its Declaration of Independence, and that holding onto the West Bank as occupiers will corrupt the soul of the people of Israel.

We must acknowledge as well that there are antidemocratic trends growing within Israel itself including the illegal, aggressive, and sometimes violent activities of some settlers vis à vis misappropriation of Palestinian-owned land and their relationship with neighboring Palestinians, the hostile approach to democracy held by the ultra-Orthodox political parties and rabbis, and the acquiescence of middle-right Israeli political parties and their Diaspora Jewish supporters to extremist trends based on reasons of political self-interests.

An old UJA advertisement once read "We never promised you a rose garden." Anyone with eyes wide open understands the truth of this statement. Indeed, the situation between Israelis and Palestinians and within their respective societies is complex and difficult. nevertheless, unless this conflict is settled, I fear for the Zionist enterprise altogether. In the 1970s there was an American Zionist movement called *Ein b'reira* (There is no alternative). That message is even more to the point today.

Note

1. Warren Goldstein, "An Open Letter to Archbishop Desmond Tutu," *International Jerusalem Post*, november 12–18, 2010.

Source: John L. Rosove, "The International Delegitimization Campaign against Israel and the Urgent Need of a Comprehensive, Two-State, End-of-Conflict Peace Agreement," *CCAR Journal: The Reform Jewish Quarterly*, Fall 2011, 90–109.

The Tapestry of
the Jewish People

How I Became a Reform Jew

Neshama Carlebach

I grew up Jewish. Simply Jewish.

My late father, Rabbi Shlomo Carlebach, raised us in an observant Ortho-dox household. Our lives were filled with beautiful ritual and we celebrated the wonder of a familial spiritual connection.

That said, we also danced along the fine line of progressive Judaism. My father's Torah was an expression of the beauty of Judaism. He taught the world to love and cherish Shabbat even on a Tuesday and to love Jewish rituals in an open hearted, expansively spiritual way that often set him apart and alienated him from many established religious groups.

My father's true goal was to raise Jewish life above the rote performance of ritual acts. He wanted the light and redemptive message of the Torah to make all of humanity deeper more empathetic, loving and capable of kindness. He often said that effecting global healing was the reason we were in the world to begin with.

Though it sometimes got him in trouble with the Orthodox establishment, my father was an active member and lover of all interfaith experiences. He attended many different houses of worship, sang with people of all colors, faiths and backgrounds, and attended conferences where he spoke about finding true unity for all of God's children.

Significantly, he encouraged women to learn and read Torah. At his syna-gogue he created the space for women to physically dance with the the Torah and stand all the way up, next to the ark on holidays.

For this passion and commitment, my father's life was complicated. Within the Orthodox world, he was a visionary who stood alone and was too often lonely.

As the daughter of this great man, I bear witness to the intolerance, cruelty and ostracism he suffered for daring to step outside the "*daled amot*" (personal space) of observant Jewish life. As his child, I suffered alongside him when he tried to give me a platform to sing, the outcry from my Orthodox brothers and sisters invariably drowning out my voice and suffocating my love for Jewish tradition.

Strengthened by my father's love and vision, I persisted. It was not easy being taunted and called names, hearing angry voices and seeing the enraged faces of those who believed genuinely believed that what I called prayer was an affront to God. Looking back, I believe that the ugliness I saw was not motivated by a desire to hurt me personally but by a deep misunderstanding of the message of our Torah and what it means to be a Jew in the modern world.

Looking back, I feel sadness and sorrow for this narrow vision, this narrow place, an Egypt of the mind *mitzrayim*. I know, as my father knew, that the redemption of the world will come from the opposite impulse: expansive love and inclusivity. Isn't that what *klal Yisrael* (the whole of the Jewish community) is about?

I have just experienced *klal Yisrael*, the people of Israel, in an amazing way, having returned from a most remarkable event the Biennial convention of the Union for Reform Judaism (URJ). Five thousand people strong, it is one of the most spirited and important events in the Jewish world, and the largest spirituality-oriented gathering of Jews in North America.

Before I arrived at the convention, I felt honored and excited at the opportunity to be able to offer my music and heart to those with whom I don't often have the chance to connect my Reform brothers and sisters. The Conservative Jewish world has been a warm and loving home away from home for me (and I had the dazzling experience of joining "The Conversation of the Century" by headlining at the centennial of the United Synagogue of Conservative Judaism this past October in Baltimore). Many of the Conservative Jews I know share practices and beliefs close to the openminded Orthodoxy I experienced as a child. But Reform synagogues have always been "the shuls I didn't attend."

That world was far away from mine or so I thought.

Boarding the plane for the West Coast, I did not know what to expect; I certainly had no inkling of the personal transformation that awaited me. So, it is with an overflowing heart and soul that I must report, as I did on the stage on Saturday night, that my soul made an *aliyah* (coming up) at the URJ's Biennial.

Simply put, I had no idea how extraordinary Reform Judaism was. The *tikkun olam* (social justice) mandate is so strongly bound up with the movement, and in the most joyous of ways. I was overwhelmed by the music, by the *davening* (prayer) and yes, my Orthodox friends, by the everpresent light of Torah. To give you an idea of the stellar caliber of Reform Judaism, here is a link to a keynote address given by Rabbi Rick Jacobs, the URJ president.

In his passionate talk, Rabbi Jacobs spoke about the commitment to a path of progressive change, to inclusivity, social justice, nurturing the next generation, egalitarian values and spiritual relationship to all that the Torah stands for. Standing among 4,999 other delegates, I almost couldn't believe what I was hearing. I found myself moved to tears, inspired and grateful. And when Rabbi David Ellenson, the outgoing head of Hebrew Union College-Jewish Institute of Religion spoke on Shabbat morning, his warmth and scholarship opened my eyes as well as my heart.

Having felt like a refugee from Orthodoxy for the past couple of decades, I feel like I found a new family with values I can get behind. And so, at my show on Saturday night, I told the audience I was making *aliyah* to the Reform movement. I know that statement made a great sound byte, but I meant every word. To be clear, when one makes *aliyah*, they take all parts of themselves with them. I have not abandoned anything that is intrinsic to me; I've simply expanded myself and been elevated. I've been blessed.

Last week, I touched something brand new and yet deeply familiar. It reminded me of my father'seachings. It gave me a feeling of homecoming. And perhaps that is the best that we can aspire to: a homecoming. Let us return again and again to the land of our souls. Let us transcend our differences and discover that we are one people, regardless of our label, movement or denomination. Let us make *aliyah* every day to who we are, to what we are, to where we are born and reborn again.

Neshama Carlebach, daughter of the late Jewish singer-songwriter Rabbi Shlomo Carlebach, is a singer who performs at venues throughout the world.

Source: Neshama Carlebach, "How I Became a Reform Jew," ReformJudaism.org blog, December 18, 2013, http://www.reformjudaism.org/blog/2013/12/18/how-i-becamereform-jew.

Historical Reflections on 350 Years of American Jewish History

Rabbi Gary Phillip Zola, Ph.D.

In September of 2004, North American Jewry will commence a yearlong celebration marking the 350th anniversary of Jewish communal settlement in North America. This anniversary memorializes the arrival, in 1654, of approximately two dozen bedraggled Jews who disembarked from the *St. Catrina*, a modest sea vessel that carried them to New Amsterdam, a Dutch colony that later became Manhattan Island. Most of these Jewish refugees came to New Amsterdam from Recife, another Dutch colony on the east coast of Brazil. Dutch Jewish colonists began settling in Recife shortly after that small fortified town had been captured by the Netherlands in 1630. After Portuguese and Brazilian forces recaptured the colony in January of 1654, Recife's Jews had no choice but to find a new home lest they be subjected to the perils of the Inquisition by the Portuguese authorities.[1]

The specific historical details pertaining to the Jewish departure from Recife and the subsequent peregrinations of its exiles remain somewhat obscure. Most scholars agree that many of the Jewish exiles from Recife ultimately made their way to New Amsterdam on board the *St. Catrina*, though Recife emigrés may have had their numbers swelled by another band of refugee Jews who joined them at some point along their twisted route to New Amsterdam. We do know, however, that when the *St. Catrina* arrived in New Amsterdam and shed its passengers into the New World, the sea-weary Jewish refugees were met by a handful of Jewish colonists who were already sojourners in New Amsterdam.

These Jews had come to the Dutch colony earlier that same year with the permission (and possibly even the encouragement) of the directors of the Dutch West India Company.[2]

This event—the coming of a few dozen Jewish refugees to the Dutch colony of New Amsterdam in the fall of 1654—may not seem like a momentous historical event in and of itself. However, American Jews have been commemorating this episode for a century. This custom developed at the dawn of the twentieth century, when a number of American Jews began to take an interest in the history of Jewish life in America. It was at this time that throngs of East European Jewish immigrants were swelling the Jewish population in the United States. The dramatic upsurge in the number of Jewish inhabitants worried many German and central European Jews, who arrived in the United States during the last half of the nineteenth century. Many of these German Jews feared that the masses of East European Jewish greenhorns would reflect negatively on the status of the American Jew. One way of addressing this concern was to show the world that Jewish life in America had deep roots.

To do so, a group of prominent New York Jews organized a celebration marking the anniversary of Jewish communal settlement on these shores. The occasion highlighted the fact that 250 years had passed since Jews first received official permission to reside in the New Netherlands. Documentary evidence relating to the arrival of Jews in the New World proved to be a very useful discovery. America's role as the great haven for Jewry served as a focal point of this first national commemoration.[3]

A year-long American Jewish Tercentenary was commemorated fifty years later (1954–1955) with a nationwide series of events and observances focusing on an overall theme: "Man's Opportunities and Responsibilities Under Freedom." This universalistic motif clearly expressed U. S. Jewry's sense of being at home in America in the post-World War II era. At that time, academic study of American Jewry was still in its infancy, but the tercentenary successfully underscored the importance of preserving and reconstructing the history of Jewish life in the American nation.[4]

Another half-century has now passed, and from the fall of 2004 through the fall of 2005 the United States will observe the 350th anniversary of Jewish communal life in North America. Years from now, historians will undoubtedly compare and contrast the evolving character and content of these three historical commemorations. For the present time, however, this milestone occasion challenges students of the American Jewish experience to reflect thoughtfully on the significance of this anniversary. What broad lessons can be drawn from the study of 350 years of Jewish life in America? At the same time, we consider an equally important question: What do these past 350 years teach us about the character of this nation? In an attempt to respond to these milestone considerations, this essay will touch briefly upon three broad motifs that exemplify the uniqueness of the American Jewish experience.

* * *

First, the American Jew has played a pivotal role in actualizing the democratic experiment that continues to unfold in the New World. In the United States of America, the Jewish community has been an active participant in the incessant dialectic that has defined and refined the nation's understanding of the core values that are expressed in phrases like "inalienable rights," "land of liberty," and "equal justice under the law." Many assume erroneously that the political and civil rights that are the birthright of U.S. Jewry at the dawn of the twenty-first century were foreordained with the ratification of the Federal Constitution (1787) and Bill of Rights (1789). In a sense, those great charters constituted a metaphoric promissory note that future generations of Americans would need to indemnify. From the dawn of this republic, Jews have been vocal participants in the debate over how the nation should interpret the free exercise clause of the First Amendment to the Constitution. As the dean of American Jewish historians, Jacob Rader Marcus (1896–1995) emphasized, the Jew in the New World has consistently compelled the general community to make good on the Constitution's avowal that this republic guarantees liberty and justice to all citizens.[5]

An early pioneer of American civil liberties was a Jew named Asser Levy (d. 1681). Levy came to New Amsterdam just a few months prior to the arrival of the Jewish refugees from Recife in 1654.[6] The colony's governor, Peter Stuyvesant, and its ruling council did not want these tattered Jewish refugees from Recife to remain. Stuyvesant complained to the directors of the Dutch West India Company back home in Amsterdam. He argued that the Jews were "anti-Christs," and he assured his superiors that these impoverished Jews undoubtedly would be a financial burden to the already struggling colony. By initially refusing them permission to acquire property, to trade with other Dutch colonies, or to serve in the local militia (and thereby avoid paying the colony a tax for homeland security), Stuyvesant made remaining in New Amsterdam a very unappealing option for the first Jewish minyon in North America.

However, New Amsterdam's Jewry resisted Stuyvesant's plan. Anticipating the New World Jew's characteristic determination to secure equal footing under the law, these pioneering Jews contacted influential Jews back home in Amsterdam (many of whom were prominent stockholders in the Dutch West India Company).[7] They urged their coreligionists in the Netherlands to appeal Stuyvesant's decision to the trustees of the Dutch West India Company. Evidently, the character of New World capitalism trumped Mr. Stuyvesant's Old World prejudices; the directors of the Dutch West India Company told Stuyvesant that he must allow the Jews to "travel and trade . . . live and remain [in New Netherlands] provided the poor among them shall not become a burden to the company or the community, but be supported by their own nation."[8] Since that time, as Jacob Rader Marcus emphasized, American Jewry has never failed to meet its own communal needs. In doing so, American Jewry has founded and sustained a diverse array of social welfare organizations that render services to Americans in need.[9]

Above all, the Jews in New Amsterdam were dogged in pursuit of equal footing under the law. Asser Levy and a coreligionist, Jacob Barsimson, requested the right to stand guard along with the colony's other burghers in 1655. A few years later, in 1660, Mr. Levy, working as a butcher, asked for and received permission "to be excused from killing hogs, as his religion does not allow him to do it."[10]

In addition to Asser Levy, there were other Jewish colonists in New Amsterdam who advocated for civil liberties during this opening chapter of the American Jewish experience. In 1655, Abraham de Lucena, Jacob Cohen Henriques, Salvador Dandrada, Joseph d'Acosta, and David Frera petitioned the director general and the Council of New Netherlands for permission to travel, trade with neighboring colonies, and own real estate. It appears that these particular petitions were not granted. Asser Levy remained in New Amsterdam until the British took control in 1664, and he continued fighting for civil rights in New York. In 1678, he was given permission to build a slaughterhouse and acquire a butcher's license. He became a burgher in the colony, and this entitled him to serve on a jury. As a jury member in the English colony of New York, he proved the adage that every dog has its day for he served on a jury for a case in which none other than Peter Stuyvesant was the defendant.[11]

Early American history is replete with examples of Jews who objected vigorously to those who sought to perpetuate Old World political and civil disabilities in the New World. Jews like Asser Levy and his contemporaries wanted more than toleration. They conceived of themselves as full-fledged citizens, and they conducted themselves as such. These impulses intensified during the decades that led up to the Revolutionary War when colonial Jews listened with keen interest to the enlightenment rhetoric that characterized the discourse of the intellectuals who advocated American independence from the British Empire. These colonial Jews believed that the expressions of liberty ushering forth from the lips of those who founded the American republic were sincere. Their faith was rewarded when these progressive and noble sentiments became enshrined in the nation's founding documents. Once the War of Independence had been won, American Jews became even more determined to vanquish political and civil disabilities that lingered on despite the adoption of the Constitution and the Bill of Rights.[12]

Jacob Henry's (1775?–1847) famous soliloquy before North Carolina's House of Commons in 1809 is emblematic of this trend. Henry insisted that he was entitled to occupy the congressional seat he won without professing an oath of office on the New Testament. Like many Jews in the early national period, Henry believed that the spirit of the Federal Constitution would ultimately overpower those state constitutions that preserved religious and civil disabilities for non-Christians:

> Shall this free Country set an example of persecution which even the returning reason of enslaved Europe would not submit to?... Are you prepared to plunge at once from the sublime heights of moral legislation, into the dark and gloomy caverns of superstitious ignorance? Will you drive from your shores and from the shelter of your constitutions, all who do not lay their oblations on the same altar, observe the same ritual, and subscribe to the same dogmas? If so, which amongst the various sects into which we are divided, shall be the favored one...?[13]

Moreover, many people are stunned when they discover that American Jews were once expelled from American soil. In a thoughtless response to exaggerated and inaccurate complaints about Jews who were undermining the Union's war effects by smuggling goods and provisions into the South, General Ulysses S. Grant expelled all the Jews living in the Military Department of Tennessee (which included the states of Kentucky and parts of Mississippi) under the authority of martial law. The reaction of American Jews to this development is as remarkable as was Grant's astonishing decree.[14]

Within hours of the promulgation of the general's order, outraged Jewish citizens launched a protest against what one of them called "the grossest violation of the Constitution and our rights as citizens under it."[15] One Jew from Paducah, Kentucky, a man named Cesar J. Kaskel, rushed to Washington, D.C. to secure an audience with President Abraham Lincoln. Kaskel's recounting of that historic encounter constitutes one of the great moments of American Jewish history. After Kaskel told the president that General Grant had banished the

Jews from the Military Department of Tennessee, "Honest Abe" smiled wryly and summarized all that he had heard with a question: "So, the children of Israel have been expelled from the happy land of Canaan?" "Yes," Kaskel rejoined, "and that is why we come unto Father Abraham's bosom, asking protection." "And that protection," Lincoln told him, "they shall have at once." And then, the sixteenth president sat down at his big table and canceled the major general's order.[16]

Was this a great victory for the few hundred Jews in the Department of Tennessee? Indeed, it was. Yet, it is possible to argue that the president's action was an even greater victory for the character of the American nation. The history of this country is replete with countless examples of American Jews who assumed that the Constitution's lofty ideals of equality and justice under the law were applicable to one and all. In laying claim to these rights and winning them for themselves, these Jewish citizens helped to define the meaning of political and civil liberty in this country.

* * *

With the ideals of equal rights and equal opportunity continuously serving as a collective lodestar, American Jews always have interrelated with their fellow citizens as peers. Without question, there always have been (and there always will be) those who despised Jews and other minorities as unwanted aliens. Nevertheless, the Constitution of the United States established a *de jure* atmosphere in which American Judaism and the American Jew could lay claim to a religious status that was authoritatively equal to that of any man or woman in America. This licit standing engendered another unique and remarkable feature of the American Jewish experience: the distinctive bond of friendship that overwhelmingly characterizes the relationship between the Jew and the non-Jew.[17]

One would search in vain throughout the annals of Jewish life in the Diaspora to find another setting in which the social, cultural, political, and economic bonds between Jew and non-Jew are so extensive and thoroughgoing as they have been consistently in the American nation. To be sure, one can cite numerous instances in which Jews, as individuals, had established personal relationships with non-Jews in many Old World Diaspora contexts. Generally speaking, Jewish corporate existence in the Old World Diaspora constituted a distinct entity that functioned as a body that stood apart from the rest of society.[18]

As a direct consequence of the Constitution's guarantee of religious freedom and, concomitantly, its outlawing the possibility of an established national religion, American Jews—individually and collectively—have achieved an unprecedented level of social integration and acceptance. As Isaac Harby

(1788–1828) of Charleston, South Carolina, noted, American Jews were "a portion of the people" in every conceivable way.[19] This distinctive feature of American life has made it possible for Jews, a tiny minority of the general population, to weave themselves as a major thread in the fabric of American culture. From the dawn of the Republic, America's Jews insisted that they were at home in this nation.[20]

These sentiments were not lopsided. The words and deeds of non-Jewish neighbors nurtured this spirit of American Jewish "athomeness." For example, one of the signers of the Declaration of Independence, a man named Dr. Benjamin Rush (1745–1813), was on the streets of Philadelphia in 1787 when the citizenry celebrated the ratification of the new Federal Constitution with a street parade. In his reminiscences, Rush remarked that for him a most "agreeable" highpoint of that joyous procession was when the Roman Catholic father, the Protestant minister, and the Jewish "priest" walked together arm-in-arm down the boulevard. The Jewish priest to whom Dr. Rush referred was the Reverend Jacob R. Cohen (1738?–1811), minister of Philadelphia's Mickve Israel Congregation.[21]

Three decades later, a Jew from England settled in the pioneering town of Cincinnati, Ohio. His name was Joseph Jonas (1792–1869), and he was one of the first Jews in the community. In his memoirs, Jonas remembers that when he first arrived on the banks of the Ohio, a Quaker woman traveled quite some distance to see a real Jew with her own eyes. She bid Jonas to turn about in a circle so she could examine him from every angle. Finally, she offered up her assessment of the man in one poignant declaration: 'Thou art a Jew, but I see that thou art different from no other man.' In many ways, this Quaker woman's remark has become the touchstone of Jewish life in America.[22]

When Mickve Israel Congregation in Philadelphia began to solicit funds to erect a building of its own in the last quarter of the eighteenth century, the list of contributors included several nonJews—including the name of Benjamin Franklin. Examples of Christian financial contributions to synagogues and Jewish activities abound in American Jewish history. On countless occasions when churches burned down, the local synagogue invited the homeless Christians to use its facility on Sundays. From time to time, that courtesy was reciprocated when a Jewish congregation had lost its house of prayer. In the last half of the twentieth century, we find one or two instances wherein Jewish and Christian congregations co-own and share one building. Surely, this is a phenomenon that (as Senator Joseph Lieberman declared in accepting the vice-presidential nomination of the Democratic National Party in 2000) could happen only in America.[23]

In his final Will and Testament, a wealthy New Orleans businessman named Judah Touro (1775–1854) left what was at the time one of this country's most impressive philanthropic bequests. He returned the favor of Mr. Franklin's modest contribution to Mickve Israel by bequeathing large donations to an array of Christian philanthropies along with money to benefit his own people. Touro was one of many Jews who had no hesitation identifying with the humanitarian efforts of non-Jewish philanthropies.[24]

Nearly one hundred years after Touro's death, President Harry S. Truman had a good friend named Edward (Eddie) Jacobson (1891–1955). Jacobson and Truman worked together long before the latter entered politics. This personal friendship was a camaraderie based on affection, and the bond may very well have affected the course of Jewish history in the twentieth century. It was Jacobson, the Jewish haberdasher, who prodded his old buddy and former business partner, the president of the United States, to agree to an important face-to-face meeting with Zionist leader Chaim Weizmann (1874–1952) against the better judgment of many of Truman's advisors. Evidently, Jacobson won the day by comparing Weizmann to one of the president's personal heroes: Andrew Jackson! In any event, many have argued that this meeting proved to be an important factor in the political intrigue that led President Truman to recognize the newly declared State of Israel promptly.[25]

This is not to say that anti-Semitism has never manifested itself on these shores. We have already noted that Peter Stuyvesant may very well have been the first of an endless array of North American bigots who have found Jews to be miserable blemishes on the nation's winsome complexion.[26] Even the optimistically inclined Jacob Marcus observed that America's anti-Semitic paroxysms—especially those that compounded (as it were) the Holocaust's inhumanity—have deeply dishonored this country's glory:

> Poor Uncle Sam!…; in 1943 when he finally reached Central Europe, the good citizens of German cremated him. The Messiah did not die alone; Benjamin Franklin, Thomas Jefferson, Abraham Lincoln perished with him. President Franklin Delano Roosevelt, the Congress, the State Department held life and death in their hands; they chose death.[27]

All this is true and valid. Nevertheless, no history of the American Jewish experience can possibly contain a litany of oppression and heartache, because the predominant features of Jewish life in the American nation have been social acceptance, equal footing, civil liberty, and religious freedom. American anti-Semitism—in its various manifestations—has essentially been an Old World curio. In contrast to Europe, the fundamental story of the Jew in the United States cannot be described by the phrase "a people apart (from the nation)," but rather "a people, a part (of the nation)." Some historians have even asserted that American society's disposition to Jews has been characterized largely by philo-Semitism.[28] The depth and breadth of Jewish social integration and cultural influence in the United States literally have no parallel in any other Jewish community in the Diaspora.[29]

* * *

There is, however, a dark side to the benevolent political and social conditions that have been sketched above. Although Jews have flourished unquestionably under these favorable and unique American circumstances, many have pointed out that the same cannot be said of American Judaism. In America, equality, pluralism, and unfettered familiarization seem inevitably to lead Jewry toward acculturation, assimilation and, ultimately, to complete dissipation. The consequences of Jewish assimilation in America threaten the corporate survival of Jewish life.

Gloomy prognostications about the survivability of American Judaism are as old as the American Republic. In a letter to family members still living in Posen, the best-known Jewish financier of the American Revolution, Haym Salomon (1740–1785), noted that there was *"wenig Yiddishkeit"* (very little Judaism) in America.[30] One hundred and fifty-three years ago, in 1846, a newly arrived immigrant named Isaac Mayer Wise (1819–1900) reflected on the prospects for Jewish life in America:

> There were only three men in private life who possessed any Jewish or Talmudical learning… Otherwise, ignorance swayed the scepter [and] darkness ruled. And when I comprehended the real position of affairs, I understood why two physicians had advised me to have nothing to do with the Jews… and I began to waver in my intentions of pursuing a rabbinical career.[31]

Three decades later, in 1872, another pessimistic American Israelite named W. M. Rosenblatt wrote an article entitled "The Jews: What They Are Coming To?" Lamenting what he called "the [nonchalant] sentiments of the rising generation on the subject of intermarrying and circumcision," Rosenblatt predicted that "within fifty years," Jewish life in America would be defunct and the only remnant would be "the history of their perils."[32]

Even though the mass migration of East European Jewry to the United States in the last decades of the nineteenth century made Mr. Rosenblatt a false prophet, post-World War II assimilation has intensified levels of anxiety over the future viability of American Judaism. In 1964, Thomas B. Morgan's now famous cover story in *Look* magazine suggested that, by the onset of the twenty-first century, American Jewry might very well become a guttering communal flame.[33] The title of Morgan's article provoked widespread alarm, and American Jews have been worried about "The Vanishing American Jew" ever since. After 350 years of American Jewish history, we continue to pose American Jewry's perennial question about its ultimate durability: can the American Jew survive and thrive in a friendly Diaspora, in this land of equal rights and social integration?[34]

The answer to this enduring concern brings us to a third noteworthy American Jewish legacy. American Judaism, with its seemingly open-door reception to voluntary annihilation, has managed for more than three and a half centuries to position itself in a remarkable state of suspended animation between the universal and the particular, between accommodation and resistance to acculturation, between being just like everyone else and being just different enough to ensure the continuation of a uniquely Jewish experience in the midst of a host environment that has been so overwhelmingly embracing. How has this come to be?

At least a partial answer to this question may be traced to the fact that, in every generation of this nation's history, there arose a cadre of Jewish individuals who were ardently, even fanatically committed to sustaining Jewish life amidst the most challenging conditions. When the *St. Catrina* landed in New Amsterdam, the Jews on board must have been surprised and pleased to learn that one of the Amsterdam Jews who had arrived in the colony a few weeks earlier had actually carried a *Sefer Torah* with him to the Dutch colony. Common sense dictates that the Jew who carried this Torah across the Atlantic to a remote and roughhewn colony did so for a reason. It seems logical to assume that this man wanted to pray as a Jew and to preserve his Jewish heritage in New Amsterdam.[35]

In the early decades of the eighteenth century, a Jewish congregation was founded in New York. It was called Shearith Israel, "The remnant of Israel." Nearly forty years before the American Revolution, Shearith Israel established the very first Jewish day school on these shores. Even in the boondocks, an ocean away from the security and convenience of a major center of Jewish life, we find American Jews striving to provide their children with a Jewish education.[36]

In 1838, a quintessentially American approach to Jewish education was launched by a Philadelphian named Rebecca Gratz (1781– 1869). This pioneering female educator was a pious and dedicated Jew. She surmised that the novel Sunday School concept that Christians were using with dawning success could be refitted for effectual use by American Jewry. Shortly thereafter, a highly regarded poet, Penina Moïse (1797–1880), replicated Gratz's Sunday School innovations at Kahal Kadosh Beth Elohim in Charleston. At the same time, Gratz, Moïse, and many other American Jews lamented the complete absence of educational texts that could be used to instruct Jewish learners. Isaac Leeser (1806–1868), this nation's most outstanding proponent of traditional Judaism during the nineteenth century, provided American Jewry with its first English translation of the Hebrew Scriptures. He also founded the Jewish Publication Society (JPS) in 1845, and though the JPS would have two abortive starts before it would be permanently established in America, Leeser understood that the Jewish community needed access to suitable pedagogic resources in order for meaningful Jewish learning to occur in this country.[37]

Early in the twentieth century, Samson Benderly (1876–1944) and a circle of his distinguished disciples applied the modern educational strategies of the Progressive Era—what was at the time called "new psychology"—to the needs of Jewish learning in America. These modern Jewish educators opened a new chapter in the history of Jewish education in this country. Their efforts resulted in the creation of a nationwide network of educational bureaus, camps, innovative curricula, teacher training, and so forth. This host of educational innovations provided American Jewry with trail-blazing forms of Jewish learning that, eventually, were exported to Jewish communities around the globe.[38]

Isaac Mayer Wise stands out as the most vocal nineteenthcentury advocate of an indigenous strategy for American Jewish education. From his first days in America, Wise began to agitate for the establishment of a school by which American-born men (and women!) could prepare themselves to teach Judaism. Wise invested a lifetime of energy into this vision, which was realized in the creation of the Hebrew Union College (HUC) in 1875.[39]

Along the way, Wise encountered many critics. Some insisted that American Jewry lacked the intellectual resources needed to produce qualified rabbis. How could a small, ill-equipped religious school in Cincinnati compete with the great rabbinical schools of Europe? What American congregation, they asked, would select an HUC ordinee if it could have an ordinee who studied at one of the great talmudic centers in Lithuania or Belorussia? What congregation would want to engage a graduate of such a fledgling school when men trained in Eishishok, Minsk, Vilna Volozhin, Slobodka, Telz, Lomza, Radzyn, Novogrudok,

Slutsk, Malch, and Bryansk were available? Yet Wise never wavered in his primary conviction: if American Jewry was to flourish, it would need to produce its own indigenous supply of American rabbis, educators, and communal workers.[40]

Had Wise given up on his idea and had the Hebrew Union College never come into existence, consider how that decision would have affected the subsequent history of American Jewish life. American Jewry never would have known the school's first four rabbinical graduates—Israel Aaron (1860–1912), the founder of Buffalo's Zion House, a pioneering center for the settlement of East European immigrants; Henry Berkowitz (1857–1924), the founder of the Jewish Chautauqua Society in 1893; Joseph Krauskopf (1858–1923), the founder of the National Jewish Farm School (today known as the Delaware Valley College); and David Philipson (1862–1949), pioneering historian and author.[41]

It is also vitally important to note that when HUC opened in 1875, a young woman named Julia Ettlinger studied together with the school's male students. Though she did not complete the course of study (she left after the first year), she did play a role in blazing a trail that ultimately led to the ordination of women rabbis. It is beyond the scope of this essay to describe the extraordinarily important role that women rabbis are playing in revitalizing and advancing Jewish life and learning in America. Their story, too, is uniquely American, and the remarkably important contributions that American Jewish women have made over the course of 350 years of American Jewish history constitute a story that we have only just begun to recover.[42] American Jewry's relentless determination to provide indigenous institutions of learning that are uniquely suited to educate another generation in Jewish letters is a third significant theme that reverberates through the annals of American Jewish history.

* * *

In Hebrew, the number 350 may be written with a triliteral root that means "to tell" or "to count." The lesson in this happenstance is that, in and of themselves, dates and historical anniversaries have no intrinsic or self-evident significance. They acquire significance when they prompt us to engage in historical analysis. This is precisely what Dr. Marcus meant when he wrote: "Interpretation of facts is imperative, for history is the precipitate of interpretation."[43]

The 350th anniversary of the establishment of Jewish communal life in North America becomes significant when it motivates us to examine the past and gain perspective from it. An interpretive *retelling* or *recounting* of events past inevitably leads to a greater appreciation of those who occupied our space in years gone by. They were people with dreams and hopes and visions. Some of these forebears dedicated their lives to the advancement of Jewish life in the American nation. Today, we are inheritors of all that has been bequeathed to us. However, it is important to bear in mind Goethe's familiar admonition: "What you have inherited from your forebears, you must earn for yourself before you can really call it yours."[44]

"Jews glory in their survival," Marcus often observed, "they refuse to disappear." Undoubtedly, his views on this subject were influenced by the Jewish historians he studied—men such as Nachman Krochmal (1785–1840), Isaac Marcus Jost (1793–1860), Heinrich Graetz (1817–1891), and Simon Dubnow (1860–1941)—all of whom believed in the Jewish people's immortality. Marcus was dogged in his insistence that the study of the past maximized the likelihood that Jews would become "proud exponents of the best in our Jewish heritage." Historical cognizance would kindle a spark of pride that, in turn, would ignite a renaissance in American Jewish life: "Oh, that we could realize . . . our debt to the past; the debt we owe of continuing the great work that has been going on for the past three thousand years."[45]

This, then, is a transcendent motivation for using the 350th anniversary of Jewish communal settlement in North America to examine critically the character of the American Jewish experience. If we successfully preserve the past and convey its meaning to our peers, we will ultimately succeed in safeguarding our future.

Notes

1. On the history of the Jewish community in New Amsterdam, see Jacob Rader Marcus, *The Colonial American Jew, 1492–1776* (Detroit: Wayne State University Press, 1970), 215–16, and passim; Samuel Oppenheim, "The Early History of the Jews in New York, 1654–1664," in *Publications of the American Jewish Historical Society*, vol. 32 (1909), 37–43; Arnold Wiznitzer, "The Exodus from Brazil to New Amsterdam of the Jewish Pilgrim Fathers 1654," *Publications of the American Jewish Historical Society*, vol. 44 (1954), 88, 90.

2. Egon and Frieda Wolff, "The Problem of the First Jewish Settlers in New Amsterdam 1654," *Studia Rosenthaliana*, vol. 15 (August 1981), 176–77; and Leo Hershkowitz, "New Amsterdam's Twenty-Three Jews—Myth or Reality," in Shalom Goldman, ed., *Hebrew and the Bible in America* (Hanover, N.H.: University Press of New England, 1993), 172–73. See idem, *By Chance or Choice: Jews in New Amsterdam 1654*, located in The Jacob Rader Marcus Center of the American Jewish Archives, Cincinnati, Ohio.

3. On the beginnings of American Jewish history, see Robert Liberles, "Postemancipation Historiography and the Jewish Historical Societies of America and England," in *Reshaping the Past: Jewish History and the Historians* (Studies in Contemporary Jewry, vol. 10), Jonathan Frankel, ed. (New York: Oxford University Press, 1994), 186–204. The "Executive Committee" for celebrating the 250th anniversary of Jewish Settlement in America published a volume on the occasion. See, *The Two Hundred and Fiftieth Anniversary of Jews in the United States: Addresses*

Delivered at Carnegie Hall, New York, on Thanksgiving Day MCMV Together with Other Selected Addresses and Proceedings (New York: The New York Co-operative Society, 1906).

4. Arthur A. Goren, "A 'Golden Decade' for American Jews: 1945–1955," in *The Politics and Public Culture of American Jews* (Bloomington: Indiana University Press, 1999), 186–204.

5. See Jonathan D. Sarna, "The Impact of Nineteenth-Century Christian Missions on American Jews," in *Jewish Apostasy in the Modern World*, ed. Todd M. Endelman (New York, 1987), 239; on the "slow and gradual development" of political equality for the Jew in the United States, see Stanley F. Chyet, "The Political Rights of the Jews in the United States: 1776–1840," in *American Jewish Archives*, vol. 10 (April 1958), 14–75; Oscar and Mary F. Handlin, "The Acquisition of Political and Social Rights by the Jews in the United States," *American Jewish Year Book* 56 (1955), 43–98; and Jacob Rader Marcus, "Three Hundred Years in America," in Gary Phillip Zola (ed.), *The Dynamics of American Jewish History: Jacob Rader Marcus's Essays on American Jewry* (Hanover, N.H.: Brandeis University Press, 2004), 125–26.

6. Some argued that Asser Levy arrived with the Recife refugees on the *St. Catrina*. See Morris U. Schappes (ed.), *A Documentary History of the Jews in the United States, 1654–1875* (New York: Schocken Books, 1971). Historian Leo Hershkowitz disputes this contention, claiming that Levy came to New Amsterdam on a Fluyt called the *Peachtree (Pereeboom)*, which left Amsterdam on July 8, 1654. See idem, *By Chance or Choice: Jews in New Amsterdam 1654*, located in The Jacob Rader Marcus Center of the American Jewish Archives, Cincinnati, Ohio. For additional background on Asser Levy, see Maurits Prins, "Asser Levy," *Judaism*, vol. 41, no. 4 (1992), 395–400; Leo Hershkowitz, "Asser Levy and the Inventories of Early New York Jews," *American Jewish History* vol. 80, no. 1 (1990), 21–55; and Malcolm H. Stern, "Asser Levy: A New Look at Our Jewish Founding Father," *American Jewish Archives*, vol. 26 (1974), 66–77.

7. Jonathan Israel, "The Republic of the United Netherlands until 1750: Demography and Economic Activity," *The History of the Jews in the Netherlands*, edited by J. C. H. Blom, R. G. Fuks-Mansfeld, and I. Schöffer (Oxford: Littman Library of Jewish Civilization, 2002), 85–115.

8. Directors of the Dutch West India Company to Peter Stuyvesant, 26 April 1655, in Schappes, 4–5.

9. Jacob Rader Marcus, *The Jew in the American World: A Source Book* (Detroit: Wayne State University Press, 1996), 164–65.

10. On Levy, see L. Huhner, *Publications of the American Jewish Historical Society*, vol. 8 (1900), 9–23; and Schappes, 1–13.

11. Schappes, 15–16. Jacob Rader Marcus, *The Colonial American Jew: 1492–1776*, vol. 2 (Detroit: Wayne State University Press, 1970), 247.

12. Leo Pfeffer, "Jews and Jewry in American Constitutional History," in *Jews, Judaism and the Constitution* (Cincinnati: American Jewish Archives, 1982), 21–34.

13. Schappes, 122–24.

14. On Grant's Order No. 11, see Bertram W. Korn, *American Jewry and the Civil War* (Philadelphia: Jewish Publication Society, 1951), 121–55.

15. Ibid., 124.

16. Ibid., 124–25.

17. Egal Feldman, *Dual Destinies: the Jewish Encounter with Protestant America* (Urbana: University of Illinois Press, 1990).

18. David Vital's recent tome titled *A People Apart: A Political History of the Jews in Europe, 1789–1939* (New York: Oxford University Press, 1999) powerfully drives this point home.

19. For Harby's famous quote, see Joseph L. Blau and Salo W. Baron (eds.), *The Jews of the United States 1790–1840: A Documentary History*, vol. 2 (New York: Columbia University Press), 318–22.

20. Abraham J. Karp, *Haven and Home: A History of the Jews in America* (New York: Schocken Books, 1985).

21. Howard M. Sachar, *A History of the Jews in America* (New York: Alfred Knopf, 1992), 32. On Cohen, see Edwin Wolf 2nd and Maxwell Whiteman, *The History of the Jews of Philadelphia from*

Colonial Times to the Age of Jackson (Philadelphia: Jewish Publication Society of America, 1975), s.v. index.

22. Jacob Rader Marcus, *Memoirs of American Jews, 1776–1865* (Philadelphia: Jewish Publication Society, 1955), I, 203.

23. Jacob Rader Marcus (ed.), *The Jew in the American World* (Detroit: Wayne State University Press, 1996), 105, 107–8.

24. Schappes, 333–41.

25. Edward Jacobson, "Two Presidents and a Haberdasher—1948," in *American Jewish Archives*, vol. 20 (1968), 3–15.

26. Leonard Dinnerstein, *Antisemitism in America* (New York: Oxford University Press, 1994).

27. Jacob Rader Marcus, "Testament," as quoted in Gary Phillip Zola (ed.), *The Dynamics of American Jewish History*, 148.

28. Malcolm H. Stern stressed this important point in his article "The 1820's: American Jewry Comes of Age," in Bertram W. Korn (ed.), *A Bicentennial Festschrift for Jacob Rader Marcus* (New York: Ktav Publishing House, 1976), 539–49. See also Harry Golden, *Jewish Roots in the Carolinas; A Pattern of American Philo-Semitism* (Greensboro, N.C.: Deal Printing Company, 1955).

29. Jacob Rader Marcus, *United States Jewry, 1776–1985*, vol. 4 (Detroit: Wayne State University Press, 1993), 776–68.

30. Arthur Hertzberg, *The Jews in America: Four Centuries of an Uneasy Encounter: A History* (New York: Simon and Schuster, 1989), 55.

31. Isaac Mayer Wise, *Reminiscences* (Cincinnati: Leo Wise & Company, 1901), 21, 24.

32. W. M. Rosenblatt, "The Jews: What They are Coming To," in *The Galaxy* (January 1872), 47–60.

33. *Look*, May 5, 1964.

34. In the wake of the Council of Jewish Federations' (CJF) *Jewish Population Study* of 1990, ominous essays peppered the pages of the AngloJewish press and a cornucopia of books with the grimmest of prospects appeared. Most of these books bespeak their perspective in the title: Alan Dershowitz's volume, *The Vanishing American Jew: In Search of Jewish Identity for the Next Century* (Boston: Little, Brown, 1997); writer Anne Roiphe's *Generation Without Memory*, Rabbi David Forman's *Israel —On Broadway; America — Off Broadway*, and former statesman Elliott Abrams' book entitled *Faith or Fear: How Jews Can Survive in a Christian America* (New York: Free Press, 1997).

35. Jonathan D. Sarna, *American Judaism: A History* (New Haven & London: Yale University Press, 2004), 10.

36. David de Sola Pool and Tamar de Sola Pool, *An Old Faith in the New World; Portrait of Shearith Israel, 1654–1954* (New York: Columbia University Press, 1955); and David de Sola Pool, *Portraits Etched in Stone: Early Jewish Settlers, 1682–1831* (New York: Columbia University Press, 1952).

37. On Gratz, see Dianne Ashton, *Rebecca Gratz: Women and Judaism in Antebellum America* (Detroit: Wayne State University Press, 1997); on Moïse, see Solomon Breibart, "Penina Moïse, Southern Jewish Poetess," in Samuel Proctor, Louis Schmier, and Malcolm H. Stern, *Jews of the South: Selected Essays from the Southern Jewish Historical Society* (Macon, Ga.: Mercer University Press, 1984), 31–43; on Leeser, see Lance Jonathan Sussman, *Isaac Leeser and the Making of American Judaism*, (Detroit: Wayne State University Press, 1995); on the Jewish Publication Society of America, see Jonathan D. Sarna, *JPS—The Americanization of Jewish Culture, 1888–1988* (Philadelphia: Jewish Publication Society of America, 1989).

38. Lloyd P. Gartner, *Jewish Education in the United States: A Documentary History* (New York: Teachers College Press, 1969); and Judah Pilch (ed.), *A History of Jewish Education in America* (New York: American Association for Jewish Education, 1969); on Benderly, see Nathan H. Winter, *Jewish Educationin a Pluralist Society: Samson Benderlyand Jewish Education in the United States* (New York: New York University Press, 1966).

39. Michael A. Meyer, *Hebrew Union College-Jewish Institute of Religion —A Centennial History, 1875–1975* (Cincinnati, Hebrew Union College Press: 1992).

40. On Isaac M. Wise's career, see Sefton D. Temkin, *Isaac Mayer Wise, Shaping American Judaism* (Oxford, England: Published for the Littman Library by Oxford University Press, distributed in the United States by B'nai B'rith Book Service, 1992). See also Israel Knox, *Rabbi in America: The Story of Isaac M. Wise* (Boston: Little, Brown and Company, 1957); Max B. May, *Isaac Mayer Wise: A Biography* (New York: G.P. Putnam's Sons, 1916); and David Philipson and Louis Grossman (eds.), *Selected Writings of Isaac M. Wise* (Cincinnati: The Robert Clarke Company, 1900).

41. On Aaron, see *The Universal Jewish Encyclopedia*, s.v. Aaron, Israel; on Berkowitz, see Max E. Berkowitz, *The Beloved Rabbi* (New York: The Macmillan Company, 1932); on Krauskopf, see William W. Blood, *Apostle of Reason: A Biography of Joseph Krauskopf* (Philadelphia: Dorrance, 1973); on Philipson, see Douglas J. Kohn, "The Dean of American Rabbis: A Critical Study of … David Philipson" (Rabbinical Thesis, Hebrew Union College-Jewish Institute of Religion, 1987).

42. Gary Phillip Zola, *Women Rabbis: Exploration & Celebration: Papers Delivered at an Academic Conference Honoring Twenty Years of Women in the Rabbinate, 1972–1992* (Cincinnati: HUC-JIR Rabbinic Alumni Association Press, 1996).

43. Jacob Rader Marcus, *The Colonial American Jew, 1492–1776*, 3 vols. (Detroit: Wayne State University Press, 1970), I, xxvi–xxvii.

44. Goethe quote as cited in Rabbi Sidney Greenberg (ed.), *A Treasury of the Art of Living* (Hollywood, Calif.: Wilshire Book Company, 1963), 245.

45. Jacob Rader Marcus, *The American Jew, 1585–1990: AHistory* (Brooklyn: Carlson Publishing, Inc., 1995), 383; and idem, "America: The Spiritual Center of Jewry" and "Testament" as quoted in Zola, *Dynamics of American Jewish History*, 42 and 150.

Source: Gary Phillip Zola, "Historical Reflections on 350 Years of American Jewish History," *CCAR Journal: The Reform Jewish Quarterly*, Fall 2004, 7–24.

Denominations of American Judaism

RENEWAL
https://aleph.org/what-is-jewish-renewal

RECONSTRUCTIONIST
https://www.jewishrecon.org/about-us

REFORM
(see earlier chapters and www.urj.org)

CONSERVATIVE
http://www.uscj.org/JewishLivingandLearning/JewishObservance/
TheIdealConservativeJew.aspx

ORTHODOX
http://www.myjewishlearning.com/article/orthodox-judaism-today/

1885 Pittsburgh Conference

Convening at the call of Kaufmann Kohler of New York, Reform rabbis from around the United States met from November 16 through November 19, 1885 with Isaac Mayer Wise presiding. The meeting was declared the continuation of the Philadelphia Conference of 1869, which was the continuation of the German Conference of 1841 to 1846. The rabbis adopted the following seminal text:

1. We recognize in every religion an attempt to grasp the Infinite, and in every mode, source or book of revelation held sacred in any religious system the consciousness of the indwelling of God in man. We hold that Judaism presents the highest conception of the God-idea as taught in our Holy Scriptures and developed and spiritualized by the Jewish teachers, in accordance with the moral and philosophical progress of their respective ages. We maintain that Judaism preserved and defended midst continual struggles and trials and under enforced isolation, this God-idea as the central religious truth for the human race.

2. We recognize in the Bible the record of the consecration of the Jewish people to its mission as the priest of the one God, and value it as the most potent instrument of religious and moral instruction. We hold that the modern discoveries of scientific researches in the domain of nature and history are not antagonistic to the doctrines of Judaism, the Bible reflecting the primitive ideas of its own age, and at times clothing its conception of divine Providence and Justice dealing with men in miraculous narratives.

3. We recognize in the Mosaic legislation a system of training the Jewish people for its mission during its national life in Palestine, and today we accept as binding only its moral laws, and maintain only such ceremonies as elevate and sanctify our lives, but reject all such as are not adapted to the views and habits of modern civilization.

4. We hold that all such Mosaic and rabbinical laws as regulate diet, priestly purity, and dress originated in ages and under the influence of ideas entirely foreign

to our present mental and spiritual state. They fail to impress the modern Jew with a spirit of priestly holiness; their observance in our days is apt rather to obstruct than to further modern spiritual elevation.

5. We recognize, in the modern era of universal culture of heart and intellect, the approaching of the realization of Israel s great Messianic hope for the establishment of the kingdom of truth, justice, and peace among all men. We consider ourselves no longer a nation, but a religious community, and therefore expect neither a return to Palestine, nor a sacrificial worship under the sons of Aaron, nor the restoration of any of the laws concerning the Jewish state.

6. We recognize in Judaism a progressive religion, ever striving to be in accord with the postulates of reason. We are convinced of the utmost necessity of preserving the historical identity with our great past.. Christianity and Islam, being daughter religions of Judaism, we appreciate their providential mission, to aid in the spreading of monotheistic and moral truth. We acknowledge that the spirit of broad humanity of our age is our ally in the fulfillment of our mission, and therefore we extend the hand of fellowship to all who cooperate with us in the establishment of the reign of truth and righteousness among men.

7. We reassert the doctrine of Judaism that the soul is immortal, grounding the belief on the divine nature of human spirit, which forever finds bliss in righteousness and misery in wickedness. We reject as ideas not rooted in Judaism, the beliefs both in bodily resurrection and in Gehenna and Eden (Hell and Paradise) as abodes for everlasting punishment and reward.

8. In full accordance with the spirit of the Mosaic legislation, which strives to regulate the relations between rich and poor, we deem it our duty to participate in the great task of modern times, to solve, on the basis of justice and righteousness, the problems presented by the contrasts and evils of the present organization of society.

Source: "1885 Pittsburgh Conference," CCAR, http://ccarnet.org/rabbis-speak/ platforms/ declaration-principles/.

Reform Judaism:
A Centenary Perspective

ADOPTED IN SAN FRANCISCO—1976

The Central Conference of American Rabbis has on special occasions described the spiritual state of Reform Judaism. The centenaries of the founding of the Union of American Hebrew Congregations and the Hebrew Union College–Jewish Institute of Religion seem an appropriate time for another such effort. We therefore record our sense of the unity of our movement today.

One Hundred Years: What We Have Taught

We celebrate the role of Reform Judaism in North America, the growth of our movement on this free ground, the great contributions of our membership to the dreams and achievements of this society. We also feel great satisfaction at how much of our pioneering conception of Judaism has been accepted by the Household of Israel. It now seems self-evident to most Jews: that our tradition should interact with modern culture; that its forms ought to reflect a contemporary esthetic; that its scholarship needs to be conducted by modern, critical methods; and that change has been and must continue to be a fundamental reality in Jewish life. Moreover, though some still disagree, substantial numbers have also accepted our teachings: that the ethics of universalism implicit in traditional Judaism must be an explicit part of our Jewish duty; that women have full rights to practice Judaism; and that Jewish obligation begins with the informed will of every individual. Most modern Jews, within their various religious movements, are embracing Reform Jewish perspectives. We see this past century as having confirmed the essential wisdom of our movement.

One Hundred Years: What We Have Learned

Obviously, much else has changed in the past century. We continue to probe the extraordinary events of the past generation, seeking to understand their meaning and to incorporate their significance in our lives. The Holocaust shattered our easy optimism about humanity and its inevitable progress. The State of Israel, through its many accomplishments, raised our sense of the Jews as a people to new heights of aspiration and devotion. The widespread threats to freedom, the problems inherent in the explosion of new knowledge and of ever more powerful technologies, and the spiritual emptiness of much of Western culture have taught us to be less dependent on the values of our society and to reassert what remains perenially valid in Judaism's teaching. We have learned that the survival of the Jewish people is of highest priority and that in carrying out our Jewish responsibilities we help move humanity toward its messianic fulfillment.

Diversity Within Unity, the Hallmark of Reform

Reform Jews respond to change in various ways according to the Reform principle of the autonomy of the individual. However, Reform Judaism does more than tolerate diversity; it engenders it. In our uncertain historical situation we must expect to have far greater diversity than previous generations knew. How we shall live with diversity without stifling dissent and without paralyzing our ability to take positive action will test our character and our principles. We stand open to any position thoughtfully and conscientiously advocated in the spirit of Reform Jewish belief. While we may differ in our interpretation and application of the ideas enunciated here, we accept such differences as precious and see in them Judaism's best hope for confronting whatever the future holds for us. Yet in all our diversity we perceive a certain unity and we shall not allow our differences in some particulars to obscure what binds us together.

1. *God*—The affirmation of God has always been essential to our people's will to survive. In our struggle through the centuries to preserve our faith we have experienced and conceived of God in many ways. The trials of our own time and the challenges of modern culture have made steady belief and clear understanding difficult for some. Nevertheless, we ground our lives, personally and communally, on God's reality and remain open to new experiences and conceptions of the Divine. Amid the mystery we call life, we affirm that human beings, created in God's image, share in God's eternality despite the mystery we call death.

2. *The People Israel*—The Jewish people and Judaism defy precise definition because both are in the process of becoming. Jews, by birth or conversion, constitute an uncommon union of faith and peoplehood. Born as Hebrews in the ancient Near East, we are bound together like all ethnic groups by language, land, history, culture, and institutions. But the people of Israel is unique because of its involvement with God and its resulting perception of the human condition. Throughout our long history our people has been inseparable from its religion with its messianic hope that humanity will be redeemed.

3. *Torah*—Torah results from the relationship between God and the Jewish people. The records of our earliest confrontations are uniquely important to us. Lawgivers and prophets, historians and poets gave us a heritage whose study is a religious imperative and whose practice is our chief means to holiness. Rabbis and teachers, philosophers and mystics, gifted Jews in every age amplified the Torah tradition. For millennia, the creation of Torah has not ceased and Jewish creativity in our time is adding to the chain of tradition.

4. *Our Religious Obligations:* Religious Practice—Judaism emphasizes action rather than creed as the primary expression of a religious life, the means by which we strive to achieve universal justice and peace. Reform Judaism shares this emphasis on duty and obligation. Our founders stressed that the Jew's ethical responsibilities, personal and social, are enjoined by God. The past century has taught us that the claims made upon us may begin with our ethical obligations but they extend to many other aspects of Jewish living, including: creating a Jewish home centered on family devotion: lifelong study; private prayer and public worship; daily religious observance; keeping the Sabbath and the holy days: celebrating the major events of life; involvement with the synagogues and community; and other activities which promote the survival of the Jewish people and enhance its existence. Within each area of Jewish observance Reform Jews are called upon to confront the claims of Jewish tradition, however differently perceived, and to exercise their individual autonomy, choosing and creating on the basis of commitment and knowledge.

5. *Our Obligations:* The State of Israel and the Diaspora—We are privileged to live in an extraordinary time, one in which a third Jewish commonwealth has been established in our people's ancient homeland. We are bound to that land and to the newly reborn State of Israel by innumerable religious and ethnic ties. We have been enriched by its culture and ennobled by its indomitable spirit. We see it providing unique opportunities for Jewish self-expression. We have both a stake and a responsibility in building the State of Israel, assuring its security, and

defining its Jewish character. We encourage aliyah for those who wish to find maximum personal fulfillment in the cause of Zion. We demand that Reform Judaism be unconditionally legitimized in the State of Israel.

At the same time that we consider the State of Israel vital to the welfare of Judaism everywhere, we reaffirm the mandate of our tradition to create strong Jewish communities wherever we live. A genuine Jewish life is possible in any land, each community developing its own particular character and determining its Jewish responsibilities. The foundation of Jewish community life is the synagogue. It leads us beyond itself to cooperate with other Jews, to share their concerns, and to assume leadership in communal affairs. We are therefore committed to the full democratization of the Jewish community and to its hallowing in terms of Jewish values.

The State of Israel and the Diaspora, in fruitful dialogue, can show how a people transcends nationalism even as it affirms it, thereby setting an example for humanity which remains largely concerned with dangerously parochial goals.

6. *Our Obligations:* Survival and Service—Early Reform Jews, newly admitted to general society and seeing in this the evidence of a growing universalism, regularly spoke of Jewish purpose in terms of Jewry's service to humanity. In recent years we have become freshly conscious of the virtues of pluralism and the values of particularism. The Jewish people in its unique way of life validates its own worth while working toward the fulfillment of its messianic expectations.

Until the recent past our obligations to the Jewish people and to all humanity seemed congruent. At times now these two imperatives appear to conflict. We know of no simple way to resolve such tensions. We must, however, confront them without abandoning either of our commitments. A universal concern for humanity unaccompanied by a devotion to our particular people is self-destructive; a passion for our people without involvement in humankind contradicts what the prophets have meant to us. Judaism calls us simultaneously to universal and particular obligations.

Hope: Our Jewish Obligation

Previous generations of Reform Jews had unbound confidence in humanity's potential for good. We have lived through terrible tragedy and been compelled to reappropriate our tradition's realism about the human capacity for evil. Yet our people has always refused to despair. The survivors of the Holocaust, being granted life, seized it, nurtured it, and, rising above catastrophe, showed humankind that the human spirit is indomitable. The State of Israel, established and maintained by the Jewish will to live, demonstrates what a united people can accomplish in history. The existence of the Jew is an argument against despair; Jewish survival is warrant for human hope.

We remain God's witness that history is not meaningless. We affirm that with God's help people are not powerless to affect their destiny. We dedicate ourselves, as did the generations of Jews who went before us, to work and wait for that day when "They shall not hurt or destroy in all My holy mountain for the earth shall be full of the knowledge of the Lord as the waters cover the sea."

Source: "Reform Judaism: A Centenary Perspective; Adopted in San Francisco—1976," CCAR, http://ccarnet.org/rabbis-speak/platforms/reformjudaism-centenary-perspective/.

A People and/or A Religion;
My Jewish Journey;
Next Steps and *Siyum*

Source Texts

Deuteronomy 10:19

[19]You too must befriend the stranger, for you were strangers in the land of Egypt.

Ruth 1:16-18

[16]But Ruth replied, "Don't urge me to leave you or to turn back from you. Where you go I will go, and where you stay I will stay. Your people will be my people and your God my God. [17]Where you die I will die, and there I will be buried. May the Eternal deal with me, be it ever so severely, if even death separates you and me." [18]When Naomi realized that Ruth was determined to go with her, she stopped urging her.

Babylonian Talmud, *Y'vamot* 47a-b

Our Rabbis taught: A person who wishes to convert at this time is told: "Why do you want to convert? Don't you know that the people of Israel at this time are afflicted, pushed about, swept from place to place, and tossed about, and that tribulations come upon them?" If he answers: "I know and I am not worthy [to be one of them]," then we immediately accept him. We inform him of the punishment for not observing "Gleanings," "Forgotten Sheaves," "Corner of the Field," and "Tithe for the Poor," and we further tell him the punishment for violating the *mitzvot*. We say to him: "Be aware that up until now you could eat forbidden animal fat without being liable for the penalty of *karet*, you could profane Shabbat without incurring the punishment of stoning. But from now on, [you are liable]. . . . Just as we tell him of the punishment for non-observance of the mitzvot, so too we describe the reward to him. . . . We are neither too lengthy with the descriptions nor too detailed. If he accepts, then he is immediately circumcised. . . . When he heals, we immerse him immediately, while two scholars stand by him and inform him of some of the lighter and some of the weightier mitzvot. When he has completed the immersion, he is considered as a Jew in all respects. . . .

Sifrei, Numbers 108

Rabi says: The people of Israel entered the covenant [of the Torah] through three things: circumcision, immersion, and the presentation of offerings. Converts must do likewise.

Tanchuma Buber, Lech L'cha 6:32a

Dearer to God than all of the Israelites who stood at Mount Sinai is the convert. Had the Israelites not witnessed the lightning, thunder, quaking mountain, and sounding trumpets they would not have accepted the Torah. But the convert, who did not see nor hear any of these things, came and surrendered himself to God and took the yoke of heaven upon himself. Can anyone be dearer to God than such a person?

Welcoming Converts

Rabbi Barry Block

Welcoming converts is a mitzvah!

Jewish tradition regards Abraham and Sarah as the first converts. Raised in idolatrous families, they respond to God's call to travel to the land of God's choosing, that they might be a blessing. Like Abraham and Sarah, those desiring conversion to Judaism in our own day are embarking on a journey—albeit a spiritual, rather than a geographical, sojourn.

Abraham and Sarah are also understood to be the first Jews to receive converts. Torah teaches that when they set out for the Promised Land, our patriarch and matriarch brought "the souls that they had made in Haran" (Genesis 12:5). The medieval commentator Rashi understands those "souls" to be proselytes whom Abraham and Sarah "had brought under the wings of the *Shechinah* [Divine Presence]. Abraham converted the men and Sarah converted the women and Scripture accounts it unto them as if they had made them."[1] We may even say that receiving converts is the first mitzvah ascribed to our original patriarch and matriarch, concluding that welcoming converts is a most exalted religious obligation.

We may puzzle, then, at an unfortunate reality: many people, including many Jews, believe that Judaism does not especially welcome converts. Yes, in addition to Abraham and Sarah, the *Tanach* tells of Ruth, the Moabite, who becomes a loyal daughter of Israel and ultimately an ancestor of King David. Yes, the Talmud, written in the earliest centuries of the Common Era, lays

---

1 Rashi to Genesis 12:5, translation by A. M. Silbermann.

579

out a procedure for receiving converts.[2] Still, the suspicion remains that Jews don't enthusiastically welcome converts.

In 1978, in an address to the Board of Trustees of the UAHC, Rabbi Alexander Schindler, then the president of the UAHC (now URJ) explained the sad historical reality that led Jews to be reluctant to receive converts:

> After Christianity became the established religion of the Roman Empire, and later, again, when Islam conquered the world, Jews were forbidden to seek converts or to accept them. The death penalty was fixed for the gentile who became a Jew and also for the Jew who welcomed him [or her]. Many were actually burned at the stake, and the heat of the flames cooled our conversionist ardor. Even so, it was not until the sixteenth century that we abandoned all proselytizing efforts; only then did our rabbis begin their systematic rejection of those who sought to join us.[3]

Centuries of necessity-driven discouragement of conversion continue to weigh on the Jewish people, even now, as we live in free lands, where men and women of conscience can and do feely choose to adopt new religions. Rabbi Schindler urged Reform Jews to adopt a new attitude, to embrace converts with joy, and to serve as their guides along the way: "Newcomers to Judaism, in short, must embark on a long-term naturalization process, and they require knowledgeable and sympathetic guides along the way, that they may feel themselves fully equal members of the synagogue family."[4]

Rabbis play a special role in receiving prospective Jews-by-choice. The rabbi is charged with providing a warm welcome while at the same time maintaining standards for conversion. Rabbis are conscious of this dual role and of the vulnerability that many conversion candidates understandably feel in relation to the authority figure who must ultimately accept them for conversion. In the words of the CCAR's "Guidelines for Working with Prospective *Gerim*," "Relationships between rabbis and prospective *gerim* [converts] pose a particularly sensitive set of circumstances of which rabbis must remain aware."[5] Therefore, rabbis eagerly seek lay partners to serve as mentors and guides, providing the most unfettered embrace of the conversion candidate.

---

2 See, especially, BT *Y'vamot* 46–47.
3 Address of Rabbi Alexander M. Schindler, president of the UAHC, to the Board of Trustees on December 2, 1978, in Houston, Texas.
4 Ibid.
5 "Guidelines for Working with Prospective *Gerim*," CCAR, June 2001, "Initial Contact," https://www.ccarnet.org/rabbis-communities/professional-resources/guidelines-for-rabbisworking-with-prospective-gerim/.

Rabbis will typically meet privately with individuals soon after being approached about conversion. The rabbi will then describe the requirements for conversion, emphasizing that each person is on an individual journey and that the timetable for the process cannot be predicted at the outset.[6] Throughout the rabbi's work with a prospective convert, the rabbi may raise questions about the candidate's fitness for conversion. While many people are aware of a traditional requirement that prospective converts be turned away three times before being accepted,[7] the CCAR has affirmed, "The Reform Movement . . . has formally rejected the traditional practice of strongly discouraging prospective *gerim* [converts] three times."[8]

Many people choosing Judaism are initially inspired by Jewish theology. Exploring Judaism through family or friends, through books or the Internet, they find that our faith fits the belief system they have always held. In the case specifically of Reform Judaism, others are attracted to our movement's commitment to social justice, often exemplified by a local rabbi and congregation.

Still, the process of becoming a Jew is essentially one of beginning to live as a Jew by taking on the performance of mitzvot. The ancient Rabbis called that requirement *kabbalat ol hamitzvot*, literally, "acceptance of the burden of the commandments." Reform Judaism views the performance of mitzvot not as a burden, but rather as an opportunity to come closer to God and the people of Israel, bringing the world closer to the messianic ideal.[9]

Conversion is a journey. The preparation includes intellectual learning, spiritual direction, and participation in the community.[10] Each encounter—in an introduction to Judaism course, in the rabbi's study, or in community celebration—introduces the prospective convert new opportunities to explore mitzvot that will most meaningfully enrich that person's life.

In each area of Jewish observance—from Shabbat and holy days to personal ethical conduct, from affixing a mezuzah to the doorpost of one's home to considering some degree of Jewish dietary discipline, from *tzedakah* (righteous charitable giving) to selecting ritual garb for worship—becoming a Jew requires studying traditional Jewish text and practice, discussion with one's supervising rabbi, and prayerfully considering how mitzvot will best ennoble the individual's journey.[11]

6 Ibid.
7 *Ruth Rabbah* 2:1.
8 "Guidelines for Working with Prospective *Gerim*," "Initial Contact," 1b.
9 Ibid., 6.
10 Ibid., 2–4.
11 Ibid., 6.

When the conversion candidate and the rabbi agree that the time is right, the performance of mitzvot will mark the individual's entry into the covenant, the *b'rit*, with God. Each person seeking to become Jewish will appear before a *beit din* (Jewish court), made up of three knowledgeable Jews, arranged by the supervising rabbi. Upon acceptance by the *beit din*, male candidates will usually be asked to enter *b'rit milah*, the covenant of circumcision. Those previously circumcised enter *b'rit milah* through a ritual called *hatafat dam b'rit*, drawing a drop of blood from the site of the original, non-ritual, circumcision.[12]

The crowning moment of the conversion process is immersion in the mikveh, the ritual bath. Witnessed by an appropriate person of the same gender, the candidate enters the mikveh with blessing. Rabbi Rachel Cowan, describing her own immersion in the *mikveh*, writes "that it had helped me reach a new level in a spiritual journey that would last the rest of my life."[13] The person who emerges from the mikveh is a Jew in every respect.[14]

Each Jew-by-choice will receive a Hebrew name, chosen by the individual in consultation with the rabbi. That name will include *ben* (son of) or *bat* (daughter of) *Avraham v'Sarah* (Abraham and Sarah). The connection to the original matriarch and patriarch of Judaism emphasizes that the new Jew is to be considered a lineal descendant of the first man and woman to choose to follow the God of Israel.

The first conversion ceremony I ever attended was my aunt's, in 1968, ten years before Rabbi Schindler called for renewed enthusiasm for conversion. I was only five years old, but two aspects of the event remain emblazoned on my mind: First, I do recall that the ceremony was joyous and attended by our entire family. By contrast, though, I was told that we must never speak of the fact that my aunt had converted to Judaism. Her conversion was to be kept secret, making me imagine it to be shameful.

Today, conversion is celebrated publicly. Some time after the private moment at the mikveh, the new Jew is welcomed by the congregation—with an *aliyah* (blessing over the Torah), with a public blessing before the holy ark, or with a full conversion ceremony in the presence of all gathered for Shabbat worship. The congregation is inspired by the devotion of the newest Jew in its midst, reminding all assembled that whether we be Jews by conversion or "by birth,"

12 Ibid., 8.
13 Rachel Cowan, "A Personal Story of Conversion," in *Embracing Judaism*, by Simcha Kling (New York: Rabbinical Assembly, 1987), page 179.
14 BT *Y'vamot* 47b.

we can all be "Jews-by-choice," Jews who continually choose to perform mitzvot and embrace our covenant.

Source: Rabbi Barry Block, "Welcoming Converts," in *Navigating the Journey: The Essential Guide to the Jewish Life Cycle*, ed. Rabbi Peter Knobel (New York: CCAR Press, 2017).

Peace at Home:
The Virtue of *Sh'lom Bayit*

Better a piece of dry bread and tranquility with it, than a house full of feasting with strife. (Proverbs 17:1)

> The prosperity and success of the wicked, however impressive, is only illusion. Far better is the fortune of those who are *tzadikim* (righteous ones), even if they have only a crust of bread, because they have peace in their homes, while the wicked are in a state of discord, either with their families or with other people. Family harmony and peace are the essence of true success in life, and can be attained even with a piece of dry bread.
>
> —*Malbim* (Rabbi Meir Leibush ben Yehiel Michel Weiser, 1809–1879)

Parents and Children

Start softly. A discussion that begins with accusation or criticism triggers the natural inclination to fight back, drastically reducing the chances of resolution. A soft start, by contrast, invites constructive conversation. The importance of a soft start and soft reply is established in Jewish tradition. In Proverbs 15:1, we read: "A soft answer turns away wrath"; and in *Pirkei Avot* 1:15: "Receive everyone with a cheerful expression." Beginning softly does not mean abandoning a parent's responsibility to set limits or to discipline the child; it means only that we do not begin with blame.

When problem-solving in the context of an unequal relationship like parent–child, the *principle of justice* still applies. The rule is that inequalities in authority should be justified by the purpose and function of the relationship. In other words, parental authority is justified by the responsibility to care for, keep safe, and raise children properly. It would be grossly unfair to grant such a major responsibility without the authority to carry it out. At the same time, the person with more power should not take advantage of it in a self-serving or cruel way. Such advantage-taking is known in Rabbinic parlance as *honaat rei·a*— a serious moral violation and one of the sins in the Yom Kippur confession.

Being a kind and just parent during their early years helps build a foundation of respect that will endure through the difficult teen years. Agreeing to abide by *a covenant of respect* can help keep parent–teenager discussions on track. The covenant of respect means that teens follow the biblical commandment to honor their parents—which includes accepting parental authority and parental rights to set appropriate limits (Talmud, *Kiddushin* 29–32). Parents, in turn, would follow the Rabbinic injunction to honor all people (*Pirkei Avot* 4:1), which involves listening to their child's point of view with an open mind.

—William K. Berkson (b. 1944), adapted

If your wife is short, bend over to hear her whisper.

—*Talmud Bava M'tzia* 59a

When his disciples asked Rabbi Adda bar Ahavah, "To what do you attribute your long life?" he replied, "I never lost my temper in the midst of my family."

—*Talmud Taanit* 20b

Diversity is built into the human condition; our tradition regards it as a blessing. Says the Talmud (*B'rachot* 58a): "Just as the faces of human beings are different, so their minds and personalities are different." Disagreements are inevitable in any close relationship. But the prophet Zechariah taught, "Love truth and peace" (8:19). In other words: balance the quest for truth with the striving for peace. Don't let brutal honesty lead you to hurt the ones you love. Don't insist on being right at the expense of a loving, harmonious relationship with your partner or spouse.

When the temple was destroyed, it was replaced not by another Temple but by the home, later named a *mikdash m'at*, a sanctuary in miniature. The Rabbis established an extraordinary equivalence:

Temple = home	priests = us around the table
altar = table	sacrifice = bread

And because the altar could not be built from hewn stones (it would take a tool of violence to shape them), so, too, a tool of violence is not used to cut the bread on the Shabbat table. How many of us tear the challah with our hands (instead of using a knife) at the Friday night dinner?

Just as the Temple had to be a place of peace and wholeness, it is our hope that our home will also be a place of peace, not a place of hurt, competition, or violence. We reinforce these wonderful principles not only through grand gestures and statements but also through the regular practice of law and ritual.

—Rabbi Shira Milgrom (b. 1951)

For Reflection

Sh'lom bayit does not mean a "quiet house" but a home in which people are at peace with one another. How can I bring more peace into my home and into my relationships? Am I refraining from discussing important matters in order to maintain peace in my home?

Source: Rabbi Edwin Goldberg, Rabbi Janet Marder, Rabbi Sheldon Marder, and Rabbi Leon Morris, eds., *Mishkan HaNefesh: Machzor for the Days of Awe*, vol. 2, Yom Kippur (New York: CCAR Press, 2015), 402–403.

Questions You Might Be Asked
by the Beit Din

I. What have been the key events of your religious journey up to today?
   a. Please describe your spiritual Journey to Judaism.
   b. Describe the road of Jewish education that you have undertaken since beginning this process.
   c. How does your family feel about your decision to become Jewish?
   d. What aspects of your previous religious identity will you miss the most?
   e. Which Jewish values and beliefs do you find the most appealing and persuasive?
   f. What are some of the books that have particularly influenced your religious outlook?
   g. Is there a time in Jewish history that you've found to be especially compelling?
   h. Who are your Jewish heroes?
   i. Is there a biblical character or story that you find especially resonant or meaningful?
   j. Who have been your mentors in Jewish living, and why?

II. What kind of Jewish life do you lead today?
   a. Is there a specific mitzvah that you have taken on that you've found to be particularly delightful or meaningful?
   b. Describe a typical Shabbat in your household.
   c. Describe some ways in which you make the mitzvah of *tzedaka*h a priority.
   d. What standard of Jewish food practices do you keep today?
   e. Is there a specific mitzvah or aspect of Jewish life that you have found to be particularly difficult to accept?

   f. How would a visitor know that your home is a Jewish home?

   g. What is your relationship with the Land of Israel?

   h. Describe your involvement in your synagogue.

III. What is the quality of your spiritual life?

   a. What is your commitment to prayer and religious services?

   b. What are the moments in your life when you felt particularly close to God?

   c. What questions and issues of Jewish life and belief continue to challenge you?

   d. Do you have a favorite Jewish prayer?

   e. What Jewish holiday is most meaningful to you?

IV. What kind of Jewish life will you be leading tomorrow?

   a. Should you be blessed with children, how will you provide them with a Jewish education?

   b. Is there a new Jewish experience that you are looking forward to?

   c. What are your plans for future Jewish study?

V. Concluding Question

Please let the בית דין know about the Hebrew name you have chosen for yourself, and why you have selected this name.

Is there anything you would like to add?

Do you have any questions for the בית דין?

Source: Rabbi Donald Goor, ed. *For Sacred Moments: The CCAR Life-Cycle Guide* (New York: CCAR Press, 2015).

Dear Reader,

Thank you for joining us on this journey. We look forward to continued learning together.

The Editors

⸙

Babylonian Talmud, *Taanit* 7b

Much I have learned from my teachers, more from my colleagues,
but most from my students.